Baltic Yearbook of International Law, Volume 17 (2017/2018)

Baltic Yearbook of International Law

VOLUME 17, 2017/2018

Editors-in-Chief

Lauri Mälksoo, Ineta Ziemele, Dainius Žalimas

Managing Editor

Ligita Gjortlere, M.Sci.Soc., Riga Graduate School of Law

Language Editor:

Christopher Goddard, MEd

Editorial Board

Egidijus Bieliunas (Judge at the General Court of the Court of Justice of the EU) – *Tanel Kerikmäe* (Professor at the Tallinn University of Technology) – *Egils Levits* (President of the Republic of Latvia, former Judge at the Court of Justice of the EU) – *Lauri Mälksoo* (Professor of International Law, University of Tartu) – *Mārtiņš Mits* (Judge at the European Court of Human Rights; Associate Professor, Riga Graduate School of Law) – *Rein Müllerson* (Member of the *Institut de droit international*; Professor Emeritus of the Tallinn University) – *Vilenas Vadapalas* (Attorney at Law; former judge of the General Court of the Court of Justice of the EU) – *Dainius Žalimas* (President of the Constitutional Court of Lithuania; Professor at the Faculty of Law, Vilnius University) – *Ineta Ziemele* (President of the Constitutional Court of Latvia; Professor at the Riga Graduate School of Law) – *Pēteris Zilgalvis* (Head of Unit, Digital Innovation and Blockchain, Digital Single Market Directorate, DG CONNECT)

The titles published in this series are listed at *brill.com/balt*

Advisory Board

Gudmundur Alfredsson (Professor, University of Akureyri; Visiting Professor, University of Strasbourg) – *Theo van Boven* (Professor Emeritus of International Law, University of Maastricht) – *James Crawford* (Judge at the International Court of Justice, the Hague) – *Andrew Drzemczewski* (Visiting Professor at Middlesex University; former staff member of the Council of Europe) – *John Dugard* (Professor Emeritus of Public International Law, University of Leiden; Professor Emeritus of Law, University of the Witwatersrand, Johannesburg) – *Asbjørn Eide* (Founder of the Norwegian Institute of Human Rights, University of Olso) – *Christine Gray* (Professor Emeritus in International Law, University of Cambridge) – *Mahulena Hofmann* (Professor, SES Chair at the University of Luxembourg) – *Göran Melander* (Professor Emeritus of International Law, University of Lund) – *Allan Rosas* (Judge at the Court of Justice of the EU) – *Bruno Simma* (Arbitrator, Iran-United States Claims Tribunal; former Judge, International Court of Justice) – *Brigitte Stern* (Professor Emeritus of International Law, University of Paris I) – *Rüdiger Wolfrum* (Professor, former Director, Max Planck Institute for Comparative Public Law and International Law)

Baltic Yearbook of International Law, Volume 17 (2017/2018)

Edited by

Lauri Mälksoo
Ineta Ziemele
Dainius Žalimas

BRILL
NIJHOFF

LEIDEN | BOSTON

Typeface for the Latin, Greek, and Cyrillic scripts: "Brill". See and download: brill.com/brill-typeface.

ISSN 1569-6456
E-ISSN 2211-5897
ISBN 978-90-04-41392-4 (hardback)

Copyright 2020 by Koninklijke Brill NV, Leiden, The Netherlands.
Koninklijke Brill NV incorporates the imprints Brill, Brill Hes & De Graaf, Brill Nijhoff, Brill Rodopi, Brill Sense, Hotei Publishing, mentis Verlag, Verlag Ferdinand Schöningh and Wilhelm Fink Verlag.
All rights reserved. No part of this publication may be reproduced, translated, stored in a retrieval system, or transmitted in any form or by any means, electronic, mechanical, photocopying, recording or otherwise, without prior written permission from the publisher.
Authorization to photocopy items for internal or personal use is granted by Koninklijke Brill NV provided that the appropriate fees are paid directly to The Copyright Clearance Center, 222 Rosewood Drive, Suite 910, Danvers, MA 01923, USA. Fees are subject to change.

This book is printed on acid-free paper and produced in a sustainable manner.

Contents

Editorial Note IX
Ineta Ziemele and Lauri Mälksoo

PART 1
Special Theme: 100 Year Anniversary of the Baltic States

1. Principles and Pragmatism in State Succession: Bargaining in the Economic Affairs Commission of the Tartu Peace Conference 3
   Hent Kalmo

2. On the Borders of Law, History and Politics: Estonian Statesman Jüri Jaakson's Views and Life in Context 24
   Jaanika Erne

3. One Hundred Years of Faith: The Baltic States' Contribution to International Justice 39
   Rytis Satkauskas

4. A Century of the Baltic States' Independence: Some Similarities and Differences with Bulgaria 60
   Gabriela Belova and Nikolay Marin

5. Finland's Continuation War (1941–1944): War of Aggression or Defence? War of Alliance or Separate War? Analyzed from the International – Especially Legal – Perspective 77
   Lauri Hannikainen

6. Application of Domestic Criminal Statutes in regard to International Crimes 122
   Andres Parmas

7. Case Law of the European Court of Human Rights as a Source of Human Rights Law 143
   Ineta Ziemele

PART 2
Annual Conference of European Society of International Law in Riga (2016)

8   Human Dignity in an Age of Autonomous Weapons: Are We in Danger of Losing an 'Elementary Consideration of Humanity'?   169
       Ozlem Ulgen

9   Vulnerability as a Virtue: An Attempt to Transpose the Care Ethic in International Law   197
       Marion Blondel

PART 3
Elements of Practices of the Baltic States in International Law

10   Republic of Estonia Materials on International Law 2016   225
       Edited by *René Värk*

11   Republic of Latvia Materials on International Law 2016   291
       Edited by *Kristaps Tamužs*

12   Republic of Lithuania Materials on International Law 2017   334
       Edited by *Andrius Bambalas and Saulius Katuoka*

Editorial Note

With this volume, the Baltic Yearbook of International Law celebrates the 100th Anniversary of the three Baltic States: Estonia, Latvia and Lithuania. Following World War I, pro-independence national forces in the territories of today's Estonia, Latvia and Lithuania had the opportunity and the will to proclaim the establishment of their respective States. Lithuania was the first to do so on 18 February 1918, followed by Estonia, whose declaration of independence was adopted on 24 February 1918, while the Declaration Establishing a Provisional Government of Latvia and the Political Platform was adopted on 18 November 1918. These respectively mark the founding dates of the three Baltic States.

The history of Baltic statehood gives rise to many international law questions starting with secession from the Russian Empire and the creation of three new States in 1918 and, of course, the restoration of their independence in 1990–1991, following long decades of Soviet occupation, their accession to the EU and NATO in 2004. The Baltic Yearbook of International Law published its first volume in 2001. Since then it has addressed many issues linked to the statehood of the Baltic States. Even so, new research is still being done and new questions are coming up. For example, Lithuania opened the Soviet KGB archives but only in 2017 published the files therefrom. Latvia has had a very complex debate about these archives, which were finally made public at the end of 2018. The archives of the Soviet secret service illustrate one page in the complex history of the Baltic States. Moreover, the archives left behind in the Baltic States after the withdrawal of the Soviet armed forces are not complete. Does their publication contribute to reconciliation and the right to truth?

Territorial questions have also given rise to disputes. Latvia has signed and ratified its border agreement with the Russian Federation while Estonia and Russia have not yet ratified their border treaties (concerning borders at land and at sea). In 2015 the three Baltic ministers of justice signed a common declaration on cooperating in calculating the damage caused to the Baltic States during the Soviet occupation, though this declaration was not followed by formal claims. In other contexts, issues of minority rights and protection – that have been with the Baltic States since the 1920s – certainly returned in the 1990s. Furthermore, since the Baltic peoples were born in 1918 as Baltic nations with explicit reference to the right of peoples to self-determination, the question has arisen whether the Baltic case is a precedent in the context of this right as well. Or one can more generally ask, by the example of the Baltic States, how small States operate in the context of conflicting geopolitical claims, and how international law is relevant in those contexts. In other words, multiple questions of international law arise in relation to the past and present of the Baltic States. These legal issues show that international law has a normative capacity to preserve claims and disputes in force for a long time until they have been settled one way or another.

It is highly symbolic that the Baltic Yearbook of International Law, having been founded and hosted for many years by the Raoul Wallenberg Institute at Lund University in Sweden, has now, since 2018, come home and has taken up residence at the Riga Graduate School of Law (RGSL) in Latvia, in the very heart of the three Baltic States. Established in 1998, RGSL has emerged as a leading legal education and research institute in the Baltic region, providing education in English. RGSL offers numerous study programmes in the area of International and European Law at bachelor and master's level. RGSL benefits from partnerships with numerous leading European universities and cooperates closely with the University of Latvia, the major shareholder. In addition to its growing resident faculty, RGSL also benefits from the involvement of a large number of eminent scholars and practitioners based in the local environment, elsewhere in Europe, and overseas. A primary objective of RGSL is to contribute to the development of Latvia and the wider region by educating new generations of motivated and highly skilled young scholars and professionals capable of promoting the ongoing process of European integration. Research and education in the area of international and European law are integral to the realisation of this objective. In 2016 the RGSL hosted the annual conference of the European Society of International Law on the theme "How International Law Works in Times of Crisis", thus being the first university in Eastern Europe to do so. Proceedings of the conference are published by several publications. First, the papers presented at the panel on Minority Rights in Times of Crisis appeared in a special issue of the International Journal on Minority and Group Rights (vol. 24, issue 3, August 2017). Second, this anniversary volume of the Yearbook publishes articles by Ozlem Ulgen and Marion Blondel presented during the RGSL-ESIL annual conference which address important moral issues in the age of rapid technological development. The fact that we see these issues addressed from an international law standpoint shows, against all odds, that a value discourse has entered the international political arena. The story of the Baltic States is also the story about the rule of law in international law.

The Baltic Yearbook of International Law launched a call for papers across the Baltics and beyond on the theme of the 100th Anniversary of independence. For this reason, the articles published in this volume carry a historical dimension. Hent Kalmo examines how the theory of State succession was approached and applied at the peace negotiations between Soviet Russia and Estonia in early 1920. Gabriela Belova and Nikolay Marin draw parallels in their article with the 100-year history of Bulgaria, pointing to similarities in the development of the Baltic States and Bulgaria. Undoubtedly, history is shaped by people. Lawyers have played an important role in the processes leading to establishing the Baltic States and their independent legal systems. Jānis Čakste, the first President of the Republic of Latvia, was a lawyer. The article by Jaanika Erne looks at the influence of Jüri Jaakson, a prominent Estonian lawyer of the turn of the nineteenth and twentieth centuries, on the formation of an independent Estonian legal system. She highlights the many influences that lie at the roots of the country's legal system, which she notes was European in character even at the outset. Rytis Satkauskas illuminates an interesting perspective on the Baltic States with regard to their contribution to the formation of twentieth-century international case law. All three States accepted the jurisdiction of the Permanent Court of Justice – Lithuania and Estonia in October 1921 and Latvia in January 1922. The cases of *Railway traffic between Lithuania and Poland*, *Interpretation of the Statute of the Memel Territory* and the *Panevežys-Saldutiškis railway* belong to the foundations of modern international law. Satkauskas traces the principles that were discerned by the Court in those cases and that continue to form the backbone of the legal system. It is particularly interesting to compare and contrast the story of the Baltic States with that of Finland. The Baltic Yearbook is pleased to carry an article by Lauri Hannikainen on World War II in Finland, its legal analysis and broader conclusions.

Additionally, the Baltic States offer interesting materials concerning international law nowadays – for example, Andres Parmas discusses the implementation of international criminal law in Estonia, and raises some noteworthy practical (and conceptual) questions as to the interplay between international and domestic law in the context of criminal law. Finally it has to be noted that protection of human rights has been very high on the agenda of the Baltic States having freed themselves from Soviet occupation. They have acceded to human rights treaties and have been active participants in relevant human rights fora. The article by Ineta Ziemele explores the legal nature of the case law of the European Court of Human Rights and pushes the boundaries of examining the nature of judicial decisions as a source of law to reflect the growing importance of international and national courts.

The Baltic States have now left their first hundred years behind them. Collaboration between Baltic intellectuals from different jurisdictions in terms of common publishing already has a long tradition – for example, there springs to mind the academic and literary journal *Baltische Monatsschrift* that was published throughout the nineteenth and early twentieth centuries, mostly in Riga but occasionally also in Tallinn (Reval, as it once was). In this spirit, we hope to continue to play a part in global international law scholarship in future decades as well.

Ineta Ziemele

*Lauri Mälksoo**

---

[*] Editing of parts of this volume was supported by a grant from the Estonian Research Council, IUT20-50.

PART 1

Special Theme: 100 Year Anniversary of the Baltic States

∴

CHAPTER 1

Principles and Pragmatism in State Succession: Bargaining in the Economic Affairs Commission of the Tartu Peace Conference

Hent Kalmo

Abstract

The conventions of legal argumentation have the tendency to reinforce the notion that the development of international law is a principled affair. This article will examine the elaboration of one particular treaty – the Tartu Peace Treaty signed between Estonia and Soviet Russia in 1920 – in order to see to what extent it lends support to the idea that treaties grow out of principles. The Tartu Peace Treaty perfectly illustrates the point that the contents of a treaty can be entirely indeterminate with regard to their underlying principles. My conclusion is not that, in this case, pragmatism triumphed over principles: that the negotiating parties refrained from debates over abstract principles and took the more pragmatic route of finding an array of concrete solutions. Whilst it is true that the end result – the Treaty as it finally stood – was detached from any single foundational idea, it was not obtained by putting principles aside. The Tartu Peace Conference rather offers us a particularly good example of how principles can be used as rhetorical ploys.

Keywords

Tartu Peace Treaty – State succession – legal argumentation

1 Introduction: The Tartu Peace Treaty as an Incompletely Theorized Agreement

Anyone seeking to justify some act under international law is induced, by the very nature of the discipline, to invoke some rule or principle in its support. Most frequently, the argument takes the form that the relevant legal materials, such as the provisions of a treaty, express or exemplify a rule. Things are relatively uncontroversial whenever the materials explicitly set out a rule of general application. But such enunciatory character is often absent – especially in the field of international law, where State practice plays such a prominent role as adducible authority. The materials might be dealing with particular circumstances, without any explicit indication as to the rule that is being applied. For example, when the rights and obligations of a defunct State are allocated in a treaty, the text could simply contain a distribution of individual titles and obligations and leave the reader completely in the dark as to the principles from which the distribution flows. Nonetheless, when such a treaty is later invoked as a precedent, its provisions are still presented as if expressing some rule or principle situated upstream. The conventions of legal argumentation thus have the tendency to reinforce the notion that the development of international law is a principled affair.

This article will examine the elaboration of one particular treaty – the Tartu Peace Treaty signed between Estonia and Soviet Russia in 1920 – in order to see to what extent it lends support to the idea that treaties grow out of principles. My emphasis will be on the economic provisions which sorted out the proprietary consequences of the Czarist Empire's demise. As I shall show, there already existed a large body of doctrine on State succession by the time the Tartu Peace Treaty was signed. This doctrine was mostly premised on the assumption that a set of clear principles existed in this area. Yet it is impossible to fit the Tartu Peace Treaty into the elaborate classification of succession cases that emerged from the pre-war scholarship. The Treaty, although far from lacking detail, left open the question that was considered the most fundamental of all – the question as to whether the independence of Estonia was a case of break-up or one of secession from a continuing Russian State. More generally, the Tartu Peace Treaty perfectly illustrates the point that the contents of a treaty can be entirely indeterminate with regard to their underlying principles. My conclusion is not that, in this case, pragmatism triumphed over principles: that the negotiating parties refrained from debates over abstract principles and took the more pragmatic route of finding an array of concrete solutions.[1] Whilst it is true that the end result – the Treaty as it finally stood – was detached from any single foundational idea, it was not obtained by putting principles aside. The Tartu Peace Conference rather offers us a particularly good example of how principles can be used as rhetorical ploys.

---

1 As suggested by the notion of 'incompletely theorized agreements'; *See* Cass R. Sunstein, *Legal Reasoning and Political Conflict*, 2nd edition, Oxford University Press, 2018, p. 64.

2 Pre-WWI Doctrine on State Succession: in Search of Principles

The First World War was more than any preceding conflict a crucible of new States. One might think that that presented international lawyers with an excellent opportunity to showcase the relevance of their discipline. Yet, puzzlingly, the dominant scholarly view on the eve of the War had been that the emergence of a new State is an event which lies outside the scope of law. As Georg Jellinek put it in a pre-war *locus classicus* on the topic, international law addresses itself to existing States and not to 'State-creating powers'.[2] The rules of the parent State were also unavailable as a standard of legality, argued Jellinek, for using them would amount to subjecting the break-away State to foreign law. Nor could the law of the nascent State itself be pressed into service: "A State cannot establish law for its own emergence, for, in order to create law, it first needs to exist."[3] As this seemingly exhausted all avenues for bringing the birth of a new State into the realm of legal imagination, the conclusion remained that the process has a purely factual character. This conclusion was widely accepted. It was hardly deemed to be a cause for embarrassment. On the contrary, to characterize State creation as a non-legal occurrence was a way to affirm the positivist credentials of international law scholarship. Few needed reminding that it had been a central tenet of the natural law tradition that the creation of a new political community is a legal transaction. When the doctrine of social contract fell into discredit, it was perceived to be imperative to tie an enquiry into whether something admits of legal qualification to the question as to which set of positive rules is applicable.[4] And if none could be found, an avowed positivist would only prove their scientific rigour by conceding that there was nothing a lawyer could say about the matter.

Nonetheless, if only for practical purposes, it was often necessary to recognize some form of continuity between newborn States and their sovereign peers or predecessors. By the early 1900s, there was little virgin land where a purely original State could form, as was noted in the literature. The process was therefore likely to be derivative and happen either on the ruins, or at the expense, of an existing State.[5] Under such circumstances, the fact of secession or disintegration might represent an absolute beginning in terms of validity, but

---

2 Georg Jellinek, *Allgemeine Staatslehre*, Berlin, 1922, p. 273.
3 *Ibid.*
4 For the view that a positive rule needs to exist to confer validity on the social contract, *see e.g.* Conrad Bornhak, *Allgemeine Staatslehre*, Berlin, Carl Heymanns Verlag, 1896, pp. 16–17.
5 Arrigo Cavaglieri, *La dottrina della successione di stato a stato e il suo valore giuridico*, Pisa, Archivio giuridico, 1910, p. 6.

the emergent State still had to be seen as having a past in order to justify transferring to it some rights and duties of the mother State. Consider the creation of independent Belgium in 1830 as a case in point. The secession of the southern provinces from the United Kingdom of the Netherlands was invoked as an example showing that 'it is impossible to find a legal relationship between the old and new sovereign power'.[6] But what about the debts of the former Kingdom of the Netherlands? Or responsibility for damage caused during the armed revolt in the period immediately preceding Belgian independence?[7] The claim of radical discontinuity, however unassailable in the eyes of theorists, was an unhelpful starting point for discussing such practical issues. It would not have recommended itself to the five Powers (Austria, France, Great Britain, Prussia and Russia) who met in a conference to mull over the consequences of the Belgian Revolution. Unsurprisingly, the participants of the London Conference emphasised continuity over discontinuity. They noted that "when united to Holland, and as an integral part of the Kingdom of the Netherlands, Belgium had to fulfil its part of the European obligations of this Kingdom [...] Its separation from Holland cannot liberate it from this part of its obligations..."[8] As on many such occasions, uppermost in their minds was debt apportionment. The Conference decided that Belgium should assume 'in fair proportion' the debts contracted since the beginning of its union with Holland.[9] Similar arrangements were made for the liquidation of the debt of the Westphalian Kingdom in the wake of its dissolution in 1813.[10] Other knots had to be untied at the time of a sovereign breakup: trading privileges, rights to colonies, public buildings, the fate of archives, and so on. They all tended to prompt the question as to the nature of the legal relationship between the old State and the new.

As the 19th century progressed, legal scholars set out to erect a coherent doctrine of State succession on such past precedents. It was increasingly

---

6   Heinrich Pohl, *Die Entstehung des belgischen Staates und des Norddeutschen Bundes. Eine Staatsrechtliche Studie*, Freiburg i. B., C.A. Wagners Universitäts-Buchdruckerei, 1905, p. 39.
7   For this aspect, see Patrick Dumberry, *State Succession to International Responsibility*, Leiden, Boston: Martinus Nijhoff Publishers, 2007, p. 161.
8   'Protocole de la Conférence tenue au Foreign Office, le 20 Décembre, 1830', British and Foreign State Papers (1830–1831), London, James Ridgway, 1833, p. 749.
9   See 'Draft articles on succession of States in respect of State property, archives and debts, adopted by the International Law Commission at its thirty-third session', p. 89.
10 For the diplomatic practice of debt apportionment around the turn of the 19th century, see Fr. J. Haas, *Ueber das Repartitions-Princip der Staatsschulden bei Länderzerstückelungen*, Bonn: T. Habicht, 1831.

assumed that settled principles exist in this area. Hugo Grotius was cited to the effect that, if a State is split up, "anything which may have been held in common by the parts separating from each other must either be administered in common or be rateably divided".[11] When confronted with a separation, one first had to establish whether what had occurred was merely loss of territory by a continuing State or division of a State into several distinct sovereign units. In the former case, it was asserted, the identity of the mother State would not be affected, nor would its treaty obligations or rights of property.[12] In other words, it was enough to determine whether the old State was extinct to obtain answers to a whole array of practical queries, such as what is the relationship of the new State to the property belonging to the parent State. Little concern was caused by the fact that the legal nature of the separation process had sometimes been hotly contested by the participants in the cases adduced as instances of established principles.[13] For example, to return to the Belgian Revolution of 1830, the Netherlands viewed the splitting away of the southern provinces as a mere diminution of its territory, whereas the new Belgian State considered it as the demise of the United Kingdom of the Netherlands. Both had their sights on the practical consequences of post-independence State identity. The Netherlands claimed that parties should refrain from setting off mutual debts, that is, property ought to be apportioned according to its location. Belgium, by contrast, viewed the parties as having undertaken to liquidate all former joint property with compensation being due *pro rata*.[14] The participants of the London Conference offered their good offices for mediating between these conflicting views. They justified their intervention by noting that "experience ... had only too often demonstrated to them the complete impossibility of the Parties directly concerned agreeing on such matters, if the benevolent solicitude of the five Courts did not facilitate agreement."[15] In a way which bolstered the impression of later writers that State succession is subject to clear rules,

---

11 Cited in William Edward Hall, *A Treatise on International Law*, Third edition, Oxford, Clarendon Press, 1890, p. 89, fn 1.
12 *Halleck's International Law or Rules Regulating the Intercourse of States in Peace and War*, Vol. 1, London: C. Kegal Paul & Co, 1878, p. 76.
13 Although some authors recognized that it was not always easy to distinguish between a split-off and a State's extinction, they assumed that there was one correct, scientifically ascertainable way to characterize the situation; *see e.g.* S. Kiatibian, Conséquences juridiques de la transformation des États sur les traités, Paris, A. Giard & E. Brière, 1892, p. 73.
14 Max Huber, *Die Staatensuccession. Völkerrechtliche und Staatsrechtliche Praxis im XIX. Jahrhundert*, Leipzig, Verlag von Duncker & Humblot, 1898, p. 138.
15 'Draft articles on succession of States in respect of State property, archives and debts, adopted by the International Law Commission at its thirty-third session', p. 88.

the five Powers then proceeded to apply "principles which, far from being new, were those that have always governed the reciprocal relations of States."[16]

When in doubt, there was an obvious source from where to import principles by way of analogy: private law. The Belgian situation bore a strong resemblance to a divorce. Belgium had been united to Holland upon the defeat of Napoleon in 1814 and, at the time of separation after sixteen years of joint existence, there were both its former debts and the debts contracted during the period of union to be considered. Another seemingly straightforward analogy was with inheritance. In the words of Friedrich Martens, the consequences following from the 'death' of a State "are reminiscent of relationships arising between private persons under the rules of inheritance…"[17] Even the direct applicability of private law rules was not excluded in some circumstances if public property and governmental powers were seen as being transmissible from one reigning monarch to the next.[18] Contracts of succession, signed by heirs, had been a regular presence within the Holy Roman Empire.[19] Admittedly, writers on constitutional law were keen to establish the autonomy of their discipline by decrying the persistence of private law categories such as inheritance in treatments of the State.[20] The same defensive attitude gradually took hold of international law scholarship, although the latter remained more conciliatory in this respect. In one of the earliest extended discussions of State succession, Johann Caspar Bluntschli took the analogy with inheritance seriously. The common element justifying the analogy, according to Bluntschli, was that the former bearer of rights and obligations disappears, in one case through death in another through extinction, while rights and obligations are

---

16 Ibid.
17 Фёдор Мартенс, Современное международное право цивилизованных народов, Том 1, Санкт-Петербург, Типография Министерства Путей Сообщения (А. Бенке), 1882, p. 274.
18 This view was defended *e.g.* with regard to the princes reigning in the States belonging to the German Confederation; see Romeo Maurenbrecher, *Die deutschen regierenden Fürsten und die Souverainität. Eine publistische Abhandlung*, Frankfurt am Main, Verlag von Franz Barrentrapp, 1839, p. 109. Some two centuries earlier, Hugo Grotius had taken it to be a "clear legal principle that the person of the heir is considered the same as the person of the deceased in all that concerns the continuation of ownership of both public and private property." Stephen C. Neff (ed.), *Hugo Grotius on the law of war and peace*, Cambridge University Press, 2012, p. 176 (2, 9, 12).
19 For examples, see Hermann Schulze (ed.), *Die Hausgesetze der regierenden deutschen Fürstenhäuser*, Erster Band, Jena, Verlag von Friedrich Mauke, 1862.
20 C.F. Gerber, *Ueber öffentliche Rechte*, Tübingen, Verlag der H. Laupp'schen Buchhandlung, 1852, p. 9.

transmitted to other persons "who can be seen to be, in some sense, carrying on its personality."[21] The crucial difference was that whereas succession by inheritance is based on the family relationship between heirs and the deceased, State succession depends on substantial continuity in the form of partial or total passage of land and people from one State to another. Important consequences flowed from this for the distribution of property. In the private system of inheritance, the governing principle is familial closeness. "Remaining State property, on the other hand, possesses a natural link to people and territory and the public needs of both. Distribution is therefore to be effected according to principles of public law."[22] What this meant in more concrete terms was that all public buildings and institutions devolved upon the State in whose territory they were located, without any compensation being due to co-successors unless the buildings and institutions in question had also served the public needs of their populations and if costs needed to be incurred to replace them. For anything divisible, such as public funds, the most equitable basis of apportionment was population share. "There does not exist a more natural distribution ratio", wrote Bluntschli, "and a more solid standard for division than population… To find a just and generally understandable solution, one has to return to the simple and original elements of the State, which are, after all, the people that it unites."[23]

Perhaps the most ambitious treatment of the topic of State succession in pre-war scholarship came from the pen of the young Max Huber, an admirer of Bluntschli.[24] Huber also brought inheritance and State succession under a common heading. The two differed, he wrote, in that the heir is merely a legal successor, whilst a new State is a real continuation of its predecessor. Another distinguishing characteristic was that only States make themselves successors, independently of the will of their predecessor, by taking possession of the object of succession.[25] Rather than being an orderly affair, State succession could be a messy carve-up where might (continuing possession of territory) was right. As another scholar later put it, "[e]ach part takes such territory as it can

---

21   J.C. Bluntschli, *Das modern Völkerrecht der civilisierten Staaten*, Nördlingen, C.B. Beck, 1868, p. 80.
22   *Ibid.*, pp. 80–81.
23   *Ibid.*, p. 82.
24   On Huber's life and early scholarly work, *see* Paul Guggenheim, 'Nachruf. Max Huber', *Juristenzeitung*, Vol. 15, 1960, pp. 187–188; Dietrich Schindler, 'Max Huber – His Life', *The European Journal of International Law*, Vol. 18, 2007, pp. 83–84.
25   Max Huber, *Die Staatensuccession. Völkerrechtliche und staatsrechtliche Praxis im XIX. Jahrhundert*, Leipzig, Duncker & Humblot, 1898, p. 20.

grasp."[26] The fragments resulting from a break-up were assimilated to annexing foreign powers who had, so to speak, conquered the territory in their possession, as if, for example, Poland had partitioned itself without any external interference. More than a mere metaphor was involved here. This comparison provoked the question as to whether a successor could enjoy any rights to property outside the territory under its control, given that such rights were usually denied to conquerors. One writer described it as the most unquestionable maxim of international law that if some State funds are "situated not in the conquered territory, but either in an unconquered or in a neutral country, [...] they are not within the *imperium* of the Conqueror."[27] The more general rule was that "neither moveable nor immoveable, corporeal nor incorporeal property situate within [...] an unconquered land, can be considered as among the acquisitions of the Conqueror."[28] In the background of these Statements was the view that, although *occupatio bellica* is a legal method of acquiring ownership of un-owned property – and upon the extinction of the parent State its property becomes *res nullius* – it is a 'legal impossibility' to take possession of mere claims.[29] The pairing of State succession with post-war partition thus suggested that, not only would each party take as much territory and moveable property as it could grasp, but that it would have to content itself with what it had actually been able to seize. Indeed, when taken to its limits, the idea of State succession as appropriation of *bona vacantia* entailed the conclusion that there was, strictly speaking, no such thing as State succession: what happened in legal terms was that, subsequent to the withdrawal of the former sovereign power, the self-styled successors had rushed into the void to divide the spoils to which none of them had any pre-existing right.[30]

Huber himself took a slightly different tack. In his view, once an aggressive or peaceful division of territory had taken place, a much more tidy distribution of rights and obligations would begin, the details of which were largely similar to those of private inheritance law. He drew up an elaborate tree-like schema

---

26 Arthur Berriedale Keith, *The Theory of State Succession with Special Reference to English and Colonial Law*, London, Waterlow and Sons Limited, 1907, p. 99.
27 Sir Robert Phillimore, *Commentaries upon International Law*, Volume 3, 2nd edition, London, Butterworths, 1873, p. 826.
28 *Ibid.*, p. 827 (emphasis omitted).
29 B.W. Pfeiffer, *Das Recht der Kriegseroberung in Beziehung auf Staatscapitalien*, Cassel, 1823, pp. 62–63; S. Kiatibian, *supra* note 14, p. 7.
30 See Gilbert Gidel, *Des effets de l'annexion sur les concessions*, Paris, L. Larose & Forcel, 1904, pp. 79–80. *See also* D. O'Connell, 'State Succession and the Theory of the State', C.H. Alexandrowicz (ed.), *Studies in the History of the Law of Nations*, The Hague, Martinus Nijhoff, 1972, p. 48.

of legal configurations, covering all possible succession scenarios, each having their own peculiar principles. For example, one would be dealing with a case of partial succession if a territorial fringe of a continuing State gained independence. On the other hand, if an existing State undergoes complete fragmentation and is extinguished as a result, universal succession follows. The latter extends to the very legal personality of the former State. The implications for property rights would be vastly different. In the case of mere separation, that is, partial succession, the territorial principle would apply exclusively, so that the new State would acquire merely what is located within its borders: public buildings, roads, harbours, money, archives, and so on. The emergent State would have no claim to compensation for what lies beyond its borders. Complete break-up, accompanied by universal succession, represents a much more intricate situation. The application of the territorial principle would now constitute only the first of two stages of division. Since all co-successors would have a share in the central property of the extinct parent State, another standard, the liquidation principle, would begin to operate in the second stage, assigning proportional payments for such communal things as gold reserves and the like that are not connected with any territory as its inseparable appendage.[31] Huber, like Bluntschli before him, assumed that some things are, by their very nature, moored in State territory, while others – possibly just as immovable in physical terms, such as federal buildings – have a communal character and therefore belong to the compensable mass of property. The precondition for any obligatory compensation, however, was that the division is between formally equal co-successors rather than a newly independent State and its parent. In the latter case, if any payments were made under a treaty to the newly independent State for its exclusion from centralised property, it was a gesture of goodwill, not something required by international law.

Some contemporaries were baffled by the assurance with which scholars enounced such comprehensive rules regarding points for which State practice offered few if any precedents. "All this cannot conceivably be regarded as law", remarked one author in commenting on a passage in which Huber had first laid down a principle and then spelled it out in detail.[32] Heinrich Triepel went so far as to speak of the wholesale invention of the international law of inheritance. It was an 'aberration', he claimed, an especially outrageous example of the indiscriminate importation of private law ideas which writers had poured like water into the empty vessel of positive international law.[33] But

---

31   Huber, *supra* note 26, p. 38, pp. 75–76.
32   Keith, *supra* note 27, p. 100.
33   Heinrich Triepel, *Völkerrecht und Landesrecht*, Leipzig, C.L. Hirschfeld, 1899, p. 216.

even if it was true that there existed a similarity between doctrines in private and international law, it was not obvious that one had been the source and the other the recipient. Some writers argued that both areas of law shared a common source: rules and doctrines were similar because they embodied the logical consequences of principles governing universal legal institutions such as contract.[34] The same was said of succession, which was understood as a general notion underlying both private inheritance and State succession under international law. Hersch Lauterpacht would later take up this line of reasoning to mount a more general attack on the kind of isolationist approach to international law promoted by the likes of Triepel. Should it be the case that States themselves draw on general principles underlying both international and private law in signing treaties, then it would run counter to the positivists' own credo to deny the relevance of such principles, argued Lauterpacht.[35] Succession he took to be a particularly clear example of a situation where the operation of general principles produces an analogy between municipal and international rules:

> [T]he problem of succession, so far as it is treated as a problem of law, is identical in private and international law. The fundamental fact in both cases is that there take place both substitution and continuation of rights and duties, and that legal stability and acquired rights are not destroyed in consequence of the subject of law ceasing to exist.[36]

A revolution produces an abyss between the old and new constitution. It is international law, wrote Lauterpacht, which "constitutes the bridge between two facts otherwise totally disconnected."[37] If this bridge did not exist, the former State's rights and duties would be distributed at the whim of the successors. But this is not what the practice of States teaches us, according to Lauterpacht. The replacement of one sovereign power with another was supposedly a much more principled affair.

Although sceptical voices were by no means absent, scholarship on international law before and after the First World War thus tended to subscribe to the notion that State succession is a rule-governed process. Not that co-successors were precluded from reaching an agreement to distribute property according

---

[34] Georg Jellinek, *Die rechtliche Natur der Staatenverträge. Ein Beitrag zur juristischen Construction des Völkerrechts*, Wien, Alfred Hölder, 1880, pp. 51–52.
[35] Hersch Lauterpacht, *Private Law Sources and Analogies of International Law*, Longmans, Green and Co, 1927, pp. 31–32.
[36] *Ibid.*, p. 125.
[37] *Ibid.*, p. 13.

to their own preferences. International law was most directly concerned with the fate of third-party rights, such as sovereign debt held by foreigners or treaties signed by the extinguished State. Many writers, however, took the view that rules of international law also extended to matters of concern only to successors themselves, such as the allocation of rights to archives. As seen above, Max Huber declared it to be a rule of positive law that a break-away State can neither lay claim to community property outside its borders nor demand compensation for it. His assumption appears to have been that, if the emergence of a State falls into a particular category, for example into that of secession, a predetermined set of consequences would come into effect, covering both internal issues and legal relationships with third parties. Not everyone had as expansive a view of the law as it stood. Some scholars laid more emphasis on the possibility open to successor States to fill in gaps and dispose things as they saw fit. The signing of a succession treaty was to be expected in most cases of dissolution, noted one writer on the eve of World War I, because buildings, gold reserves and the like are unlikely to be evenly dispersed across the territory of the extinguished State, so that redistribution becomes necessary.[38] Yet he also believed that past treaties had followed well-defined principles and standards, albeit rarely in pure form, but rather combining several standards. For example, he found the territorial and liquidation principles distinguished by Huber often mixed in various proportions.

3   Tartu Peace Treaty Negotiations

The economic provisions of the Tartu Peace Treaty, signed between the Republic of Estonia and the Soviet Republic of Russia in February of 1920, might be seen as an illustration of precisely such mixing of principles. Both the territorial and liquidation principles appear to have been taken into account by the Estonian and Russian diplomats who met in late 1919 and proceeded to untangle the legal consequences of the Czarist Empire's demise. Under Article 11 of the Treaty, Russia surrendered "any claim to the transfer, or repayment of the value, of property of the former Russian Empire, of whatever nature, whether real or other estate, situated in Esthonia and forming the common property of the whole nation." Estonia, for her part, was not "entitled to bring against Russia any claim based on her former status as a part of the Russian Empire." This looks like a straightforward application of the territorial principle.

---

[38]   W. Schönborn, 'Staatensukzessionen', Fritz Stier-Somlo (ed.), *Handbuch des Völkerrehts*, 2. Band, Stuttgart, Verlag von W. Kohlhammer, 1913, p. 118.

Yet Article 12 added that "notwithstanding these agreements [...] Russia grants to Esthonia fifteen million gold roubles". In this latter provision, the liquidation principle seems to be at work, since, supposedly, the sum of fifteen million gold roubles was to be paid as a consequence of 'liquidating' some form of common property. However, the Treaty does not say whether this lump sum corresponded to Estonia's share in the gold reserves, was meant to provide compensation for something or represented the balance of the netting of mutual payment obligations. No authoritative justification was offered for the allocation of rights and duties. Nor does the Treaty specify whether the signatory States saw themselves as co-successors of the Russian Empire. In other words, from reading the letter of the provisions it is far from clear which principles are being applied. Does the Treaty reflect the assumption that the Soviet Republic of Russia never had any claim to the property of the former Russian Empire located in Estonia? Or, alternatively, does it presume that Soviet Russia had such claims – in virtue of the liquidation principle, for example – and now simply 'surrenders' them (as the wording of the Treaty runs)? Even assuming that State succession follows a well-defined legal pattern, as suggested by the doctrine outlined above, the Tartu Peace Treaty, whilst seemingly signed to clarify the signatory States' legal ties with the former Russian Empire and therefore a *pactum successorium*, remains ambiguous regarding both the category of succession (Is it a case of secession or dissolution?) and the principles implemented in determining outstanding relationships.

A study of the negotiations which led to the Treaty also fails to bring the case unequivocally under the prevailing doctrinal classification. The economic provisions of the Tartu Peace Treaty emerged largely from a special commission which convened alongside the plenary sessions of the Tartu Peace Conference in December of 1919 and January 1920. Its mundane business has been overshadowed by the high drama surrounding the border negotiations and the signing of the armistice agreement on 31 December 1919. In fact, the commission came into being precisely at the moment in mid-December when negotiations over the border had reached a deadlock, both sides having declared that no further concessions would be made. The plenary conference then turned its attention to economic matters. In this area, the main objective of the Estonian delegation was to obtain a division of the central gold reserves of Tsarist Russia. Jaan Poska, who led the Estonian delegates, viewed the item as being of crucial importance. He calculated that the ongoing talks presented a unique opportunity to force the Soviets to come to terms on an issue whose resolution they were likely to drag out endlessly once their immediate objective of securing peace had been achieved. In a preparatory meeting on the morning of the day the issue would be discussed with the Russian side, Poska remarked to his co-delegates that unless agreement on gold was forthcoming, the talks should be interrupted.[39] Such an unyielding attitude regarding the gold question appears to have been unpopular among the Estonian delegation. Other members were much more pessimistic about the prospect of gaining a significant share of the central gold reserves, considering that obtaining even one million roubles would be a satisfactory result.[40] Everything points to the conclusion that it was Poska who was the source of the intransigence discernible in the Estonian position *vis-à-vis* this matter.

It remained to work out a line of reasoning to support Estonian claims. Poska, a practising lawyer who had some familiarity with international law – he had studied under Karl Magnus Bergbohm at Tartu[41] – never publicly presented the matter as crudely as to offer peace for gold. He rather confronted the Soviets with a two-pronged legal argument in the ensuing plenary. Poska first remarked that, as a general rule, a new State will be vested with the right to property inside its territory. But on top of that comes a claim to central property, he added. The latter was to be shared among all the States which had formed out of the Tsarist Empire. There was no question of accepting the Russian view that a division on the basis of *uti possidetis* would express their surrendering a right to property in Estonian territory and therefore an act of goodwill. "We look at things a little differently", said Poska. "We don't see it so that the Russian government unilaterally leaves to Estonia this or that kind of property and, in this way, does a favour to it."[42] If Russia had rights to buildings erected at the public expense in Estonia, so had Estonia to those in Petrograd and Moscow, or to the Trans-Siberian Railway for which the Estonian population had also paid its share of tax-money. The Soviet side retorted that, given the size of its population, Estonia's share in all former public property would not in any case exceed one percent, and it would thus be far better off simply keeping what it had within its borders, especially since this included an oversized Tallinn port. Ants Piip, a member of the Estonian delegation who had recently become a professor of international law at Tartu, took up the challenge, asserting that the cost of the Tallinn port paled in comparison with the tens of millions of roubles sucked out of Estonia in Tsarist times. More back and forth ensued, until it was decided that the technical nature of the issues warranted the creation of a special commission on economic affairs.

---

39 ERA.957.10.26, p. 22.
40 Ants Piip, "Tartu rahu," *Mälestused iseseisvuse võitluspäevilt, Vabadussõda 1918–1920*, Tallinn, Rahvaülikool, 1930, p. 415.
41 Eduard Laaman, *Jaan Poska: Eesti riigitegelase elukäik*, Eesti Raamat, 1935, p. 13.
42 ERA.957.10.29, p. 26.

The commission had its first meeting on the following day, on 13 December. The Russians again started by tabling their proposal to refrain from all mutual settlement of accounts. This was not at all meant as a consequence of some theory regarding State succession. On the contrary, Abram Ioffe, the head of the Soviet delegation, had explicitly presented it in the plenary as a departure from the legal situation obtaining after past secessions. He had mentioned Bulgaria's separation from Turkey in the 1870s as a precedent for the rule that a part of the public debt devolves on the seceding State. "We will pay", Poska replied. "But we will release you from that [obligation]", said Ioffe.[43] When the Russians returned to their proposal to stick to the *status quo* with respect to property in the economic affairs commission, their main justification was that this would enormously simplify matters, and indeed that it would be impossible to quickly collect the information needed to itemise and substantiate accounts. The Estonians objected to the *status quo* solution. They were seeking to obtain as large a portion as possible of the central gold reserves and, if feasible, also secure the recovery of at least some of the ships and factories taken to Russia in the course of the war. Agreeing to the existing territorial distribution of property would not get them there. Their objections were not prompted by a conviction that the territorial principle was an inappropriate standard to use in the case of secession or dissolution. This was not the meaning behind Poska's ready willingness to pay *pro rata* for the Tsarist public debt. It was rather that their rejection of implementing an exclusively territorial solution committed them to something resembling the liquidation principle, requiring the apportionment of all public property, wherever located. The Estonian delegation took themselves to be facing a choice: they could either lay claim to a share in centralized financial assets (pension funds, gold reserves, and the like) along with a share of the sovereign debt, or, alternatively, they would be freed from the obligation to reimburse a fraction of the sovereign debt, but would, in this case, also have to relinquish their claim to a proportional share of all centralized financial assets. The data the delegation possessed indicated that Estonians' claims to central assets (in the form of deposits, bonds, and the like) exceeded the proportion of Czarist sovereign debt that would devolve on Estonia.[44] This was the consideration which motivated their – apparently puzzling – unwillingness to be released from joint debt obligations.

And if this was to be their position, some regard had to be paid to consistency. Only to a moderate degree, though. The Estonian side clearly never contemplated the scenario that the liquidation principle would ever be seriously

---

43 ERA.957.10.29, p. 33.
44 See Asutawa Kogu III istungjärk: protokollid nr. 98 – 119, Tallinn, Täht, 1920, column 278.

applied. Upon mentioning public buildings in Petrograd and Moscow, Poska asked: "How much do they cost?" It stretches credulity to believe that he meant this question to be taken literally, as an opening for a vast exercise in real estate assessment encompassing everything from universities in Estonia to the Trans-Siberian Railway. The Estonians' commitment to the liquidation principle was substantially interchangeable with the demand that *something* be given to them over and above what they already had. Once the other side's offer satisfied them, it became quite irrelevant what its legal basis was. It was enough to write into the Treaty that, notwithstanding the general territorial settlement, 'Russia grants to Esthonia fifteen million gold roubles' – not to mention the fact that this under-theorised solution harmonized perfectly with the Soviet interest to avoid setting any precedents which might tie its hands in negotiations with other successor States. Ioffe declared at one point that, although they might be willing to part with a portion of the gold in their possession, they would not recognise any Estonian right to it. "Either side will approach the matter according to its own conception", replied Piip. "We will view it as being within our rights, whereas you will approach it according to your own conception."[45] The plan, he said, was to "consider a series of concrete cases practically, without any reference to principles."[46]

However, in mid-December, the negotiators were still a long way from agreement on a lump sum payment. The Estonians were apparently of several minds about the advisability of leaving out principles and concentrating on piecemeal bargaining. The nature of the negotiating process forced them to develop a position which would go beyond a mere statement of demands. The border talks – which continued to run in parallel to the wrangling over gold – also did not take the form of a continual exchange of unjustified offers, along the lines of the tatonnement process described by economists. Both sides went out of their way to show that the border they proposed was reasonable, geographically, militarily, ethnically appropriate, and so on, as if the other side truly cared about such things. In reality, it was primarily a way to steer the talks clear of the ever-threatening danger of rupture. The language of 'reasonableness', pervasive throughout the two-month negotiating period, was not empty rhetoric. It was the oil that kept the wheels turning until the final signing of the Treaty. Similar considerations explain why, in the economic commission, the Estonians kept pushing on with dogged persistence with the idea that all public property must be taken into account in sharing the legacy of the Tsarist Empire, while simultaneously dropping hints that it was ultimately a question

---

45   ERA.957.10.41, p. 20.
46   ERA.957.10.41, p. 22.

not of legal principle but of what and how much they would get under the Treaty. Poska repeatedly noted that the lump sum covering all Estonian claims should not be 'arbitrary'.[47] He was resisting the Russian proposal to avoid any discussion of rights which might go into the calculation of the sum. On the face of it, this looks like the attitude of a man of principle who cares about legal correctness, even when the latter tips the balance in the end against the Estonian side. Yet he was happy to adopt the Russian approach when a compromise about the lump sum was finally reached in late January. There is no doubt that Poska was a master tactician with a singularly good feel for the art of the deal. Everything suggests that he was insisting on things being done by the book, as it were, with an eye to the prospect of extracting a much larger share of gold than was initially offered by the Russian side.

And so it happened that the liquidation principle was launched like a trial balloon into the discussion in the economic affairs commission where both sides were at pains to show how immensely beneficial its implications would be for them. The Russian members continued to remark on the disproportionate share of publicly-funded buildings and institutions situated in Estonia, such as the two universities which, they argued, represented far more than one percent of their total number in the Russian Empire. The Soviet expert Isidor Gukovsky contended that it was a well-known law of economics, mentioned in all textbooks, that the fringes of large States tended to become enriched at the expense of the centre. Conveniently oblivious to the Leninist line of branding the Tsarist policy of assimilation as a rape of nations, Gukovsky offered the policy of Russification as an example of such channelling of resources to the periphery. When the Estonians protested that Russification 'did not create cultural values', Gukovsky, ever the skilled tactician, countered that this was to introduce a criterion of valuation completely unrelated to the accrual of costs (and this latter principle was what the Estonians themselves were appealing to in speaking of their taxes being used, for example to erect buildings in the Russian capital). The Estonians also tried out other lines of argument. Ants Piip, who was to play the leading role among the Estonian delegation in the economic affairs commission, attempted to tweak the territorial principle to his side's advantage. He tentatively agreed that this should be the governing principle, but remarked that it did not necessitate the maintenance of the situation as it stood at the end of the war. Indeed, as Piip depicted it, the territorial principle even required the return of all evacuated property (factories, libraries, ships, and so on) which had belonged to the 'economic unit' that Estonia

---

47   ERA.957.10.41, p. 51.

now represented.[48] There was a double flexibility within the territorial principle that could be exploited. First, while possession was undoubtedly a pivotal criterion, it was not obvious which moment was decisive: was it *status quo post bellum* or *status quo ante bellum*? Secondly, an essential relationship to a given territory did not inevitably mean being situated in that territory at a given moment. Bluntschli, for example, had put land, people and their 'public needs' on a par as elements underlying the phenomenon of State succession. Piip portrayed the notion of 'economic unit' in the same light: the newly independent State of Estonia had not come into the possession of a random collection of moveable and immoveable things, but of an organic whole. The Russians would have none of this. Ioffe's response was that all parts of Russia had suffered from the war and lost property. Evaluating who had lost more was precisely the kind of debate they hoped to avoid with their proposal to refrain from all mutual claims.

This last point deserves attention. The Soviet defence of its no-mutual-claims position suggests that it might at times be misleading to speak of a territorial principle in the context of State succession. The Soviet line had very little to do with the idea, *à la* Bluntschli or Huber, that some categories of property have a special relationship with territory while others are endowed with a cross-border character which comes alive as a criterion of apportionment when a State breaks up into fragments (but not when it loses a province). There are admittedly good reasons to treat at least some types of property located in a territory as inseparable from the State that holds sovereignty over it. "The political inconvenience of having a foreign Government the owner of railways, etc.",[49] to use the words of one pre-war writer on State succession, would be among such reasons. By contrast, the Soviet position at the Tartu Peace Conference was only indirectly concerned with territory. Its rationale was analogous to that of the *uti possidetis* principle. The main argument was that disputes would have no end once any contestation of actual possession as it resulted from the war were to be allowed. To designate this *uti possidetis* stance as the territorial principle is justified to the extent that possession and territory very largely mapped onto one another, though not always in an unequivocal manner. There were territorially situated claims in the form of sovereign bonds held by the Estonian population. The Soviet delegation fought hard to have all such private claims also negated. Its position thus came to resemble strongly the conquest theory of succession described above. Yet they also explicitly rejected the link between title-conferring possession and the right of conquest.

---

48 ERA.957.10.41, p. 7.
49 Keith, *supra* note 27, p. 52.

There was a moment in the discussion when an Estonian expert stated – in response to Ioffe's remark that Russia had left to Estonia such public Tsarist property as naval ships – that the vessels in its possession were a prize of war. Ioffe was quick to jump on his young interlocutor's imprudent argument. "If you adopt the point of view of conquest, then you're welcome to conquer everything you demand."[50] He would expand on this riposte in a later session: "The Treaty we are signing does not rest on the principle of victory and defeat [...] If you insist on the principle of military loot, then don't demand what you haven't seized. One of two options: you either adopt a military or a legal point of view."[51]

Since it was unsure what the legal point of view required, and how the situation was to be legally characterized at all (the break-up of Russia or Estonia's secession from a State still in existence), private law analogies were invoked by both sides. In an early session one of the Estonian experts introduced what he described as a 'helpful metaphor': If a son leaves the family home with nothing but the clothes he is wearing and the family property is later divided – the Estonian expert asked – will it be said that he has already had his share in the form of what he possessed at the moment of departure? Ioffe, a seasoned Soviet diplomat who had come through the immeasurably tougher ordeal of the Brest-Litovsk peace talks two years earlier, was clearly delighted to play this simplistic game of metaphors. He said that the son might even have received too much if the family was numerous and had, say, only three expensive suits one of which had been put on the back of the departed son. The Estonians kept at it. They would continually return to a comparison with inheritance, although the latter was so ambiguous in its implications as to be no more favourable to themselves than to the Russians on its face. What exactly went into the estate that was supposedly being divided? The Estonians argued that it covered all former State patrimony. This, however, raised the earlier question, namely whether what they had within their territory was not already a fair share. It was more than a fair share, the Russians had insisted. Ioffe added – with regard to the Estonian claim of the need to compensate war-time loss of property – that inheritance could only comprise what actually exists at the time of division. This again offered a chance for the Estonians to advance their position by claiming that, indeed, patrimony in existence was what counted, but at the moment the estate was opened, not several years later. To press the point home, the Estonian delegates went on undiplomatically to describe a scenario where the heir solely in possession of the estate ruins it, to the damage

---

50   ERA.957.10.41, p. 14.
51   ERA.957.10.41, p. 48.

of other heirs. The Russians retorted that, if Estonia was incapable of taking possession of its share of the inheritance at the moment the Czarist patrimony became available for division, this was because it was a minor at the time and was therefore to bear the consequences for any damage that happened later.[52]

It is easy to see how this discussion could have rambled on. The Estonians could have argued that its having been a minor at the time of division was precisely the reason why their country should not bear the consequences of its co-heirs' actions, or that an independent State is never a minor, and so on. However, it is worth pausing to reflect on what the negotiators were doing by thus drawing out at length the analogy of State succession to inheritance. They were clearly not applying any municipal law of inheritance. No statute was cited. Perhaps it might be said that they were appealing to general principles at the basis of inheritance law. As we saw, this is how Hersch Lauterpacht perceived the role of private law analogies in international law. There was much talk of equity and justice in the commission on economic affairs. One reading could be that what the members of the commission were in effect doing was to articulate such ill-defined notions according to the deep structure shared by inheritance law and the law of State succession. Yet what principles did inheritance law yield them, other than a vague requirement of fair division? A better explanation appears to be that the analogy was helping the negotiations along on a much more detailed level. This may sound paradoxical because it is precisely at the level of detail that all private law analogies fail. Whilst the situation of a new unrecognised State may bear some resemblance to the legal status of a minor or the assets of a former State to the patrimony of a deceased person, no one believes that the analogy continues to make sense at the level of detailed rules. But in the context of negotiations, where analogies were continually being developed and turned around to undermine the side that first proposed them, the focus indeed quickly shifted from foundational principles *à la* Lauterpacht to much more concrete rules. For example, in the early sessions of the commission, the debate revolved mostly around the question whether the share of Tsarist property within territory held by Estonia was disproportionate compared to what was in the possession of the rest of former Russia. The introduction of the inheritance analogy prompted a reformulation of the main outstanding issues as being about the moment the estate was opened.[53] It seems incorrect to say that this change in vocabulary reflects an

---

52   ERA.957.10.41, p. 56.
53   The Estonian side contended it was when ties with Russia were ultimately cut by a declaration of sovereignty, *i.e.* in November 1917. Since the German front had only reached the larger Estonian islands by this time, a large part of what would soon be evacuated

agreement by the parties to apply inheritance law or draw on its underlying principles. Rather, they were carrying on the earlier discussion, which had been in danger of reaching a deadlock, by moving to new ground where negotiating positions had not yet been marked down and where concessions were thus easier to make.

4 Conclusion

The language of principles was pervasive at the Tartu Peace Conference. Yet this language was used in a way that tends to throw into doubt the idea that the area of State succession, or international law more generally, is governed by fundamental principles. At least, it raises questions about what can be meant by 'governed'. What I have tried to show was that legal principles proved inseparable from the process of negotiation. Even in the absence of any need for window-dressing for an outside audience, claims, however concrete, had to be justified *somehow* if they were not to appear as arbitrary or an expression of brute force. The use of the language of law was not an indication that the parties were seeking to conform to the rules of international law. There was simply no other language in which they could speak to each other without making the negotiating process overtly, and needlessly, conflictual. Hence what might be characterized as the pragmatic use of principles by both sides. Concrete demands and draft provisions were almost invariably presented as expressions of some general principle to which the other side could not refuse its assent. Both the Estonians and Russians employed the tactic of seeking first to obtain agreement on some abstract principle in order to manoeuvre the other side into accepting some if its demands in the name of consistency. When the language of principles had done its work, both sides were happy to abandon it and sign a document that was detached from all assumptions about the rules that governed their patrimonial relationships. The Tartu Peace Treaty is thus a good

---

eastward was still in Estonia, and could therefore be reclaimed under the inheritance analogy. The Tartu delegates finally arrived at a compromise which fixed the decisive date on 23 February 1918, a day before Estonia was declared an independent republic. The Tartu Peace Treaty accordingly provided that Russia surrendered, in addition to what was in Estonian territory at the moment of signing the Treaty, all rights held by the Russian State over the real or personal property of individuals formerly subject to it, and all her rights over vessels 'as far as such property [...] may have been situated there at the time of the German occupation, i.e., on February 23, 2018.' (Art. 11) The Estonian defence of the liquidation principle had borne fruit which was dressed up as a backdated application of the territorial principle.

example of how the rules of international law can be so overburdened with inconsistent justifications at the point of creation that they lose all justification at the level of principles.

Acknowledgements

The research for this paper has been funded by the European Union's Horizon 2020 research and innovation programme under the Marie Sklodowska-Curie grant agreement No 709386.

CHAPTER 2

On the Borders of Law, History and Politics: Estonian Statesman Jüri Jaakson's Views and Life in Context

Jaanika Erne

Abstract

Focusing on the life and work of the Estonian politician and Statesman Jüri Jaakson (1870–1942), the article gives an overview of the changing historical and social context that has influenced the formation of Estonian law. Estonia's historical diversity can be regarded as events of transformation and disruption that have resulted in vague concepts.

The article consists of three interrelated parts, taking into account that law and society are interconnected and that politics is constructed through language. The first part builds on Jüri Jaakson's presentation at the first Estonian Lawyers' Days in 1922, and shows how historical events have influenced political and legal conceptualisation. The second part shows how Jüri Jaakson's own biography tragically reflects the changing Estonian historical context that he himself considered diverse and controversial. Finally, in the third part, some normative assertions have been made in an attempt to show that any legal term always relates to a certain social and political context.

Although the author's aim has not been to frame a doctrine or provide instruction, but rather, with the help of Jüri Jaakson's thoughts situated in the context of his time, to offer a moral measure for understanding the developments that could influence small states, it offers a measure for understanding why societies require (new) conceptualisation and re-conceptualisation. Conceptualisation is understood as constructing something new that we cannot identify in the past, while reconceptualisation is understood as change, also resulting from discontinuity and/or interruption. Because there are no unchangeable social categories or meanings, continuity can at best mean a situation where the research objects have remained more static over a concrete period.

Methodologically this article is an attempt to connect legal research with a conceptual historical approach.

Keywords

autonomy of legal conceptualization – social and historical contexts – transformation of legal – political and linguistic structures

1 Introduction

Focusing on the life and public work of the Estonian politician and statesmen Jüri Jaakson (1870–1942), this article gives an overview of the changing historical and social context that has influenced the formation of Estonian law. Estonia's historical diversity can be regarded as events of transformation and disruption that have resulted in vague concepts.

The article consists of three interrelated parts, taking into account that law and society are interconnected and that politics is constructed through language. The first part builds on Jüri Jaakson's presentation at the first Estonian Lawyers' Days in 1922,[1] and shows how historical events have influenced political and legal conceptualisation. The second part shows how Jüri Jaakson's own biography tragically reflects the changing Estonian historical context that he himself considered diverse and controversial. Finally, in the third part, some normative assertions have been made in an attempt to show that any legal term always relates to a certain social and political context. My legal research has been directly influenced by all the major changes of paradigm, related, on the one hand, with internal developments, and, on the other hand, with international developments following the restoration of Estonian independence, including the transition from the Soviet legal system to Estonian law, and subsequent adaptation to European law.

The article also explains why continuity in conjunction with the principle of primacy of EU law would be necessary. According to the general principles of EU law, the terms used in EU law should be understood in accordance with the EU legislator's intention. However, it can sometimes be difficult to understand that intention due to the changing nature of politics that shapes the EU *acquis*. Due to constant change, society requires (new) conceptualisation or re-conceptualisation. Conceptualisation is understood in this article as constructing something new that we cannot identify in the past, while reconceptualisation is understood as change, also meaning discontinuity and/or interruption. Because there are no unchangeable social categories or meanings, continuity at best means a situation in which research objects have remained more static over a concrete period.[2]

Methodologically this article is an attempt to connect legal research with a conceptual historical approach.

---

1 Jüri Jaakson, 'Referaat. Meie tsiviilõiguste puudustest ja nende puuduste kõrvaldamisest. Esimene Õigusteadlaste päev Tartus 19. ja 20. aprillil 1922.a.', [*Protokollid*] // *Õigus* , (1922–7) pp. 193–208.
2 *See* Tiiu Jaago, 'Discontinuity and Continuity in Representations of 20th Century Estonian History' 6 *Culture Unbound* (2014) pp. 1071–94.

This article is devoted to those people who search for a balance between science, politics and law. The author's aim has not been to frame a doctrine or provide instruction, but Jüri Jaakson's thoughts, situated in the context of his time, could rather offer a moral measure for understanding the developments that could influence small states.

2 Jüri Jaakson's Views on the Conceptualisation of Estonian Law Prior to the Formal Statehood Period

Jüri Jaakson (1870–1942), University of Tartu alumnus, member of the 'Ühendus' student corporation, lawyer and politician, and Estonian *Riigivanem* (Head of State) from 16 December 1924 to 15 December 1925, named Estonia's linguistic and political development – which began long before the period of formal statehood in 1918 – very diverse ("motley").[3] It can be inferred from Jüri Jaakson's presentation in 1922[4] that when defining Estonian political history, he was influenced by foreign regimes' governance of Estonian territory, each of which influenced the formation of Estonian law and shaped Estonia's legal understandings and conceptualisations. New eras, and new governors and harmonisers added new layers to the Estonian legal language, which sometimes resulted in contradictions because of the different legal systems involved.[5]

Jüri Jaakson explained historical influences on Estonian law by describing different governing regimes as they occurred from the 12th century: when the Germans brought German legal concepts to Estonian territory the concepts developed differently in Estonia according to different models of governance. For example there were two independent legal systems in 13th-century Estonia, one in cities (*Stadtrecht*) and the other in the countryside (*Ritter-* and *Landrecht*). Because of their more advanced economic development the cities, especially Riga and Tallinn, were politically independent with their own governors and jurisdiction. Riga and Tallinn both belonged to the Hanseatic League and played important roles in trade relations between Western and Eastern Europe.[6] Riga borrowed its laws from the city of Hamburg, leading to other

---

[3] I first used the word 'motley' when translating Jaakson's Estonian-language metaphor *kirju* for an article published in 2010, introducing similar problems from a different angle: Jaanika Erne, 'Political and Legal Problems Related to Estonian Private Law Reforms Prior to the Formal Statehood Period and during the Early Formal Statehood Period' 4 *Nordic Journal of International Law* (2010) pp. 543–562.
[4] *Supra* note 1, Jaakson.
[5] *Ibid.*
[6] *Ibid.*

Livonian cities adopting this Riga-Hamburg law. Tallinn borrowed its laws from the city of Lübeck, and other Estonian cities borrowed their laws from Tallinn.[7] But while the cities at that time were politically independent, with their own governors, the Estonian countryside was governed by the Livonian Order and the bishops, and by vassals who had received their land from the Order and the bishops. There was a constant struggle between the vassals, on the one hand, and the Order and the bishops, on the other hand, concerning the territorial applicability of laws in the Estonian countryside.[8] At the same time, laws in the Livonian and Estonian cities differed because of their different belonging to Livonia and Estonia before the formation of the Livonian Confederation. In 1561, Livonia (the Baltic provinces) lost its independence to Sweden, and thereafter to other foreign states.

Surrendering to foreign countries, the local governors (in both countryside and cities) wished to maintain all their rights and privileges.[9] But the new governors were neither able nor willing to allow this because of evolving economic and political life, which required the advancement of laws rather than stagnation. In addition, the new governors had from the beginning looked for ways to connect the surrendering provinces with their states and to spread their legal order in the provinces.[10] For these reasons, the legal order of the governing states greatly influenced the development of Estonian law. Since the Estonian areas lacked their own legislative power, all laws for those areas were adopted by the legislative powers of the governing states which, as a rule, were not aware of Estonian law. Consequently, every new law adopted in Estonian territory carried with it the influence of the governing state. In this context the influence of Swedish law was most significant, especially in rural areas. The cities, for example the leading cities of Riga and Tallinn, remained connected with Hamburg and Lübeck during the period of Swedish governance, so they were better able to resist the influence of Swedish law and continued to independently develop their own laws where possible.[11] For example, Tallinn recodified Lübeck law during the Swedish era. In addition, Russian law had a great influence on Estonian laws, although not on Estonian civil law. Similarly when Estonia was governed by Poland for a short period, Estonian laws were influenced by Polish law.[12]

---

7   *Ibid.*
8   *Ibid.*
9   *Ibid.*
10 *Ibid.*
11 *Ibid.*
12 *Ibid.*

Roman law has significantly influenced the development of Estonian civil law. Estonia received Roman law in the 16th and 17th centuries, thus much later than Western Europe. Despite the period of Swedish rule in Estonia, Roman law was received following the German method.[13] The main reasons for the reception of Roman law in Western Europe were the insufficiency and fragmentary nature of local laws.[14] These were also the main reasons in Estonia, where the failure of local laws to keep up with rapid economic development, and the fact that each province had its own laws, presented major obstacles to the emerging international trade. Roman law was adopted both in an attempt to assist in remedying these shortcomings,[15] and because it was hoped that adoption of Roman law would stop the intrusion of Swedish law.[16] Estonian governors felt a closer spiritual connection with Germany and so wanted Roman law to displace Swedish law because Roman law came from Germany.[17]

It can be inferred from the foregoing that there were two mainstreams in Estonian civil law prior to the formal statehood period – one influenced by German law and one by Roman law. While German law mainly influenced family law, with both Roman and German law influencing the right of succession, Roman law influenced property law and the law of obligations. According to Jaakson, the effect of Swedish and Russian law was felt on only a few legal institutions.[18]

During the reign of Emperor Nicholas I, Count Speransky was entrusted with the task of organising Russian laws, which led to the question of redrafting Baltic laws.[19] Speransky delegated this work to Reinhold von Samson-Himmelstierna, an Estonian lawyer and Livonian District Magistrate. Speransky had completely abandoned the idea of working out a new code when arranging Russian laws. Rather, he was committed to collecting and systematising only existing laws.[20] Similarly, Samson-Himmelstierna had guidelines to collect and systematise only existing laws when systematising Baltic laws.[21] He was neither allowed to leave any valid laws out, nor to add any law that was not valid.[22] These guidelines also fully corresponded to the will of the governors of

---

13 Ibid.
14 Ibid.
15 Ibid.
16 Ibid., p. 197.
17 Ibid.
18 Ibid.
19 Ibid.
20 Ibid.
21 Ibid.
22 Ibid.

both the Estonian countryside and cities. Being concerned that something could disappear from their rights and privileges, they demanded that nothing should be excluded from, nor added to, valid laws. Samson-Himmelstierna composed three draft laws on the basis of Estonian law – the Baltic Institutions, the Baltic Classes, and the Baltic Civil Law. The first two of these drafts were confirmed by Nicholas I, Emperor of Russia, in 1845, and entered into force a year later, while the third draft, the Baltic Civil Law, was not confirmed.[23]

In 1856, the Russian governors tasked Friedrich Georg von Bunge, a former Professor at the University of Tartu's faculty of law, with finishing Samson-Himmelstierna's work on the codification of Baltic civil law and the composition of the new draft Baltic Civil Law. The sources that were made available to Bunge consisted of the work done within the area so far, including Samson-Himmelstierna's project with comments by revisers. Similarly to Samson-Himmelstierna, Bunge received guidelines stipulating inclusion of only valid laws without changes. Bunge used many textbooks, especially Roman law textbooks. Professor A. Nolde later established that Bunge had literally copied a great amount of Baltic civil law from Roman law textbooks written by Mühlenbruch, Glück, Mackeldey, Unterholzner and other authors. According to Jaakson, Bunge had aimed to avoid useless changes of legal terms and constructions from these textbooks because he considered them authoritative.[24]

In addition to Roman law textbooks, Bunge used textbooks on German law, and his own textbooks on Baltic law, Samson-Himmelstierna's draft, the Prussian *Allgemeines Landrecht* of 1794, the Austrian Civil Code of 1811, and the Saxon draft Civil Code (*Entwurf eines bürgerlichen Gesetzbuches für das Königreich Sahen*) published in 1860.[25]

Bunge's draft was revised by judges and other lawyers in various Baltic cities, including Professors Melkov and Rummel from Tartu.[26] The revisers of Bunge's draft also followed guidelines stipulating inclusion of valid law without any changes. Diversity and lack of consistency were among the most common shortcomings of the Baltic Civil Law.[27] However, those who revised Bunge's work managed to make the best of these shortcomings.

The draft, which was composed by Bunge in German, was later translated into Russian by academic Bytschkov under Baron von Korf's supervision, was

---

23   Ibid.
24   Ibid.
25   Ibid.
26   Ibid.
27   Ibid.

adopted by Imperial decree of 12 November 1864, and entered into force as a new law on 1 July 1865.[28]

Bunge had been instructed to use the Russian civil law system when preparing the draft in an attempt to create a certain degree of consistency between Russian and local laws. The latter, according to Speransky's guidelines, could only include Russian laws if they were based solely on local peculiarities. As the Russian civil law system was deficient, Bunge did not carefully follow these instructions; rather, he followed the guidelines that he felt were applicable to him.[29]

Jüri Jaakson explains these historical processes as a particularity. Although particularity is also characteristic of other states, in Jaakson's opinion, legal pluralism most characterized Estonia.[30] The reader of this article may agree or disagree, having now an overview of the historical development of different legal systems on Estonian territory in the form of country law, and city law, and the differences between them in Livonia and Estonia. Jaakson also shows how everyone who participated in codifying the draft civil law tried to accurately include the smallest local legal peculiarities. However, these codifiers and revisers did not understand that the territory's civil law and its uniformity were suffering because of such concentration on detail. This situation was made even worse by the fact that apart from Baltic Civil Law, Estonian and Livonian peasants' rights, as well as the Russian Civil Law and Russian peasants' rights, were valid at Petserimaa and east of Narva. The borders of individual territorial areas were unclear during the medieval era, and became even more confused during the period of formal statehood.

The February Bourgeois Democratic Revolution, the first revolution in 1917 in Russia, brought major changes not only to political life but also to bourgeois life in general. The principles upon which the entire social system was based, and which had been purposefully codified in Russian laws (on which the Estonian legal system essentially depended), were set aside and replaced by new principles that often contradicted the previous ones.[31] The February Revolution demanded legal reconceptualisation from Estonian lawyers. Even more crucial was the period after the Great October Socialist Revolution, accompanied by the birth of each of the three Baltic States, whose new treaties and secondary legislation contained new legal norms. On the one hand, laws in the Baltic States were reformulated because of Russia's revolutionary changes,

---

28   *Ibid.*
29   *Ibid.*
30   *Ibid.* For discussion, *see for example* Jan Klabbers/Toukko Piiparinen (eds.), *Normative Pluralism: An Exploration* (Cambridge: Cambridge University Press, 2013).
31   *Supra* note 1 Jaakson.

which meant that they could no longer base laws on 'old' Russian law; while on the other hand, new norms were created for the new-born states.

One can conclude that new eras and new rulers added new norms to Estonian laws, resulting in plurality, fragmentation and incoherence in those laws. Because of the differences, any harmonisation of these laws was not an easy task. Jaakson explains that, when drafting the new Baltic Civil Code, Bunge had tried to unify different regulations from the various legal institutions and to remove possibly conflicting provisions. Often, unification of German and Roman laws in this way was impossible.[32]

3 Jüri Jaakson's Life in the Context of the Estonian Formal Statehood Period

Jüri Jaakson's life recalls Estonian history, which Jaakson himself called diverse and contradictory. In the following, I have tried to situate Jüri Jaakson's biography into the general context of his time.

Born on 16 January 1870, Jüri Jaakson graduated from the University of Tartu in 1896 with a first class diploma.[33] From 1897 to 1901, Jaakson worked as an assistant attorney in Viljandi, then from 1901 to 1902 as an assistant attorney and from 1902 to 1914 as a sworn advocate in Riga. From 1902 to 1905, he was chairman of the board of the Estonian Society at Riga 'Imanta', from 1904 to 1920 a member of the board of governors and chairman of the Estonian Alexandr School, and from 1906 to 1914 the founder and chairman of the board of the Estonian education and assistance society (*Eesti Hariduse ja Abiandmise Selts*) in Riga.[34] When World War I began in 1914 and military activity spread to Latvian territory, Jüri Jaakson came from Riga to Estonia, married Olga Vilhelmine Behrens in May 1915, and worked from 1915 to 1918 as a board member and assistant director of Tallinn City Bank.[35]

After the 1917 February Revolution, the Russian Provisional Government replaced the Estonian governors with new regional commissars (*guberniya* commissars).[36] While Estonian territory in the Russian tsarist state had been divided between two administrative regions, Estonia and Livonia, after the

---

32   Ibid.
33   Richard Kleis (ed.), *Eesti avalikud tegelased: eluloolisi andmeid* (Tartu: Eesti Kirjanduse Selts, 1932) p. 60.
34   Ibid.
35   Ibid.
36   In turn, the October Revolution turned the subdivisions into *guberniya soviets* (губернский совет). See also Seppo Zetterberg, *Viron historia* (Helsinki: Suomalaisen Kirjallisuuden Seura, 2007).

overthrow of tsarist governance the two regions were merged and established as an autonomous administrative unit. In the spring of 1917, Jüri Jaakson participated in drafting the law on the provisional local authority and administration of the governorate of Estonia (which was later adopted through the Russian provisional government's decree on the Estonian provisional authority) and a resolution of 5 July 1917 for its implementation.

On 5 March 1917, Jaan Poska was appointed as the representative of the Russian provisional government in the governorate of Estonia. In response to claims for Estonian national autonomy, the Russian provisional government adopted a decree on administration of an Estonian province (*guberniya* and the provisional organisation of self-government: '*Eestimaa kubermangu omavalitsuse ja administratsiooni ajutise korraldamise seadus*')[37] on 30 March 1917, allowing provisional autonomy until 1919, and merging the Estonian governorate and the northern part of the governorate of Livonia into a new joint administrative unit of Estonia. Regional commissar Jaan Poska's powers were extended over the entire new Governorate of Estonia, and the *Maapäev* (the Estonian Provincial Assembly) was established as the highest body of the governorate with members elected by universal suffrage.[38] Although power was conferred on the *Maapäev* to arrange all local administrative matters through acts, these acts had to correspond to Russian law and other hierarchically higher acts.[39] From 1917 to 1918, Jüri Jaakson was assistant to Jaan Poska,[40] the Estonian regional commissar of Russia's then provisional government;[41] from 1917 to 1919 he was a member of the Estonian Provincial Assembly, and from 1917 to 1918 the first assistant chairman of the Estonian Provincial Assembly.[42] Estonian politicians at that time solved important national questions and strategic problems,[43] such as claiming Estonian national autonomy in 1917, and the 1918

---

37 Jaak Pihlak, 'Viljandi kihelkond ja Vabaduse Risti vennad'. *Viljandi Muuseumi aastaraamat* 1998 at http://muuseum.viljandimaa.ee/?op=body&id=227 (12.4.2016) pp. 156–265, 181.
38 *Supra* note 36 Zetterberg.
39 See Artur-Tõeleid Kliimann, Õiguskord [Legal Order], (Tartu: Akadeemilise Korporatsiooni Kirjastus, 1939).
40 *Supra* note 33 Kleis p. 60.
41 *Supra* note 36 Zetterberg.
42 *Ibid.*
43 The role of the Baltic States in foreign policy has been disputable – have these states done anything or can they rather be viewed as passive objects in history and geopolitics, caught between the Great Powers? See Magnus Ilmjärv, *Hääletu alistumine* (Tallinn: Argo, 2010).

decision to declare Estonian independence for fear of the Bolsheviks, at a time when Germany was occupying Estonia.[44]

Estonians had wished for more than just limited autonomy[45] and this wish had created tension within society. The Estonian Knighthood (*Eestimaa rüütelkond*[46]) called the provisional government's decisions invalid because they had not been approved either by the Knighthood's provincial assembly or by the Russian State Duma, and allegedly contradicted the 1721 Uusikaupunki Peace Treaty.[47] On 9 October 1917, the Petrograd Soviet Executive Committee appointed the Military Revolutionary Committee to organise and direct the transfer of power to the Bolsheviks in Petrograd on 25 October 1917. Following the example of Petrograd, the Estonian Military Revolutionary Committee was established in Tallinn on 22 October 1917 under the joint leadership of Ivan Rabtšinski and Viktor Kingissepp. In October 1917, the Bolsheviks achieved a majority in the Soviet-led Estonian Congress in Tallinn, ending the powers of the Russian provisional government and its regional commissar Jaan Poska. Power in Estonia was transferred to the Bolsheviks in the representation of Jaan Anvelt and Viktor Kingissepp. Jaan Anvelt was elected as Chairman of the Soviet Executive Committee. At the same time, the Estonian Provincial Assembly continued its existence, and adopted the 'decision on supreme power' on 15 (28) November 1917,[48] which constitutionalised a new legal framework. The Estonian Provincial Assembly's activities were suspended by the Bolsheviks.

In December 1917, the Estonian Knighthood declared Estonia's separation from Soviet Russia and declared itself the supreme local authority; the Livonian Knighthood did the same a few weeks later. At the end of January 1918, an authorised representative of the Livonian Knighthood forwarded the declarations of independence of the Estonian and Livonian Knighthoods to the representative of Soviet Russia in Stockholm, which prompted the Bolsheviks to arrest them and deport them to Russia. The Bolsheviks also arrested Estonian politicians,[49] among whom Jüri Jaakson was imprisoned in January 1918.[50]

---

44   Some other examples: turning to Russia for assistance against Germanisation, or expecting military support from Germany after the Soviet attack in 1939. *See supra* note 36, Zetterberg.
45   *Supra* note 36, Zetterberg.
46   EAA (*Eesti Ajalooarhiiv*, Estonian History Archive), p. 854.
47   *Supra* note 36, Zetterberg.
48   Maanõukogu 28. novembri 1917.a otsus kõrgeimast võimust. – *Maanõukogu protokollid 1917–1919* (Tallinn, 1935).
49   *Supra* note 36, Zetterberg.
50   *Ibid*.

It was feared that, if governed by the Bolsheviks, Estonia would fall under Russian rule, although at the same time it was feared that Estonia would be absorbed into Germany. These fears resulted in the decision by the Elders of the Estonian Provincial Assembly to declare Estonian independence at a time when German troops were expected to occupy Estonia.

On 24 February 1918, the Manifesto to the Peoples of Estonia (the Estonian Declaration of Independence)[51] was issued in Tallinn, proclaiming an independent and democratic Republic of Estonia, under the leadership of the Estonian provisional government headed by Konstantin Päts, while Jüri Vilms became Estonia's first deputy prime minister and Jaan Poska was appointed Estonia's minister of foreign affairs.

On 25 February 1918, the invading Germans took over all power in Tallinn, ending Bolshevik activities. According to the Brest-Litovsk Treaty, signed on 3 March 1918, Soviet Russia formally gave Estonia over to the German military administration. However, Germany did not recognise Estonian independence and the Estonian provisional government went underground, where it communicated with the Western powers. Great Britain recognized Estonian independence (*de facto*) on 3 May 1918, France on 18 May 1918, and Italy on 29 May 1918. After the weakening of the German military position in autumn 1918 and the armistice of 11 November 1918, the Estonian provisional government regained power under Jaan Poska's leadership, and on 13 November 1918 representatives of the German government ceded power to representatives of the Estonian government. Latvia proclaimed independence on 18 November 1918 and the following day an agreement to transfer power on Estonian territory was concluded between the representative of the German government, August Winnig, and the Latvian provisional government in Riga. This agreement legally meant *de facto* recognition of Estonian independence by Germany. In December 1918, Germany formally handed over power to the Latvian Government.

The Estonian provisional government convened the Estonian Provincial Assembly in order to prepare sessions of the Estonian Constituent Assembly, which was engaged in drafting the Estonian constitution. The Estonian Provincial Assembly began its activity on 20 November 1918, and delegated its power to the provisional government. Jüri Jaakson was the general commissioner of the provisional government in 1918, tasked with taking over government agencies from the German occupying powers.[52]

---

51 Maapäeva Vanemate Nõukogu 24. veebruari 1918.a manifest. – RT (*Riigi Teataja*, The State Gazette) 1918, 1.
52 *Supra* note 36, Zetterberg.

Between 1918 and 1920, Jüri Jaakson worked as the Minister of Justice (*kohtuminister*) for the provisional government in Otto Strandman and Jaan Tõnisson's cabinets.[53] At that time, in November 1918, the Red Army began an attack against Estonia. On 15 November 1918, some Estonians formed the Estonian Provisional Revolutionary Committee in Petrograd, declaring the Estonian Socialist Soviet Republic on 29 November. Together with the Russian Council of People's Commissars they recognised the Commune of the Working People of Estonia (*Eesti Töörahva Kommuun*), which ended its activities in 1919. At the beginning of April 1919, elections to the constituent assembly took place, and a commission on constitutional affairs was formed. On 4 June 1919, the constituent assembly adopted the provisional order of governance of Estonia (*Eesti Vabariigi valitsemise ajutine kord*). On 15 June 1920 the Estonian constitution was adopted, entering into force on 21 December 1920, the day on which the provisional order of governance of Estonia and the powers of the Constituent Assembly came to an end. (Jaakson was a member of the Constituent Assembly in 1919–1920). On 2 February 1920, peace negotiations between Estonia and Russia resulted in the Peace Treaty of Tartu, by which Russia *de jure* recognised Estonian independence and forever abandoned its rights to Estonian territory. This was followed on 12 July 1920 by the peace treaty between Russia and Lithuania,[54] and on 11 August 1920, by the Treaty of Riga, between Russia and Latvia.[55]

In the years between 1920 and 1926, Jüri Jaakson was a member of the II and III *Riigikogu* (Estonian parliament). In December 1924, the Communists attempted to seize power in Tallinn. The *Riigikogu* appointed a government consisting of farmers, the Labour Party, social democrats, the People's Party and the Christian People's Party: almost all that time Estonian political parties were represented, divided into rightist, leftist and centrist, and some parties had been formed in 1917.[56] Jüri Jaakson was a member of the Estonian People's Party, headed by Jaan Tõnisson, which represented intellectuals, the bourgeoisie, and peasants[57] and had been formed in 1905.[58] Jüri Jaakson was a People's Party politician and Elder of State[59] in 1924–1925, during which time the government acted uniformly in questions of internal politics,[60] with national

---

53   *Supra* note 33, Kleis, p. 60.
54   League of Nations (LN) Treaty Series, Vol. III, pp. 105–137.
55   LN Treaty Series, Vol. II, pp. 195–231.
56   *Supra* note 36, Zetterberg, *supra* note 3, Erne.
57   *Supra* note 33, Kleis 60.
58   *Supra* note 36, Zetterberg.
59   *Supra* note 33, Kleis 60.
60   *Supra* note 36, Zetterberg.

defence, restoration of the National Defence League, creation of a military-political Baltic Union, and patriotic education as priorities. In response to an attempted *coup d'état* by the Soviet Union and the Communist International (the Third International, Comintern), and the attempted formation of the Soviet Government of Estonia, which could have turned to the Red Army for assistance, the government declared a state of war and convened a war tribunal, which passed 155 death sentences.

In 1921, Estonia became a member of the League of Nations, with Jüri Jaakson representing the country between 1929 and 1936 at meetings of the League's financial committee in Geneva. Between 1926 and 1940, Jaakson acted as President of the Bank of Estonia.[61]

During approximately the same period, 1931–1937, Jaakson emphasised Estonian independence by participation in international banking meetings.[62] In 1936, he established an endowment of 20,000 Kroons to the Hugo Treffner Gymnasium.[63] He acted as a member of the 1937 II chamber of the Estonian National Assembly. Between 1935 and 1938 he was a member of the National Economic Council,[64] and between 1938 and 1940 of the *Riigikogu's* National Council (*Riiginõukogu*). Finally, between 1920 and 1932 Jaakson was a member of the I–IV *Riigikogu*.[65]

At that time Estonian security policy was built on territorial alliances and belief in the League of Nations as the collective guarantor of global peace.[66] Since the first two did not materialise, and the League of Nations turned out to be rather a weak bystander, Estonia based its foreign policy on neutrality. As the Soviet Union was considered the main threat to Estonian security, there was growth in support for Germany, from where military assistance was expected in the case of a Soviet attack.

On the other hand, on 28 March 1939 the Russian Council of People's Commissar of Foreign Affairs, Maksim Litvinov, responded to increasing German influence with a note to the Estonian envoy to the Soviet Union, August Rei, reminding him of the Tartu Peace Treaty and the non-aggression pact of 1932, and with the announcement that the Soviet Union would not remain passive if a third party tried to destroy Estonian or Latvian independence. Russia was

---

61 *Ibid.*
62 Peeter Tarvel/Hans Kruus/Jaan Olvet (eds.), *Eesti biograafilise leksikoni täienduskõide* (Tartu, Tallinn: Loodus, 1940) p. 102.
63 *Ibid.*
64 *Ibid.*
65 *Supra* note 33, Kleis, p. 60.
66 *Supra* note 36, Zetterberg.

ready to demonstrate this by bringing the Red Army to the Baltics.[67] The note was taken as a warning to Germany.[68] The Estonian and Latvian foreign ministers signed a non-aggression treaty with Germany on 7 July 1939 within the framework of their neutrality policy. On 23 August 1939, Germany and the Soviet Union concluded the non-aggression treaty known as the Molotov-Ribbentrop Pact, which included an additional secret protocol that assigned Estonia to the Soviet Union's sphere of influence.[69]

Nine months into World War II, on 17 June 1940, Red Army troops entered Estonia and a new government was formed under the control of a representative of the Soviet Union.[70] On the same day, Jüri Jaakson was released from the office of President of the Bank of Estonia.[71] On 21 July 1940, the name of the country was changed from Estonia to the Estonian Soviet Socialist Republic, and the government asked that Estonia become part of the Soviet Union; land was confiscated, large-scale industry was nationalised, a new constitution was drafted, and the President removed from office. The government remained in office until 25 August 1940, when the *Riigivolikogu* (parliamentary body), which had been transformed into the provisional Supreme Soviet of Soviet Estonia, drafted a constitution for Estonia that was a copy of the Soviet Union's constitution.[72] In March 1941, Jüri Jaakson's wife and daughter were resettled in Germany (*Nachumsiedlung*),[73] while Jaakson stayed in Estonia. When the purging of 'public enemies' began in Estonia in June 1941,[74] Jaakson was arrested by the NKVD (the People's Commissariat for Internal Affairs) and deported to Russia, where he was tried for the war tribunal – accused of having set up a war tribunal under his leadership as an Elder of State – which had executed 155 people. He was sentenced to death and executed by firing squad in Sverdlovsk Oblast in 1942.[75]

With the exception of August Rei, who escaped to Sweden in 1940, and Otto Strandman, who allegedly shot himself dead on 5 February 1941 when the NKVD came to arrest him, all other Estonian heads of state were arrested and executed in Tallinn or deported to Soviet prison camps where they died or

---

67   *Ibid.*
68   *Ibid.*
69   *Ibid.*
70   *Ibid.*
71   *Supra* note 37, Pihlak, p. 181.
72   *Supra* note 36, Zetterberg.
73   *Supra* note 37, Pihlak, p. 181.
74   *Supra* note 36, Zetterberg.
75   *Ibid.* See also, *supra* note 37, Pihlak, p. 182.

were executed.[76] The German occupation that began in 1941 was unable to change anything for these people.

4 Conclusions with Regard to Estonia's International and Transnational Participation

This article was an attempt to show why contextualisation could be useful for understanding and explaining Estonian legal developments. The article recalled those moments in Estonian history where external influence resulted in legal diversity and in fragmentation of Estonia's internal developments. The article began with the (re)conceptualisations that came with external influence on Estonian legislative developments prior to the formal statehood period, and indicated the diverse origins and contents of the laws that affected Estonian territory. Thereafter, the article analysed legislative developments in the context of the formal statehood period from 1918 to World War II.

The problems relating to meaning and to the (re)conceptualisation of laws that were shown in the article have not disappeared, but are still extant in the context of changes related to the restoration of Estonian independence in 1991, accompanied by several other factors: the transition from Soviet to Estonian law; the later accession of Estonia to the European Union; Estonia's membership in other international organisations; and Estonia's participation in other forms of international and transnational cooperation.

I hope that the article is an effective, although sad, example of normative contexts that frame positivist developments.

---

76   *Supra* note 36, Zetterberg.

CHAPTER 3

One Hundred Years of Faith: The Baltic States' Contribution to International Justice

Rytis Satkauskas

Abstract

One hundred years on from the establishment of the first World Court provides an excellent occasion to assess the evolution of International Justice and its role in setting new standards of inter-State behaviour. Faith in the rule of law and international justice in the institutionalised world order by Lithuania, Latvia and Estonia was based on the public mood in the aftermath of the First World War, as well as distinctly practical security interests. Early acceptance of the Court's jurisdiction in turn contributed to the formation of international law with three cases and interpretation by the Court of numerous rules of international law.

Keywords

interpretation – compulsory jurisdiction – Poland – dispute – Wilna – Lithuania – Permanent Court – International Justice – Legacy – Statute of the Memel Territory case – autonomy – sovereignty – diplomatic protection – Railway Traffic case – Railway Panevezys-Saldutiskis

1   Introduction

Call it experiment and failure, or call it necessity, hope for the future: one hundred years ago, the League of Nations was created. Conceived in Versailles,[1] just like the three Baltic States, it took its shape in the form of a Covenant signed on 28 June 1919. The preamble of the Covenant referred to international law as the actual rule of conduct among governments, and to the maintenance of justice "in the dealings of organised peoples with one another".

---

1   On the debate *see* S. Sarè, *The League of Nations and the debate on disarmament (1918–1919)*, Edizioni Nuova Cultura, 2013, pp. 37–75.

As Howard Ellis noted in 1929, "There was very little new in the League, although the League was new"; it was an attempt by the powers to seek peace and ensure it.[2] The League was not designed, however, to replace the sovereignty of its members; it did not become an international government to secure implementation of the rules of international coexistence by means of coercion. It was understood that if coercion were the sole guarantee of implementing a norm of conduct, that norm would lose its meaning. "If the nations of the future are in the main selfish, grasping and warlike, no instrument or machinery will restrain them", stressed the British Foreign Office commentary to the Covenant of the League, "It is only possible to establish an organisation which may make peaceful cooperation easy and hence customary, and to trust in the influence of custom to mould opinion". The Permanent Court of International Justice (PCIJ), established in accordance with Article 14 of the Covenant, became an inseparable part of the new world order. Even though the Statute of the Court did not provide for its compulsory jurisdiction in any dispute between States, it encouraged the world community to extend it gradually by accepting the optional clause to the Statute.

The Second Assembly of the League admitted Estonia, Latvia and Lithuania as members on 22 September 1921. By that time, the Statute of the PCIJ had been ratified by a sufficient number of States to bring it into force and the Court held its inaugural meeting on 30 January 1922. All three Baltic States had signed the Statute of the Court by this date: Lithuania (5 October 1921), Estonia (18 October 1921) and Latvia (21 January 1922).

The three Baltic States remained faithful supporters of the World Court until its final days and their own occupation. Official correspondence and government deliberations reveal a strong realisation that there was no other option but to follow the ideas of the rule of law and peaceful settlement of disputes in international relations. International justice provided at least titular security guarantees for the young nations.

This faith on the part of the Baltic governments to rely on international justice was rewarded by the outcomes of three cases, successfully settling issues related to the general political conditions of the time. As often happens in a neighbourhood, one of the cases against Lithuania was brought by the Estonian government while Latvian interests were involved in two of these cases.

In its advisory opinion in *Railway traffic between Lithuania and Poland*, the Court refused to legitimise factual Polish control of Vilnius by affirming that there was no international obligation upon Lithuania to open railway traffic

---

2   C. Howard-Ellis, *The Origin, Structure & Working of the League of Nations*. Boston, Houghton Mifflin Company, 1929, reprinted 2003 by The Lawbook Exchange, p. 68.

with the occupied part of its territory and even if there was one, Lithuania would be entitled not to apply it in the case of an emergency affecting its vital interests.

Similarly, considering the *Interpretation of the Statute of the Memel Territory* case, the Court accepted the argument that Lithuania was to enjoy full sovereignty over the Memel territory ceded to it by the Allied Powers. The autonomy of Memel was only to operate within the limits fixed and expressly specified. The Court found it difficult to accept the submission of the four complaining powers that the Lithuanian Government should be left with no protection against a violation of the statute of the autonomous territory by its governing bodies.

Finally, in the *Panevėžys-Saldutiškis railway* case, the Court found that the Lithuanian preliminary objection regarding non-exhaustion of the remedies afforded by municipal law was well founded and declined to entertain the Estonian claim concerning property rights to former Tsarist property in Lithuanian territory.

The three Baltic cases at the PCIJ, all of them relating to different aspects of the territorial rearrangements following the First World War, provide valuable material for both historical examination of international relations in Europe and legal analysis of the Court's judgments.

The Permanent Court of the League of Nations was resurrected in 1946, in the form of the International Court of Justice (ICJ), the principal judicial body of the United Nations. It took much longer for Lithuania, Latvia and Estonia to reappear on the international stage, in the triumph of international law against brute force and injustice. Despite waves of hostility against international adjudication,[3] the three Baltic States remain determined to settle their future disputes in the Court. Just recently, on 30 November 2017, Latvia's Parliament adopted a law recognising the compulsory jurisdiction of the ICJ,[4] joining 72 other countries, among them 23 EU members, including Estonia and Lithuania, in recognising the Court's jurisdiction to handle their disputes.

The Court's jurisprudence is undoubtedly of major significance for the development of the theory and practice of peaceful dispute settlement between States; at the same time it has contributed extensively to the formation and development of international law. By 1946, it became difficult to compile a statement of the application of international law to given facts without some

---

[3] *See e.g.* A. Giustini, 'Compulsory Adjudication in International Law: The Past, The Present, and Prospects for the Future', *Fordham International Law Journal*, Vol. 9, Issue 2, 1985, pp. 213–256.
[4] No 2017/252.2, 'Latvijas Vēstnesis', 252 (6079), 19 December 2017. The declaration deposited to the United Nations on 24 September 2019 https://www.icj-cij.org/en/declarations/lv.

recourse to the case law of the PCIJ and parallel inter-State arbitrations. The Court itself began the practice of citing its earlier decisions whenever relevant, thus contributing to the development of consistency and stability in judicial decisions.

This article aims to reinstate the importance of the decision by the Baltic States to recognise the compulsory jurisdiction of the first permanent international tribunal. Firstly, it recalls doubts and reflections from the time when international justice was more an aspiration than reality, the faith of the Baltic governments in Wilson's ideals and their determination to rely on international law. Second, it provides an overview of the international norms applied by the Court and their role in the formation of international law.

2   The World Court

> What we seek is the reign of law,
> based upon the consent of the governed,
> and sustained by the organized opinion of mankind.
>   WOODROW WILSON

In the aftermath of WWI a new world institutional order was to be constituted by the Allied powers to ensure global peace and security, to change once and for all the nature of relations among sovereign nations and guarantee the equal participation of the members of the international community in deciding global issues. The main role for ensuring global peace and security of States was foreseen as a new mechanism for peaceful settlement of disputes between States. The PCIJ was to become the judicial body of the new world organisation, with a mandate of adjudicating inter-State claims in a peaceful manner.

The fundamental principle of international relations stipulates the sovereign equality of States and the implied principle of consent to any rule of an international character.[5] As Kelsen puts it, "State sovereignty under international law is its legal independence from other States".[6] The same principle applies to the settlement of disputes. One would recall in this respect the advisory opinion on the *Status of Eastern Carelia* where the PCIJ affirmed that "no

---

[5] I. Brownlie, *Principles of Public International Law*, Oxford University Press, 6th ed., 2003, p. 287.
[6] H. Kelsen., 'The Principle of Sovereign Equality of states as a Basis for International Organization', *Yale Law Journal*, Vol. 53, 1944, p. 208.

state can, without its consent, be compelled to submit its disputes... to arbitration, or any other kind of pacific settlement".[7]

There was certainly some scepticism and even open sarcasm as to the future of the new system. The League of Nations itself warned that "This scepticism would constitute a very great danger to the young institution and would jeopardise the blessings that the world is entitled to expect from its creation and activities". There was also a modest belief, though, that it would be able "to create little by little, by practical and successive solutions, a conscience of justice within the community of nations, and to make that community love the conception of justice".[8]

The concept of justice or perceived legal value of an international norm is essential in ensuring the effectiveness of any legal system. Implementation of a legal norm could not be achieved by coercion exclusively, and in an international system, lacking a sanctions mechanism, it becomes even more significant. The authority of a legal norm in such a system depends to a very high degree on the moral authority of the institution in charge of applying and interpreting the norm.

Procedurally, States were allowed to express their consent to the compulsory jurisdiction of the Court by signing optional clause declarations, triggering reciprocal obligations among declarant States. This had become a universally recognised practice by the end of the twentieth century,[9] but at the time of establishment of the PCIJ it was regarded as a novelty.[10]

The Statute was drafted to enable the United States of America to participate even if it did not join the League, but to no avail.[11] On the other hand,

---

7   *Status of Eastern Carelia*, Advisory Opinion, 1923 P.C.I.J. (ser. B) No. 5, p. 19 (Jul. 23). The Court felt no need to provide evidence of the existence of such a rule, or to elaborate on its precise content.

8   League of Nations, *The Permanent Court of International Justice*, Geneva 1921, p. 20. See also J.B. Scott, *The project of a Permanent Court of International Justice and resolutions of the Advisory Committee of Jurists*, Endowment, Washington, 1920, p. 245. A. Hammarskjöld 'The Place of the Permanent Court of International Justice within the System of the League of Nations', *International Journal of Ethics*, Vol. 34, No. 2, January 1924, pp. 146–156.

9   See N. Kebbon, 'The World Court Compulsory Jurisdiction under the Optional Clause' (1989) 58 *Nordic Journal of International Law* 257; L. Gross, 'Compulsory Jurisdiction under the Optional Clause: History and Practice' in L.F. Damrosch (ed.), *The International Court of Justice at a Crossroads*, New York, 1987, pp. 19–41.

10 The Court's Statute followed the scheme of the 1907 Draft Convention Relative to the Institution of a Court of Arbitral Justice. See F.A. Boyle, *Foundations of World Order: The Legalist Approach to International Relations* (1898–1922), Duke University Press, 1999, p. 220.

11 See M. Pomerance, *The United States and The World Court as a 'Supreme Court of the Nations': Dreams, Illusions and Disillusion*, Martinus Nijhoff Publishers, 1996, p. 506.

some 48 other countries, mostly in Europe, did sign the Protocol and accepted the optional clause by 1921.[12] In 1939, the League had 54 members and the same number of governments had accepted compulsory jurisdiction.[13] A PCIJ publication of 1932 also lists 420 bilateral and multilateral agreements conferring on the Court the competence to decide on future disputes relating to their application.[14] Remarkably, at the time the Court was inaugurated, a bigger than ever part of the international community was in a position to declare a belief in international justice.

3 Post-war Geopolitics

> International law does in fact exist.
> LÉON BOURGEOIS

One hundred years ago, new countries appeared from the ruins of the Russian and Austro-Hungarian empires to become a part of the new world order.[15] According to Articles 116–117 of the Treaty of Versailles, the Brest-Litovsk Treaties were abrogated, Germany agreed to recognise new States coming into existence in the territory of the former Russian Empire and to respect their independence as permanent and inalienable.

In the Baltics, the war was not over with the Peace Treaty. During the first years of their independence Estonia, Latvia and Lithuania had to defend their statehood. The new republics were fighting German militarists, Bolsheviks and White Russian volunteers plundering their countries. Their armies still had to be created and public funds were scarce to say the least. The First World War left behind unresolved territorial claims, ethnic conflicts and nationality issues, revanchist moods and lack of trust among neighbours. In other words, insecurity was present and well perceived. Inexperienced governments had to work in complicated circumstances, balancing on the edge of confrontation, or confronting more powerful neighbours.

It has been claimed that Lithuania, Latvia and Estonia were the weakest independent countries in Europe, the most vulnerable chain in the international

---

12 League of Nations Economic Intelligence Service, *Statistical Year-Book of the League of Nations 1938/39*, Geneva 1939, p. 306.
13 PCIJ Series E, no. 15, 4th edition, 7th add., 1939, p. 275.
14 PCIJ, Series D, no. 6, 4th ed., 1932.
15 See M. MacMillan, *Paris 1919: Six Months That Change the World*, Random House, New York, 2003, p. 570.

community.[16] The Allied powers did not rush to recognize the new republics, barely in control of their territories. Their first request to join the League was declined in December 1920. The new world system of institutions and rule of law was their strongest guarantee of security, if not the only one.

While Latvia and Estonia struggled to expel the Red Army, on 19 April 1919 the Lithuanian capital was overrun by Polish forces in their pursuit of the Bolsheviks. Only by a treaty of 12 July 1920 was the Vilnius region attributed to Lithuania. Peace Treaties with Russia established the borders in the East but the issue of borders between the Baltic States or with Poland was not addressed.

One of the main goals of the Lithuanian State was to acquire access to the sea. This was based on the interests of State security (military supplies by sea) as much as economic interests. The administrative line dividing Tsarist governorates left the coastal region to Latvian Courland. Lithuania and Latvia decided to submit the question to international arbitration. The successful solution to this complicated question contributed to their belief in international law and justice.[17] Once the borders were established, all related nationality and property questions still had to be settled.

The city of Klaipėda (Memel) under the mandate of the Allied powers,[18] with its Lithuanian speaking population, remained in the sights of Lithuanian political leaders. On 11 November 1921 the Lithuanian Parliament (*Seimas*) declared that "The economic interests of the Klaipėda region and nationalistic aspirations of the main part of its population are so in line with those of the Republic of Lithuania which makes unification into one Lithuanian State unavoidable and mutually beneficial". The Seimas further requested the government to implement these provisions. It had become clear by that time that the solution for the future of the city of Memel was to be found in accordance with international law and by applying the right to self-determination of the population.

The most urgent solution, however, was needed for the armed conflict with Poland. The Polish army crossed the line established by the Council of the Allied powers and at the request of the Polish side[19] a conciliation procedure was triggered within the League's Council in accordance with Article 15 of the

---

16   V. Žalys, *Lietuvos diplomatijos istorija (1925–1940)*, Vol. I, Versus Aureus, Vilnius, 2007, p. 25.
17   See R. Satkauskas, 'Lithuanian-Latvian Border Arbitration 1920–1921', *Baltic Yearbook of International Law*, Volume 8, Issue 1, 2008, pp. 197–225.
18   Arts 28 and 99 of the Treaty of Versailles.
19   *Journal officiel de la Société des Nations*, Supplement No. 4, 1920, 'Documents relatifs au differend centre la Pologne et la Lituanie', Document No. 4, p. 44.

Covenant.[20] Negotiations were broken by the mutiny of General Żeligowski while the only weapon in Lithuanian hands was protest and outrage.[21] Even if the League's dispute settlement mechanism did not look perfect, it was the only available response to military force. Not surprisingly, Lithuania rushed to declare its total loyalty to the League of Nations.[22]

Historians often refer to the Lithuanian-Polish conflict as one of the biggest challenges for the League of Nations.[23] Lithuania requested urgent intervention, but the response was slow and declaratory.[24] Only on 28 October 1921 did the Council order a plebiscite in the occupied territory and replacement of Polish troops by an international contingent – a plan that also failed.[25] No peaceful solution had been achieved by both parties to the conflict by the outbreak of World War II. Nevertheless, it is hard to deny that the engagement of international settlement mechanisms prevented escalation of the territorial conflict into a full scale war.[26]

The League of Nations' recommendations adopted under the conciliatory procedure had no binding effect on the parties to the dispute and could not be implemented without their agreement.[27] It was clear among the Lithuanian elite that only an impartial and compulsory decision by an authoritative international court in accordance with international law could help to halt the military threat to Lithuania's statehood.

Public opinion, at least in Europe, was looking into achieving peace through compliance and for the first time popular expectations were reducing the

---

20 The conciliation procedure was cancelled by Council resolution of 13 January 1922. *Journal officiel de la Société des Nations*, février 1922, pp. 99–100.
21 P. Klimas, *Lietuvos diplomatinėje tarnyboje 1919–1940 m.*, Mintis, Vilnius, 1991, p. 35.
22 Letter from the Agent of the Lithuanian Government A. Voldemaras of 16 September 1920 to the President of the Council L. Bourgeois, *supra* note 19, Document No. 20, p. 60.
23 *See more* in G. Vilkelis, *Lietuvos ir Lenkijos santykiai Tautų Sąjungoje*, Versus Aureus, Vilnius, 2006, p. 232; F.P. Walters, *A History of the League of Nations*, Oxford University Press, London, 1952, pp. 105–109.
24 P. Gerbet, *Le rêve d'un ordre mondial. De la SDN à l'ONU*, Imprimerie nationale, Paris, 1996, p. 56.
25 *Journal officiel de la Société des Nations*, février 1922, pp. 99–100.
26 F. Nansen, *The Suffering People of Europe*, Nobel Lecture of 19 December 1922. https://www.nobelprize.org/prizes/peace/1922/nansen/lecture/.
27 In its Advisory Opinion of 21 November 1925 on *Interpretation of Article 3, Paragraph 2, of the Treaty of Lausanne* the Permanent Court agreed that the 'Council can only make recommendations, which, even made unanimously, do not of necessity settle the dispute'. PCIJ, Series B, no. 12, 1925, p. 27.

intensity of political disputes, thus facilitating a judicial settlement. The First World War turned a distant dream into an urgent task.[28]

In these circumstances Lithuania, Latvia and Estonia had no choice but to declare their faith in the new institutional order and accept the existing rules and procedures.[29] Peaceful settlement of disputes and the rule of law undoubtedly served the interests of these small countries. Their faith in the League was not overwhelming or illusory. However, they understood the price of peace and stability: it was clear that any military conflict in Europe would have catastrophic consequences for the Baltic States.

4 The Commitment

> Our wish is that law and justice in relations among nations will become compulsory for all countries.
> *Lithuanian Government*

Lithuania, Latvia and Estonia were among the first countries to recognise the compulsory jurisdiction of The Hague Court. The Lithuanian representative signed the Protocol of Signature of the Statute on 5 October 1921, followed by Estonia on 18 October 1921 and Latvia on 21 January 1922. The protocol entered into force respectively on 16 May 1922, 2 May 1923, and 12 February 1924. Declarations of acceptance of compulsory jurisdiction were deposited by Estonia in 1923 (for five years), 1928 (ten years) and 1938 (ten years), Latvia in 1923 (five years), 1929 (five years) and 1935 (five years). Lithuania accepted the Court's jurisdiction for five-year periods in 1922, 1930 and 1935. Thus, for most of the time of the functioning of the Court the three Baltic States remained bound to submit their disputes with other States to the PICJ.

While presenting the draft law on ratification of the statute in the parliament, Lithuanian Deputy Foreign Minister Petras Klimas underlined: "As to the compulsory jurisdiction of the Court, the protocol so far remains signed only

---

28 See S. Wertheim 'The League of Nations: a retreat from international law?', *Journal of Global History* (2012), 7, pp. 210–232.

29 See V.O. Lumans, *Latvia in World War II*, Fordham University Press, 2006, p. 547; R. Putins Peters 'The Baltic states and the League of Nations: A study of opportunities and limitations' *Journal of Baltic Studies*, Vol. 10, 1979 – Issue 2, pp. 107–114, E. Medijainen, 'Eesti ja maailm. Identiteediotsingud 1905–1940', In: *Eesti identiteet ja iseseisvus* A.A. Bertricau (ed.), Tallinn: Avita, 2001, p. 120; V. Made, *Eesti ja Rahvaste Liit* [Estonia and the League of Nations], Tartu: University of Tartu Press, 1999, pp. 110–119.

by a few countries, such as the Netherlands, Switzerland, Sweden, Denmark, Finland, Bulgaria, Luxembourg, Norway and similar. The Lithuanian State deems it necessary to sign both protocols, including the optional one, establishing the compulsory competence of the Court for five years".[30]

This position was based on the rules of equality of nations and the rule of law in relations among States. P. Klimas observes: "We must note the progress achieved in relation to the universality of the compulsory jurisdiction of the Court, even if progress is not such as to be expected after the lessons of the Great War".[31] The parliament agreed with the reflection of the founders of the Court project that States with their own consistent practice must contribute to the peaceful solution of disputes to achieve the universality of international justice. The Statute of the PCIJ did not establish compulsory jurisdiction but allowed for its constant development by the members of the international community.[32]

Legalistic considerations certainly played a leading role in accepting the Court's jurisdiction. Faith in the ideals of the League was perceived as a crucial argument in the struggle for a place in the international community. "Formal inauguration will take place in the Hague on 15 February this year, and the Government is certain that by that day it will be able to announce on behalf of Lithuania both the ratification of the statute and the optional declaration accepting the Court's compulsory jurisdiction", insisted the Lithuanian Foreign ministry in its submission to the Parliament:

> We must hope that the Court of International Justice, composed of the best and most prominent lawyers (…), will indeed seek justice in international relations and will be able to put justice as their basis. We feel huge satisfaction in taking part in the implementation of this great concept, because we live this concept and greatly suffer from lack of this concept in reality. We wish that law and justice in relations among nations will become compulsory for all countries, big and small, and for once nobody be allowed to break the law of nations and to impose injustice by violence based on size and force.[33]

The Estonian Government noted in its explanatory memorandum to the Draft Law on Ratification of the Statute that the permanent organisation of the

---

30 Lithuanian Central State Archives LCVA, F. 383, Ap. 7, B. 311, p. 101.
31 Lithuanian Central State Archives LCVA, F. 383, Ap. 7, B. 311, p. 106.
32 Lithuanian Central State Archives LCVA, F. 383, Ap. 7, B. 311, p. 107.
33 Lithuanian Central State Archives LCVA, F. 383, Ap. 7, B. 311, p. 111.

Court gave reason to assume that it would be able to deliver justice better than any international body before it.[34] A rules based order would put all countries on an equal footing.[35] As to the declaration of acceptance of the Court's jurisdiction, it was underlined that legally binding decisions were necessary to ensure peace.[36]

At the same time, the practical aspects of acceding to the Court in ensuring State security were clearly identified. The Lithuanian Foreign Minister noted in a letter of 25 January 1922 that "ratification is becoming urgent in relation to our case with Poland".[37] In the week following recognition by Lithuania of compulsory jurisdiction the Registrar received a note proposing to jointly submit the Polish-Lithuanian dispute to the PCIJ.[38] In accordance with Article 36 paragraph (c) and (d) of the Statute, Lithuania suggested that the Court address the issue of breach of Treaty of Suwałki of 7 October 1920 and determine the nature and amount of reparations.[39] Urgent involvement of international institutions was essential to stop imminent annexation.

Poland, while a party to the Statute of the Court, had not by that time accepted its compulsory jurisdiction and rejected the Lithuanian demand without hesitation. In its response of 15 March 1922 the Polish Government specified, that "ongoing events deprived the request of any legal basis".[40]

Another attempt to refer the question to the Court failed in 1923. In a telegram dated 10 February and a letter of 8 March, the Lithuanian government requested the Council to refer to the PCIJ questions regarding the binding force of the recommendations of a Council report.[41] Finally, the case did reach the Court in 1931.

In retrospect, one might ask whether the jurisprudence of the PCIJ failed to convince States from going to war. The clearest answer to these doubts rests in the wording of the Statute of the ICJ, forming part of the Charter of the United

---

34 National Archives of Estonia, ERA 80.1.800 p. 8.
35 National Archives of Estonia, ERA 80.1.345, p. 240, ERA 80.1.800 p. 71.
36 National Archives of Estonia, ERA 80.1.345, p. 241.
37 Lithuanian Central State Archives LCVA, F. 383, Ap. 7, B. 311, p. 92.
38 Lithuanian Central State Archives LCVA, F. 383, Ap. 7, B. 311, p. 80.
39 Lietuvos Respublikos Vyriausybės raštiškas ekspozė Tautų Sąjungai atsiklausus nuolatinio tarptautinio teismo patariamosios nuomonės, Kaunas, 1931, p. 90.
40 Lietuvos Vyriausybės 1922 m. vasario 20 d. nota., Lietuvos Respublikos Vyriausybės raštiškas ekspozė Tautų Sąjungai atsiklausus nuolatinio tarptautinio teismo patariamosios nuomonės, Kaunas, 1931, p. 91.
41 *Journal officiel de la Société des Nations*, juin 1923, pp. 585, 500, 669–700; *See also* League of Nations, Report of the Fourth Assembly of the League on the Work of the Council, on the Work of the Secretariat on the Measures taken to Execute the Decisions of the Assembly. Geneva 23 June 1923, p. 25.

Nations and establishing a clone of the First World Court. The vision of the League's founders has triumphed in paving the way for the growth of a global society bound by a common consciousness and common values.[42]

5 Legacy of the Court

> It is for the Court itself to make out what is international law.
> ÅKE HAMMARSKJÖLD

The League swiftly became an engine for the generation of new claims, elaboration of new practices and the emergence of new norms.[43] The whole need for a universal international organisation was to make the law, and ensure its implementation. Whilst helping to resolve some serious international disputes, many of them consequences of the First World War, the decisions of the PCIJ often clarified previously unclear areas of international law and contributed to its development.[44]

The role of precedents in international law is a matter of considerable controversy and debate. According to the Statute of the Court of Justice, the decision of the Court has no binding force except as between the parties and in respect of that particular case. On the other hand, the impact of the Court's rulings for determining rules of law is now universally recognized. Hersch Lauterpacht summarised the 'law making' functions of the Court's jurisprudence into applying general principles of law and filling gaps by interpreting existing rules in order to avoid *non liquet*.[45] In the words of Alain Pellet, "while staying within the general existing legal framework the Court constantly and consistently (even if rather prudently) adapts the law to the new circumstances and needs of international society, notably when it is clear that a more orthodox interpretation would lead to a dead-end or is no longer acceptable by

---

42 *See more* Ch. J. Tams, *The Development of International Law by the International Court of Justice*, Oxford University Press, 2013, p. 430; Ch. J. Tams, M. Fitzmaurice (eds.), *Legacies of the Permanent Court of International Justice*, Martinus Nijhoff Publishers, 2013, p. 413.
43 S. Pedersen, *The Guardians: The League of Nations and the Crisis of Empire*, Oxford University Press, 2015, p. 405.
44 Handbook ICJ, https://www.icj-cij.org/files/publications/handbook-of-the-court-en.pdf.
45 H. Lauterpacht, *The Development of International Law by the International Court*, Cambridge University Press, 1982, pp. 158–172.

the international society, or because there appears to be gaps in the existing applicable rules".[46]

The three Baltic cases at the PCIJ provided the Court with the opportunity to look at a wide range of international rules. The resulting interpretations contributed substantially to the further development of international law.

One of the most significant parts of the advisory opinion in the *Railway traffic case*[47] relates to the obligation to start negotiations in accordance with the recommendation of the Council of the League of Nations, to put to an end to the territorial dispute and "establish such relations between the two neighbouring States as will ensure 'the good understanding between nations upon which peace depends'". As explained by the Court, the engagement incumbent on the two governments in conformity with the Council's Resolution means not only to enter into negotiations but also to "pursue them as far as possible, with a view to concluding agreements". An obligation to negotiate, however, "does not imply an obligation to reach an agreement", nor in particular does it imply making arrangements before an agreement is reached.

The advisory opinion in the dispute between Lithuania and Poland contributed to international jurisprudence with two important rules of general international law. First, the obligation to negotiate is not a mere formality: the negotiations should be carried out in good faith with a view to reaching an agreement. Second, the negotiating parties have no obligation to accept unfavourable conditions if no compromise has been reached. Lack of good faith on the part of a negotiating State could be considered as a breach of international law and could form a basis to claim compensation. However, the agreement to start negotiations, the so called *pactum de negotiando*, does not impose a duty to accept the terms of agreement as proposed by the other side.

Even though these general rules do not appear in the 1969 codification of the international law of treaties, they are universally followed by State practice. The Court's interpretation in the *Railway traffic* case of the Lithuanian-Polish agreement to negotiate is consistently referred to in decisions of tribunals[48] and international doctrine. Direct confirmation of this customary

---

46   A. Pellet, 'Decisions of the ICJ as Sources of International Law?', *G. Morelli Lectures Series Decisions of the ICJ as sources of International Law*, Rome: International and European Papers Publishing, 2018, p. 47.

47   *Railway Traffic between Lithuania and Poland* (Railway Sector Landwarów-Kaisiadorys), Lithuania v. Poland, Advisory Opinion, 15th October 1931, (1931) PCIJ Series A/B no 42.

48   *See North Sea Continental Shelf, (Federal Republic of Germany v. Denmark; Federal Republic of Germany v. Netherlands)*, Judgment of 20 February 1969, 1969, I.C.J. Reports, Nos. 51 & 52, pp. 47–48 para. 87; *Pulp Mills on the River Uruguay* (Argentina v. Uruguay), Judgment,

rule is, for example, found in the latest decision of the ICJ in the *Obligation to Negotiate Access to the Pacific Ocean (Bolivia v. Chile)*.[49]

This advisory opinion may also be seen in the light of the debate as to the binding force of so called soft law – documents adopted by international organisations but having no treaty status. The Court confirmed in that instance that the Governments of Lithuania and of Poland were bound by their acceptance of the Council's resolution. Even though there was no disagreement by the parties as to the nature of the engagement and the question deserved only a few lines in the Court's decision, this confirmation goes in line with today's assertions that even non-binding international documents may create commitments by applying the principles of good faith and estoppel.[50] A State is considered to have accepted the international obligation contained in a declaration because the international community has well-founded expectations for that State not to breach its promises.

Another important rule of international law, applied in the *Railway traffic* case, relates to implementation of international commitments in a *force majeure* situation. The Court had to decide whether an international obligation continues to exist if circumstances have essentially modified its contents. The Lithuanian position, based on emergency measures to avoid *de facto* acceptance of the territorial changes, was supported by the Court. According to the Court, "regard is had to the present political relations between Lithuania and Poland" and therefore Lithuania has "a ground for refusing to open this sector for traffic or for certain categories of traffic, in case of an emergency affecting her safety or vital interests".[51] The circumstances precluding the wrongfulness

---

I.C.J. Reports 2010 (I), p. 68, para. 150; *Application of the International Convention on the Elimination of All Forms of Racial Discrimination (Georgia v. Russian Federation)* Judgment of 1 April 2011. *Georgia v. Russian Federation*, I.C.J. Reports 2011 (I), p. 84. See more in K. Wellens, *Negotiations in the Case Law of the International Court of Justice: A Functional Analysis*, Routledge, 2016, p. 358.

49 *Obligation to Negotiate Access to the Pacific Ocean (Bolivia v. Chile)*, Judgment of 1 October 2018, p. 32, para. 91. https://www.icj-cij.org/files/case-related/153/153-20181001-JUD-01-00-EN.pdf.

50 See more in M.D. Öberg, 'The Legal Effects of Resolutions of the UN Security Council and General Assembly in the Jurisprudence of the ICJ', *The European Journal of International Law* Vol. 16, 2005, no. 5, pp. 879–906; H. Thierry, 'Les résolutions des organes internationaux dans la jurisprudence de la Cour Internationale de Justice', *Collected Courses of the Hague Academy of International Law*, Vol. 167, Brill, 1980, pp. 385–441 ; A. Pellet, 'La formation du droit international dans le cadre des Nations Unies', *European Journal of International Law*, Vol. 6, 1995, pp. 417–418; S.M. Schwebel, 'The Legal Effect of Resolutions and Codes of Conduct of the United Nations', in S.M. Schwebel, *Justice in International Law – Selected Writings of Stephen M. Schwebel*, Cambridge University Press, 1994, p. 503.

51 Paras 53 and 54.

of an act by a State are codified today in the fifth chapter of the Articles on State Responsibility (Articles 20–27).[52] The interpretation of the customary law by the Permanent Court[53] appears totally in line with later jurisprudence and the reasoning of the International Law Commission. It is worth noting that the Court did not consider in detail the question of legitimate reprisals; the value of the case in this respect remains in the Lithuanian submission, which argues their legitimacy.

The main focus of the Permanent Court's judgments in the case concerning *Interpretation of the statute of the Memel Territory*[54] in formation of international law is somehow hard to grasp. As time passes new arguments and nuances of the Court's decisions are invoked by international lawyers. It appears clear, however, that many rules of international law, applied in this case, were later expanded by subsequent jurisprudence and codified in international conventions.

First, the Court pointed out – when considering the Lithuanian preliminary objection – its position, expressed in earlier decisions, that "the preparatory work cannot be adduced to interpret a text which is, in itself, sufficiently clear". The historical circumstances of the drafting of an agreement have only subsidiary value as a means of treaty interpretation. Nevertheless, the parties' positions at the time of adoption of the treaty were considered in the Memel Territory case as in other PCIJ cases. The will of the parties to accept an international agreement at the time of its conclusion is an important element in determining the contents of the agreement, which is exactly the sense incorporated in Article 32 of the 1969 Vienna Convention on International Treaties. Not surprisingly, this rule of international law was further developed in many subsequent decisions and the works of the most eminent lawyers.[55]

---

52   Draft Articles on the Responsibility of States for Internationally Wrongful Acts, adopted by the ILC in its 53rd Session (2001), and submitted to the General Assembly as a part of the Commission's report covering the work of that Session, UN Doc. A/56/10 (2001), UN Doc. A/RES/56/83 (2001) ('ILC Articles'). Arts 23 and 25 of the ILC Articles are generally seen as general principles of law and as a codification of customary international law respectively.

53   F. Paddeu, *Justification and Excuse in International Law: Concept and Theory of General Defences*, Cambridge University Press, 2018, p. 604.

54   *Interpretation of the statute of the Memel Territory*, Judgment of 11 August 1932 (Series A/B, No. 49).

55   See U. Linderfalk, *On the Interpretation of Treaties: The Modern International Law as Expressed in the 1969 Vienna Convention on the Law of Treaties*, Springer Science & Business Media, 2007, p. 414; H. Lauterpacht, 'Some Observations on Preparatory Work in the Interpretation of Treaties', *Harvard Law Review*, Vol. 48, No. 4, 1935, pp. 549–591; E. Bjorge *The Evolutionary Interpretation of Treaties*, Oxford University Press Oxford, 2014, p. 280.

However, the main conclusion in this case concerned the separation of powers between authorities of an autonomous territory, and the sovereign. In its remarkable decision *a contrario*[56] on the merits the Court held that given the terms of the Statute "it is impossible to adduce the silence of the Statute in regard to any matter in order to restrict the sovereignty of Lithuania in favour of the autonomy of Memel, or to deny to the former the exercise of certain rights simply because they are not expressly provided for in the Statute of Memel". Moreover, as the judgment stresses, "the purpose of the Statute was not to confer rights on Lithuania, but to fix the limits of the autonomy which the Parties to the Convention of Paris of 1924 intended to establish in favour of the Memel Territory". Therefore, the sovereignty of Lithuania prevailed. As the Court explained, "the sovereign powers of the one and the autonomous powers of the other are of quite a different order in that the exercise of the latter powers necessitates the existence of a legal rule which cannot be inferred from the silence of the instrument from which the autonomy is derived, or from an interpretation designed to extend the autonomy by encroaching upon the operation of the sovereign power". It may be observed that the Court rejected the 'pragmatic' but vague idea of the division of sovereign powers. As proved in the Court's jurisprudence, the new entity either had full sovereignty (e.g. the Free City of Danzig) or depended on the sovereignty of another State (e.g. Memel Territory, Upper Savoy and the District of Gex). Thus, in the case of concurring sovereigns priority should be conferred upon the strongest one.

The issue of the relationship between autonomous powers and a sovereign State has clearly remained of significant interest to international lawyers until today even if (and especially because) this subject has remained mainly governed by customary rules.[57] Whether speaking about secessionist movements, limits of political autonomy or other issues of sovereignty, the *Memel Territory* case provides an important example of legal reasoning.[58]

Thirdly, the Court found that the Lithuanian Government was not internationally responsible for the acts of the executive power of the autonomous territory. According to the modern theory of State responsibility, the conduct of any State institution amounts to an act of that State under international law, whatever position that institution holds in the organisation of the State, and

---

[56] Y.A. Abdulqawi, D. Peat, 'A Contrario Interpretation in the Jurisprudence of the International Court of Justice', *Canadian Journal of Comparative and Contemporary Law*, Vol. 3–1, 2017 http://www.cjccl.ca/2017-volume/.

[57] See M. Suksi, *Sub-State Governance through Territorial Autonomy: A Comparative Study in Constitutional Law of Powers, Procedures and Institutions*, Springer, 2011, p. 685.

[58] See e.g. L. Langer, 'Out of Joint? – Hong Kong's International Status from the Sino-British Joint Declaration to the Present', *Archiv des Voelkerrechts*, Vol. 46, 2008, pp. 309–344.

therefore may incur international responsibility.[59] Nevertheless, the Lithuanian Government was not held responsible for the acts of the President in appointing the new members of the Directorate in violation of the Statute. This lack of attribution was due to the *ultra vires* situation, when the circumstances prove that the act in question did not emanate from the authority of the State and was not in its interest.[60]

One more unusual interpretation in the *Memel Territory* case relates to the non-retroactivity of the judgment. In accordance with general principles of law, the judicial interpretation of a treaty has a retroactive effect: in other words, the treaty is to be considered to have the same meaning from its very entry into force. However, contrary to its own position in the *Access to German Minority Schools in Upper Silesia* case,[61] the Court decided that:

> on the proper construction of the Statute the Governor ought not to have taken certain action which he did take. It does not thereby intend to say that the action of the Governor in dissolving the Chamber, even though it was contrary to the treaty, was of no effect in the sphere of municipal law. This is tantamount to saying that the dissolution is not to be regarded as void in the sense that the old Chamber is still in existence, and that the new Chamber since elected has no legal existence.[62]

This "dynamic" interpretation of the international agreement should be considered in the light of the formulation of the questions, presented to the Court by the applicant powers. The Court underlines: "the intention of the Four Powers was only to obtain an interpretation of the Statute which would serve as a guide for the future".[63] Therefore, a declaration of the nullity of the existing Chamber *in abstracto* was not justified.

Two main parts of the Permanent Court's judgment in the *Panevezys-Saldutiskis Railway* case[64] correspond to the objections presented on behalf of the Lithuanian government. The first objection disputed the right of Estonia to exercise diplomatic protection in this case, maintaining that a claim must be

---

59 *Application of the Convention on the Prevention and Punishment of the Crime of Genocide*, I.C.J. Reports 2007, 205 (para. 392).
60 I. Brownlie, *System of the Law of Nations: State Responsibility*, Part I, p. 135; R. Kolb, *Good Faith in International Law*, Bloomsbury, 2017, p. 184.
61 Advisory Opinion No. 19 of 15 May 1931, PCIJ, Ser. A./B., No. 40, 1931.
62 Para 152.
63 *ibid.*
64 *Panevezys-Saldutiskis Railway* (Estonia v. Lithuania), 1939 P.C.I.J. (ser. A/B) No. 76, Judgment of 28 February 1939.

national not only at the time of presentation of the complaint but also at the time of the injury. The second invoked a specific condition for the exercise of diplomatic protection – exhaustion of local remedies before submitting a dispute to international justice.

International regulation of diplomatic protection is receiving growing attention both in jurisprudence and in academic circles. Not surprisingly, the United Nations International Law Commission included this topic in 1996 as one of three topics appropriate for codification and progressive development. Ten years later the Commission adopted the Draft Articles on Diplomatic Protection,[65] submitting them for elaboration by a convention. On many provisions of the Draft Articles, the *Panevezys-Saldutiskis Railway* case served as a starting point for the Commission's work and represented the necessary *opinio juris* revealing the rules of customary law, *lex lata*, as referred to by Emmanuel Addo.[66] The Order of 30 June 1938[67] by which the preliminary objection was joined to the merits of the case also deserves a special mention.

The first article of the ILC's Draft Articles describes diplomatic protection in the words of the Permanent Court's 1939 judgment (first mentioned in the *Mavrommatis Palestine Concessions* case),[68] that is, as the invocation by a State, through diplomatic action or other means of peaceful settlement, of the responsibility of another State for an injury caused by an internationally wrongful act by that State to a natural or legal person that is a national of the former State with a view to implementation of such responsibility. We can see that the conditions for the exercise of diplomatic protection as they appear in the new codification are based on customary rules, reflected in international jurisprudence. Not surprisingly, the Permanent Court's decision in the dispute between Lithuania and Estonia occupies a central role in the Commission's commentaries on these provisions.

The Lithuanian submission on the continued nationality rule was not addressed by the Court in its 1939 judgment, because the identity of the Estonian company was not established. In his comment on the case, Patrick Dumberry summarises the Court's judgment on the requirement to prove the identity of the claimant, the main contribution of the case being the proven existence of

---

65 Draft Articles on Diplomatic Protection with commentaries [2006]. Report of International Law Commission on the work of its Fifty-Eighth Session (2006). General Assembly, Official Records, 61st Session, Supplement No. 10 (A/61/10), pp. 16–100.
66 *Yearbook of the International Law Commission*, 1998, vol. I, 2521st meeting – 29 April 1998, p. 11. http://www.un.org/law/ilc/index.htm.
67 *Panevezys-Saldutiskis Railway* (Est. v. Lith.), 1938 P.C.I.J. (ser. A/B) No. 75 (Order of June 30).
68 *Mavrommatis Palestine Concessions* (Greece v. U.K.), 1924 P.C.I.J. (ser. B) No. 3 (August 30), p. 12.

succession to the private property rule, as affirmed in the separate opinion of judges De Visher and Rostworowski.[69] Article 5 of the 2006 ILC Draft Articles, however, confirms and develops the Lithuanian position of continuous nationality.

The Permanent Court upheld the second preliminary objection and rejected the Estonian claim because of non- exhaustion of domestic remedies. This procedural rule is based on the customary principle of non- intervention.[70] Today, it is accepted as a customary norm, affirmed by the ICJ in the *Interhandel*[71] and *ELSI*[72] cases, and codified in the ILC Draft Articles (Article 14). In addition, the Court underlined that it is not for it to judge the application of domestic law in the national sphere, which is to be ensured by national courts. Thus, "the question whether or not the Lithuanian courts have jurisdiction to entertain a particular suit depends on Lithuanian law and is one on which the Lithuanian courts alone can pronounce a final decision".[73]

Coming back to the decision to join the preliminary objection to the merits of the case, this was based on the risks of adjudicating on questions which appertain to the merits of the case or of prejudging their solution without having exact information as to the legal contentions respectively adduced by the parties and their arguments. The question of joining preliminary objections to the merits arises in most of the judicial cases.[74] In some recent cases, it has deserved special attention: for example, in the *South China Sea* case, the arbitral tribunal joined Chinese objections to the merits despite the provision by the latter of an extensive argument and additional information.[75] It is true, on one hand, that the institute of preliminary objections implements the principle of the sovereign equality of States and ensures the voluntary character of the court's jurisdiction. On the other hand, implementation of compulsory

---

69   P. Dumberry, *State Succession to International Responsibility*, Brill, 2007, pp. 390–401.
70   A.A. Cançado Trindade, 'Origin and Historical Development of the Rule of Exhaustion of Local Remedies in International Law', *Revue Belge de Droit International*, No. 2, 1976, p. 521.
71   *Interhandel* case (*Switzerland v. United States of America*) Preliminary objections, I.C.J. Reports 1959, p. 27.
72   *Case Concerning Elettronica Sicula S.p.A.* (*ELSI*), I.C.J. Reports 1989, p. 15 at para. 59.
73   *Panevezys-Saldutiskis Railway, supra* note 63, p. 19.
74   H. Thirlway, *The International Court of Justice*, Oxford University Press, 2016, p. 240 ; G. Abi-Saab *Les exceptions préliminaires dans la procédure de la Cour internationale : Etude des notions fondamentales de procédure et des moyens de leur mise en œuvre*, Paris, Pedone, 1967, p. 280.
75   S. Talmon, 'Objections Not Possessing an 'Exclusively Preliminary Character' in the South China Sea Arbitration', *Journal of Territorial and Maritime Studies*, vol. 3, 2016, Bonn Research Papers on Public International Law, Paper No. 10/2016, 16 June 2016; Special Issue on Jurisdiction and Admissibility in the South China Sea Arbitration, *Chinese Journal of International Law*, vol. 15, 2016, pp. 217–430.

jurisdiction cannot depend on the will of a State to settle a specific dispute. The Court therefore must justify such a move in each individual case. In his seven-part long separate opinion concerning the ICJ decision on Chile's preliminary objection in the *Obligation to Negotiate Access to the Pacific Ocean* case[76] judge Cançado Trindade underlines the practice of the Permanent Court and in particular the *Panevezys-Saldutiskis Railway* case. The principle of sound administration of justice (*la bonne administration de la justice*) has always been the basis of international justice. The International Court invoked the Order of 30 June 1938 for many years, including when deciding the famous *Barcelona Traction* case (1964–1970). Then, in the 1972 Amended Rules of the Court confirmed the exceptional character of the joinder.[77]

6 Conclusion

> International Law is what international lawyers make of it.
> MARTTI KOSKENNIEMI

While many refer to the League of Nations as an experiment, very few make the same reference to the United Nations. Building on the experiences of its predecessor the UN embraced, strengthened and universalised the institutional framework of a multilateral world order.

At the end of the Cold War, the 1945 Charter's aim of saving succeeding generations from the scourge of war was as appealing to the Baltic peoples as ever. Despite the loss of global momentum in accepting the compulsory jurisdiction of the ICJ, Estonia,[78] and later Lithuania and Latvia, declared their commitment to settling their international disputes in the Court.

The acceptance of compulsory jurisdiction raises support for the institution of international justice underlining the determination to pursue policies based on international law rather than force, economic influence, political pressure and intimidation.[79] The Court provides a forum for exchanging legal views and

---

76   *Obligation to Negotiate Access to the Pacific Ocean (Bolivia v. Chile)*, Judgment of 24 September 2015.
77   See more in U. Villani, 'Preliminary Objections in the New Rules of the International Court of Justice', *The Italian Yearbook of International Law*, Vol 1, 1975, pp. 206–221. The recently released new rules of the court retain flexibility of the Court in deciding on the preliminary nature of the objections.
78   https://vm.ee/en/restoration-effect-estonias-international-treaties.
79   In the words of Judge Trindade, the foundation of compulsory jurisdiction ultimately lies in confidence in the rule of law at international level: A.A. Cançado Trindade, 'Reflection

constructs a *modus vivendi* for the parties to a conflict. Neither the *Panevezys-Saldutiskis Railway* judgment, nor the *Railway Traffic* advisory opinion resolved the disputes between the parties. The Court did not pronounce on the legality of Polish control of Vilnius, and it did not settle the financial claims related to the operation of the Panevezys-Saldutiskis line. Instead, The Court provided a mechanism for peaceful settlement of disputes, channelling the arguments of the parties to the legal path.

Apart from its main function – peaceful settlement of international conflicts to achieve international peace and security – one of the most important aims of the International Court is to contribute by its jurisprudence to the development of international law. It is true that each situation is determined on its own merits: in the *Panevezys-Saldutiskis Railway* case the Court even mentions expressly that the decision should not constitute a precedent; nevertheless, existing jurisprudence is always taken into consideration.[80]

The commitment of governments to submit disputes to the International Court provides it with an opportunity to decide on the contents of the law and its sphere of application, thus contributing to formation of the law. As Alain Pellet notes, "It remains that, in the absence of a world legislator, there is no exaggeration in thinking that the Court, limited as it is by the hazards of its seizing, is one of the most efficient, if not the most efficient, vehicle for adaptation of general international law norms to the changing conditions of international relations".[81]

It is clear that the international community today is not the same as it was in the 1920s. The number of States has multiplied, new forms of interstate relations, new norms of international law have partly replaced the importance and direct applicability of the rules invoked in the Permanent Court's jurisprudence. On the other hand, many of the customary norms revealed in its decisions have been finally incorporated in multilateral conventions and universally accepted by State practice. Legal arguments invoked by the court and given interpretations have influenced every further development of international law. Looking at the decisions of the Permanent Court today is more than simply looking into the past: they can provide answers applicable for the future.

---

    on a Century of International Justice: Developments, Current State and Perspectives', *Teisė*, vol. 97, 2015, p. 220.

80   As judge Guillaume notes, there are good and bad precedents and the best are not always immediately adopted. G. Guillaume, 'The Use of Precedent by International Judges and Arbitrators', *Journal of International Dispute Settlement*, Vol. 2, No. 1 (2011), p. 23.

81   A. Pellet, 'Article 38', *The Statute of the International Court of Justice: A Commentary*, A. Zimmermann, K. Oellers-Frahm (eds.), Oxford University Press, 2006, p. 790.

CHAPTER 4

A Century of the Baltic States' Independence: Some Similarities and Differences with Bulgaria

Gabriela Belova and Nikolay Marin

Abstract

The article scrutinizes the Baltic States and their century of independence which have been the focus of interest of various sciences. On the occasion of the commemoration of the 100th anniversary of the proclamation of the independence of the Baltic States – Estonia, Lithuania and Latvia – some parallels could be drawn with the historical, economic and political development of these countries and Bulgaria. These parallels are not only found in the political and legal period but are contained in different stages, which shows the interesting legal and political nature of the Baltic States and some of their common problems and events with the countries of Eastern Europe and, in particular, the example with Bulgaria. The article has also drawn attention to a significant problem that the three Baltic States and Bulgaria have to deal with, namely the demographic crisis. This problem is particularly important in the light of migratory pressures that the countries outlining the external borders of the European Union are facing and it involves systematic and long-term efforts.

Keywords

Baltic States' independence – Bulgaria and the Baltic States – diplomatic relations – foreign policy co-operation

1   Introduction

The Baltic States and their century of independence have been the focus of interest of various sciences. The creation of independence is always an important event, which consists of highly complex reasons for entering into real political relations. Undoubtedly the independence of States is a significant issue or case in any period of development of Public International Law. Baltic independence is a special case because it concerns establishing statehood for three similar but not identical States with rich customs, traditions and contribution to the development of the European political system after the First World War. There are some similarities with Bulgaria as well as differences. The 100th anniversary of the independence of the Baltic States is an event of utmost significance for the formation and development of Public International Law due to its complex character. The emergence of newly independent States in all cases constitutes a series of processes. Some common features, though in a different aspect, with Bulgaria are present.

On the occasion of the commemoration of the 100th anniversary of the proclamation of the independence of the Baltic States – Estonia, Lithuania and Latvia – some parallels could be drawn with the historical, economic and political development of these countries and Bulgaria. These parallels are not only found in the political and legal period but are contained in different stages, which shows the interesting legal and political nature of the Baltic States and some of their common problems and events with the countries of Eastern Europe and, in particular, the example with Bulgaria. The focus on Bulgaria is not by accident, but rather because it involves a number of common political and legal dimensions both after the First World War, after World War II and after the end of the Cold War. From a diplomatic point of view, it is worth focusing on the common foreign and political priorities for the Baltic States and Bulgaria such as membership in Euro-Atlantic organizations such as NATO and the EU.[1] These countries also interact after the accession phase, with Estonia being part of the trio of the EU Council Presidency together with Bulgaria and Austria in the period June 2017 until December 2018.

2 Brief Historical Overview: Bulgaria and the Baltic States in the 1920s

First of all, the 1920s was an extremely important and difficult period in the history of the Baltic States and Bulgaria, but at the same time, all of them became members of a recently established universal international organization, namely the League of Nations.[2] In this regard, it is hard to overlook the contribution of a small country like Bulgaria, which was also in the whirlpool of the world's processes. The Bulgarian engineer Nikola Dimkov, in his book "The Star

---

1   Lanham, Walter C. Clemens Jr., The Baltic Transformed: Complexity Theory and European Security, Maryland: Rowman and Littlefield Publishers, Inc., 2001; Demokratizatsiya. Summer 2003, Vol. 11 Issue 3, pp. 460–462.
2   Annuaire statistique de la Société des Nations, 1934.

of Consent",[3] published in 1916, first gave the idea of creating a world organization for peace and security, and the principles it offers lie at the heart of the future League of Nations.

2.1 Bulgaria

With regard to Bulgaria, the end of the First World War buried hopes for the realization of the national ideal. Moreover, even after its outbreak the war soon became unpopular with most Bulgarians, who suffered great economic hardship and also disliked fighting their fellow Orthodox Christians in alliance with the Muslim Ottomans.[4] It could be said that the Russian Revolution of February 1917 had a great effect in Bulgaria, spreading anti-war and anti-monarchist feelings among the troops and in the cities. In September 1918, Tsar Ferdinand abdicated in favour of his son Boris III in order to suppress anti-monarchic revolutionary tendencies. Under the Treaty of Neuilly (November 1919) Bulgaria ceded its Aegean coastline to Greece and nearly all of its Macedonian territory to the newly created Kingdom of Serbs, Croats and Slovenes, was forced to recognize its existence and had to give Dobruja back to Romania. The country had to reduce its army to no more than 22,000 men and pay huge reparations. Bulgarians generally refer to the results of the treaty as the 'Second National Catastrophe'.[5]

2.2 Estonia

Unlike Bulgaria, Estonia won the Estonian War of Independence against both Soviet Russia and the German Freikorps and *Baltische Landeswehr* volunteers. Independence was secured with the Tartu Peace Treaty, signed on 2 February 1920.[6]

Soon the first Estonian constitution was adopted by the Constituent Assembly on 15 April 1920. Established as a parliamentary democracy, legislative power was held by a 100-seat parliament or Riigikogu.

The Republic of Estonia was recognised (*de jure*) by Finland on 7 July 1920, Poland on 31 December 1920, Argentina on 12 January 1921, by the Western

---

3   Димков, Н. „Звезда на съгласието" – българският проект за ООН / Ред. Даниела Василева. – Варна: Данграфик, 2001.
4   Гърдев, Борислав „България и световната криза (1913–1918 г.)" Мемоари за катастрофите.
5   Gilbert, Felix. *The End of the European Era 1890 to the Present*, Weidenfeld &Nicolson, London, 1971, p. 159.
6   Krepp, Endel. *The Estonian War of Independence 1918–1920: on the Occasion of its 60th anniversary from the Treaty of Brest-Litovsk to the Treaty of Peace at Tartu.* Stockholm: Estonian Information Centre.1980.

Allies on 26 January 1921 and by India on 22 September 1921. In 1921 Estonia became a full member of the League of Nations and developed successful economic relations with many countries, including the Soviet Union. The backbone of the Estonian economy became agricultural exports to the West, due to tens of thousands of small farm holdings being established as a result of land reforms that ended the Baltic German economic dominance.[7] The Estonian Kroon was introduced in 1928. At the same time, Estonian politics during the 1920s was dominated by unstable coalition governments, with a government lasting on average a period of 11 months.

The 1920s also saw the development of national culture, with emphasis on the Estonian language, history, education and ethnography. National minorities were granted cultural autonomy – something that the Bulgarian population in the lands given to neighbouring countries under the peace treaty cannot acknowledge.[8]

Diplomatic relations between Bulgaria and Estonia were established in 1920 as they also resulted from the warm attitude of the Bulgarian people towards the contribution of the Estonian people to liberation from Turkish slavery – over 4000 Estonians participated in the Russo-Turkish War 1877–1878.[9] Estonian Plenipotentiary Minister Otto Strandman (with headquarters in Warsaw) was accredited in the same capacity in Bulgaria as well.[10] At that time, Bulgaria did not send a diplomatic representative to Estonia. In the period between the two world wars, there was an active Bulgarian consulate in Tallinn. In 1938, an Association for Friendship between Estonia and Bulgaria was established in Tallinn, and one of its founders was the then Bulgarian consul. The Friendship Association aims to support rapprochement between Estonia and Bulgaria and familiarization with Bulgarian culture in Estonia.

2.3   Latvia

During the 1919 Paris Peace conference, Latvia had unsuccessfully lobbied for international *de jure* recognition of its independence by the Allied countries.[11] The Allies still hoped for a quick end of the Soviet regime and establishment of

---

7   *Ibid.*
8   Серафимов, Виктор. „Особеност На Процедурата По Прекратяване На Международни Договори", Сб. „Научни Трудове На Института На Държавата И Правото При Българската Академия На Науките, Том XII. 2015.
9   Беляев Н., Русско-турецкая война 1877–1878, Москва, 1957.
10 Матеева М. „История на дипломатическите отношения на България", Български бестселър, София, 2005, с. 199.
11 Bleiere, Daina. *History of Latvia: 100 years*. Riga, Domas spēks 2014.

a democratic Russian State which would grant Latvia a large degree of autonomy. The internal situation was also unstable, as during 1919 three different governments (Latvians, Germans-White Russians, Soviets) were fighting for control.[12]

According to Latvian diplomats, during that time the USA and France were against recognizing Latvia, Italy and Japan supported recognition while the United Kingdom gave limited support and waited for events to play out.

On 11 August 1920, under the Latvian–Soviet Peace Treaty, Soviet Russia relinquished authority over the Latvian nation and claims to Latvian territory as "Russia recognizes without objection the independence and sovereignty of the Latvian State and forever renounces all sovereign rights held by Russia in relation to the Latvian nation and land on the basis of the previous State legal regime as well as any international agreements, all of which lose their force and effect for all future time as herein provided. The Latvian nation and land shall have no obligations arising from their previous possession by Russia".[13]

In 1920 Latvia, together with Lithuania and Estonia, tried to join the League of Nations but was denied membership.[14]

As the Soviet victory in the Russian Civil War became clear and after heavy lobbying by Foreign Minister Zigfrīds Anna Meierovics, the Allied Supreme War Council, which included the United Kingdom, France, Belgium, Italy and Japan, recognized Latvia's independence on 26 January 1921. Recognition from many other countries soon followed. Latvia also became a member of the League of Nations on 22 September 1921. The USA recognized Latvia only in July 1922 but by 1940 Latvia was recognized by 42 countries.[15]

On 21 May 1922, Bulgaria recognized Latvia and established diplomatic relations with it at a delegation level. The Deputy Minister of Latvia in Italy, Pierre Seyah, was also accredited in Bulgaria. He handed his letters of credence to Sofia on 26 June 1928. Bulgaria appointed its plenipotentiary minister Vladimir Robev, based in Warsaw, for its representative in Latvia, too. He served his credentials in Riga at the end of 1931. As is known, on 5 October 1939, based on the secret protocol to the Molotov-Ribbentrop Pact, the Soviet Union forced Latvia to sign a separate Mutual Assistance Treaty. The treaty with Latvia provided for the establishment of Soviet Air Force, Naval and Army bases in Western Latvia and the stationing of up to 25,000 troops, more than the peacetime strength of

---

12   Bilmanis, Alfreds. *A History of Latvia*. Westport, Conn., Greenwood Press. 1977.
13   Peace Treaty between Latvia and Russia, 9 September 1920, Art. II, https://en.wikisource.org/wiki/Peace_Treaty_between_Latvia_and_Russia_1920.
14   Annuaire statistique de la Société des Nations, 1934.
15   Bleiere, *supra* note 11.

the Latvian forces. On 16 June 1940 without factual basis, a Soviet ultimatum accused Latvia of breaching the Mutual Assistance Treaty and demanded that *within six hours* Latvia should admit an unlimited number of Soviet troops to Latvia and to form a new government. Knowing that Lithuania had been invaded by the Red Army the day before and that its troops were massed along the eastern border and mindful of the Soviet military bases in Western Latvia, the government acceded to the demands. Logically, after Soviet troops entered Latvia and announced the country in July as a Soviet Socialist Republic, diplomatic relations between Latvia and Bulgaria were interrupted.[16]

2.4 Lithuania

After the end of the First World War, Lithuania has the greatest uncertainty about its status and perhaps the most unresolved issues about its development on the international stage.[17] In March 1921, plans for a plebiscite were abandoned. Neither Lithuania, which was afraid of a negative result, nor Poland, which saw no reason to change the *status quo*, wanted the plebiscite.[18] The parties could not agree in which territory to carry out the vote and how Żeligowski's forces (Polish authorities) should be replaced by international governance conducted by the League of Nations. The League of Nations then moved on from trying to resolve the narrow territorial dispute in the Vilnius Region to shaping the fundamental relationship between Poland and Lithuania. During 1921, Belgian Paul Hymans suggested several Polish–Lithuanian federation models, all rejected by both sides. In January 1922, a parliamentary election to the Wilno Diet (*Sejm wileński*) resulted in a landslide Polish victory. In its first session on 20 February 1922, the Diet voted for incorporation into Poland as the Wilno Voivodeship. The Polish **Sejm** accepted the resolution of the Diet. The League of Nations ended its efforts to mediate the dispute. After Lithuanians seized the Klaipėda Region in January 1923, the League saw recognition of the Lithuanian interest in Klaipėda as adequate compensation for the loss of Vilnius. The League accepted the *status quo* in February 1923 by dividing the neutral zone and setting a demarcation line, which was recognized in

---

16   Матеева М. „История на дипломатическите отношения на България", Български бестселър, София, 2005, с. 295.
17   Eidintas A., Bumblauskas A. *The History of Lithuania*. 2016. Revised 2nd edition. Alfonsas Eidintas, Alfredas Bumblauskas, Antanas Kulakauskas, Mindaugas Tamošaitis. Translated and edited by Skirma Kondratas and Ramūnas Kondratas. Publishing House "Eugrimas", 2015. Published on behalf of the Ministry of Foreign Affairs of the Republic of Lithuania. Translated from the second Lithuanian edition (2013). Revised English translation by Skirma Kondratas and Ramūnas Kondratas.
18   Erlickas, J. *History of Lithuania*. Tyto alba 2000.

March 1923 as the official Polish-Lithuanian border. Lithuania did not recognize this border.

Some historians have asserted that if Poland had not prevailed in the Polish–Soviet War, Lithuania would have been invaded by the Soviets, and would never have experienced two decades of independence. Despite the Soviet–Lithuanian Treaty of 1920, Lithuania was very close to being invaded by the Soviets in summer 1920 and being forcibly incorporated into that State, and only the Polish victory derailed this plan.[19]

The dispute over Vilnius remained one of the biggest foreign policy issues between Lithuania and Poland. Lithuania broke off all diplomatic relations with Poland and refused any actions that would recognize Poland's control of Vilnius even *de facto*. For example, Lithuania broke off diplomatic relations with the Holy See after the Concordat of 1925 established an ecclesiastical province in Wilno, thereby acknowledging Poland's claims to the city. Poland refused to formally recognize the existence of any dispute regarding the region since that would have lent legitimacy to the Lithuanian claims.[20] Despite several attempts to normalize relations, the situation of 'no war, no peace' lasted until Poland demanded reestablishment of diplomatic relations by issuing an ultimatum in 1938. These tensions were one of the reasons why Józef Piłsudski's Międzymorze federation was never formed. The Soviet Union gave Vilnius to Lithuania after the Soviet invasion of Eastern Poland in September 1939.

3   The Period after the Collapse of the Socialist System

3.1   *Diplomatic Relations between Bulgaria and the Baltic States*

After the end of the Cold War, these four countries started their development on the path to democracy.[21] Initially, they joined the Council of Europe:

---

19   Eidintas / Bumblauskas. *Supra* note 17.

20   It is interesting to note that railroad traffic and telegraph lines could not cross the border, and mail service was complicated. For example, a letter from Poland to Lithuania needed to be sent to a neutral country, repackaged in a new envelope to remove any Polish signs, and only then delivered to Lithuania.

21   Bremmer, Ian, *Nations and Politics in the Soviet Successor States*. 1993. Available at: https://newbooksinpolitics.com/political/nations-and-politics-in-the-soviet-successor-states/; *see also* Mälksoo, M. 'Enabling NATO Enlargement: Changing Constructions of the Baltic States' in Trames: *A Journal of the Humanities & Social Sciences*. 2004, Vol. 8 Issue 3, pp. 284–298; Clemmesen, Michael H., Kvaernø, Ole, 'Debate: NATO Enlargement-With or Without a Baltic Dimension?', *Baltic Defence Review*. Jan 2001, Vol. 5 Issue 1, pp. 44–55; Labarre, F., 'NATO-Russia relations and NATO enlargement in the Baltic Sea Region', *Baltic*

Bulgaria on 7 May 1992, a year later on 14 May 1993 Estonia and Lithuania became members of the organization and lastly, Latvia joined on 10 February 1995. In the next decade, on 29 March 2004, the four countries together became NATO members. Membership in the European Union for the three Baltic States became a reality on 1 May 2004,[22] whereas for Bulgaria this occurred on 1 January 2007. It should be borne in mind that the initial scenario for the enlargement of the Union was in the '6 + 6' format. Estonia fell into the first group with Poland, Hungary, the Czech Republic, Slovenia and Cyprus, while Lithuania, Latvia and Bulgaria were in the so-called Helsinki Group together with Romania, Slovakia and Malta. The countries' varying degrees of progress ultimately led to two enlargements in 2004 and 2007 under the '10 + 2' scheme. Unlike Bulgaria, in 2003 EU referendums on EU membership were held in the three Baltic States, with a high level of support declared – 91.9% in Lithuania, 66.8% in Estonia and 57.5% in Latvia.[23] The reasons for such an approach in Bulgaria – not to hold a referendum – are not very clear given that the country, according to polls, has one of the highest levels of pro-European sentiment among the candidate countries.[24] This remained the case throughout the whole pre-accession process, despite some unpopular decisions on the closure of Kozloduy NPP units, as was the case with Lithuania's Ignalina NPP. Regrettably, in contrast to distinguished Lithuanian diplomats, the Bulgarian negotiators failed to agree on acceptable conditions for the closure of the first Kozloduy NPP units, which made the social costs of this transaction extremely high.

The main reason for the non-inclusion of Bulgaria in the first enlargement group in 2004 was its weaker socio-economic development, as well as its non-attractiveness for foreign investment.[25] The slow pace of reform in the judicial system led to the introduction, after Bulgaria and Romania's accession, of a monitoring mechanism in both countries. According to Bulgarian scholars, the Cooperation and Verification Mechanism (CVM) for Bulgaria and Romania

---

Defence Review No. 6, Volume 2001, Vol. 6 Issue 2, pp. 46–69; Kara-Murza, V. 'Russia and the Baltics Once Friend, Now Foe', *World Affairs*. Jan/Feb 2015, Vol. 177 Issue 5, pp. 16–23.

[22] Ulrich, B. 'From Soviet Republics to EU Member States. A Legal and Political Assessment of the Baltic States' Accession to the EU', *Review of Central & East European Law*. June 2011, Vol. 36 Issue 2, pp. 203–206.

[23] Morawa, A. *Constitutional Evolution in Central and Eastern Europe: Expansion and integration in the EU*. London, Routledge, 2013. See also Mihkelson, Marko, 'Baltic-Russian Relations in Light of Expanding NATO and EU', *Demokratizatsiya*. Spring 2003, Vol. 11, Issue 2, p. 270.

[24] Белова Г. „Европейска интеграция", СИЕЛА, София, 2008.

[25] Dickinson, D. Mullineux A., *Financial and Monetary Integration in the New Europe: Convergence between the EU and Central and Eastern Europe (Elgar Monographs)*, 2002. ISBN-10: 1840642467, ISBN-13: 978-1840642469.

could be assessed as a tool for both pressure and support which aimed to achieve irreversibility of the expected reforms and strengthen the rule of law in the newly acceded countries.[26] Additionally, unlike the Baltic countries, at the time of their accession to the EU Bulgaria and Romania were marked by high levels of widespread political corruption. Endemic corruption and an inefficient judiciary exercise a negative influence and undermine the rule of law and the human rights protection, which are among the Copenhagen criteria for accession to the EU.[27]

3.1.1   Bilateral Relations Bulgaria – Estonia

Diplomatic relations between Bulgaria and the Baltic States were restored in the aftermath of the changes that marked the collapse of the socialist bloc. On 10 September 1991, a joint declaration was signed in Moscow to restore diplomatic relations between Bulgaria and Estonia. The declaration was signed by Bulgaria's Foreign Minister Victor Valkov and Estonian Foreign Minister Leonard Mary. The Declaration states: "Guided by the desire to develop mutual relations and cooperation on the basis of respect for the principles of international law and the Charter of the United Nations, the two States have agreed to establish diplomatic relations at embassy level with effect from the date of signature of this joint declaration".[28] By the end of 1998, no diplomatic representatives had been exchanged between Estonia and Bulgaria. It was not until the beginning of 1999 that Alexander Yordanov was accredited as Bulgarian ambassador to Estonia based in Warsaw (Poland). As its ambassador to Bulgaria, Estonia accredited its Warsaw ambassador Peter Revstynski, who handed over his credentials in Sofia on 13 December that year.

Bilateral relations are held on a high political level. Several high-level visits have been carried out: visits by the chairs of the national parliaments; Sofia has seen visits by Estonian Foreign Minister Paet and Interior Minister Pomerants. In turn, Tallinn was visited by Bulgaria's Foreign Minister Mladenov, Finance Minister Djankov, Interior Minister Tsvetanov and Prime Minister Borisov. In 2006, Estonian Prime Minister Andrus Ansip opened the embassy of the Republic of Estonia in Sofia. Bulgaria had an embassy in Tallinn from 2008 to 2011, and after it was closed Bulgaria has covered Estonia from its embassy in Helsinki. Bulgaria and Estonia have many twin cities such as Gorna Orjahovitsa

---

26   Ковачева, Д., „Стратегически подходи и политики на ЕС за противодействие на корупцията", сп. Правна мисъл, кн. 1, 2015 г. с. 18–19.

27   Ковачева, Д., „Противодействие на корупцията. Международноправни аспекти", Институт за държавата и правото, БАН, София., 2016, с. 164–175.

28   Матеева М. „История на дипломатическите отношения на България", Български бестселър, София, 2005, с. 200.

and Narva, Smolyan and Võru, Kubrat and Türi. In the last decade, official visits to Estonia have been made by the Minister of Foreign Affairs Nikolay Mladenov (2010 and 2012), Deputy Prime Minister and Minister of Finance Simeon Djankov (2010), Deputy Prime Minister and Interior Minister Tsvetan Tsvetanov (2010), President Rosen Plevneliev (2013) and Deputy Prime Minister and Minister of Education and Science Meglena Kuneva (2016). Significant agreements have been concluded on defence, readmission of persons, exchange and protection of classified information, border management and police and criminal cooperation, and double taxation.

However, the development of relations still has room in all areas, given our team co-operation during the EU presidency in 2017–2018. In 2017 at a trilateral meeting in Brussels the Presidency trio (Estonia, Bulgaria and Austria)'s program was adopted.[29] This puts a strong accent on the security and consolidation of the EU's outer borders,[30] economic growth and competitiveness, as well as stabilization of regions neighbouring the bloc.[31] Estonia pointed out that it would have 'a short and focused program' and unprecedented engagement on the implementation of a Digital Single Market for All by the end of 2018, with efforts focused on the increased use of e-solutions and free movement of data, as well as development of cross-border e-services and e-commerce.[32]

As European Commissioner Mariya Gabriel[33] says, the future of Europe and of the world will inevitably be digital. For the first time, the EU should have a dedicated digital funding programme with a budget of €9.19bn in the Digital Europe programme[34] proposed by the Commission to shape and support the

---

[29] Илиева И., Хармонизация на българското законодателство срещу дискриминацията с правото на Европейския съюз, в: Научни трудове на Института за държавата и правото, 2017, т. XVI, с. 65–87.

[30] Попова, Ж., Право на Европейския съюз, трето основно преработено и допълнено издание, Ciela, С., 2015 г., с. 490.

[31] Marin N., Dimitrov P. 'Economic Effects of the Membership of the Republic of Bulgaria in the European Union', *Kutafin Law Review*, Vol. 5 April 2018, Issue 1, pp. 209–221.

[32] Белова Г., Марин Н., Георгиева Г. и Й. Кочев, Нови моменти в защитата на личните данни в Европейския съюз, в: Научни трудове на Института за държавата и правото, 2017, т. XVI, с. 54–65. *See also* Hristova A. & G. Georgieva 'New Research and Technology Development: Some Legal and Ethical Issues', *Kutafin Law Review*, Vol. 4, 2017, Issue 2, pp. 389–397.

[33] The Bulgarian citizen Mariya Gabriel in 2017 was appointed to the European Commission to fill a spot left vacant by the departure of Kristalina Georgieva.

[34] EU Commissioner Mariya Gabriel: 9 billion euro from next EU budget to show citizens how important digital skills are, http://www.focus-fen.net/news/2018/06/25/431785/eu-commissioner-mariya-gabriel-9-billion-euro-from-next-eu-budget-to-show-citizens-how-important-digital-skills-are.htm. See also Kochev Y. 'The Digital Single Market in the

digital transformation of Europe's society and economy. This financing gap is particularly evident in capacity building, deployment and use of computing and data handling, cybersecurity, and artificial intelligence.

3.1.2 Bilateral Relations Bulgaria – Latvia

On 26 August 1991, Bulgaria recognized Latvia's independence and on 10 September a joint declaration was signed with similar content to that with Estonia, by Bulgaria's Foreign Minister Victor Valkov and Latvia's Yannis Yurkans. In 1997, Latvia accredited its diplomatic representative to Poland, Albert Kreischakis (chargé d'affaires), to Bulgaria. The next Ambassador, Ayvars Vovers, was awarded the Third Order of Madara Horseman on his final departure from the country. The First Ambassador of the Republic of Bulgaria to the Republic of Latvia is Alexander Yordanov.

A Free Trade Agreement between Bulgaria and Latvia was signed on 16 October 2002 in Riga. Following the entry of Latvia to the EU in 2004, a free trade agreement with the EU was implemented.

In the period 3–5 December 2003, during the first state visit of Latvian President Vayra Vike-Freiberga to Bulgaria, at the invitation of President Georgi Parvanov, the following were signed: Agreement on the Promotion and Mutual Protection of Investments, and Agreement on the avoidance of double taxation and prevention of income tax evasion. A Cooperation Agreement has also been concluded between the Chambers of Commerce of Bulgaria and Latvia. In 2005, an Agreement was signed between the two governments on Cooperation in the Field of Education, Science and Culture to strengthen cultural ties between the two nations.

3.1.3 Bilateral Relations Bulgaria – Lithuania

Unlike Estonia and Latvia, Bulgaria did not establish diplomatic relations with Lithuania in the 1920s. For the first time, Bulgaria recognized Lithuania's independence on 26 August 1991. On 10 September the same year, a joint declaration on the establishment of diplomatic relations was signed in Moscow by Viktor Valkov and Lithuanian Foreign Minister Algirdas Saudargas. For its first ambassador to Bulgaria, Lithuania accredited its ambassador to Poland, Anthony Valionis, who presented his credentials in Sofia on 5 April 1996.[35] The first Bulgarian ambassador to Lithuania was again Alexander Yordanov. On 10

European Union: Obstacles and Trends', Kutafin Law Review, Vol. 4, 2017, Issue 2, pp. 449–457.

35 Костов, Валентин „Двустранните отношения между Литва и България": Интервюта; Превод от англ. Мария Ангелова. 2009.

April 1996, a contract for friendly relations and cooperation was signed in Sofia between the two governments. Subsequently, an Agreement between the Bulgarian Ministry of Defence and the Lithuanian Ministry of National Defence (2000) was signed and during an official visit to Sofia by Lithuanian President Valdas Adamkus (21–22 November 2005) an Agreement was concluded for mutual protection and promotion of investments. During an official visit by Bulgarian Deputy Prime Minister and Minister of Foreign Affairs Ivaylo Kalfin to Vilnius on 9 May 2006, an Agreement for the avoidance of double taxation and the prevention of income and capital deviation was signed. An official visit in Sofia by a parliamentary delegation headed by Lithuanian Parliament (Seimas) leader Viktoris Muntignas was carried out in 2007 and an official visit to Sofia was undertaken by the Lithuanian Minister of Foreign Affairs, Petras Vayeetunas on 9–11 June 2008. During a state visit to Vilnius by Bulgarian President Georgi Parvanov (16–18 March 2009) a Protocol on Cooperation between the foreign ministries of both countries was signed as well as a Cooperation Agreement in the field of Tourism between the two governments. Two months later, Memoranda of Understanding between the defence ministries of both countries were signed in Brussels, and in November 2009 in Sofia – between their interior ministries, too. In 2009, the 85th anniversary of the establishment of diplomatic relations between the two countries was celebrated.

3.2   Common Economic Challenge – the Currency Board

In the 1990s, a currency board was introduced in Bulgaria as well as in the three Baltic States. According to some economists, the experience of transition economies shows that several motives determine the establishment of a currency board: (1) it is a way to build up credibility for a newly created national currency, and it enhances monetary sovereignty after the country leaves the rouble zone (Estonia); (2) it is done to follow other countries with similar economic structures, where this monetary regime has been implemented and operates successfully (Lithuania); and (3) it is done to replace a discretionary central bank in order to restore confidence in the national currency and to overcome deep financial crisis (Bulgaria).[36] While Estonia initiated the introduction of a currency board, and, thus, at first had a disagreement with the International Monetary Fund (IMF), Lithuania, and especially Bulgaria, on the

---

36   Nenovsky N. 'The Currency Board in Estonia, Lithuania and Bulgaria: Comparative Analysis', https://www.researchgate.net/publication/46531621. *See also* Kern, K. & Löffelsend, T., 'Sustainable Development in the Baltic Sea Region. Governance beyond the Nation State', *Local Environment*. Oct 2004, Vol. 9, Issue 5, pp. 451–467. Hilmarsson, H. 'The Baltic States and the Challenge of Being a Small Donor', ISSN 1392-3137. TILTAI, 2012, Vol. 58, Issue 1, pp. 1–14.

other hand, took steps toward currency board establishment mainly under pressure from the IMF.

However, the introduction of a Currency Board in the Baltic States clearly yielded results from Estonia as of the beginning of 2011, and from 1 January 2014 Latvia and Lithuania on 1 January 2015 were admitted as members of the Eurozone.[37]

A report by the Bulgarian Chamber of Commerce states that regarding Bulgaria, together with the three Baltic States, the currency board system was included in the so-called BELLs group (Bulgaria, Estonia, Lithuania, Latvia) as opposed to the PIGS[38] group made up of the four over-indebted economies from the periphery of the EU.

The three Baltic States in the BELLs group are the closest analogues of the monetary and fiscal policy implemented in 1997 in Bulgaria. At the same time, the high fiscal sustainability and creditworthiness of the BELLs countries and the benefits of the long-term policy of a fixed exchange rate have been achieved at the cost of huge 'internal bleeding' – the so-called Internal Devaluation (ILO and UNCTAD, 2014), limited opportunities for restructuring the economy, depressed labour markets, a demographic and emigration crisis, including due to delay in joining the Eurozone.[39]

The accession of the three Baltic States to the Eurozone in the period 2011–2015 (for which preparations began in 2005) allowed the effects of the global economic crisis, the so-called 'property bubble' and worsening political and economic relations with the Russian Federation to be overcome or significantly mitigated. A bare analysis also shows numerous positive effects both for CEE economies from the first wave of joining the Eurozone (Slovenia, Slovakia) and for the second wave (Estonia – 2011, Latvia – 2014, and Lithuania – 2015), for which there are more similarities to the economic and demographic situation in Bulgaria.[40]

Bulgaria is now a step closer to the euro after the 19 finance ministers of the Eurogroup agreed that Sofia should become the 20th country in the Eurozone

---

37 The Eurozone is a monetary union of 19 of the 28 European Union (EU) Member States which have adopted the euro (€) as their common currency and sole legal tender.
38 The PIGS acronym originally refers to the economies of the Southern European countries of Portugal, Italy, Greece, and Spain.
39 Доклад „Присъединяването на България към Еврозоната – очаквания, времева рамка, подготовка и необходими реформи", https://www.bia-bg.com/standpoint/view/21567.
40 *Ibid.*

by July 2019.[41] Eurozone ministers said that Bulgaria should "thoroughly implement the reforms monitored by the Commission under the Cooperation and Verification Mechanism in the areas of judicial reform and the fight against corruption as well as organised crime in light of their importance for the stability and integrity of the financial system". The Bulgarian press commented that Bulgaria is the first country scheduled to be admitted to the Eurozone after the introduction of the banking union: "The Eurozone is at a crossroads.... Either it respects the formal accession criteria or the Member States make a political decision.... That entails a big risk for the EU because Bulgaria has fulfilled the accession criteria for some years now. Not allowing it to join the Eurozone would convey the impression of a lack of principles and equal rights in the monetary union and in the EU as a whole".[42]

3.3 Similar Demographic Problems

Another common problem for Bulgaria and the Baltic States, which can be highlighted, is the demographic crisis that even provokes public debate about national extinction.

The fall of the Berlin wall was followed by a massive exodus of the population of Eastern European countries. As a result of the new 'resettlement of peoples', human losses to Eastern Europe were much greater than those of both world wars.[43] Over the past 30 years, Bulgaria and Lithuania have lost 20.8% of their population and Latvia 25.3% of its population.[44] Depopulation of Eastern Europe is connected not only to the outflow of labour resources: after 1989, the era of wild capitalism began in the former 'socialist countries', accompanied by the collapse of social and medical systems, a sharp increase in mortality, especially among men, with a simultaneous fall in the birth rate. The EU rules on free movement of labour have made it much easier for Bulgarians to work in the other Member States. The most significant outflow was observed in Lithuania: over 300,000 people out of 3 million left the country.

The UN projects that Bulgaria's population will fall from 7.1 million to 5.2 million by 2050, making it the world's fastest-shrinking country (the next nine

---

41   The Eurogroup backs Bulgaria to join the Eurozone by July 2019, https://www.neweurope.eu/article/eurogroup-backs-bulgaria-join-eurozone-july-2019.
42   'Postponement bad for EU image', *Trud BG*, 18 May 2018.
43   On the topic of contemporary challenges for public law and in particular for criminal law cf. V. Vachev, 'Racjonalizacja prawa wykroczeń – potrzebna jest reforma' (in) *Węzłowe problemy prawa wykroczeń – czy potrzebna jest reforma?* – M. Kolendowska-Matejczuk, V. Vachev (eds.), Warszawa 2016, p. 63.
44   'Eastern Europe experiencing deep demographic crisis', https://www.novinite.com/articles/190919/Eastern+Europe+Experiencing+Deep+Demographic+Crisis.

are also in Eastern Europe). This demographic catastrophe, concentrated in the countryside, finds its cruellest expression in Bulgaria's neglected northwest, the poorest region of the poorest country in the European Union.

In 2017 a total of 57,175 babies were born in this country which has a population of 7.1 million people. Thus, Bulgaria marked a record-low birth-rate since 1945. The babies born in 2017 were nearly 8,000 fewer compared to the previous year. Meanwhile, nearly 108,000 Bulgarians passed away in 2017, as shown by data from the National Statistical Institute.[45] Moreover, many Bulgarians left the country to study and work abroad. It turns out that in 2017 only the population of Bulgaria decreased by 65–70,000 people which equals the population of a medium-sized Bulgarian town. Highly-developed European countries usually take measures when their population is ageing. Bulgaria, however, has taken partial and modest measures, because the authorities do not want to further strain already tense relations between the different ethnic groups, namely the Bulgarian and Roma populations.

Similarly, in 2000, Latvia's population stood at 2.38 million. At the start of this year, it was 1.95 million. No other country has had a more precipitous fall in population – 18.2 percent according to UN statistics. Only Latvia's fast-shrivelling neighbour, Lithuania with a 17.5 percent decrease, comes close.

To be sure, economic migration is not the only reason for the country's declining population. The small Baltic republic's comparatively low birth rate and high mortality rate are also contributing factors.

Against the backdrop of Bulgaria, Latvia and Lithuania, Estonia stands out in respect of its demographic situation. In 2015 the country experienced population growth. Improved well-being has increased immigration to Estonia, in particular from third countries. Prof. Bagdonas from Fatih University, Istanbul emphasizes that this challenge to the EU stemmed from the inability to maintain some of the existing rules due to their cost, and the inability to change those rules due to self-imposed structural normative constraints and disagreements about the nature of the required changes.[46] The year 2015 was significant in that, for the first time in 25 years, the number of people who took up residence in Estonia exceeded the number of those who left. But it should be noted that the population mainly increased as a result of net immigration by

---

[45] 'Demographic catastrophe in Bulgaria to result in economic collapse', bnr.bg/en/post/100917894/demographic-catastrophe-in-bulgaria-to-result-in-economic-collapse.

[46] Bagdonas, Ąžuolas 'The EU Migration Crisis and Baltic Security', *Journal on Baltic Security* Vol. 1, Issue 2, 2015. *See also* Ivanova, D. 'Migrant Crisis and the Visegrád Group`s Policy', Volume 22: Issue 1, DOI: https://doi.org/10.1515/kbo-2016-0007, 2016, pp. 41–45.

European Union citizens, with citizens of Russia and Ukraine making up the bulk of non-EU immigration.

4   Conclusion

The three Baltic States and Bulgaria have many common aspects in terms of their political, diplomatic and economic development both in the 1920s and in the period after the collapse of the socialist system. In the 1920s, these four countries were focused mainly on the idea of newly gained independence and realization of their national ideals as well as on enhancing their international reputation and membership of the League of Nations. The independence of the Baltic States has been a crucial political event that underlines the right of self-determination of peoples and has a significant impact upon the formation of the contemporary political and legal system. This article has examined a number of common areas related to the implementation of official diplomatic relations in different periods which shows the connectivity, common issues but particular specificities as well.

The period after the end of the Cold war leads to an overlap in the foreign policy priorities of the Baltic States and Bulgaria, namely accession to Euro-Atlantic organizations such as NATO and the EU.[47] In the pre-accession period, Bulgaria initially fell into the so-called Helsinki Group, along with Lithuania and Latvia, and also had to resolve a problem with its Kozloduy nuclear power plant as did Lithuania with its Ignalina plant.

The introduction of a currency board in the BELL group countries (Bulgaria, Estonia, Latvia and Lithuania) was judged by economists as a success, which led to the three Baltic States being included in the eurozone (during the period 2011–2015). Similarly, despite some criticisms, the currency board system represents the advantage that outlines the near future of Bulgaria's accession to the eurozone.

It should be noted that both the Baltic States and Bulgaria are external borders of the European Union. This means that they have a key role in the promotion of European values and the strong engagement of solidarity among Member States in resolving common political problems. An expression of Bulgaria's political relations with the Baltic States was the case in 2015 when Prime Minister Boyko Borisov delegated powers to Lithuanian president Dalia

---

47   Mölder, H. 'NATO's Role in the Post-Modern European Security Environment, Cooperative Security and the Experience of the Baltic Sea Region', *Baltic Security & Defence Review*, Volume 8, 2006, Vol. 8, pp. 7–33.

Grybauskaite to represent the Republic of Bulgaria during an EU summit. Mr. Borisov was prompted to leave Brussels and fly back home due to an incident on the Bulgarian-Turkish border. Further improvement of co-operation between the Baltic States and Bulgaria could be achieved through development of more active bilateral relations and establishment of diplomatic representation on a reciprocal basis.

Last but not least, this article has drawn attention to a significant problem that the three Baltic States and Bulgaria have to deal with, namely the demographic crisis. This problem is particularly important in the light of migratory pressures that the countries outlining the external borders of the European Union are facing and it involves systematic and long-term efforts.

CHAPTER 5

Finland's Continuation War (1941–1944): War of Aggression or Defence? War of Alliance or Separate War?

Analyzed from the International – Especially Legal – Perspective

Lauri Hannikainen

Abstract

In September 1939, after having included a secret protocol on spheres of influence in the so-called Molotov-Ribbentrop Pact, Germany and the Soviet Union invaded Poland and divided it between themselves. It was not long before the Soviet Union approached Finland by proposing exchanges of certain territories: 'in our national interest we want to have from you certain territories and offer in exchange territories twice as large but in less crucial areas'. Finland, suspicious of Soviet motives, refused – the outcome was the Soviet war of aggression against Finland by the name of the Winter War in 1939–1940. The Soviet Union won this war and compelled Finland to cede several territories – about 10 per cent of Finland's area.

After the Winter War, Finland sought protection from Germany against the Soviet Union and decided to rely on Germany. After Germany attacked the Soviet Union in June 1941, Finland joined the German war effort in the so-called Continuation War and reoccupied the territories lost in the Winter War. Finnish forces did not stop at the old border but occupied Eastern (Soviet) Karelia with a desire eventually to annex it. By that measure, Finland joined as Germany's ally in its war of aggression against the Soviet Union in violation of international law. In their strong reliance on Germany, the Finnish leaders made some very questionable decisions without listening to warnings from Western States about possible negative consequences.

Germany lost its war and so did Finland, which barely avoided entire occupation by the Soviet Army and succeeded in September 1944 in concluding an armistice with the Soviet Union. Finland lost some more territories and was subjected to many obligations and restrictions in the 1947 Paris Peace Treaty, dictated by the Allies.

This article analyses, according to the criteria of international law, Finland's policy shortly prior to and during the Continuation War, especially Finland's secret dealings with Germany in the months prior to the German attack against the Soviet Union and Finland's occupation of Eastern Karelia in the autumn of 1941. After Adolf Hitler declared that Germany was fighting against the Soviet Union together with Finland and Romania, was the Soviet Union entitled – prior to the Finnish attack – to resort to armed force in self-defence against Finland? And was Finland treated too harshly in the aftermath of World War II? After all, its role as an ally of Germany had been rather limited.

Keywords

war of aggression – armed force in self-defence – occupation – Finland in World War II – Finland as an ally of Germany – the 1947 Paris Peace Treaty – the Kellogg-Briand Pact

1   Introduction

1.1   *Finland's First Two Decades of Independence*

The first decades of Finland's independence were turbulent times.[1] The autonomous Grand Duchy of the Russian Empire declared its independence on 6 December 1917. The revolutionary Bolshevik regime of Russia gave its formal recognition to Finland's independence on 31 December – in the name of peoples' right to self-determination. Recognitions were soon received from others of Finland's neighbours and a number of other European States, such as Germany and France. In early 1918 a civil war broke out in Finland, when the Reds, representing the lower classes, rebelled against the bourgeois White government. The Reds were inspired, encouraged and materially helped by the Bolshevik regime.[2]

The bloody civil war lasted until mid-May and resulted in the victory of the White side, with the help of military intervention by Germany, which took place upon invitation by the Whites. The Reds were severely punished and masses of Red prisoners died in the camps due to poor nourishment and epidemic diseases.[3]

---

[1] Finland was under the sovereignty of Sweden for many centuries and under the Russian Empire's sovereignty from 1809 until 1917.

[2] See L. Hannikainen, 'The Finnish Civil War 1918 and its Aftermath', in L. Hannikainen & R. Hanski & A. Rosas (eds.), *Implementing Humanitarian Law Applicable in Armed Conflicts – The Case of Finland*, (Martinus Nijhoff Publishers, Dordrecht, 1992), pp. 9–12; J. Kekkonen, *Kun aseet puhuvat*, (Art House, Helsinki, 2016), pp. 95–99.

[3] Kekkonen, *ibid*, pp. 41–174.

Finland was not satisfied with its eastern boundary. It demanded sovereignty over the whole of Karelia – even Eastern Karelia that had belonged to Russia for a long time. The Karelians belong to the Finno-Ugric tribe. Finland considered itself as the mother country of Karelia. Finland organized military interventions to Eastern Karelia in 1918–19; however, all were unsuccessful.[4]

The disagreements between Finland and Bolshevik Russia were settled by the Peace Treaty of Tartu (Dorpat) in 1920.[5] Finland had some freedom of choice on whether it would like to have sovereignty over a part of Eastern Karelia or over the Pechenga region in the north. Finland opted for Pechenga as this secured Finnish access to the Arctic Ocean. Eastern Karelia remained under Russia.[6] Russia gave, however, a unilateral declaration assuring that it would grant autonomy to Eastern Karelia.[7] This declaration was not a part of the Peace Treaty and was not strictly binding. The question about the potential threat of the vicinity of the border to the security of St Petersburg (Leningrad) was not on the table as an important matter (see Figure 1).

In 1921 anti-Bolshevik forces in Eastern Karelia revolted against Bolshevik power. Finnish fighters played a substantial role in the resulting armed conflict – one of the leading figures of the revolting forces was the Finnish Major Paavo Talvela. The revolt was suppressed by the Bolsheviks.[8] The Finnish action violated the Tartu Peace Treaty.

Finland became a member of the League of Nations in 1921, whereas Russia (the Soviet Union since 1922) remained outside. Finland attempted to bring the case of Eastern Karelia to the leading organs of the League and was to some degree successful but, ultimately, this effort failed.[9]

In these two neighbouring countries, their civil wars had ended differently. In Russia, the Bolsheviks were able to defeat the White forces, whereas in Finland the Whites were victorious. No surprise that relations between these neighbouring countries remained cool, even somewhat hostile.

---

4 Hannikainen, *supra* note 2, pp. 32–40, and J. Niinistö, *Heimosotien historia 1918–1922* (SKS, Helsinki, 2005), pp. 10–85 and 148–183.
5 Treaty of Peace between Finland and Russia, 3 *LNTS* 5.
6 See J. Niinistö, *Bobi Sivén, Karjalan puolesta* (SKS, Helsinki, 2001), pp. 149–165.
7 J. Kallenautio, *Suomi katsoi eteensä – Itsenäisen Suomen ulkopolitiikka 1917–1955* (Tammi, Helsinki, 1985), pp. 62–66.
8 See T. Nygård, *Suur-Suomi vai lähiheimolaisten auttaminen*, (Otava, Helsinki, 1978), p. 87, Niinistö, *supra* note 4, pp. 246–261, and H. Seppälä, *Suomi miehittäjänä 1941–1944* (SN-kirjat, Helsinki, 1989), pp. 13–14.
9 Permanent Court of International Justice: *Finland v. Russia, Advisory Opinion on the Status of Eastern Carelia*, Advisory Opinion No. 5, 1923, www.worldcourts.com (visited on 19 February 2010).

In the early 1930s, the Soviet Union wanted to strengthen its security through non-aggression treaties with its neigbouring States. Finland and the Soviet Union concluded their Non-aggression Treaty in 1932; its binding force was extended until 1945 in an additional Protocol in 1934.[10] If the parties were not able to settle their disputes through diplomatic negotiation, they had to submit them to international mediation before a specific mediation board. Under the Protocol, it was not permitted to denounce the treaty before 1945. The Soviet Union was accepted into membership of the League of Nations in 1933. Notwithstanding the bilateral treaty, Finnish-Soviet relations were quite strained. In Moscow, Finland was regarded as one of the most anti-Soviet European States whose face was turned towards Germany, which after the takeover by the Nazis became the ideological arch enemy of the Soviet Union.[11] The atmosphere became very tense towards the end of the 1930s.

1.2   Scope of this Article

In this article I plan to analyse and draw conclusions regarding Finland's role in the Continuation War: the primary question is whether it was a war of aggression or of defence under international law. The related secondary question is whether it was a war of alliance with Germany or something else, for example, a war of co-belligerents in which both had their own separate goals and cooperated only to a limited extent – or was it simply Finland's separate war against the Soviet Union? In my legal analysis, I take a broad view and try to discuss all relevant factors in order to make the analysis rich and, hopefully, to be able to arrive at well-reasoned conclusions. I also discuss the treatment Finland received after the Continuation War from the victorious Allied powers.

Historians have extensively examined the Continuation War and the events preceding it, but no international legal analyses have been done for over 75 years. During the Continuation War, the Finnish government requested the leading Finnish expert in international law, Professor Rafael Erich, to write a legal analysis in support of Finland. I will naturally analyse Erich's report. Finnish historians have focused on analysing the question whether the Continuation War was a war of alliance or something less. I fully understand that historians do not want to become judges on what has happened, but focus in

---

10   See *Suomen Asetuskokoelman Sopimussarja* 13/1932 and 58/1934. The original language of the treaty and of the protocol was French.
11   Kallenautio, *supra* note 7, pp. 146–148.

their studies to finding out what happened and how and why. To a limited degree, some historians have addressed some legal aspects of the present theme, but I have found no attempts to analyze the aggression/defence theme in legal terms.

My main method in this article is decidedly normative, primarily and as much as possible legal and secondarily moral. The reason for this choice can be found from the previous paragraph. If historians have written numerous studies about the Continuation War, but no international legal expert has endeavoured to examine objectively the questions formulated in the first paragraph of this section, surely it is reasonable for me to choose the normative approach? This method is commonplace in legal research: to analyse legal norms and to try to end up with a well-reasoned conclusion – in this case, to interpret whether, in the first months of the Continuation War, Finland violated the Kellogg-Briand Pact and was guilty of an aggressive war, or not. Since I am not a judge but a scholarly analyst, I prefer to examine the case in a broader international and political perspective.

Is the approach chosen here relevant more than seventy years after the Continuation War? Historians have examined this war extensively and engaged in a lively discussion. I want to enrich the picture by adding the perspective of normative international law in this discussion.

I start my legal analysis from the late autumn of 1939. Since the Soviet Union grossly violated international law in the Winter War, was not Finland justified in resorting to armed force and besides taking back the territories lost at the end of the Winter War also justified in proceeding even further to the East for the purpose of obtaining reparation for the gross violation of its sovereignty and perhaps to secure better possibilities to defend itself against the Soviet Union?

In this article, I examine Finnish and foreign historians' writings about the Continuation War. Additionally, the views of foreign non-academic experts, such as diplomats, are discussed. Since especially leading Western powers and Sweden closely followed the developments of the Continuation War and Finland's policies, it is advisable to include the views of their representatives in this study. The legal analysis will of course resort to international instruments and writings by international legal experts.

Among my leading history sources, I mention the book *Finland in World War II* (2012) in which 14 Finnish and one German younger generation historians analyse Finland's role from different angles – however, not from the legal angle. Regarding international law, besides certain conventions and treaties, my main source is Professor Ian Brownlie's excellent book *International Law and the Use of Force by States*, 1963. I also resort to a number of other legal experts but regret that none of them has analysed the Continuation War in any depth.

Analyses by contemporary historians have poorly penetrated the conscience of the leadership of Finland and the public at large, who continue to maintain highly patriotic interpretations of Finland's role in the Continuation War – pointing to Finland's separate war from Germany.

This article goes on as follows: Part 2 discusses Finland's complicated path to the Continuation War, its waging of – and difficult exit from – the war, including the main provisions of the Paris Peace Treaty. Part 3 contains analysis, primarily legal analysis. The article ends with concluding observations.

2   Finland's Path to the Continuation War, Waging the War and Exiting from the War

2.1   *The Winter War*

Nazi Germany attacked Poland on 1 September 1939, starting World War II. A week beforehand, Germany and the Soviet Union had concluded a non-aggression treaty – the so-called Molotov-Ribbentrop treaty – to the astonishment of other States. This instrument had a secret protocol that defined the spheres of influence of the parties.[12] Pursuant to the protocol, the Soviet Union invaded the eastern part of Poland in later September. In the protocol, Finland fell within the sphere of influence of the Soviet Union. Notwithstanding the conclusion of the treaty, both parties knew that they were ideological arch enemies. Neither could they trust the other party to honour the treaty.

Soon the Soviet Union approached Finland and proposed territorial changes. Namely, Finland should: (1) move the border westward in the Karelian isthmus (located between the Baltic Sea and Lake Ladoga), because the Soviet Union wanted to ensure the security of Leningrad; (2) cede a number of islands in the Baltic Sea; (3) cede a part of Pechenga; and (4) lease the town of Hanko and its surroundings on the southern coast of Finland to the Soviet Union for the establishment of a naval military base.

---

12   Secret Supplementary Protocols of the Molotov-Ribbentrop Non-Aggression Pact, September 1, 1939, quoted in *History and Public Policy Program Digital Archive*, Library of Congress of the United States, http://digitalarchive.wilsoncenter.org/document/110994, (visited on 3 March 2018).

As compensation, Finland would get territory from the western part of Eastern Karelia, twice the size of the area it was proposed that Finland should give up. Finland was ready to make limited compromises – one being to transfer the border in the Karelian isthmus westward, but not so far as to lose the second biggest town in Finland: Vyborg. Finland refused to lease Hanko. The Finnish choices were understandable, because Vyborg was very important for Finland and a Soviet military presence near Helsinki would be a threat to Finland's security and independence.

The Finnish line was drawn by Foreign Minister Eljas Erkko, with the strong support of Prime Minister Paavo Cajander and many other leading politicians. Erkko believed that Finland should not adopt a compromising line, with the exception of limited concessions. When the negotiations came to a dead end in November (Finland interrupted them), Erkko was convinced that after an intermission the Soviet Union would be ready to continue negotiations even though it spiced its demands with threats of military action.[13] To his surprise, the Soviet Union gave up the negotiations and launched an armed attack against Finland at the end of November and declared the creation of a puppet regime for Finland, composed of Finnish Communists.[14] This meant a threat that the Soviet leadership aimed at conquering Finland and making it a socialist country – either a close ally or a part of the Soviet Union.

After fierce fighting, the Soviet Union compelled Finland into signing a peace treaty in March 1940.[15] The Soviet Union did not occupy Finland and had to give up its support to the puppet regime. In the peace treaty Finland lost ten per cent of its territory, including eastern parts of Finnish Karelia where a part of the most important industry of Finland was located. The border in the Karelian isthmus was moved westward (Finland lost Vyborg) and the Soviet Union

---

13 See Kallenautio, *supra* note 7, pp. 178–187, and H. Meinander, 'Finland and the Great Powers in World War II: Ideologies, Geopolitics, Diplomacy', in *Finland in World War II – History, Memory, Interpretations*, T. Kinnunen & V. Kivimäki (eds.), (Brill, Leiden 2012), pp. 49–91 and 58–59. Professor H. Ylikangas in *Suomen historian solmukohdat* (WSOY, Helsinki 2007), pp. 254–264, considers that Soviet territorial demands were rather modest – especially compared with the outcome of the Winter War. From abroad Finland was warned about Soviet readiness to attack Finland.

14 On the Winter War in general, *see* P. Tuunainen, 'The Finnish Army at War: Operations and Soldiers, 1939–45', in Kinnunen & Kivimäki , *supra* note 13, pp. 140–151.

15 Treaty of Peace between Finland and the Union of Soviet Socialist Republics, *Finnish Treaty Series* no. 3/1940.

built its naval base in the Hanko area (see Figure 2). Diplomatic relations were soon resumed between the parties.

Finland had been the victim of a blatantly aggressive war, in violation of the Covenant of the League of Nations, the Tartu Peace Treaty and the bilateral Non-Aggression Treaty. The Finns defended their country stubbornly and successfully, but the opponent had so many more troops that ultimately the Finnish defence was not enough to continue fighting. Finland received considerable material and moral support internationally, and the League of Nations expelled the Soviet Union from membership.[16] A voluntary Swedish air squadron participated in the defence of northern Finland. Sweden did not declare itself neutral – non-belligerent, though. Volunteers from many countries came to fight for Finland's defence. The biggest group came from Sweden (8,000) with the slogan: *'Finlands sak är vår'*.[17]

Thus, in the Winter War the Soviet Union grossly violated international law. Even though it reached its goals, it lost an excessively large number of soldiers due to inefficient organization and maintenance. One Soviet officer was said to have stated bluntly that the Soviet Union occupied enough land to bury its dead. One may have some understanding towards the Soviet Union's worry about the security of Leningrad, but the way the Soviet Union behaved was thuggish and manifestly illegal.[18]

The Finnish foreign policy leadership made a political mistake by misevaluating the Soviet Union's next moves in November 1939. It should be noted that such leading personalities as the military hero Marshal C.G. Mannerheim, and the leader of the Finnish delegation at the 1920 Tartu negotiations, J.K. Paasikivi – both future presidents of Finland – had supported a more compromising line for Finland in the negotiations.

Nearly all inhabitants from the territories lost by Finland to the Soviet Union – 420,000 – moved to Finland and had to be resettled. They lost their homes and property. It was a huge task for Finland to resettle such a big population.

---

16   See I. Brownlie *International Law and the Use of Force by States* (Oxford University Press, 1963) pp. 105–107.
17   O. Bring, *Neutralitetens uppgång och fall*, (Atlantis, Stockholm, 2008), pp. 197–201, and Swedish Airforce Museum, Vinterkriget: Den svenska hjälpen, a factsheet, 7 November 2017.
18   See A. Upton, *Välirauha*, (Kirjayhtymä, Helsinki, 1965), pp. 20–25 and pp. 13–19, (original title, *Finland in Crisis 1940–1941*).

FINLAND'S CONTINUATION WAR (1941–1944)

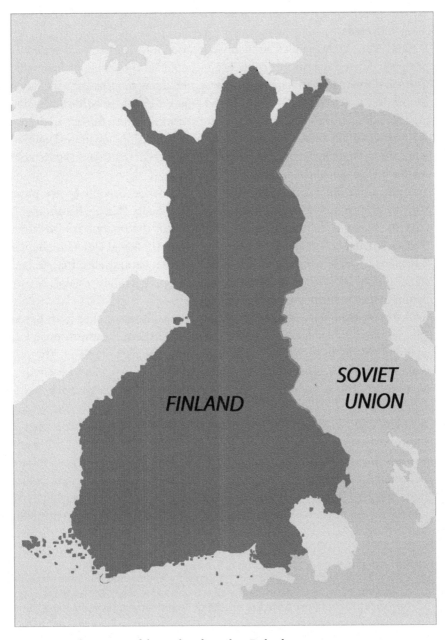

FIGURE 5.1 The territory of the newly independent Finland, 1920

2.2 The Inter-war Period: From Survival Worries to Greater Finland Dreams

Finland had barely avoided foreign occupation and had suffered much. Its prospects for the near future grew even dimmer in the spring of 1940 when Germany occupied Denmark and Norway, and a few months later the Soviet Union, as a countermove,[19] occupied and annexed the three Baltic States. Blatant violations of international law again. From Finland's foreign trade perspective, Germany then controlled the movement of shipping in the Denmark Strait. Thus, factually Finland's possibilities for foreign trade were restricted to trade with Sweden and Germany.

In the months following the peace treaty, the Soviet Union required punctual observance from Finland of the terms of the treaty. During the summer of 1940, its demands increased beyond the terms of the treaty – it also issued threats. Finland had ample reason to suspect that the Soviet Union might plan the same fate for it as for the Baltic States.[20] Since it became clear that Finland could not rely on Sweden or Britain for any substantial military help, the only option to seek security from was Germany.

In August 1940, the Finnish leadership received a secret offer from Berlin. The German Army wanted to transfer troops to Northern Norway through Finland and offered in exchange to sell modern weaponry to Finland. The proposal was immediately accepted and led to a warming of the Finnish-German relationship. The treaty on the transfer of German troops was concluded in September.[21]

In late autumn 1940, the parties to the Molotov-Ribbentrop Pact met in Berlin. After the meeting the Germans, informing the Finns about the secret protocol to the Molotov-Ribbentrop Pact, said that Foreign Minister Molotov had wanted Germany's confirmation that Finland would continue to belong to the sphere of influence of the Soviet Union. Molotov wanted consent – or at least non-expression of opposition – that the Soviet Union was entitled to

---

19   According to Kallenautio, *supra* note 7, p. 215, the Soviet Union was convinced that in the near future it would end up in a war against Germany. See also A. Beevor, *Toinen maailmansota*, (WSOY, Helsinki, 2012), p. 17 (original title: *The Second World War*), and Ylikangas, *supra* note 13, p. 270.
20   See P. Visuri, *Mannerheimin ja Rytin vaikeat valinnat*, (Docendo, Jyväskylä, 2013), p. 38.
21   Meinander, *supra* note 13, p. 68, and Upton, *supra* note 18, p. 193. The entry into force of the treaty took place with exchange of notes. President Ryti signed the treaty for Finland. The conclusion of the treaty alarmed the leaders of the Soviet Union, who suspected – correctly – that it would be used as a pretext to station German soldiers in Finland.

FINLAND'S CONTINUATION WAR (1941-1944)

solve the Finnish question in the way it wanted – even to invade Finland. However, Adolf Hitler had refused his consent to any occupation.[22] Whether this information was fully correct is uncertain. According to Ylikangas, Molotov did not refer to the use of armed force but simply to solving the question of Finland in accordance with the pact.[23] Molotov's main concern may have been that Germany should not send its armed forces to Finland. Germany also informed Finland about the Barbarossa Plan, that is, to commit a wholesale armed attack on the Soviet Union. Through this information Germany aimed to open negotiations with the Finns about closer military cooperation.

Secret negotiations were conducted between the high military representatives of Germany and Finland during the first half of 1941. In late March, the Finnish leadership was informed that the offensive would probably begin on 22 June. According to contemporary historians, apparently in February-March but certainly at the latest in May 1941, the Finnish leadership decided to join Germany's attack against the Soviet Union, if it were to take place.[24] In his comprehensive study, Jokipii concludes that in March the Finnish leadership took the decisive step in its mind in favour of close cooperation with Germany.[25]

Decisive negotiations were conducted during May-June, the most important round taking place in Helsinki between 3 and 6 June. Surprisingly few documents are available about the results of these negotiations between military men. In his biography on J.K. Paasikivi, Tuomo Polvinen writes that in the negotiations in May it was aggressive war, not defensive war, that was on the agenda. When Finland's chief negotiator, General Erik Heinrichs, returned to Finland he brought with him a clearly formulated proposal for participation in an aggressive war. The proposal was accepted by the inner circle of the Finnish leadership. When President Risto Ryti informed the cabinet about the danger

---

22 See Upton, *supra* note 18, pp. 233-236 and 346; Vilhelm Assarsson, *Stalinin varjossa*, (WSOY, Porvoo-Helsinki, 1963), p. 50 (original title: *I skuggan av Stalin*); Wipert von Blücher, *Suomen kohtalonaikoja – Muistelmia vuosilta 1935-44*, (WSOY, Porvoo-Helsinki, 1951) p. 214; Michael Jonas, *Kolmannen valtakunnan lähettiläs – Wipert von Blücher ja Suomi*, (Ajatus Kirjat, Gummerus Kustannus Oy, Helsinki, 2010), p. 175 (original title: *Wipert von Blücher und Finnland – Alternativpolitik und Diplomatie im 'Dritten Reich'*).
23 Ylikangas, *supra* note 13, p. 278.
24 M. Jokipii, *Jatkosodan synty – Tutkimus Saksan ja Suomen sotilaallisesta yhteistyöstä 1940-41* (Otava, Helsinki, 1987), pp. 622 and 634-637, and *Jatkosodan pikkujättiläinen*, J. Leskinen & A. Juutilainen (eds.), (WSOY, Helsinki, 2007), pp. 19 and 43.
25 Jokipii, *ibid.*, p. 636.

of war and the need for partial mobilization, he did not mention the results of the negotiations with Germany.[26]

According to Meinander, in the spring and summer of 1941 Germany was strongly present in the public life of Finland. In April, a German industry exhibition was arranged in Helsinki during which the Nazi swastika and Finnish flags flew together. Many German lecturers visited Finland and strengthened the belief of the Finns that Germany was the unchallenged master of Europe. Visions of a so-called Greater Finland, the old nationalist dream of expanding Finnish territory far eastwards into Eastern (Soviet) Karelia, were no longer just daydreams. Meinander goes on:

> Despite their Western sympathies, both President Ryti and Marshal Mannerheim were convinced in the spring of 1941 that Germany could beat the Soviet Union in a swift *Blitzkrieg*. In May 1941, President Ryti discreetly asked two scholars to write a scientifically formulated study, in which it was 'proven' that Soviet Eastern Karelia belonged to Finland both for geographical and cultural reasons. One month later a leading Finnish historian received a similar request from the president, who also needed political and strategic arguments for such an expansion. Both books were written to persuade decision-makers in Berlin of the future territorial claims in the east, and they were consequently published in Germany.[27]

Indeed, the books mentioned did not hide the Finnish belief that a reorganization of borders would take place in Europe and that Finland desired a meaningful role in that process. Visuri mentions that the books went along with Nazi views about *Lebensraum* and racial relations, applying them to Finland's circumstances.[28] The books were translated into several languages. One of them, written by Professor Jalmari Jaakkola, concluded that in the European reorganization of borders Finland and the Finno-Ugric people living in the Soviet Union should be treated justly. Finland should be entitled to fulfil its national and historic task of uniting all the Finno-Ugric peoples in one State. Finland should also be entitled to moral, legal and economic compensation for the barbaric aggression by the Soviet Union in 1939 and 1941. Thus, the Soviet Union should cede to Finland – besides those territories which it seized in the 1940 peace treaty – also Eastern Karelia and the Kola peninsula. An exchange of

---

26 T. Polvinen, *J.K. Paasikivi, Valtiomiehen elämäntyö 3, 1939–1944*, (WSOY, Porvoo, 1995) pp. 294–295.
27 Meinander, *supra* note 13, pp. 70–71.
28 Visuri, *supra* note 20, p. 30.

populations should also take place, with Finland receiving the Finnish (Finno-Ugric) population from the Soviet Union and the Soviet Union receiving the foreign (Russian) population from Finland. The vocabulary used by Jaakkola was openly nationalistic.[29]

In the course of the first months of 1941 the Soviet leadership became convinced that Germany's and Finland's relationship had become close. As a result, the Soviet Union changed its policy towards Finland, becoming more conciliatory, even making a number of proposals to that effect but not receiving any positive response. Finland, on the contrary, withdrew its ambassador, J.K. Paasikivi, from Moscow in May and did not appoint a new ambassador.[30]

In May-June 1941, a great number of German troops arrived in northern Finland so that when Germany attacked the Soviet Union on 22 June, some 200,000 German troops were there. It was agreed that the Finnish army units stationed in northern Finland were subordinated to the command of the regional German Supreme Commander. A number of joint military projects, mainly mine-laying operations, were taken, especially in the Baltic Sea area. Finland granted six airfields for use by the German Air Force.[31] Finland was ready to support Germany's war of aggression against the Soviet Union and to participate in it.

Nazi Germany attacked the Soviet Union (to its surprise) on 22 June 1941 with aggressive purpose and massive force, starting the biggest war ever between two States, Operation Barbarossa. Adolf Hitler declared that Germany was fighting together with Finland and Romania. At the time of the attack, Finland had already mobilized its armed forces, which were better equipped than ever. However, Finland did not want to be labelled as Germany's aggressive ally and therefore held back its attack for a few weeks.[32] Finland did not issue an official declaration of neutrality but a more informal one.[33] On 22 June Pavel Orlov, the Ambassador of the Soviet Union in Helsinki, in an interview with United Press stated that the Soviet Union wished that Finland would maintain peace with his country. The Soviet Union was ready to regard Finland as neutral as long as no military action was taken against his country from Finnish territory.[34] That was a difficult requirement, because Germany was using Finnish airfields in support of its bombing flights to the Soviet Union and at least two bands of Finnish guerrilla troops had crossed the border in the north for bombing

---

29 J. Jaakkola, *Finlands östproblem*, (Runar Schildts förlag, Helsingfors, 1941), pp. 95–97.
30 Paasikivi was considered by the Finnish leadership as too lenient towards the Soviet Union. See Upton, *supra* note 18, pp. 320–324 and 331–333, and Visuri, *supra* note 20, p. 49.
31 Jokipii, *supra* note 24, pp. 355–475 and 640–644.
32 Meinander, *supra* note 13, p. 69.
33 Jokipii, *supra* note 24, pp. 550 and 606.
34 *Ibid.*, pp. 605–606.

purposes.[35] In Pechenga the German-Finnish police force occupied the Soviet consulate.[36] Colonel Keijo Mikola estimates that even though formally Finland was outside the war until 25 June, its military cooperation with Germany must be interpreted in practical terms as wartime cooperation.[37]

Three days after Operation Barbarossa had begun (that is, on 25 June), the Soviet air force bombed a number of airfields in Finland, especially those which had been used by Germany in its bombing of Soviet territory, and some other targets.[38] The Soviet leadership calculated that Finland had agreed to become an ally of Germany.[39] Joint military projects between Germany and Finland in June 1941, the great number of German troops in Finland and the subordination of Finnish forces in the northern half of Finland under German command convinced the Soviets that it was advisable to bomb Finnish targets in self-defence without waiting for a Finnish attack.

The Soviet attack gave Finland a handy ground to declare to the world and to its own people that Finland had again been subjected to an armed attack. The Finnish people were astonished and believed that Finland had been subjected to a Soviet attack in a similar way as at the beginning of the Winter War. Negotiations and their results, as well as joint preparations, with Germany had been kept secret from publicity. Nor, too, was the Parliament well informed in this respect.[40]

Sweden and Britain were fully aware of the game that Finland was playing and[41] warned: you may be entering a road where you may have to face unpleasant surprises. They proved to be right.

On 10 July, Finland attacked in full force over its eastern border. Compared with the size of its population, Finland attacked with a large army – 470,000 soldiers. Over 100,000 other persons were connected to the Finnish military effort. In August, the number of troops rose to 520,000. Thus, about 16 per cent

---

35 Ibid., pp. 643–644, and P. Rantanen, *Suomi kaltevalla pinnalla*, (Atena, Jyväskylä, 2012), p. 310.
36 Visuri, *supra* note 20, p. 58.
37 K. Mikola, "Vuosien 1940–1941 saksalais-suomalaisen yhteistoiminnan tarkoitusperien ja muotojen tarkastelua", *Tiede ja ase*, No. 25, 1967, p. 143.
38 Jokipii, *supra* note 24, p. 603.
39 Aleksander Warma, the Estonian ambassador to Finland between 1939–1944, stated in his memoirs that after the outbreak of war between Germany and the Soviet Union there was no doubt that Finland's active entry into the war on the German side would be a matter of a few days. A. Warma, *Lähettiläänä Suomessa 1939–1944*, (Otava, Helsinki, 1973) p. 180.
40 Jokipii, *supra* note 24, pp. 353, 513, 620 and 624.
41 Ibid., p. 513, and Rantanen *supra* note 35, p. 299.

of the Finnish population participated directly in the Finnish war effort – according to Meinander it was a higher percentage than any of the other belligerent States so far in World War II. It appeared that Finland would be ready to go rather far to the east.[42] This was proved by the orders given by Marshal Mannerheim, the Commander in Chief of the Finnish Armed Forces.

In an order on 29 June, Mannerheim stated to the troops: "I invite you to a holy war against the enemy of our nation. ...in order to create a safe future for Finland we proceed to a crusade together with the powerful military forces of Germany against our enemies". In the so-called Scabbard Order on 10 July, Mannerheim stated in connection with the Finnish attack: "The freedom of Karelia and a greater Finland are glimmering in front of us in the enormous avalanche of world historic events.... Your victory will liberate Karelia, your deeds will create a great and happy future for Finland".[43] According to Jokipii, this statement adequately corresponded to the prevailing mood in the Finnish Military Headquarters.[44] President Risto Ryti in his radio speech on 26 June accused the Soviet Union in strong words for its policy against Finland and its latest blatant attack. This time, however, Finland was not left alone in its defence but was operating together with the military forces of the Third Reich.[45]

In northern Finland, Finnish forces openly crossed the border on 1 July and from then on took joint military action with German forces.[46] Whereas in southern and central Finland the crossing of the border took place to the territories lost by Finland as a result of the Winter War, in the north the attack over the border took place to territories which had long belonged to Russia.[47]

When the Finnish people recovered from the shock of the Soviet attack, they were strongly in favour of Finland's close relationship with Germany and even the attack to the east. The bitterness caused by the Winter War and the 1940 peace agreement, the fear of, and hatred of, violent socialism and the Russians,[48] and the possibility of reconquering the lost territories and creating

---

42   Meinander, *supra* note 13, p. 71.
43   The texts of Mannerheim's military orders can be found in www.mannerheim.fi/pkaskyt/s_paiva.htm – (visited on 19 February 2010; these military orders are in Finnish).
44   Jokipii, *supra* note 24, p. 448.
45   http://heninen.net/sopimus/ryti1941_f.htm – (visited on 9 August 2017).
46   Visuri, *supra* note 20, p. 58.
47   V. Kivimäki, 'Rintamamiesten Suur-Suomi', in *Luvattu maa*, S. Näre & J. Kirves (eds.), (Johny Kniga, Helsinki, 2014), p. 265.
48   It was common in Finland to call Russians by the derogatory name 'Russki' (ryssä). It was not uncommon that the bodies of dead Russian soldiers were called 'corpses' (ryssän raatoja) – like those of animals – instead of bodies, see V. Kivimäki &T. Tepora, 'Meaningless Death or Regenerating Sacrifice? Violence and Social Cohesion in Wartime Finland', in Kinnunen & Kivimäki, *supra* note 13, p. 258.

a Greater Finland with the help of Germany were in the minds of most Finnish people. The belief that the Soviet Union could be decisively defeated grew. In the autumn of 1941, the hopes of a Greater Finland seemed to become true and a kind of religious belief in Finland as a nation under the special protection of God spread among the people. The crusade against mankind's common enemy seemed to succeed.[49] The aggressive mood was particularly strong among higher military officers and the clergy within the military.[50] A strong belief in success prevailed for quite a long time because the government imposed strict censorship on the media.

2.3 The Reasoning behind Mannerheim's and Ryti's Choices

It is clear that Marshal Mannerheim, who continued to serve as the Commander in Chief, and President Ryti were the two persons who made the decisive war-related decisions in Finland – Mannerheim on the military side and Ryti on the political side. In addition, only three cabinet members belonged to the leading group that decided on relations with Germany and other important foreign policy matters.[51]

From the foregoing pages, the development of the thinking of Mannerheim and Ryti appears to be quite clear. In order to protect Finland's survival, the best solution seemed to be to rely on Germany. When negotiations with the Germans proceeded, Mannerheim and Ryti decided to join Finland with Germany's attack against the Soviet Union. They became convinced that Germany would defeat the Soviet Union decisively, apparently in a short time.[52] The Germans promised that besides recovering the territories lost as a result of the Winter War, Finland could invade other territories east of Finland, especially Eastern Karelia. Thus, the Finns drafted several alternative designs about additional territories to be occupied. It appeared advisable to attack eastwards in full force as a co-belligerent of Germany.

However, other possibilities were also in sight – unpleasant ones. The Finnish leadership had reason to worry that Germany might – after all – make a deal with the Soviet Union and sacrifice Finland to the Soviets. Or the Soviets would attack Finland, for example the Åland Islands or Finland's southern

---

49 O. Silvennoinen, 'Kumpujen yöhön', in Näre & Kirves, *supra* note 47, pp. 29–31. *See* Upton, *supra* note 18, pp. 368 and 379–380.
50 Kivimäki, *supra* note 47, p. 267.
51 The prime, foreign and defence ministers. During the first part of 1941 the Finnish chief negotiator in the military negotiations, General Erik Heinrichs, also participated in the inner circle's decision making.
52 Jokipii, *supra* note 24, pp. 542 and 619–622, Ylikangas, *supra* note 13, p. 271; Leskinen & Juutilainen, *supra* note 24, p. 74, Visuri, *supra* note 20, p. 30, Upton, *supra* note 18, p. 403.

coast or Pechenga in the north. Or Finland would end up with war on two fronts. It was in Finland's interest to tie itself so closely to Germany that it would not sacrifice Finland.[53]

Why did Mannerheim and Ryti adopt the line advocated by the supporters of the Greater Finland ideology? They were fully aware of the fact that Finland's population was only 3.7 million compared with the Soviet Union's population of 180 million. On what grounds did they think that even in the case of Germany's decisive victory the Russians would not come back later and accuse Finland of robbing Russia of its territories – taking military action to get them back? Did Mannerheim and Ryti calculate that Germany would completely destroy the Soviet Union and divide it (and Russia) into several vassal States or colonies? Presumably they must have thought so since they brushed aside all warnings.

2.4 Finland in the Continuation War

After the Finnish Army crossed the existing border on 10 July, it quite rapidly reconquered the territories lost in the 1940 peace treaty. This was done in early September, and without delay the Finnish Army continued its attack eastwards. On 1 October 1941, Finnish forces occupied the capital of Eastern Karelia, Petrozavodsk (Äänislinna), and by December Finland had occupied all of Eastern Karelia with the exception of certain territories in the north. Then the Finns stopped their advance and did not attempt to occupy any further areas.[54]

The Finnish army was a valuable addition to the German offensive to the east. Germany drafted 3.7 million soldiers for its attack. The third participant in the assault on the Soviet Union, Romania, only sent 150,000 soldiers at the beginning. The German leaders respected the quality of Finnish military forces' action. This respect could be seen in the discussions and cooperation between the two States in 1941–1944.

When the Finnish army reached the 1939 border, Britain and the United States called on Finland not to proceed further. Finland wanted to maintain decent relations with these States, but did not comply with their demands.

---

53 H.P. Krosby *Suomen valinta 1941*, (Kirjayhtymä, Helsinki, 1967), p. 179; Leskinen & Juutilainen, *supra* note 24, pp. 41 and 134, Rantanen, *supra* note 35, pp. 290–292. Edwin Linkomies, Finland's Prime Minister in 1943–1944, wrote in his memoirs that Ryti wished that Germany would attack the Soviet Union. E. Linkomies, *Vaikea aika*, (Otava, Helsinki, 1970), p. 86.

54 On the Continuation War in general, *see* Tuunainen, *supra* note 14, pp. 153–169, and Meinander, *supra* note 13, pp. 71–76.

Then it clumsily terminated its diplomatic relations with Britain.[55] In any case, Finland emphasized to the West that its warfare and goals were separate from those of Germany – it was fighting a separate war.

The Swedish ambassador in Helsinki, Mr Westman, was so openly critical about Finland's war policy that the Finnish government requested the Swedish government to recall Westman and to send a new ambassador to Helsinki.[56]

One cannot say that the Western States would have believed Finnish assurances, but yet they adopted a 'wait and see' attitude. However, when Finland was clearly going to invade nearly the whole of Eastern Karelia and signed the Anti-Komintern Pact with Germany, Italy and Japan in late November,[57] Britain declared war on Finland on its Independence Day, 6 December.

On the very same day, the Finnish Parliament declared its decision to bring the territories lost during the Winter War under the sovereignty of Finland once again. Mannerheim was not happy with that decision, because he thought the border should not be so near Leningrad.[58]

One day later, on 7 December, the Japanese attacked Pearl Harbour and a few days later Germany declared war on the United States. The Finnish leaders' worries even increased because the United States' joining the war significantly increased the strength of the group of States fighting against Germany – the Allies. The United States continued, however, to maintain diplomatic relations with Finland.

During 1941, Finland was successful in its warfare but yet it lost more men than in the Winter War. The Soviet army appeared to be stronger than in 1939–40. Germany, on the other hand, was not as successful in its attack as was expected. The war was not a Blitzkrieg but would be lasting longer and might not even end in victory. Mannerheim and Ryti had to admit that their evaluation about the forthcoming war had not been correct. Finland had drafted virtually all the men between the ages of 19.5 and 45 for the war effort exactly at harvest time. The outcome was that the harvest was smaller than usual. The need to release men from the army for the purposes of the labour market became

---

55   J.H. Magill, *Tasavalta tulikokeessa*, (Weilin & Göös, Mikkeli, 1981), p. 93, and Leskinen & Juutilainen, *supra* note 24, p. 126.
56   M. Reimaa, *Pohjoismaisia yhteyksiä Saksan vallan varjossa 1940–1944*, (Docendo, Jyväskylä, 2015), pp. 157–159.
57   Finland's accession to the Anti-Komintern Pact was interpreted internationally as general acceptance of the policies of Germany, Italy and Japan. About Finland's accession to the Pact, see Jonas, *supra* note 22, pp. 221–228.
58   *See* Visuri, *supra* note 20, p. 71.

imperative. Besides, Finland was highly dependent on Germany for food and military equipment.[59]

The Finns also had other worries. Meinander describes some of them as follows:

> During the winter of 1941–42, Marshal Mannerheim ... received alarming reports about how the Germans had gravely missed their chance to win over the population of the conquered areas in the Soviet Union by treating them with horrific brutality. This not only destroyed the credibility of the anti-communist arguments in the Nazi propaganda but also cast a shadow on their Finnish brother-in arms, who had emphasized that they, too, fought a war against communism and for the freedom of the Karelian people.[60]

Jonas decribes the fading of Finland's expectations:

> The heightened Finnish expectations towards Germany and a swift victory in the east cooled early on. After the Soviet Union failed to collapse as projected and survived the winter of 1941–42 greatly strained, though nonetheless basically intact, Helsinki's military-political leadership adjusted their projections accordingly. Mannerheim's early and 'boundless pessimism', surfacing from late 1941 onwards, transpired even to the German side and led the way to a whole series of increasingly gloomy perceptions on the part of the Finnish government and the country's better informed public. Helsinki's deepening scepticism and the risk that their essential ally in the northeast could break ranks left Berlin anxious....[61]

The Finnish leadership decided that it was advisable to limit Finland's future participation in the war. Finland refused to participate by active military means in the strangulation of Leningrad and cutting off the Murmansk railway.[62] Finland had exceeded its capabilities and had to diminish the size of its army. Participation in the strangulation of Leningrad would result in big losses.

---

59 Ylikangas, *supra* note 13, p. 297, Upton, *supra* note 18, p. 349–350, and Leskinen & Juutilainen, *supra* note 24, p. 154.
60 Meinander, *supra* note 13, p. 74. See also Assarsson, *supra* note 22, p. 90.
61 M. Jonas, "The Politics of Alliance: Finland in Nazi Foreign Policy and War Strategy", in Kinnunen & Kivimäki, *supra* note 13, pp. 120–121. See also H.O. Lunde, *Finlands val 1941–1944 – Samarbetet med Hitler-Tyskland*, (Fischer & Co, Sweden, 2014), p. 194, (original title: *Finland's War of Choice: The Troubled German-Finnish Coalition in WW II*, 2011).
62 Lunde, *ibid.*, pp. 196–197.

Germany tried to put pressure on Finland but when Finland did not yield, Germany gave up challenging the Finnish decision.

The period from the beginning of 1942 until the spring of 1944 can be characterized as stationary warfare at the front between Finland and the Soviet Union. Only sporadic fighting took place. In the course of this period, the position of Germany weakened – the decisive blow was the failure of the German forces at Stalingrad in early 1943, followed by the unsuccessful summer offensive against the Kursk salient later the same year. The Finnish leadership drew the conclusion that Germany would lose the war and that Finland would have difficult times ahead. It was advisable to be ready to pull out of the war at a suitable time, if the terms of an armistice were decent. However, Finland continued its occupation of Eastern Karelia because it was regarded as an asset for Finland in its defence, and perhaps it could be beneficial for Finland in the peace negotiations.

In any case, it was clear that Finland had to prepare for a defensive war, if it could not accomplish a peace agreement. The Finns knew that it would be difficult to withdraw from the war for a number of reasons, one of the main reasons being Finland's heavy dependence on Germany. In March 1944 secret negotiations for an armistice were arranged in Moscow. The Finnish negotiator, J.K. Paasikivi, returned with a proposal which the Finnish government rejected. Paasikivi was furious and argued that Finland would not receive better terms later.[63] It appears that Paasikivi was right.

In June 1944, Soviet armed forces attacked Finland in full force through the Karelian isthmus. Finland had to withdraw its forces rapidly from Eastern Karelia. The Soviet attack threatened to be so strong that the Finnish defence might collapse. Finland had to agree with Germany not to make a separate peace with the Soviet Union in order to receive much needed aid from Germany. Finland was successful in choosing the form of agreement. Namely, President Ryti made the agreement in his own name with Foreign Minister Ribbentrop: as long as he was in power, Finland would not make a separate agreement with the Soviets.[64] Germany was satisfied with this pledge and continued to provide Finland with food and military aid, including anti-tank weapons and air support which, together with a German infantry division, proved to be essential for Finnish fighting capacity and spirit.[65] After brave

---

63 J. Tarkka, 13. artikla, (WSOY, Porvoo, 1977), pp. 50–51.
64 M. Jokisipilä, *Aseveljiä vai liittolaisia? Suomi, Hitlerin Saksan liittosopimusvaatimukset ja Rytin-Ribbentropin sopimus*, (Suomalaisen Kirjallisuuden Seura, Helsinki, 2004), pp. 261–367, Visuri, *supra* note 20, pp. 248–258, and Jonas, *supra* note 22, pp. 359–377.
65 *See* Meinander, *supra* note 13, p. 81, and Jokisipilä 2004, pp. 379–381.

fighting, the Finns were able to prevent a Soviet breakthrough. Then the Soviet leadership decided to transfer a part of its forces from the Finnish front to Central Europe.[66]

In September 1944, the Finnish leadership found it advisable to agree to the peace terms demanded by the Soviet Union. Ryti withdrew from the presidency and was succeeded by Mannerheim. Finland considered that it was no longer bound by the agreement concluded by Ryti in his own name.[67] The terms of the peace were quite harsh.

Understandably, the Germans were furious about the 'betrayal' by Finland, but the Finns replied that all State leaders' primary obligation was to secure the survival of their country.[68] The German forces withdrew towards the north and burnt most of the dwellings in Lapland on their way to northern Norway, in revenge.

Under the terms of the Armistice Agreement, Finland was to lose Pechenga and to lease to the Soviet Union a military base on the Finnish south coast near Helsinki (see Figure 3).[69] Finland also had to disarm the German military forces in Finland and to hand over their personnel to the Soviet Union as prisoners of war. Very soon after the Agreement was signed in September 1944, the Allies sent their Control Commission to Finland to supervise Finland's faithful observance of the terms of the Agreement. The Soviets played a leading role in this. The Commission left Finland in 1947.[70]

The 1947 Peace Treaty of Paris with Finland added many other obligations for Finland. The other parties to the Treaty were all those Allied States that had been at war with Finland (even if only formally).[71] The Treaty set many restrictions on Finland's armed forces (Articles 13–22) and ordered Finland to deliver machines and other articles worth USD 300,000 million as compensation to the Soviet Union (Article 23). Finland also had to hand over to the Soviet Union all German-owned property (Article 26) and to dissolve all fascist and military-type organisations which had conducted hostile propaganda against the Soviet Union or other Allied States (Article 8).

---

66 Meinander, *ibid.*, pp. 82–83, and Tuunainen, *supra* note 14, pp. 159–167.
67 Jokisipilä, *supra* note 64, pp. 414–419.
68 Blücher, *supra* note 22, pp. 416–417.
69 *Finnish Treaty Series* 4/1944. The parties were the Soviet Union, Britain and Finland.
70 See R. Allison, *Finland's Relations with the Soviet Union 1944–84*, (The MacMillan Press LTD, London, 1985), pp. 129–132; P. Visuri, *Suomi suurvaltojen puristuksessa 1944–1947*, (Docendo, Jyväskylä, 2015), pp. 89–94.
71 UNTS No 53 (1948).

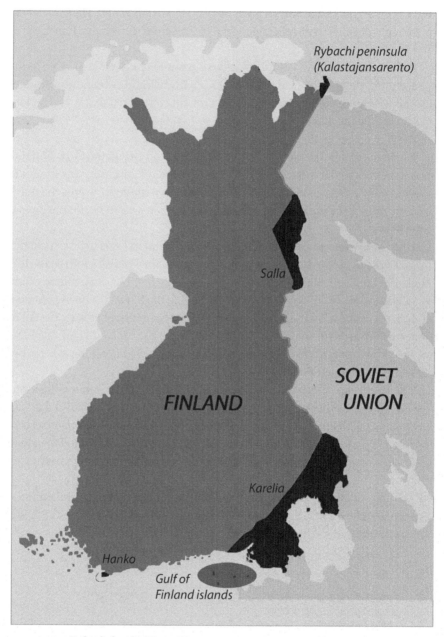

FIGURE 5.2 Finland after the Winter War, 1940

FINLAND'S CONTINUATION WAR (1941–1944)

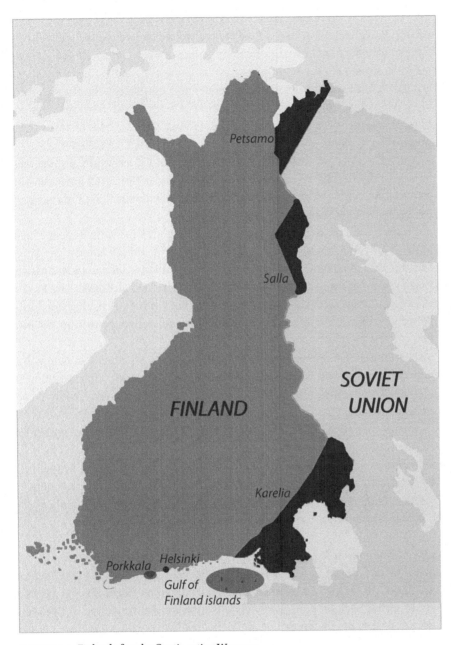

FIGURE 5.3 Finland after the Continuation War, 1944

2.5 Finland's Occupation of Eastern (Soviet) Karelia, 1941–1944

Having previously written a scholarly article on the occupiers' behaviour in Eastern Karelia, here I explain the main points of the article.[72] As early as July 1941, Mannerheim issued non-public military orders establishing a provisional military administration for Eastern Karelia and on placing the Russian population in concentration camps (they were not extermination camps). Eastern Karelia covered over 170,000 square kilometres, that is, half of the size of present-day Finland.

Finland's expressed reasons for its occupation of Eastern Karelia were, firstly, to save the Karelian people from extinction under the harsh Soviet leadership and, secondly, to secure Finland a more easily defensible border against its aggressive neighbour.

When the Finns arrived in Eastern Karelia, there were only 85,000–87,000 inhabitants there, mostly women, children under 15 and the elderly. The Finns had the idea of placing the non-Finno-Ugric population in camps in order to transfer them later to the German-occupied territories of Russia. The Finno-Ugric population was given better treatment than ethnic 'aliens'. It was a disappointment for the occupier that it had no common language with many local Finno-Ugric people.

The Finnish occupier did not succeed in placing all 'aliens' in camps but only about a half (up to 22,000). It failed severely in camp administration in 1941–42. The camps were overcrowded and nourishment and medical care were inadequate. The mortality rate was at least 18 per cent, perhaps even as high as 25 per cent. The main causes of the high mortality were epidemics, overcrowding, hunger and hard work.

My article concluded that Finland had violated the 1907 Hague Regulations Respecting the Laws and Customs of War on Land. Finland's treatment of 'alien' persons was unworthy of a democratic State. Fortunately, Finland did not transfer the 'alien' population to German-occupied territories.

2.6 Some (non-legal) Concluding Observations Concerning Part 2

As in the autumn of 1939, in 1941 the Finnish leadership made a problematic evaluation about the war scene. They overestimated the capability of Germany to defeat the Soviet Union. Many experts in other countries shared this view. However, the Finns belonged to those who took forceful action in that belief.

---

72   L. Hannikainen, 'Military Occupation of Eastern Karelia by Finland in 1941–1944: was international law pushed aside?', in *Searching for a 'Principle of Humanity' in International Humanitarian Law*, K.M. Larsen, C.G. Cooper and G. Nystuen (eds.), (Cambridge University Press, 2013), pp. 183–205.

As early as in the course of autumn 1941 the Finnish leaders had to admit that they had been at least partially wrong. At the beginning of 1943 they had to admit that they had been fundamentally wrong.

When the Finnish army crossed the borders in July-August 1941, it did so with maximum force. Finland was ready to occupy foreign territory. However, in the course of the autumn it became clear that Finland had exceeded its capabilities and had to diminish the size of its army. Its policy had led to shortage of food. Finland had suffered much during the Winter War and after that war it had to resettle over 400,000 persons from the territories lost to the Soviet Union. In the summer of 1941 Finland's food situation was fairly good, but not so good as to enable virtually all men between the ages of 19.5 and 45 to be drafted to the military for the harvest period. The harvest succeeded only partially – the outcome was shortage of food, which hit hard, especially persons confined in camps, where thousands of inmates died as result of hunger and epidemic diseases.[73]

In the defensive war in 1944 Finland was barely able to retain its independence. The Finnish soldiers fought bravely and with success.

3 Legal Analysis (in a Broad Sense)

3.1 *How Did International Law Regulate the Inter-state Use of Armed Force Prior to World War II?*

Before World War I, international law granted a broad right to resort to war if a State considered that another State had violated its rights and did not agree to compensation. The leading term in State relations was 'balance of power', a term of power politics that had next to no connection to law.[74] When the League of Nations was established in 1919, its Covenant set substantial limitations on its members to resort to inter-State war but did not prohibit it altogether. If member States were not able to settle their dispute by peaceful means, they had no right to resort to war but were obligated to submit the dispute to the League's dispute settlement procedures. If the League was not able to resolve the dispute, a party was not unequivocally prohibited from resorting to war, but it had to wait for three months before it could do so. If the League Council reached a unanimous report on the dispute, then the member had no right to resort to war. If a member violated the provisions described

---

73 Blücher, *supra* note 22, pp. 260–261.
74 See Brownlie, *supra* note 16, pp. 3–50.

above, the Council was to recommend appropriate measures to the parties – the League's sanctions were not excluded.[75]

It was soon realized that the League's partial ban of war would not work in practice. In 1928, a short treaty was concluded by the name of the General Treaty for the Renunciation of War, generally called the Kellogg-Briand Pact. The Pact condemned recourse to war for the solution of international controversies and as an instrument of national policy (Article 1) and went on: "The High Contracting Parties agree that the settlement or solution of all disputes or conflicts of whatever nature or of whatever origin they may be, which may arise among them, shall never be sought except by pacific means" (Article II).[76] This was all – the Pact said nothing about what should be done if a State party violated the Pact, or about the right to withdraw from it. The Pact prohibited foremostly wars of aggression, whereas wars of defence were not prohibited.[77] The Pact received a handsome number of ratifications. Only four States from Latin America refrained from ratifying the Pact due to the reason that it was too vague as it said nothing about what to do if a State party resorted to a war of aggression. Like many other States, these four States ratified the 1933 Anti-War Treaty of Non-Aggression and Conciliation (Anti-War Pact). Besides condemning wars of aggression, the Anti-War Pact stipulated that no territorial acquisitions obtained by force of arms would be recognized by the parties. The provisions of the Kellogg-Briand Pact and the Anti-War Pact were referred to in numerous other international treaties and other instruments.[78] It was clear that the new prohibition was not just one rule among other new rules of international law but a rule of primary importance.

After the entry into force of the Kellogg-Briand Pact, no State denounced it or denied its obligatoriness.[79] When a given State violated the Pact, the League of Nations and/or States reacted against the violation. As regards the Soviet Union, on various occasions it reaffirmed the obligatory force of the Pact.[80]

The Preamble to the Pact contains one sentence, however, that should be commented upon. It reads as follows: "[a]ny signatory Power which shall

---

75   The Covenant is reprinted, for example, in *Blackstone's Internal Legal Documents*, 7th ed. edited by Malcolm D. Evans (Oxford: Oxford University Press, 2005), pp. 1–7.
76   94 *LNTS*, p. 57.
77   About the legality of defensive war, *see* Brownlie, *supra* note 16, pp. 235–250. Inside its own territory a State has always had a sovereign right to use armed force against a foreign trespasser.
78   About the Covenant, the Kellogg-Briand Pact and Anti-War Pact as well as other instruments and State practice, *see ibid.*, pp. 51–111.
79   *Ibid.*, pp. 80 and 83.
80   *Ibid.*, pp. 76, 78 and 104.

hereafter seek to promote its national interests by resort to war should be denied the benefits furnished by this treaty". That meant at least that the aggressor State was denied the right to the fruits of its aggression, such as occupation of a foreign territory. There were opinions according to which a State's resort to aggressive war released other States from obligations towards that State and permitted other States to withdraw from the Pact.[81] The practice of States after the Pact's entry into force made it clear, however, that they were for a different interpretation. No State withdrew from the Pact or spoke in favour of having been released from the Pact's obligations. If other States had reacted to German aggression by denouncing the Pact or by declaring that they were no longer bound by the Pact towards Germany, the Pact would soon have collapsed as a significant treaty. They did not do so.

After the Winter War, Finland could have developed the interpretation that it was no longer obligated towards the Soviet Union under the Pact and could even resort to war against it, but it did not do so. It knew that this kind of interpretation had not won any significant support in the international community.

One may conclude that when World War II broke out all existing States had expressed their legal consent to the prohibition of aggressive war. In the international community led by the League of Nations, the Kellogg-Briand Pact's outlawry of wars of aggression was comprehensive in character.[82] Reservations for self-defence did not weaken the Pact.[83] Brownlie argues that besides their treaty obligation(s) all existing States had the obligation – on the basis of customary international law – to refrain from aggressive war.[84] In fact, the Pact was meant to have an even wider scope: to outlaw all resort to war that was not defensive.

As regards the right of self-defence, Friman concludes that in the interwar era States used the term 'defence' in its natural meaning, namely as a response to imminent or actual violence.[85] The League's bodies rejected arguments for

---

81 See L. Oppenheim, *International Law – A Treatise, Vol. II – Disputes, War and Neutrality*, sixth ed., H. Lauterpacht (ed.) (Longmans, London, 1946), p. 157, and H. Wehberg, *The Outlawry of War* (Carnegie Endowment for International Peace, Washington, 1931), pp. 87–88.

82 Wehberg, *ibid.*, at 81, and K. Skubiszewski, 'Use of Force by States. Collective Security. Law of War and Neutrality', in *Manual of Public International Law*, Max Sörensen (ed.) (St Martins Press, New York, 1968), p. 744.

83 Some States made dubious reservations to the Kellogg-Briand Pact but they did not create any major problems during World War II.

84 Brownlie, *supra* note 16, pp. 110–111.

85 J. Friman, *Revisiting the Concept of Defence in the Jus ad Bellum,* (Hart, Oxford, 2017), p. 28. In support, see J.L. Brierly, *The Law of Nations* (Clarendon Press, Oxford, 1955), p. 316.

wider self-defence.[86] As regards humanitarian armed intervention, it is true that the Pact did not prohibit small-scale interventions short of war. One could argue that a State's large-scale humanitarian intervention was not prohibited due to its noble, non-selfish purpose – to protect a persecuted group or one in mortal danger in another State. However, Ronzitti concludes that in the era of the League and the Pact, States practically never tried to justify the use of force by referring to humanitarian intervention.[87]

What did it mean that a State had ratified the Kellogg-Briand Pact, or any other treaty? It meant that this State was bound by the treaty and obligated to respect it in good faith. The State had no choice to decide whether to respect the treaty or not.[88] However, keeping in mind that the Kellogg-Briand Pact was very short and categorical, did the new prohibition have a sufficiently definite content for reliable interpretation? One can answer that whereas it is commonplace for the spheres of rules of law to be somewhat ambiguous, this may have been to some extent true also with the prohibition of aggression, but its nucleus was certainly obligatory.[89] The most undisputed cases of 'war of aggression' were the use of armed force on a large scale and with an aggressive purpose, such as to seize territory from another State, to occupy a State with the purpose of controlling it, or to put into power a government favourable to the occupying power.

In 1933, two conventions for the definition of aggression were concluded. Altogether, twelve States became parties to these. In one of them both Finland and the Soviet Union were parties. It contained a list of different forms of aggression, such as invasion of foreign territory and attack by land, naval or air forces. The aggressor was the State which was the first to resort to force. No aggression could be justified by the internal condition of a State, including alleged defects in its administration or due to revolutions, counter-revolutions or civil war.[90] However, the 'first resort' formula received criticism as it totally

---

86 See S.C. Neff, *War and the Law of Nations*, (Cambridge University Press, 2008), pp. 303–307.
87 N. Ronzitti, *Rescuing Nationals Abroad through Military Coercion and Intervention on Grounds of Humanity*, (Martinus Nijhoff, Dordrecht, 1985), p. 91. See also K. Simonen, *The State versus the Individual – The Unresolved Dilemma of Humanitarian Intervention* (Martinus Nijhoff Publishers, Leiden, 2011), p. 6; S. Chesterman, *Just War or Just Peace? Humanitarian Intervention and International Law* (Oxford University Press, 2001), p. 43; A. Cassese, *International Law*, second ed. (Oxford University Press, 2005), p. 299.
88 Lord McNair, *The Law of Treaties* (Clarendon Press, Oxford, 1961), Chapter XXX.
89 Brownlie, *supra* note 16, pp. 91 and 111, and Oppenheim, *supra* note 81, pp. 158–159 and 161.
90 The Conventions were signed on 3 and 4 July 1933, LNTS No. 3391 and No. 3414. See Brownlie, *supra* note 16, pp. 347 and 247–248.

FINLAND'S CONTINUATION WAR (1941-1944)　　　　　　　　　　　　　　　　105

condemned anticipatory self-defence and, thus, "could become a trap for the innocent".[91] This may have been the reason why the two conventions did not receive more ratifications.[92]

However, there was a period during World War II (1940-1942) when the prohibition of aggressive war was so mercilessly violated, especially by Germany but also by some other States – the Soviet Union being a leading State in that list – that one could reasonably doubt the sanctity of the prohibition of aggressive war. It was during that period when the Finnish Continuation War began. After that period, the victorious Allied Powers confirmed, however, that the prohibition had been in force all the time.

When international military tribunals were established in the aftermath of World War II for prosecuting the German and Japanese political and military leaders, one of the three categories of international crimes listed in their statutes was crimes against peace. Article 6 (a) of the Charter of the International Military Tribunal in Nuremberg read as follows:

> *Crimes against peace*: namely planning, preparation, initiation or waging of a war of aggression, or a war in violation of international treaties, agreements or assurances, or participation in a common plan or conspiracy for the accomplishment of any of the foregoing;

The Nuremberg Charter was enacted and entered into force in 1945[93] and was meant to apply to individual German war criminals. However, the Tribunal itself made it plain that it regarded the Charter as an expression of international law as of 1939 and war of aggression as the supreme international crime, since it contained within itself the accumulated evil of the whole.[94] It referred specifically to the Kellogg-Briand Pact as the leading source of the prohibition of aggressive war. The crime of aggressive war was applied only to major war criminals.

Historians writing about the Continuation War have only very seldom used the term 'aggressive war' but have often analyzed whether Finland acted in

---

91　S. Alexandrov, *Self-Defense against the Use of Force in International Law* (Kluwer Law International, The Hague, 1996), p. 73.

92　A. Rifaat, *International Aggression*, (Almqvist & Wiksell International, Stockholm, 1979), pp. 90-91.

93　UNTS, Vol. 82, at 279.

94　*Trial of the Major War Criminals before the International Military Tribunal, Nuremberg, 14 November 1945 – 1 October 1946*, Vol. I, (Nuremberg, 1947), p. 186.

alliance with Germany – 'alliance' being the key word. The alliance choice would point to co-responsibility for participation in a war of aggression.[95]

What was meant by the notion of 'alliance'? In the era prior to creation of the League of Nations, it was quite common for States to create alliances by treaties for defensive or aggressive purposes. The existence of an alliance was clear if it had been created by treaty. However, if no treaty or comparable joint declaration was made, how to find out whether there was an alliance or not? Then one had to draw a conclusion based on the intensity of cooperation: such factors as whether the States had identifiable common goals in their warfare; how much by way of common fighting operations they had; how much they helped each other. One concrete sign pointing to an alliance was if States had created joint military structures, such as placing their armed forces under a single commander.

3.2 The 1947 Paris Peace Treaty and Finland's Use of Armed Force

The preamble to the 1947 Paris Peace Treaty stated that Finland participated as an ally of Hitlerite Germany in the war against the Soviet Union, the United Kingdom and other Allied States and that Finland had to bear its share of responsibility for the war. The Treaty did not say specifically that Finland resorted to a war of aggression, but the reference to an alliance with Germany and the whole tone of the Treaty setting punitive-type obligations on Finland logically permit the conclusion that Finland was considered as having participated in a war of aggression. One may argue that statements in preambles have only limited legal significance, but in this Treaty the statement of Finland's responsibility forms the basis of its articles with many definite legal obligations.

In a strict legal analysis one could conclude that there is no longer any need for an extensive analysis, since the Peace Treaty was and is valid under international law and obligatory on Finland. Finland has not tried to propose to the parties to the Peace Treaty a re-evaluation of its role in the Continuation War. With the end of the Cold War, many articles lost their significance but not all. The Treaty remains in force.

In the post-Cold War era Finnish leaders have disregarded the statement in the preamble and have emphasized that Finland was conducting its own separate defensive war against an aggressive Soviet Union.[96] The same view is

---

95   Nor does the Paris Peace Treaty use the words of Art. 6 (a). The Treaty is discussed in more detail in the next section.
96   See T. Kinnnen & M. Jokisipilä, 'Shifting Images of "Our Wars": Finnish Memory Culture of World War II', in Kinnunen & Kivimäki, note 13, pp. 455–467. They explain the views of

shared by the majority of the Finnish people. On the other hand, the majority of contemporary Finnish history professors consider that Finland was fighting against the Soviet Union in alliance with Germany.[97] All in all, in contemporary discussion the Peace Treaty sits on the sidelines. For this reason, I find it advisable to write this article.

3.3 Only a Quick Look at Criminal Law

In this article I do not analyze the criminal trial of Finnish leaders' war guilt but limit myself just to describing it briefly. The Allied Powers had decided that criminal trials had to be arranged for all 'satellites' of Germany. The Allies seemed to recognize that the Finnish leaders were no major war criminals but had tried to safeguard the independence of their country. Then, unfortunately, they became so carried away by the expected superiority of Germany that they joined Finland in Germany's war of aggression.

General Andrei Zhdanov, the Chief of the Allied Control Commission, said that Finland received favourable treatment in three respects: (1) no death penalties were demanded, (2) only the members of a small central circle were to be indicted, and (3) Finland was permitted to arrange the trial itself. Tarkka's assessment is that Finland succeeded in choosing the least bad alternative.[98] When the Commission and the new Finnish government were negotiating about the trial to be arranged, the Commission made it known that the Finns themselves could make preparations for the trial and arrange the trial before a national court, though under the supervision of the Commission.[99]

The tone of the criminal categories formulated by the Finns was in passive terms: permitting things to take place and not actively seeking peace.[100] Definitely, there was no reference to the crime of aggressive war. Since there were no military leaders among the accused, tactically a large part of the responsibility could be pushed on to the shoulders of military leaders.

Presidents Tarja Halonen and Martti Ahtisaari (later Nobel Peace Prize laureate) and of ex-Prime Minister Paavo Lipponen. In 2005, President Halonen gave a deliberately concise portrayal of Finland's role in World War II to a prestigious audience in Paris without saying a word about Finland's cooperation with Hitler or the offensive warfare of the Continuation War. Also ex-President Mauno Koivisto released Finland from any responsibility by stating that all war-related decisions made by Finland's leaders during World War II were right. See Leskinen & Juutilainen, *supra* note 24, p. 42.

97   See *Helsingin Sanomat* (newspaper), on 19 October 2008, Part A.
98   Tarkka, *supra* note 63, pp. 184 and 245.
99   T. Polvinen, *Jaltasta Pariisin rauhaan*, (WSOY, Porvoo 1981), pp. 131–140.
100 Tarkka, *supra* note 63, pp. 181–182.

In the trial the national court was to decide on the guilt of ex-President Ryti, six ministers and Finland's ambassador to Germany.[101] It was an openly political trial. Marshal Mannerheim was not among the accused, because the Soviet Union calculated that he would be more valuable by assuring the Finnish people that realism dictated the need to consent to the terms of the Armistice Agreement and to consent to a more Soviet-friendly foreign policy.[102]

The trial resulted in prison sentences of between two and eight years. However, the Control Commission was dissatisfied and demanded more severe sentences. The court had to raise them – to between two years and ten years (Ryti).[103]

I draw one conclusion for my analysis below: the Allies did not regard the Finnish leaders as bearing criminal responsibility for participation in aggressive war. So, if not the leaders, then hardly the Finnish State either.

3.4   Legal Analysis of Finland's Arguments
3.4.1   The Soviet Danger
3.4.1.1   Finland's Arguments

Finland's first argument is not a legal one but is important for understanding its policy. Even after the Winter War the Soviet Union behaved aggressively towards Finland and might well have started a new war in order to invade the whole of Finland. Finland decided to do its utmost to gain powerful support against the Soviet Union. Germany was very powerful in Europe and Finland was dependent on Germany in economic terms. Finland was not Nazi-minded and knew that Germany had behaved aggressively, but nevertheless felt that Germany was the best available choice in its search for security. Finland did not engage in any warfare of destruction but respected the law of war.

Finland was caught between two dictatorships: the Stalinist Soviet Union and Nazi Germany. It knew what had happened to Poland, which had refused to ally with either of those powers: they invaded it and divided it between themselves.[104] Finland succeeded in creating a cooperative relationship with Germany, but in the first half of 1941 it had no certainty about how Germany's

---

101   I. Tallgren, "Martyrs and Scapegoats of the Nation? The Finnish War-Responsibility Trial, 1945–1946", in *Historical Origins of International Criminal Law*, Vol. 2, M. Bergsmo & C. Wui Ling & Yi Ping (eds.), (Torkel Opsahl Academic Publishers, Brussels,2014), pp. 516–527, and J. Tarkka, *Hirmuinen asia – Sotasyyllisyys ja historian taito*, (WSOY, Helsinki, 2009), pp. 167–301.
102   Visuri, *supra* note 20, pp. 277–278; Jonas, *supra* note 22, p. 417.
103   Tarkka, *supra* note 63, pp. 212–221.
104   A.J.P. Taylor, *The Origins of the Second World War*, (Fawcett Publications, Greenwich, 1961), p. 190.

relations with the Soviet Union would develop – a war or some deal between those two strong powers, possibly affecting Finland's independence. In its uncertainty Finland decided to follow Germany in order to improve its chances not to be left alone against the Soviet Union. True, Finland also wished that with help from Germany it could correct the injustice of the Winter War by reacquiring the territories lost and obtaining compensation for the injustices and hardships it had suffered, caused by the Soviet Union. In addition, it was important to have a safer border with the Soviet Union – the border of three isthmuses.

According to Krosby, Germany was the best choice, because if Finland had decided to avoid allying with either Germany or the Soviet Union, it would have been drawn into the war anyway. Germany was the only realistic choice.[105]

3.4.1.2 *Analysis*

It is true that Finland was in a difficult position in the vicinity of two dictatorships. However, it knew that reliance on Germany could involve dangers and that as a small State it had to carefully deliberate its policy moves. It must have known that a liberal interpretation of the Kellogg-Briand Pact – permitting derogations – would constitute a dangerous policy for a small State.

3.4.2 Finland's Relationship with Germany

3.4.2.1 *Finland's Arguments*

Finland was not an ally of Germany but the relationship between these two States was based on looser cooperation. There did not exist any treaty on alliance. The two States undertook a number of joint operations, but their goals were different. Germany gave material help to Finland but that neither created an alliance nor made Finland a satellite of Germany. Finland had its own limited goals and warded off Germany's proposals for military action beyond Eastern Karelia. It refused to participate in the strangulation of Leningrad and in efforts to cut the Murmansk railway. Finland had a problem in withdrawing from the war after it had reached its goals, because Germany would have reacted by forcible means.[106]

3.4.2.2 *Analysis*

a) Secret Negotiations

German-Finnish negotiations and preparations for attack were conducted in secrecy. From 1941, no treaties or memorandums of understanding were made

---

105 Krosby, *supra* note 53, pp. 232–237.
106 Meinander, *supra* note 13, p. 75.

public to outsiders. One of Finland's main legal arguments in support of its separate war was that there was no treaty of alliance between itself and Germany. According to Visuri, in their mutual correspondence Hitler and Ryti confirmed the results of the military negotiations without specifying the contents of these results. Visuri takes this correspondence as proof of the existence of extremely secret inter-State treaties without regard for national constitutional law.[107] It is quite logical that if two States plan to engage in a gross violation of international law, they agree about it through an informal secret agreement.

b)   Weighty Proof of an Alliance

Cooperation between the two States was so close that it speaks for an alliance whose purpose was to attack the Soviet Union. The strongest cases of proof (most of them have been reported above) were the following:
- The number of German troops in Finland prior to Germany's attack of 22 June reached as many as 200,000.
- Finland's armed forces located in Northern Finland were subordinated under the German commander in chief. This meant that Finnish forces there were part of the German attack against the Soviet Union – in the north the attack began on 1 July. Thus, the relationship between these two States was very close. Admittedly, however, in military terms the role of this unified northern army remained quite limited.
- Elsewhere in Finland, German armed forces were subordinated under the command of Marshal Mannerheim.
- The Germans and Finns were in agreement about the direction of Finland's attack on Soviet territory. According to Polvinen, the Germans wanted to tell the Finns when they should attack and in what direction. Thus, on 9 July Mannerheim received an announcement from the Germans that the attack should begin during the following day. He was dissatisfied with the late date of the announcement. However, the Finnish forces were re-grouped rapidly and Finland began its attack on 10 July as proposed by the Germans.[108]
- When Finland attacked on 10 July, it did so with maximum force – even exceeding its capabilities, as could be seen in late 1941 and 1942. Finland invaded a substantial area of a foreign territory and if Germany had been as successful in its attack as Finland expected, Finland did not exclude even more invasion. By exceeding its actual capabilities Finland made itself in material terms even more dependent on Germany. According to Jokisipilä, Finland received considerable material help from Germany – without this

---

107   Visuri, *supra* note 20, pp. 52 and 55–56.
108   T. Polvinen, *Barbarossasta Teheraniin*, (WSOY, Porvoo, 1979), pp. 15–16.

help Finland's backbone would have broken.[109] One may conclude that Finland was heavily dependent on Germany for food and other materials, especially military equipment.[110]
- Finland gave certain airfields over to the use of the German Air Force.
- In maritime areas cooperative measures were taken.
- At the request of Germany, in the early months of 1941 Finland permitted the establishment of a so-called SS-battalion for volunteers to join. The battalion participated in the anti-Soviet war in the ranks of the German army outside Finland.[111]
- In November 1941, Finland joined the Anti-Komintern Pact that had been created by Germany, Japan and Italy against the international communist movement and the Soviet Union.
- Finland recognized without delay the new satellite States which Germany created in occupied territories.[112]
- President Ryti made the agreement in his own name with Foreign Minister Ribbentrop: as long as he was in power, Finland would not make a separate agreement with the Soviets. This meant the admission that relations between the two States were indeed close.
- The Finns surrendered to the Germans over two thousand Soviet prisoners of war and the Germans surrendered to the Finns about an equal number of Finno-Ugric prisoners of war.[113]

The Allies were of the opinion that Finland, Hungary and Romania were Germany's allies, even satellites. To Finland they gave somewhat better status than the two other allies.[114]

Among historians, Jonas writes that Finland's inclusion in Operation Barbarossa leaves virtually no doubt that the German-Finnish attack against the Soviet Union was at the very least a joint military venture with the shared

---

109 M. Jokisipilä, "'Kappas vaan, saksalaisia!" Keskustelu Suomen jatkosodan 1941–1944 luonteesta', in *Sodan totuudet*, Markku Jokisipilä (ed.), (Ajatus Kirjat, Gummerus Kustannus Oy, Helsinki, 2007), p. 162. In support of this view, *see* Ylikangas, *supra* note 13, p. 297. *See also* Jonas, *supra* note 22, pp. 231–232 and pp. 206–207. According to him, Finland's complete dependence on German help took the steam out of Finland's claim concerning a separate war.
110 Leskinen & Juutilainen, *supra* note 24, p. 145, and Upton, *supra* note 18, pp. 349–350.
111 A. Swanström, *Hakaristin ritarit*, (Atena, Jyväskylä, 2018), pp. 31–42.
112 Jonas, *supra* note 22, p. 216.
113 O. Silvennoinen, 'Limits of Intentionality – Soviet Prisoners of War and Civilian Internees in Finnish Custody', in Kinnunen & Kivimäki, *supra* note 13, pp. 513–514.
114 Jokipii, *supra* note 24, pp. 626–628 and p. 652, and Visuri, *supra* note 20, p. 25. The Nuremberg Tribunal in 1946 (*supra* note 21, p. 214) estimated that Germany drew Hungary, Romania and Finland into war against the Soviet Union.

purpose of conducting a war of aggression. Preparations for war between Germany and Finland were more intensive than between Germany and its other allies.[115] Kivimäki and Lunde think that the idea of Finland's separate war against the Soviet Union comes close to absurdity.[116] Jokipii is of the opinion that cooperation between Germany and Finland in 1941 was so close that it is not possible to speak of Finland's separate war against the Soviet Union but rather intensive co-belligerency which fulfilled the criteria of an alliance – even if without a formal treaty.[117] Jokisipilä writes that if the relationship between Finland and Germany had to be described in one word, it is difficult to use any other word than alliance, taking into consideration the degree of Finland's dependence on Germany and the intensiveness of their cooperation. He points out, however, that Finland was not a satellite of Germany but had its own goals and interests.[118]

One may conclude that the evidence of Finland's close relationship with Germany speaks for an alliance.

3.4.3 Did the Soviet Union Start Aggressive War on 25 July?
3.4.3.1 *Finland's Arguments*
Finland was subjected to an armed attack by the Soviet Union on 25 June 1941 (and in the following days). The message of the 1933 Convention for Definition of Aggression was clear: the first to use armed force is the aggressor. It was the Soviet Union which – as in 1939 – started the war.

3.4.3.2 *Analysis*
When Germany started its massive attack against the Soviet Union on 22 June, Adolf Hitler stated in the radio proclamation to the German people that an attack unprecedented in history in its extent and size had begun. He went on that German forces stood in a common front with Finnish and Romanian forces against the Bolshevik Soviet Union for safeguarding Europe.[119] Romania joined the attack immediately. Should the Soviet leaders who knew a lot about

---

115 Jonas, *supra* note 61, pp. 112–113, and Jonas *supra* note 22, p. 207.
116 Kivimäki, *supra* note 50, p. 6, and Lunde, *supra* note 61, p. 390.
117 Jokipii, *supra* note 24, pp. 355–516, 548–550 and 612–628. Visuri, *supra* note 20, is of the same opinion, pp. 22–25 and 55–56.
118 Jokisipilä, *supra* note 109, p. 173.
119 See https://research.calvin.edu/german-propaganda-archive/hitler4.htm – (visited on 22 November 2018); and Visuri, *supra* note 20, pp. 53–55.

German-Finnish cooperation suspect that Hitler was exaggerating Finland's role? Hardly so.[120]

Hitler's declaration in itself could serve as a sufficient reason for the Soviet Union to take military measures against Finland. The German attack on the Soviet Union was massive and threatened the existence of the Soviet Union – a matter of life or death. It is the inherent right of every State to defend itself against an attack endangering its existence. For Finland to avoid a Soviet attack it would have been important to (1) contest Hitler's declaration (2) declare neutrality according to Finnish law, (3) emphasize to the Soviets that the German forces in Finland were meant only for Finland's defensive purposes, and (4) assure that no military action would be taken across the border. The Soviet ambassador offered such a possibility to Finland, but Finland could not give any convincing answer.

What, then, of the criterion of the 1933 Convention – the decisive role of the first use of armed force? As reported above, prior to 25 June Finland took small-scale military action and had given airfields over for German use against the Soviet Union. In this case that was sufficient to constitute first use of armed force.

I conclude that the Soviet Union had weighty reasons to argue that it had the right to use armed force in self-defence against Finland starting on 25 June.[121] Finland was playing a double game.

3.4.4   Did Finland have the Right to Occupy Eastern (Soviet) Karelia – and Ultimately to Annex it?

3.4.4.1   *Finland's Arguments*

The Soviet Union had pursued an anti-Karelian policy in Eastern Karelia, the traditional territory of the Karelians. In particular the years 1936–1938 of the Great Terror were horrifying. Ethnic minorities were then persecuted as they were regarded as unreliable in comparison with Russians. Eastern Karelia was severely affected – many Karelians were executed or imprisoned in labour camps.

In November 1941, Professor Rafael Erich, who was the leading Finnish expert in international law, submitted to the Finnish government (upon its request) his memorandum in which he presented legal arguments in favour of Finland's right to occupy Eastern Karelia and ultimately to take it away from

---

[120] In his radio speech to the Finnish people on 26 June Ryti confirmed that Finland was fighting together with the German army.
[121] I share this view with Jonas 2012, *supra* note 61, p. 113. See also Varma, *supra* note 39, at 180.

the Soviet Union. The Soviet Union had illegally seized a part of Finland's territory for itself – and thereafter pursued an aggressive policy.

Erich went on to say that the Soviet Union had disregarded its obligations under the Tartu Peace Treaty concerning Eastern Karelia. Whereas in 1920 the Finno-Ugric Karelians formed the majority of the population of Eastern Karelia, in 1941 they formed only a minority as the result of changes to administrative borders, transfer of other nationalities – primarily Russians – to, and compulsory transfer of Karelians away from, the territory. In the Tartu Peace Treaty, Soviet Russia obligated itself to recognize the right of national self-determination to the Karelian population in the form of territorial autonomy (Articles 10 and 11). In addition, in Tartu it gave a unilateral declaration specifying the contents of territorial autonomy. In Erich's view, the Soviet government had completely disregarded its obligations and prevented any meaningful autonomy for the Karelians.[122]

In conclusion, in Erich's view Finland had the right to demand indemnity from the Soviet Union as result of the violations suffered by it in accordance with general international legal principles. Because of the harsh policy of the Soviet Union in terms of denying any meaningful territorial autonomy to the Karelians and of reducing the Karelians, who had a strong ethnic bond with the Finns, to a minority position in their own territory, suitable compensation would be the annexation of Eastern Karelia to Finland. In Finland their rights would be respected and the Finnish nation would achieve its unity and its natural borders.[123]

3.4.4.2 Analysis
A   Domestic Developments in Eastern Karelia

The basic starting point was that Eastern Karelia had for several centuries been under the sovereignty of Russia, having both Karelian and Russian populations.

In the Tartu negotiations the outcome was that Eastern Karelia remained under the sovereignty of Russia, but the Peace Treaty referred to its right of internal self-determination (that is, territorial autonomy). Whereas Soviet Russia recognized this status, it did not recognize that Finland had any right to act

---

122   Statement (in Finnish) by Rafael Erich on 26 November 1941, *Horellin kokoelma* PK 1350/5, SA. *See* also A. Laine, *Suur-Suomen kahdet kasvot*, (Otava, Helsinki,1982), pp. 56–58.
123   Erich, *ibid.*, especially pp. 62–64 and 11–12.

as the supervisor of the Karelian cause. However, in 1921 Soviet Russia agreed to a procedure according to which Finland could pose questions – before a Finnish-Soviet mixed committee – to the Soviets, who had to give answers.[124] The Finns were unhappy with this compromise.

Finland actively kept up the cause of the Karelian population in the international arena and nationally. The Soviet side warded off Finland's efforts to persuade the League of Nations to take a stand on Eastern Karelia. The Soviets accused Finland in strong words of participation in the Karelian uprising in 1921 – violating the sovereignty of the Soviet State and the Tartu Peace Treaty.

Soviet Russia established the Karelian Labour Community in 1920 to realize the territorial autonomy of Eastern Karelia. In 1923 this was developed into the Karelian Autonomous Socialist Soviet Republic, an autonomous unit within the Russian Socialist Soviet Republic. The structure and political orientation of the Soviet State was very different from that of Finland, in whose view the administration in Eastern Karelia did not fulfil the requirements for genuine autonomy. Notwithstanding the accusations of the Finnish government, the leadership of Soviet Karelia – Finnish communists who had fled from Finland at the end of the 1918 Civil War – made efforts, according to Churchill and Nygård, to protect the interests of the Karelian population.[125] When in the mid-1930's the political atmosphere internationally and in the Soviet Union became tense, the Finnish leadership in Eastern Karelia was accused of discriminating against the Russian inhabitants.[126] The Finnish leaders were replaced by Russian leaders and the Russian language was lifted to the leading position. The years of the 'Great Terror' were very hard in the Soviet Union – for both Russians and ethnic minorities alike.

Already in the 1920s the Soviet leadership decided to increase the number of Russian inhabitants in Eastern Karelia, because it suspected that Finland would continue to have imperialist designs in mind. Population transfers diminished the number of Karelians.

According to international law, the State had an exclusive right to decide its own political and economic systems, including the constitutional order, unless it had international conventional obligations restricting this right. The Soviet

---

124 Nygård, *supra* note 8, pp. 86–87.
125 S. Churchill, *Itä-Karjalan kohtalo 1917–1922*, (WSOY, Porvoo, 1970), p. 193, and Nygård, *supra* note 8, p. 86.
126 A. Ylärakkola, *Edvard Gylling – Itä-Karjalan suomalainen rakentaja*, (Otava, Helsinki, 1976), pp. 281–288, and Nygård *supra* note 8, pp. 221–222.

Union was a federal State whose smaller parts had broader or more limited rights of autonomy.[127]

B   Analysis on Finland's Arguments

As regards the possible legitimacy of external armed humanitarian intervention, among the basic preconditions one was that a population or a part of it in a given country were in great and immediate danger for their life, and another was that the intervening State(s) had to limit its intervention solely to saving or protecting the lives of those persons in danger. In the late summer of 1941, the situation was as follows: Germany had started a massive aggressive war against the Soviet Union and its attack was progressing well. In the territories occupied by Germany, the local populations were in mortal danger. Eastern Karelia was outside the area of the German attack. According to the joint German-Finnish plan, Finland was to occupy Eastern Karelia.[128] When the Finnish occupier arrived in Eastern Karelia, it realized that the Soviet Union had moved the great majority of the inhabitants away. Those remaining were elderly, children and mothers. They were not in any great danger but were better off than civilians in many other regions of the Soviet Union. The Finnish military administration treated local Russians and other 'aliens' in Eastern Karelia very harshly. One may conclude that (1) the preconditions for armed humanitarian intervention did not appear to exist in Eastern Karelia and (2) the Finnish occupier treated a significant part of the local population inhumanely.

One of Finland's arguments to occupy – and eventually to annex – Eastern Karelia was to have a safer border easier to defend from future attacks. However, such an argument was impossible for the international community to accept. Occupation of alien territories for future defence purposes would foster armed conflicts when States subjected to occupation of their territories would resort to force in order to seize back the territories lost.

Other arguments were Finland's right to occupy Easter Karelia were to obtain indemnity for the hardships caused by the Soviet Union to Finland in the

---

[127] The two 1933 Conventions for the Definition of Aggression stipulated that no aggression could be justified by the internal condition of a State, including alleged defects in its administration or due to revolutions, counter-revolutions or civil war – *LNTS* No. 3391 and No. 3414. One of these conventions bound both Finland and the Soviet Union.

[128] Brownlie, (*supra* note 16, p. 338), writes that humanitarian intervention was in the nature of a police measure whose result could not be the change of sovereignty over the territory concerned.

Winter War and to protect Karelians from harsh Communist rule. The annexation of Eastern Karelia had been the Finnish goal since Finland's independence in 1917. The statements and activities by Mannerheim and Ryti in 1941 were very outspoken. Germany's massive aggression against the Soviet Union made it easy for Finland to invade Eastern Karelia.[129]

From the perspective of the Kellogg-Briand Pact it is impossible to accept Finland's occupation war as legal. It served as an instrument of Finland's national policy. Finland should have raised the question of indemnity at the end of the war in Europe when peace settlements were due.

One may conclude that Finland did not have the right to occupy and annex Eastern Karelia.

3.4.5 Concluding: Did Finland Participate in a War of Aggression?

On the basis of the foregoing, Finland participated in Germany's war of aggression against the Soviet Union. Finland's guilt, in the opinion of the Allied Powers, did not amount to criminal guilt for aggressive war but less, as analyzed above. Finland's participatory role meant that Finland was in alliance with Germany. Finland's aggressive role was limited to the second half of 1941. Then Finland attacked with maximum force in accordance with the wishes of Germany, invaded Eastern Karelia and was of great help to Germany in the northern front. After that time Finland's role turned gradually to defensive war and a looser alliance with Germany.

It is not correct to characterize Finland's role in the Continuation War as a separate war or as a defensive war only. If someone were of the opinion that the best term to characterize Finnish-German co-operation would be co-belligerency, that does not mean that Finland was not guilty of aggressive war.

3.4.6 Was Finland Treated too Harshly in the Settlement of the Continuation War?

3.4.6.1 *Finland*

Finland was treated unreasonably harshly in the Paris Peace Treaty. It lost even more territory, had to pay a high sum in war reparation, many restrictions were set on its armed forces and it had to convict its leading politicians. The Soviet

---

129 Jonas (*supra* note 22, p. 203) writes critically that the ideological motive for a crusade against Bolshevism only partially concealed the most evident features of a war of invasion whose end goal was a Greater Finland that included Soviet Karelia.

Union kept all those territories that it seized from Finland in the 1940 peace treaty, and acquired even more.

3.4.6.2 Analysis: Was the Paris Peace Treaty Just and Reasonable? If not...

a)　　　　Aggravating Factors

First, Finland participated in the German-led aggressive war against the Soviet Union. It was convinced that Germany would decisively defeat the Soviet Union and take power in Europe. The distress of the Soviet Union offered Finland a suitable moment to realize the dream of creating a Greater Finland by occupying Eastern (Soviet) Karelia.

Second, Germany's war against the Soviet Union was not just a 'normal' armed contention between the armies but it was also a war of destruction and extermination. Finland did not participate in the war of destruction but helped it indirectly by keeping its forces in Eastern Karelia and near Leningrad. The Finnish leaders must have understood that a Europe led and terrorized by the Nazis would be a horror continent.[130]

Third, the Finnish occupier treated Russian civilians in Eastern Karelia harshly.

b)　　　　Mitigating Factors

First, the Soviet Union had treated Finland in a grossly illegal and unjust way. Second, Finland's aggressive role was limited to the second half of 1941 only. In 1942–1944, it took mainly only defensive action. Thus, in the war against the Soviet Union Finland's role was limited. Third, Finland did not participate in the strangulation of Leningrad or in military efforts to cut the Murmansk railway. Fourth, since the leaders of the Soviet Union were not brought to justice for the aggressive war against Finland, why were Finland and the Finnish leaders penalized?

c)　　　　Concluding Analysis

Finland's participation in Germany's war of aggression was considered to have been such a bad sin that in the eyes of the Allies Finland lost the right to demand compensation for the wrongs committed by the Soviet Union in the

---

130　Polvinen writes that in the anarchical circumstances of World War II, States saw the safeguarding of their own interests as the highest principle. *See* T. Polvinen, *Suomi suurvaltojen politiikassa 1941–1944*, (WSOY, Porvoo, 1964), p. 282.

Winter War. According to Tarkka, in the opinion of the Western Allies Finland learned a healthy lesson without suffering heavy consequences.[131]

After Finland's acceptance of the Armistice Agreement, it assumed that in the final peace settlement it could try to get through some relief for the terms of peace. At the 1946 Paris Peace Conference, Finland asked for a reduction in the amount of war reparations and for redrawing the border around Vyborg. However, the Soviet Union rejected these claims decisively and was able to prevent their acceptance. The leading Western Powers had many disagreements with the Soviet Union and concentrated on those important for political interests. They considered that Finland had to manage in bilateral negotiations with the Soviet Union.[132]

What was positive for Finland in the existing circumstances was that it could organize the criminal trial of its wartime leaders before a national court. The prison penalties were from two years to ten years. The eight prisoners were confined in a Finnish prison and Finland had a wide possibility to decide on their release. The outcome was that none of them remained in prison more than three years.[133]

In spite of the relatively mild trial of the Finnish leaders, it can well be argued in light of the many obligations imposed on Finland in the Paris Peace Treaty that Finland was treated *too harshly*. After all, the sins of the Finns were in the circumstances of World War II of rather limited scope.

4   Concluding Observations on Finland's Role in the Continuation War

Finland was subjected to a war of aggression by the Soviet Union in 1939 and lost a part of its territory. After this Winter War, it sought protection from Germany against the Soviet Union and decided to rely on Germany. After Germany attacked the Soviet Union, Finland reoccupied the territories lost in the Winter War. The Finnish forces did not stop at the old border but attacked Eastern (Soviet) Karelia and occupied it with a wish eventually to annex it. By that measure, Finland joined as Germany's ally in its war of aggression against the Soviet Union in violation of international law. In their strong reliance on

---

131   Tarkka, *supra* note 63, p. 63.
132   *See* T. Polvinen, *supra* note 99, pp. 183–244.
133   Tarkka, *supra* note 101, pp. 263–279 and 293–301.

Germany, the Finnish leaders made some very questionable decisions without listening to warnings from Britain, the United States and Sweden about possible negative consequences. One may say that Finland became the victim of its own ambitions. The leadership must have known about the sinister plans of Germany to make Operation Barbarossa a war of destruction and extermination.

When Finland attacked over the border against the Soviet Union in July 1941 (harvest time), it did so with maximum armed force, actually exceeding its capabilities. The outcome was a famine with sorry results in the following months and a high degree of dependency on Germany for material help. This dependency later complicated Finland's possibilities to withdraw from the war.

The Finnish leaders must soon have recognized that they had overestimated the military strength of Germany and, indeed, underestimated the strength of the Soviet Union. Germany lost the war and so did Finland. After heroic fighting, Finland avoided military occupation and was able to maintain its independence. Finland's military performance was commendable: in the war in Europe there were only three belligerent States whose capital was not occupied: London, Moscow and Helsinki.

After the Continuation War, Finland's fate was in the hands of the Allied Powers. The preamble to the 1947 Paris Peace Treaty stated that Finland had participated as an ally of Germany in the war against the Soviet Union and other Allied States and bore its share of responsibility for that war. The terms of peace were harsh. Finland again lost the territories retaken in 1941 and even some more territories. It had to pay war reparations to the Soviet Union and was subjected to many restrictions, especially concerning its military forces. In addition, Finland had to lease a naval base near to Helsinki (Porkkala) for 50 years to the Soviet Union and to prosecute and penalize a small number of its high political leaders in a national trial under the control of the Allied Control Commission.

Finland had to pay quite dearly for the problematic decisions of its leaders. As a small State it should have refrained from invading Eastern Karelia. Apparently Germany would have complied with the Finnish choice not to proceed further to the east, because objectively Finland had suffered greatly in the Winter War and had to resettle the population of 420,000 inhabitants of the territories lost to the Soviet Union. Hitler was of the opinion that after the Winter War Finland was quite weak.[134]

Small States have to deliberate very cautiously the consequences of their foreign policy decisions. Powerful States can escape at least partially the negative

---

134   Leskinen & Juutilainen, *supra* note 24, p. 134.

consequences of their erroneous decisions, whereas small States may suffer much more, perhaps even fatally.[135] Ziemke well concludes that Finland, on one hand, fell into a war between two superpowers and, on the other hand, became the victim of its own ambitions.[136]

The most important result for Finland was, however, that it was able to maintain its independence – even if somewhat limited *de facto* – and its democratic system. Notwithstanding, the Finns were left dissatisfied with the harsh treatment of their country in the peace process after the Continuation War. No sanctions had been directed against the Soviet Union that had attacked and forced Finland to surrender territories to it. Nothing much could be done about that, however, since the leading Western powers participated actively in the peace settlement of 1944–47 and were satisfied with the treatment of Finland.

After World War II, European nations concentrated on rebuilding their countries – life had to go on. Finland had to listen carefully to the views of the Soviet Union and had internal political difficulties, but altogether it fared well. It duly paid the war reparations, was able by 1952 to organize the Summer Olympic Games, and by 1956 received back from the Soviet Union the Porkkala naval base. Porkkala's return was of great importance, because it was located near to Helsinki and formed a real threat to Finland's independence. Finland began to develop as a modern Western European welfare State.

---

135 See *ibid.*, p. 33, and Polvinen *supra* note 26, p. 312.
136 E. Ziemke, *The German Northern Theater of Operations 1940–1945*, (United States Department of the Army, Washington D.C., 1959), pp. 203–204. Jokipii's view is similar to that of Ziemke, *supra* note 109, p. 171. *See also* Magill *supra* note 55, p. 87.

CHAPTER 6

Application of Domestic Criminal Statutes in regard to International Crimes

Andres Parmas

Abstract

In order for an international crime to be prosecuted in a domestic court, norms prescribing punishability have to be adopted in the legal system of the respective State. The article analyses issues that come up with autonomous transposition of international criminal law norms into the domestic legal order, based on the example of the Estonian Penal Code. It also seeks to offer an explanation as to why it is necessary to be aware of these issues and what the strategies would be to overcome problems with transposition. Both issues of the special part as well as the general part are touched upon.

Keywords

international criminal law – Estonian Penal Code – transposition of international norms

1   Introduction

International criminal law can be applied either directly via international(-ized) criminal tribunals or the ICC or indirectly through domestic judicial bodies. It is a well-known fact that this second method of application is dominant and only a small fraction of all international crimes are prosecuted before international institutions.[1] In order for an international crime to be prosecuted in a domestic court, norms prescribing punishability have to be adopted in the legal system of the respective State. What this effectively means is the need to transpose into the domestic legal order definitions of crimes (but also some

---

1   See e.g. G. Werle, *Principles of International Criminal Law.* 2nd ed., p. 117. TMC Asser (2009). See also A. Cassese. *International Criminal Law.* 2nd ed., p. 343. Oxford University Press (2010).

general principles of responsibility) from international law, either international treaties (for example, the Rome Statute) or customary international law (for example, the definition of crimes against humanity).

There are in principle four ways to introduce international crimes into a national legal order. First of all, it is possible to directly apply international law (or so that national law simply refers to international law). The second possibility is to incorporate an international law norm, unamended, into the national legal system. The third option is to construct an independent national legal norm criminalising the conduct concerned.[2] Naturally there exists the option that an international crime is prosecuted and punished as an ordinary crime under domestic law. To illustrate the first group, Sections 4 and 6 of Canada's War Crimes and Crimes against Humanity Act refer to customary international law, international treaty law or general principles of international law as the normative basis for international crimes punishable in Canada.[3] Another example of this group is from the United Kingdom, where Section 50 of the International Criminal Court Act refers to Articles 6–8 of the Rome Statute.[4] The Israeli Crime of Genocide (Prevention and Punishment) Law of 1950,[5] on the other hand, represents national legislation that copies word for word the text of Article 2 of the Genocide Convention.[6] As an example of the third option, Estonian penal law could be referred to. To at least some extent Danish law adheres to the fourth approach mentioned above.[7] This alternative, however, has been criticised as demonstrating unwillingness to actually recognise

---

2   *See e.g.* M. Bergsmo (ed.). *Importing Core International Crimes into National Law*. 2nd ed., pp. 7–8. Torkel Opsahl Academic EPublisher (2010). Available at: https://www.legal-tools.org/doc/398270/pdf/, last visited 30.01.2019. See a somewhat different systemisation of transposition in G. Werle. *Principles of International Criminal Law*, pp. 76–78. TMC Asser Press (2005); *or* H. Kreicker. 'Völkerstrafrecht in Ländervergleich', pp. 27–34. In Nationale Strafverfolgung völkerrechtlicher Verbrechen. Band 7. A. Eser, U. Sieber, H. Kreicker (Hrsg.). Duncker & Humblot (2006).

3   *See* Canadian War Crimes and Crimes against Humanity Act. Available: https://laws-lois.justice.gc.ca/eng/acts/C-45.9/page-1.html, last visited 30.01.2019.

4   *See* International Criminal Court Act 2001. Available at: https://www.legislation.gov.uk/ukpga/2001/17/section/50, last visited 30.01.2019.

5   *See* Crime of Genocide (Prevention and Punishment) Law. Available at: https://ihl-databases.icrc.org/applic/ihl/ihl-nat.nsf/6fa4d35e5e3025394125673e00508143/835deccea9b97f85c1257 5ae0043f781/$FILE/Law%20no.%2031.pdf, last visited 30.01.2019.

6   *See* Convention on the Prevention and Punishment of the Crime of Genocide. Adopted by the UN General Assembly on 9 December 1948. Available at: https://treaties.un.org/doc/publication/unts/volume%2078/volume-78-i-1021-english.pdf, last visited 30.01.2019.

7   *See e.g.* A. Laursen. 'A Danish Paradox?: A Brief Review of the Status of International Crimes in Danish law'. *Journal of International Criminal Justice*, Vol. 10 (2012), pp. 1000–1001.

the different quality of an internationally protected legal interest (as compared to 'ordinary' legal goods) and to criminalise its violation.[8]

Choice of method of transposition will also define the technique of later application of the respective norms. When international law is applied directly, reference is made to an international norm or the text of an international norm has been copy-pasted into domestic law, so it is fairly easy to establish the boundaries of the applicable norm. In contrast, if autonomous domestic norms are being defined or compliance with international law is sought through application of ordinary criminal law, the situation becomes more ambiguous.[9]

This article – based on the example of the Estonian Penal Code – analyses issues that come up with autonomous transposition of international criminal law norms into the domestic legal order. It also seeks to offer an explanation as to why it is necessary to be aware of these issues and what the strategies would be to overcome problems with transposition. Both issues of the special part – that is, definitions of international crimes – as well as the general part are touched upon below.

2   General Remarks on Transposing International Criminal Law into the National Legal Order

Implementing international crimes into domestic legal systems through autonomous definitions might bring to the domestic legal system norms that are not in full conformity with the corresponding original international norms. The domestic norm might turn out to be either narrower or wider in scope than the international norm. This of course can happen because of deliberate policy considerations; but it can also happen involuntarily, because of faulty translation, use of improper terminology, as a result of structuring norms differently from international law, and so on. Be that as it may, domestic definitions of international crimes that substantially deviate from corresponding international definitions will cause problems in their application both domestically[10] and also taking into consideration the international obligations of the

---

8   See e.g. R. Cryer, et al. *An Introduction to International Criminal Law and Procedure*. 2nd ed., pp 73–74. Cambridge University Press (2010). *See also* concurring practice of the ICTR: *The Prosecutor v Bagaragaza*, ICTR-05-86-AR11bis. Appeals Chamber decision of 30.08.2006.
9   See Kreicker, *supra* note 2, pp. 27, 30, 31.
10 See e.g. on some disputable Estonian court practice in T. Kerikmäe, A. Parmas. 'Correspondents' reports: a guide to state practice concerning international humanitarian law:

country that applies a domestic statute whose terminology is not in accordance with the respective international norms.[11]

If the domestic definition of an international crime is wider than the definition in international law, it means that the domestic definition will entail elements which are not found in the corresponding international norm (either a wider circle of acts, protected persons or potential victims, lower *mens rea* standard, and so on). In order to establish if a domestically criminalised act is also punishable under international law, one must not be guided merely by the title of the crime, but must check the elements of the offence. Should the elements differ from the international norm and not have a corresponding element in the international norm, then in regard to these elements one can only speak about a domestic offence. The fact that such elements have been put under the title of an international crime and have been amalgamated together with other elements that correspond to elements of an international crime does not change this legal reality. In such cases the punishability under international law of an act criminalised in a domestic criminal code is at least partly only an illusion.

Application of such a norm might infringe the *nullum crimen sine lege* principle if the underlying act has been committed outside the territory of the country concerned.[12] On the other hand, there are no hindrances to utilising the territoriality principle (Article 6 of the Estonian Penal Code) in regard to offences that extend the grounds of responsibility in comparison to the law of the offender's country of nationality or international law.[13] If the act has been committed outside the territory of a country, it might of course be possible to apply the active or passive personality principle (Article 7(1) of the Estonian Penal Code). However, these jurisdictional principles usually require the existence of an identical norm in the place where the act was committed. This means that whether the State can exercise its jurisdiction over a certain offence or not will depend on the law of the place where the act was committed.[14]

Estonia', p. 490. In: *Yearbook of International Humanitarian Law*. Vol. 3 (2000). TMC Asser (2002).

11 See Kreicker, *supra* note 2, pp. 15, 31–32.

12 *See* for further discussion H. Kreicker. 'Deutschland', p. 68. In A. Eser, H. Kreicker (Hrsg.) *supra* note 2. Edition iuscrim (2003).

13 In this vein the Estonian Supreme Court has explained that the mere fact that the offender is a citizen of another country is not a reason to exempt him from criminal responsibility. *See* case *Penart*, 18.12.2003 Supreme Court judgment no 3-1-1-140-03, para. 12. Available at: https://www.riigikohus.ee/et/lahendid?asjaNr=3-1-1-140-03, last visited 30.01.2019. *See also* Kreicker, 'Völkerstrafrecht in Ländervergleich', *supra* note 2, pp. 15, 47–48.

14 *See* on the nationality principle *e.g.* H. Satzger. *International and European Criminal Law*, C.H.Beck, Hart, Nomos (2012), pp. 20–21. In recent Estonian judicial practice, the

According to the State protection principle, if the act harms the vital interests of a country, it is also possible to apply domestic penal law to acts committed outside the territory of a country notwithstanding the existence of an identical norm (Article 9 of the Estonian Penal Code). In terms of international crimes that have been defined more extensively than in international law, the State protection principle might justify the use of a country's domestic criminal jurisdiction if citizens or residents of that country have fallen victim to such a crime. Hence it operates somewhat as an extended form of passive personality principle.[15] The universality principle (Article 8 of the Estonian Penal Code) could apply to such a crime only if the elements of the domestic criminal offence fully coincide with the corresponding international norm.[16]

It appears that the domestic judge is put in a very difficult position in terms of applying domestic jurisdiction to international crimes that have been defined more widely than the corresponding international norms. First, the domestic judge has to analyse to what extent the domestic and international norms overlap and to what extent one can only speak of purely domestic law. After that the judge has to decide which jurisdictional principle applies at a given time and only then is it possible to decide how widely to apply the norm. Clearly, this is a blurry legal situation. Perhaps this is also the reason why, in the legal system of some countries, the preference has been to stick to internationally recognised definitions when defining international crimes (for example, the German VStGB.)[17]

If domestic definitions of international crimes are narrower than corresponding international norms, other problems arise in their application. First and foremost, if some of the internationally required elements are not covered in domestic criminal law, it will possibly mean breach of international obligations by the State concerned, such as its inability to follow the duty to either

---

conditions of application of the active personality principle have been discussed at the sharpest in the case of *Kender*, 11.10.2017 judgment of Tallinn Circuit Court no 1-15-11024. Available at: https://www.riigiteataja.ee/kohtulahendid/detailid.html?id=215770780, last visited 30.01.2019.

15   This view is implicitly supported by the commentary to the Estonian Penal Code. See J. Sootak '§ 9', para. 17. In J. Sootak, P. Pikamäe. Karistusseadustik. *Kommenteeritud väljaanne.* Juura (2015).

16   See in that regard G. Werle, *supra*, note 1, pp. 59–60. See also A. Parmas, J. Sootak. 'Landesbericht. Estland', p. 288. In *Jurisdiktionskonflikte bei grenzüberschreitender Kriminalität. Ein Rechtsvergleich zum Internationalen Strafrecht*. Universitätsverlag Osnabrück (2012).

17   *See* with reference to further discussion thereon H. Gropengiesser. 'The Criminal Law of Genocide. The German Perspective'. *International Criminal Law Review* 5 (2005), p. 336.

prosecute a certain offence or to extradite the offender.[18] For a State party to the ICC this means that the country is unable to fulfil its duty to exercise its criminal jurisdiction over those responsible for international crimes.[19] But it also means that the country cannot fully utilize its own criminal jurisdiction even if it would otherwise be willing to do so.

Transposing the definitions of international crimes into a domestic legal order in too narrow a fashion might entail some quite unexpected results in the domestic adjudication process. The constitutions of several countries contain a provision according to which the universally recognised principles of international law form part of the domestic legal order.[20] At the same time in countries following the civil law tradition usually both the constitution and the penal code entail a provision stipulating that no one shall be held responsible on account of an action which did not constitute a criminal offence at the time it was committed. In the light of these two constitutional norms a situation might arise where a domestic judge has to choose whether to give preference to the constitutional principle that generally accepted principles and norms of international law prevail or whether the principle that all criminal offences have to be defined in the domestic criminal code should prevail.[21] Most probably a domestic judge is not ready to decide such issues. On the other hand, it

---

18   *See further* on the principle *aut dedere aut iudicare* R. Cryer *et al.*, *supra*, note 8, pp. 69 and 72; G. Werle, *supra*, note 1, pp. 63–64. *Also* ILC 1996 Draft Code of Crimes against the Peace and Security of Mankind, Art. 9 and commentaries thereto. Available at: http://legal.un.org/ilc/texts/instruments/english/commentaries/7_4_1996.pdf, last visited 31.01.2019.

19   *See* H. Satzger, *supra*, note 14, p. 279; S.A. Williams, W.A. Schabas. 'Art 17', p. 606. In O. Triffterer (ed.). *Commentary on the Rome Statute of the International Criminal Court*. C.H.Beck, Hart, Nomos (2008).

20   *E.g.* according to Art. 6(2) of the Georgian Constitution the legislation of Georgia must correspond to universally recognised principles and rules of international law. The Constitution of Georgia. Adopted on 24 August 1995, last amended 27 December 2006. Available at: http://www.parliament.ge/files/68_1944_951190_CONSTIT_27_12.06.pdf, last visited 30.01.2019; Art. 25 of the German Basic Law (*Grundgesetz*) stipulates that the general rules of international law are an integral part of federal law. They take precedence over the laws and directly create rights and duties for the inhabitants of federal territory. Basic Law of the Federal Republic of Germany. Available at: https://www.gesetze-im-internet.de/englisch_gg/englisch_gg.html, last visited 30.01.2019; According to Art. 3 (2) of the Estonian Constitution generally recognised principles and rules of international law are an inseparable part of the Estonian legal system. The Constitution of the Republic of Estonia. Available at: https://www.riigiteataja.ee/en/eli/530102013003/consolide, last visited 30.01.2019.

21   *But see* for a different opinion in Germany https://www.jura.uni-bonn.de/fileadmin/Fachbereich_Rechtswissenschaft/Einrichtungen/Institute/Voelkerrecht/Dokumente_fuer_Webseite/Grenzen_JZ_1_2013__S_12-21.pdf, last visited 30.01.2019.

is problematic from the point of view of the defendant's defence rights even to find oneself in the midst of such a dilemma.

3 Concrete Examples from Estonian Legislation with some Comparative Remarks

3.1 *Special Part*

3.1.1 Genocide

Article 90 of the Estonian Penal Code defines the circle of protected groups in the crime of genocide as follows: "[...] with the intention to destroy, in whole or in part, a national, ethnic, racial or religious group, a group resisting occupation or any other social group [...]".[22] Hence the list of protected groups differs from the widely accepted international standard. It includes one more specific group and the list is left open. Naturally, broadening the definition of genocide in domestic law in comparison to that of international law is not only the brainchild of the Estonian legislator: quite a number of States have nationally broadened the circle of protected groups. It is noteworthy that such developments often occurred in the previous decade and that formerly socialist Eastern-European States have been more apt to extend the definition. Evidently, this is substantially due to the rich palette of different mass-murder and persecution campaigns which were conducted in these States during the socialist regime. In Poland, for example, a political group, or a group with a different perspective on life is included as a protected group;[23] in Lithuania a social or political group is included;[24] the Slovenian Penal Code extends protection to any identifiable group or community on political, racial, national, ethnic, cultural, religious, gender as defined in paragraph 3, or other grounds that are universally recognized as impermissible under international law;[25] in Belarus, Burkina Faso and France 'other groups' are added to the list of

---

22 Penal Code of Estonia. English translation available: https://www.riigiteataja.ee/en/eli/520122018001/consolide, last visited 12.01.2019.

23 Penal Code of Poland of 6 June 1997, Art. 118. Available at: https://www.legislationline.org/documents/section/criminal-codes/country/10/Poland/show, last visited 30.01.2019.

24 Criminal Code of the Republic of Lithuania, Art. 99. Available at: https://e-seimas.lrs.lt/rs/legalact/TAD/TAIS.366707/format/ISO_PDF/, last visited 31.01.2019.

25 Penal Code of Slovenia of 20 May 2008 (as last amended on 24 May 2017), Arts 100 (2) and 101 (8). Available at: https://www.legislationline.org/documents/section/criminal-codes, last visited 31.01.2019.

protected groups;[26] the Penal Code of Côte d'Ivoire prescribes protection of political groups in addition to the traditionally protected groups;[27] under the Finnish Penal Code the circle of protected groups covers 'another comparable group'.[28] The Georgian legislator has followed the same path when defining the circle of protected groups to comprise, along with national, ethnic, racial, religious groups, also groups that are united by any other hallmarks.[29]

The road chosen by Estonia and several other States, where domestic regulation of genocide is wider than required by international treaties or customary international law, certainly raises problems in applying domestic norms.[30]

If a State wishes to prosecute somebody for genocide on the basis of universal jurisdiction, the question arises whether it can fully apply its domestic law. The solution to this problem can be manifold. At first, if in the State where genocide was committed the targeted group was identified on some feature other than their nationality, ethnicity, religion or race, but objectively the victims are also determinable on one of those grounds; there might be a possibility for prosecution under universal jurisdiction.

Such a situation is very likely to occur in a civil war that is regarded by the central government merely as an anti-terrorist operation and where the opponents are not regarded as a group entitled to protection under the Genocide Convention, but as plain criminals, terrorists or a political group. The Soviet Union, for example, punished – according to official rhetoric – political criminals, bandits and enemies of the working class in the occupied Baltic States. In reality, however, the aim was to destroy the Estonian, Latvian and Lithuanian nations as groups with a distinct identity by selectively eliminating national

---

26 Уголовный кодекс Республики Беларусь, принят Палатой представителей 2 июня 1999 года, Статья 127. Available at: http://www.pravo.by/webnpa/text.asp?RN=HK9900275, last visited 31.01.2019; Law No 043/96/ADP of 13 November 1996 – Penal Code, Section 313. Available at: http://www.preventgenocide.org/fr/droit/codes/burkinafaso.htm, last visited 31.01.2019; Penal Code of France, Section 211-1. Available at: https://www.legifrance.gouv.fr/affichCode.do;jsessionid=9D45B5EEA2BBE13B7FF6413DB2D55525.tplgfr22s_3?idSectionTA=LEGISCTA000006165393&cidTexte=LEGITEXT000006070719&dateTexte=20190131, last visited 31.01.2019.

27 Penal Code of Côte d'Ivoire, Section 137. Available at: http://www.apdhci.org/images/documents_pdf/instruments_ivoiriens_des_droits_de_homme/code_penal_ci.pdf, last visited 31.01.2019.

28 Rikoslaki, 19.12.1889/39, Luku 11, 1 §. Available at: https://www.finlex.fi/fi/laki/ajantasa/1889/18890039001#L11, last visited 31.01.2019.

29 Criminal Code of Georgia, Art. 407. Available at: https://matsne.gov.ge/en/document/download/16426/157/en/pdf, last visited 31.01.2019.

30 See J. Sootak, A. Parmas. 'Developing the Definition of the Crime of Genocide through National Criminal Laws', pp. 71–72. In *Festschrift in Honour of Raimo Lahti*. K. Nuotio (ed.). Helsinki University Print (2007).

figureheads of these nations, and to melt these groups into the amorphous mass of *'homo sovieticus'*.[31]

A more complex situation will develop if, according to the universal jurisdiction principle, it is sought to prosecute for genocide a person whose victims can indeed not be included under any protected group in the sense of the internationally accepted concept of the crime of genocide. Is the prosecution of such persons according to a wider domestic norm legitimate? Apparently not. The obligation to base prosecution for the crime of genocide, according to the universal jurisdiction principle, on the internationally accepted definition of this crime derives from the *nullum crimen nulla poena sine lege* postulate, since a person can only be accountable for conduct that was explicitly criminal at the time and place of its perpetration. That viewpoint is supported by the Princeton Principles of Universal Jurisdiction. Article 2(1) of the Principles indeed does not explain what exactly is meant by crimes allowing universal jurisdiction, but its commentary refers unequivocally to the Genocide Convention.[32] Therefore, for example Belarusian criminal law has to be criticised, as Section 6(3) of its Criminal Code provides exclusive universal jurisdiction in the case of the crime of genocide notwithstanding the fact that the crime is defined more extensively in Belarus than accepted on the international level. What was said above does not necessarily mean that in a situation like this the application of domestic jurisdiction would be entirely precluded. Let us once more refer to the Estonian Penal Code: the surrogate adjudication jurisdictional principle established in Article 7, which enables prosecution of an alien offender who has been detained in Estonia and is not extradited. The provision referred to has been constructed on the identical norm principle and thus only a person whose conduct was punishable where the act was committed, or if no penal power is applicable at the place where the act was committed, can be prosecuted under that norm.

3.1.2 The Crime of Aggression

Unlike the definition of the crime of genocide, an attempt has actually been made to define the crime of aggression in Estonia's Penal Code in accordance

---

31 *See* more thoroughly L. Mälksoo. 'Soviet Genocide? Communist Mass Deportations in the Baltic States and International Law', *Leiden Journal of International Law* Vol. 14, Issue 4 (2001), pp. 784–785.

32 Princeton Principles on Universal Jurisdiction. Commentary on the Princeton Principles, p. 47. Available at: http://www1.umn.edu/humanrts/instree/princeton.html, last visited 31.01.2019.

with international law.[33] It is supposed to follow the amendments to the Rome Statute agreed in Kampala in 2010 (Article 8bis of the Rome Statute).[34] This goal, however, has not been achieved, for two reasons. For one, a mistake has sneaked into the text of Article 91 of the Penal Code, where the offence is defined. Along with that, Article 91 of the Estonian Penal Code is a good example of what can unintentionally happen if the aim were to keep the original meaning of the international norm but at the same time to use original vocabulary to express that meaning.

The Estonian legislator amended the existing definition of the crime of aggression in Article 91 of the Penal Code in 2014. According to the new text, a punishable act is defined as follows: "(1) Participation in the management, execution or preparation of an act of aggression controlling or directing the activities of the State or threatening with an act of aggression by a representative of the State [...]". This does not make much sense. In the draft law proposed by the Ministry of Justice the definition was "participation in the leading,[35] execution or preparation of an act of aggression *by a person* controlling or directing the activities of the State or threatening with an act of aggression by a representative of the State".[36] Hence, it appears that the legislator has made an error, omitting the phrase 'by a person' from the adopted text of the amendment. The result of the error is that the bulk of Article 91 of the Estonian Penal Code is effectively inapplicable for the time being. A prosecution for the crime of aggression in the Estonian courts would mean requiring the Estonian judge to turn directly to customary international law in order to establish the content of the punishable act.

Punishable individual conduct in Article 91 of the Estonian Penal Code is defined as "participation in the leading, execution or preparation of an act of aggression". The reason for choosing this formulation remains unclear. The explanatory memorandum to the draft law only States that the "formulation of

---

33   See discussion on Estonian regulation of the crime of aggression: A. Parmas. 'Chapter 26. Estonia'. In *The Crime of Aggression. A Commentary*, C. Kreß, S. Barriga (eds.), pp. 895–922. Cambridge University Press (2016).

34   Amendments to the Rome Statute of the International Criminal Court. Kampala, 11 June 2010. Available at: https://asp.icc-cpi.int/iccdocs/asp_docs/RC2010/AMENDMENTS/CN.651.2010-ENG-CoA.pdf, last visited 31.01.2019.

35   Actually in the official translation of the Penal Code here the term 'management' is used, which might be misleading and perplexing. Therefore, this author prefers to translate the original Estonian term *'juhtimises'* as 'leading', which is also in line with the language used in Art. 8 *bis* of the Rome Statute.

36   The original draft law is available (in Estonian) at: http://eelnoud.valitsus.ee/main/mount/docList/2c861e08-9718-4cec-83f5-a88a63e8cd68?activity=1#JD3B88Dm, last visited 31.01.2019.

the definition stems from the amendments to the Rome Statute".[37] The new wording is likely to produce problems in interpretation. In particular, how to distinguish between leading and executing an act of aggression is open to question given that the responsibility for the crime of aggression is already by its very nature confined to persons who are in effect running the aggressive campaign of one State against another State. This is by definition a leadership crime.

Comparatively speaking, there seems to be some considerable inconsistency in defining punishable individual conduct of the crime of aggression throughout domestic penal codes that include this offence. According to Article 110 of the Lithuanian Penal Code, it is punishable to cause aggression or to be in command thereof.[38] The Finnish Criminal Code Chapter 11, Article 4a stipulates that the person responsible for the crime of aggression is the one who can effectively rule or lead the State's political or military actions and who commits an attack that is manifestly contrary to the UN Charter.[39] The Latvian Criminal Code Section 72 stipulates that it is criminal to prepare or trigger military aggression or to participate therein, to conduct a war of aggression in violation of international agreements or to conspire to commit such acts.[40] At the same time several other countries have basically retained the Nuremberg formulation of a crime against peace in their domestic statutes. In that vein according to Article 353 of the Russian Criminal Code it is punishable to plan, prepare, unleash or wage aggressive war.[41] The Ukrainian, Armenian, Azerbaijani, Polish and Belarusian criminal codes and to a large extent the Georgian Penal Code follow the same example.[42]

In terms of a collective act, it might seem, at least at first glance, that Estonia has adhered to the definition of the crime of aggression agreed in Kampala.

---

37 See Explanatory Memorandum to the draft law amending the Penal Code and other related legal acts (SE 554), at 3.2.2., available (only in Estonian) at: www.riigikogu.ee/tegevus/eelnoud/eelnou/78433b29-8b2f-4281-a582-0efb9631e2ad/, last visited 31.01.2019.
38 Criminal Code of the Republic of Lithuania, Art. 110.
39 Rikoslaki, *supra* note 28, Luku 11, 4a §.
40 The Criminal Law of the Republic of Latvia, Section 72. Available at: https://www.legislationline.org/documents/section/criminal-codes, last visited 31.01.2019.
41 Уголовный кодекс Российской Федерации, Статья 353. Available at: http://pravo.gov.ru/proxy/ips/?docbody&nd=102041891
42 Armenian Criminal Code, Art. 384. Available at: https://www.legislationline.org/documents/action/popup/id/8872/preview, last visited 31.01.2019; Уголовный кодекс Азербайджанской Республики, Статья. 100. Available at: https://online.zakon.kz/Document/?doc_id=30420353, last visited 31.01.2019; Penal Code of Poland, *supra* note 23, Art. 117; Criminal Code of Georgia, Art. 404; Уголовный кодекс Республики Беларусь, Статья 122.

The Estonian legislator has set a similar objective threshold for a punishable act as in Article 8bis of the Rome Statute. Still, the meaning of "the use of armed force by one State, in violation of international law, against another State" in Article 91(3) of the Estonian Penal Code needs some further clarification. Although the commentary to the Penal Code refers to Article 8 *bis* of the Rome Statute,[43] the formulation is different from "an act of aggression which, by its character, gravity and scale, constitutes a manifest violation of the Charter of the United Nations" as used in Article 8 *bis* of the Rome Statute. The first version of the new definition of the crime of aggression proposed by the Ministry of Justice still followed the formula agreed in Kampala and stipulated that for the purposes of Article 91 of the Penal Code only "an act of aggression which, by its character, gravity and scale, constitutes a manifest violation of the Charter of the United Nations" is relevant.[44] However, in the course of the consultation process, the draft law was amended into its current version. Curiously, the justification for changing the text was the will to bring it into accordance with Article 8 *bis* of the Rome Statute![45] It appears that the drafters overlooked the logic behind Article 8 *bis* of the Rome Statute and therefore came to the wrong conclusions. As the crime of aggression actually has two origins in international law, both binding on Estonia – the customary law definition of the crime and Article 8bis of the Rome Statute – it could have made sense at least to try to combine the requirements of both of these sources. In the light of the above, this departure from the Kampala description of the minimum standard for the collective act is clearly open to criticism.

The issue is not merely of theoretical significance. The above-discussed construction rather causes practical problems for applying the definition of the crime of aggression under Article 91 of the Penal Code. An Estonian judge would find it difficult to find guidance in setting the minimum standard of an act of aggression punishable as a criminal offence. Different sets of rules of international law pose different standards as to what should be deemed illegal use of force. According to the definition of aggression in Article 1 of GA Resolution 3314, aggression is the use of armed force by a State against the sovereignty, territorial integrity or political independence of another State, or in any

---

43 J. Tehver, '§ 91', p. 330. In J. Sootak and P. Pikamäe (eds.) *supra* note 15.
44 *See* draft law amending the Penal Code and related acts, as presented for consultation to other government bodies, Art. 1 (46), *supra* note 36 [only available in Estonian].
45 *See* the remarks by the Ministry of Foreign Affairs on proposed changes to Art. 91 in the coordination table to the draft law amending the Penal Code and other related legal acts (SE 554 [only in Estonian]. Available at: http://eelnoud.valitsus.ee/main#AgeZUuFw, last visited 31.01.2019.

other manner inconsistent with the UN Charter.[46] At the same time, Article 8 *bis*(1) of the Rome Statute speaks of "an act of aggression which, by its character, gravity and scale, constitutes a manifest violation of the Charter of the United Nations". Besides that, any unjustified use of armed force by one State against another State (for example, shooting a single bullet over the border) is contrary to Article 2(4) of the UN Charter. This begs the question: what standard binds the Estonian judge? The task of determining which aggressive acts are in violation of international law is not simply difficult for a domestic judge, but in most cases is probably an unrealizable task. This is the reason why, for example, the German legislator has chosen a middle way, where from one side it has opted for the Kampala definition. According to VStGB Article 13 (1) a collective act is defined as war of aggression or any other act of aggression which, by its nature, gravity and scope, constitutes a manifest violation of the UN Charter. Paragraph 3 of the same article, however, adds a further condition when stipulating that an act of aggression is the use of armed force by a State, directed against the sovereignty, the territorial integrity or the political independence of a State, or in an otherwise incompatible manner with the UN Charter.[47]

3.1.3   War Crimes

As a third example, where the domestic legislator has transposed international crimes in a considerably narrower fashion than the related international norms, the definitions of war crimes in the Estonian Penal Code have to be pointed out.

Unlike its predecessor, the Estonian Penal Code that was adopted in 2001 was supposed to entail comprehensive definitions of war crimes.[48] Although Estonia had already signed the Rome Statute for the ICC at the end of 1999, the cumbersome system of defining war crimes in the Statute was not followed by the Estonian legislator. First, no distinction has been drawn in the Estonian Penal Code between war crimes punishable during an international and a non-international armed conflict.[49] The offences were grouped based on the legal values protected through definitions of the offences. The trouble, however, is

---

46   UN General Assembly 14 December 1974 Resolution 3314 (XXIX). Definition of Aggression. Available at: https://documents-dds-ny.un.org/doc/RESOLUTION/GEN/NR0/739/16/IMG/NR073916.pdf?OpenElement, last visited 31.01.2019.

47   Völkerstrafgesetzbuch, § 13. Available at: https://www.gesetze-im-internet.de/vstgb/BJNR225410002.html, last visited 31.01.2019.

48   The original text of the 2001 Estonian Penal Code (in Estonian) is available at: https://www.riigiteataja.ee/akt/73045, last visited 31.01.2019.

49   J. Tehver, *supra* note 43, '§ 94', pp. 335–336.

that the Estonian legislator was not meticulous enough to think through whether all internationally recognised definitions of war crimes were covered by the articles in Chapter VIII Section 4 prescribing war crimes in the Estonian Penal Code. The result was that in the original version of the Code, several acts that are punishable as war crimes in international law were completely omitted, whereas in the case of several other offences the elements of the crime were defined more narrowly than in corresponding international law.

For example, the Estonian Penal Code did not provide definitions of war crimes involving conscripting minors (Article 8 paragraph 2 (b) (xxvi) of the ICC Statute); treacherous attack (Article 8 paragraph 2 (b) (xi) of the ICC Statute); human shields (Article 8 paragraph 2 (b) (xxiii) of the ICC Statute) and attacking a combatant *hors de combat* who has not yet surrendered at discretion. The war crime of declaring that no quarter will be given was only punishable as an ordinary crime of threat under Article 120 of the Estonian Penal Code. Most of the internationally recognised war crimes against property were only partly covered by the relevant articles of the Estonian Penal Code, leaving large areas of violations only punishable as ordinary property offences. The war crime of illegally restricting the judicial rights of the nationals of a hostile party was only punishable as the ordinary crime of violation of equality under Article 152 of the Estonian Penal Code.[50]

None of these errors referred to above were based on any policy considerations but were merely miscalculations or results of poor analysis. Although all these errors have now been amended, it shows how easily it could happen that an autonomous domestic definition of an international norm goes awry. One of the reasons for that is clearly the large number of different war crimes definitions in international law that are partly overlapping and that apply in some instances only to international armed conflicts, but in other instances to non-international armed conflicts as well. The long and cumbersome list of war crimes presented in Article 8 of the Rome Statute is not helpful in that sense either.

3.2 *General Part*

Apart from the definitions of international crimes, international criminal law has gradually evolved also to regulate issues of general principles of criminal

---

[50] *See* more thoroughly A. Parmas; T. Ploom. 'Prosecution of international crimes: Estonia'. In: A. Eser, U. Sieber, H. Kreicker (eds.). *National Prosecution of International Crimes. Nationale Strafverfolgung Völkerrechtlichen Verbrechen.* Vol. 5, pp. 89–188. Duncker & Humblot (2005).

responsibility (the general part). This means that when stipulating the underlying rules for determining criminal responsibility in the domestic legal order, the legislator also has to take into account the related international rules. At least for now a State is mostly free to choose the doctrine of the general part itself, as long as it covers the classic concepts of criminal law such as jurisdiction, commission and complicity, inchoate forms of crime, subjective elements of the offence, guilt, mistake, omission and justifications and excuses.

Although for the most part the institutes of the general part have not been prescribed with enough precision in international law, there are some exceptions. At least the concepts of superior responsibility and the (non-)defence of superior orders have obtained clear enough shape in international law so that domestic legal systems are no longer completely free to define these institutes at their own discretion. Bearing that in mind, one has to admit that in regulating both of these institutes the Estonian legislator has also not been up to the task.

3.2.1   Superior Responsibility

The responsibility of a superior is prescribed in Article 88 (1) of the Estonian Penal Code, which stipulates that for a criminal offence provided for in Chapter 8, a representative of State powers or military commander who issued an order to commit a criminal offence, consented to the commission of a criminal offence or failed to prevent the commission of a criminal offence although it was in their power to do so or who failed to submit a report of a criminal offence while being aware of the commission of a criminal offence by their subordinate(s) are also to be punished in addition to the principal offender. As we have seen, Estonian regulation of the superior orders doctrine is in many ways problematic and hardly reconcilable with customary international law[51] or Article 28 of the Rome Statute. In a nutshell the most outstanding issues of Article 88 (1) of the Estonian Penal Code lie in the following.

Unlike as stipulated in Article 88 (1), not only State representatives should be covered as non-military superiors, but the regulation should also extend to non-military superiors as such (both *de iure* and *de facto*), notwithstanding their (non)status in the State power hierarchy. There is considerable case-law from the ICTY and ICTR where superior responsibility has been applied to

---

51 *See e.g.* K. Ambos. Chapter 21. 'Superior Responsibility'. In A. Cassese, P. Gaeta, J.R.W.D. Jones (eds.). *The Rome Statute of the International Criminal Court. A Commentary.* Vol. I. Oxford University Press (2002) pp. 824–841.

non-military superiors.[52] In fact, as long ago as the Nuremberg follow-up cases, non-military superiors not belonging to a State power hierarchy (managing doctors, industrialists), were found guilty based on superior responsibility.[53] Certainly, the exact preconditions for the responsibility of military and non-military superiors may vary. In particular, great care has to be taken in establishing that there exists actual effective control by a superior over their subordinates, namely in relation to those acts towards which the superior has a guarantor position, that is to say, that fall within the sphere of competence of the superior.[54]

Moreover, Article 88 (1) of the Estonian Penal Code in a problematic way combines very different grounds for liability: (1) order to commit a crime (which might – as the facts of the concrete case may be – constitute joint commission of a criminal offence or commission through another; it might also constitute only instigation to commit a criminal offence); (2) consent (which in turn might constitute aiding a crime by omission, but might also fall under mere tolerance of a crime and therefore merge together with failure to prevent or report a criminal offence – consequently superior responsibility proper); (3) failure to prevent or report the commission of a criminal offence (elements of superior responsibility proper). This means that, effectively, the Estonian legislator has put together direct liability, accessory liability and the *sui generis* liability of superiors, thereby hopelessly blurring all these grounds of liability. The idea of superior responsibility is to make superiors answer for crimes committed by their subordinates if they have culpably violated their duty of control over subordinates.[55]

If a superior gives an order to commit a crime or aids or abets a crime, this should be distinctly categorized as such. Hence, one could say that problems with regulating the responsibility of superiors in Estonian penal law are similar to what lay before the German legislator in 2002: a combination of all forms of omission by superiors in one article is incompatible with the distinction between the concepts of perpetration and complicity (*Täterschaft und Teilnahme*). Failure to prevent crimes – tolerating or ignoring atrocities – should

---

52   See with reference to case-law: W.A. Schabas. *The International Criminal Court. A Commentary on the Rome Statute*, pp. 459–460. Oxford University Press (2010).

53   See with reference to respective case-law: K. Ambos. *Der Allgemeine Teil des Völkerstrafrechts. Ansätze einer Dogmatisierung*, p. 101. Duncker & Humblot (2002).

54   T. Wu, Y. Kang. 'Criminal Liability for the Actions of Subordinates. The Doctrine of Command Responsibility and its Analogues in United States Law'. *Harvard International Law Journal* Vol. 38 (1997), p. 295; *also* R. Arnold. Article 28, p. 841. In O. Triffterer, *supra* note 19.

55   G. Werle, *supra*, note 1, p. 128; *see also* A. Cassese. *International Criminal Law*. 2nd ed., p. 242. Oxford University Press (2008).

be clearly brought out as one ground of liability, whereas mere dereliction of the duty to supervise or to report crimes already committed is another ground of liability.[56]

According to the doctrine of superior orders, a superior is responsible for not preventing crimes by their subordinates that are only about to be committed; not suppressing crimes that are in the process of being committed; or not reporting crimes that have already been committed.[57] In the Estonian Penal Code these aspects have been embraced only partly. The text of Article 88 (1) of the Penal Code shows that it only covers non-suppression (*ei ole takistanud*) and non-reporting of crimes. Therefore, one important element of a superior's duties – the duty actually to prevent their subordinates from even starting to commit a crime – has unfortunately been omitted altogether.

If the duties of a superior have been incompletely stipulated in the Estonian Penal Code, then other vital elements that would enable attributing dereliction of those duties to a superior in the first place are missing altogether from Article 88 (1) of the Penal Code. A superior can only be responsible for crimes committed by subordinates under their effective control.[58] However, this element is not even explicitly stipulated in Article 88 (1). On top of effective control over subordinates as such, further criteria need to be addressed: these are the elements of "failure to exercise proper control over subordinates", which is missing from Article 88 (1); and "failure to take necessary and reasonable measures", which is formulated inadequately (although it was in their power). If some means and measures are in the power of a superior, this does not necessarily mean that not utilizing those means and measures could – in the concrete circumstances – be seen as failure to take necessary and reasonable measures. There exist recognizable limits to application of the command responsibility doctrine – otherwise the liability of superiors for acts by subordinates would be tantamount to vicarious liability, where the crime of the subordinate (once committed) would be attributed to the superior irrespective of their personal circumstances or efforts to avert commission of the crime or its

---

56 *See* for discussion: M. Neuner. 'General Principles of International Criminal Law in Germany', pp. 127–135. In M. Neuner (ed.). *National Legislation Incorporating International Crimes*. Berliner Wissenschafts-Verlag (2003). *See also* the German Solution in Völkerstrafgesetzbuch, *supra* note 48: § 4 (*Verantwortlichkeit militärischer Befehlshaber und anderer Vorgesetzter*), § 14 (*Verletzung der Aufsichtspflicht*) and § 15 (*Unterlassen der Meldung einer Straftat*).
57 W.A. Schabas. *supra*, note 52, p. 464.
58 *See* as a landmark case on this matter ICTY trial chamber judgment of 16 November 1998 in *Delalic et al.* No IT-96-21-T, paras. 377–378. Available at: http://www.icty.org/x/cases/mucic/tjug/en/981116_judg_en.pdf, last visited 31.01.2019.

consequences. Nor is command responsibility a form of strict liability, since the mental element involving the knowledge of the accused must be well proven.[59] It is also inexplicable why not preventing an offence has to be in the power of the superior according to the formulation of Article 88 (1), but not reporting does not.

Another misconception that has found its way into Article 88 (1) of the Penal Code, concerns the *mens rea* required for responsibility. According to Estonian law it is necessary that the superior (both military and non-military) act with indirect intent (*dolus eventualis*) when failing in their duty to suppress a crime by their subordinate; or that the superior acts with awareness (*dolus directus* II) when failing to fulfil the duty to report a crime already committed. This is not the *mens rea* standard required for superior responsibility in international law. According to Article 28 of the Rome Statute the mental element required for military commanders is "either knew or, owing to the circumstances at the time, should have known", whereas it is "either knew, or consciously disregarded information which clearly indicated" for non-military superiors. The conclusion drawn from such formulations is that with regard to military commanders both negligent and intentional omissions are criminal, but in the case of non-military superiors only (quasi-)reckless and intentional behaviour is criminal.[60] Here again, the issue is further complicated by the fact that basically all forms of liability have been packed together into Article 88 (1) of the Penal Code, because different forms of conduct involve different mental requirements.

As appears from the above, the Estonian legislator has tried to be innovative and pragmatic when formulating the regulation on superior responsibility in the Penal Code. Unfortunately, the result is completely unsuccessful and does not follow either the doctrine of superior orders as having crystallized in customary international law or in Article 28 of the Rome Statute, leaving lumps of superior omissions uncovered that should be punishable under the superior responsibility doctrine in international law.

3.2.2 Superior Orders

The doctrine of superior orders has also been inadequately transposed into the Estonian legal system. According to Article 88 (2) of the Estonian Penal Code,

---

[59] I. Bantekas, S. Nash. *International Criminal Law*. 3rd ed., Routledge-Cavendish (2007) p. 37.

[60] *See* for further discussion: K. Ambos. *Treatise on International Criminal Law*. Volume I, pp. 220–227, esp. p. 224 (military commanders), and pp. 227–228 (non-military superiors). Oxford University Press (2013).

commission of a criminal offence as provided in Chapter 8 pursuant to the order of a representative of State powers or a military commander does not preclude punishment of the criminal offender. However, in the context of Article 33 of the Rome Statute it is debatable whether there is a difference in the origin of the orders – either these stem from a (military or civilian) superior belonging to a formal government power hierarchy – the problem lies in the formulation of Estonian law.[61] Namely, superior orders have been formulated in Article 33 of the Rome Statute as follows: the fact that a crime within the jurisdiction of the Court has been committed by a person pursuant to an order from a government or a superior, whether military or civilian, will not relieve that person of criminal responsibility unless: (a) the person was under a legal obligation to obey the orders of the government or the superior in question; (b) the person did not know that the order was unlawful; and (c) the order was not manifestly unlawful. According to paragraph 2 orders to commit genocide or crimes against humanity are manifestly unlawful. Article 88 (2) of the Penal Code has been formulated the other way round – not outlining in which (exceptional) instances orders from a superior can be relied on, but excluding it as a full defence altogether. This corresponds to the language of the ICTY and ICTR, where superior orders have been excluded as a full defence.[62] It appears from the language of Article 88 (2) of the Estonian Penal Code that there is no restriction on referring as a defence to an order from a non-military, non-State authority to commit an international crime, which surely could not have been the intention of the legislator. This in turn means that the Estonian legislator has failed to understand that, in an armed conflict, unofficial non-military superiority chains not (directly) deriving from any State structure might also play a significant role and it might be necessary to assess the relevance thereof as a defence of 'orders given' in such superior-subordinate relationships. This is already the case in the context of international armed conflicts, let alone in the context of non-international conflicts, where it is inevitable that the whole political leadership of the parties to the conflict that oppose the governing regime are representing non-State powers.

---

61   See e.g. A. Zimmermann. 'Superior orders', pp. 968–969. In A. Cassese, P. Gaeta, J.R.W.D. Jones (eds.), *supra* note 51; *but also* K. Ambos. Treatise *supra* note 60, pp. 380–381.

62   Updated Statute of the International Criminal Tribunal for the former Yugoslavia. Adopted 25 May 1993 by UN SC Resolution 827, last amended 7 July 2009 by UN SC Resolution 1877, Art. 7 (4). Available at: http://www.icty.org/x/file/Legal%20Library/Statute/statute_sept09_en.pdf, last visited 31.01.2019; Statute of the International Criminal Tribunal for Rwanda. Adopted 8 November 1994 by UN SC Resolution 955, last amended 13 October 2006 by UN SC Resolution 1717, Art. 6 (4). Available at: http://legal.un.org/avl/pdf/ha/ictr_EF.pdf, last visited 31.01.2019.

As a legal policy issue, it should be assessed whether Estonia actually would like to follow the absolute illegality standard or the manifest illegality standard as set by Article 33 of the Rome Statute. In academic literature about superior orders, the approach of manifest illegality taken in Article 33 of the Rome Statute has been criticized as an unfounded deviation from well-established customary international law.[63] On the other hand, this standard has also been supported and has been adopted in several States,[64] whereas some States have even taken a longer leap and recognize the defence of superior orders on a much more extensive scale than stipulated in Article 33 of the Rome Statute.[65]

4   Conclusion

The above is not in any way meant to discourage domestic legislators from choosing the method of autonomous norm-making when transposing international law into domestic law. Nor should it be taken as a warning to avoid at all costs a result where domestic statutes would differ from corresponding international norms. Indeed, quite the contrary. Taking into account the rigidity of law-making in substantive international criminal law, advancing domestic legislation is perhaps one of the most realistic ways to come to a point one day where a real evolution of one or the other international norm would become possible. So far it would be possible to test advanced norms in domestic proceedings, to create case-law, but also enhance academic discussion.

Additionally, autonomously defined norms might better suit the domestic legal system. They are easier for the participants in legal proceedings to comprehend and clearer in their application (at least from the domestic point of view). On the other hand, it is vital to create a clear understanding about in what respects domestic norms deviate from corresponding international

---

[63] *See e.g.* P. Gaeta. 'The Defence of Superior Orders: The Statute of the International Criminal Court Versus Customary International Law'. *European Journal of International Law*, Vol. 10 (1999), pp. 172–191, esp. pp. 190–191; A. Cassese, *supra* note 51, p. 270. However, there are also contradicting opinions: *e.g.* A. Zimmermann, *supra* note 61, p. 965; H.-H. Jescheck. 'The General Principles of International Criminal Law Set Out in Nuremberg, as Mirrored in the ICC Statute'. *Journal of International Criminal Justice*. Vol. 2 (2004), p. 46.

[64] *E.g.* German law follows the manifest illegality standard: Völkerstrafgesetzbuch, *supra* note 48, § 3 (*Handeln auf Befehl oder Anordnung*). *See* a comparative overview in H. Kreicker. Völkerstrafrecht im Ländervergleich, *supra* note 2, pp. 242–245.

[65] *E.g. see* the Russian solution, where the defence is extensive: Уголовный кодекс Российской Федерации, Статья 42; the same is true for Belarus: Уголовный кодекс Республики Беларусь, Статья 40.

norms, so that prosecutors, defence counsels and judges would have some guidance in an otherwise strange and unexplored territory.

However, when creating autonomous norms in transposing international law into the domestic legal order, one has to take into account the *nullum crimen* principle and how it would actually be possible to apply the transposed norms. In the context of the State's participation in the ICC, would it contribute to exercise of the complementarity principle? Do the transposed norms meet the requirements that devolve on the State from international law? These are the questions that the domestic legislator should always ask before implementing international criminal law.

CHAPTER 7

Case Law of the European Court of Human Rights as a Source of Human Rights Law

Ineta Ziemele

Abstract

The European Court of Human Rights with its case law has been for decades a particularly important actor in developing human rights law in Europe and beyond. At the same time the question as to the legal nature of its case law has not received a single answer. Most traditionally, the answer to this question has been that case law is binding on all States parties to the Convention at least to the extent that it contains *lex interpretata* as part of the Court's authoritative interpretation of the Convention entrusted to it by the founding States of the Convention regime. In accordance with the Convention's Article 46, judgments of the Court are binding on the respondent State. At the same time, judgments are followed more generally by the Contracting Parties while the Court's case law has added to the original – admittedly open-ended – text of the Convention. This article explores the impact of civil law tradition, Anglo-Saxon tradition and the theory of sources of international law on better conceptualization of the legal nature of the case law of the Court. It arrives at the conclusion that at least for the time being, there is a coherent tendency in more advanced legal systems to acknowledge that the courts and judges do occasionally make law. The example of the European Court of Human Rights goes along with these developments. It is argued that case law is a material source of law while the overall consolidation of the Convention system begs for the conclusion that the Court's case law has become a formal source of law.

Keywords

general rule of interpretation – Articles 38.1 (d) – material source of law – formal source of law – European consensus

1 Introduction[1]

Since its establishment, the European Court of Human Rights (hereinafter – the ECtHR or the Court) has broadened the scope and content of the European Convention on Human Rights (hereinafter – the Convention) and has advanced human rights law in Europe. In turn, this has inevitably impacted international human rights law. Former judge of the Court Boštjan Zupančič describes the expansion very aptly: "Half a century ago the Court was faced with [an] open space; it filled in the intermediate layers of case-law. The real substance of the Convention now lies in casuistic jurisprudence".[2] Another former judge, Vice-President Christos Rozakis, has described the nature of this development as follows: "[t]he Court undoubtedly operates rather more as a common law court than a continental European (civil law) court".[3]

On the one hand, the Court has been criticised for its casuistic jurisprudence.[4] Questions have also been raised about its activist stance.[5] On the other hand, some have argued that the Court could have been bolder in its pronouncements, especially if it were to follow properly its own principle of the Convention as a constitutional instrument. In other words, the Court's case law and working methods have attracted comments and views from all possible perspectives and continue to do so in all circles, including governments, lawyers and academics. Furthermore, an interesting study could also be made looking at the composition of the Court over time and its stance with regard to the development of case law.[6] One would probably notice some differences in attitude with each new composition of judges, an issue that might raise further concerns as to the legitimacy and authority of the Court's case law, especially now, when the term of judicial office at the Court is nine years.

---

1   The article reflects and expands material delivered in a course at the European University Institute during the 27th Session of the Academy of European Law Summer School.
2   Cited in Dragoljub Popovic, 'The Role of Precedent in the Jurisprudence of the European Court of Human Rights', in D. Spielmann, M. Tsirli, P. Voyatzis (eds.) *The European Convention on Human Rights, a living instrument. Essays in Honour of Christos L. Rozakis* (Bruylant 2011) p. 472.
3   *Ibid.*, p. 483.
4   On this point, *see* Stephen Greer, *The European Convention on Human Rights. Achievements, Problems and Prospects* (Cambridge University Press, 2006), p. 193.
5   Marc Bossuyt, 'Judicial Activism in Strasbourg', in K. Wellens (ed.) *International Law in Silver Perspective. Challenges Ahead* (Brill/Nijhoff, 2015), p. 31 *et seq.*
6   Nina-Louisa Arold Lorenz, Xavier Groussot *and* Gunnar Thor Petursson, The European Human Rights Culture – A Paradox of Human Rights Protection in Europe (*The Raoul Wallenberg Institute Human Rights Library, Brill, 2014) Volume: 44.*

Irrespective of which side one takes or which view one holds on the role of international courts, much scholarly work has focused on the findings of the Court in individual cases and the methodology of the Court's adjudication, that is, the question whether the Court is equipped with the necessary interpretative tools and uses them in a coherent and consistent manner. Given the wide impact of the Court's case law it is important to subject to scrutiny all the elements forming the basis for the legitimacy and authority of the Court's judgments such as the qualifications and election of judges, working methods and the coherence of case law. These issues are closely linked to the question at the heart of this article: the legal character of the Court's judgments.

Some scholarly writings and relevant governmental work have posed a question about the binding nature of the Court's judgments beyond the respondent State. Most traditionally, the answer to this question has been that case law is binding on all States parties to the Convention at least to the extent that it contains *lex interpretata* as part of the Court's authoritative interpretation of the Convention entrusted to it by the founding States of the Convention regime. In accordance with the Convention's Article 46, judgments of the Court are binding on the respondent State. At the same time, judgments are followed more generally by the Contracting Parties while the Court's case law, as noted at the outset, has added to the original – admittedly open-ended – text of the Convention.

Despite a wealth of literature on the Convention and the Court's case law, it still holds true that there is no clear and coherent theory explaining this phenomenon or, put differently, the legal nature and legitimacy of the Court's case law.[7] Questions linger as to whether the Court has advanced human rights law through its development in accordance with its competence or wheher at times it has acted *ultra vires*. I submit that the answer to these questions will depend on the view one takes on the theory of sources of international law insofar as relevant to the ECtHR.

This article will elaborate upon the proposition that ECtHR case law is a source of human rights law. This proposition may respond to some of the questions about the binding nature of the Court's case law and developments of human rights law that have taken place within the Convention system and beyond. The article will consist of two parts. The first part will place the debate on international judicial decisions as a source of international law within the broader context of the evolution of the international legal system as well as within a comparative context. I will therefore examine the distinction drawn between formal and material sources of international law. Before discussing

---

7   For a similar criticism, *see* Greer, *supra* note 3, p. 194.

sources of international law, I will pay attention to the common law doctrine of *stare decisis* and the civil law doctrine of *jurisprudence constante* as well as the notion of judge-made law since these legal constructs have influenced the theory of sources of international law, especially in so far as concerns judicial decisions.

In the second part of the article I will suggest that the legal nature of ECtHR case law can be depicted through a better understanding of the methodology of adjudicating cases by the Court and in that context by addressing the challenge of far reaching case law and the question of the legitimacy of the Court in expanding human rights in Europe – a question that forms part of the study into the legal nature of case law. I will explain that ECtHR case law also represents a degree of law making by the Court. The analysis hereinafter is an insider's view since the author has been a judge at the ECtHR.

2 Relevance of Common Law v. Civil Law Traditions

The doctrines of *stare decisis* and *jurisprudence constante* have offered a frame for reflection within the European Court of Human Rights, too. In the context of the debate about the legal nature of case law, a number of judges have taken the view that the Court has reached the stage where it can be said that its case law enjoys the binding force of precedent.[8] The question arises whether this is a relevant reflection apt to answer the legality and legitimacy questions concerning the Court's case law within the international legal system.

Saïda El Boudouhi, when examining the views of Sir Gerald Fitzmaurice and Sir Robert Jennings on international judicial decisions as a source of international law, has pointed out that their belonging to the common law tradition is only partly determinative of their stance on this issue. This background does contribute to drawing their attention to the importance of judicial decisions[9] and possibly to being more open to the idea of a more active role for the courts in international law-making. This is because the difficult question of the role of the courts and judges in determining the law does not arise – or at least is indeed quite different – in the common law systems. It is generally known that:

---

8 Popovic, *supra* note 2, p. 483.
9 Saïda El Boudouhi, "Les décisions judiciaires comme source du droit international chez Fitzmaurice et Jennngs", *Grandes pages du droit international. Les sources* (Paris: Editions A. Pedone, 2016) p. 355.

> [t]he common law is a legal system that has developed out of the practice and decisions of the various courts. [...] The development of the law has been entrusted to the jurisdiction of the courts, which make decisions based on the principle of *stare decisis*, applying legal principles developed through the precedents of the respective courts.

Therefore, judicial decisions are a source of law. They contain binding legal norms.

In democratic civil law systems, the question of the function of a judge and questions about the legal nature of judicial decisions and judicial pronouncements in these decisions have been addressed against the backgound of the principle of separation of powers and the democratic function of the legislator to pass generally binding legal norms. Nevertheless, legal systems and the understanding of the role of the judiciary have been evolving towards recognition of the case law of the courts as a source of law. In the German, French and other civil law systems it is recognized that so-called judge made law stemming from case law is also part of legal regulation, while the source of validity and legitimacy of such law continues to be debated in modern legal theory and practice in different jurisdictions.[10] Comparative law study shows that as a result of developments in legal thinking and practice, in some legal systems there is even a normative prohibition against considering judicial decisions as a source of general law, for example, in a specific area of law, while other systems have normative permission.[11] These legislative choices show that the legislator acknowledges the important legal effect of judicial decisions as well as the ongoing theoretical controversies to the point that it has to legislate on the limits of judicial impact in a law-making area. Part of the judicial activism critique is situated within the above developments.

In the civil law tradition, reliance by the courts on their previous rulings is important because it ensures their authority and credibility, in addition to reinforcing their legitimacy. It is true that civil law jurisdictions do not recognize the doctrine of precedent but they do recognize that rulings may form binding case law and as such can operate as a source of law.

Today it is acknowledged that the presumption of sharp differences between common law and civil law systems concerning the role of judges may no longer correspond to legal reality and there has certainly been some mutual

---

10 See Ginta Sniedzīte, *Tiesnešu tiesības* [Judge made law] Rīga: Latvijas Vēstnesis, 2013, pp. 91–94.
11 Sniedzīte, *ibid.*, p. 91.

convergence over time. One can agree with the following observation by El Boudouhi:

> Plus précisément, la convergence entre les deux systèmes tient à deux phénomènes simultanés: d'une part, si les jurisdictions de tradition civiliste ne sont pas tenues par la règle du précédent, elles n'en conaissent pas moins le principe de la jurisprudence constante, qui les mène à ne s'écarter d'une solution passée que si cela est justifié. D'autre part, la règle du précédent pour les jurisdictions de common law ne signifie pas qu'elles sont toujours tenues de suivre leur jurisprudence passée....[12]

As for international law, Jennings and Fitzmaurice both concluded at the time that the *stare decisis* doctrine is not part of international law. But this does not mean that it could not become a part of international law at some point in the future since there are elements in judicial practices that could serve as the basis for such a development.[13]

Some scholarly writings on the Convention and its case law have engaged with the doctrine of precedent in order to understand the legal nature of the Court's case law. One of the reasons must be the Court's own pronouncements. In *Rees v the United Kingdom*, the Court identified its stance on precedent by stating that:

> The Court is not bound by its previous judgments. However, it usually follows and applies its own precedents, such a course being in the interests of legal certainty and the orderly development of the Convention case-law. Nevertheless, this would not prevent the Court from departing from an earlier decision if it was persuaded that there were cogent reasons for doing so.[14]

With some alterations in the wording this approach has remained valid and has been followed, after the reform of the system, by the full time Court. In *Mamatkulov and Askerov v Turkey* the Court said: "While the Court is not

---

12 El Boudouhi, *supra* note 9, p. 355. *"More precisely, convergence between the two systems is due to two simultaneous phenomena: on the one hand, if the courts of the civil tradition are not bound by the rule of precedent, they do not any the less recognize the principle of stable jurisprudence, which leads them to deviate from a past solution only if justified. On the other hand, the rule of precedent for common law jurisdictions does not mean that they are always required to follow their past jurisprudence...".* [ed.transl.]
13 *Ibid*, pp. 356–359.
14 *Rees v. the United Kingdom*, Series A – 106 (1986), para. 35.

formally bound to follow its previous judgments, in the interests of legal certainty it should not depart, without good reason, from its own precedents".[15] In the light of the Court's position, former judge Dragoljub Popović has come to the conclusion that "following precedents has been and still remains a firm and unchanged attitude of the Court".[16]

At this point, it is important to distinguish, on the one hand, between the *stare decisis* doctrine as a basis for law making by courts leading to the development of human rights law and, on the other hand, the need to follow previous judgments for reasons of legal certainty which among other things serve the authority of the Court. The latter cannot serve as a basis for assuming automatically that the Court has or has been given a norm-creating function. So far the proposition that the case law of the Court may follow precedent does not provide an answer to the question whether the Court's case law is a source of law. Even if some scholars and judges have suggested that the *stare decisis* doctrine exists in the practice of the ECtHR, that is not an entirely correct reading of the Court's position.[17] The Convention does not spell out the theory of precedent and the Court itself has stated that it is not legally bound to follow its case law even if it normally does so for reasons of legal certainty. In other words, the founders of the Convention system have not created a system of precedents. However, the way the system works resembles the system of precedent. At the same time, the Court itself emphasizes that it can, if it so chooses, depart from case law. One has to agree that the Convention system does not place particular restrictions on the Court in this regard.

Arguably, too, the ECtHR is inspired even more by the concept of *jurisprudence constant*, which should not be surprising given that the majority of judges come from the civil law tradition. It can surely be confirmed that the Court indeed takes particular care not to change its case law without good reason. However, if it does so, it attempts to provide an explanation.[18] In the majority of cases, though, the Court does not consider that it changes the case law. The Court often resorts to distinguishing the facts of cases in order to arrive at a different conclusion – a method of great importance in common law. All in all, the Court has undoubtedly been inspired by the principles and methodology that domestic courts follow in both common law and civil law traditions. The consistency of case law as a means of ensuring legal certainty is one of the guiding principles in the Court's adjudicating function. It would be difficult to

---

15   *Mamatkulov and Askerov v Turkey*, ECtHR 2005-I.
16   Popović, *supra* note 2, p. 482.
17   A contrario, Sniedzīte, *supra* note 9, p. 86 with references.
18   *Kudla v Poland* [GC] 26.10.2000. § 148.

argue, however, that this explains the development of human rights law, which brings about new obligations upon States. The principle is essential for upholding the authority of the Court and its judgments but it cannot alone provide the legal basis for the proposition that case law is a source of law.

Moreover, the difficulty with applying the *jurisprudence constante* doctrine to the Court's function and its case law is linked to the differences between the nature and operation of constitutional and international legal orders and the difficulties that the doctrine of *jurisprudence constante* still presents even in domestic legal systems. In international law, unlike in domestic legal systems, the exercise of any public authority by international courts beyond the mere dispute resolution function within the limits of their attributed competence has to be carefully argued because, as Donald H. Regan has put it, "in the international sphere the problems are magnified by the absence of a legislature or a true world community".[19] The role of the international courts in developing rules of international law, if accepted especially in the absence of a judicial hierarchy and in view of the plurality of international courts, requires a conception of a coherent theory which addresses the concerns of legitimacy and accountability.[20]

Having pointed out that the doctrine of precedent has no application with respect to the Court's case law and that the concept of *jurisprudence constante* in the horizontal legal system needs further explanation and adaptation in international law, I will now turn more properly to relevant notions and legal provisions in international law for an understanding of the legal character of judicial decisions.

3   Relevant International Law

Under Article 38. 1 (d) of the Statute of the International Court of Justice (hereinafter – ICJ), the Court "shall apply" "[...] judicial decisions as subsidiary means for the determination of rules of law". The key notions in this article are: 'decisions as subsidiary means' and 'the determination of rules'. According to the Oxford Dictionaries, the ordinary meaning of the verb 'to determine' means to establish something, for example, rules, as in our case. In other words, the

---

[19] *See* Donald H. Regan, 'International Adjudication: A Response to Paulus – Courts, Custom, Treaties, Regimes, and the WTO', in S. Besson and J. Tasioulas (eds.) *The Philosophy of International Law* (Oxford University Press 2010) p. 229.

[20] *See further*, Karel Wellens, 'The International Court of Justice, Back to the Future', in K. Wellens *supra* note 4, p. 143; Andreas Paulus, "International Adjudication", in S. Besson and J. Tasioulas (eds.) *supra* note 19, p. 224.

ICJ could establish rules but in the light of the prevailing view in the theory of sources of international law only as a subsidiary action to that of the law making process carried out typically by States in international law *qua* treaties or custom.[21] It is noteworthy that Article 38.1 (d) refers to both judicial decisions and teachings of the most highly qualified publicists. It has been said that this wording, too, evidences that these sources of law are of a subsidiary nature only. It has even been said that: "They do not actually qualify as sources of law but rather as means to establish the existence of sources of law".[22] Even if the structure of the article would not evidently support the conclusion of the existence of primary and subsidiary sources, the text of point (d) does so. At the same time it is recognised that "[c]onsidering judgments of international courts merely as an interpretation of a given international agreement does not do justice to their role".

At the same time "international courts and tribunals as a rule are not considered to have norm-creating functions, although the line between interpretation and law-making is sometimes fluid".[23] Thus in the context of customary international law, the ICJ as well as other international courts would very often have a particularly important role to play because it is the courts that would identify the practice which makes law.[24] Especially in view of the customary nature of international law, the role of international courts cannot be underestimated.[25] It is therefore a fair summary to say that "a judicial decision, in almost all cases, by definition adds something to the corpus of law on the subject of the dispute: if the law had been crystal clear before the decision, it is reasonable to suppose that the case would never have been fought".[26]

There are several notions at play that require further commentary. Authors have divided sources of international law into formal and material sources and attribute to Article 38.1 (d) the status of a material source of law.[27] "*C'est le rôle qu'elle joue dans l'interprétation du droit ou dans sa suppléance en cas de vide*

---

21 A study by Shahabuddeen examined the exact meaning of these same words, suggesting that they could open ways for the determination of rules by the ICJ based on its own jurisprudence. For a discussion on this point, see Hugh Thirlway, *The Sources of International Law* (Oxford University Press, 2014), p. 122.

22 See Rudiger Wolfrum, 'Sources of International Law', in R. Wolfrum (ed.), *The Max Planck Encyclopedia of Public International Law* (Oxford University Press 2012) vol. IX, p. 301.

23 *Ibid.* pp. 307–308.

24 Jean Combacau et Serge Sur, *Droit international public*, 5e ed. (Montchrestien Paris 2001) p. 44.

25 James Crawford, *Chance, Order, Change: The Course of International Law* (Hague Academy of International Law 2014) p. 57.

26 Thirlway, *supra* note 21, p. 118 with references.

27 Thirlway, *ibid.*, p. 117.

juridique qui lui permet d'acquérir ce caractère".[28] Here we can draw parallels with the evolution in jurisdictions of the civil law tradition which also gradually recognized that domestic courts' stable and coherent case law becomes a source of law and the courts evidently fill gaps in the legal system. It has to be noted that in some civil law jurisdictions the theory of sources of law has developed further and has accepted the case law of the highest national courts among formal sources of law.[29] While it is true that international courts cannot take part in law making in the classic sense of the term, those who have analysed the work and the influence of judicial decisions could not have avoided noticing how transparent the line is between mere application of law and its development – a development that has raised the question whether judicial decisions are merely a material source of international law.

This analysis has to be placed in the context of modern law making in international law with many more international actors and frameworks within which States and other actors interact – a context which has clearly affected the nature of law-making at an international level. There is also increased activity in international adjudication between States as well as between States and other actors which contributes to the changed nature of law-making. Von Bogdandy and Venzke point out that:

> [The courts] exceed the confines of concrete cases and bear on the general legal structures. The practice of international adjudication creates and shifts actors' normative expectations and as such develops legal normativity.[30]

For these reasons d'Aspremont suggests that the identification of law in international law has moved away from formal sources in the direction of effect-based, impact-based, or process-based asessment.[31]

Despite a clearly pluralist context of law making and an ever growing density of international regulation, the system remains largely decentralised and

---

28 David Riché, 'Retour sur la distinction entre sources matérielles et formelles du droit international chez Georges Scelle, Lazare Kopelmanas et Sir Gerald Fitzmaurice', in *Grandes pages du droit international. Les sources, supra* note 1, p. 429 et seq. *"It is the role that it plays in interpreting the law or substituting for it in the event of a legal vacuum that allows it to acquire that character"*. (ed.transl.)

29 Daiga Rezevska, 'Judikatūra kā tiesību avots: izpratne un pielietošana', *Latvijas Republikas Augstākās tiesas Biļetens* Nr. 1/2010, p. 31.

30 Armin Von Bogdandy and Ingo Venzke, 'Beyond Dispute: International Judicial Institutions as Lawmakers', 12 *German Law Journal* 2011, p. 979.

31 For a discussion of Jean d'Aspremont theory, *see* Thirlway, *supra* note 21, pp. 206–215.

lacking in a proper hierarchy of sources of law. Yet there is a logic to it and it does operate through collective judgment.[32] Questions on the nature of the international legal system and its sources continue to be debated and international law scholars keep finding new arguments to rebut criticism of international law as a primitive legal system.[33] At the same time, it is still generally accepted that, as David Lefkowitz put it:

> no international law scholar will dispute the claim that international law currently lacks a single basic rule that serves both of the functions that Hart assigns to a rule of recognition: validating norms as law and systematizing them, in particular by establishing relations of superiority and subordination between laws of various types.[34]

This clearly distinguishes international law from domestic law – a difference that remains relevant for discussion of the proposition that judicial decisions are a source of law and even a formal source of law in international law.

Within a democratic legal system, stemming from a basic norm, there are ways and means to validate what courts and judges do and to systematize what they do. Judges enjoy democratic legitimacy and abide by general principles of democracy and rule of law, and their decisions, that is, case law, will have a rather clearly determined place in the hierarchy of legal sources and the necessary legal authority. There is no doubt that a clear system of sources, and of their legitimacy, permit us to consider the case law of domestic courts as a source of law since judicial decisions will comply with the normativity characteristic whichever way it is conceived in any given domestic legal order.

In international law, explanations of the normativity, legitimacy and legality of legal rules do not relate to a basic norm such as the will of the people. Explanations, however, do exist, even if at times conflicting, but no one really seriously doubts that international law has all the characteristics it takes to be a normative legal system. According to Samantha Besson:

> As a matter of fact, international law's normativity has increased and diversified over the years, and with it have emerged difficult questions

---

32   Crawford, *supra* note 25, p. 8.
33   *See* David Lefkowitz's answer to H.L.A. Hart's criticism. 'The Sources of International Law: Some Philosophical Reflections', in S. Besson and J. Tasioulas (eds.), *supra* note 19, p. 196 et seq.
34   *Ibid.*, p. 198.

pertaining to international legal norms' universality, objectivity, and hierarchy.[35]

When discussing where and how to find a rule of recognition in international law, Besson suggests that the rule of recognition is not to be equated with the existence of a hierarchy of sources of international law. She says: "[a]ll that is required is that the rule of recognition itself is protected through entrenchment from secondary rules of change, i.e., from the sources of primary law in a given legal order". She arrives at the conclusion that Article 38.1 of the ICJ Statute and the list of sources possess that character since she does not see that changing it would be possible.[36] There are other propositions as to the foundational rules that hold the legal system together, such as the rules on the law of treaties. While it is true that the idea of a basic norm in domestic law is different – given that it emanates from the will of the people – international law may have and does have its own justification. Moreover, it clearly has rules that States and other actors abide by and continue to develop. There is merit to the proposition, existing in legal theory, that legal sources in each given legal system are determined by a dominant legal thought, belonging to the specific family of legal tradition and the stage of development of the particular legal culture and institutions.[37] Besson's thesis that Article 38.1 of the ICJ Statute has become the backbone of the normativity of the international legal system can certainly be accepted in view of the current state of development of that system.

The questions should be asked whether legal thinking and legal practice at the current stage of development of international law may indicate that judicial decisions under Article 38.1 (d) have become a primary or formal source of law along with treaties or custom. It has been said that international adjudication "consists in the resolution of a dispute between two or more parties by a neutral third party, ideally a court or an arbitral tribunal, in an adversarial procedure on the basis of international law".[38] This has been the classic understanding of the judicial function in a system of law characterized by its bilateral nature. But in a world which has moved beyond its bilateral nature, the courts have a new role. Even if the ongoing debate about that new role of the courts is very lively, it is recognized that "[a] judgment of the Court does not

---

35   Samantha Besson, 'Theorizing the Sources of International Law', in S. Besson and J. Tasioulas (eds.) *supra* note 19, p. 174.
36   *Ibid.*, 181–182.
37   Rezevska, *supra* note 29, p. 28.
38   Andreas Paulus, "International Adjudication", in S. Besson and J. Tasioulas (eds.) *supra* note 19, p. 210.

simply decide a particular dispute, but inevitably also contributes to the development of international law". Indeed, the Court takes account of these two functions.[39] Today it is correct to say that "the regulation of community interests [...] comes under the jurisdiction of international courts" which admittedly is a particularly difficult task because of the variety of value systems continuously represented in the world.[40] Today one notices that greater demand emerges from within the courts and from a more multifaced community so that the courts would also perform their judicial function considering broader goals and aims such as strengthening the international rule of law.[41] The growing importance of a broader judicial function beyond mere dispute resolution in international law is compatible with the view of judicial decisions as a source of law proper. Parallels can be drawn with the function of constitutional courts in jurisdictions where they have been established. Constitutional courts have the role of consolidating the legal system and overseeing its internal coherence in the light of the constitutional values that the people have set for themselves. International law has gradually evolved into a legal system geared towards certain values. As noted, this system is no longer purely bilateral in nature. Those international courts that have been established have the function of ensuring the internal coherence of the area of international law that they oversee. Growing interest and demands with regard to the court's formation, functioning and compliance of the proceedings with the principles of a fair trial attest to the importance that various actors attribute to the role of international courts.[42]

A belief or understanding that the international judiciary have to comply with a set of principles that lie at the basis of independent and impartial tribunals and that the proceedings would respect fair trial principles, such as equality of the parties, can indeed be traced back to early international adjudication proceedings.[43] The idea of independent courts could even be traced back to the ancient world, which knew the principle of dispute settlement by independent judges between the Greek city-states.[44] In other words, the development

---

[39] Karel Wellens, "The International Court of Justice, Back to the Future", in K. Wellens (ed.) *supra* note 5, p. 149.

[40] Paulus, *supra* note 20, pp. 212–213.

[41] Wellens, *supra* note 5, p. 142.

[42] Arman Sarvarian, Filippo Fontanelli, Rudy Baker & Vassilis Tsevelokos, *Procedural Fairness in International Courts and Tribunals*, BIICL 2015.

[43] Bin Cheng, *General Principles of Law as applied by International Court and Tribunals*, (Cambridge University Press, 1994), pp. 257–258.

[44] Sanita Osipova, *Eiropas tiesību priekšvēsture. Senās Ēģiptes, Divupes, Izraēlas, Griekijas tiesības*. (Rīga: Tiesu namu aģentūra, 2017), pp. 351–354.

of legal and political thought over a long time has led to the establishment of international courts as we know them today. The strengthening of the role of international courts has even acquired a label: judicialization of international law.[45] It may well be that this development deserves a special name; but – approached from the perspective of the growing importance of the rule of law in international law – the role of an independent judiciary evidently goes hand in hand with that process. Thus it is that the current stage of development of the international community dictates a different view on international courts, including the issue of judicial decisions as a formal source of law.

These developments and elements are relevant for the proposition that the case law of the courts where it is established may certainly be a formal source of law. Nevertheless, in international law the nature of judicial decisions as a formal source of law is inevitably different compared to domestic judicial decisions. Even though this is not a study of all international courts, I submit that the competence and specific characteristics of each court and the legal regime that it oversees will be an important factor for determining the nature of its judicial decisions. Within this broader reflection, the legal nature of the case law of the ECtHR has to be assessed.

4   Legal Nature of ECtHR Case Law

The ECtHR was established "to ensure the observance of the engagments undertaken by the High Contracting Parties in the Convention and the Protocols thereto [...]".[46]

Article 32 of the European Convention on Human Rights delimits the jurisdiction of the ECtHR. It provides that:
1.   The jurisdiction of the Court shall extend to all matters concerning the interpretation and application of the Convention and the Protocols thereto which are referred to it as provided in Articles 33, 34, 46 and 47.
2.   In the event of dispute as to whether the Court has jurisdiction, the Court shall decide.

The wording regarding the competence of the ECtHR and of the ICJ in their respective texts is not identical. The ECtHR text focuses on interpretation of the Convention and the Court's function to ensure observance of Convention

---

45   Andreas Follesdal & Geir Ulfstein, 'International Courts and Tribunals: Rise and Reactions', in A. Follesdal & G. Ulfstein (eds.) *The Judicialization of International Law. A Mixed Blessing* (Oxford University Press 2018), p. 1.
46   Art. 1.

obligations through the complaints mechanism. In other words, the primary aim, at least through the relevant wording, is to ensure respect for the Convention provisions. Settlement of a dispute is the means to achieve the primary aim. This to some degree contrasts with the original aim of the ICJ, namely, to decide upon the disputes submitted to it and in that process to apply international law.

The Convention sets a value system in Europe and reflects a certain agreement on that system. In that regard, the problem of acceptance of the judicial function with regard to broader community interests by and large does not arise. States in the region have agreed on their common interests and have set up a judicial mechanism to follow it up. The Statute of the Council of Europe stipulates that "every member of the Council of Europe must accept the principles of the rule of law and of the enjoyment by all persons within its jurisdiction of human rights and fundamental freedoms, and collaborate sincerely and effectively in the realisation of the aim of the Council" which is "to achieve a greater unity between its members for the purpose of safeguarding and realising the ideals and principles which are their common heritage and facilitating their economic and social progress".[47]

In this regard, this is almost an ideal situation in international law in that a group of States have legislated on a set of values and have entrusted a court with the important function of ensuring that these are observed. It does not mean that in exercising this function the Court need not follow the rules and principles which would typically ensure the authority of the Court and its rulings within a democratic legal system. To the contrary, it is particularly important that the composition of the Court, its rules of procedure and the reasoning in the rulings meet the highest standards of independence and impartiality of the Court.

Since the international legal system, unlike constitutional systems, does not contain a fully-fledged principle of separation of powers nor that of democratic legitimacy stemming from the will of the people, the international courts, including the ECtHR, have to ensure, through the exercise of their functions, that what they do is legitimate.[48] Besson has identified these requirements in general but they are also applicable to the Court specifically, that is: clarity, publicity, certainty, equality, transparency, and fairness.[49] Where

---

47   Statute of the Council of Europe, Arts. 1 (a) and 3.
48   On another aspect of judicial function, see Arina Melse, *Inherent Powers of the European Court of Human Rights: Part of the Judicial Function of an International Public Authority*, PhD thesis, University of Copenhagen and Riga Graduate School of Law, 2017.
49   Besson, *supra* note 19, p. 172.

the composition of the Court, rules of procedure and rulings comply with these principles of the rule of law, the Court can exercise its function of upholding human rights in Europe with the appropriate authority and legitimacy. Within international law, it is this authority in combination with the function entrusted to the Court that will explain the legal nature of the Court's case law.

At this stage it is appropriate to engage with the argument that the Convention is a "constitutional instrument of European public order in the field of human rights", creating a "network of mutual bilateral undertakings (and) objective obligations".[50] The question has to be asked whether the qualification of the Convention as a constitutional instrument adds any particular dimension to the specific aims and the particular judicial function attributed to the Court by the Convention. Saying that the Convention is a constitutional instrument does not resolve the democratic challenge faced by this Court – like other international courts.[51] This qualification as such does not grant the Court law-making powers. Moreover, the Court has come up with this qualification itself through its case law.[52] What meaning the Court considers giving to this notion has remained rather obscure. There is no agreement among States parties to the Convention that it would be a constitutional instrument in the meaning normally assigned to the notion of a constitution. It is therefore that this pronouncement by the Court does not offer a new legal basis for the Court's case law where it allegedly goes beyond the text of the Convention.

In its recent work on reservations to treaties, the International Law Commission (hereinafter – the ILC), when addressing the issue of reservations to such treaties as human rights treaties, reiterated the qualification of such treaties as "a treaty containing numerous interdependent rights and obligations" which had already been used in the early works of the ILC in the field of treaty law.[53] As already pointed out, the Convention is a regional human rights treaty which creates a set of these mutual obligations among the States parties because those States agreed on certain values which will be upheld together and through the mechanism of the Court. Thus the Convention has created an objective regional regime in the field of human rights in the sense that each

---

50   Greer, *supra* note 4, p. 195.
51   Geir Ulfstein, 'The International Judiciary', in J. Klabbers, A. Peters and G. Ulfstein (eds.) *The Constitutionalization of International Law* (Oxford University Press 2009) pp. 151–152.
52   *Loizidou v Turkey* [GC] 18.12.1996.
53   Art. 3.1.5.6., Guide to Practice on Reservations to Treaties. *Yearbook of International Law Commission*, 2011, vol. II, Part Two.

pair of States cannot agree otherwise on the Convention issue.[54] It is left to the Court through a clear methodology to apply, interpret and develop this regime of interdependent rights and obligations.

Another difference between the role of the ECtHR and the ICJ may be relevant for a better understanding of the challenges in assessing the legal nature of their respective judicial decisions. That is, unlike the ICJ, the ECtHR does not determine a rule within the legal system of an essentially customary nature. The ECtHR applies written law. Consequently, an argument can be made that for the application of the Convention, the ECtHR does not have to look at state practice on issues that appear not to have been defined within the Convention. This perspective offers a particularly narrow view on the role of the courts. As pointed out, since its early days the Court has not taken such a narrow positivist approach to the text of the Convention. This has indeed at times created controversies among those who would define the scope of the Convention primarily guided by the text of the treaty. The Court has justified the development of Convention law by reference to the object and purpose of the Convention which, admittedly, it has understood rather broadly.[55] To sum up, the nature of the Convention rights and obligations, the broader aims of the Convention system, the overall development of the international legal system and higher expectations with respect to the work of the ECtHR and the other international courts and tribunals, as well as the evidently growing impact of ECtHR case law even beyond the 47 Contracting Parties are all relevant factors to be taken into account in re-conceptualizing the legal nature of the Court's case law. However, it is still necessary to assess just how much the Court allegedly goes beyond the scope of the Convention text and its Protocols. In order to answer this question one needs to understand the Court's adjudication methodology.

4.1 *The Principles of Interpretation of the Convention*
Since the early days, the Court and the Commission at the time have for the purposes of interpreting the Convention resorted to the general rule of interpretation of international treaties codified in the 1969 Vienna Convention on the Law of Treaties Articles 31–33 (hereinafter – VCLT). It has been argued that

---

54 Alexander Orakhelashvili, 'Restrictive Interpretation of Human Rights Treaties in the Recent Jurisprudence of the European Court of Human Rights', *European Journal of International Law* (2003), Vol. 14 No. 3, p. 531.
55 *Golder v. the United Kingdom*, 21 February 1975, §29, Series A no. 18. Separate opinion of Judge Sir Gerald Fitzmaurice.

emphasis on the object and purpose of the Convention has led the Court to teleological interpretation of the Convention and allowed for its development or evolution with time. However, this was by no means an evident choice as shown by a fierce disagreement between Judge Fitzmaurice and the majority in the *Golder* case.[56]

The object and purpose of the treaty is only one element in the interpretation exercise carried out by the Court. The Court early on developed a few other tools of interpretation whose content admittedly has not always been clear. In the *Demir and Baykara* case the Court recalled that:

> In accordance with the Vienna Convention, the Court is required to ascertain the ordinary meaning to be given to the words in their context and in the light of the object and purpose of the provision from which they are drawn (see [...] Article 31 § 1 of the Vienna Convention). Recourse may also be had to supplementary means of interpretation, either to confirm a meaning determined in accordance with the above steps, or to establish the meaning where it would otherwise be ambiguous, obscure, or manifestly absurd or unreasonable.[57]

The Court interprets the Convention in accordance with modern-day conditions; this approach goes back to the *Tyrer* case.[58] Often within the case before it the Court has had to admit that there is either a growing acceptance of the social phenomenon among European States or in international instruments. The Court has provided sufficient detail as to how it views other sources of international law and the rules thereof, as well as their relation with the Convention. It clearly does not apply the Convention in a vacuum but interprets the Convention by taking cognizance of other relevant rules of international law that either give rise to new obligations for member States relevant for the Convention's purposes, or inform the scope of the Convention rights as such. For the Court, State practice takes several different forms, all of which are relevant for the interpretation of the Convention.

The Court clearly pays attention to any common trends that may be reflected in domestic legislation, domestic case law, international case law, other international treaties, and statements by governments. It also seeks information

---

56   See, e.g., *Golder v. the United Kingdom*, 21 February 1975, §29, Series A no. 18; *Johnston and Others v. Ireland*, 18 December 1986, §§51 et seq., Series A; and *Witold Litwa v. Poland*, no. 26629/95, §§57–59, ECtHR 2000-III.
57   *Demir and Baykara v. Turkey* [GC] 12.11.2008, § 65.
58   *Tyrer v. the United Kingdom* (1978) Series A no 26, para. 31.

in scholarly writings, but to a lesser extent. This information will most of the time be considered to reflect the so-called European consensus, a concept which is the Court's creation. The case law shows that the Court provides effective protection of Convention rights by taking into account relevant developments in European States, determining them as relevant international rules or subsequent practice in the sense of Article 31 (3) (b) and (c) VCLT.

The Court has developed its own principles of interpretation such as effective protection of Convention rights as well as the principles of proportionality, subsidiarity and autonomous meaning. It has been suggested that the principles of democracy, rule of law and legality also form part of the interpretation and application of the Convention. This approach sits particularly well within the discourse which examines the Convention as a constitutional instrument for Europe.[59]

It has to be said that the Court may appear to change or expand upon the scope of rights provided for in the Convention. This occurs, firstly, when the Court reads into the Convention provisions the content of other applicable rules of international law *qua* Article 31 (3) (c) VCLT; and secondly, when the Court sees that, through consistent subsequent practice, States have expanded upon the interpretation of the scope of a Convention provision *qua* Article 31 (3) (b) VCLT. It seems that the Court's consistent perspective that the Convention is part of a wider legal system, and that it has to be interpreted in accordance with the general rule of interpretation of a treaty and in harmony with other branches and rules of international law, has by and large allowed it to interpret the Convention progressively but within the scope of existing international law. It has to be underlined that where the Court has found within the scope of a right an aspect that originally was not there but which is now part of international law and is binding upon the States parties to the Convention, it is difficult to sustain the argument that the Court has amended the Convention. Where one takes the view that the international legal system is internally coherent, this approach by the Court makes sense and contributes to overall coherence beyond the Convention system. In that context no legislative activity can be detected; it is merely application of the Convention within the broader international legal system.

Questions will continue to arise in relation to the sufficiency and exact relevance of the evidence of State practice. Questions will also arise, as in *Demir and Baykara*, whether the Court correctly interprets the meaning of the concepts in Article 31 (3) (b) and (c) such as 'the agreement of the parties' and 'in relations between the parties'. It is in this regard that a looser approach can be

---

59 Greer, *supra* note 4.

noticed in the Court's case law – an approach that needs to be explained and justified. In this context, the importance of the reasoning in the Court's judgments cannot be overstated. For example, in *Demir and Baykara* while the Court found that Turkey had indeed not ratified the relevant Articles 5 and 6 of the European Social Charter (revised) with respect to the right to form trade unions and the right to collective bargaining, it nevertheless relied on the fact that an overwhelming majority of the States Parties had accepted these rights also in relation to municipal civil servants and thus accepted that Article 11 also contains – in addition to the right to form trade unions – the right to collective bargaining by municipal civil servants. The Court explained its view as concerns the criterion of 'a party' to an agreement or subject to a rule as follows:

> it is not necessary for the respondent State to have ratified the entire collection of instruments that are applicable in respect of the precise subject matter of the case concerned. It will be sufficient for the Court that the relevant international instruments denote a continuous evolution in the norms and principles applied in international law or in the domestic law of the majority of member States of the Council of Europe and show, in a precise area, that there is common ground in modern societies.[60]

In other words, the Court indeed embraces an evolutive approach to the Convention. Moreover, it does so through interpretation based on a general rule of interpretation as well as resort to the concepts of the Convention as a living instrument and the European consensus.

4.2   *The European Consensus*

Resort to the concept of a European consensus in the case law of the ECtHR may also make an international lawyer think about both subsequent State practice and regional customary law. In 2008, during a seminar at the opening of its judicial year, the ECtHR prepared its own background paper on 'consensus', which was the theme of the seminar. In that paper, two conceptual propositions were the subject of reflection. First, that consensus can be seen as "an element in the development of customary law" and, second, that:

> consensus in the context of the European Convention on Human Rights is generally understood as being the basis for the evolution of Convention standards through the case-law of the European Court of Human

---

60   *Demir and Baykara v Turkey*, *supra* note 56, ECtHR 2008-V § 86.

Rights. [...] Consensus legitimises progress and facilitates its reception into domestic law.[61]

The paper did not explain whether, within the first proposition, a European consensus might be seen as an element of State practice which lies at the core of the development of customary law. It did not link consensus to the element of subsequent practice in the law of treaties. Nor did the paper explain the second option, which primarily emphasizes the role of the Court in the evolution of human rights standards. In *A. B. and C* the Court explains how it understands 'European consensus'. Referring back to the *Tyrer* case, the Court says:

> The existence of a consensus has long played a role in the development and evolution of Convention protections beginning with *Tyrer v. the United Kingdom* [and] ... the Convention being considered a 'living instrument' to be interpreted in the light of present-day conditions. Consensus has therefore been invoked to justify a dynamic interpretation of the Convention [...].[62]

This passage confirms that, in the view of the Court, a European consensus gives space for evolutive and dynamic adjudication. The Court here does not engage with Article 31 of the VCLT. European consensus appears to have an autonomous meaning in the context of *Tyrer* and *A, B and C* or other similar cases. I have concluded that the Court has attempted to read an autonomous scope into the notion of European consensus, probably and at least partly because some elements of Article 31 of the VCLT may have appeared too rigid for effective protection of human rights. There has also been great reluctance to engage with the notion of customary law when the Court examines relevant state practice. As noted, nothing prevents the Court from deciphering regional custom proper, similar to the manner of the ICJ. In that case ECtHR case law would be considered a subsidiary source of law. But the Court has chosen to advance human rights law through several autonomous concepts. Therefore, the Court does engage in law-making. In other words, when the Court does not stay within the general rule of interpretation – for example, by determining the relevant rule of a regional custom – but instead develops the scope of the

---

61   See 'The role of consensus in the system of the European Convention on Human Rights', *Dialogue between judges* (European Court of Human Rights, 2008), pp. 17–18.

62   *A, B and C. v Ireland* ECtHR 2010-VI § 234. Other references in the judgment are to the following cases: *Marckx v. Belgium* (1979) Series A no 31, para 41; *Dudgeon v. the United Kingdom* (1981) Series A no 45, para. 60; *Soering v. the United Kingdom* (1989) Series A no 161, para. 102; *L. and V. v. Austria* ECtHR 2003–1 29, para. 50.

Convention through an autonomous concept of European consensus, that case law is a primary or formal source of law. At the same time, it is important to emphasize that the general rule of interpretation of a treaty does not prevent some evolutive interpretation.[63] It would also be misleading to think that the Court has in fact considerably expanded the scope of the Convention through some sort of law-making. One area could be identified, namely, issues related to Article 14, but not much more.[64] The fact that there is criticism indicates that the Court should take particular care to better explain the different steps it takes in interpreting the Convention provisions in accordance with the general rule of interpretation, to distinguish between cases or, to the contrary, treat like cases alike.

5 Conclusions

As far as concerns discussion of international courts in scholarly writings, three main paradigms are addressed, that is, their proliferation and forum shopping, the legitimacy of judicial decisions, and the fragmentation of international law.[65] Questions and criticism addressed towards the case law of the ECtHR come up against each one of these paradigms. For an examination of the legal character of ECtHR case law as a formal source of law, the nature of the debate within these paradigms is relevant. It is true that historically the Convention with its implementation mechanism was not meant either to focus on individual justice or to go beyond adjudicating a dispute between Constracting Parties.[66] Placed within the historical context of post-war Europe and in view of the stage of development of international law at that time, the Convention's original purpose – to preserve peace between States based on resolving disputes in terms of their compliance with the treaty – evidently belongs to the co-operation model of States at the time.

However, today the case law of the Court is the basis for observations that the Convention has gone beyond its original purpose. Instead, and as explained before, the Court provides individual justice and has over the decades engaged in law-making with the purpose of guaranteeing the human rights of individuals with regard to their governments, a purpose that requires interpreting the Convention so as to permit its development with time. The role of the Court, as

---

[63] *See* more on this Ineta Ziemele, "European consensus and international law" in A. Van Aaken and I. Motoc (eds.) *ECtHR and General International Law*, Oxford University Press, 2018.
[64] Marc Bossuyt, "Judicial Activism in Strasbourg", in K. Wellens (ed.), *supra* note 5.
[65] A. Follesdal & G. Ulfstein (eds.), *supra* note 45.
[66] Greer, *supra* note 4, pp. 316–317.

it has evolved over time, discloses the changing nature of the international legal system, the plurality of actors and calls for a more democratic law-making process. The question of the authority and credibility of the ECtHR is raised in this context. In a plural and horizontal system in which judicial decisions are, first of all, a secondary source of law but gaining in importance, as evidenced by ECtHR case law, the legitimacy and authority of such decisions is of paramount importance. Thus the importance of a clear methodology of adjudication, that is, of the power of reasoning. I have explained that the Court uses all the legal tools that the international legal system offers for the purposes of interpreting the Convention. Where the Court goes beyond the general rule of interpretation, it most likely sets forth a new rule in European human rights law and thus it is in this instance that case law becomes – or has the effect of – a source of law proper. Admittedly, it is difficult to maintain a distinction between case law that interprets the Convention and case law that develops the Convention. In other words, it is difficult to draw a distinction between case law as a material source of law and case law as a formal source of law. At least for the time being, there is a coherent tendency in more advanced legal systems to acknowledge that the courts and judges do occasionally make law. The example of the ECtHR goes along with these developments.

There has been a rather lenghty discussion among scholars about the effect on the international law system of the existence of allegedly self-sufficient areas of legal regulation such as human rights law, in other words, the fragmentation debate. Within a horizontal legal system, it is quite normal to have various pockets of legal regulation developing at different speeds – a fact which does not have to lead to fragmentation of international law. Where these legal regimes continue to accept that their validity and normativity stems from the same basic source which stands as the basis of international law as such and that the interpretation and application of norms is guided by the same rule of interpretation, fragmentation as a potentially disruptive phenomenon would not arise.[67] We cannot exclude, however, that those areas which due to active normative processes in those areas would provide for new and denser regulation can impact other areas in which agreement is slow to come. Certainly, human rights law is a highly active domain that evidently impacts reflections in other areas of international law, including the theory of sources of international law.

---

67 For somewhat similar reflections, *see* A. Pellet, 'The ILC Adrift? Some Reflexions from Inside', in Mixa Pogačnik (ed.) *Challenges of Contemporary International Law and International relations. Liber Amicorum in Honour of Ernest Petrič* (Evropska Pravna Fakulteta v Novi Gorici, 2011) pp. 299–312.

PART 2

*Annual Conference of European Society of
International Law in Riga (2016)*

∴

CHAPTER 8

Human Dignity in an Age of Autonomous Weapons: Are We in Danger of Losing an 'Elementary Consideration of Humanity'?

Ozlem Ulgen

Abstract

Military investment in robotics technology is leading to development and use of autonomous weapons, which are machines with varying degrees of autonomy in target, attack, and infliction of lethal harm (that is, injury, suffering or death). Examples of autonomous weapons include weapons systems involving levels of automation and remotely controlled human input, unmanned armed aerial vehicles (UAV), remotely-controlled robotic soldiers, bio-augmentation, and 3D printed weapons. Autonomous weapons generally fall into one of two categories: semi-autonomous, involving some degree of autonomy in certain critical functions such as acquiring, tracking, selecting, and attacking targets, along with a degree of human input or remote control (for example, UAV or 'drones'); and autonomous, involving higher levels of independent thinking as regards critical functions without the need for human input or control (for example, US Navy X-47B UAV with autonomous take-off, landing, and aerial refuelling capability). The trend is clearly towards developing autonomous weapons. Development of new weapons aimed at reducing costs and casualties is not a new phenomenon in warfare. Technological advances have created greater distance between the soldier and the battlefield. A bullet fired from a rifle handled by a human has been superseded by a missile fired from a remotely controlled or autonomous machine. So what makes autonomous weapons different? What particular challenge do they pose international law? Although autonomous weapons may be employed to attack non-human targets, such as state infrastructure, here I am primarily concerned with their use for lethal attacks against humans.

In this chapter I focus on autonomous weapons (both semi-autonomous and fully autonomous) and their impact on human dignity under two of Kant's conceptual strands: (1) human dignity as a status entailing rights and duties; and (2) human dignity as respectful treatment. Under the first strand I explore how use of autonomous weapons denies the right of equality of persons and diminishes the duty not to harm others. In the second strand I consider how replacing human combatants with autonomous weapons debases human life and does not provide respectful treatment. Reference is made to contemporary development of Kant's conceptual strands in ICJ and other international jurisprudence recognising human dignity as part of 'elementary considerations of humanity' in war and peace.

Keywords

Kantian human dignity – autonomous weapons – Kantian ethics – international humanitarian law

1   Human Dignity as an Elementary Consideration of Humanity[1]

New military weapons technology such as autonomous weapons challenge our understanding of what is permissible and impermissible in warfare. Autonomous weapons are characterised by varying degrees of autonomy in the critical functions of acquiring, tracking, selecting, and attacking targets; and, to some extent or even fully, removal of human involvement from the decision-making process to use lethal force. Apart from whether these weapons comply with specific international humanitarian law principles (for example, distinction, proportionality, and unnecessary suffering), their characteristics may conflict with a fundamental ethical tenet of humanity that permeates the law, namely, human dignity.

Critics of human dignity refer to it as 'a deceptive facade' and 'an empty space' open to exploitation and potentially threatening to personal autonomy.[2] Proponents, it is argued, should at least identify which strand of human dignity they are referring to (for example, status, inner value, right, or relating to treatment of human beings) so that we can make sense of its content and meaning. Considering human dignity is a pervasive idea in international human rights law and many constitutions,[3] these criticisms seem unconvincing.

---

[1] This was originally presented as a paper at Agora 1 New Forms of Warfare and Armed Conflict of the 12th Annual Conference of the European Society of International Law in Riga, Latvia, on 8 September 2016.

[2] Michael Rosen, 'Dignity: The Case Against' in Christopher McCrudden (ed.), *Understanding Human Dignity* (Oxford University Press, 2014) 143.

[3] 1948 Universal Declaration of Human Rights, Preamble and Arts. 1, 22, 23(3); 1966 International Covenant on Civil and Political Rights, Art. 10; 1966 International Covenant on Economic, Social and Cultural Rights, Art. 13; 1965 Convention on the Elimination of All Forms of Racial Discrimination, 1979 Convention on the Elimination of All Forms of Discrimination

In international humanitarian law, human dignity has been referred to as 'the basic underpinning and ... the very raison d'être of international humanitarian law and human rights law ... in modern times it has become of such paramount importance as to permeate the whole body of international law.'[4] It is given expression as an elementary consideration of humanity in the Martens Clause; a fundamental principle of customary international law protecting civilians and combatants in all circumstances not regulated by international law.[5] Indeed, the ICJ has pointed to the significance of the Martens Clause as 'an effective means of addressing rapid evolution of military technology'.[6]

In the 1949 *Corfu Channel Case* the ICJ referred to Albania's international obligation to warn approaching British warships of the imminent danger posed by a minefield in Albanian territorial waters as based on 'elementary considerations of humanity, even more exacting in peace than in war.'[7] The 1996 ICJ Advisory Opinion on the *Legality of the Threat or Use of Nuclear Weapons* recognised that many rules of humanitarian law (for example, the distinction between civilians and combatants, prevention of unnecessary suffering, proportionality) are 'so fundamental to the respect of the human person and "elementary considerations of humanity"' that they have received wide acceptance through treaty ratification and customary international law.[8] In the most recent case of *Costa Rica v. Nicaragua*, Judge Cançado Trindade reasserted the 'autonomous legal regime' of provisional measures, and how the principle of

---

Against Women, 1984 Convention Against Torture and Other Cruel, Inhuman or Degrading Treatment or Punishment, Preamble; 1989 Convention on the Rights of the Child, Preamble and Arts. 23, 28, 37, 39, 40; 2006 Convention on the Rights of Persons with Disabilities, Preamble and Arts. 1, 3(a), 8(1)(a), 16(4), 24(1)(a), 25(d); 1978 Spanish Constitution, s 10(1); 1949 German Basic Law, arts 1(1) (as a duty), 79(3) (amendment to the duty is inadmissible); 1996 South African Constitution, s 1 (as a constitutional value), s 10 (as a right); see also Paolo Carozza, 'Human dignity in constitutional adjudication' in Tom Ginsberg and Rosalind Dixon (eds.), *Comparative Constitutional Law* (Edward Elgar, 2011).

4 *Prosecutor v. Furundžija*, Judgment, Case No IT-95-17/1-T, Trial Chamber (10 December 1998), para. 183.
5 Additional Protocol I to the Geneva Conventions of 12 August 1949 (1977) ('API'), Art. 1(2); Hague Convention respecting the Laws and Customs of War on Land ('Hague Convention IV') (1907); Hague Convention with respect to the Laws and Customs of War on Land ('Hague Convention II') (1899).
6 *Legality of the Threat or Use of Nuclear Weapons, Advisory Opinion of 8 July 1996, ICJ Reports 1996*, para. 78.
7 *Corfu Channel, Merits Judgment, Judgment of April 9 1949, ICJ Reports 1949*, 4, 22.
8 *Nuclear Weapons*, supra note 6, para. 79. See also paras. 92 and 95 on the principle of humanity.

humanity has expanded their scope of protection beyond the inter-state dimension.[9]

These examples point to two interrelated aspects of human dignity: first, it is a status of human beings who have equal and inherent moral value and, second, rules (whether conceptualised as values, rights, or duties) flow from such a status relating to how human beings should be treated during war and in peace.[10] Kant's moral theory on ethical conduct provides a rationale and justification for rules based on human dignity as a status and as respectful treatment of human beings.

2   The Kantian Notion of Human Dignity

In his search for a moral theory on human conduct Kant put forward the idea of human dignity as a fundamental principle. In *Groundwork of the Metaphysics of Morals* (1785) he establishes the rationale and key elements of human dignity, and in his later work *The Metaphysics of Morals* (1797) tries to give practical illustration of its effect. Both works reveal Kant's understanding of human dignity as a special status conferred on humans from which certain rights and duties flow. This special status is based on the human capacity for rational thinking to create and abide by rules, and the capacity to identify what Kant refers to as 'ends'.[11] 'Ends' here means reasons or justifications for having the rules and abiding by them. Linked to rational thinking is 'autonomy of will', which refers to the human capacity to freely and rationally adopt and abide by rules.[12] These characteristics endow human beings with an overriding value known as human dignity. Dignity is an 'unconditional and incomparable worth' with 'intrinsic value' meaning it is not dependent on other factors for its existence, recognition, or respect. It is self-evident, priceless so cannot be replaced with an equivalent, and is 'the sole condition under which anything can be an end in itself'.[13] Waldron criticises Kant for respecting something within a

---

9   *Certain Activities carried out by Nicaragua in the Border Area (Costa Rica v. Nicaragua)*, Judgment of 16 December 2015, ICJ Reports 2015, Separate Opinion of Judge Cançado Trindade.

10 Carozza expresses these as the 'status claim' and 'normative principle' under international human rights law: Paolo Carozza, 'Human Dignity' in Dinah Shelton (ed.), *The Oxford Handbook of International Human Rights Law* (Oxford University Press, 2013), ch. 14.

11 Immanuel Kant, *The Moral Law: Kant's Groundwork of the Metaphysic of Morals* (H.J. Paton tr., Hutchinson & Co 1969) 90-91, paras. 64-66 [428-429].

12 *Ibid.*, 101-102, paras. 87-88 [440].

13 Kant, *supra* note 11, at 90-91, paras. 65-67 [428-429]; 96-97, paras. 77-79 [435-436].

person rather than a person him or herself.[14] But Kant's approach develops human dignity as a higher norm capable of applying to all humans, irrespective of recognition or not of their personhood, and entitling them to participate in law-making and governance with certain moral expectations.

Kant's notion of human dignity is inclusive and does not admit distinctions or exclusions on the basis of wrongdoing. If a person commits a wrong they do not lose their human dignity, which is something intrinsic and inherent to them. However, Kant's conception of what it takes to live in a moral society, referred to as 'the kingdom of ends', incorporates the need for state coercive force and punishment. Specifically in relation to wrongdoers who commit murder, he allows for the possibility of a death sentence, which seems at odds with human dignity. But because there is no equivalent to human dignity, once a life is taken through murder it can never be replaced so that the just thing to do is to take the life of the perpetrator. This is retributive punishment under strict conditions: there must first be a finding of wrongdoing; the sentence must be judicially prescribed; and the wrongdoer must not be mistreated.[15] Human dignity is upheld by punishing but not mistreating the wrongdoer for taking a life. Thus, human dignity is conceived as both a status and higher norm governing how we treat each other. Below I will explain how and why autonomous weapons are contrary to the status and higher norm aspects of human dignity.

3   Autonomous Weapons and Human Dignity as a Status

Kant's reference to humanity as an objective end and humans as rational agents with autonomy of will help explain how human dignity represents a status. Below I will explain the meaning and content of each of these elements and how autonomous weapons impact on them.

3.1   *From Humanity as an Objective End to Relative Ends*

What Kant refers to as humanity as an objective end is part of his process of establishing human dignity as a fundamental principle. Kant distinguishes 'relative ends' from 'objective ends'. Relative ends are values based on personal desires, wants, hopes, and ambitions. They are easily replaced and replaceable.

---

14   Jeremy Waldron, 'Dignity, Rank, and Rights' The Tanner Lectures on Human Values (University of California, Berkeley, 21-23 April 2009).

15   Immanuel Kant, *The Metaphysics of Morals* (Mary Gregor tr. and ed., Cambridge University Press, 1996) 105-109.

Objective ends, however, cannot be replaced with an equivalent. They are reasons for morals governing human conduct which are capable of universalisation and valid for all rational beings. Objective ends are superior because they possess a particular moral value: dignity. Humanity as an objective end is expressed in Kant's maxim, 'Act in such a way that you always treat humanity, whether in your own person or in the person of any other, never simply as a means but always at the same time as an end.'[16] What does it mean to treat someone as 'an end' rather than 'as a means'? Rational beings have intrinsic worth and a self-determining capacity to decide whether or not to do something. They are not mere objects or things to be manipulated, used or discarded on the basis of relative ends (for example, personal wants, desires, hopes, and ambitions). Human dignity gives a person a reason for doing or not doing something. That reason takes precedence over all others. It means setting moral and rational limits to the way we treat people in pursuit of relative ends.[17]

3.1.1 Treating Human Targets as Mere Objects

How does this relate to autonomous weapons? First, autonomous weapons are used for a relative end (that is, the *desire* to eliminate a human target in the *hope* of preventing harm to others). Relative ends, as we know from Kant's formulation, are lesser values capable of being replaced by an equivalent. This is not to say that preventing harm to others *per se* is a relative value. In fact, it is an objective end because it is something that all rational beings could freely and rationally agree to and abide by. But killing a human being in the *hope* that it will prevent further harm is insufficiently morally grounded to override human dignity and may be reckless if alternatives and consequences are not considered. Utilitarians may counter that balancing interests involves consideration of the greater good, which in this instance is to prevent harm to others.[18] As Mill argued in relation to consequences, 'All action is for the sake of some end, and rules of action, it seems natural to suppose, must take their whole character and colour from the end to which they are subservient.'[19] The double effect doctrine of harm, which differentiates between intended harm and

---

16 Kant, *supra* note 11, at para. 67 [429].
17 For elaboration of Kant's humanity principle as an objective end representing human dignity, see Thomas E. Hill, Jr, *Dignity and Practical Reason in Kant's Moral Theory* (Cornell University Press, 1992) 43-44.
18 Jeremy Bentham, *An Introduction to the Principles of Morals and Legislation* (Batoche Books, Kitchener [1781] 2000).
19 John Stuart Mill, *Utilitarianism* (Reprinted from *Fraser's Magazine*, 7th edition, Green and Co, published by "The Project Gutenberg EBook of Utilitarianism, by John Stuart Mill" [1879] 2004) 8-9.

unintended yet foreseeable harm, could also be used to justify action that results in unintended harm.[20] Indeed, consequentialist thinking and the utilitarian calculus are reflected in the proportionality principle under Article 51 API, requiring assessment of whether an attack is expected to cause excessive incidental loss of civilian life in relation to the concrete and direct military advantage anticipated.

However, such aspects of utilitarianism cannot overcome the problem of applying a quantitative assessment of life for prospective greater good that treats the humans sacrificed as mere objects, and creates a hierarchy of human dignity. In Germany, where the state has a constitutional duty to respect and protect human dignity for all, such an approach was rejected by the Constitutional Court in 2006 when it declared void and unconstitutional aviation security legislation allowing shooting down of hijacked planes. To sacrifice the lives of passengers and aircrew was to treat them as mere objects and call into question their quality and status as human beings with dignity.[21] Thus, unless autonomous weapons can only be used to track and identify rather than eliminate a human target, they would extinguish a priceless and irreplaceable objective end possessed by all rational beings: human dignity. Perhaps the problem lies in utilitarianism setting the 'end' as preservation of human life rather than preservation of human dignity. Mill's formulation that actions take 'their whole character and colour from the end' is another way of saying the ends justify the means. But if the 'end' is set as maximum preservation of human dignity in a broad sense (and not restricted to your own combatants) this cannot be achieved by autonomous weapons and would not satisfy rule-consequentialism or utilitarianism.

3.1.2   Undermining the Existential Reason for Rules

Second, using autonomous weapons to extinguish life removes the reason for having morals in the first place: human dignity of rational beings with autonomy of will to apply rules of warfare. In doing so, a relative end is given priority over an objective end. Heyns warns:

> it presents a very bleak picture of the international order if ethical norms are explicitly excluded from consideration. An approach that ignores ethical norms presents the spectre of an order that will find itself increasingly unsupported by the fundamental values of the people whose

---

20   Fiona Woollard, *Doing and Allowing Harm* (Oxford University Press, 2015).
21   Bundesverfassungsgericht, February 15, 2006, 115, BVerfGE 118, paras. 121-124, available at www.bverfg.de/e/rs20060215_1bvr035705en.html (last visited 23 April 2017).

interests it is supposed to serve. Human rights norms such as the right to life and dignity have to be given contents in terms of ethical standards.[22]

From a positivist or natural law theory approach, there is a basic existential reason for rules: to ensure states, peoples, and individuals can survive within the international legal order.[23] But a rule that allows for life to be extinguished anywhere in the world by an autonomous weapon undermines the existential reason. Judge Weeramantry expanded on this point in relation to nuclear weapons in the *Legality of the Threat or Use of Nuclear Weapons*:

> members of the international community have for the past three centuries been engaged in the task of formulating a set of rules and principles for the conduct of that society – the rules and principles we call international law. In so doing, they must ask themselves whether there is a place in that set of rules for a rule under which it would be legal, for whatever reason, to eliminate members of that community or, indeed, the entire community itself. Can the international community, which is governed by that rule, be considered to have given its acceptance to that rule, whatever be the approach of that community – positivist, natural law, or any other? Is the community of nations, to use Hart's expression, a "suicide club"?[24]

3.1.3 Creating a Hierarchy of Human Dignity

Third, without face-to-face killing certain humans are deemed more valuable and priceless than others, which creates a hierarchy of human dignity. This may appear to idealise or romanticise warfare as involving chivalrous, primitive physical contact between men.[25] And surely modern warfare increasingly

---

22 Christof Heyns, 'Autonomous weapons systems and human rights law' (Presentation made at the informal expert meeting organised by the state parties to the Convention on Certain Conventional Weapons 13-16 May 2014, Geneva, Switzerland) 8; Christof Heyns, 'Autonomous weapons systems: living a dignified life and dying a dignified death' in Nehal Bhuta, Susanne Beck, Robin Geiß, Hin-Yan Liu, Claus Kreß (eds.), *Autonomous Weapons Systems Law, Ethics, Policy* (Cambridge University Press, 2016).
23 H.L.A. Hart, *The Concept of Law* (Oxford University Press, 1961).
24 *Nuclear Weapons, supra* note 6, Dissenting Opinion of Judge Weeramantry, 521.
25 I am grateful to Marco Sassóli for raising this point during the ESIL conference. See also Marco Sassóli, 'Autonomous Weapons and International Humanitarian Law: Advantages, Open Technical Questions and Legal Issues to be Clarified' (2014) 90 *International Legal Studies* 308.

involves distancing of combatants through the use of bombs and precision-guided missiles so that autonomous weapons are part of the same development? To clarify, face-to-face killing is not used here in the sense of caricaturing warfare as literally pitting men against each other through physical contact. Rather, it is intended to evoke the human essence of warfare; that there is human moral and legal agency in targeting and lethal force decisions and actions. Existing semi-autonomous weapons with some degree of autonomy in certain critical functions tend to be restricted in terms of types of operations, targets, and contexts (for example, air defence weapon systems programmed to detect and shoot projectiles within close range of target base, border control defensive weapon systems programmed to detect and destroy incoming rockets, naval ship-based automatic machine guns programmed to detect and destroy incoming missiles).[26] Even with some removal of human involvement in relation to certain critical functions, these weapons remain dependent on human input and are designed to fire automatically when pre-determined parameters are detected. They are not designed to act independently in dynamic or changing situations.

So unlike other weapons, autonomous weapons, especially those with full autonomy in all the critical functions, present a more challenging impact by removing the human essence of warfare. Military personnel, remote pilots, commanders, programmers, and engineers are immune from rational and ethical decision-making to kill another human being and do not witness the consequences. By replacing the human combatant with a machine the combatant's human dignity is not only preserved but elevated above the human target. This can also be seen as a relative end in that it selfishly protects your own combatants from harm at all costs, including violating the fundamental principle of humanity as an objective end.[27]

Characterising the protection of your own combatants as a relative and selfish end may offend utilitarian perspectives on the necessities and realities of warfare. Strawser distinguishes fully autonomous from semi-autonomous weapons, finding the former 'morally impermissible' but the latter, especially UAV, permissible due to a moral duty to protect soldiers who should not be put

---

26   See, e.g., German NBS Mantis, available at http://www.army-technology.com/projects/mantis/ (last visited 23 April 2017); Israeli Iron Dome, available at http://www.army-technology.com/projects/irondomeairdefencemi/ (last visited 23 April 2017); American Phalanx, available at http://www.navy.mil/navydata/fact_print.asp?cid=2100&tid=487&ct=2&page=1 (last visited 23 April 2017).

27   Hill pursues an interesting line of enquiry as to whether Kantian human dignity allows for this sort of hierarchy in relation to terrorists and hostage situations, Hill *supra* note 17, at ch. 10.

at unnecessary risk. UAV, he argues, do not violate the demands of justice, do not make the world worse, or expose your own combatants to potentially lethal risk unless incurring such a risk aids in the accomplishment of good in some way that cannot be gained via less risky means.[28] From a national interest and utilitarian perspective, this moral duty to protect soldiers sounds logical and sensible, but it fails to recognise that the inherent asymmetry in human dignity status introduced by autonomous weapons (whether fully or semi-autonomous) leads to insecurity and unpredictability in warfare which makes neither the combatant nor target safe. Even using a semi-autonomous weapon means a combatant is not in direct harm's way or at risk of losing his life. With a fully autonomous weapon a machine completely replaces the human combatant in all the critical functions. In either case, protection of the combatant relates to life not dignity as status and respectful treatment. This in itself does not seem a valid reason for using autonomous weapons because potential loss of combatant lives in war is expected and an unavoidable risk (unless the state is negligent in preparing and equipping troops). In fact, replacing combatants with autonomous weapons undermines the former's dignity by not recognising their professional training and military ethics of courage and respect for human targets, as reflected under international humanitarian law.[29] There would also appear to be no reason for having armies.

3.2 The Cycle of Irrationality and Irrational Agents

We have already established that Kant considers humanity as formed by rational beings with the capacity to create, amend, and abide by moral rules. Individuals engaged in immoral conduct are not excluded from humanity and, therefore, cannot lose their human dignity. Autonomy of will is key to Kant's conception of the rational being because it means individuals are not coerced to create, amend, and abide by moral rules.[30] Autonomy of will does not refer to the capacity to achieve personal objectives, which are relative ends. It is about freely and willingly accepting rules that achieve objective ends (for example, preventing harm to humans in order to respect their human dignity). But the introduction of fully autonomous weapons with autonomy in all the critical functions actually makes us irrational agents who relinquish our autonomy of will. Humans are removed from the rational thinking process of

---

28　Bradley Jay Strawser, 'Moral Predators: The Duty to Employ Uninhabited Aerial Vehicles' (2010) 9(4) *Journal of Military Ethics* 342-368.

29　Geoffrey Best, *Humanity in Warfare* (Columbia University Press, 1980). See also Rain Liivoja, 'Chivalry without a Horse: Military Honour and the Modern Law of Armed Conflict' (2012) 15 *Estonian National Defence College Proceedings* 75-100.

30　Kant, *supra* note 11, at 107-109, paras. 97-101 [446-448].

when and how to use lethal force, and abdicate a key characteristic of humanity to a machine. This begs the question whether we need rationality at all if it can be so easily delegated to machines.

'Human central thinking activities'[31] are critical during warfare and involve the ability to feel, think and evaluate, and the capacity to adhere to a value-based system in which violence is not the norm governing human relations. This uniquely identifies how humans engage in qualitative analysis through exercising judgment and reasoning. A combination of knowledge, experience, environment, and critical evaluation skills influence 'human central thinking activities' enabling difficult decisions to be made on the extent and timing of force. Pre-programmed machines perform cost effective and speedy peripheral processing activities based on quantitative analysis, repetitive actions, and sorting data. But they do not possess the human attributes to appraise a given situation, exercise judgment, refrain from taking action, or to limit harm. Stating that there will be human control over autonomous weapons is not enough to allay concerns about removing 'human central thinking activities' from the lethal force decision-making process. The type of human control is critical. A human operated on/off switch to trigger an attack does not demonstrate exercising rational thinking. There is also the problem of automation bias in semi-autonomous weapons whereby the human operator accepts what the machine approves as legitimate targets. Sharkey refers to the need for 'meaningful human control', which means allowing human deliberation about a target before initiating an attack.[32]

Without this rational capacity, do we then revert to a state of nature? Human targets are denied the status of rational agents with autonomy of will, and arbitrarily deemed irrational agents subject to extrajudicial killings or subhumans not worthy of human face-to-face contact. Remember that under the Kantian notion of human dignity immoral conduct does not lead to loss of human dignity, so no matter what the human target has or has not done they still have human dignity. By excluding the human target from human dignity on the basis of their alleged immoral conduct there is no opportunity to convince them of the validity of moral laws or to engage non-lethal methods. In fact, an opportunity is lost to build what Kant refers to as the 'kingdom of ends' in which rational beings create and abide by moral rules recognising human

---

[31] Ozlem Ulgen, 'Autonomous UAV and Removal of Human Central Thinking Activities: Implications for Legitimate Targeting, Proportionality, and Unnecessary Suffering' (forthcoming) 1-45.

[32] Noel Sharkey, 'Towards a principle for the human supervisory control of robot weapons' (2014) 2 (May-August) *Politica & Società* 1-16.

dignity. By violently ousting human targets for perceived irrational and immoral conduct, autonomous weapons perpetuate a cycle of irrationality in which humans become irrational agents.

4 Autonomous Weapons and Human Dignity as Respectful Treatment

Kant's approach to ethical conduct is rooted in rational beings with autonomy of will having an inclination towards respect for moral rules. This inclination derives from rationality and recognition of the intrinsic worth of human dignity. It is not based on self-interest or coercion. It follows from the status of human dignity that respecting the rights of others amounts to recognition of human dignity.[33] What are these rights? Respectful treatment of yourself and others is a manifestation of human dignity or humanity as an objective end. For example, human dignity resides in individuals taking care of their own moral worth through avoiding immoral conduct and constantly striving to move from a state of nature to an improved rightful or lawful condition. Individual morality is moderated by self-restraint and openness.[34] Too much self-restraint is contrary to human dignity (for example, denial of basic human needs for some greater good). Too much openness in seeking personal pleasure at the expense of others is also contrary to human dignity (for example, avarice, arrogance). As regards respecting others, Kant expresses this as a negative formulation. We restrain our words and deeds towards others and thereby respect their human dignity. Kant's writings on human value, state powers of punishment, and rights in war provide a basis for understanding human dignity as respectful treatment.

4.1 Mistreatment of Rational Beings and Wrongdoers

Not mistreating human beings is Kant's negative formulation of the duty to respect human dignity in others. All humans, including wrongdoers, are rational beings with autonomy of will deserving respect for their human dignity. Recall that dignity means recognition of another's worth that has no price and cannot be exchanged for an equivalent. If we do not respect a wrongdoer's

---

[33] Waldron refers to dignity as a 'status-concept' whereby humans with moral and/or legal standing control their own conduct, account for their actions, and demand that others recognise and accommodate such status. See Jeremy Waldron, 'How Law Protects Dignity' (2012) 71(1) *Cambridge Law Journal*, 201-202. See also Waldron, *supra* note 14.

[34] Kant, *supra* note 15, at 173-218.

dignity or treat them less favourably we are judging them as worthless and, in Kant's terms, with contempt. For Kant a dangerous wrongdoer is no object of contempt and no less worthy of respect because he remains a human being even if his deeds are unworthy.[35] In relation to how to treat such a person, Kant refers to certain 'disgraceful punishments' that cannot be justified because they 'dishonour humanity itself ... [and] ... make a spectator blush with shame at belonging to the species that can be treated that way.'[36] Examples include quartering a man, having him torn by dogs, cutting off his nose and ears. These are severe acts against physical integrity and dignity of the person which, read in conjunction with Kant's remarks about a judicially prescribed death sentence without mistreatment, provide illustrations of the duty not to mistreat humans. More subtle illustrations of mistreatment, referred to as 'vices', include arrogance, defamation, and ridicule.[37]

4.1.1 'Outrages upon personal dignity' and Inhumane Treatment

Kant's notion of human dignity conceptualises the generic category of 'wrongdoers' to help us understand that even if a person is suspected of wrongdoing or has done wrong, or is an enemy combatant, they are still entitled to status and certain treatment. Kant's 'disgraceful punishments' are today transposed into international humanitarian law through prohibition of certain acts and forms of conduct. Common Article 3 of the Geneva Conventions provides fundamental guarantees (applicable to both non-international and international armed conflicts) that civilians and *hors de combat* 'shall in all circumstances be treated humanely'.[38] Article 3(1)(a) prohibits violence to life and person, in particular murder of all kinds, mutilation, cruel treatment and torture. Article 3(1)(c) prohibits 'outrages upon personal dignity, in particular humiliating and degrading treatment'. The Elements of Crimes for the International Criminal Court defines 'outrages upon personal dignity' as acts which humiliate, degrade, or otherwise violate the dignity of a person to such a degree 'as to be generally recognised as an outrage upon personal dignity'.[39]

---

35 Kant, *supra* note 15, at 210.
36 *Ibid.*
37 Kant, *supra* note 15, at 211-213.
38 The majority decision in *Military and Paramilitary Activities in and against Nicaragua (Nicaragua v. USA), Merits Judgment of 27 June 1986, ICJ Reports 1986*, 14 held that Common Art. 3 expresses 'minimum rules applicable to international and non-international conflicts' (para. 219), and these rules reflect 'elementary considerations of humanity' (para. 218).
39 Elements of Crimes for the International Criminal Court, Article 8(2)(b)(xxi) (war crime of outrages upon personal dignity covering all persons including the dead); Art. 8(2)(c)(ii)

Common Article 3 fundamental guarantees are also provided for enemy combatants under Articles 1(2) and 75 of API. Enemy combatants are afforded protection under 'the principles of international law derived from established custom, from the principles of humanity and from the dictates of public conscience'; and if they do not benefit from more favourable treatment under the Geneva Conventions or API, they must be 'treated humanely in all circumstances'. The law's moral basis derives from 'principles of humanity' and 'the dictates of public conscience' which, although not defined, are intended to overcome any ambiguities or uncertainties by anchoring the law back to what would be in the interest of humanity. This moral basis prevents the assumption that something which is not prohibited in law is therefore permissible, and applies regardless of developments in weapons technology.[40] It has normative force to provide additional protection by appropriately controlling military behaviour.[41]

These provisions establish obligations to take account of others' interests, including the human dignity of enemy combatants. Use of autonomous weapons to kill 'wrongdoer' human targets completely bypasses such obligations and represents a modern-day example of Kant's 'disgraceful punishments' amounting to 'outrages upon personal dignity'. The human target is treated as an inanimate object without any interests; easily removed and destroyed by a faceless and emotionless machine. No value is placed on the life taken. No 'human central thinking activities' are involved in the interpretation and application of international humanitarian law on prevention of unnecessary suffering, taking precautionary measures, and assessing proportionality. The lack of human discretion in these decisions violates Articles 35, 51, 57 API.[42]

There is currently no prohibition on the use or development of autonomous weapons but this does not make them permissible when judged against human dignity as a principle of humanity. Autonomous weapons would devalue humanity by treating humans as disposable inanimate objects rather than

---

(war crime of outrages upon personal dignity of *hors de combat*, civilians, medical personnel, or religious personnel).

[40] Yves Sandoz, Christophe Swinarski and Bruno Zimmermann (eds.), *ICRC Commentary on the Additional Protocols of 8 June 1977 to the Geneva Conventions of 12 August 1949* (ICRC 1987), paras. 55-56.

[41] *Nuclear Weapons, supra* note 6, Dissenting Opinion of Judge Shahabudden, 405-409.

[42] Eliav Lieblich and Eyal Benvenisti, 'The obligation to exercise discretion in warfare: why autonomous weapons systems are unlawful' in Bhuta (et al.) *supra* note 22, argue that autonomous weapons systems violate the duty to exercise discretion under international humanitarian law because they have pre-determined decision-making capability which does not respect the individual by considering their case/position carefully and exercising discretion where necessary.

ends with intrinsic value and rational thinking capacity. All individuals targeted and killed by such weapons are entitled to respect for their human dignity. Whether or not they are designated enemy combatants or terrorists, they have rational capacity, possess a moral value of dignity which cannot be replaced by an equivalent, and cannot lose such status through immoral acts. If an autonomous weapon is capable of causing unnecessary suffering in the human target this would constitute mistreatment. For example, certain types of Hellfire missiles used on UAV cause burning in targets and incineration of bodies.[43] The AGM-114N MAC ('metal augmented charge') variant uses a thermobaric warhead that can 'suck the air out of a cave, collapse a building, or produce an astoundingly large blast radius out in the open.'[44] It contains a 'fluorinated aluminium powder layered between the warhead casing and the PBXN-112 explosive fill. When the PBXN-112 detonates, the aluminium mixture is dispersed and rapidly burns. The resultant sustained high pressure is extremely effective against enemy personnel and structures.'[45]

4.1.2 Does It Matter whether Mistreatment Comes from Man or Machine?

It may be argued that international humanitarian law allows use of lethal force against an enemy so that death resulting from use of autonomous weapons is not unlawful *per se*. But this avoids moral and legal considerations of methods and means of warfare, which stand at the heart of human dignity as respectful treatment. To say that human targets are indifferent as to whether they are killed by autonomous weapons or soldiers undermines human dignity in the person and runs contrary to evidence of the effects and repercussions of American UAV strikes in Pakistan and Yemen.[46] Apart from causing civilian

---

[43] See e.g., American UAV strike of 23 January 2013 killing four individuals, including two civilians: Joseph Cox, 'The Yemeni Man Suing BT for America's Deadly Drone Attacks' *Vice News* (23 May 2014) available at www.vice.com/en_uk/read/the-yemeni-man-suing-bt-for-american-drone-strikes (last visited 23 April 2017); Glenn Greenwald, 'Burning Victims to Death: Still a Common Practice' *The Intercept* (4 February 2015) available at https://theintercept.com/2015/02/04/burning-victims-death-still-common-practice/ (last visited 23 April 2017).

[44] 'US Hellfire Missile Orders, FY 2011-2017' available at www.defenseindustrydaily.com/us-hellfire-missile-orders-fy-2011-2014-07019/ (last visited 23 April 2017).

[45] 'AGM-114N Metal Augmented Charge (MAC) Thermobaric Hellfire' available at www.globalsecurity.org/military/systems/munitions/agm-114n.htm (last visited 23 April 2017).

[46] Dieter Birnbacher, 'Are autonomous weapon systems a threat to human dignity?' in Bhuta (et al.) *supra* note 22, asserts that victims whose human dignity is at stake are indifferent as to whether they are killed by manned or unmanned weapons, although concedes that use of autonomous weapons systems in certain circumstances (e.g. causing unrelieved

casualties, UAV strikes have caused loss of livelihood due to fear of venturing outside, and severe psychological harm officially diagnosed as PTSD.[47] 'Decapitation strikes' intended to weaken the organisational capability of al-Qaeda and the Taliban by removing key players or leaders have not achieved that objective, and UAV strikes in Pakistan have fuelled recruitment into militant organisations and solidified resistance against the Pakistani State.[48] Victims' accounts of targeted killings in Yemen reveal extreme physical, psychological and economic harm: targeted vehicles continue burning with victims inside; clothes fused to survivors' skin; skin burned off; local population living in fear and terror from hearing planes; women suffering miscarriages; children frightened to go outside; dependents of individuals killed unable to support themselves economically; local population suffering shock after strikes; inability to sustain a living from the land due to fear of being outside.[49]

Cases of combatants committing war crimes amounting to 'outrages upon personal dignity' may appear to bolster the argument supporting use of autonomous weapons (that is, the latter will act more rationally and be less prone to human flaws leading to atrocities). The 'irrational soldier' argument maintains that soldiers are susceptible to emotions and unpredictability which can be eliminated by use of autonomous weapons.[50] Human emotions and negative human characteristics (for example, susceptibility to fatigue and capacity for revenge) are said to debilitate soldiers' performance and ethical judgment to the extent of enabling commission of war crimes and atrocities. Replacing soldiers with autonomous weapons will somehow guarantee rational thinking which does not lead to violations of international humanitarian law or war crimes.

---

mental pain for civilian victims, severely restricting their freedom, and potentially treating victims as means to an end) potentially violates human dignity.

[47] Stanford International Human Rights and Conflict Resolution Clinic and Global Justice Clinic, *Living under drones: death, injury, and trauma to civilians from us drone practices in Pakistan* (NYU School of Law, September, 2012), ch. 3; UK Defence Committee, *Written evidence from the All Party Parliamentary Group on Drones (APPG)* (HC 2013-14) para. 24 (Dr Peter Schaapveld's, forensic psychologist, evidence on drones in Yemen).

[48] Jenna Jordan, 'Attacking the Leader, Missing the Mark: Why Terrorist Groups Survive Decapitation Strikes' (Spring 2014) 38(4) *International Security* 7; Saira Yamin and Salma Malik, *Mapping Conflict Trends in Pakistan* (United States Institute of Peace, Peaceworks No. 93, February 2014) 7.

[49] *Reprieve Complaint to the UK National Contact Point under the Specific Instance Procedure of the OECD Guidelines for Multinational Enterprises in respect of BT plc* (15 July 2013) 4-5.

[50] Ronald Arkin, *Governing Lethal Behaviour in Autonomous Robots* (CRC Press, 2009); Ronald Arkin, 'Lethal Autonomous Systems and the Plight of the Non-combatant' (work was supported in part by the U.S. Army Research Office under Contract #W911NF-06-1-0252).

But such an argument makes questionable assumptions about human and robotic rational thinking capacities and conduct in warfare, disregarding human agency in the creation and failures of autonomous weapons. It assumes humans have no capacity for preventing unethical conduct and that machines will act more ethically than humans. There are many different reasons why combatants commit war crimes, not necessarily related to inherent human flaws.[51] Human emotions, as part of 'human central thinking activities', play a vital role in navigating complex social environments in combat, especially where it is necessary to perceive and interpret human behaviour (for example, children playing ball rather than throwing a hand grenade, someone running with a stick rather than a gun, a young man of military age in the vicinity of an attack).[52] The judgment, reasoning, and discretion exercised by a human cannot be performed by a machine. Far from advocating replacement of human combatants with machines, war crimes cases serve as barometers of public conscience on acceptable conduct in warfare. They promote human dignity by recognising that only human action justifies lethal force and, therefore, requires human accountability and responsibility.

In *R v. Blackman* a British acting colour sergeant in the Royal Marines, in command of a group of the Royal Marines serving as part of the British armed forces in Afghanistan, was found guilty of murder and sentenced to life imprisonment for shooting in the chest a seriously wounded Afghan insurgent. The insurgent was entitled to be treated with dignity, respect, and humanity, yet Sergeant Blackman treated him 'with contempt and murdered him in cold blood'.[53] The sergeant had failed to ensure medical assistance was quickly provided, allowed soldiers under his command to manhandle the wounded insurgent causing him additional pain, ordered those providing first aid to stop, and waited for the military surveillance helicopter to be out of sight before shooting

---

[51] Daniel Munoz-Rojas and Jean-Jacques Frésard, *The Roots of Behaviour: Understanding and Preventing IHL Violations* (Geneva: International Committee of the Red Cross, 2004), found that advanced technologies which permit killing at a distance or on the computer screen prevent the activation of neuro-psychological mechanisms which render the act of killing difficult, and violations are usually coupled with moral disengagement. See also Hugh Gusterson, *Drone: Remote Control Warfare* (MIT Press, 2016) 66-77, on the impact of UAV 'voyeuristic technology' and 'remote narrativization'.

[52] Marcello Guarini and Paul Bello, 'Robotic Warfare: Some Challenges in Moving from Non-civilian to Civilian Theaters' in Patrick Lin, Keith Abney and George Bekey (eds.), *Robot Ethics: the ethical and social implications of robotics* (MIT Press, 2012).

[53] *R v. Sergeant Alexander Wayne Blackman* (UK Military Court, Bulford, Judge Advocate General Jeff Blackett, Sentencing Remarks, 6 December 2013) Case Reference: 2012CM00442, available at www.judiciary.gov.uk/wp-content/uploads/JCO/Documents/Judgments/r-v-blackman-marine-a-sentencing+remarks.pdf (last visited 23 April 2017).

the insurgent. The sergeant was filmed saying, 'There you are, shuffle off this mortal coil, you cunt ... It's nothing you wouldn't do to us,' then turned to his fellow soldiers and stated, 'Obviously this doesn't go anywhere, fellas ... I've just broke [sic] the Geneva Convention,' while the insurgent continued to writhe as these remarks were made.[54] Whilst mitigating factors pointed to human flaws in combat (for example, the effect of fellow soldiers' injuries and deaths, combat stress) these were not extraordinary or unexpected risks to sufficiently displace military ethics and respect for humanity:

> ... thousands of other Service personnel have experienced the same or similar stresses. They exercised self discipline and acted properly and humanely; you did not. ... while this sort of offence is extremely rare, if not unique, those Service personnel who commit crimes of murder, or other war crimes or crimes against humanity while on operations will be dealt with severely. This is a message of deterrence but it is also to reassure the international community that allegations of serious crime will be dealt with transparently and appropriately.[55]

Although murder is separate from and not an 'outrage upon personal dignity',[56] the sergeant's acts and omissions preceding the killing can be characterised as 'animated by contempt for the human dignity of another person'[57] and,

---

54 *R v. Alexander Wayne Blackman* [2017] EWCA Crim 190 (15 March 2017), para. 22. See also Steven Morris, 'Judges Allow Partial Release of British Marine Shooting Video', *The Guardian* (1 February 2017), available at www.theguardian.com/uk-news/2017/feb/01/judges-allow-partial-release-of-british-marine-shooting-video (last visited 23 April 2017). On appeal his conviction was substituted for manslaughter on grounds of diminished responsibility due to new evidence adduced that he had suffered from adjustment disorder, see *R v. Alexander Wayne Blackman* [2017] EWCA Crim 325 (28 March 2017). His sentence was reduced to seven years which, allowing for time already spent in prison, resulted in him serving three and a half years in prison and being released in April 2017. His previous dismissal with disgrace was substituted for dismissal. For criticism about the Court Martial Appeal Court's application of the defence of diminished responsibility and sentencing leniency, particularly given the defendant's manifest premeditation and awareness of his actions, see Kevin Jon Heller, 'Bad Criminal Law in the Alexander Blackman Case (With Addendum)' *Opinio Juris* (31 March 2017) available at http://opiniojuris.org/2017/03/31/bad-criminal-law-in-the-alexander-blackman-case/?utm_source=feedburner&utm_medium=email&utm_campaign=Feed%3A+opiniojurisfeed+%28Opinio+Juris%29 (last visited 23 April 2017).

55 *R v. Sergeant Alexander Wayne Blackman*, supra note 53.

56 *Prosecutor v. Kvočka and others*, Judgment, Case No IT-98-30/1-T, Trial Chamber (2 November 2001), para. 172.

57 *Prosecutor v. Aleksovski*, Judgment, Case No IT-95-14/1-T, Trial Chamber (25 June 1999), paras. 54-56.

therefore, falling into the particular category of inhumane treatment. This case makes clear the importance of interaction and interrelatedness between warring parties in the application of international humanitarian law. The court emphasised that military personnel acting with brutality and savagery lose the support and confidence of those they seek to protect, and provoke the enemy to act more brutally in retribution or reprisal. With use of autonomous weapons there is no interaction and interrelatedness between warring parties, which creates a dangerous human accountability and responsibility gap.

4.1.3 Mistreatment of the Deceased

'Outrages upon personal dignity' and inhumane acts may be committed against the dead in warfare, and the Geneva Conventions establish extensive state obligations to search for the dead and prevent their being despoiled or ill-treated.[58] International criminal tribunal cases provide examples of the types of acts and conduct that constitute outrages against the personal dignity of the deceased, and consideration must be given as to how autonomous weapons may affect this aspect of human dignity.

In the *Trial of Max Schmid* a German medical officer was found guilty of wilfully, deliberately and wrongfully mutilating the deceased body of a US serviceman, and sentenced to ten years imprisonment.[59] In *Prosecutor v. Niyitegeka* the Minister of Information in the Rwandan Interim Government was convicted, among other crimes, of other inhumane acts as crimes against humanity. He was jubilant at the capture of a prominent Tutsi and rejoiced when he was killed, decapitated, castrated, his skull pierced through the ears with a spike, and his genitals hung on a spike for the public to see. Niyitegeka's jubilation, especially in light of his leadership role in the attack, supported and encouraged the attackers and thereby aided and abetted the commission of crimes. He subsequently ordered men to undress the deceased body of a Tutsi woman and insert a sharp piece of wood into her genitalia. The Trial Chamber considered the order an aggravating factor for its 'cruel and insensitive disregard for human life and dignity' and found that both incidents 'would cause mental suffering to civilians, in particular, Tutsi civilians, and constitute a serious attack on the human dignity of the Tutsi community as a whole'.[60]

---

58 Art. 15 Geneva Convention I of 12 August 1949; Art. 18 Geneva Convention II of 12 August 1949; Arts. 13, 120-121 Geneva Convention III of 12 August 1949; Art. 16 Geneva Convention IV of 12 August 1949; Art. 34 API.

59 *Trial of Max Schmid, Case No 82, UN War Crimes Commission Law Reports of Trials of Criminals, 19 May 1947*, 151-152.

60 *Prosecutor v. Niyitegeka*, Judgment, Case No ICTR-96-14-T, Trial Chamber (16 May 2003), paras. 465 and 499.

These criminal acts cannot simply be explained as consequences of combat because they go beyond what is necessary to achieve a military objective and offend humanity. Although Kantian human dignity is predicated on the individual, *Prosecutor v. Niyitegeka* suggests there is a communitarian aspect to human dignity concerning mistreatment of deceased human targets. 'Civilians', 'Tutsi civilians', 'the Tutsi community as a whole' were all deemed to be affected as a group of protected persons, as an ethnic group, and as part of humankind. 'Collective human dignity' is important in communities where humaneness and personhood are achieved through association with others. Social honour, group moral standing, and the capacity to form communal relations are aspects of the '*ubuntu*' tradition in sub-Saharan Africa.[61] To the extent that '*ubuntu*' regards dignity as conceived and maintained by communities it offers a perspective on what it means to be part of humankind. It would, for example, be wrong to punish or otherwise harm an innocent person, even when it would save more innocent lives, because this fails to treat the person in accordance with the way he has exercised his capacity for community. But this communitarian aspect has a problematic potential to exclude individuals on the basis that they are not 'innocents' or do not meet communitarian standards. What happens to the enemy combatant who is not part of any community or is unable to form communal relations? Does he lack personhood and human dignity? Would this then justify using autonomous weapons against him? Kantian human dignity avoids this dilemma by advocating humane treatment of wrongdoers and enemy combatants.

Beyond this particular problematic potential, the communitarian aspect offers a way of understanding how autonomous weapons offend the 'collective human dignity' of mankind. Lack of face-to-face contact (understood as human moral and legal agency) between human combatants and human targets renders state obligations to search for and prevent mistreatment of the dead redundant. The weapon is programmed to administer lethal force without concerns about how the target dies or what happens after death. There is no obligation for the weapon to search for the dead or prevent mistreatment, which itself could be considered a form of mistreatment. Death caused by conventional combat (that is, human combatants *in situ*) whether on land, at sea, or in the air appears to be accorded greater protection against outrages upon personal dignity than death by autonomous weapons.

---

61 On 'collective human dignity' see Mica Werner, 'Individual and collective dignity' in Marcus Düwell, Jens Braarvig, and Roger Brownsword (eds.), *The Cambridge Handbook of Human Dignity* (Cambridge University Press, 2014), ch. 35; Thaddeus Metz, 'Dignity in the ubuntu tradition' in Marcus Düwell (et al.) *ibid.,* ch. 32.

4.2 Preconditions for Punishment of Wrongdoers and Treatment of Enemy Combatants

Some ambiguities exist in Kant's formulation of dignity which may raise difficulties in its application to those targeted and killed by autonomous weapons. What if those targeted have killed humans? Do they lose rational capacity? Should they be afforded dignity? There are two possible answers here.

The first focuses on rational capacity as a *potential* rather than actual human characteristic and, therefore, dignity cannot be lost by committing immoral acts. This corresponds to the principle of equality based on innate humanity of all persons so that if you kill the person committing an immoral act, you kill yourself.[62] The second answer provides a potential exception under punishment of such individuals. Kant regards retributive punishment, specifically the death penalty for murderers, as a matter of justice. Life and death are not the same and there is no substitute for taking a life other than death. But this exception has preconditions: punishment and sentence must be imposed by a judge, and even if the wrongdoer is facing an imminent death sentence 'he must still be freed from any mistreatment that could make the humanity in the person suffering it into something abominable.'[63] Kant gives an example of mistreatment as dangerous physical experiments on a murderer for greater medical good. These can never be consented to by the murderer or society because they are contrary to the murderer's human dignity and 'justice ceases to be justice if it can be bought for any price whatsoever.'[64]

Kant's non-mistreatment precondition is pervasive in today's international humanitarian law. Even in situations where security or repressive measures are necessary against certain individuals, the dictates of humanity require that the law provides protection from mistreatment in order to preserve human dignity.[65] For example, Articles 13 and 14 Geneva Convention III and Article 11(1) API require prisoners of war to be treated humanely at all times; not be subjected to physical mutilation or to medical or scientific experiments, even with their consent; to be protected from acts of violence or intimidation and against insults and public curiosity; and to be entitled in all circumstances to 'respect for their persons and their honour'. Thus, even if those targeted by autonomous weapons have killed human beings, they are still entitled to humane treatment.

---

62   Kant, *supra* note 15, at 105.
63   Kant, *supra* note 15, at 106.
64   Kant, *supra* note 15, at 105.
65   Jean S. Pictet (ed.), ICRC *Commentary on Geneva Convention III 12 August 1949* (ICRC 1960) 140.

The preconditions (that is, judicial punishment and sentence, no mistreatment) keep human dignity intact by not legitimising cruel and arbitrary treatment of wrongdoers as human outcasts without any moral rights. Human dignity is innate, priceless, and an objective end in itself. But the difference with autonomous weapons is that there is no due process to determine guilt or innocence. There is no prior determination of punishability and a judge is not imposing a sentence. Although lawful killing of enemy combatants in armed conflict generally does not require a prior judgment because it is not about punishment, autonomous weapons as a means of killing represent a form of punishment without preconditions because they undermine human dignity and deny the possibility of interaction and interrelatedness between warring parties. By targeting and attacking the wrongdoer the autonomous weapon is a means of avoiding judicial pronouncement and authorisation of punishment. The human target is treated as a means to an end without human dignity and subhuman treatment of efficient disposal is justified.

The non-existence of preconditions is contrary to Kant's ideal state of the 'kingdom of ends' (a commonwealth of persons who legislate universal laws that are rational and based on humanity as an end in itself). Kant is not advocating a world superstate but recognises the need for some form of state apparatus to enable legislating in this kingdom of ends. State apparatus necessarily includes coercive and punishment powers. Those who go against the moral rules can be punished, but not in a way that mistreats them or is contrary to human dignity. There must be an opportunity for the wrongdoer to avoid the punishment, which in any case must be judicially prescribed and administered. As we have already seen, Kant considers the death penalty a legitimate sentence for murderers but only under judicially prescribed conditions and only if the murderer is not mistreated in any other way.[66]

4.3 Limitations on Methods and Means of Warfare

Kant's idea of individual and state morality is based on a trajectory from a state of nature to a rightful or lawful condition. It forms the basis for his views on rights in war. Kant describes war as 'barbaric' and to be expected while states remain in a state of nature.[67] A state of rightfulness would involve states voluntarily coming together in a congress to uphold perpetual peace. Conceding that the state of nature will involve war, he then discusses rights in war. Where there is an 'unjust enemy' states are entitled to unite against and deprive the enemy state of its power. An 'unjust enemy' is one 'whose publicly expressed

---

66   Kant, *supra* note 15, at 105-109.
67   Kant, *supra* note 15, at 118-120, paras. [6:349-6.351].

will (whether by word or deed) reveals a maxim by which, if it were made a universal rule, any condition of peace among nations would be impossible and, instead, a state of nature would be perpetuated.'[68]

4.3.1   Kantian 'just war' Impact on jus in bello

Kant's reference to just war theory is somewhat problematic in merging *jus ad bellum* and *jus in bello* considerations. But it is understandable for the period in which he was writing. Early modern writers of the 16th to 18th centuries were busy expanding Aquinas' classical just war theory, which was conceived as a limited enforcement measure requiring three conditions: a sovereign authority to wage war; a just cause (broadly defined as a prior or threatening injury by the enemy); and an intention to do justice and attain just peace.[69] By the 18th century it encompassed all-out war among sovereigns and legitimised broadly defensive action which did not necessarily limit violence against an enemy.[70] Vitoria recognised that both warring parties could legitimately claim to be fighting a just cause, and therefore had the right to derive benefit from *jus in bello*. Gentili considered war lawful if it was waged by a sovereign and formally declared. Grotius introduced the concept of 'state of war' which meant *jus in bello* applied to belligerents and *jus in pace* (that is, normal laws) applied in peacetime. Unlike these writers, Kant, even with his opposition to war, saw the necessary evil in having a limited form of self-help as conceived under classical just war theory. But he seems to be sabotaging it from within by setting limitations on methods and means of warfare to include proportionality in the conduct of hostilities, and humane treatment of enemy combatants. It is at this juncture that Kant's understanding of *jus in bello* proves significant for autonomous weapons.

Modern just war theory has nothing to say on methods and means of warfare, but requires us to conceive of the slippery-slope 'just cause' war.[71] It is

---

68   Kant, *supra* note 15, at 119, para. [6:349].
69   Randall Lesaffer, 'Too much history. From war as sanction to the sanctioning of war' in Mark Weller (ed.), *The Oxford Handbook of the Use of Force in International Law* (Oxford University Press, 2015); Mary Ellen O'Connell, 'Peace and War' in Bardo Fassbender and Anne Peters (eds.), *The Oxford Handbook of the History of International Law* (Oxford University Press, 2014), ch. 11.
70   Lesaffer *ibid.*
71   Michael Walzer, *Just and Unjust Wars: A Moral Argument With Historical Illustrations* (Basic Books, 1977). For example, Strawser, *supra* note 28, argues for a duty to use UAV in order to prevent harm to soldiers fighting a just war: 'for any just action taken by a given military, if it is possible for the military to use UAV platforms in place of inhabited aerial vehicles without a significant loss of capability, then that military has an ethical obligation to do so' at 346.

highly contentious and subjective as to what constitutes a 'just cause' and all parties to a conflict may conceivably claim they are pursuing a just cause that justifies use of autonomous weapons. The utilitarian argument for protecting your own soldiers fails to recognise the need for interaction and interrelatedness in warfare in order for some basic common rules to apply to all parties and limit harm. A dual-harm prevention approach is necessary in the conduct of warfare; one that takes account of combatants and targets so as to lay foundations for common understanding and de-escalation of war. Kantian cosmopolitan ethics places human beings at the centre of norms and laws governing warfare so that irrespective of combatant or target status, both are entitled to human dignity. Seeking to justify any methods and means of warfare on the basis of a just cause disregards the impact on humans.

4.3.2 Restraint to Preserve Human Dignity and Conditions for Peace

Kant wrote in a period of rapid state formation with states as the primary global force for power, but his definition of 'unjust enemy' could extend to non-state actors with transnational effects. Thus, whatever the political or religious motives of Islamist suicide bombings, such arbitrary attacks are not capable of universalisation as a moral rule because they guarantee mutual self-destruction, perpetuate war, and are fundamentally opposed to humanity in the Kantian sense of rational beings with autonomy of will. This being so, such attacks threaten state freedoms so that states are entitled to unite and deprive Islamist groups of power. But even when discussing permissible actions against unjust enemies Kant maintains a perspective of rational and proportionate conduct aimed at preserving peace and respecting human dignity. Thus, states are not entitled to divide the enemy's territory among themselves or to eliminate the state because this would be an 'injustice against its people.' Distinguishing an unjust enemy state from its people enables prohibiting acquisition of land by force and respect for human dignity by treating humanity as an objective end and not simply as a means.

A state that is injured by the actions of an unjust enemy cannot resort to any means of self-defence but 'those means that are allowable to any degree that it is able to, in order to maintain what belongs to it.'[72] Kant offers no further explanation as to why there should be restraint on methods and means of warfare, but the same reasoning used to justify forms of state punishment against wrongdoers can apply here. Resorting to any means of retaliation, irrespective of its impact on peoples or the degree to which it is necessary, would continue the state of nature and deny the existence of rational beings with autonomy of

---

[72] Kant, *supra* note 15, at 119, para. [6:349].

will. He identifies poisoning, using your own citizens as spies, and using your own citizens or foreigners as assassins or poisoners as impermissible methods and means of self-defence because these are 'underhanded means as would destroy the trust requisite to establishing a lasting peace in the future.'[73] So Kant's rationale for restraint on methods and means of warfare is based on preserving human dignity as well as ensuring conditions exist for perpetual peace among states. At its core is interaction and interrelatedness between rational beings and wrongdoers, and injured states and unjust enemies.

Such interaction and interrelatedness is evident in today's international humanitarian law. For example, poison and poisoned weapons are prohibited under Article 23(a) of the Regulations annexed to the 1899 Hague Convention II and the 1907 Hague Convention IV and their use constitutes a war crime under Article 8(2)(b)(xvii) of the 1998 Rome Statue of the International Criminal Court. A spy captured out of the uniform of his armed forces whilst engaging in espionage loses combatant status and POW rights, but must still be treated humanely according to the fundamental guarantees under Article 75 API.[74]

Restraint in action towards human targets is reflected in Articles 35 and 36 API, the principle of proportionality, and prevention of unnecessary suffering. If we accept that humanitarian law exists to regulate conduct in warfare in order to limit unnecessary suffering then it certainly is not controversial to expect less lethal methods and means, where possible, to be used. Capturing enemy combatants where feasible is an example and arguably a duty derived from custom and treaty law.[75] Current use of remotely operated UAVs involves pursuing individuals to their death without prior criminal investigation, due process, or attempts at their capture. The same lethal capability and lack of non-lethal options would exist with autonomous weapons, especially those with autonomy in all the critical functions. The elimination capability of autonomous weapons creates injustice against targeted individuals, physical and psychological collateral damage to communities in targeted areas, and perpetuates a state of nature.

---

73   Kant, *supra* note 15, at 117, para. [6:347].
74   Regulations annexed to the 1899 Hague Convention II and the 1907 Hague Convention IV, Art. 29; Art. 46 API.
75   See, e.g., ICRC *Interpretive Guidance on the Notion of Direct Participation in Hostilities under International Humanitarian Law* (Geneva, Switzerland, May 2009); Ryan Goodman, 'The Power to Kill or Capture Enemy Combatants' (2013) 24(3) *EJIL* 819-853. For an opposite view see, W. Hays Parks, 'Part IX of the ICRC 'Direct Participation in Hostilities' Study: No Mandate, No Expertise, and Legally Incorrect' (2010) 42 *NYU J Int'l L & Politics* 794; Michael Schmitt., 'Wound, Capture, or Kill: A Reply to Ryan Goodman's 'The Power to Kill or Capture Enemy Combatants'' (2013) 24(3) *EJIL* 855-861.

But could restraint needs be overridden by utilitarian considerations of the costly resourcing and financing of conventional warfare and, therefore, justify replacing combatants with efficient machines? It is claimed that time and money can be saved by investing in autonomous weapons technology to engage in combat situations with precision and efficiency.[76] Autonomy in unmanned air systems, for example, is seen as a means to decrease the number of personnel needed to operate them.[77] It may require only one person to control multiple unmanned systems with automated processing and analysis of information. Autonomous weapons might also be used to substitute or expand existing ground forces.[78] These practical, cost-benefit reasons for supporting autonomous weapons sit rather uncomfortably with more pressing concerns about legitimate targeting, proportionality, and preventing unnecessary suffering.

Cost-benefit reasoning was used to justify fire-bombing of German and Japanese cities during the Second World War and, eventually, nuclear bombing of Hiroshima. In a critical essay about nuclear warfare Rawls rejects this reasoning because it 'justifies too much, too easily, and provides a way for a dominant power to quiet any moral worries that may arise. If the principles of war are put forward at that time, they easily become so many more considerations to be balanced in the scales.'[79] In the same way, cost-benefit reasoning in the use of autonomous weapons 'too easily' provides justification and a way to 'quiet any moral worries'. Indeed, the cost-benefit approach is not entirely convincing given the extensive financial resourcing that will be necessary to ensure weapons are predictable, reliable, and operationally compliant with international humanitarian law.[80] There is also concern that a cost-benefit analysis is susceptible to efficiency-driven, short-term decisions which in the long-run may lead to combatant casualties and breaches of international humanitarian law.[81]

---

76   UK Ministry of Defence, Development, Concepts and Doctrine Centre, *The UK Approach to Unmanned Aircraft Systems, Joint Doctrine Note 2/11* (30 March 2011) paras. 102-103.
77   US Department of Defense, *Unmanned Systems Integrated Roadmap FY2011-2036* (2011) 44.
78   US Department of Defense, *Unmanned Systems Integrated Roadmap FY2013-2038* (2013) 19 and 68.
79   John Rawls, 'Fifty Years after Hiroshima' in Samuel Freeman (ed.), *Collected Papers: John Rawls* (Harvard 1999) 565-572.
80   Alan Backstrom and Ian Henderson, 'New capabilities in warfare: an overview of contemporary technological developments and the associated legal and engineering issues in Article 36 weapons reviews' (2012) 94(886) *International Review of the Red Cross* 483-514, 508-509.
81   See, e.g., *Smith and Others v. Ministry of Defence* (2013) UKSC 41 negligence claims brought by military personnel against the UK Ministry of Defence for failures to provide target identity devices that allow automatic confirmation as to whether a vehicle is a friend or

Closely related to the cost-benefit argument is the claim that due to the sophistication and superior capability of autonomous weapons in precision targeting, there are less likely to be civilian casualties and combatants will be taken out of harm's way. Apart from the speculative calculus, such a utilitarian rationale provides no interaction and interrelatedness between human combatants and human targets. It enables the former to treat the latter as irrational agents unworthy of human dignity. It is a one-sided justification made to the wider world without any relation to the individual target. What justification can be offered to the individual who is automatically treated as a lesser human? If there is no interaction and interrelatedness then there is potentially no restriction on the use of such means to conduct warfare. It may prove difficult to maintain the principle of distinction and categories of persons (for example, *hors de combat*, POWs, civilians).[82]

5   Conclusion

Assessing autonomous weapons against the Kantian notion of human dignity exposes their undesirability. First, ethical conduct of individuals and states should be determined by an inclusive moral theory; one providing justification for morals as well as legitimate responses to immoral conduct. Morality is rooted in something fundamental and objective: the human dignity of each person. Kant believed all humans, including wrongdoers, have rational capacity and autonomy of will which gives them an intrinsic value of dignity. This entitles humans to set and abide by rules, and to expect others to make rational choices. A rule that permits death by autonomous weapons cannot be universalised because rational beings cannot freely and rationally agree that it respects human dignity. Autonomous weapons create a hierarchy of human dignity whereby human targets are unequal and unworthy of face-to-face human contact and, therefore, excluded from an inclusive moral theory. Their life is deemed less worthy than human combatants replaced by autonomous weapons, and they are treated as mere relative ends that can be subjected to efficient disposal.

---

foe, and situational awareness equipment that permits tank crews to locate their position and direction of sight accurately.

82   Nagel argues that absolutist restrictions in warfare are based on a requirement that they be capable of specific justification to the person harmed rather than just to the world at large: Thomas Nagel, 'War and Massacre' (1972) 1 *Philosophy and Public Affairs* 128, 133-138.

Second, Kant's belief in not harming or killing others is not absolute and does allow for punishment with preconditions (for example, judicial punishment and sentence, no mistreatment, limitations on methods and means of warfare). Human targets who have committed immoral acts maintain moral worth and human dignity so they cannot be mistreated or subject to punishment that dishonours humanity. Yet autonomous weapons do both. They treat humans as disposable inanimate objects and legitimise extrajudicial killing without giving the human an opportunity to avoid death. Although Geneva law prohibits inhumane treatment, lack of face-to-face killing and efficient disposal of human life make provisions against outrages upon the personal dignity of the dead redundant.

Rather than creating Kant's 'kingdom of ends' autonomous weapons perpetuate a cycle of irrationality and irrational agents; humans abdicate rational thinking on lethal force to a machine and human targets are violently ousted as irrational agents. It is a world of relative ends where there is no interaction and interrelatedness between human combatants and human targets. The perceived benefits of autonomous weapons are one-sided without any relation to the individual target. If there is no interaction and interrelatedness then there is potentially no restriction on the use of such means to conduct warfare, and it may prove difficult to maintain the principle of distinction and categories of persons.

Acknowledgements

I am most grateful to Claus Kress, Ineta Ziemele, and George Ulrich for their insightful comments on an earlier draft.

CHAPTER 9

Vulnerability as a Virtue: An Attempt to Transpose the Care Ethic in International Law

Marion Blondel

Abstract

The utilisation of the concept of vulnerability in international law has risen exponentially. This contribution intends to analyse the issues underlying this phenomenon. Vulnerability is frequently used in a functional manner in order to enhance the protection of individuals. Therefore, even if vulnerability has been initially developed as a non-legal concept, it has now become integrated into legal discourse. As it inevitably supposes the contributions of other disciplines such as moral philosophy and legal sociology, vulnerability reshapes the ways in which individuals are protected by law. Hence, the reconsideration of several concepts, especially individual autonomy and international responsibility, paves the way for better protection of individuals.

Keywords

vulnerability – care – capability – autonomy – identity – pluralism – responsibility

The utilisation of the concept of vulnerability in international law has risen exponentially. This contribution intends to analyse the issues underlying this phenomenon. Vulnerability is frequently used in a functional manner in order to enhance the protection of individuals. Therefore, even if vulnerability has been initially developed as a non-legal concept, it has now become integrated into legal discourse. A more thorough study of the consequences of this integration is thus necessary. As it inevitably supposes the contributions of other disciplines such as moral philosophy and legal sociology, vulnerability reshapes the ways in which individuals are protected by law. Hence, the reconsideration of several concepts, especially individual autonomy and international responsibility, paves the way for better protection of individuals.

For Aristotle, vulnerability is one of the human virtues. It is linked to the finite and fragile characters of existence and it defines all those human beings that cannot escape their own condition. At first glance, associating this ontological argument related to the individual's vulnerability with law can be surprising. Nonetheless, numerous studies published on vulnerability show an increasing interest in legal doctrine pertaining to this subject.

Often as a result of sociological research renewing the debate on precariousness, fragility and exclusion, used in international economic institutions and asserting itself in the field of human development,[1] 'the expansion of vulnerability's metaphor has been huge'.[2] International law, as a transcript of social phenomena, was not spared by this 'tidal wave':[3] reference to the vulnerable person gradually became inevitable in the search for protection of the individual, both in domestic[4] as in international law,[5] substituting itself gradually for other notions.[6]

However, despite its frequent use, international instruments and case law[7] do not provide a clear definition of this concept as they only enumerate vulnerable persons.[8] Therefore, one can solely infer a definition of the vulnerable

---

1   Hélène Thomas, *Les vulnérables, la démocratie contre les pauvres* (éd. du Croquant, Terra, 2010) 78.
2   Susann Sontag, *Le sida et ses metaphores* (Paris, C. Bourgeois, 1989).
3   Marc-Henri Soulet, 'La vulnérabilité, une ressource à manier avec prudence', in Laurence Burgorgue-Larsen (ed.), *La vulnérabilité saisie par les juges en Europe*, (Journée d'étude organisée par l'IREDIES, Paris, Pedone, Cahiers Européens n°7, 2014) 8.
4   *Cf.* for the French Right: Loi n°2003–239 du 18 mars 2003 pour la sécurité intérieure; For the German Right: Gesetz zur Reform des Rechts der Vormundschaft und Pflegschaft für Volljährige, 12 September 1990; For the English Right: Youth Justice and Criminal Evidence Act 1999, para. 2 ch. 1.
5   The notion is used in international refugee law: *cf.* Council Directive 2003/9/EC of 27 January 2003 laying down minimum standards for the reception of asylum seekers, regarding children in armed conflict [2003] OJ L31/18; *cf.* General Assembly Resolution A/RES/54/263 of 25 May 2000, Optional Protocol to the Convention on the Rights of the Child on the involvement of children in armed conflict.
6   The notion of vulnerable person replace those of 'poverty' or 'exclusion' in the field of social sciences, *cf.* Marc Henri Soulet, 'La vulnérabilité, une ressource à manier avec prudence', *in* Burgorgue-Larsen, *supra* note 3, at 11.
7   L'auteure emploie la règle de proximité.
8   Cf. for example : Directive 2013/33/EU of the European parliament and of the Council of 26 June 2013 laying down standards for the reception of applicants for international protection (recast), art. 21: 'Member States shall take into account the specific situation of vulnerable persons such as minors, unaccompanied minors, disabled people, elderly people, pregnant women, single parents with minor children, victims of human trafficking, persons with serious illnesses, persons with mental disorders and persons who have been subjected to torture, rape or other serious forms of psychological, physical or sexual violence, such as victims of female genital mutilation, in the national law implementing this Directive'. Cf. Directive 2004/83/EC of 29 April 2004 on minimum standards for the qualification and status of third country nationals or stateless persons as refugees or as persons who otherwise need

person in international law: this is a person in danger of being exposed to a grave risk on account of their particular weakness.[9] Vulnerability is thus an open concept illustrating a progressive and current trend in scientific research tending to abandon the compartmentalization of disciplines. Its intrinsic conceptual characteristics that enable it to grasp/pinpoint several problematic aspects of social reality and its plastic qualities are likely to explain the spread of this concept as well as the capacity of different disciplinary approaches to grasp it.

Beyond its plasticity, which conveys unified representations whilst it concerns very different situations, the reference to vulnerability in international law reflects the contemporary concerns of a world in 'crisis' – whether as an economic, climatic or identity crisis. In a troubled context of fear or hope for deep change, it stands out as a central reference, a corollary of the notions of risk and insecurity. Since the end of the 1970s, the *crisis* confers a new political dimension on the notion of risk, 'changing it even into an ideology of security'.[10] Safety gradually becomes 'a major claim of populations',[11] a collective requirement. This phenomenon, maintained by persistent threats – in particular, terrorist threats – is essentially observed in industrialized societies, focused on the acquisition and enjoyment of material assets, which, at the same time, promote the values of individualism. It is moreover striking that sociological writings related to vulnerability generally analyze capitalist societies.[12] Widely conveyed by political and media speeches, the notions of crisis – and of the risks involved – are massively invading numerous fields such as politics, economy, ecology, and law. Vulnerability is also analyzed as a western concept. Institutions considered to have stemmed from western powers, such as the European Court of Human Rights,[13] the International Criminal Court,[14] the

---

international protection and the content of the protection granted.; XIV Ibero-American Judicial Summit, Brasilia Regulations regarding Access to Justice for Vulnerable People, Brasilia, 2008, §3.

9 Marion Blondel, La personne vulnérable en droit international, Thèse de doctorat, Université de Bordeaux, 2015 (à paraître).

10 David Le Breton, *Sociologie du risque*, (Paris, PUF, coll. Que sais-je ?, n°3016, 2012) 57.

11 Frank Furedi, *The Culture of Fear: Risk Taking and the Morality of Low Expectation*, (London, Cassel, 2002).

12 Cf. Viviane Châtel and Shirley Roy (eds), *Penser la vulnérabilité: visages de la fragilisation du social* (Presses universitaires de l'Université du Québec, 2008).

13 Cf. Lucius Caflisch, 'Approche légale d'ancien juge à la Cour Européenne des Droits de l'Homme', in Conférence Les 4 Vents, *Les droits de l'Homme, un luxe occidental ?*, (Université de Fribourg, 2008).

14 Serge Sur, 'Le droit international pénal entre l'Etat et la société internationale', Actualité et droit international, *Revue d'analyse juridique de l'actualité internationale* (publication

International Court of Justice and more widely the United Nations (UN),[15] use this reference first and foremost. Just like the notion of crisis, vulnerability concerns firstly rich societies as it is considered to be an evil 'in progress':[16] it is not a matter of helping a victim, but preventing the risk that leads to the creation of a victim. Hence, taking into account the vulnerable person implies a perfected institutional system, able to anticipate the realization of risk or limit its effects, for instance by insurance mechanisms.[17]

This occidental context modernizes classical legal theory. The latter is based on a conception of the individual as a 'non substantial and non sensitive being',[18] whose neutrality leads to his enfoldment by binding legal statuses. Yet, 'this traditional epistemological posture is pushed aside by a desire of individuation, of recognition of the being's peculiarities, demanding a consideration of its feelings by the law'.[19] Its satisfaction would lead to a new function of law: to contribute to the being's fulfilment. This movement considers that the human being is not only endowed with reason but is also capable of emotions. The human being's vulnerability supposes nothing less than a modernized legal conception of the individual and its protection. The exponential use of the notion of vulnerable person therefore seems to be a sign of a new mission of protection assigned to international law. In reality, protection of the individual is a classic foundation of domestic and international law. Following the idea that 'whilst helplessness still seems to concern the same type of phenomena, the words however transform',[20] the notion of vulnerability could be

---

du RIDI, octobre 2001) 8, para. 2. For example, in March 2013, the president of the African Union claimed that the ICC prosecute only African people.

15   Cf. United nations Charter of 26 June 1945, Ch. XII: international trusteeship system. The ICJ and the United nations use to use the notion of 'civilized nations', which implies that there were 'uncivilized nations', seemed as 'the legacy of the period, now passed away, of colonialism': *North sea continental shelf cases, Federal Republic of Germany vs Netherlands*, separate opinion of judge Ammoun (ICJ, 20 February 1969, Rec. 1969) 133. See also Georges Fischer, 'Les réactions devant l'arrêt de la Cour internationale de Justice concernant le Sud-Ouest africain' (AFDI, vol.12, 1966, Paris, CNRS) 148.

16   If vulnerabilty can be assumed as 'a world of loss', it is because there is a 'have': Guillaume Le Blanc, *Que faire de notre vulnérabilité ?* (Montrouge, Bayard, 2011) 49.

17   Cf. Deepa Narayan and others, *Voices of the Poor: Crying Out for Change* (New York, Oxford University Press, 2000).

18   Vincente Fortier and Sébastien Lebel-Grenier (eds), *Les sentiments et le droit, Rencontres juridiques Montpellier- Sherbrooke* (Sherbrooke, Éditions Revue de droit de l'Université de Sherbrooke, 2012).

19   *Ibid.*

20   Florence Faberon, 'Vulnérabilité dans le droit de l'aide et de l'action sociale', in Elisabeth Paillet and Pascal Richard (eds), *Effectivité des droits et vulnérabilité de la personne* (CERC, Bruylant, 2014) 51.

understood 'as a new ornament for an already well-established notion'.[21] However, this notion can also be conceived as a new instrument used to strengthen the individual's protection. Thus, vulnerability converges with the current emphasis placed on individuals by international legal society.

The ambivalence of vulnerability is linked to the notion of a *crisis* of international law. This notion can be understood in a negative sense, which relates to the idea of a precarious and decisive moment for the international legal order. It can also be apprehended in a more constructive sense, as a decision answering an upheaval that has happened in life's ordinary course. In this second perspective, it seems essential that the use of vulnerability does not embody a simple 'latest intellectual trend'.[22] In fact, vulnerability equates to an injunction: its observation, particularly in the *faces*[23] of children asking for asylum at Europe's doorstep, must lead to a real conceptualization of this type of individual protection. Taking into consideration its vulnerability embodies the need to refine the apprehension of social reality, by stressing certain particular aspects ignored until now.

Used within a liberal international society, this notion must however not fall into ideological faults which would risk annulling its protective effects, or would contribute to stressing the vulnerability of the person. Vulnerability's rhetoric can indeed contribute to a euphemism – even to a performativity – for social problems and disparities. In this respect, women often constitute invisible victims. They are not only vulnerable because they are placed in precarious situations in increasingly neoliberal systems; their vulnerability is also symbolically predetermined as it precedes their coming into the world and structures the way they act and identify with others and themselves. It is precisely because of this symbolic predetermination that guides and disciplines their gender, and other aspects of their lives before being able to consciously resist, that they are vulnerable.[24] For example, the representation of women within the UN – whose announced objective is the promotion of gender

---

21   Cf. Laurence Boisson de Chazournes, 'De la "responsabilité de protéger" ou d'une nouvelle parure pour une notion déjà bien établie' (RGDIP, n°1, 2006) 11–18.

22   Marc-Henri Soulet, 'La vulnérabilité, une ressource à manier avec prudence', in Burgorgue-Larsen (ed.), *supra* note 3, at 7.

23   Emmanuel Levinas, *Totality and Infinity* (translated by Alphonso Lingis, Duquesne U. Press, 1982) 48–5: 'The way in which the other presents himself, exceeding the idea of the other in me, we here name face' (Levinas derives the primacy of his ethics from the experience of the encounter with the Other. For Levinas, the irreducible relation of the 'face-to-face' experience is a privileged phenomenon in which the other person's proximity and distance are both strongly felt).

24   Judith Butler, 'Vulnerability and Resistance Revisisted' (public lecture at trinity College, 5 February 5 2015).

equality[25] – is unbalanced even today compared to men's.[26] Certain authors believe that this observation illustrates that international law, an androcentric law, structurally relegates women to a position of vulnerability, confirming a representation of the world and its dominant legal structure.[27]

Yet, vulnerability as an ontological trait – although traditionally assigned to women – can suggest a new conceptualization of the protection of the individual in international law. Considering vulnerability as a virtue[28] in international law leads to development of an ethical reading of the individual's protection to suggest legal solutions allowing human beings to live a better life. Virtue, in the Aristotelian sense, is not pure knowledge or an isolated action; it is a habit, a stable and lasting disposition of the will, acquired by exercise, to act well.[29] In order to effectively protect the vulnerable person in international law, it seems necessary to recognize vulnerability as an essential factor, and to make it a 'habit' in international legal practice. However, if vulnerability is to be taken into consideration in a durable manner, the liberal theoretical framework in which it is currently integrated must be adapted.

Indeed, the appeal to vulnerability in international law is of little use if the values on which the latter is based (competition, individual success, accumulation of assets) go against the requirements the former supposes. That is why effective protection of the vulnerable can be achieved by utilization of a care ethic in international law.[30] Having understood the ontological vulnerability of

---

25 Cf. United nations, Resolution adopted by the General Assembly on 22 September 2010, 'Keeping the promise: united to achieve the Millennium Development Goals', A/RES/65/1§72, 16–20, Millennium Development Goal 3 – Promote gender equality and empower women.

26 In 1995, 7% of senior officials were women; in 2013, they occupied one quarter of positions in the United Nations General Secretariat. Cf. Stéphanie Hennette-Vauchez, 'Le droit international malgré elle' in Hilary Charlesworth, Sexe, genre et droit international, (IREDIES, Paris, Pedone, coll. Doctrine (s), 2013) 3–42.

27 Juliette Gaté and Diane Roman, 'Droits des femmes et vulnérabilité, une relation ambivalente', in Paillet and Richard, supra note 20, at 229; Diane Roman, 'Les stéréotypes de genre : "vieilles lunes" ou nouvelles perspectives pour le droit ?' in Stéphanie Hennette-Vauchez, and others (eds), Ce que le genre fait au droit (REGINE, Paris, Dalloz, coll. À droit ouvert) 2013.

28 Etymologically, 'virtue' comes from virtus (derived from the word 'vir' which designates the male human individual) and denotes masculine force and, by extension, 'value', 'discipline'. Cf. Aristot'e, Nicomachean Ethics, Book 1, Ch 11, 1100b 20–35, (Flammarion 2004), 85–86; Martha Nussbaum, 'Aristote et la fragilité de la bonté' (Bulletin de la Société française de philosophie, 1987, vol.81, n°4) 117–144.

29 Aristotle, Nicomachean Ethics, Book 2, Ch 1, 1103b-1105a, (Les Echos du Maquis, 2014) 42–43.

30 See the Preamble of the 2011 ILO Convention (n°189) on domestic workers, Convention concerning decent work for domestic workers (entry into force: 5 September 2013): 'Considering that domestic work continues to be undervalued and invisible and is mainly

the individual, *care* ethics – firstly formulated in the 1980s in America – postulates that human bonds cannot be resumed to trade exchanges. The *care* ethic is generally defined 'as a generic activity which includes all our actions to maintain, perpetuate and repair our world, so that we can live in it as well as possible'.[31] It involves 'a complex set of practices, which extend from very intimate feelings such as "maternal thoughts" to extremely wide actions such as designing public education systems'.[32] The interpretation of *care*, according to Joan Tronto, confers on it a real political dimension[33] which allows establishing the operational effectiveness of the notion of a vulnerable person in international law: pulling away from 'romantic'[34] revolutionary theories, the author tries to concretize *care* in current society, postulating that 'if we seriously considered *care*, even traditional liberal thought would be transformed'.[35] Solicitude was depreciated for a long time as it was linked to the – often feminine – private and emotional sphere. It also contradicted such praiseworthy qualities in our society as the advocated values of individual success and autonomy. It is thus an issue of 'rethinking our conceptions of human nature and abandoning the dilemma of autonomy or dependence',[36] postulated by contemporary international law, in order to build 'a more elaborate feeling of human interdependence'[37]

International law can be an instrument for realization of *care*. This postulate leads to suggesting the idea of 'strength of vulnerability'.[38] Indeed, 'not only [vulnerability] pushes to action, creates possibilities, but it is also a synonym of otherness, it initiates introductions and creates solidarity'.[39] A person's vulnerability reveals a link of interdependence between human beings, who share a common vulnerability, allowing *care* to express itself.[40] Vulnerability also arouses reaction, even revolt, especially in times of crisis. While the

---

carried out by women and girls, many of whom are migrants or members of disadvantaged communities and who are particularly vulnerable to discrimination in respect of conditions of employment and of work, and to other abuses of human rights'.

[31] Berenice Fischer and Joan Tronto, 'Toward a Feminist Theory of Caring', in Emily Abel and Margaret Nelson (eds), *Circles of care*, (Albany, Suny Press, 1990) 40.
[32] Joan Tronto, *Le risque ou le care ?*, (Paris, PUF, coll. Care studies, 2012) 31.
[33] Joan Tronto, *Un monde vulnérable : pour une politique du 'care'*, (Paris, La découverte, 2009) 9.
[34] *Ibid.*, 21.
[35] *Ibid.*
[36] *Ibid.*, 141.
[37] *Ibid.*
[38] Elisabeth Paillet, 'Avant-propos', in Paillet and Richard, *supra* note 20, at 5.
[39] *Ibid.*
[40] Cf. Sandra Laugier, *Tous vulnérables ? Le care, les animaux et l'environnement* (Paris, Payot et rivages, coll. Petite bibliothèque Payot 2012).

incapable person is the object of assistance, the vulnerable subject is an actor, mobilizing tools 'allowing the protection of the person by itself, by favouring autonomy and responsibility'.[41] So, vulnerability relates on the one hand to the concept of solicitude, which expresses the capacity to care about an identified vulnerable subject, that is, 'a relational ethic structured by the attention to others'.[42] On the other hand, it relates to the notion of care, which includes a set of activities or social practices that together problematize the fact of taking and receiving care. Applying the notion of the vulnerable person in international law within the *care* framework leads to analysis of the existing interdependent relation between people (I.) and of the conception of the vulnerable person's autonomy (II.).

1 Vulnerability as a Relation

Vulnerability's ontological dimension is intrinsically linked to the notion of otherness. The utilization of vulnerability in international law leads to a reappraisal of the individual's legal protection. By taking into account the factors of dependence and responsibility, a relational dimension is included in this protection. 'To recognize that we share vulnerability is recognizing the dignity of others, in a relation of equal to equal'.[43] For Paul Ricœur, a person's vulnerability can only be perceived within a relationship with others: the action, the individua's voice cannot exist without others, which is straightaway included in the possibility for the *self* to accomplish itself. Intersubjectivity – in particular by means of social, political and legal institutions – is thus a fundamental condition for the realization of capabilities.[44] This corresponds to the spirit of '*care*', which can be translated to 'solicitude'. This 'attentive care provided to one person, and to what concerns it'[45] firstly implies recognizing their existence, their identity (A). But *care* is also inseparable from the notion of burden:[46]

---

41 Bénédicte Lavaud Legendre, 'La paradoxale protection de la personne vulnérable par elle-même: les contradictions d'un "droit de la vulnérabilité" en construction'» (RDSS, 2010) 520.
42 Fabienne Brugère, *L'éthique du 'care'* (Paris, PUF, coll. Que sais-je ?, 2014) 3.
43 Premières Rencontres scientifiques sur l'autonomie de la Caisse nationale de solidarité pour l'autonomie, *Évaluer pour accompagner* (Paris, 2009) 8.
44 Paul Ricoeur, *Soi-même comme un autre* (Paris, Seuil, coll. 'Points essais', 1997); Amartya Sen, *Ethique et économie* (Paris, PUF, coll. Quadrige, Grands textes, 1993).
45 Centre National de Ressources Textuelles et Lexicales, CNRS, ATILF, Portail lexical, Lexicographie, Sollicitude.
46 Nel Noddings, *Caring: A Feminine Approach to Ethics and Moral Education* (Berkeley, University of California Press, 1984) 9.

'to care implies more than a simple desire or temporary interest, but much rather the compliance to a form of transfer of responsibility'.[47] Taking into consideration vulnerability supposes a form of commitment, which can be translated in international law as a broadened concept of responsibility (B).

1.1 An Aspiration to Recognition

The reference to vulnerability can paradoxically lead to the effacement of certain populations on the legal scene, even to the performativity of their vulnerability. In contrast, its analysis through the *care* prism should reveal them. It is indeed the purpose of the 'caring about' of the care ethic developed by Joan Tronto, who aims to recognize the existence of the vulnerable person's need, which supposes a form of attention to its reality. Firstly, protection of the vulnerable person implies fulfilment of its identity. This can equate to legal recognition of its existence, of rights and to acceptance of the expression of those rights. Vulnerability then reveals itself to be an instrument for promotion of pluralism on an international scale. Indeed, evaluating the need for people's protection can only be done within the framework of a 'democratic process where the addressees are taken seriously, instead of being delegitimized because they are in necessity'.[48] The concept of *care*, the active process of putting those who take care and those who benefit from it into relation with one another is thus essentially democratic.[49]

This search for pluralism constitutes an aspiration of contemporary international law. In a general way, the UN promotes the actual participation of all populations to the democratic process.[50] The treatment of native populations is in this respect significant. With the 1989 Convention of the International Labour Organization (ILO) on Native and Tribal Populations in Independent Countries[51] and the 2007 UN Declaration on the Rights of Native People,[52] recognition of a nation's multicultural composition and legal pluralism is

---

47 Tronto, *supra* note 31, at 143.
48 *Ibid.*, 186.
49 This democratic requirement is essential to avoid a perpetuation of the domination of the healer – which imposes on the nursed – classic plan of colonization.
50 Cf. Human Development Report 2002 Deepening Democracy in a Fragmented World Published for the United Nations Development Programme, New York, Oxford, Oxford University Press, 2002; United Nations, General Assembly, Resolution adopted by the General Assembly on 16 September 2005, World Summit Outcome, A/RES/60/1.
51 Convention concerning Indigenous and Tribal People in Independent Countries, 1989, n°169, entry into force: 5 September 1991.
52 Resolution adopted by the General Assembly, United Nations Declaration on the Rights of Indigenous People of 13 September 2007, doc. AG/RES/61/295.

gradually being introduced in certain constitutions.[53] Native peoples are invited to expose their views on social, economic and cultural questions and to participate in the democratic process from which they were previously excluded.

At the regional level, the 1995 Framework Convention for the Protection of National Minorities on the initiative of the Council of Europe, expresses 'that a pluralistic and really democratic society not only has to respect the ethnic, cultural, linguistic and religious identity of every person belonging to a national minority, but also to create conditions appropriate to allow to express, to protect and to develop this identity'.[54] Additionally, the Charter of Fundamental Rights of the European Union supports that 'the Union contributes to the preservation and to the development of these common values while respecting the diversity of the cultures and traditions of the peoples of Europe'.[55] At the jurisdictional level, we can mention the activism of the Court of San Jose for taking into consideration the cultural specificity of native peoples because of their 'situation of special vulnerability'.[56] In its ruling *Yatama against Nicaragua*,[57] having recalled that democracy is a fundamental element of the Inter-American system of human rights,[58] the Court insisted that every citizen must be able to take part in elections, if he respects the legal requirements, thus excluding any non justified restrictions of this right by the state.[59] On this basis, the judges took into consideration the Indian sense of identity by obliging the state to offer a legal framework allowing the representatives of this native community – qualified explicitly as a vulnerable group by the Court – to become part of the political representation. If the ethic of care calls for considerating the particular needs of individuals, particularly in terms of representation, it seems that international law is compatible with this objective.

1.2   A Widened Conception of Responsibility

The concept of individual vulnerability induces a renewed understanding of responsibility in international law as Joan Tronto's care ethics can be linked

---

53   Constitutions of Ecuador of 2008 and Bolivia of 2009 – proclaiming the foundation of a "social State of multinational right".
54   Framework Convention for the Protection of national Minorities and explanatory Report, February 1995, Preamble.
55   Charter of Fundamental Rights of the European Union, 18 December 2000, (2000/C 364/01), Preamble.
56   *Community Yakye Axa v. Paraguay*, Merits, Reparations and Costs (IACHR ser. C n°125, 17 June 2005) 63.
57   *Yatama v. Nicaragua*, Preliminary Objections, Merits, Reparations and Costs (IACHR ser. C n°127, 23 June 2005).
58   *Ibid.*, 191–193.
59   *Ibid.*, 199.

with the responsibility to protect doctrine. In international law, responsibility can traditionally be defined as a 'set of new legal relations resulting from an internationally illicit fact of a subject of international law (essentially a State or an international organization but also, in some cases, a national liberation movement or a private person)'.[60] Yet, within the framework of *care*, responsibility has 'at the same time a different connotation and a different context'..[61] Care exceeds the limits of legal reasoning by promoting global responsibilization, both institutional and individual. In this respect, vulnerability can contribute to the establishment of a link between the legal and ethical spheres on the ground of responsibility. This illustrates a renewed understanding of international responsibility with regard to the individual, which we can detect in certain contemporary instruments of international law.[62] Acknowledgment of a person's vulnerability is not foreign to the reflections relative to responsibility in contemporary international law.[63] The principle of responsibility to protect,[64] as a corollary of the notion of human safety, is based on this observation.[65] It is in this context that the reference to vulnerability best brings to light the possibility of the link between *care* and international law on the ground of responsibility. The principle of responsibility to protect distinguishes itself from classic designs of international responsibility. Its concept 'affects

---

60   Jean Salmon (ed.), *Dictionnaire de droit international public* (Bruxelles, AUF, Bruylant, 2001) 995.
61   Tronto, *supra* note 31, at 178.
62   Cf. Universal Declaration on Bioethics and Human Rights of 19 October 2005 'confirms, every human being has a claim to our care that must be respected' : The Principle of Respect for human Vulnerability and personal Integrity, Report of the International Bioethics Committee of UNESCO (IBC), 2013, para. 5.
63   United Nations, International Law Commission, Report on the work of its fifty-third session (23 April–1 June and 2 July–10 August 2001), 24 October 2001, A /56/10/Corr.1, 29–470; Alain Pellet, 'The definition of responsibility in international law', in James Crawford, and others (eds), *The Law of International Responsibility* (Oxford University Press, 2010) 3–16; Brigitte Stern, 'Les dilemmes de la responsabilité internationale aujourd'hui', in Chriastian Poncelet (ed.), *Vers de nouvelles normes en droit de la responsabilité publique* (actes du colloque, le 11 et 12 mai 2001).
64   Resolution adopted by the General Assembly on 16 September 2005, 'World Summit Outcome', doc. A/60/1. 2005, 24 October 2005; Resolution 1674 (2006) adopted by the Security Council on 28 April 2006, 'Protection of civilians in armed conflict', doc. S/RES/1674(2006), confirmed by Resolution 1738 (2006) adopted by the Security Council on 23 December 2006, 'Protection of civilians in armed conflict', doc. S /RES/1738 (2006). At regional level: European Parliament resolution on the situation in Darfur, 28 September 2006; European Parliament resolution on the situation in Darfur, 15 February 2007.
65   International Commission on Intervention and State Sovereignty, *The Responsibility to Protect*, Report, December 2001, International Development Research Centre, para. 1.19/ para. 3.23.

and obliges to look for its sense in other domains such as morality and politics'.[66] That is also a reason why this principle faces so much criticism.[67]

Operating in the field of state international responsibility and being highly controversial, the responsibility to protect doctrine involves ethical, legal and political features. Therefore, it can converge with *care* ethics in order to improve the protection of vulnerable persons. Utilizing this doctrine in particularly serious circumstances can overshadow the compensatory and punitive character of the classic responsibility concept. This also coincides with the definition of 'taking care' developed by Joan Tronto: 'taking care' implies 'to undertake responsibility pertaining to an identified need, [...] to recognize that one can act in order to fulfill these unsatisfied needs'.[68] Thus, responsibility acquires a proactive character: 'one is responsible for his own acts as for the individuals placed under one's care [...] It is an obligation that requires a positive action going beyond the compensatory and punitive framework'.[69] The notion of individual vulnerability therefore raises the question of the opportunity and the possibility to renew the notion of responsibility leading to development of a proactive understanding of the latter, operating *ex ante* rather than *ex post*. It triggers the establishment of preventive obligations which define an internationally wrongful act by linking it to breach of other obligations. For instance, the first article of the Convention on the Prevention and Punishment of the Crime of Genocide stipulates that states must 'undertake to prevent and to punish' genocide.

By contributing to rethinking the concept of responsibility in international law, vulnerability also affects the determination of debtors. It involves extending the addressees of international responsibility. This is in agreement with *care*'s design, which notices that *solicitude* is 'too often [...] defined as a necessary relation between two individuals, most of the time between a mother and her child'.[70] Care has to be analysed as 'a practice and a measure', which 'absorbs a big part of human activity':[71] it postulates a responsibility that exceeds the private sphere to extend to the political and legal spheres. Within the principle of responsibility to protect, the responsibility to take care of the vulnerable

---

66 Hassan Abdelhamid and others (eds), *Sécurité humaine et responsabilité de protéger, l'ordre humanitaire international en question* (Agence universitaire de la Francophonie, Paris, Editions des archives contemporaines, 2009) 97.
67 Cf. Anne Peters, "The Security Council's Responsibility to Protect", (*International Organizations Law Review* 8 2011), 1–40.
68 Tronto, *supra* note 31, at 148.
69 Paul Ricoeur, *Le Juste* (Paris, Editions Esprit, 1995) 42.
70 Tronto, *supra* note 31, at 144.
71 *Ibid.*, 145.

mainly falls on the state, because of its sovereignty.[72] This indeed implies inflexible obligations, as the guarantee of its population's human safety. This conception of responsibility fits with the 'to take care' requirement of the *care ethic*, which suggests meeting the needs of the vulnerable by carrying out material work, involving implementation of specific skills.[73] The objective here is effectiveness of protection, according to the idea that 'intending to care for another and even to assume responsibility towards them, but failing to provide adequate care is after all not answering the need'.[74] Non-intervention is then only blameworthy if the agent actually had the means to bend the course of events, that is, responsibility solely falls on the person actually capable of implementing it.[75] However the state is generally the best guarantor of the protection of vulnerable persons placed under its jurisdiction against serious violations of international law. It disposes of numerous means such as, in particular, the faculty of incorporating protective international instruments in its domestic law, establishing national institutions of protection or of effective judicial appeals.

But the principle of responsibility to protect also implies that in the case of a state's lack of action, the international community has grounds to intervene. Particularly, 'new international institutions and non-governmental organizations, concerned with the monitoring and promotion of worldwide implementation of human rights', can then provide protection for the vulnerable.[76] If implementation of the principle of responsibility to protect is debated,[77] international humanitarian law actually gives an illustration of *care giving*: by

---

72 Address by the Secretary-General of the United Nations at the opening of the World Conference on human rights Vienna, 14 June 1993, document A/Con.157/22: 'the State should be the best guarantor of human rights. It is the State that the international community should principally entrust with ensuring the protection of individuals'. International Commission on Intervention and State Sovereignty, *The Responsibility To Protect*, Report, December 2001, International Development Research Centre, §1.A: 'State sovereignty implies responsibility, and the primary responsibility for the protection of its people lies with the state itself'.

73 Alice Le Goff, 'Care, participation et délibération: Politiques du care et politique démocratique', in Marie Garrau and Alice Le Goff (eds), *Politiser le care? Perspectives sociologiques et philosophiques* (Le bord de l'eau, coll. Diagnostics, 2012) 104.

74 Tronto, *supra* note 31, at 179.

75 *Ibid.*, 180.

76 International Commission on Intervention and State Sovereignty, The Responsibility to Protect, Report, December 2001, International Development Research Centre, para. 1.27. Cf. 'there is growing recognition worldwide that the protection of human security, including human rights and human dignity, must be one of the fundamental objectives of modern international institutions' (para. 1.28).

77 Nabil Hajjami, *La responsabilité de protéger* (coll. de droit international, Bruylant 2013).

applying a sectoril approach, it appoints the most competent bodies for every mission of protection in order to optimize the efficiency of the help brought to populations.

But a transcription of the care ethic into international law seems to involve a more global empowerment of individuals. The Report of the International Committee of Bioethics on the principle of respect for human vulnerability and for personal integrity tries to extend application of UNESCO's Universal Declaration on Bioethics and Human rights, expressing that if 'article 1.2 of the Declaration clearly addresses States [...], States and governments are not the only addressees of article 8. [...] It is rather necessary to boost awareness of the responsibility that all sectors of society share'.[78] The idea is to build a culture of *care*, which seems to be difficult to exclusively establish 'from the top': individuals have to take their share of responsibility in the protection of their fellow men.[79]

However, if individuals are to take on responsibility for other individuals, the former have to become conscious of the existence of the latter. According to Emmanuel Levinas, in current Western society, exacerbation of the *Me* and dilution of solidarity tend to lead to the disappearance of the *Other*. In this perspective, vulnerability is 'the experience of the non-human, which consists in being an object for others'.[80] This indifference to *Others* is the foundation of vulnerability: excluded from my world, denied in its humanity, the *Other* has nothing in common with Me, the social link is annihilated. Yet, as far as international law embodies a societal choice, 'a continuous and progressive passage of moral norms and of the social environment's aspirations in international norms takes place'.[81] That is why *care* requires empowerment of the individual. At this stage, that responsibility can only be moral and has to be used as basis for a legal transcription: if *care* becomes a societal choice, its manifestations will establish material sources of law and they can lead to the enactment of rules of conduct.

---

78   The Principle of Respect for human Vulnerability and personal Integrity, Report of the International Bioethics Committee of UNESCO (IBC), 2013, para. 5.
79   It is the sense of the 'responsibility for others' developed by Emmanuel Levinas, according to whom concern for the other is that of the human being: Emmanuel Levinas, *Humanisme de l'autre homme* (Paris, Le livre de poche, 1996) 109.
80   Viviane Châtel, 'Agir en situation de vulnérabilité: Un essai de problématisation?', in Viviane Châtel and Marc-Henri Soulet (eds), *Agir en situation de vulnérabilité* (Sainte-Foy, Québec, Les Presses Universitaires de Laval, coll. Sociologie contemporaine, 2003) 24.
81   Paul Reuter, *Principes de droit international public* (RCADI, 1961, t.103) 480.

2 Vulnerability as Autonomy

International law traditionally supposes the person's[82] autonomy, understood as the individual's power to judge and act independently. Indeed, in contemporary Western society, 'the prevailing paradigm is unquestionably the adult individual acting in autonomy and thus at its own risk'.[83] In a capitalist context, this perception of the individual seems today to be understood as the antithesis of *care*, 'any type of dependency (being) treated as an unbearable weakness'.[84] It is possible that the appearance of vulnerability in the legal sphere will entail a progressive change in this perception, consistent with the ethics of *care*. This way, vulnerability and dependency would be viewed as natural characteristics of the human being, which 'complicate the traditional concept of autonomy'.[85] Indeed, theories of *care* depart from the Kantian conception of autonomy (conceived as the capacity for rational self-determination), interpreting it as the ability to have one's voice heard and engaging in acts that express that voice. This ability being only possible to the extent that individuals have the type of relationship to one another that the theory of *care* expects. Thus, analysis of the vulnerable person in international law, within the framework of *care* ethics, supposes to redefine the autonomy of the person (A). In turn, redefining entails a new definition of protection of the person: it is no longer a question of assisting a vulnerable person but of allowing that person to take an active part in their own protection (B).

2.1 *A Redefinition of the Concept of Autonomy*

Vulnerability implies that autonomy is no longer to be considered as a prerequisite, but rather as the object of a progressive conquest. It is Paul Ricœur's concept of the 'capable man'[86] that highlights the relational dimension of autonomy. A perfect illustration of this re-reading of the concept of autonomy of the person is shown in the law of incapacity, as initiated notably by Recommendation n° R(99)4 of the Council of Europe[87] and the Convention on the

---

82 Cf. Robert Kolb, *Théorie du droit international* (second éd., Bruxelles, Bruylant, coll. de droit international, 2013, Pt 3) para. 7.
83 Bjarne Melkevic, 'Vulnérabilité de la personne et effectivité des droits de l'homme: une question de potentialité', in Paillet and Richard, *supra* note 20, at 181.
84 Tronto, *supra* note 31, at 169.
85 Marie Garrau and Alice Le Goff, *Care, justice et dépendance: Introduction aux théories du care* (Paris, PUF, 2010) 7.
86 Paul Ricœur, 'Devenir capable, être reconnu' (Esprit, n°7, juillet 2005).
87 Principles concerning the legal protection of incapable adults – Recommendation n°R (99) 4 and explanatory memorandum (1999).

International Protection of Adults of 13 January 2000.[88] Where the principles of freedom and equality in dignity and in rights of the Universal Declaration of Human Rights are translated in civil law by the recognition of the complete and equal capacity of all individuals, which guarantees freedom to act autonomously, the dialectical nature of vulnerability 'forces to handle jointly what could be considered at first sight as inflexible opposite situations, autonomy and dependence'.[89] The introduction of vulnerability implies a dynamic balance between these two situations.[90] The works of the International Committee of Bioethics in connection with UNESCO's 2005 Universal Declaration on Bioethics and Human Rights[91] well illustrate this evolution. The Report on the Principle of Respect for Human Vulnerability and for Personal Integrity thus provides that taking into account

> vulnerability acknowledges that we all may lack at some point the ability or the means to protect ourselves [...]. We are all confronted with the possibility of disease, disability and environmental risks. At the same time, we live with the possibility that harm, even death, can be caused by other human beings.[92]

This emphasis on the ontological and relational aspects of vulnerability allows redefining choices of protection. Thus, the Report can be linked to *care* ethics: calling on the need for 'solicitude',[93] the Report suggests that 'acknowledging the reality of vulnerability might provide a bridge between the moral "strangers" of a pluralistic society, thereby enhancing the value of solidarity rather than mere individual interests'.[94] In this way, international law takes into account the 'importance of compassion and empathy [...]. Sensibility is valued as a dimension of humanity, excluding any radical distinction between the vulnerable and autonomous subjects'.[95] Reference to vulnerability therefore allows for a different understanding of the relations between one another, no

---

88   Convention of 13 January 2000 on the International Protection of Adults, Hague, Conference on Private International Law, art. 1.
89   Marc-Henri Soulet, 'La vulnérabilité, une ressource à manier avec prudence', in Burgorgue-Larsen, *supra* note 3, at 26.
90   Cf. *Aristote, Eudemian ethics*, Book III, Ch 1, 1228a.
91   Universal Declaration on Bioethics and Human Rights, 19 October 2005.
92   The Principle of Respect for human Vulnerability and personal Integrity, Report of the International Bioethics Committee of UNESCO (IBC), 2013, para. 6.
93   *Ibid.*, para. 5.
94   *Ibid.*, para. 9.
95   Céline Ruet, *La vulnérabilité dans la jurisprudence de la Cour européenne des droits de l'homme* (RTDH, n°102, 2015, Nemesis) 321.

longer based on individual autonomy, but on the idea of solidarity, of a shared autonomy.[96]

To guarantee the best possible protection, the sharing of autonomy can be analytically structured 'by the model of interlocution, with first emphasis being placed on the first person, "I", the second emphasis being one in which "you" puts the accent on the face-to-face encounter [...]; finally, the third person characterizes the last form of the sharing of autonomy, where the status of the person is guaranteed as a possible "he" or "she"'.[97] The protective measure thus has to aim at encouraging a person's initiative, and at assisting and reassuring them when necessary. Thus, a more complex understanding of the individual takes shape as their 'unity [is] not residing in autonomy alone, but in a community of sensibility where the individuality factor does not exclude the possibility of being part of a group. The introduction of vulnerability does not seem to result in a clear-cut separation between categories of subjects, autonomous and vulnerable: one's duties towards vulnerable persons become clearer and the idea of assisting the autonomy of such vulnerable persons is developing'.[98] For instance, the Universal Declaration on Bioethics and Human Rights insists on the necessity to afford special protection to persons unable to express their consent, particularly in the context of research or medical practice where 'the person concerned should be involved to the greatest extent possible in the decision-making process of consent, as well as that of withdrawing consent'.[99] The protective measure must allow a person, for example by way of representation, to maintain their place in society. In this respect, the International Committee of Bioethics emphasises in particular the importance of women's participation in any type of decision-making.[100]

Reference to vulnerability also implies an understanding of autonomy as the freedom to live one's life as one chooses. Following the millions of casualties caused by the two World Wars, international law was influenced by a movement of subjectivisation, refocusing on the individual and on the ways individual needs are to be fulfilled. In this context, the concept of autonomy evolves and requires today 'a little more than legal capacity, that is, in fact, the

---

96 Benoît Eyraud, *Protéger et rendre capable. La considération civile et sociale des personnes très vulnérables* (éd. Erés, coll. Études, recherches, actions en santé mentale en Europe, 2013).
97 *Ibid.*, 379.
98 Ruet, *supra* note 95, at 340.
99 Universal Declaration on Bioethics and Human Rights, 19 October 2005, art.7.
100 The Principle of Respect for human Vulnerability and personal Integrity, Report of the International Bioethics Committee of UNESCO (IBC), 2013, para. 42.

ability to move freely'.[101] In this way, reference to vulnerability supports the concept of personal autonomy, which appeared in the early 2000s in the European legal order.[102] This concept is defined as 'the faculty for the human being to live his or her life as he or she intends it, [...] to decide freely on the choices to be made in the construction of his or her personality, and to claim such choices so that they are legally recognized and protected in the context of his or her relations with others'.[103] The use of the concept of personal autonomy indeed allows 'to legally register personal identities and behavior which could have previously socially disadvantaged certain persons, such as those in a vulnerable situation'.[104] An example of this can be found in the dispute concerning the Roma/Gypsies before the European Court of Human Rights. In 1996, in the case of *Buckley against the United Kingdom*,[105] the Court refused to recognize that the traditional lifestyle of the members of a minority, living in a caravan, could affect enforcement of town planning regulations by invoking article 8 of the Convention. Their vulnerability was only mentioned by the partially dissenting opinion of Judge B. Repik. However, in the 2004 case of *Connors against the United Kingdom* the Court found on the contrary that 'the vulnerable position of gypsies as a minority means that some special consideration should be given to their needs and their different lifestyle [...]. To this extent, there is thus a positive obligation imposed on the Contracting States by virtue of Article 8 to facilitate the gypsy way of life'.[106] In this context, the concept of personal autonomy aims at promoting social equality by legally protecting certain groups due to their vulnerability. It then contributes to the construction of a plural society.

2.2 An Encouraged Participation

The concept of vulnerability implies that of resilience, of the idea of the individual's struggle to full autonomy. The ethics of *care* according to Joan Tronto refuses to consider 'those who are in need [...] as a passive element of the

---

101 Cour de cassation, Rapport annuel 2009, *Les personnes vulnérables dans la jurisprudence de la Cour de cassation*, Paris, La documentation française, 58.
102 *Pretty v. UK*, App n°2346/02 (ECHR, 2002).
103 *Ibid.*
104 Hélène Hurpy, *Fonction de l'autonomie personnelle et protection des droits de la personne humaine dans les jurisprudences constitutionnelles et européennes* (Bruxelles, Bruylant, 2015).
105 *Buckley v. UK*, Appl. n°20348/92 (ECHR, 1996).
106 *Connors v. UK*, Appl. n°66746/01 (ECHR, 2004) 84.

process'.[107] On the contrary, it makes reference to the theory of capabilities[108] to assert *care* as an active process of protection, where the vulnerable person participates in their own resilience. While the unable person is the object of care, the vulnerable person becomes an actor. As opposed to marginalization, exclusion, poverty, all of which are concepts involving a lack, pointing to what the individual may lack, vulnerability emphasizes the individual's ability to react. 'It is in this way an intrinsically enabling term'.[109] It seems that international law adopts this participative approach to protection. This can be illustrated by the United Nations' Convention on the Rights of Persons with Disabilities,[110] the negotiation and drafting of which involved organizations representing these very persons. Moreover, Article 4 of this treaty states that this role must be preserved; it requires Member States to 'closely consult' and 'actively involve' disabled persons in the decision-making process concerning them.[111]

This enabling approach is today translated by the term 'empowerment'. Literally meaning to 'strengthen or acquire power', the term has been used in international development law since the 1990s,[112] generally in the context of the struggle against poverty[113] or more specifically gender issues.[114] Moreover, one of the first formulations in this domain stems from the DAWN network.[115]

---

[107] Tronto, *supra* note 31, at 186.

[108] Cf. Martha Nussbaum, Amartya Sen, *The Quality of Life* (Oxford, Clarendon Press, UNU-WIDER Studies in Development Economics, 1993); Amartya Sen, *Commodities and Capabilities* (Oxford, Oxford University Press, 1999).

[109] Marc-Henri Soulet, 'La vulnérabilité, une ressource à manier avec prudence', in Burgorgue-Larsen, *supra* note 3, at 24.

[110] United Nations Convention on the Rights of Persons with Disabilities, December 2006. Cf. International Day of Disabled Persons, 2004, 'Nothing about us without us!'.

[111] United Nations Convention on the Rights of Persons with Disabilities, December 2006, art. 3§4. cf. art. 33.3: 'Civil society, in particular persons with disabilities and their representative organizations, shall be involved and participate fully in the monitoring process'.

[112] The term has been used since the end of the 1970s in domains such as social psychology or public health. Cf. Barbara Simon, *The Empowerment Tradition in American Social Work: a History* (New York, Columbia University Press, 1994).

[113] Kwok-Fu Wong, *Empowerment as a Panacea for Poverty, Old Wine in new Bottles? Reflections on the World's Bank's Conception of Power* (Progress in Development Studies, vol.3, 2003) 307–322.

[114] Gita Sen, Caren Grown, *Development, Crisis and alternative visions: Third World Women's Perspectives* (New York, Monthly Review Press, 1987). This question is still on the agenda: 'Promote gender equality and the empowerment of women' is actually the third of eight Millennium development goals, adopted in 2000 during the Millennium summit.

[115] The network 'Development Alternatives with Women for a New area' consists of researchers, activists and feminist politicians, at the origin of 'the empowerment approach' in the field of development.

Critical towards programmes concerning 'women and development' organized by the UN between 1976 and 1985, the network analysed the mechanisms underlying development and the methods used to draw out minorities from the social and economic structures maintaining them in poverty.[116] At the end of the Second World War, the idea of development was based on Western conceptions, emphasising the search for economic growth, the principle of free trade, and adherence to a multilateral commercial and monetary system. Thus, development law is not neutral, because it inevitably implies preconceived economic and cultural ideologies which are often transcribed in adopted legal principles.[117] Thought of as an answer to this issue, empowerment is from the beginning a critical concept. It does not conceive poverty as a lack of material resources, but as a process of exclusion from economic and social power (*disempowerment*).[118] It can therefore be used within the framework of human safety, which refocuses the purpose of development on the individual rather than on the state.

Empowerment can then be analysed as a method for achieving resilience. According to the World Bank, 'in its most general sense, empowerment is the extension of the freedom of choice and action. [It is] the increase of assets and capabilities of poor people allowing them to participate, to negotiate, to influence, to check and to hold the institutions that condition their lives accountable'.[119] Hence, empowerment is 'the process of strengthening the capacity of individuals or groups to make voluntary choices and to transform these choices into actions and results'.[120] The idea is to influence the context in which the vulnerable person evolves as this context often has the effect of perpetuating vulnerability. Indeed, the ontological essence of vulnerability highlights the fact that incapacity to exercise real power over one's life would be at the origin of existential suffering contributing to performativity of a situation of vulnerability.[121]

---

116 Gita Sen, Caren Grown, *Development, Crisis and alternative Visions: Third World Women's Perspectives*, United Nations Convention on the rights of persons with disabilities, *supra* note 110, at 19.

117 Emmanuelle Jouannet, *Le droit international libéral-providence. Une histoire du droit international*, (Bruxelles, Bruylant, coll. de droit international, 2011) 322.

118 John Friedman, *Empowerment: the Politics of Alternative Development*, (Cambridge, Blackwell, 1992).

119 Anne-Emmanuelle Calvès, *"Empowerment": Généalogie d'un concept clé du discours contemporain sur le développement* (Revue Tiers Monde, vol.4, 2009) 742.

120 Ruth Alsop and others, *Empowerment in Practice: from Analysis to Implementation* (Washington DC, The World Bank, 2006).

121 Margot Breton, *On the Meaning of Empowerment and Empowerment-oriented Social Work* (Social Work with Groups, vol.17, n°3, 1994) 23–27; Seymour Sarason, *Psychology Misdirected: The Psychologist in the Social Order* (New York, The Free Press, 1981).

VULNERABILITY AS A VIRTUE 217

This necessity 'to strengthen or acquire some power'[122] is present in international humanitarian law. For instance, nowadays, protection of displaced persons within camps bypasses their participation in the construction of infrastructures but also in the daily management of the camp. In particular, the operational instruments of the Norwegian Refugee Council insist on the fact that:

> Participation, especially in governance, mitigates those effects by giving people back some power – building self-reliance and a sense of achievement, influence and control – restoring some of the dignity that has been taken away. It gives people an opportunity to make choices that restore some sense of normality, enabling them to be the subject, and not the object of their own lives. Participation and involvement creates opportunities for people to solve their own problems and can lead to growing self-esteem and help them overcome trauma.[123]

This participation in the decision-making process can become a reality through representation by traditional or elected leaders or heads, by means of camp committees, the idea being to lay the foundations of a kind of local governance.[124] In this respect, the importance of women's participation is widely put forward by the international instruments of empowerment.[125]

A particular manifestation of empowerment in international law is related to the idea of contractualization. Similarly to the domestic level, 'contractual procedures pertain to the idea that it is not only necessary to insert but still "insert with".[126] The contract can, indeed, be an instrument allowing a rebalancing, at least formally, of the relation: in recognizing the vulnerable person as a legitimate contracting party, capable of taking part in their own protection, the contract marks a break with the unilateral decision-making process regarding assistance. This idea is linked to the ethics of *care* as 'to take care […] is not assistance, but it defines a social logic of intervention in the life of others which implies being conscious of the vulnerability of weakened lives'.[127] This formal appreciation of the vulnerable person is not trivial as far as 'in the law,

---

122 Calvès, *supra* note 113, at 735.
123 Norwegian Refugee Council, *Camp management toolkit, 2008*, 79.
124 *Ibid.*
125 *Cf.* Office of the Special Adviser on Gender Issues and Advancement of Women, gender mainstreaming an overview, United Nations, New York, 2002; Fourth World Conference on Women, Report of the fourth world Conference on women, Beijing, 4–15 September 1995, 17 October 1995, A/CONF.177/20.
126 Faberon, *supra* note 20, at 58.
127 Tronto, *supra* note 31, at 179; See also Fabienne Brugère, *L'éthique du care* (Paris, PUF, 2011).

there is always a psychological dimension'.[128] We find numerous illustrations of this contractual trend in relations with the vulnerable person in international law. In international humanitarian law, it can be shown by the employment and empowerment of refugees and displaced persons within camps. This contributes to reconstruction of their self-esteem, and to their resilience following the traumas they have undergone.[129] In another sense, European law also works in this direction: The Head office for development and cooperation (EuropeAid) insists on the necessity of assuring legal enabling as well as access to justice for 'disadvantaged individuals or marginalized groups' and sets up numerous projects promoting empowerment of vulnerable people.[130] Therefore, empowerment tries to restore the individual's place as a legal subject in society.

However, empowerment presents certain dangers. At first, its vagueness, aiming at flexibility and at the operational effectiveness of protection, can render identifying the legal answer difficult. International law is increasingly using the notion of empowerment, without really determining what it consists in or how to evaluate it. Indicators used to measure it, such as the Indicator of the participation of women (*Gender Empowerment Measure*) of the UN Development Programme,[131] do not generally specify the ways implemented to achieve a result although these ways are elements leading to the empowerment. This approach finds itself in the Millennium Objectives, where the empowerment of women prescribes an objective, implemented by standard measures applicable to all. However, the essence of empowerment is to leave those on the ground to define objectives and methods of action.[132] The danger of a managerial reading of empowerment is that taking vulnerability into consideration could finally aim at a commitment to respect a predefined model of success, potentially leading to the disappearance of their particular identity. From this perspective, empowerment joins a 'movement transferring to the individual the task to build itself and to remain a responsible subject'.[133] This way,

---

128   Faberon, *supra* note 20, at 59–60.
129   Norwegian Refugee Council, 'Camp management toolkit, camp management project 2004', 24.
130   Cf. European Commission with UN Women, 'Promoting gender justice and empowerment of young women', Kyrgyzstan, July 2015; European Commission, 'High-Level Event on Women's Economic Empowerment and Sustainable Development' (2 March 2015, Riga).
131   UNDP, *Human Development Report 2004*, Economica, 217–237.
132   Resolution adopted by the General Assembly 55/2. United Nations Millennium Declaration, 8 September 2000, para 20.
133   Marc-Henri Soulet, 'La vulnérabilité comme catégorie de l'action publique', in Burgorgue-Larsen, *supra* note 3, at 50.

vulnerability maintains the illusion of individual merit whilst it conceals the part played by structural factors.

The success of empowerment supposes a context favourable to the deployment of capabilities. So, effective protection of the vulnerable can be based on a well-balanced sharing of responsibilities. This idea can relate to human safety logic, which seems to constitute a conceptual framework for empowerment allowing implementation of this sharing. Human safety establishes the link between protection by states and empowerment of individuals. Thus, human safety combines a top-down approach, charging states – but also international and regional organizations and civil society – to establish systematic, complete protection based on prevention, and an ascending approach aimed at developing the capacity of individuals to make choices and to act on their own behalf.[134] This way, protection allows offering a development framework for individuals' capabilities and empowerment leads to non-intervention in how they organize them.[135] So, these protective measures in the strict sense and empowerment of the vulnerable mutually strengthen themselves and thus inevitably operate together. The mission of international law should be that of achieving this balance, by establishing a favourable normative frame allowing the individual to completely fulfill their capabilities. In this sense, respect for the personal autonomy of the vulnerable can be strengthened for example by the mechanism of positive discrimination. For illustrative purposes, confronted with national reluctance relating to recognizing the right of minorities,[136] the Parliamentary Assembly of the Council of Europe (PACE) recommends implementing positive discrimination, in particular within the representative organs of the state, in order 'to associate more widely one or several minorities in the management of national affairs'.[137] Autonomy becomes a way to legally recognize vulnerable groups not represented within states until then. If this division of powers can follow several paths,[138] PACE urges 'every State to put in place

---

[134] Commission pour la Sécurité Humaine, *La sécurité humaine maintenant: rapport de la Commission sur la sécurité humaine* (Paris, Presses de Sciences po, 2003) 31.

[135] Martha Nussbaum, 'Aristotelian Social Democracy', in Bruce Douglass et al. (eds), *Liberalism and the Good* (London, Routledge, 1990) 214.

[136] Cf. for example for France: Conseil constitutionnel, *Décision du 6 mai 1991* (RGDIP, 1991) 797–798.

[137] Parliamentary Assembly, Political Affairs Committee, Report on Positive experiences of autonomous regions as a source of inspiration for conflict resolution in Europe, 3 June 2003, doc. 9824, para. 20; *Young, James and Webster v. UK*, App n°7601/76, 7806/77 (ECRH, 1981) 63.

[138] Ruth Lapidoth, *Autonomy, Flexible Solutions to Ethnic Conflicts* (Washington, United States Institute of Peace Press, 1997).

constitutional or legislative norms allowing for a transfer or allocation of powers for the benefit of these minorities'.[139]

3   Conclusion

Reference to the concept of vulnerability can have an ambivalent effect in the context of 'crisis'. On the one hand, vulnerability can eclipse individuals' demands relating to their legal existence and their need for specific protection. On the other hand, as this concept implies the contribution of new factors in protection of the individual, vulnerability can be grasped as a driving and resilient mechanism facing the 'crisis', thus justifying utilization of *care* ethics in international law.

As far as the ethics of *care* is the result of research in social sciences pertaining to the vulnerability of the person, it can be regarded as the framework in which the latter concept can be used in international law. The proposal to transpose the care ethic in international law implies a profound change in its aspirations and means. The reference to vulnerability calls for rethinking its conceptions of protection of persons, taking into account still marginal elements in the international legal sphere such as alterity, capacity, or even empowerment. While international law does not explicitly include this ethics of care, it is possible to distinguish some markers in the principle of responsibility to protect, which the UN is seeking to implement, as well as in some of the most recent international protection instruments.

This proposition thus requires international law makers to use their imagination. According to Paul Ricœur, imagination is a tool for the subject to represent the world, and thus to intervene in it. As an instrument for transposing social aspirations,[140] law undoubtedly has a role to play in the realization of *care*. For instance, *caring about* native populations in the ILO Convention on Native and Tribal Populations in Independent Countries[141] and the UN Declaration on the Rights of Native People[142] have led to recognition of a nation's

---

[139] Parliamentary Assembly, Political Affairs Committee, Report on Positive experiences of autonomous regions as a source of inspiration for conflict resolution in Europe, 3 June 2003, *supra* note 137, para. 136.

[140] Georges SCELLE, *Manuel de droit international public* (Paris, Montchrestien, coll. Domat, 1948) 6.

[141] Convention concerning Indigenous and Tribal People in Independent Countries, 1989, n°169, entry into force: 5 September 1991.

[142] Resolution adopted by the General Assembly, United Nations Declaration on the Rights of Indigenous People of 13 September 2007, doc. AG/RES/61/295.

multicultural composition and legal pluralism in certain constitutions.[143] Native populations are invited to expound their views on social, economic and cultural questions and to participate in the democratic process from which they were previously excluded.

Care is also an active process of protection, leading to participation by the vulnerable in their own resilience. To give an example, the UN Convention on the Rights of Persons with Disabilities[144] is an illustration of 'empowerment' in international law.

Moreover, the realization of *care* can be conceived as a priority at the international level because globalization does not allow the state to apply a care ethic alone if others pursue development of the liberal model. International law is therefore bound to change the world, thus fulfilling one of its inherent missions.

---

143 Constitutions of Ecuador of 2008 and Bolivia of 2009 – proclaiming the foundation of a "social State of multinational right".
144 United Nations Convention on the rights of persons with disabilities, December 2006. Cf. International Day of Disabled Persons, 2004, "Nothing about us without us!".

PART 3

Elements of Practices of the Baltic States in International Law

∴

CHAPTER 10

Republic of Estonia Materials on International Law 2016

Edited by René Värk

[*Editorial Notes:*[1]

1. Republic of Estonia Materials on International Law 2016 (REMIL 2016) have been classified according to Recommendation (97)11 P12 June 1997 of the Committee of Ministers of Council of Europe, as applied by the British Yearbook of International Law from 1997, with certain minor amendments.

2. The REMIL mostly concern the opinions of Estonian institutions and officials. Where not expressly stated otherwise, the institutions and officials mentioned in the REMIL are those of Estonia. Often, different officials expressed views on the same issues. In order to prevent undue repetition, the editor has selected materials from the highest possible level. Some materials are quoted at length due to their importance or because they provide useful insights into the relevant aspects of Estonian history, politics and geopolitical concerns, and so on.

3. There were several recurring topics in speeches and statements by officials, for example, cyber issues, human rights, migration, online freedom of expression, the conflict in Ukraine, and the unpredictability of Russia. In many cases, nothing new was added compared to the speeches and statements of previous years and therefore the editor has not included them or has limited their inclusion in the materials.

4. The European Court of Human Rights handed down five judgments on the merits against Estonia and found violations in three cases. The violations concerned Articles 3, 6, and 10. Eight applications were declared (partially) inadmissible or struck out of the list.]

---

1 The editor has compiled the State practice report in a private capacity. Research and writing were supported by grant IUT20-50 from the Estonian Research Council.

Index[2]

Part One: *International Law in general*
I   Nature, basis, purpose
    A   In general
    B   *Jus cogens*
    C   Soft law
II History

Part Two: *Sources and Codification of International Law*
I   Sources of international law
    A   Treaties
    B   Custom
    C   General principles of law
    D   Unilateral acts, including acts and decisions of international organisations and conferences
    E   Judicial decisions
    F   Opinions of writers
    G   Equity
    H   Comity (*comitas gentium*)
II Codification and progressive development of international law

Part Three: *The Law of Treaties*
I   Definition, conclusion and entry into force of treaties
    A   Definition
    B   Conclusion, including signature, ratification, and accession
    C   Reservations, declarations, and objections
    D   Provisional application and entry into force
II Observance, application, and interpretation of treaties third States
III Amendment and modification, derogation
IV Invalidity, termination and suspension of the operation
    A   General rules
    B   Invalidity
    C   Termination and suspension of operation, denunciation, and withdrawal
    D   Procedure
    E   Consequences of invalidity, termination, or suspension of operation

---

[2] The Baltic Yearbook presents the Index of State practice reports only in front of the first State report – Ed.

v   State succession in respect of treaties (see Part Five)
vi Depositaries, notifications, corrections, and registration
vii Consensual arrangements other than treaties

Part Four: *Relationship between International Law and Domestic Law*
i   In General
ii Application and implementation of international law in domestic law
iii Remedies under domestic law for violations of international law

Part Five: *Subjects of International Law*
i   States
    A   Status and powers
        1   Personality
        2   Sovereignty and independence
        3   Non-intervention
        4   Domestic jurisdiction
        5   Equality of States
        6   State immunity
        7   Other powers, including treaty-making power
    B   Recognition
        1   Recognition of States
        2   Recognition of governments
        3   Types of recognition
            (a) *de facto/de jure*
            (b) conditional/unconditional
        4   Acts of recognition
            (a) implied/express
            (b) collective/unilateral
        5   Effects of recognition
        6   Non-recognition (including non-recognition of governments) and its effects
        7   Withdrawal of recognition
    C   Types of States
        1   Unitary States
        2   Personal and real unions
        3   Protected States
    D   Formation, identity, continuity, extinction, and succession of States
        1   Conditions for statehood
        2   Formation

3 Identity and continuity
4 Extinction
5 Succession
   (a) Situations of State succession
       (i) Union with or without the demise of the predecessor State
       (ii) Dismemberment
       (iii) Separation
       (iv) Newly independent States
   (b) Effects of State succession
       (i) Territory and other areas under national jurisdiction
       (ii) Nationality
       (iii) Succession in respect of treaties
       (iv) Archives
       (v) Debts
       (vi) Property
       (vii) Responsibility
       (viii) Other rights and obligations

II International organisations
   A In general
      1 Status and powers
         (a) Personality
         (b) Privileges and immunities of the organisation
         (c) Powers, including treaty-making power
      2 Participation of States and international organisations in international organisations and in their activities
         (a) Admission
         (b) Suspension, withdrawal, expulsion, and deportation
         (c) Obligations of membership
         (d) Representation of States and international organisations to international organisations, including privileges and immunities
      3 Legal effect of the acts of international organisations
      4 Personnel of international organisations
      5 Responsibility of international organisations (see Part Thirteen)
      6 Succession of international organisations
   B Particular types
      1 Universal organisations
      2 Regional organisations

            3   Organisations constituting integrated (e.g. economic) communities
            4   Other types
III   The Holy See
IV   Other subjects of international law and other entities or groups
      A   Mandated and trust territories
      B   Dependent territories
      C   Special regimes
      D   Insurgents
      E   Belligerents
      F   Others (indigenous peoples, minorities, national liberation movements, and the like)

Part Six: *The Position of the Individual (including the Corporation) in International Law*
I   Nationality
II   Diplomatic and consular protection (see Part Thirteen)
III   Aliens
IV   Members of minorities
V   Stateless persons
VI   Refugees
VII   Immigration and emigration, extradition, expulsion, asylum
      A   Immigration and emigration
      B   Extradition
      C   Expulsion
      D   Asylum
VIII Human rights and fundamental freedoms
      A   General concept
      B   Under the United Nations treaty system
      C   Under the Council of Europe treaty system
      D   Other aspects of human rights and fundamental freedoms
IX   Crimes under international law
X   Responsibility of the individual (see Part Thirteen)

Part Seven: *Organs of the State and their Status*
I   Heads of State
II   Ministers
III   Other organs of the State
IV   Diplomatic missions and their members
V   Consulates and their members
VI   Special missions

VII Trade and information offices, trade delegations, and the like.
VIII Armed forces
IX   Protecting powers

Part Eight: *Jurisdiction of the State*
I   Bases of jurisdiction
     A   Territorial principle
     B   Personal principle
     C   Protective principle
     D   Universality principle
     E   Other bases
II   Types of jurisdiction
     A   Jurisdiction to prescribe
     B   Jurisdiction to adjudicate
     C   Jurisdiction to enforce
III Extra-territorial exercise of jurisdiction
     A   General
     B   Consular jurisdiction
     C   Jurisdiction over military personnel abroad
     D   Other (artificial islands, *terrae nullius*, and so on)
IV   Limitations upon jurisdiction (servitudes, leases, and so on)
V   Concurrent jurisdiction

Part Nine: *State Territory*
I   Territory
     A   Elements of territory
         1   Land, internal waters, lakes, rivers, and land-locked seas (see also Parts Ten and Eleven)
         2   Sub-soil
         3   Territorial sea (see Part Eleven)
         4   Airspace (see Part Twelve)
     B   Good neighbourliness
II   Boundaries and frontiers
     A   Delimitation
     B   Demarcation
     C   Stability
III Acquisition and transfer of territory
     A   Acquisition
     B   Transfer

Part Ten: *International Watercourses*
I   Rivers and lakes
   A   Definition
   B   Navigation
   C   Uses for purposes other than navigation
   D   Protection of the environment
   E   Institutional aspects
II   Groundwaters
III   Canals

Part Eleven: *Seas and Vessels*
I   Internal waters, including ports and bays
II   Territorial sea
III   Straits
IV   Archipelagic waters
V   Contiguous zone
VI   Exclusive economic zone, exclusive or preferential fisheries zones
VII   Continental shelf
VIII   High seas
   A   Freedoms of the high seas, including overflight
   B   Visit and search
   C   Hot pursuit
   D   Piracy
   E   Conservation of living resources
IX   Islands, rocks and low-tide elevations
X   Enclosed and semi-enclosed seas
XI   International sea bed area
XII   Land-locked and geographically disadvantaged States
XIII   Protection of the marine environment
XIV   Marine scientific research
XV   Cables and pipelines
XVI   Artificial islands, installations, and structures
XVII   Tunnels
XVIII   Vessels
      A   Legal regime
         1   Warships
         2   Public vessels other than warships
         3   Merchant vessels

    B   Nationality
    C   Jurisdiction over vessels
        1   Flag State
        2   Coastal State
        3   Port State
        4   Other exercises of jurisdiction

Part Twelve: *Airspace, Outer Space, and Antarctica*

I   Airspace
    A   Status
    B   Uses
    C   Legal regime of aircraft
II   Outer space and celestial bodies
    A   Status and limits
    B   Uses
    C   Legal regime of spacecraft
III   Antarctica
    A   Limits and status
    B   Uses
    C   Protection of the environment

Part Thirteen: *International Responsibility*

I   General concept
II   General issues of international responsibility
    A   The elements of responsibility (such as wrongfulness of the act, imputability)
    B   Factors excluding responsibility (self-defence, necessity, reprisals)
    C   Procedure
        1   Diplomatic protection
            (a)   Nationality of claims
            (b)   Exhaustion of local remedies
        2   Consular protection
        3   Peaceful settlement of disputes (see Part Fourteen)
    D   Consequences of responsibility (*restitutio in integrum*, damages, satisfaction, guarantees)
III   Responsible entities
    A   States
    B   International organisations
    C   Entities other than States and international organisations
    D   Individuals and groups of individuals (including corporations)

Part Fourteen: *Peaceful Settlement of Disputes*
I   The concept of an international dispute
II Means of settlement
    A   Negotiations and consultations
    B   Good offices
    C   Enquiry (fact-finding)
    D   Mediation
    E   Conciliation
    F   Arbitration
        1   Arbitral tribunals and commissions
        2   Permanent Court of Arbitration
    G   Judicial settlement
        1   International Court of Justice
        2   Other courts and tribunals
    H   Settlement within international organisations
        1   United Nations
        2   Other organisations
        I   Other means of settlement

Part Fifteen: *Coercive Measures Short of the Use of Force*
I   Unilateral measures
    A   Retorsion
    B   Counter-measures
    C   Pacific blockade
    D   Intervention (see also Part Five)
    E   Other unilateral measures
II Collective measures
    A   United Nations
    B   Outside the United Nations

Part Sixteen: *Use of Force*
I   Prohibition of the use of force
II Legitimate use of force
    A   Self-defence
    B   Collective measures
        1   United Nations
        2   Outside the United Nations
    C   Others
III Use of disarmament and arms control

Part Seventeen: *The Law of Armed Conflict and International Humanitarian Law*
I   International armed conflict
    A   Definition
    B   The law of international armed conflict
        1   Sources
        2   The commencement of international armed conflict and its effects (such as diplomatic and consular relations, treaties, private property, nationality, trading with the enemy, *locus standi personae in judicio*)
        3   Land warfare
        4   Sea warfare
        5   Air warfare
        6   Distinction between combatants and non-combatants
        7   International humanitarian law
        8   Belligerent occupation
        9   Conventional, nuclear, bacteriological, and chemical weapons
        10   Treaty relations between combatants (cartels, armistices, and the like)
        11   Termination of international armed conflict, treaties of peace
II   Non-international armed conflict

Part Eighteen: *Neutrality and Non-Belligerency*
I   The laws of neutrality
    A   Land warfare
    B   Sea warfare
    C   Air warfare
II   Permanent neutrality
III Neutrality in the light of the United Nations Charter
IV   Policy of neutrality and non-alignment
V   Non-belligerency

Part Nineteen: *Legal Aspects of International Relations and Co-operation in Particular Matters*
I   Part Eighty-four General economic and financial matters
    A   Trade
    B   Loans
    C   Investments
    D   Taxes

    E   Monetary matters
    F   Development
II   Transport and communications
III   Environment
IV   Natural resources
V   Technology
VI   Social and health matters
VII   Cultural matters
VIII   Legal matters (such as judicial assistance, crime control, and others)
IX   Military and security matters

Part Five: 11.A. 4. Subjects of International Law – International Organisations – in general – Personnel of International Organisations

5/1

On 21 September, Estonia in collaboration with Costa Rica, Finland and the United Nations Elders organized a side event of the General Assembly, focusing on selecting the next Secretary-General for the organization. Ministry of Foreign Affairs Under-Secretary Väino Reinart pointed out the achievements that have been made this past year to make selection of the Secretary-General more transparent:

> [United Nations] member states, the international community, civil society and the media have put pressure on the [United Nations] so that after 70 years of secrecy, those outside the Security Council could also have an overview of the selection. ... Currently everyone has an overview of the nine candidates for the position of Secretary-General. Public hearings with them also took place for the first time.

According to Reinart, the more open process unfortunately does not reflect the attitude of the Security Council as they do not inform other United Nations members of the results:

> The Security Council has to change with time as well and become more open.

Reinart also emphasized that the Secretary-General has to be independent in filling high-level United Nations positions:

Estonia supports removing the option of reappointment after the first term to guarantee the Secretary-General's independence and to avoid the period of the re-selection campaign.

Estonia belongs to the Security Council working methods ACT (Accountability, Coherence, Transparency) Group. The initiative, launched by Switzerland, is to make the Security Council's decision-making and operational mechanisms more reliable, transparent and effective and give the member States an opportunity to be actively engaged in the process. In the past two years, Estonia, as a member of the ACT leading the issue of transparency, has been actively engaged in making the selection process of the Secretary-General more open.

(Available at the website of the Ministry of Foreign Affairs, <https://vm.ee/en/news/reinart-selecting-un-secretary-general-should-be-more-open-without-option-reappointment-after>, visited on 30 August 2018)

Part Six: VII.A. Immigration and Emigration, Extradition, Expulsion, Asylum – Immigration and Emigration

6/1

On 21 September, President Toomas Hendrik Ilves gave a speech at the opening of the 71st Session of the General Assembly of the United Nations and addressed various challenges facing the international community, which included refugees and migrants:

> During the last fifteen years, the number of migrants and refugees worldwide has grown faster than the world's population. I raise this not only because this is a crisis, but also because I myself am a child of refugees. What we face is not, I underline, an unprecedented crisis in the world. We have faced far worse refugee crises and we have prevailed. In the Europe of 1946, Germany alone had 12 million internal refugees and another 12 million displaced persons of 20 different nationalities. Other countries in the post-war shambles and ruin of Europe at the time were not in much better shape. Yet, we prevailed, or our grandparents did: in three years UNRRA, the UN Relief and Rehabilitation Administration, spent – in today's money – some 50 billion Euros to resolve that refugee crisis. It took political will and courage and far more money to solve that crisis than we are willing to spend today.
>
> Migration is our common challenge. A sustainable solution to this complex problem lies in addressing its causes. Yet we also must fulfil our

commitments under international conventions on the protection of refugees. These commitments already exist; they are not some vague future goal we pledge to.

Migrant children are at the heart of migration influx. Children on the move or otherwise affected by migration are by far the most vulnerable group, who, lacking agency, face limited access to justice, social and health services. And hence often suffer horrible abuse.

One significant challenge is to provide education to the children in refugee camps. Deprivation of education will damage the prospects of refugee and asylum-seeking children, leave them behind and at the same time, increase the risk of the kind of alienation that often leads later to extremism. We have seen this where refugee camps have been in place for long, sometimes for generations, begetting a continuing crop of disaffected, alienated and radical youth who feel they have nothing to lose.

(Available at the website of the President of the Republic, <https://vp2006-2016.president.ee/en/official-duties/speeches/12557-address-by-the-president-of-the-republic-of-estonia-toomas-hendrik-ilves-at-the-general-debate-of-the-71st-united-nations-general-assembly/>, visited on 30 August 2018)

Part Six: VIII.C. The Position of the Individual (including the Corporation) in International Law – Human Rights and Fundamental Freedoms – Under the Council of Europe Treaty System

6/2

On 19 January, the European Court of Human Rights handed down judgment in the case of *Kalda* v. *Estonia*, where the applicant complained that the prison authorities had refused to grant him access to certain websites and thus violated his right to receive information "without interference by public authority" (Article 10). The Chamber found the following:

1. Alleged Violation of Article 10 of the Convention

[...]

2. The Court's assessment

41. The Court has consistently recognised that the public has a right to receive information of general interest. Within this field, it has developed case-law in relation to press freedom, the purpose of which is to impart information and ideas on such matters. The Court has also found that the function of creating forums for public debate is not limited to the press. That function may also be exercised by non-governmental organisations, the activities of which are an essential element of informed public debate (see, for example, *Österreichische Vereinigung zur Erhaltung, Stärkung und Schaffung* v. *Austria*, no. 39534/07, §§ 33–34, 28 November 2013, with further references).

42. Furthermore, the Court has held that the right to receive information basically prohibits a Government from preventing a person from receiving information that others wished or were willing to impart (see *Leander* v. *Sweden*, 26 March 1987, § 74, Series A no. 116). It has also held that the right to receive information cannot be construed as imposing on a State positive obligations to collect and disseminate information of its own motion (see *Guerra and Others* v. *Italy*, 19 February 1998, § 53, *Reports of Judgments and Decisions* 1998-I).

43. In the present case, however, the question in issue is not the authorities' refusal to release the requested information; the applicant's request concerned information that was freely available in the public domain. Rather, the applicant's complaint concerns a particular means of accessing the information in question: namely, that he, as a prisoner, wished to be granted access – specifically, via the Internet – to information published on certain websites.

44. In this connection, the Court reiterates that in the light of its accessibility and its capacity to store and communicate vast amounts of information, the Internet plays an important role in enhancing the public's access to news and facilitating the dissemination of information in general (see *Delfi AS* v. *Estonia* [GC], no. 64569/09, § 133, ECHR 2015; *Ahmet Yıldırım* v. *Turkey*, no. 3111/10, § 48, ECHR 2012; and *Times Newspapers Ltd* v. *the United Kingdom (nos. 1 and 2)*, nos. 3002/03 and 23676/03, § 27, ECHR 2009).

45. Nevertheless, the Court notes that imprisonment inevitably involves a number of restrictions on prisoners' communications with the outside world, including on their ability to receive information. It considers that

Article 10 cannot be interpreted as imposing a general obligation to provide access to the Internet, or to specific Internet sites, for prisoners. However, it finds that in the circumstances of the case, since access to certain sites containing legal information is granted under Estonian law, the restriction of access to other sites that also contain legal information constitutes an interference with the right to receive information.

46. The Court observes that it is not in dispute that the restriction on prisoners' use of the Internet was based on the Imprisonment Act, which limits prisoners' Internet access to the official databases of legislation and the database of judicial decisions. Internet access beyond the authorised websites was prohibited. The Court is thus satisfied that the interference at issue was 'prescribed by law' within the meaning of Article 10 § 2 of the Convention.

47. Furthermore, the Court accepts the Government's argument that the interference in question served the aims of the protection of the rights of others and the prevention of disorder and crime.

48. As regards the issue of whether the interference was 'necessary' within the meaning of Article 10 § 2, the Court notes that according to the Government, granting prisoners access to a greater number of Internet sites would have increased security risks and required the allocation of additional material and human resources in order to mitigate such risks. By contrast, the applicant was of the opinion that allowing access to three more websites (in addition to those already authorised) would not have given rise to any additional security issues. Possible security issues were already effectively managed by the Ministry of Justice, which blocked any links or other such features on already authorised websites that could cause security concerns; there was no reason, according to the applicant, why this should be different in the case of the three requested additional websites.

49. The Court reiterates that under section 31-1 of the Imprisonment Act, prisoners are granted limited access to the Internet – including access to the official databases of legislation and the database of judicial decisions available on the Internet.

50. The Court notes that the websites of the Council of Europe Information Office in Tallinn, the Chancellor of Justice, and the *Riigikogu*, to

which the applicant wished to have access, predominantly contained legal information and information related to fundamental rights, including the rights of prisoners. For example, the website of the *Riigikogu* contained bills together with explanatory memoranda to them, verbatim records of the sittings of the *Riigikogu*, and minutes of committee sittings. The website of the Chancellor of Justice (who is also an ombudsman in Estonia) contained his selected legal opinions. The Court considers that the accessibility of such information promotes public awareness and respect for human rights and gives weight to the applicant's argument that the Estonian courts used such information and the applicant needed access to it for the protection of his rights in the court proceedings. The Court has also taken note of the applicant's argument that legal research in the form of browsing through available information (in order to find relevant information) and making specific requests for information were different matters and that the websites were meant for legal researches rather than making specific requests. Indeed, in order to make a specific request one would need to be aware of which particular information is available in the first place. The Court also notes that the domestic authorities have referred to alternative means of making available to the applicant the information stored on the websites in question (for example, by mail – see paragraph 17 above), but did not compare the costs of these alternative means with the additional costs that extended Internet access would allegedly incur.

51. The Court further notes that in the Rules of the Committee of Ministers for the supervision of the execution of judgments and of the terms of friendly settlements, publication of the Court's judgments in the language of the respondent State is mentioned as an example of the general measures to be taken in order to execute judgments (see paragraph 22 above). The Court notes, in this connection, that when the applicant lodged his complaint with the domestic courts, the Estonian translations and summaries of the Court's judgments were only available on the website of the Council of Europe Information Office and it was only later that this information was published elsewhere – in the online version of *Riigi Teataja* (see paragraph 40 above).

52. The Court cannot overlook the fact that in a number of Council of Europe and other international instruments the public-service value of the Internet and its importance for the enjoyment of a range of human rights has been recognised. Internet access has increasingly been understood as a right, and calls have been made to develop effective

policies to attain universal access to the Internet and to overcome the 'digital divide' (see paragraphs 23 to 25 above). The Court considers that these developments reflect the important role the Internet plays in people's everyday lives. Indeed, an increasing amount of services and information is only available on the Internet, as evidenced by the fact that in Estonia the official publication of legal acts effectively takes place via the online version of *Riigi Teataja* and no longer through its paper version (see paragraph 7 above). The Court reiterates that the online version of *Riigi Teataja* also currently carries Estonian summaries and Estonian translations of the Court's judgments (see paragraph 40 above).

53. Lastly, the Court reiterates that under the Imprisonment Act the prisoners have been granted limited access to the Internet via computers specially adapted for that purpose and under the supervision of the prison authorities. Thus, the Court observes that arrangements necessary for the use of the Internet by prisoners have in any event been made and the related costs have been borne by the authorities. While the security and economic considerations cited by the domestic authorities may be considered as relevant, the Court notes that the domestic courts undertook no detailed analysis as to the security risks allegedly emerging from the access to the three additional websites in question, also having regard to the fact that these were websites of State authorities and of an international organisation. The Supreme Court limited its analysis on this point to a rather general statement that granting access to additional Internet sites could increase the risk of detainees engaging in prohibited communication, thus giving rise to the need for increased levels of monitoring. The Court also considers that the Supreme Court and the Government have failed to convincingly demonstrate that giving the applicant access to three additional websites would have caused any noteworthy additional costs. In these circumstances, the Court is not persuaded that sufficient reasons have been put forward in the present case to justify the interference with the applicant's right to receive information.

54. The Court concludes that the interference with the applicant's right to receive information, in the specific circumstances of the present case, cannot be regarded as having been necessary in a democratic society.

There has accordingly been a violation of Article 10 of the Convention.

(*Kalda* v. *Estonia*, app. no. 17429/10, 19 January 2016, Judgment of the Chamber)

6/3

On 26 April, the European Court of Human Rights handed down judgment in the case of *Kashlev v. Estonia*, where the applicant complained that the Court of Appeal had convicted him only on the basis of the case file without examining any witnesses at its hearing (Article 6 §§ 1 and 3 (d)), and that he had had no possibility to appeal against his conviction and directly submit his arguments to a higher court since the judgment convicting him had been delivered by the Court of Appeal and the Supreme Court had decided not to examine his appeal (Article 2 of Protocol No. 7). The Chamber found the following:

1. Alleged Violation of Article 6 §§ 1 and 3 (d) of the Convention

[...]

2. *The Court's assessment*

(a) General principles

37. The Court reiterates that in the interests of a fair and just criminal process it is of capital importance that the accused should appear at his trial (see *Poitrimol v. France*, 23 November 1993, § 35, Series A no. 277-A; *Lala v. the Netherlands*, 22 September 1994, § 33, Series A no. 297-A; and *De Lorenzo v. Italy* (dec.), no. 69264/01, 12 February 2004), and the duty to guarantee the right of a criminal defendant to be present in the courtroom – either during the original proceedings or in a retrial – ranks as one of the essential requirements of Article 6 (see *Stoichkov v. Bulgaria*, no. 9808/02, § 56, 24 March 2005, and *Hermi v. Italy* [GC], no. 18114/02, § 58, ECHR 2006-XII).

38. However, the personal attendance of the defendant does not take on the same crucial significance for an appeal hearing as it does for the trial hearing (see *Kamasinski v. Austria*, 19 December 1989, § 106, Series A no. 168). The manner of application of Article 6 to proceedings before courts of appeal depends on the special features of the proceedings involved; account must be taken of the entirety of the proceedings in the domestic legal order and of the role of the appellate court therein (see *Monnell and Morris v. the United Kingdom*, 2 March 1987, § 56, Series A no. 115; *Ekbatani v. Sweden*, 26 May 1988, § 27, Series A no. 134; and *Hermi*, cited above, § 60). Nevertheless, the Court has held that where an appellate court is called upon to examine a case as to the facts and the law and to make a full assessment of the question of the applicant's guilt or innocence, it

cannot, as a matter of fair trial, properly determine those issues without a direct assessment of the evidence given in person by the accused who claims that he has not committed the act alleged to constitute a criminal offence (see *Ekbatani*, cited above, § 32, and *Popovici* v. *Moldova*, nos. 289/04 and 41194/04, § 68, 27 November 2007).

39. Furthermore, the Court reiterates that the guarantees in paragraph 3 (d) of Article 6 are specific aspects of the right to a fair hearing set forth in paragraph 1 of that provision, which must be taken into account in any assessment of the fairness of proceedings. In addition, the Court's primary concern under Article 6 § 1 is to evaluate the overall fairness of the criminal proceedings (see *Taxquet* v. *Belgium* [GC], no. 926/05, § 84, ECHR 2010, and *Al-Khawaja and Tahery* v. *the United Kingdom* [GC], nos. 26766/05 and 22228/06, § 118, ECHR 2011).

40. While Article 6 of the Convention guarantees the right to a fair hearing, it does not lay down any rules on the admissibility of evidence or the way it should be assessed, which are therefore primarily matters for regulation by national legislation and the domestic courts (see, amongst others, *Schenk* v. *Switzerland*, 12 July 1988, §§ 45–46, Series A no. 140, and *García Ruiz* v. *Spain* [GC], no. 30544/96, § 28, ECHR 1999-I). The Court's only concern is to examine whether the proceedings have been conducted fairly (see *Gäfgen* v. *Germany* [GC], no. 22978/05, § 162, ECHR 2010, with further references, and *Al-Khawaja and Tahery*, cited above, § 118).

41. All the evidence must normally be produced at a public hearing, in the presence of the accused, with a view to adversarial argument. There are exceptions to this principle, however. As a general rule, paragraphs 1 and 3 (d) of Article 6 cannot be interpreted as requiring in all cases that questions be put directly by the accused or his lawyer, whether by means of cross-examination or by any other means, but rather that the accused must be given an adequate and proper opportunity to challenge and question a witness against him, either when the witness makes his statement or at a later stage (see *Al-Khawaja and Tahery*, cited above, § 118). The use in evidence of statements obtained at the police inquiry and judicial investigation stages is not in itself inconsistent with the provisions cited above, provided that the rights of the defence have been respected (see *Saïdi* v. *France*, 20 September 1993, § 43, Series A no. 261-C).

42. Lastly, the Court reiterates that neither the letter nor the spirit of Article 6 of the Convention prevents a person from waiving of his own free

will, either expressly or tacitly, the entitlement to the guarantees of a fair trial (see *Kwiatkowska v. Italy* (dec.), no. 52868/99, 30 November 2000). However, such a waiver must, if it is to be effective for Convention purposes, be established in an unequivocal manner and be attended by minimum safeguards commensurate with its importance (see *Poitrimol*, cited above, § 35). In addition, it must not run counter to any important public interest (see *Håkansson and Sturesson v. Sweden*, 21 February 1990, § 66, Series A no. 171-A; *Hermi*, cited above, § 73; and *Sejdovic v. Italy* [GC], no. 56581/00, § 86, ECHR 2006-II).

(b) Application of these principles to the present case

43. The Court considers that the issue to be examined in the present case is whether the proceedings against the applicant, taken as a whole, were fair in the light of the specific features of these proceedings.

44. The Court notes at the outset that the applicant, assisted by a lawyer, took part in the hearing at first instance. He was heard at the County Court hearing where all relevant witnesses were also examined. It is not in dispute that the defence could and did put questions to the witnesses before the County Court.

45. Furthermore, the Court notes that after the applicant's acquittal by the first-instance court the prosecutor lodged an appeal with the Court of Appeal. A copy of the appeal was served on the applicant and his lawyer and both of them were summoned to the Court of Appeal hearing. However, the applicant informed the court in writing of his wish not to take part and asked for the case to be examined in his absence. The Court notes that it has not been argued that the applicant – who was not in detention – was hindered from seeking legal advice concerning the nature of the proceedings before the Court of Appeal or their possible outcome, including the possibility that the first-instance acquittal judgment would be overturned and the applicant convicted by the Court of Appeal as requested by the prosecutor. The Court further notes that, according to the record of the Court of Appeal hearing, the applicant's lawyer – who was present – submitted that he was aware of the applicant's wish not to take part. The Court thus considers that the applicant unequivocally waived his right to take part in the hearing before the Court of Appeal (see, generally, *Hermi*, cited above, § 73, with further references; compare and contrast *Popovici*, cited above, § 73, where the Government failed to

adduce any evidence in support of their submission that the applicant had refused to attend the hearing in question). The Court does not therefore need to further examine the question of whether the special features of the proceedings concerned would have allowed an appellate court to decide the case without a direct assessment of the evidence given by the applicant in person. In that respect the present case differs from a number of cases the Court has dealt with where the defendant in criminal proceedings had not been heard by an appellate jurisdiction since no oral hearing had been held at all (see *Igual Coll* v. *Spain*, no. 37496/04, § 7, 10 March 2009; *Marcos Barrios* v. *Spain*, no. 17122/07, § 10, 21 September 2010; and *García Hernández* v. *Spain*, no. 15256/07, § 8, 16 November 2010), had not been heard in person regardless of the hearing having taken place (see *Lacadena Calero* v. *Spain*, no. 23002/07, § 10, 22 November 2011) or had been able to address the court but had not been heard during the trial (see *Constantinescu* v. *Romania*, no. 28871/95, § 58, ECHR 2000-VIII, and *Popa and Tănăsescu* v. *Romania*, no. 19946/04, §§ 28 and 50, 10 April 2012).

46. As regards the question of whether the Court of Appeal was required to re-examine the witnesses – who had already been examined at the County Court hearing – in person, the Court underlines again that the applicant, who was assisted by a lawyer, was aware of the content of the prosecutor's appeal (see paragraph 12 above). The applicant was equally aware of the Court of Appeal's powers to convict him. In this context, the Court considers it significant that the applicant did not request in any manner the examination of witnesses at the appellate court's hearing (compare *Destrehem* v. *France*, no. 56651/00, §§ 45–47, 18 May 2004, where the Court, in finding a violation, relied on the fact that the applicant had requested summoning the witnesses but in spite of that request the court of appeal nevertheless had overturned the first-instance judgment without summoning the witnesses; contrast with *Flueraş* v. *Romania*, no. 17520/04, § 60, 9 April 2013).

47. It is true that the Court has found that one of the requirements of a fair trial is the possibility for the accused to confront the witnesses in the presence of a judge who must ultimately decide the case, because the judge's observations on the demeanour and credibility of a certain witness may have consequences for the accused (see *Hanu* v. *Romania*, no. 10890/04, § 40, 4 June 2013). At the same time, according to the Court's settled case-law, the admissibility of evidence or the way it should be

assessed are primarily matters for regulation by national legislation and the domestic courts (see among many other authorities, *Al-Khawaja and Tahery*, § 118; *García Ruiz*, § 28; and *Schenk*, §§ 45–46, all cited above). Exceptions to the principle that all evidence against the accused must normally be produced in his presence at a public hearing with a view to adversarial argument are possible but must not infringe the rights of the defence, which, as a rule, require that the accused should be given an adequate and proper opportunity to challenge and question a witness against him, either when that witness makes his statement or at a later stage of the proceedings (see *Solakov v. 'the former Yugoslav Republic of Macedonia'*, no. 47023/99, § 57, ECHR 2001-X, and *Al-Khawaja and Tahery*, cited above, § 118, with further references to *Lucà v. Italy*, no. 33354/96, § 39, ECHR 2001-II). The Court considers that if it has been accepted that the defendant's ability to put questions to witnesses against him during the pre-trial proceedings can meet the requirements of Article 6 §§ 1 and 3 (d) and that the testimony of such witnesses can be admissible as evidence, those requirements are, *a fortiori*, met when the witnesses in question have been examined before the first-instance court in the presence of the defendant who could put questions to them and the appellate court admits those statements as evidence. The Court notes that it has not been argued that the proceedings before the first-instance court in the present case did not meet the fair trial requirements of Article 6 §§ 1 and 3 (d).

48. Furthermore, the Court has had regard, in the present case, to the reasoning related to the radically different assessment of the witness statements by the domestic courts. It reiterates in this connection that it is not its task to act as an appellate court or, as is sometimes said, as a court of fourth instance, for the decisions of domestic courts. It is the role of the domestic courts to interpret and apply the relevant rules of procedural or substantive law. The domestic courts are best placed to assess the credibility of witnesses and the relevance of evidence to the issues in the case (see, among many other authorities, *Vidal v. Belgium*, 22 April 1992, § 32, Series A no. 235-B; *Edwards v. the United Kingdom*, 16 December 1992, § 34, Series A no. 247-B; *Melnychuk v. Ukraine* (dec.), no. 28743/03, ECHR 2005-IX; and *Karpenko v. Russia*, no. 5605/04, § 80, 13 March 2012). In the instant case, the Court notes that there is nothing in the case file which might lead to the conclusion that the domestic courts acted in an arbitrary or unreasonable manner in assessing the evidence, establishing the facts or interpreting the domestic law. On the contrary, the Court

considers that adequate safeguards against arbitrariness were in place in the proceedings against the applicant. The Court notes that the difference in the County Court's and Court of Appeal's assessment of the evidence mainly resulted from the courts' different approach to the coherence or discrepancies within and between the testimony of individual witnesses and their interpretation of the circumstances of the offence as a whole. The Court also notes in this connection that the Court of Appeal, following the Supreme Court's pertinent case-law (see paragraph 24 above), provided – as required by the Supreme Court – particularly thorough reasoning as to why it had come to a conclusion different from that of the County Court, and indicated what mistakes the latter had made, in the Court of Appeal's view, in assessing the evidence. The Court observes, in particular, that the Court of Appeal disagreed with the County Court's rejection of certain witness statements and identification reports as evidence and, having taken into account that evidence, arrived at a conclusion different from that of the County Court (see paragraphs 10 and 15et seq. above).

49. The Court further notes that an appeal against the Court of Appeal judgment could be lodged with the Supreme Court. The applicant, through his lawyer, made use of that possibility and the Supreme Court was thus able to verify whether its case-law in that area had been followed by the Court of Appeal. While deciding whether to examine the applicant's appeal, it had in substance a possibility to assess the appellate court's approach. The Court considers that the requirements deriving from the Supreme Court's case-law and its verification in the present case that those requirements had been met constituted further safeguards for the applicant's defence rights.

50. The Court finds that because of the existence of the above safeguards against arbitrary or unreasonable assessment of evidence or establishment of the facts, the present case is different from a number of previous cases where the Court found a violation of the Convention (contrast, for example, *Flueraş*, cited above, and *Hanu,* cited above; see also the cases referred to in paragraph 45 above). In those cases the domestic law or binding case-law did not contain any rules comparable to those in the instant case.

51. In conclusion, given that the applicant unequivocally waived his right to take part in the Court of Appeal hearing, that the defence was able to

put questions to the witnesses before the first-instance court in proceedings the compatibility of which with the fair trial guarantees enshrined in Article 6 §§ 1 and 3 (d) has not been put into question, that the applicant, who was assisted by a lawyer, did not request the examination of witnesses at the appellate court's hearing, that the Court of Appeal followed the requirement of domestic law to provide particularly thorough reasoning for departing from the assessment given to the evidence by the first-instance court, including the indication of mistakes made by it, and that an appeal against the Court of Appeal judgment to the country's highest court allowed the latter to verify whether the requirements of domestic law, including those of a fair trial, had been met, the Court finds that the applicant's right to a fair trial was not breached in the present case.

There has accordingly been no violation of Article 6 §§ 1 and 3 (d) of the Convention.

11. Other Alleged Violations of the Convention

[...]

53. This complaint falls to be examined under Article 2 of Protocol No. 7 to the Convention. The Court considers that the Contracting States dispose in principle of a wide margin of appreciation to determine how the right secured by Article 2 of Protocol No. 7 to the Convention is to be exercised. Thus, the review by a higher court of a conviction or sentence may concern both points of fact and points of law or be confined solely to points of law. In several member States of the Council of Europe such a review is limited to questions of law or may require the person wishing to appeal to apply for leave to do so (see, for example, *Pesti and Frodl v. Austria* (dec.), nos. 27618/95 and 27619/95, ECHR 2000-I (extracts); *Kristjansson and Boasson v. Iceland* (dec.), no. 24945/04, 10 April 2007; and *Dorado Baúlde v. Spain* (dec.), no. 23486/12, 1 September 2015). Moreover, the second paragraph of Article 2 of Protocol No. 7 specifically refers to exceptions to the right to appeal in criminal matters in cases where the person concerned was convicted following an appeal against acquittal. The Court finds therefore that there is no appearance of a violation of the provision cited. It follows that this part of the application must be rejected as manifestly ill-founded, pursuant to Article 35 §§ 3 (a) and 4 of the Convention.

(*Kashlev* v. *Estonia*, app. no. 22574/08, 26 April 2016, Judgment of the Chamber)

6/4

On 21 June, the European Court of Human Rights handed down judgment in the case of *Lähteenmäki* v. *Estonia*, where the applicant complained that the reasoning of the domestic courts in the judgments refusing to award her compensation violated her right to be presumed innocent (Article 6 § 2) and that the domestic courts had failed to take into account the evidence she had submitted to them (Article 6 § 1). The Chamber found the following:

1. Alleged Violation of Article 6 § 2 of the Convention

[...]

2. The Court's assessment

45. Once it has been established that there is a link between the two sets of proceedings, the Court must determine whether, in all the circumstances of the case, the right to the presumption of innocence has been respected. The Court in *Allen* explained that where Article 6 § 2 applies, the compatibility of the proceedings with that Article will depend on their nature and context, and the language used by the decision-maker will be of critical importance (cited above, §§ 125–126). However, considering the nature and context of particular proceedings, even the use of some unfortunate language may not be decisive (see *Allen*, cited above, § 126, and the case-law cited therein; *A.L.F.* v. *the United Kingdom*, (dec.), no. 5908/12, § 24, 12 November 2013; *Adams* v. *the United Kingdom*, (dec.), no. 70601/11, § 41, 12 November 2013; and *Vella* v. *Malta*, no. 69122/10, § 61, 11 February 2014).

46. In the present case, the Court must assess whether the language that the domestic courts employed was compatible with the presumption of innocence. The Court must assess this taking into account the context of the ruling ordering discontinuance of the criminal proceedings against the applicant, and the nature of the task that the domestic courts were required to carry out in the civil proceedings.

47. Turning to the context of the discontinuance of the criminal proceedings, the Court observes the following. Firstly, the discontinuance

decision was delivered by an independent and impartial court which held a hearing to examine the prosecutor's request to discontinue the proceedings (see paragraph 7 above). Both the applicant and the defence counsel of her own choosing were able to take part in that hearing. Secondly, at that hearing the prosecutor explicitly stated that the applicant had committed offences of minor importance. Thirdly, the prosecutor explicitly described the applicant's guilt as negligible, because she had participated in the commission of the offence at the instigation of the co-accused. Fourthly, the applicant and her counsel explicitly agreed with the reasons for and conditions of the discontinuance of the proceedings that the prosecutor had put forward. Fifthly, the applicant has not questioned the compatibility of criminal proceedings with the requirements of a fair trial. Nor has the Court any reason to do so.

48. The Court has taken note of the applicant's argument that she had consented to the discontinuance because she had been raising a small child alone and had sought to avoid the additional costs and discomfort which could have been caused by protracted proceedings. However, it also observes that the fact that the applicant had been raising a small child alone was taken into account by the prosecutor as one of the reasons for requesting the discontinuance of the proceedings. Moreover, the applicant never voiced those considerations in the domestic proceedings, nor did she otherwise complain in those proceedings that she had had to give her consent to the discontinuance because of some external constraint.

49. The Court has also taken note of the applicant's argument and the Government's counter-argument related to the nature and consequences of the discontinuance of criminal proceedings under Article 202 of the CCrP (see paragraphs 39 and 41 above). The Court observes that this disagreement concerns a question of interpretation of domestic law. It is primarily a matter for the national authorities, in particular the courts, to interpret and apply domestic law. The Court is required to verify whether the way in which domestic law is interpreted and applied produces consequences that are consistent with the principles of the Convention, as interpreted in the light of the Court's case-law (see *Scordino v. Italy* (no. 1) [GC], no. 36813/97, §§ 190–91, ECHR 2006-V). It has to examine the circumstances of how this provision was applied in the applicant's case. That is to say that the Court has to examine how exactly the criminal proceedings against the applicant were discontinued in practice (see

paragraphs 47 and 48 above). Nevertheless, it can be gleaned from the plain wording of the article in question (see paragraph 19 above) that the discontinuance required, among other things, an assessment of whether or not an offence had been committed and the conclusion that the guilt of the accused had been negligible. It also required the consent of the accused and that the ruling ordering discontinuance be delivered by a judge acting at the request of a prosecutor. Domestic case-law shows that, while discontinuance under this provision does not amount to conviction, it does not amount to an acquittal either, and that discontinuance has some inculpatory effect (see paragraphs 20–23 above). The Court is satisfied that the applicant, who was represented by a defence counsel of her own choosing, was aware, or at least ought to have been aware, of the potential nature of the discontinuance in accordance with this provision.

50. Turning to the nature of the task that the domestic courts were required to carry out in the civil proceedings, the Court observes at the outset that the applicant instituted those proceedings after the criminal proceedings against her had been discontinued in the circumstances referred to in paragraphs 47 to 49 above. In those proceedings it had been established that the applicant's car had been involved in a staged accident and that the applicant had submitted false information about the event to the insurance company and the authorities. The applicant's civil action also followed the performance of the obligations imposed on her in the ruling ordering discontinuance of the criminal proceedings. It is because of this and the circumstances referred to in paragraphs 47 to 49 above that the present case differs from cases where the subsequent proceedings followed on from a discontinuance of criminal proceedings because of insufficient evidence (*Capeau v. Belgium*, no. 42914/98, ECHR 2005-I) or because of want of proof and the prosecution having been time-barred (*Grabchuk v. Ukraine*, no. 8599/02, 21 September 2006). For the same reasons the present case is different from *Panteleyenko v. Ukraine* (no. 11901/02, 29 June 2006), where the proceedings were discontinued because of the insignificance of the offence, but where the decision to discontinue was taken at the pre-trial stage by a prosecutor, and the applicant at all times actively denied having committed the offence.

51. The Court further observes that in the civil proceedings the applicant had to bear the burden of proof in respect of her allegation that a genuine traffic accident had occurred. The task of the civil courts was to assess,

based on the evidence put before it in adversarial proceedings, whether on the balance of probabilities the applicant's allegations that a genuine traffic accident had happened were supported by sufficient proof. The Court does not find it unreasonable that the applicant was required to prove the truth of her allegations. The discontinuance of the criminal proceedings against the applicant could not result in a dispensation from the obligation of having to prove her insurance claim in accordance with the applicable domestic rules regarding the burden of proof.

52. With regard to the proof, the sole piece of evidence the applicant submitted in the civil proceedings by way of proof that she had not been involved in staging the accident was the ruling ordering discontinuance of the criminal proceedings against her. The applicant argued that the fact of the discontinuance of the criminal proceedings had in itself amounted to sufficient proof of her position. As is apparent from the documents submitted to the Court, the applicant did not submit any other evidence in support of her assertion that a genuine traffic accident had taken place. At the same time, the defendant in the civil proceedings, that is to say the insurance company, submitted to the courts the judgment by which the applicant's co-accused had been convicted. The defendant argued that those two decisions from the criminal proceedings, taken together, were sufficient to refute the applicant's assertion that there had been a genuine traffic accident. The domestic courts, which were required to decide whether the applicant had properly discharged her burden of proof, were thus faced with mutually exclusive arguments regarding the assessment of the same evidence. As to the evidentiary value in civil proceedings of the decisions delivered in criminal proceedings, the Court accepts that those decisions must be treated on an equal footing with other types of evidence (see paragraphs 24 and 25 above). It also notes that the findings in those decisions constituted rebuttable positions (see paragraph 26 above).

53. In the light of the circumstances related to the discontinuance of the criminal proceedings and the nature of the evidence submitted to the courts regarding the alleged occurrence of a genuine traffic accident, the Court finds that the wording of the domestic courts' reasoning cannot be deemed unacceptable. Firstly, to a large extent the language simply followed that of Article 202 of the CCrP and the Supreme Court's understanding of the same provision. Secondly, the domestic courts' judgments, and especially that of the Court of Appeal, did not refer to the

applicant as a convicted person. Thirdly, the Court of Appeal's judgment leaves no doubt that the applicant's claim was rejected due to her failure to discharge her burden of proof. The Court of Appeal's clarification of what at first sight appeared to follow from the decisions taken in the criminal proceedings was necessary in order to explain what the applicant had failed to disprove.

54. In conclusion, the Court does not consider that the language used by the domestic courts in the judgments at issue, when viewed in the context of the ruling ordering discontinuance of the criminal proceedings against the applicant, and the nature of the task that the domestic courts were required to carry out in the civil proceedings, can be said to indicate that the applicant was treated in a manner inconsistent with the presumption of innocence.

55. There has accordingly not been a violation of Article 6 § 2 of the Convention.

II. Alleged Violation of Article 6 § 1 of the Convention

[...]

58. The Court has examined this complaint and finds that the domestic courts duly considered the evidence submitted to them concerning the occurrence of the alleged insured event. The Court therefore concludes that there is no appearance of a violation of the provision cited. It follows that this part of the application must be rejected as manifestly ill-founded, pursuant to Article 35 §§ 3 (a) and 4 of the Convention.

(*Lähteenmäki* v. *Estonia*, app. no. 53172/10, 21 June 2016, Judgment of the Chamber)

6/5

On 30 August, the European Court of Human Rights handed down judgment in the case of *Mihhailov* v. *Estonia*, where the applicant complained that the police had beaten him during his arrest and while he was detained at the police station and that the authorities had not carried out an effective investigation into his allegations of ill-treatment (Article 3). The Chamber found the following:

1. Alleged Violation of Article 3 of the Convention

[...]

2. *The Court's assessment*

(a) General principles

98. As the Court has stated on many occasions, Article 3 of the Convention enshrines one of the core values of democratic societies (see, among many others, *Selmouni*, cited above, § 95, and *Bouyid*, cited above, § 81).

99. Allegations of ill-treatment contrary to Article 3 must be supported by appropriate evidence. To assess this evidence, the Court adopts the standard of proof 'beyond reasonable doubt' but adds that such proof may follow from the coexistence of sufficiently strong, clear and concordant inferences or of similar unrebutted presumptions of fact (see, among others, *Ireland v. the United Kingdom*, 18 January 1978, § 161 *in fine*, Series A no. 25; *Labita*, cited above, § 121; *Jalloh v. Germany* [GC], no. 54810/00, § 67, ECHR 2006-IX; *Ramirez Sanchez v. France* [GC], no. 59450/00, § 117, ECHR 2006-IX; *Gäfgen v. Germany* [GC], no. 22978/05, § 92, ECHR 2010; and *Bouyid*, cited above, § 82).

100. On that latter point the Court has explained that where the events in issue lie wholly, or in large part, within the exclusive knowledge of the authorities, as in the case of people within their control in custody, strong presumptions of fact will arise in respect of injuries occurring during such detention. The burden of proof is then on the Government to provide a satisfactory and convincing explanation by producing evidence establishing facts which cast doubt on the account of events given by the victim (see *Bouyid*, cited above, § 83, and the case-law cited therein). In particular, where an individual, when taken into police custody, is in good health, but is found to be injured at the time of release, it is incumbent on the State to provide a plausible explanation of how those injuries were caused, failing which a clear issue arises under Article 3 of the Convention (see *Tomasi v. France*, 27 August 1992, §§ 108–11, Series A no. 241-A, and *Selmouni*, cited above, § 87). In the absence of such an explanation, the Court can draw inferences which may be unfavourable for the Government (see, among other authorities, *El-Masri*, cited above, § 152). That is justified by the fact that people in custody are in a vulnerable

position and the authorities are under a duty to protect them (see, among other authorities, *Salman*, cited above, § 99).

101. The Court also pointed out in *El-Masri* (cited above, § 155) that although it recognised that it must be cautious in taking on the role of a first-instance tribunal of fact where this was not made unavoidable by the circumstances of a particular case (see *McKerr v. the United Kingdom* (dec.), no. 28883/95, 4 April 2000), it had to apply a 'particularly thorough scrutiny' where allegations were made under Article 3 of the Convention (see, *mutatis mutandis*, *Ribitsch v. Austria*, 4 December 1995, § 32, Series A no. 336, and *Georgiy Bykov v. Russia*, no. 24271/03, § 51, 14 October 2010), even if certain domestic proceedings and investigations had already taken place (see *Cobzaru v. Romania*, no. 48254/99, § 65, 26 July 2007). In other words, in such a context the Court is prepared to conduct a thorough examination of the findings of the national courts. In examining them it may take account of the quality of the domestic proceedings and any possible flaws in the decision-making process (see *Denisenko and Bogdanchikov v. Russia*, no. 3811/02, § 83, 12 February 2009).

102. Ill-treatment must attain a minimum level of severity if it is to fall within the scope of Article 3. The assessment of this minimum depends on all the circumstances of the case, such as the duration of the treatment, its physical or mental effects and, in some cases, the sex, age and state of health of the victim (see, among other authorities, *Ireland v. the United Kingdom*, cited above, § 162; *Jalloh*, cited above, § 67; *Gäfgen*, cited above, § 88; *El-Masri*, cited above, § 196; *Korobov and Others*, cited above, § 92; and *Svinarenko and Slyadnev v. Russia* [GC], nos. 32541/08 and 43441/08, § 114, ECHR 2014 (extracts)). Further factors include the purpose for which the ill-treatment was inflicted, together with the intention or motivation behind it (compare, *inter alia*, *Aksoy v. Turkey*, 18 December 1996, § 64, *Reports* 1996-VI; *Egmez v. Cyprus*, no. 30873/96, § 78, ECHR 2000-XII; and *Krastanov v. Bulgaria*, no. 50222/99, § 53, 30 September 2004; see also, among other authorities, *Gäfgen*, cited above, § 88; and *El-Masri*, cited above, § 196), although the absence of an intention to humiliate or debase the victim cannot conclusively rule out a finding of a violation of Article 3 (see, among other authorities, *V. v. the United Kingdom* [GC], no. 24888/94, § 71, ECHR 1999-IX, and *Svinarenko and Slyadnev*, cited above, § 114). Regard must also be had to the context in which the ill-treatment was inflicted, such as an atmosphere of heightened tension and emotions (compare, for example, *Selmouni*, cited above, § 104;

Egmez, cited above, § 78; see also, among other authorities, *Gäfgen*, cited above, § 88).

103. Ill-treatment that attains such a minimum level of severity usually involves actual bodily injury or intense physical or mental suffering. However, even in the absence of those aspects, where treatment humiliates or debases an individual, showing a lack of respect for or diminishing his or her human dignity, or arouses feelings of fear, anguish or inferiority capable of breaking an individual's moral and physical resistance, it may be characterised as degrading and also fall within the prohibition set forth in Article 3 (see, among other authorities, *Vasyukov* v. *Russia*, no. 2974/05, § 59, 5 April 2011; *Gäfgen*, cited above, § 89; *Svinarenko and Slyadnev*, cited above, § 114; and *Georgia* v. *Russia* (I) [GC], no. 13255/07, § 192, ECHR 2014 (extracts)). It should also be pointed out that it may well suffice that the victim is humiliated in his own eyes, even if not in the eyes of others (see, among other authorities, *Tyrer* v. *the United Kingdom*, 25 April 1978, § 32, Series A no. 26, and *M.S.S.* v. *Belgium and Greece* [GC], no. 30696/09, § 220, ECHR 2011).

104. The Court notes that Article 3 does not prohibit the use of force in certain well-defined circumstances. However, such force may be used only if indispensable and must not be excessive (see *Anzhelo Georgiev and Others* v. *Bulgaria*, no. 51284/09, § 66, 30 September 2014; see also *Klaas* v. *Germany*, judgment of 22 September 1993, § 30, Series A no. 269; *Rehbock* v. *Slovenia*, no. 29462/95, §§ 68–78, ECHR 2000-XII).

105. In respect of a person who is deprived of his liberty, or, more generally, is confronted with law-enforcement officers, any recourse to physical force which has not been made strictly necessary by his own conduct diminishes human dignity and is, in principle, an infringement of the right set forth in Article 3 (see, among other authorities, *Ribitsch*, cited above, § 38; *Mete and Others*, cited above, § 106; *El-Masri*, cited above, § 207; and *Bouyid*, cited above, § 100). The Court has recently emphasised in *Bouyid* (ibid., § 101) that the words 'in principle' cannot be taken to mean that there might be situations in which such a finding of a violation is not called for, because the minimum severity threshold has not been attained. Any interference with human dignity strikes at the very essence of the Convention. For that reason any conduct by law-enforcement officers *vis-à-vis* an individual which diminishes human dignity constitutes a violation of Article 3 of the Convention. That applies in particular to their use

of physical force against an individual where it is not made strictly necessary by his conduct, whatever the impact on the person in question.

106. When an individual makes a credible assertion that he has suffered treatment infringing Article 3 at the hands of the police or other similar agents of the State, that provision, read in conjunction with the State's general duty under Article 1 of the Convention to 'secure to everyone within their jurisdiction the rights and freedoms defined in ... [the] Convention', requires by implication that there should be an effective official investigation (see *Assenov and Others*, cited above, § 102, and *Labita v. Italy* [GC], no. 26772/95, § 131, ECHR 2000-IV). The minimum standards of effectiveness, as defined in the Court's case-law, were recapitulated, *inter alia*, in *El-Masri v. the former Yugoslav Republic of Macedonia* [GC], no. 39630/09, §§ 182–185, ECHR 2012; *Mocanu and Others v. Romania* [GC], nos. 10865/09, 45886/07 and 32431/08, §§ 316–326, ECHR 2014 (extracts); and *Bouyid v. Belgium* [GC], no. 23380/09, §§ 115–123, ECHR 2015).

107. Generally speaking, for an investigation to be effective, the persons responsible for carrying it out must be independent from those targeted by it. This means not only a lack of hierarchical or institutional connection but also independence in practice (see, among others, *Đurđević v. Croatia*, no. 52442/09, § 85, ECHR 2011 (extracts); *Mocanu and Others*, cited above, § 320; and, *mutatis mutandis*, *Mustafa Tunç and Fecire Tunç v. Turkey* [GC], no. 24014/05, §§ 219–234, 14 April 2015).

108. The investigation must be prompt and reasonably expeditious (see, among many others, *Mocanu and Others*, cited above, § 323). The Court assesses whether the authorities reacted promptly to the complaints at the relevant time (see *Labita*, cited above, §§ 133–135). Consideration is given to the starting of investigations and delays in taking statements (see *Virabyan v. Armenia*, no. 40094/05, § 163, 2 October 2012).

109. Any investigation of serious allegations of ill-treatment must be thorough. This means that the authorities must make a serious attempt to find out what happened and should not rely on hasty or ill-founded conclusions to close their investigation or as the basis for their decisions (see *Assenov*, cited above, § 103 et seq., and *Korobov and Others*, cited above, § 113). They must take all reasonable steps available to them to secure evidence concerning the incident, including, *inter alia*, eyewitness testimony, forensic evidence and so on (see *Korobov and Others*, cited above,

§ 113). Any deficiency in the investigation which undermines its ability to establish the cause of injuries or the identity of the persons responsible will risk falling foul of this standard (see *Mikheyev v. Russia*, no. 77617/01, § 108, 26 January 2006; *El-Masri*, cited above, § 183; and *Korobov and Others*, cited above, § 113). The mere fact that appropriate steps were not taken to reduce the risk of collusion between alleged perpetrators amounts to a significant shortcoming in the adequacy of the investigation (see, *mutatis mutandis*, *Ramsahai and Others v. the Netherlands* [GC], no. 52391/99, § 330, ECHR 2007-II; *mutatis mutandis*, *Jaloud v. the Netherlands* [GC], no. 47708/08, § 208, ECHR 2014; and *Lyalyakin v. Russia*, no. 31305/09, § 84, 12 March 2015).

(b) Application of the principles to the present case

110. The Court notes at the outset that the parties were in agreement that the police used force against the applicant and that the applicant sustained certain injuries as a result. The disagreement between the parties concerned, firstly, the issue of whether recourse to physical force both during his arrest and subsequently at the police station was made strictly necessary by the applicant's own conduct; secondly, the type and intensity of force used (including the issue of whether he was beaten); and, thirdly, the exact nature and causes of the applicant's injuries.

111. Having regard to those disputed issues, the Court considers that the burden rests on the Government to provide a satisfactory and convincing explanation as to how the applicant's injuries could have been caused as well as regarding the issues of whether the force was strictly necessary and not excessive (see *Bouyid*, cited above, § 83, as well as *Rehbock*, cited above, § 72).

112. The Court observes that the Government's position regarding the disputed issues is based exclusively on the findings and conclusions of the domestic investigation. The Court accepts that the explanation required from the Government can be said to have been provided when it is proved to the Court's satisfaction by the Government that their national authorities have conducted an effective investigation capable of establishing the circumstances and the nature of the force used (see *Cemal Yılmaz v. Turkey*, no. 31298/05, § 32, 7 February 2012).

113. The Court notes at the outset that in compliance with the procedural obligation, arising from Article 3 of the Convention, the authorities

opened and carried out a criminal investigation into the applicant's allegations. However, for the reasons that follow, the Court is not satisfied that the investigation was effective so as to meet the requirements of Article 3 of the Convention.

114. The Court considers that the authorities did not open an investigation promptly upon receipt of the applicant's complaint. In that regard, the Court notes that the initial refusal of the police officer and the prosecutor to allow the applicant to submit his complaint, as well as their directing the applicant to the other authority (see paragraph 17 above), was unlawful under domestic law, which provides that a report of a criminal offence may be submitted to an investigative body or a prosecutor's office either orally or in writing (see paragraph 69 above). Even after the complaint was finally accepted for submission, the police did not formally open an investigation into the incident until 5 May 2009, when six days had gone by (see paragraph 18 above). The Government justified that delay by saying that the complaint had been lodged the day before a public holiday and just before the weekend. The Court considers that weekends and public holidays cannot serve as an excuse for unacceptable delays in carrying out an effective investigation, as required under Article 3 of the Convention. In any event, there is no evidence in the case file of any investigative activity between 6 May 2009 when, according to the Government, the police asked the hospital to provide the applicant's medical records, and 13 May 2009 when the applicant gave a statement as a victim two weeks after the complaint had been lodged.

115. The Court considers that the delay of almost one month between opening the investigation and taking statements from the alleged perpetrators, and the delay of 10 days to more than a month between opening the investigation and questioning other police officers hampered the effectiveness of the investigation. The Court has noted that delays in questioning the potential perpetrators of a crime constitute a serious challenge to the effectiveness of an investigation, especially when there is a risk of justice being obstructed through collusion, which is particularly acute in a situation of hierarchical subordination and common service, such as that of police officers (see *Antayev and Others* v. *Russia*, no. 37966/07, § 108, 3 July 2014). In the past the Court has found a violation of the Convention where the alleged perpetrators were not kept separate after the incident, and were not questioned for nearly three days, notwithstanding the fact that no evidence indicated any collusion among them or with their colleagues. As indicated above (§ 108), the Court found

that the mere fact that appropriate steps were not taken to reduce the risk of such collusion amounted to a significant shortcoming in the adequacy of the investigation. In the present case, the Court is unaware of any measure taken by the authorities to reduce the risk of collusion among the alleged perpetrators or with the other police officers. The delays in taking statements from the police officers therefore greatly increased the risk of collusion between the suspects and among other police officers who served as witnesses.

116. The Court also finds that the authorities did not take all reasonable steps available to collect the necessary evidence. In particular, the authorities never ordered a forensic medical examination of the applicant in person to determine the exact nature and causes of his injuries. Even the assessment of the applicant's medical records and certain other documents by a forensic medical expert was ordered more than a month and delivered more than three months after the criminal proceedings were opened (see paragraphs 37 and 42 above). The Court emphasises that a forensic medical examination should have been ordered as soon as the applicant had alleged ill-treatment. The failure to do so made it almost impossible to determine exactly what injuries the applicant had sustained and how he had got them and whether his complaint about the loss of vision in his left eye (see paragraph 87 above) was related to his alleged ill-treatment.

117. The Court also points out in this context that it is hard to understand why the police did not inform the applicant about the decision to request a forensic medical expert to assess the applicant's relevant medical records and other documents or immediately send the report of that assessment to the applicant. The Court considers that that hindered the possibility for the applicant to substantiate his claims of ill-treatment and comment on the findings of the assessment. Turning to the content of the expert's opinion, the expert insisted both in writing and subsequently in his oral statements that the haematoma around the left eye could have been caused between 29 April and 1 May 2009. On the basis of that information the police investigator concluded that the applicant's allegation that the haematoma had resulted from the incident at the police station on 29 April was completely baseless and did not conform to reality. However, in the Court's view the investigator's conclusion, as based on the expert's opinion, seems unjustifiably categorical.

118. In addition, despite repeated statements by the applicant the police never took statements from Y.B., who allegedly witnessed the applicant's arrest, or from A.D., who was detained in the police station at the same time as the applicant. The authorities' failure to interview witnesses who could have had relevant information about the course of events, without giving any reasons, is regrettable. It is all the more so given the investigator's questioning of all the police officers who were involved in or otherwise incidentally witnessed some of the events. The Court also observes that the documents submitted to it do not reveal any efforts on the part of the authorities to find the elderly man present during the applicant's arrest (see paragraph 31 above), who could have been a valuable and impartial source of evidence.

119. Further, the authorities did not hold any face-to-face formal confrontations between the applicant and any of the witnesses or the suspects, as suggested by the applicant, to eliminate contradictions in their statements. The Court does not comprehend why that investigative measure, which was provided for under domestic law (see paragraph 67 above), was not used in a situation where it was appropriate and there were no practical obstacles to it (compare *Bouyid*, cited above, § 128, and *Velikanov v. Russia*, no. 4124/08, § 63, 30 January 2014, where the Court considered it relevant for the purposes of assessing the effectiveness of an investigation under Article 3 that the authorities failed to hold or arrange for a face-to-face confrontation which might have helped establish the facts; and *Perrillat-Bottonet v. Switzerland*, no. 66773/13, §§ 21, 65 and 66, 20 November 2014, where the Court considered it relevant that the authorities had held a confrontation under similar circumstances as in the present case).

120. The police investigator also did not try to clarify facts by other means (for example, by taking additional statements or putting detailed questions to the applicant, suspects and witnesses about specific aspects of the events). For instance, the investigator did not seek to establish whether the applicant was given any clear orders before the police had recourse to force in order to arrest him, whether he was warned about the consequences of failing to obey such orders, or whether the situation was tense to the point of allowing the police to dispense with those obligations. However, those aspects were of material importance for deciding whether the use of force was lawful and not an offence of abuse of authority (see paragraph 66 above).

121. The Court also points out that the investigation did not attempt to explain the discrepancy between the statements made by M.Z. during the presentation of photographs for the identification of suspects (see paragraph 44 above) and his earlier statements (see paragraph 26 above). Nor does the decision to discontinue the criminal proceedings explain why the police investigator preferred the later statements to the earlier ones.

122. Similarly, the decision does not explain why the statements about the alleged beating in the police station given by one of the persons detained there (see paragraph 22 above) were considered more credible than the conflicting statements of two other detainees who testified in the applicant's favour (see paragraphs 24 and 20 above). That is all the more incomprehensible in view of the fact that one of the detainees was not interviewed at all (see paragraph 118 above).

123. The Court also notes that the police investigator found the applicant's statements contradictory and therefore not credible. The applicant asserted twice that the same officer had beaten him at the playground, but then on the third occasion, during the presentation of the photographs for identification, he said that he did not remember whether that officer had beaten him at the playground. In the Court's view, this can hardly be characterised as the kind of contradiction which would serve to support the conclusion that the applicant's statements as a whole were not credible. The applicant's allegations have been consistent throughout the proceedings. He stated from the beginning that the police officers had beaten him at the playground and at the police station. The applicant's later statements do not contradict that position. In any event, the alleged contradiction does not at all concern the statements about the beating at the police station.

124. Moreover, those differences may, in the Court's opinion, be attributable to the time and manner in which the police investigator organised the presentation of suspects for identification by the applicant and by M.Z. In the first place, it is not evident why an attempt at identification was made at all at that stage of the investigation. By the time the photographs were presented for identification there was no longer any doubt about the identity of the possible suspects. It was clear that E.V. and S.B. were the officers who had responded to the call about an alleged breach of the peace. It was equally clear that the applicant and M.Z. accused

those officers of beating the applicant at the scene of the arrest and later in the police station and, even more importantly, the suspects themselves never denied that they had been the ones who had used force on the applicant. Be that as it may, the time between the incident and the identification might have affected the results of the identification process. The outcome might have also been influenced by the fact that the investigator presented photographs for the identification of the suspects instead of holding an identification parade with real people. Notably, the applicant stated during the identification procedure that he would have been able to recognise the officer in person, based on his features and height.

125. As regards the applicant's criticism that the authorities did not examine recordings of the police station's security cameras (see paragraph 90 above), the Government have not contested this and have not submitted any reports to the Court about any examination of those recordings. The Court is unable to understand why they were not duly examined.

126. The Court points out that the police did not immediately identify the children who were present during the applicant's arrest or the people present at the police station and then question them as witnesses. The Government have not disputed the fact that they were only heard as witnesses after the applicant had himself identified those people. The Court reiterates that the authorities must act of their own motion once a matter of importance has come to their attention and that they cannot leave it to the initiative of the person concerned to request particular investigative procedures (see, *mutatis mutandis*, *İlhan*, cited above, § 63, and *Nachova and Others v. Bulgaria* [GC], nos. 43577/98 and 43579/98, § 111, ECHR 2005-VII). In the present context the Court notes, nevertheless, that most of those people were eventually interviewed.

127. Lastly, the Court considers that the investigation did not conform to the requirement of independence.

128. The Court observes that the police officer in charge of the investigation was a police investigator from the internal control bureau of the East Police Prefecture. In that capacity she was part of the same regional substructure (the prefecture) of the police force as the suspects and other police officers implicated in the events. In essence, she was investigating the activities of her colleagues. The investigation therefore lacked the

necessary appearance of independence as it was carried out by a police officer institutionally linked to those targeted by it (compare, among others, *Đurđević v. Croatia*, cited above, § 87; *Grimailovs v. Latvia*, no. 6087/03, § 112, 25 June 2013; and *Kummer v. the Czech Republic*, no. 32133/11, §§ 85 and 86, 25 July 2013, where the Court found that the standards of an independent investigation had not been respected when, in substance, the police had been charged with investigating allegations relating to their own officers).

129. The Court notes that by the time the police investigator signed the decision to discontinue the proceedings on 20 January 2010, her position within the police force had changed. Following a merger and reform of the Police Board and the Border Guard Board on 1 January 2010, her job title had changed to senior disciplinary officer of the III department of the internal control bureau of the Police and Border Guard Board. That meant that the police investigator's post in the organisational structure had been transferred from a regional level to the central administration. However, by that time the investigative measures had already been taken and the investigation had in substance been finished. Simply changing the police investigator's position within the organisational structure could not therefore have influenced the potential undermining of the independence of the present investigation.

130. The Court has taken note of the Government's argument that the prosecutor's acceptance of the decision to discontinue the criminal proceedings guaranteed the independence of the investigation. It is true that the Court has found that shortcomings in the independence of those carrying out an investigation could, to a certain extent, be counterbalanced by effective supervision of the investigation (see, among others, *Vovruško v. Latvia*, no. 11065/02, § 51, 11 December 2012). However, the Court held in *Kummer* (cited above, § 87) that while the prosecutor was independent from the police, his role as a mere supervisor was not sufficient to make the police investigation comply with the requirement of independence. In the present case there is no evidence of active participation by prosecutors in directing or supervising the investigation which could have counterbalanced shortcomings in its independence. On the contrary, the Court observes that the prosecutors' position was tainted by the unlawful refusal to admit the applicant's initial complaint (see paragraph 114 above). There were also several dismissals by the prosecutor, on purely formal grounds, of the applicant's requests to take certain, apparently

justifiable, investigative measures, which in the end were never taken, including a forensic medical examination of the applicant in person (see paragraph 116 above) and an examination of Y.B. and A.D. as witnesses (see paragraph 118 above)). Additionally, the prosecution dismissed the applicant's appeal against the decision to discontinue the criminal proceedings (see paragraph 54 above). The Court therefore cannot accept that the prosecutors' role in the present case guaranteed an independent investigation, as required under its case-law.

131. The Court also considers it relevant that the findings of the investigation were never the object of any judicial scrutiny (see paragraphs 54, 55 and 77–79 above).

132. The cumulative effect of the those shortcomings, which concerned important aspects of the applicant's arrest and detention, is sufficient for the Court to conclude that the domestic authorities failed to carry out an effective investigation into the circumstances surrounding the alleged use of force by the police against the applicant. Thus the Government have failed to discharge their burden of proof of demonstrating that the use of force was strictly necessary and not excessive as well as providing a satisfactory and convincing explanation as to how the applicant's injuries could have been caused.

133. There has, accordingly, been a violation of Article 3 of the Convention.

(*Mihhailov* v. *Estonia*, app. no. 64418/10, 30 August 2016, Judgment of the Chamber)

6/6
On 8 November, the European Court of Human Rights handed down judgment in the case of *Pönkä* v. *Estonia*, where the applicant complained that he had not received a fair civil trial owing to the lack of an oral hearing where he and two witnesses could have given evidence (Article 6 § 1). The Chamber found the following:

I. Alleged Violation of Article 6 § 1 of the Convention

[...]

2. The Court's assessment

30. The present case concerns an alleged violation of Article 6 § 1 of the Convention in domestic civil proceedings which were conducted under the rules for the adjudication of small claims. The Court recognises at the outset that member States may find it useful to introduce a simplified civil procedure for the adjudication of small claims. Such a simplified procedure may be in the interest of the parties as it facilitates access to justice, reduces the costs related to the proceedings and accelerates the resolution of disputes. The Court also accepts that member States may decide that such a simplified civil procedure should normally be conducted via written proceedings – unless an oral hearing is considered necessary by a court or a party requests it – and that the court may refuse such a request. Such a simplified civil procedure for the adjudication of small claims must of course comply with the principles of a fair trial as guaranteed in Article 6 § 1. The domestic provisions and their application in the domestic courts must therefore ensure respect for the right to a fair trial, in particular when deciding on the necessity of an oral hearing, on the means of taking evidence, and the extent to which evidence is to be taken (see also recital 9 in the preamble to the European Parliament and Council regulation No. 861/2007 establishing a European Small Claims Procedure (see paragraph 21 above)). In this context the Court also reiterates the obligation under Article 6 § 1 for the domestic courts to give reasons not only for judgments but also for major procedural decisions issued in the course of the proceedings (see, among others, *Suominen* v. *Finland*, no. 37801/97, 1 July 2003, which concerned the reasoning underlying a decision not to admit certain evidence, and *Múčková* v. *Slovakia*, no. 21302/02, §§ 64–70, 13 June 2006, which concerned the reasoning underlying a decision not to exempt the applicant from the payment of a court fee).

31. According to the Court's established case-law, in proceedings before a court of first and only instance, the right to a 'public hearing' within the meaning of Article 6 § 1 entails an entitlement to an 'oral hearing' unless there are exceptional circumstances that justify dispensing with such a hearing (see *Göç* v. *Turkey* [GC], no. 36590/97, § 47, ECHR 2002-V and the case-law cited therein). In proceedings before two instances, at least one instance must, in general, provide such a hearing if no such exceptional circumstances are at hand (see *Salomonsson* v. *Sweden*, no. 38978/97, § 36, 12 November 2002).

32. The exceptional character of the circumstances that may justify dispensing with an oral hearing essentially comes down to the nature of the issues to be decided by the competent national court, not to the frequency of such situations. It does not mean that refusing to hold an oral hearing may be justified only in rare cases (see *Miller v. Sweden*, no. 55853/00, § 29, 8 February 2005). The Court has accepted exceptional circumstances in cases where the proceedings concerned exclusively legal or highly technical questions (see *Koottummel v. Austria*, no. 49616/06, § 19, 10 December 2009 and the case-law cited therein). Likewise, a hearing may not be required when the case raises no questions of fact or law which cannot be adequately resolved on the basis of the case-file and the parties' written observations (see *Döry v. Sweden*, no. 28394/95, § 37, 12 November 2002).

33. The Court has also held that, other than in wholly exceptional circumstances, litigants must at least have the opportunity of requesting a public hearing, even though the court may refuse the request and hold the hearing in private (see *Martinie v. France* [GC], no. 58675/00, §§ 42–44, ECHR 2006-VI). Similarly, it has attached importance to the fact that the applicants were not denied the possibility of requesting an oral hearing, although it was for the courts to decide whether a hearing was necessary, and that the decision refusing it was supported by reasons (see *Vilho Eskelinen and Others v. Finland* [GC], no. 63235/00, § 74, ECHR 2007-II).

34. In assessing whether there has been a violation of Article 6 § 1 on account of the lack of an oral hearing, the Court has also examined whether the requirements of fairness were complied with and did not necessitate an oral hearing, and in particular, whether the applicants were given an opportunity to put forward their case in writing and to comment on the submissions of the other party (see *Vilho Eskelinen and Others*, cited above, § 74; see also *Yevdokimov and Others v. Russia*, nos. 27236/05 and 10 others, § 22, 16 February 2016, where the Court reiterated that the questions of personal presence, the form of the proceedings – oral or written – and legal representation are interlinked and must be analysed in the broader context of the 'fair trial' guarantee of Article 6).

35. In the light of its established case-law, the Court will in the instant case assess whether the nature of the issues which were to be decided before the domestic courts justified dispensing with an oral hearing.

It will then examine whether the applicant had the opportunity to request a hearing and the way the domestic court approached his request.

36. Turning to the nature of the issues the domestic courts had to examine, the Court observes that the decision of the domestic court to opt for a written procedure does not contain any mention of those issues or of the question as to whether they could be examined without holding a hearing (see paragraph 12 above). Nor does the decision make any mention of the applicant's request for evidence to be taken from him and the witnesses. The Court nevertheless notes that, in so far as the applicant contested the claim against him by arguing that the police had caused the damage or that there was not sufficient evidence regarding either the occurrence or the extent of damage, he raised certain questions of fact.

37. With regard to the opportunity to request an oral hearing, the applicant had such an opportunity and he made use of it. However, it was left to the court's discretion to decide whether a hearing was in fact necessary. The Court observes that the domestic court in substance gave no reasons for deciding the case in written proceedings and dispensing with an oral hearing and the taking of oral evidence from the applicant and the witnesses (see paragraph 12 above). It merely cited a provision of the law that set a threshold amount for cases which could be examined in written proceedings and explained that such proceedings could be used if a party had significant difficulty in appearing before the court due to the length of his or her journey or for another good reason. The court did not explain why this provision was applicable in the applicant's case. It did not state explicitly why it refused to hold a hearing despite the applicant's request. The Court notes that, pursuant to Article 5 of Regulation (EC) No 861/2007 of the European Parliament and of the Council of 11 July 2007 establishing a European Small Claims Procedure – which had served as the basis for the relevant provisions of Estonian law – the domestic court would have been under an obligation to give reasons for such refusal in writing.

38. The Court has taken note of the Government's argument that the applicant did not submit an objection under Article 333 of the CCP (see paragraph 19 above) after the court's decision to examine the case in written proceedings (see paragraph 12 above). However, the Court does not see what purpose such an objection could have served. In his reply to the action the applicant had already explicitly formulated his request for the

holding of an oral hearing in order to hear testimony from him and two witnesses and given his reasons for that request.

39. The Court has also taken account of the practical problem of the applicant serving his prison sentence in Finland at the material time, whereas the civil proceedings against him took place in Estonia. It notes that 'hearing' the applicant did not necessarily have to take the form of an oral hearing in a court room in Estonia. However, it does not appear that the domestic court considered other alternative procedural options (such as the use of modern communications technology) with a view to ensuring the applicant's right to be heard orally. Moreover, the domestic court apparently did not even explain to the applicant that it had decided to replace hearing him orally with allowing him the opportunity to make written submissions (see paragraph 16 above regarding the appellate court's explanation that for hearing the applicant no court hearing had to be conducted).

40. The above considerations are sufficient for the Court to conclude that there has been a violation of the applicant's right to an oral hearing under Article 6 § 1 of the Convention.

(*Pönkä v. Estonia*, app. no. 64160/11, 8 November 2016, Judgment of the Chamber)

Part Six: VIII.D. The Position of the Individual (including the Corporation) in International Law – Human Rights and Fundamental freedoms – Other Aspects of Human Rights and Fundamental Freedoms

6/7

On 27 April, Foreign Minister Marina Kaljurand expressed concern about the situation of the Crimean Tatars:

> I consider the so-called Supreme Court of Crimea's decision yesterday to declare the governing body of the Crimean Tatar community, the Mejlis, an extremist organization, and to ban its activity, a serious violation of human rights by Russia.

Kaljurand stressed that she is deeply concerned about the vulnerable situation of the Crimean Tatars following the illegal annexation of Crimea:

We, together with the international community, call on Russia to respect the rights of indigenous peoples and to fulfil the commitments it has made in protecting human rights.

(Available at the website of the Ministry of Foreign Affairs, <https://vm.ee/en/news/kaljurand-ruling-regarding-crimean-tatars-serious-violation-human-rights>, visited on 30 August 2018)

6/8

On 21 September, President Toomas Hendrik Ilves gave a speech at the opening of the 71st Session of the General Assembly of the United Nations and addressed various challenges facing the international community, which included development and gender issues:

> The Sustainable Development Goals (SDG) and the Agenda 2030 are effective tools for advancing security and stability, economic growth, eradicating poverty, for preservation of the environment and human development. Taking this commitment seriously, Estonia was among the first countries to present our Voluntary National Review on implementation of SDGs during the High Level Political Forum.
>
> Estonia attaches great importance to the goal of achieving gender equality that can unlock the economic potential of women. More equal societies work better for everyone. Achieving gender equality is firstly the duty of the governments.
>
> Amidst current conflicts and crises it is important to ensure that women do not fall victim to gender-based violence and that they are also included in conflict resolution and peace negotiations. Therefore it is paramount to continue to implement UNSCR resolution 1325 and related resolutions on women, peace and security.

He also spoke about the right to freedom of expression in connection with journalists and in the online domain:

> Free media is an integral, even inseparable part of modern and democratic society, where governments listen to criticism, which, after all, forms part of what we call the voice of the people. Yet all around the globe we see that critical voices and even those who merely report the facts, face reprisals, jail and violence. The UN Plan of Action on the

Safety of Journalists and the Issue of Impunity must be implemented if we are to change the absurdity that reporting facts is a life-threatening activity.

As a leader in innovation in the digital world, the right to freedom of opinion and expression online and offline is for Estonia a fundamental issue. Digital technology has been a liberating force; yet some would turn it into a means to control citizens. As a co-founder of the Freedom Online Coalition, Estonia is a donor to the Digital Defenders Partnership, contributing to the protection of the rights of journalists, bloggers and human rights defenders online. In times of rapid ICT development the protection of human rights and the rule of law online must keep pace.

The right to freedom of expression also means keeping the Internet free and unrestricted. In other words, digital freedom of expression in no way differs from freedom of expression in the analogue world. Censorship, illicit filtering and the online blocking of opposition voices thwarts democracy no less than when the printed word is censored. An open Internet is an amplifier of economic growth and thus a crucial element of the sustainable development in the twenty-first century. This is a crucial conclusion of the World Bank's World Development Report 2016, titled Digital Dividends, whose preparation I co-chaired. IT can lead to transparent governance and economic growth but only if it is open and unfettered.

(Available at the website of the President of the Republic, <https://vp2006-2016.president.ee/en/official-duties/speeches/12557-address-by-the-president-of-the-republic-of-estonia-toomas-hendrik-ilves-at-the-general-debate-of-the-71st-united-nations-general-assembly/>, visited on 30 August 2018)

Part Seven: IV. Organs of the State and their Status – Diplomatic Missions and their Members

7/1

On 19 December, Foreign Minister Sven Mikser strongly condemned the brutal killing of the Russian Ambassador to Turkey, Andrey Karlov, in Ankara:

There is no justification for this kind of horrible violence.

(Available at the website of the Ministry of Foreign Affairs, <https://vm.ee/en/news/estonia-strongly-condemns-killing-russian-ambassador-turkey>, visited on 30 August 2018)

Part Sixteen: III. Use of Force – Use of Disarmament and Arms Control

16/1

On 8 February, the Ministry of Foreign Affairs issued a statement on North Korea's missile launch:

> Estonia strongly condemns the launch of a ballistic missile by the Democratic People's Republic of Korea on February 7th following a recent nuclear test. These illegal actions seriously violate UN Security Council resolutions prohibiting such activities, thus threatening regional, as well as global security, and raising tensions on the Korean Peninsula.
>
> Estonia urges the government of the Democratic People's Republic of Korea to stop their illegal nuclear and missile programmes and to return to the Six Party Talks.

(Available at the website of the Ministry of Foreign Affairs, <https://vm.ee/en/news/statement-foreign-ministry-estonia-north-korea-missile-launch>, visited on 30 August 2018)

16/2

On 9 September, the Ministry of Foreign Affairs issued a statement on North Korea's nuclear test:

> North Korea's nuclear test is a grave violation of UN Security Council Resolutions and this irresponsible activity deserves utmost condemnation. It is not only a regional, but potentially a global threat to peace and stability. The Security Council must implement additional sanctions that would lead North Korea to cease this illegal and dangerous behaviour.

(Available at the website of the Ministry of Foreign Affairs, <https://vm.ee/en/news/statement-foreign-ministry-estonia-north-korea-missile-launch>, visited on 30 August 2018)

Part Seventeen: I.B.3. The Law of Armed Conflict and International Humanitarian Law – International Armed Conflict – The Law of International Armed Conflict – Land Warfare

17/1

On 25 May, Foreign Minister Marina Kaljurand issued a statement upon the release of Nadiya Savchenko. First Lieutenant Savchenko was a member the armed forces of Ukraine who was abducted by separatists in Eastern Ukraine and then transferred to Russia where she was found guilty of illegally crossing the Russian border and the murder of two Russian journalists. Her lawyer insisted that Savchenko should have been treated as a prisoner of war. Foreign Minister Kaljurand said:

> I am pleased that Nadiya Savchenko, who was unlawfully detained by Russia, has now safely returned to her homeland. The whole process – the detention of Savchenko and her trial – was in stark contrast with the principles of justice from the very outset. The Nadiya Savchenko incident was not only the concern of Ukraine. That concern was also shared by the people of Estonia and the court case, which grossly violated international law, was continuously followed by all of Europe from start to finish.

(Available at the website of the Ministry of Foreign Affairs, <https://vm.ee/en/news/statement-foreign-minister-marina-kaljurand-upon-release-nadiya-savchenko>, visited on 30 August 2018)

17/2

On 18 October, the foreign ministers of the Member States of the European Union had a meeting focused on the humanitarian crisis in Syria. They condemned the attacks by the Syrian regime and its allies, above all Russian attacks and air raids that have increased the number of civilian casualties. Foreign Minister Jürgen Ligi noted that:

> Attacks against civilians, schools, hospitals and humanitarian convoys should be classed as war crimes. ... By supporting the Assad regime, Russia is taking part in the crimes of the Syrian regime.

Foreign ministers called for an end all violence and stop hindering the shipment of humanitarian aid.

(Available at the website of the Ministry of Foreign Affairs, <https://vm.ee/en/news/ligi-assad-regime-and-russia-have-stop-bombing-civilians-syria>, visited on 30 August 2018)

Part Seventeen: I.B.7. The Law of Armed Conflict and International Humanitarian Law – International Armed Conflict – The Law of International Armed Conflict – International Humanitarian Law

17/3

On 4 October, Foreign Minister Jürgen Ligi met with the acting Director of the United Nations Office for the Coordination of Humanitarian Affairs (OCHA). They acknowledged that both humanitarian crises and the need for humanitarian aid are growing and they are highly concerned about violations of international humanitarian law and cutting access to food and medical supplies as a method of war. The Foreign Minister strongly condemned attacks against humanitarian aid convoys and hospitals in Aleppo, Syria:

> The International community has to do everything in their power to guarantee humanitarian aid for those who need help and to stop further destabilisation of the area.

(Available at the website of the Ministry of Foreign Affairs, <https://vm.ee/en/news/foreign-minister-ligi-violations-humanitarian-law-and-impunity-are-concern>, visited on 30 August 2018)

Part Seventeen: I.B.8. The Law of Armed Conflict and International Humanitarian Law – International Armed Conflict – The Law of International Armed Conflict – Belligerent Occupation

17/4

On 16 September, the Ministry of Foreign Affairs issued a statement on the Russian Federation's plans to hold State Duma elections in the illegally annexed Crimea and Sevastopol:

> The Estonian Ministry of Foreign Affairs condemns the Russian Federation's plans to hold State Duma elections on 18 September 2016 in the illegally annexed Crimea and Sevastopol:

The plan to hold elections is yet another example of Russia violating Ukraine's sovereignty and territorial integrity.

Estonia supports the decision of the OSCE/ODIHR not to send observers to the elections in Crimea emanating from the non-recognition of the illegal annexation of Crimea and Sevastopol.

(Available at the website of the Ministry of Foreign Affairs, <https://vm.ee/en/news/statement-ministry-foreign-affairs-russian-federations-plans-hold-state-duma-elections>, visited on 30 August 2018)

Part Nineteen: VIII. Legal Aspects of International Relations and Co-operation in Particular Matters – Legal Matters (Judicial Assistance, Crime Control, and the like)

19/1

On 5 May, Foreign Minister Marina Kaljurand spoke at an international conference, held in Tallinn, focusing on the future of international law in cyberspace, and presented a vision how international law should govern cyberspace and what steps should states take:

> As a lawyer and as a diplomat I appreciate the interplay of law and politics in the international cyber security dialogue. I have personal experience of complicated diplomatic efforts to mitigate cyber-attacks against my country. Today, my Ministry is in charge of developing Estonian views on international law as it applies to State behaviour in cyberspace.
>
> Estonia has been a member of three consecutive UN Groups of Governmental Experts (UN GGE) in the United Nations First Committee.
>
> The upcoming GGE is faced with the expectation of taking us beyond already agreed positions. Whether or not each of us will be part of the next GGE, it is our privilege and duty to inform those discussions and to support an outcome that respects and responds to our common concern.
>
> For Estonia, international law is the biggest authority. We therefore strive for clarity and certainty of norms as it not only reduces the risk of

intolerable practices, but provides transparency and predictability of behaviour that allows us to focus on peace rather than on conflict.

I want to take this opportunity to elaborate on the question of peace and conflict. Seen through the Estonian lens, while we have witnessed the disruptiveness of malicious cyber activities, our focus has always been on using ICTs in support of State and societal functions; peace, growth and prosperity. We have never invested overly into military cyber capability development, although we have taken the question of cyber defence very seriously. We have promoted an atmosphere of trust and cooperation between government and industry, including critical infrastructure providers. And we have always taken into account the preferences and requests of the community of users. For Estonia ICTs are technologies of peace and development, not of conflict. I am sure this is the case for the majority of countries in the world.

However, I can understand how these technologies can be seen as a potential source of conflict by some of us. We have heard of development of offensive military cyber capabilities and doctrines. We can see the growing statistics of cybercrime, economic espionage and other malicious uses of ICTs. Estimates of cybercrime diminishing GDP vary between 0.1 and 1.6 per cent, thus depriving us of the full benefits that ICTs can offer. Terrorists exploit ICTs and social media to forward their sermon of hatred, violence and intolerance, to recruit followers and lead their misled troops.

It is essential to acknowledge that we perceive cyber threats and opportunities differently. Regardless of how clearly we can see and understand each other's perspectives, it is essential that we remain mindful of each other's views. This open and permissive attitude allows us to achieve stability and security, while taking full advantage of technological development and advances.

It is therefore essential that we need to go further than we already have.

We need to broaden our understanding of international law. We have concluded that international law, in particular the UN Charter, is applicable to international cyber security. There are other international legally binding instruments that are applicable. We need to identify and register these instruments.

I have noted that for some commentators the applicability of international humanitarian law is not settled. Let me share the Estonian position on that. While we acknowledge, and in fact hope, that cyber hostilities will never mount to the levels of use of force or armed attack, we also consider it very essential that, should that ever happen, protections of international humanitarian law are to be afforded to their fullest. Once we have affirmed these guarantees and clearly condemned any threat to peace and security in cyberspace, we can start working on details that, no doubt, need to be clarified with the view to application of particular norms.

We need to broaden our discussion on how international law applies to State activities in cyberspace. In this regard we have witnessed both uncertainty and differences. In the absence of easily observable State practice, and given the challenges of attribution, we must make extra efforts to apply the concepts and principles of sovereignty, non-intervention and State responsibility to activities in the cyber domain. And we need to be mindful of our different interpretations of some of these concepts, both due to our different traditions of international law, but also due to the fact that we are only starting to apply well-established legal norms and principles to a new reality – cyberspace.

Over the almost two decades that the UN First Committee has dealt with the issue of international cyber security, individual States have grown their expertise and experience in addressing these fundamental questions and specific threats. We need to look at what States actually do when facing cyber threats, because their actions speak of proposed standards of responsible behaviour. We need to carefully look at all the proposals, verbal and material, that States are making about how to deal with these threats.

In this regard, I also want to emphasize how important it is that we have different experiences. Our differences inform the margins of actions that each of us, or all of us together, can take in case of an incident.

But we should not stop at that – while we have clearly condemned any malicious and hostile acts in cyberspace and focused on the remedies that international law offers in case of breaches, we need to turn to preventing incidents from happening and escalating.

Here, it is important to find the incentives and common interests of all stakeholders, including governments, industry and civil society.

It is equally important to acknowledge that international law is not the only regime that we need to adjust to our needs. When it comes to prevention, it is essential to create national policies, procedures and standards that support cooperation and exchange of information.

This is why this conference looks at the future of international law by not (only) looking at international law. As the GGE has structured the conversation, when discussing how international law applies, we also identify potential gaps and inconsistencies that merit new norms, rules and principles. State behaviour is equally conditioned by legally non-binding norms. The GGE could be further informed by practices and norms that both States and industry have come to follow in their activities in cyberspace.

I would therefore propose a few additional approaches that the international community could consider.

States have the responsibility to lead a global culture of cybersecurity. The GGE has made reference to expectations that governments have towards industry and critical infrastructure operators. It is now essential to hear how governments should lead. Few corporate actors have tabled their views on this. In my view, we need to hear more. I would therefore invite the industry to consolidate and share their views on norms, rules and principles of responsible State behaviour, as well as the application of international law.

I also invite different schools of international law and international relations to discuss the urgent and practical issues of international cybersecurity and help us chart the political-normative surface we need to operate on. Let us not just suggest, but demonstrate that international law is alive, is relevant, and is useful. Let us demonstrate that we can use some of its core principles, such as good faith, and our pledge to remain bound by treaties, to modernize it to the age of smart and connected technologies.

My last point is something I hope you all consider when thinking and making decisions about international cybersecurity and international law. I would like to introduce you to a scholar of Estonian origin who spent most of his career at the service of the Russian empire at the end of the 19th century.

Professor Friedrich Frommhold Martens, a distinguished legal scholar and an assigned diplomat to the Hague Peace Conference, helped governments overcome a similar legal puzzle we are facing today. He suggested that while norms on (at that time) land warfare are still to be clarified by high contracting parties, States should afford maximum protections to anyone under the rule of law. The Martens Clause reads as follows:

> Until a more complete code of the laws of war is issued, the High Contracting Parties think it right to declare that in cases not included in the Regulations adopted by them, populations and belligerents remain under the protection and empire of the principles of international law, as they result from the usages established between civilized nations, from the laws of humanity, and the requirements of the public conscience.

I very much hope that in our thinking and discussion of the future of international law, we follow the example and spirit of Professor Martens and that we build the future of international law by not changing the law, but changing our thinking and behaviour to support the existing legal order to the fullest.

(Available at the website of the Ministry of Foreign Affairs, <https://vm.ee/en/news/statement-foreign-minister-marina-kaljurand-conference-state-practice-and-future-international>, visited on 30 August 2018)

Part Nineteen: IX. Legal Aspects of International Relations and Co-operation in Particular Matters – Military and Security Matters

19/2
On 11 February, Foreign Minister Marina Kaljurand gave an annual speech on Estonia's foreign policy in the *Riigikogu* (parliament). Among other issues, she addressed the conflict in Ukraine and its wider consequences for the European security architecture.

> In terms of foreign policy, 2015 was an extremely difficult year for Estonia and Europe, and 2016 will not be any easier. Instability on the borders of

the European Union has increased. Soon two years will have passed since the occupation of the Crimea and the beginning of military actions in Eastern Ukraine. Two years will have passed from the day on which a country once again decided to violate a security situation which was based on international law and principles. We know that a single country cannot invalidate international law and legal order. However, a single country can undermine international security and create uncertainty. We also know that one must bear liability for one's acts and omissions. In less than a year, Europe forgave Russia for the attack against and occupation of Georgia. Our duty is to stand against the same thing happening with the occupation of Crimea and military actions in Ukraine. This kind of behaviour cannot become an everyday practice. Therefore it is very important not to recognise the annexation of Crimea at an international level, just like the occupation of the Baltic Countries was never recognised. The sanctions imposed on Russia bear the message that there is a price to pay for the violation of international rules.

In recent months there have been talks about restarting a dialogue between the West and Russia. Estonia has never been opposed to a dialogue with Russia. In September, I myself met with the Russian Minister of Foreign Affairs, and in November political consultations with ministries of foreign affairs took place in Tallinn; however, I am certain that the most difficult issues must be firmly placed in the centre of the dialogue between the West and Russia. Restarting cooperation must be dependent on the fulfilment of the Minsk agreements and Russia once again honouring the principles of European security.

Until the obligations assumed are performed, the pressure of sanctions must continue and Ukraine must remain the focus of European attention. The sanctions are not a goal in themselves, but by combining their efficient implementation with diplomatic efforts and other means of foreign policy, we can achieve common European foreign policy objectives. It is essential to find a solution to the Ukrainian conflict, which would honour and ensure the sovereignty and territorial integrity of Ukraine.

In the short-term perspective, the goal should be adherence to the Minsk Protocols. We must not forget that Ukraine is the victim of Russian aggression. Over 9,000 people have been killed as a result of this. At a rough estimate, over 5 million people need humanitarian aid. About 1.1 million people have already left Ukraine, and there are 1.6 million internal migrants in Ukraine. This is the price that the people of Ukraine have paid for their freedom. This is the context within which the Ukrainian government is trying to carry out their reforms. Besides, we must not forget that the events that happened at the Maidan two years ago originated from the wish of the Ukrainian people to live as free people in a free State. They wanted to achieve something that they had failed to achieve twenty years ago. The Ukrainian people have expressed their intention to create a society that respects European values and rights. The efforts that Ukrainians are investing into integration with Europe are a huge compliment to the European Union as a whole. They prove that the image of Europe as a bearer of democratic values is indeed very strong.

(Available at the website of the Ministry of Foreign Affairs, <https://vm.ee/en/news/address-minister-foreign-affairs-mrs-marina-kaljurand-riigikogu>, visited on 30 August 2018)

19/3

On 15 March, the foreign ministers of the members of the European Union had a meeting focused on the current status of relations between the European Union and Russia. Foreign Minister Marina Kaljurand noted that:

> Relations with Russia were complicated even before the Ukrainian conflict. The developments during recent years have demonstrated that Russia must first and foremost be assessed based on its actions. ... Given the aggressive nature of Russia's foreign policy and the discrepancy in our values, the current European policy must continue.

She added that the imposed restrictions have sent a clear message to Russia indicating the European Union does not tolerate the violation of international law. Following the annexation of Crimea in 2014, the European Union imposed a limited communication policy in its relations with Russia.

(Available at the website of the Ministry of Foreign Affairs, <https://vm.ee/en/news/foreign-minister-marina-kaljurand-current-policy-european-union-relations-russia-will-continue>, visited on 30 August 2018)

19/4

On 15 July, Foreign Minister Marina Kaljurand condemned the terror attack in Nice. The attack left 86 persons dead and 434 persons injured, including two Estonian nationals dead and three Estonian nationals or residents injured:

> My thoughts today are with all the relatives of the deceased and injured victims of the barbaric terrorist attack that occurred on the evening of the French national holiday, Bastille Day. That attack was directed towards all nations that strive for freedom and equality, at our common values. The security of Europe and its citizens is our most important challenge today and we must jointly confront those who fail to respect human lives and basic values that differ from theirs. Estonia will do its utmost to make the fight against terrorism more decisive and effective. We will stand alongside other countries and international organisations in this. ... As we have been getting reports that Estonian citizens were among those injured in the attack, this tragedy indeed strongly affects us all. The Ministry of Foreign Affairs will do everything to establish the facts regarding the affected Estonian citizens and residents and render assistance to those who need it. To this end, we have been cooperating with French national and local Nice authorities.

(Available at the website of the Ministry of Foreign Affairs, <https://vm.ee/en/news/foreign-minister-condemns-brutal-terror-attack-nice>, visited on 30 August 2018)

19/5

On 21 September, President Toomas Hendrik Ilves gave a speech at the opening of the 71st Session of the General Assembly of the United Nations and addressed various challenges facing the international community, which included defence and security issues:

> Certainly the world was more stable then, before the economic crisis, the migration crisis; current conflicts in the wider Middle East or Russia's aggression against Georgia and Ukraine; before the war on truth and facts that seems to have taken over in many places. Despite our concerns at the time, we lived in a world more stable, where optimism was not yet naiveté. Today, in too many parts of the world, we find a conflict either emerging, raging or frozen. Terrorism, always a scourge, dominates our daily headlines in all parts of the world.

> Not all of today's conflicts and crises could have been prevented. Yet the effect of many could have been mitigated had we acted sooner, had the proper mechanisms to resolve them been in place. When I addressed this assembly in the wake of Russia's invasion in Georgia in 2008, I warned not to apply international law selectively. International law had been clearly

violated, yet little was done. Six years later, in 2014, we saw a repeat performance in Ukraine. Part of a sovereign State was annexed, part turned into a warzone. For the first time since World War II borders in Europe had been changed through use of force. The prohibition on the use of force to change borders lies at the heart of the UN Charter. It was blatantly violated and yet the UN could not make a difference. Russia's aggression in Ukraine continues. Territories of Ukraine and Georgia remain occupied by a foreign military, frozen conflicts remain in Nagorno-Karabakh and Transnistria.

We need global norms. Just as we need international law, we need also the mechanisms to enforce it. Unless the UN starts to do more, it will, over time, lose relevance. When we face a global challenge, the UN should be the first place to come to for a solution, not the last stop when all other options have been exhausted, knowing that nothing will happen anyway.

[...]

The on-going conflicts we see around the world will, if we do not take control, breed a terrorism that knows no boundaries. Estonia reaffirms its commitment to work together to prevent and counter terrorism. We participate in the Global Coalition to counter ISIL.

Estonia firmly supports the International Criminal Court and its quest to end impunity. Countries – whether they have joined the Rome Statute or not – must set an example of non-aggression, self-restraint, and respect for the rule of law. We believe that a commitment to fight impunity at all levels is the only way to deter those who might commit future crimes.

In 2005, the member states of the United Nations committed to the principle of Responsibility to Protect (R2P) to fight genocide, war crimes, ethnic cleansing and crimes against humanity. The brutality we see in Syria shows, however, that an effective solution lies beyond the grasp of the UN. When a government fails to live up to its commitments, when it violates the fundamental norms of civilized behaviour, let alone the tenets of the UN, the international community must act. Here the Security Council bears primary responsibility. Council members that veto or vote against actions aimed at preventing mass atrocities carry co-responsibility for those atrocities.

A primary criticism directed at the UN today is grounded on the Security Council's lack of ability – or willingness – to respond to major crises. Estonia cannot speak from first-hand experience; we so far have not served in the Council. We want, however, to bring the spirit of openness, transparency and inclusivity to the Council's work and hence are running for the seat of a non-permanent member for 2020/2021. We are convinced that the role of the General Assembly and the role of the non-permanent members of the SC must be increased. The majority of the UN member States are small countries. Small countries are, as we look at the history of conflict since World War II, almost invariably the victims of conflict, not the abettors.

There is nothing new in this. Already Thucydides concluded in the Melian dialogues in history of the Peloponnesian Wars, 'The strong do what they will, the weak what they must'. This is why we have international law: to protect the weak, to protect the small. Their voices must be better heard; their rights must be upheld.

Estonia, as a member of the Accountability, Coherence and Transparency Group (ACT), is working together with a number of countries to improve the working methods of the Security Council that would provide for badly-needed changes.

(Available at the website of the President of the Republic, <https://vp2006-2016.president.ee/en/official-duties/speeches/12557-address-by-the-president-of-the-republic-of-estonia-toomas-hendrik-ilves-at-the-general-debate-of-the-71st-united-nations-general-assembly/>, visited on 30 August 2018)

ANNEX I.A   Agreements Signed by Estonia before 2016 but Entered into Force in regard to Estonia in 2016 – Bi- and Multilateral Agreements

Title	Conclusion	Entry into Force
Arrangement between the Republic of Estonia and the Republic of Italy on Visa Representation	11.12.2015	01.01.2016
Declaration by Certain European Governments on the Launchers Exploitation Phase of Ariane, Vega, and Soyuz from the Guiana Space Centre	30.03.2007	16.01.2016

Title	Conclusion	Entry into Force
Agreement between the Government of the Republic of Estonia and the Government of Turkmenistan on Visa Exemption for Holders of Diplomatic Passports	12.12.2015	01.04.2016
Implementing Protocol between the Government of the Republic of Estonia and the Cabinet of Ministers of Ukraine on the Implementation of the Agreement between the European Community and Ukraine on Readmission of Persons	14.01.2015	13.04.2016
Agreement between the States Parties to the Convention for the Establishment of a European Space Agency and the European Space Agency for the Protection and the Exchange of Classified Information	19.08.2002	23.04.2016
Agreement between the Government of the Republic of Estonia and the Government of the State of Kuwait on Visa Exemption for Holders of Diplomatic Passports	25.09.2015	11.05.2016
Agreement between the Government of the Republic of Estonia and the Government of Uzbekistan on Visa Exemption for Holders of Diplomatic Passports	03.12.2015	05.08.2016
Agreement between the Republic of Estonia and Georgia on the Promotion and Reciprocal Protection of Investments	24.11.2009	21.11.2016
Protocol between the Republic of Estonia and Georgia to amend the Agreement between the Republic of Estonia and Georgia on the Promotion and Reciprocal Protection of Investments	02.11.2015	21.11.2016

ANNEX I.B Agreements signed by Estonia before 2016 but Entered into Force in regard to Estonia in 2016 – Conventions

Title	Conclusion	Entry into Force
Amendments to the International Convention on Standards of Training, Certification and Watchkeeping for Seafarers (STCW), 1978	22.05.2014	01.01.2016
Amendments to the Seafarers' Training, Certification and Watchkeeping (STCW) Code	22.05.2014	01.01.2016
Amendments to the Convention on the International Regulations for Preventing Collisions at Sea, 1972	04.12.2013	01.01.2016
Amendments to Annex B to the Protocol of 1988 Relating to the International Convention on Load Lines, 1966, as Amended	22.05.2014	01.01.2016
Amendments to the Annex of the Protocol of 1978 relating to the International Convention for the Prevention of Pollution from Ships, 1973 (Amendments to MARPOL Annexes I, II, III, IV and V to make the use of the III Code mandatory)	04.04.2014	01.01.2016
Amendments to the Annex of the Protocol of 1997 to Amend the International Convention for the Prevention of Pollution from Ships, 1973, as Modified by the Protocol of 1978 relating thereto (To make the use of the III Code mandatory)	04.04.2014	01.01.2016
Amendments to the Annex of the Protocol of 1978 relating to the International Convention for the Prevention of Pollution from Ships, 1973 (Amendments to MARPOL Annex I)	04.04.2014	01.01.2016
Amendments to the Annex of the Protocol of 1978 relating to the International Convention for the Prevention of Pollution from Ships, 1973 (Amendments to MARPOL Annex VI)	17.10.2014	01.03.2016
Amendments to the Annex of the Protocol of 1978 relating to the International Convention for the Prevention of Pollution from Ships, 1973 (Amendments to MARPOL Annex III)	17.10.2014	01.03.2016

Title	Conclusion	Entry into Force
Amendments to the Annex of the Protocol of 1978 relating to the International Convention for the Prevention of Pollution from Ships, 1973 (Amendments to MARPOL Annex I)	17.10.2014	01.03.2016
Amendments to the Annex of the Protocol of 1978 relating to the International Convention for the Prevention of Pollution from Ships, 1973 (Amendments to MARPOL Annex VI)	17.10.2014	01.03.2016
Protocol of Amendments to the Convention on the International Hydrographic Organization	14.04.2005	08.11.2016
Paris Agreement	12.12.2015	04.12.2016

ANNEX II.A Agreements Signed by Estonia in 2016 – Bi- and Multilateral Agreements

Title	Conclusion	Entry into Force
Agreement between the Republic of Estonia and the Republic of Belarus regulating Certain Aspects of Entry, Stay and Exit of Persons	20.04.2016	04.11.2016
Protocol Amending the Protocol between the Government of the Republic of Estonia, the Government of the Republic of Latvia and the Government of the Republic of Lithuania Concerning the Status of the Baltic Defence College and Its Personnel	14.06.2016	11.06.2017
Arrangement between the Republic of Estonia and the Republic of Portugal on Visa Representation	21.06.2016	01.07.2016
Agreement between the Government of the Kingdom of Denmark and the Government of Republic of Estonia on the Amendment to the Agreement between the Government of the Kingdom of Denmark and the Government of Republic of Estonia for the Promotion and Reciprocal Protection of Investments, signed on 6 November 1991 in Tallinn and on the Termination thereof	25.07.2016	16.08.2017

ANNEX II.A Agreements Signed by Estonia in 2016 – Bi- and Multilateral Agreements (*cont.*)

Title	Conclusion	Entry into Force
Reciprocal Defense Procurement Agreement between the Government of the Republic of Estonia and the Government of the United States of America	23.09.2016	23.09.2016
Protocol Amending the Agreement between the Government of the Republic of Estonia and the Government of the Republic of Italy on Mutual Protection of Classified Information	21.10.2016	06.01.2017
Agreement between the Republic of Estonia and the Republic of India on the transfer of sentenced persons	15.11.2016	01.03.2017
Agreement between the Republic of Estonia and Hungary on the Exchange and Mutual Protection of Classified Information	08.12.2016	01.09.2017

ANNEX II.B Agreements Signed by Estonia in 2016 – Conventions

Title	Conclusion	Entry into Force
Amendments to the Annex to the Convention on Facilitation of International Maritime Traffic, 1965	08.04.2016	01.01.2018
Amendments to the Annex of the Protocol of 1997 to Amend the International Convention for the Prevention of Pollution from Ships, 1973, as Modified by the Protocol of 1978 relating thereto (Amendments to regulation 13 of MARPOL Annex VI)	22.04.2016	01.09.2017
Amendments to the Annex of the International Convention for the Prevention of Pollution from Ships, 1973, as Modified by the Protocol of 1978 relating thereto (Amendments to MARPOL Annex IV)	22.04.2016	01.09.2017

Title	Conclusion	Entry into Force
Amendments to the Annex of the International Convention for the Prevention of Pollution from Ships, 1973, as Modified by the Protocol of 1978 relating thereto (Amendments to MARPOL Annex II)	22.04.2016	01.09.2017
Amendments to the Annex of the International Convention for the Prevention of Pollution from Ships, 1973, as Modified by the Protocol of 1978 relating thereto (Establishment of the date on which regulation 11.3 of MARPOL Annex IV in respect of the Baltic Sea special area shall take effect)	22.04.2016	01.06.2019
Protocol to the North Atlantic Treaty on the Accession of Montenegro	19.05.2016	01.06.2017
Universal Postal Convention	06.10.2016	01.01.2018
First Additional Protocol to the General Regulations of the Universal Postal Union	06.10.2016	01.01.2018
Ninth Additional Protocol to the Constitution of the Universal Postal Union	06.10.2016	01.01.2018
Protocol Relating to an Amendment to Article 50(a) of the Convention on International Civil Aviation	06.10.2016	
Protocol Relating to an Amendment to Article 56 of the Convention on International Civil Aviation	06.10.2016	
Amendments to the Annex of the Protocol of 1997 to Amend the International Convention for the Prevention of Pollution from Ships, 1973, as Modified by the Protocol of 1978 relating thereto (Amendments to MARPOL Annex VI)	28.10.2016	01.03.2018
Amendments to the Annex of the International Convention for the Prevention of Pollution from Ships, 1973, as Modified by the Protocol of 1978 relating thereto (Amendments to MARPOL Annex I)	28.10.2016	01.03.2018

ANNEX II.B   Agreements Signed by Estonia in 2016 – Conventions (*cont.*)

Title	Conclusion	Entry into Force
Amendments to the Annex of the International Convention for the Prevention of Pollution from Ships, 1973, as Modified by the Protocol of 1978 relating thereto (Amendments to MARPOL Annex V)	28.10.2016	01.03.2018

CHAPTER 11

Republic of Latvia Materials on International Law 2016

Edited by Kristaps Tamužs

[*Editorial Notes:*

Republic of Latvia Materials on International Law 2016 (RLMIL 2016) have been classified according to the Recommendation (97)11 of 12 June 1997 of the Committee of Ministers of the Council of Europe, as applied by the British Yearbook of International Law from 1997, with certain minor amendments.

The RLMIL mostly concern opinions by Latvian institutions and officials. Often, different officials expressed views on the same issues. In order to prevent unnecessary repetition, the editor has selected materials from the highest possible level. Statements by officials and in particular decisions of the courts have been occasionally edited in order to ensure brevity, focus and consistency.

There were several recurring topics in speeches given and statements made by officials, for example, the unlawful annexation of Crimea by the Russian Federation and human rights abuses in Crimea subsequent to annexation, as well as the armed conflict in Eastern Ukraine. The President as well as the Minister of Foreign Affairs also continued to express Latvia's continued support for reform of the United Nations Security Council.

Undoubtedly the most significant international law event of 2016 in Latvia was the completion of the accession process to the OECD, of which Latvia became the 35th Member State on 1 July 2016.

In 2016 the European Court of Human Rights (ECtHR) communicated eight cases to the Latvian Government and handed down two judgments by a seventeen-judge Grand Chamber, twelve judgments by a seven-judge chamber and two judgments by a three-judge committee. A further three cases were declared inadmissible by a chamber decision and two by a committee decision. The Court in committee formation also decided to strike five cases out of the

Court's list of cases. Finally, 218 cases were either declared inadmissible or struck out of the Court's list of cases by unpublished decisions of either a single-judge formation or a three-judge committee.]

Part Four: 11. Relationship between International Law and Internal Law – Application and Implementation of International Law in Internal Law

The Constitutional Court of the Republic of Latvia continued to demonstrate its commitment to the doctrine of the Latvian legal system's openness to international law by extensively invoking the provisions of various instruments of international law, including in particular the European Convention on Human Rights (ECHR).

4/1

In its judgment of 2 March 2016 in case no. 2015-11-03 the Constitutional Court *inter alia* addressed the issue of the democratic legitimatization of the Bank of Latvia. In particular regarding the issue of the independence of the Bank of Latvia, the Court indicated as follows:

> 21.2. Article 6 of the [Constitution of the Republic of Latvia] provides that the [Parliament of the Republic of Latvia] is elected in general, equal and direct elections, and by secret ballot based upon proportional representation. Thus, the [Parliament] is directly democratically legitimized. Whereas pursuant to Article 22(1) and (2) of the law 'On the Bank of Latvia', the President of the Bank of Latvia is elected to office by the [Parliament], which also appoints the Vice-president and the members of the Council of the Bank of Latvia to their offices. Thus, all members of the Council of the Bank of Latvia are indirectly democratically legitimized.
>
> The democratic legitimization of the Council of the Bank of Latvia is influenced by the pre-requisite that its members during their term of office may be dismissed from office only in the cases envisaged in Article 22 of the law 'On the Bank of Latvia'. However, the fact indicated by the applicant that during their term in office the [Parliament] has no possibility to exert political influence upon the members of the Council of the Bank of Latvia does not mean that the members of the Council of the Bank of Latvia would lack democratic legitimization. The Council of

the Bank of Latvia being outside political influence is an essential prerequisite for the independence of the national central bank, which follows not only from the [Constitution] and the law 'On the Bank of Latvia', but also from Article 130 of the Treaty on the Functioning of the European Union and Protocol no. 4 of the Statute of the European System of Central Banks and of the European Central Bank.

(An unofficial translation by the Constitutional Court is available at the website of the Constitutional Court, <http://www.satv.tiesa.gov.lv/wp-content/uploads/2015/04/2015-11-03_Spriedums_ENG.pdf>, visited on 22 September 2018)

4/2

In its judgment of 12 May 2016 in case no. 2015-14-0103 the Constitutional Court extensively relied on international human rights documents in order to establish the scope of the right to protection of personal data. The case concerned legal regulation of gathering and storing DNA profiles and biological material of persons suspected of having committed criminal offences. Some of the findings of the Court were as follows:

> 15.1. Article 96 of the [Constitution] provides that everyone has the right to inviolability of his or her private life, home, and correspondence.
>
> The right to private life means that an individual has the right to his own private space, suffering minimum interference by the state or other persons. A finding has been enshrined in the case-law of the Constitutional Court that the right to inviolability of private life protects a person's physical and mental integrity, honour, and dignity, name and identity, personal data ...
>
> Article 89 of the [Constitution] provides that the state recognises and protects fundamental human rights in accordance with the [Constitution], laws and international agreements binding upon Latvia. It follows from this Article that the legislator's aim is to harmonise the human rights provisions included in the [Constitution] with international legal provisions. International human rights provisions that are binding upon Latvia and the practice of application thereof on the level of constitutional law serve as a means of interpretation to define the content and scope of fundamental rights and principles of a state governed by the rule of law, insofar as they do not cause decrease or restriction of fundamental rights included in the [Constitution] ...

In interpreting Article 8 of the European Convention for the Protection of Human Rights and Fundamental Freedoms ..., the ECtHR has recognised that the concept of 'private life' has broad scope. Collection and storing of personal data fall within the scope of the right to inviolability of private life (*see* the judgment of the Grand Chamber of the ECtHR of 16 February 2000 in *Amann* v. *Switzerland,* application no. 27798/95, para. 65, and the judgment of 4 December 2008 in *S. and Marper* v. *the United Kingdom,* applications no. 30562/04 and no. 30566/04, paras. 68 and 69). Inviolability of private life and protection of personal data have been enshrined also in Articles 7 and 8 of the European Union Charter of Fundamental Rights.

The Constitutional Court finds that collection, processing and storing of data that characterise a person's physical and social identity fall with the scope of a person's right to inviolability of personal life.

Thus, the right to inviolability of personal life enshrined in Article 96 of the [Constitution] comprises protection of the personal data of a natural person.

...

15.3. Pursuant to Article 2(8) of the Data Protection Law sensitive personal data are personal data which indicate the race, ethnic origin, religious, philosophical or political convictions, or trade union membership of a person, or provide information as to the health or sexual life of a person.

The Constitutional Court has recognised that these data indicated in the Data Protection Law essentially comply with the data of special categories regulated by Article 8 of Directive of the European Parliament and of the Council of 24 October 1995 95/46/EC on the protection of individuals with regard to the processing of personal data and on the free movement of such data ... The finding that an individual's DNA profile are sensitive personal data has been consolidated also in the case-law of the ECtHR (*see* the judgment of the Grand Chamber of the ECtHR of 4 December 2008 in *S. and Marper* v. *the United Kingdom,* applications no. 30562/04 and no. 30566/04, paras. 75 and 76). In all cases a DNA profile is determined with the aim of identifying a concrete person or a link between several persons. The fact that only part of information that biological material comprises is used in the process of determining a DNA profile does not substantially influence recognition of a DNA profile as being sensitive personal data (*see ibid.*, para. 73). Neither the fact that a DNA profile is a computer readable outcome of genetic analysis of DNA that cannot be used without applying appropriate information technology influences recognition of a DNA profile as being sensitive personal data (*see ibid.*, para. 75).

Thus, biological material of an identified person, which is collected and analysed in the process of determining a DNA profile, as well as a DNA profile are a natural person's personal data requiring special protection.

...

16.3. ... The Constitutional Court notes that the ECtHR has emphasized the special risks and far-reaching consequences of storing biological material and DNA profiles, in view of the fact that the respective sensitive information can actually be used at any time in the future (*see* the judgment of the Grand Chamber of the ECtHR of 4 December 2008 in *S. and Marper v. the United Kingdom*, applications no. 30562/04 and no. 30566/04, para. 69). Considering the nature of these data, requiring special protection, the fact that the Petitioner succeeded in unlawfully avoiding application of the impugned norms as united legal regulation does not mean that he has not entered the scope of these norms. Moreover, the Petitioner had been in a legal situation that had caused adverse consequences to him; i.e., it was recognised that he had committed an administrative violation.

Thus, the impugned norms have caused an infringement upon the Petitioner's fundamental rights.

...

22. ... The ECtHR has recognised that crime prevention and resolving criminal offences are legitimate aims that justify storing of sensitive personal data (*see* the judgment of the Grand Chamber of the ECtHR of 4 December 2008 in *S. and Marper v. the United Kingdom*, applications no. 30562/04 and no. 30566/04, para. 100, and the judgment of 4 June 2013 in *Peruzzo v. Germany* and *Martens v. Germany*, applications no. 7841/08 and no. 57900/12, para. 40).

The Constitutional Court upholds the opinion expressed by the [Parliament] regarding the importance of sharing the results of genetic analysis, in particular, among the EU Member States. Resolving criminal offences by verifying a person's possible connection to other criminal offences is in the interests of society as a whole and each member of it.

Thus, the legitimate aim of the restriction is public security and protection of other persons' rights.

23.1. ... The ECtHR has recognised that combating crime, in particular terrorism and organised crime, to a large extent depends upon contemporary scientific methods of investigation and identification (*see* the judgment of the Grand Chamber of the ECtHR of 4 December 2008 in *S. and Marper* v. *the United Kingdom,* applications no. 30562/04 and no. 30566/04, para. 105). The importance of these methods has been highlighted also in the sixth paragraph of the Recommendation of 10 February 1992 by the Committee of Ministers of the Council of Europe 'On the Use of Analysis of Deoxyribonucleic Acid (DNA) within the Framework of Criminal Justice System', as well as in the first and the second paragraph in the Preamble of the Resolution by the Council of the European Union of 9 June 1997 no. 97/C193/02 'On the Exchange of DNA Analysis Results'.

...

23.3.1. ... The ECtHR has recognised that a state has the right to store only such volume of data that complies with the legitimate aim of data processing, and demands the existence of sufficient legal remedies, noting that the sufficiency thereof depends upon the volume of stored personal data, duration of storing, rules on destroying and using data (*see* the judgment of the ECtHR of 25 September 2001 in *P.G. and J.H.* v. *the United Kingdom,* application no. 4478798, paras. 44–47, and the judgment of 4 December 2008 in *S. and Marper* v. *the United Kingdom,* applications no. 30562/04 and no. 30566/04, paras. 103 and 107).

The Council of the European Union has pointed out to the Member States the need to abide by appropriate rules of personal data protection when engaging in mutual personal data exchange.

It is recognised in the Framework Decision that competent authorities may collect personal data only for specified, explicit and legitimate purposes in the framework of their tasks and personal data may be processed only for the same purpose for which data were collected. It also underscores that Member States should ensure that subjects are informed that personal data could be or are being collected, processed or transmitted to another member state [see the Council Framework Decision 2008/977/JOHAN of 27 November 2008 on the protection of personal data processed in the framework of police and judicial cooperation in criminal matters, para. 27 of the Preamble and Article 3(1)]. As regards processing of data, the Framework Decision does not prohibit Member States to establish even stricter measures for personal data protection than defined therein; however, it underscores the necessity to ensure that any personal data that Member States exchange among themselves are processed legally and in compliance with fundamental principles.

Consequently, in assessing the adverse consequences caused to a person, the Constitutional Court must verify whether the impugned norms comply with these principles of data protection.

The impugned norms envisage using a DNA profile only in accordance with the purpose of the DNA Law; i.e., establishing the National DNA Database. The DNA Law provides that data to be included in the National DNA Database are to be used for resolving criminal offences, searching for missing persons, and identifying unidentified bodies (human remains).

The Constitutional Court has recognised that the legitimate aim of the restriction upon fundamental rights established by the impugned norms is protection of public security and other persons' rights.

Pursuant to Article 10 of the DNA Law, the following information is included in the National DNA Database: the suspect's given name and surname, his personal identity number, nationality and DNA profile, the criminal case number, the name of the of the institution where the comparative sample has been taken, and the name and surname of the person who has taken this sample. Thus, the amount of information that is objectively needed for identifying DNA profile is stored.

Pursuant to Article 15 of the DNA Law, suspects' DNA profiles and other information included in the National DNA Database is restricted access information. Article 16 of the DNA Law provides that the right to receive information from the National DNA Database is given only to investigatory institutions, with the consent of a prosecutor, institutions of the prosecutor's office and courts for conducting pre-trial criminal proceedings, examination and adjudication of cases. Likewise, information to foreign law enforcement institutions may be issued only for these purposes (*see also* the Resolution by the Council of the European Union of 9 June 1997 no. 97/C193/02 On the Exchange of DNA Analysis Results, the ninth paragraph of the preamble).

(An unofficial translation by the Constitutional Court is available at the website of the Constitutional Court, <http://www.satv.tiesa.gov.lv/wp-content/uploads/2016/07/2015-14-0103_Spriedums_ENG.pdf>, visited on 23 September 2018)

4/3

In its judgment of 16 June 2016 in case no. 2015-18-01 the Constitutional Court dealt with a possible conflict between the constitutionally protected right to inviolability of one's private life and a legal provision that provided for publication on the internet of personal information about non-payers of alimony. The Court invoked the relevant international law instruments in the following manner:

> 10. Article 89 of the [Constitution] provides that the state recognises and protects fundamental human rights in accordance with the [Constitution], laws and international agreements binding upon Latvia. It follows from this article that the legislator's purpose is to harmonise provisions on human rights included in the [Constitution] with the provisions of international law. Norms of international human rights that are binding upon Latvia and the practice of their application on the level of constitutional law serve also as a means of interpretation to establish the content and scope of fundamental rights and principles of a state governed by the rule of law, insofar as this does not lead to decreasing or restricting fundamental rights included in the [Constitution] ...
>
> The Republic of Latvia has assumed international commitments the purpose of which is protection of a person's private life, inter alia, of personal data.
>
> Article 8(1) of the [Convention] provides that everyone has the right to respect for his private and family life. The ECtHR, in interpreting Article 8 of the Convention, has recognised that the concept of 'private life' has a

broad scope, it covers various aspects in a person's physical and social identity, and that it cannot be defined exhaustively. Information about a person and protection of his data fall within the scope of the right to protection of private life. Protection of personal data is decisive in allowing a person to exercise his rights established in Article 8 of the Convention (see the judgment of 16 February 2000 of the Grand Chamber of the ECtHR in *Amann v. Switzerland*, application no. 27798/95, para. 65, and the judgment of 4 December 2008 in *S. and Marper* v. *the United Kingdom*, applications nos. 30562/04 and 30566/04, paras. 66 and 103). The right to inviolability of private life and protection of personal data has been enshrined also in Article 7 and Article 8 of the Charter of Fundamental Rights of the European Union.

The Constitutional Court, in establishing the content of the fundamental right defined in Article 96 of the [Constitution] in interconnection with Article 8 of the Convention, has already recognised that state institutions have not only a negative obligation to abstain from any unfounded interference with the right to inviolability of private life, but also a positive obligation to take necessary measures to protect these rights. The legislator must set up such a mechanism for protection of personal data that would ensure that rules on processing would comply with the intended purpose ... Processing (collecting, storing, disclosing) data that are linked to a person's private life or characterizing a person's physical or social identity falls within the scope of a person's right to inviolability of private life ...

Thus, the right to inviolability of private life defined in Article 96 of the [Constitution] includes also protection of a natural person's data.

17. ... The Ombudsman is focusing, in particular, upon the fact that the legitimate aim of the contested norm could be reached by other measures, less restrictive upon a person's fundamental rights. ...

Article 34 of the Hague Convention [on the International Recovery of Child Support and Other Forms of Family Maintenance of 23 November 2007], which is binding upon Latvia, indicates measures that states could use to meet the obligation of collecting maintenance (for example, tax refund withholding, informing bureaus of credit history, denial, suspension or revocation of various licences). A number of states that are members of the Council of Europe (France, the United Kingdom, Norway,

Poland, Lithuania, etc.) have implemented such measures in their legal regulation.

(An unofficial translation by the Constitutional Court available at the website of the Constitutional Court, <http://www.satv.tiesa.gov.lv/wp-content/uploads/2015/07/2015-18-01_Judgment_ENG.pdf>, visited on 27 September 2018)

4/4

On 21 October 2016 the Constitutional Court adopted a decision to terminate the proceedings in case no. 2016-03-01. In this case the Constitutional Court encountered international law issues rather directly, since the case concerned the interplay between the fundamental rights guaranteed by the Latvian Constitution and a bilateral treaty between the Republic of Latvia and the Russian Federation concerning pensions payable to military pensioners. Some of the findings of the Court were the following:

> 9. ... The [institution which has adopted the contested norm – the Parliament –] notes that the contested norm should be examined in interconnection with international commitments that follow from the Agreement [between Latvia and Russia]. The Russian Federation is responsible for granting and disbursing pensions to military pensioners of the Russian Federation. Upon applying for a Latvian pension, a person, first of all, must have met the requirements of Latvian legal acts, and, secondly, must take into consideration that in this case the disbursement of a military pension granted by Russia for the same insurance periods for which Latvia's old age pension is paid will be discontinued. Thus, a person does not have the right to receive a pension from two states for the same insurance period or a period equivalent to it. None of the provisions of the Constitution guarantees the right to receive several pensions for the same insurance period. Thus, the [Parliament] expresses the opinion that the contested norm does not interfere with the applicants' fundamental rights ...

> 12. The term 'other state' has been used in the contested norm, and, thus, it is applicable to pensions granted by any state. However, the case materials reveal that drafting and adoption of the contested norm had been closely linked to the pensions granted by the Republic of Latvia and the Russian Federation for the same insurance period or a period equivalent to it.

The Constitutional Court also takes into account that all applicants are recipients of a military pension granted by the Russian Federation for whom on the basis of the contested norms the old age pension granted by Latvia has been recalculated or the disbursement thereof has been completely discontinued. The applicants and the [Parliament] ... have expressed their considerations regarding the compliance of the contested norm with the [Constitution] in close interconnection with states' obligations deriving from an international treaty, i.e., the Agreement. ...

Article 68(1) of the [Constitution] provides: 'All international agreements which settle matters that may be decided by the legislative process shall require ratification by the [Parliament]'.

Article 68(1) of the [Constitution] imposes an obligation upon Latvia's institutions of state power, including the [Parliament], in international relations to abide by not only the requirements of the [Constitution] and other national legal norms, but also those of international legal norms. An action by the [Parliament] that would be aimed at not performing international commitments or changing their scope contrary to the requirements of international legal norms would be incompatible with Article 68(1) of the [Constitution] ... Thus, in the case under review the content of fundamental rights protected by the [Constitution] must be established in conjunction with international obligations defined by the Agreement.

By concluding the Agreement the Republic of Latvia and the Russian Federation dealt with issues pertaining to social security of former military staff of the USSR residing on the territory of the Republic of Latvia.

The Constitutional Court has ruled that it is possible to regulate the issue of calculating and granting pensions as favourably as possible to a person who is not entitled to a state social insurance pension in accordance with the Pension Law by means of an international treaty ratified by the [Parliament]. By concluding bilateral international treaties in the field of social security states come to a mutual agreement regarding social protection of each party's residents, specifying the rights and obligations of each party; thus, different social security systems of two states are adjusted for social protection of residents of the particular state. Each state's social security model is adapted to the interests of its citizens, therefore an international treaty is one of the measures for protecting social security of all residents of the state...

The first sentence of Article 7(1) of the Agreement provides: 'Pensions of military pensioners shall be non-taxable and shall be disbursed by the banking institutions of the Republic of Latvia in the national currency from the resources of the Russian Federation in accordance with the terms and conditions established in the Russian Federation'.

Thus, the Russian Federation has assumed responsibility for social security of military pensioners of the former USSR in accordance with the legal acts that are in force in the Russian Federation. To ensure that all persons within the territory of Latvia could exercise their right to social security, the Republic of Latvia, in turn, has concluded the Agreement with the Russian Federation.

The Applicants themselves also note that the contested norm does not infringe upon their right to minimum social security, because they continue receiving the military pension granted by the Russian Federation...

Hence, the contested norm does not infringe upon the right to minimum social security established in the [Constitution].

13. ... in the case under examination, it is essential to take into account Article 9 of the Agreement which provides: 'Former military staff who have acquired the right to pension provision pursuant to legal acts of the Republic of Latvia in accordance with their wish, the respective competent bodies of the Republic of Latvia may grant and disburse pensions from the resources of the Republic of Latvia. Moreover, the disbursement of pensions previously granted by the Russian Federation shall be discontinued while a pension is disbursed by bodies of the Republic of Latvia'.

This norm provides for Latvia's right to grant and disburse pensions to former military staff of the USSR in accordance with legal acts of Latvia. However, it must be underscored that this is Latvia's right, not an obligation. Thus, pursuant to Article 9 Latvia enjoys discretion to leave the disbursement of pensions to former military staff of the USSR to the Russian Federation, or, upon a request by the respective person, to grant him or her a pension in accordance with the legal acts of the Republic of Latvia.

Within the limits of its discretion Latvia had granted old age pension to all the applicants, informing the Russian Federation about it.

...Pursuant to Article 9 of the Agreement, the Russian Federation had to discontinue disbursement of pensions for those periods for which a pension was granted by the Republic of Latvia; however, the Russian Federation had failed to do so.

The Ministry of Welfare notes, with good reason, that the purpose of the Agreement is not to pay double for particular periods of work and periods equivalent to them, because in those cases where the old age pension of the Republic of Latvia has been granted and is being disbursed, Article 9 of the Agreement imposes upon the Russian Federation the obligation to discontinue disbursement of the military service pension granted by the Russian Federation. Thus, by applying for Latvia's old age pension a person makes a conscious choice in favour of it, being aware that in accordance with the terms of the Agreement the disbursement of the military pension granted by the Russian Federation will be discontinued for the period while the Latvian old age pension is disbursed. To avoid duplication of periods of pension is a general principle of law in the field of international treaties on social security, provided that only one state granted a pension for the same insurance (working period or a period equivalent to it) period ... Therefore Article 9 of the Agreement must be examined in close interconnection with the purpose of applying this norm – to prevent a situation where both states are simultaneously disbursing a pension for the same insurance period.

It follows from the above that the Applicants have never had a subjective right to receive simultaneously pensions granted by several states for the same insurance period or a period equalled thereto. Such right does not follow from the terms of the Agreement, and neither does Article 109 of the [Constitution] protect it. Thus, also exclusion of overlapping insurance periods from a person's period of insurance and following recalculation of a pension does not cause a restriction upon a person's fundamental rights.

(An unofficial translation by the Constitutional Court available at the website of the Constitutional Court, <http://www.satv.tiesa.gov.lv/wp-content/uploads/2015/12/2015-25-01_Judgment_ENG.pdf>, visited on 29 September 2018)

4/5

In its judgment of 15 November 2016 in case no. 2015-25-01 the Constitutional Court was asked for a ruling on the constitutionality of legal provisions that provided for the liability of board members of legal persons for the legal persons' failure to pay tax. The Court invoked the relevant international law instruments in the following manner:

> 13. ... Pursuant to ECtHR case-law, the presumption of innocence, although it directly pertains to the field of criminal law, in general also forms the content of the right to a fair trial in the broader understanding of it. Namely, this principle falls within the scope of Article 6(1) of the Convention. This paragraph provides that in the determination of his civil rights and obligations or of any criminal charge against him, everyone is entitled to a fair and public hearing within a reasonable time by an independent and impartial tribunal established by law. Judgment shall be pronounced publicly but the press and public may be excluded from all or part of the trial in the interests of morals, public order or national security in a democratic society, where the interests of juveniles or the protection of the private life of the parties so require, or to the extent strictly necessary in the opinion of the court in special circumstances where publicity would prejudice the interests of justice.
>
> The ECtHR in explaining the concepts 'determination of a criminal charge' and 'indictment for a criminal offence' has applied the criminal limb of Article 6(1) of the Convention also to the fields of tax, customs and competition law (*see, for example,* the judgment of 24 February 1994 of the ECtHR in *Bendenoun* v. *France,* application no. 12547/86; the judgment of 7 October 1988 in *Salabiaku* v. *France,* application no. 10519/83, and the judgment of 11 February 2003 in *Ringvold* v. *Norway,* application no. 34964/97). Pursuant to the case-law of the ECtHR, disputes regarding failure to perform the obligation to pay taxes have been examined neither under the criminal limb, nor the civil limb of Article 6(1) of the Convention, since tax administration has been recognised as being a special function of the state, in the performance of which the state enjoys substantial discretion (*see, for example,* the judgment of 12 July 2001 of the ECtHR in *Ferrazzini* v. *Italy,* application no. 44759/98, paras. 27–29). However, tax disputes linked to the calculation and recovery of fees and late payment charges have been examined in the case-law of the ECtHR under the criminal limb of Article 6 of the Convention (*see* the judgment of 23 November 2006 of the ECtHR in *Jussila* v. *Finland,* application no. 73053/01, para. 38).

In *Engel and Others* v. *the Netherlands* the ECtHR held that to establish whether a particular case must be examined in accordance with the criminal limb Article 6 of the Convention it must be reviewed in accordance with three criteria: qualification of the particular offence in national legal acts, the nature and severity thereof, as well as the severity of the penalty that the person risks incurring (*see* the judgment of the ECtHR of 8 June 1976 in *Engel and Others* v. *the Netherlands,* applications nos. 5100/71; 5101/71; 5102/71; 5354/72; and 5370/72, para. 82).

For the criminal limb of Article 6 of the Convention to be applicable, it is sufficient to establish compliance with even one of these criteria (*see* the judgment of the ECtHR of 11 February 2003 in *Ringvold* v. *Norway,* application no. 34964/97, paras. 36–42, and the judgment of 8 June 1976 in *Engel and Others* v. *the Netherlands,* applications nos. 5100/71; 5101/71; 5102/71; 5354/72; and 5370/72, para. 82). Thus, if the criminal law nature of the offence were recognised or a person risked incurring such sanctions for the specific offence that as to their nature and severity would belong to the field of criminal law, the criminal law limb of Article 6(1) of the Convention would be applicable. The second and the third criteria are alternative. If an examination of each criterion separately does not lead to a clear conclusion, then a cumulative approach to the test of these criteria is permissible (*see* the judgment of 31 July 2007 of the ECtHR in *Zaicevs* v. *Latvia,* application no. 65022/01, para. 31).

Thus, to examine the compliance of the contested norms with the presumption of innocence principle included in the second sentence of Article 92 of the [Constitution], the Constitutional Court must first establish whether the contested norms regulate a field of law to which the presumption of innocence is applicable.

...

16. The ECtHR has recognised that with respect to the second criterion in appraising the nature and severity of the offence, its substance and the nature of the sanction envisaged for it should be taken into consideration. If the norm is general in nature and the sanction has both a preventive and a punitive aim, then it should be found that the particular offence may be equated to the autonomous concept of 'criminal offence' within the meaning of Article 6 of the Convention (*see, for example,* the judgment of 21 February 1984 of the ECtHR in *Ozturk* v. *Germany,* application no. 8544/79, para. 53)...

19. [T]he Constitutional Court has recognised that in certain cases the presumption of innocence allows the legislator to provide for legal presumption of a fact in legal relationships to which this fundamental right applies ... The Convention also does not, in principle, prohibit legal presumption of a fact but allows it only upon the condition that states party to the Convention apply this presumption reasonably, by taking into consideration the risks in its application and retaining a person's right to defence (*see* the judgment of 7 October 1988 of the ECtHR in *Salabiaku v. France,* application no. 10519/83, para. 28). ...

19.2. The [Parliament] notes that a legal presumption of a fact that is included in the contested norms has been established with the aim of creating an effective system of tax collection and, thus, it complies with the legitimate aim defined in Article 116 of the [Constitution] – the protection of public welfare. This aim has been recognised as being legitimate also by the ECtHR (*see, for example,* the judgment of 23 July 2002 of the ECtHR in *Västberga Taxi Aktiebolag and Vulic v. Sweden,* application no. 36985/97, para. 116). The ECtHR has also underscored the importance of public interest, since taxes are the main source of the revenue of the state (*see* the judgment of 23 July 2002 of the EtCHR in *Janosevic v. Sweden,* application no. 34619/97, para. 103). States have the right to establish their own fiscal policy and system, ensuring that taxes are paid, and it is in public interest (*see* the judgment of 22 September 1994 of the ECtHR in *Hentrich v. France,* application no. 13616/88, para. 39). ...

19.3. The ECtHR has recognised that in the field of criminal law states must abide by certain limits in applying presumptions, i.e., it must be taken into consideration what is being presumed and verified whether the presumption is rebuttable (*see* the judgment of 7 October 1988 of the ECtHR in *Salabiaku v. France,* application no. 10519/83, paras. 26–28).

It follows from the case materials that the application of the contested norms and judicial review are envisaged within the framework of an administrative procedure which ensures a high level of protection for a private person's rights and lawful interests by applying the principle of an objective investigation. However, notwithstanding the application of the principle of an objective investigation, the participants in an administrative procedure have the obligation to participate. Article 59(4) of the Administrative Procedure Law provides that the participants in an administrative procedure have the obligation to submit evidence at their disposal and to inform institutions about facts that are known to them and could be of importance in the particular case. Article 150(3) of the Administrative Procedure Law, in turn, provides that an applicant, according to his or her capacity, must participate in collecting evidence. Whereas Article 38 of the Tax Law provides: if the taxpayer disagrees with the amount of the tax payment assessed by the tax administration, it must provide evidence regarding the amount of tax liabilities. This approach to participation has been enshrined also in the ECtHR case-law in tax cases, recognising that the tax system to a large extent is based upon information provided by the taxpayer (*see, for example,* the judgment of 23 July 2002 of the ECtHR in *Janosevic v. Sweden,* application no. 34619/97, para. 103). Moreover, the contested norms provide that if a board member no longer has access to evidence needed for his defence, it is the obligation of [the State Revenue Service] to obtain it.

Thus, in some cases within the framework of administrative procedure there are grounds to request information and documents that are solely at the disposal of a private person (in this case – a board member). However, if the person objectively has no access to the evidence, then the person has the right to expect application of the principle of objective investigation.

Thereby a board member has been ensured the possibility to substantiate and to prove that he is not liable for incurring a legal person's late tax payments and that he has acted as an honest and careful manager. This substantiation and evidence, in turn, helps the SRS to perform its statutory obligations and to assess the situation impartially.

The ECtHR has recognised that member states may grant to their institutions of tax administration the right to impose even large-scale sanctions for failure to pay taxes – but only insofar as taxpayers are given the possibility to appeal against the respective decision in court. The court should have the right to examine the dispute on its merits, *inter alia*, a right to revoke the decision in full on the basis of both the facts of the case and legal considerations (*see* the judgment of 17 April 2012 of the ECtHR in *Steininger v. Austria,* application no. 21539/07, para. 55). ...

(An unofficial translation by the Constitutional Court available at the website of the Constitutional Court, <http://www.satv.tiesa.gov.lv/wp-content/uploads/2015/12/2015-25-01_Judgment_ENG.pdf>, visited on 29 September 2018)

4/6

The Constitutional Court's judgment of 9 December 2016 in case no. 2016-08-01 dealt with the issue of constitutionality of a law on alienation of a piece of private property for the purposes of building a highway. The Court invoked the case-law of the ECtHR in the following manner:

> 16.3. ... The ECtHR also has recognised that an interference with the right to peaceful enjoyment of property must strike a 'fair balance' between the demands of the general interests of the community and the requirements of the protection of an individual's fundamental rights [see the judgment of 29 March 2006 of the Grand Chamber of the ECtHR in *Scordino* v. *Italy (no. 1)*, application no. 36813/97, para. 93]. Compensation is an essential condition which must be taken into consideration in assessing whether the state has balanced the interests of an individual and those of the society in a fair and proportionate way. Deprivation of property without compensation that is reasonably linked to the value thereof usually would be considered as being a disproportionate and unjustified interference with the exercise of rights envisaged in Article 1 of the First Protocol to the Convention (*see* the judgment of 25 October 2012 of the Grand Chamber of the ECtHR in *Vistiņš un Perepjolkins* v. *Latvia*, application no. 71243/01, para. 110). Thus, the compensation that a person is entitled to in connection with an expropriation of its property for public needs must be, first of all, fair.

> ... the ECtHR has noted in a number of judgments that compensation should be reasonably linked to the market value of property; however, Article 1 of the First Protocol to the Convention does not guarantee the right to full compensation in all circumstances [*see, for example,* the judgment of 21 February 1986 of the Grand Chamber of the ECtHR in *James and others* v. *the United Kingdom*, application no. 8793/79, para. 54, and the judgment of 29 March 2006 in *Scordino* v. *Italy (no. 1)*, application no. 36813/97, para. 95].

(An unofficial translation by the Constitutional Court available at the website of the Constitutional Court, <http://www.satv.tiesa.gov.lv/wp-content/uploads/2016/05/2016-08-01_Judgment_ENG.pdf>, visited on 30 September 2018)

4/7

In its judgment of 18 February 2016 in case no. SKA-27/2016 the Administrative Cases Department of the Supreme Court of the Republic of Latvia dealt with the question of transcription of family names and in particular with the compatibility of such transcription with the Framework Convention for the Protection of National Minorities. The Court held:

[11] ... A personal name is one of the components of private and family life of a person but not all regulation in the area of personal names will necessarily constitute an interference with these rights (*see, for instance*, the decision of 7 December 2004 of the ECtHR in *Mentzen alias Mencena v. Latvia*). ...

[I]n order to respect a person's belonging to a specific family, Article 19(2) of the State Language Law provides that if a person or the parents of an underage person so wish and are able to submit documentary proof, the Latin alphabet transcription of the patronymic surname of the person is to be indicated in the person's passport or birth certificate in addition to the person's name and last name. ...

[12] In Article 11(1) of the Framework Convention for the Protection of National Minorities it is indicated that the Parties undertake to recognise that every person belonging to a national minority has the right to use his or her surname (patronym) and first names in the minority language and the right to official recognition of them, *according to modalities provided for in their legal system*. In para. 68 of the Explanatory Report to the Convention it has been explained that, in view of the practical implications of the obligation outlined in this provision, it is worded in such a way as to enable Parties to apply it in the light of their own particular circumstances. Hence, Parties may use the alphabet of their official language to write the name(s) of a person belonging to a national minority in its phonetic form.

The use of personal names is affected by various circumstances, including historical, linguistic, religious, and cultural; this is why bestowing, recognition and use of personal names is an area where the features of a state are particularly prominent and in which there is no meaningful consensus among the national legal systems of various countries. Thus states enjoy a wide margin of appreciation in this area. There is also no reason to consider that the previously mentioned national legal provisions that are applicable in this case are contrary to the aforementioned Convention.

(Available, only in Latvian, at the website of the Supreme Court, <http://www.at.gov.lv/downloadlawfile/4285>, visited on 13 October 2018; translated by the editor)

4/7

In its judgment of 20 February 2016 in case no. SKC-74/2016 the Civil Cases Department of the Supreme Court of the Republic of Latvia applied the 1980 Rome Convention on the Law applicable to Contractual Obligations in order to determine the law applicable to a contract concluded between a Polish and a Latvian company. The Supreme Court held as follows:

> [7.2] There is no dispute ... that in the specific case the parties have acted on the basis of an oral contract and have not made a choice of the law that would govern the contract pursuant to Article 3 of the Rome Convention; therefore Article 4 is applicable which provides that the contract shall be governed by the law of the country with which it is most closely connected, namely the country where the performance which is characteristic of the contract is to be effected.
>
> [8] The appeal court has erred in concluding that in the specific case the performance which is characteristic of the contract is to be effected in Latvia because the Latvian company has been paying for the goods produced and services rendered by the Polish company.
>
> [8.1] It is indicated in the judgment of the CJEU of 15 March 2011 in case C-29/10 *Koelzch* v. *Luxembourg* that the provisions of the Rome Convention are to be interpreted according to consistent and independent criteria in order to guarantee the full effectiveness of the Convention in view of the objectives which it pursues (paras. 31 and 32). ... In the aforementioned judgment of the Court of Justice of the European Union ... (para. 50), when interpreting Article 6(2) of the Rome Convention and by referring to the 1980 report of the representative of the University of Milano, Mario Giuliano, and Professor Paul Lagarde of the University Paris I on the Convention on the Law applicable to Contractual Obligations, found that the country in which the employee habitually carries out his work in performance of the contract, within the meaning of that provision, is that in which or from which, in the light of all the factors which characterise that activity, the employee performs the greater part of his obligations towards his employer. In other words, a criterion for determining the place where the contract is effected is long-term performance

corresponding to the specific character of the contract which distinguishes it from other contracts of a similar kind.

[8.2] In the opinion of the Civil Cases Department, for the purpose of uniform application of international law the aforementioned criterion is to be applied to the case under review, by finding that performance of the contract is to be considered performance of the contract by [the Polish company] for which [the Latvian company] had an obligation to pay. Such an understanding is also confirmed by the 1980 report of the representative of the University of Milano, Mario Giuliano, and Professor Paul Lagarde of the University of Paris I on the Convention on the Law applicable to Contractual Obligations where in the section on compilation of national case-law concerning the application of Article 4 it is indicated: "the performance which is characteristic of the specific contract is not effected as a payment of money, since in modern economics a payment by one of the parties as counter performance will be present in all cases. The performance which is characteristic of the contract is *that for which* the payment is to be made depending on the nature of the contract ...; this performance is usually the '*centre of gravity*' *and the socially economic function* of the contractual transaction. ..."

(Available, only in Latvian, at the website of the Supreme Court, <http://www.at.gov.lv/downloadlawfile/149>, visited on 14 October 2018; translated by the editor)

4/8

In its decision of 16 March 2016 in case no. SKC-1196/2016 the Civil Cases Department of the Supreme Court of the Republic of Latvia was called upon to resolve issues relating to recognition of foreign judgments. Insofar as is relevant, the Supreme Court held as follows:

[8.1] The application for recognition of a foreign judgment invokes as its legal basis Articles 636 to 644 of the Civil Procedure Law or, in other words, Section 77 of the Civil Procedure Law 'Recognition of foreign judgments'.

The Civil Cases Department points out that the aforementioned provisions are applicable to recognition and enforcement of a foreign judgment only if the respective procedural issue is not governed by an international treaty or a regulation ... If the issue of recognition and enforcement of a foreign judgment is governed by an international treaty or a regulation, then the aforementioned provisions of the Law of Civil Procedure are applicable only insofar as it is necessary to ensure successful procedural implementation of the international treaty or regulation in Latvia.

In general the issue of recognition and enforcement of foreign judgments in civil cases and commercial cases in the European Union with regard to judgments given in legal proceedings instituted, to authentic instruments formally drawn up or registered and to court settlements approved or concluded before 10 January 2015 is governed by Regulation No 44/2001 (see Article 66(2) of Regulation No 1215/2012); with regard to legal proceedings instituted, to authentic instruments formally drawn up or registered and to court settlements approved or concluded on or after 10 January 2015 the recognition and enforcement of foreign judgments is governed by Regulation No 1215/2012 (see Article 66(1) and Article 81 of Regulation No 1215/2012).

Furthermore, pursuant to Article 80 of Regulation No 1215/2012 references to the repealed Regulation No 44/2001 shall be construed as references to this Regulation and shall be read in accordance with the correlation table set out in Annex III. Thus, Regulation No 44/2001 and Regulation No 1215/2012 are not mutually exclusive; they operate within a united harmonious system.

At the same time, the previously mentioned regulations also supersede the conventions concluded between the Member States (see Articles 69 of Regulation No 44/2001 and Regulation No 1215/2012) that covered the issue of mutual recognition and enforcement of judgments in civil cases and commercial cases, *inter alia* the Treaty of 11 November 1992 on Legal Assistance and Legal Relationships between the Republic of Latvia, the Republic of Estonia and the Republic of Lithuania.

[8.2] In the particular case ... the applicant asks to recognise and enforce a ruling of a court of general jurisdiction on the application of interim measures in a civil case which concerns the respondent's complaint about a decision of the Vilnius Court of Commercial Arbitration of 2 September 2014 in order to ensure the enforcement of the above-mentioned award of the arbitral tribunal, directing interim measures against the applicant.

Taking into account that pursuant to Articles 1(2) (d) of Regulation No 44/2001 and Regulation No 1215/2012 these regulations are not applicable to arbitrations, the Civil Cases Department considers that prior to deciding upon the recognition or non-recognition of such a ruling of a foreign court, the primary issue to be resolved is whether such a ruling may be subject to recognition at all.

[8.2.1] The Court of Justice of the European Union has established that if the ruling concerned does not apply to civil or commercial matters, or if it is excluded from the scope of application of Regulation No 44/2001, as laid down by Article 1 thereof, that regulation cannot be applied (see the judgment of the Court of Justice of the European Union of 10 September 2009 in case C-292/08 *German Graphics Graphische Maschinen*, paras. 18–19, and compare with the judgment of 27 March 1979 in case 143/78 *Cavel*, para. 9; the judgment of 31 March 1982 in case 25/81 C.H.W., para. 12; the judgment of 17 November 1998 in case C-391/95 *Van Uden*, para. 30).

Furthermore, this regulation applies equally to provisional measures and definitive measures (see the judgment of the European Court of Justice of 27 March 1979 in case 143/78 *Cavel*, para. 9). Consequently provisional measures may not be requested in matters excluded from the scope of the regulations (see the judgment of the European Court of Justice of 31 March 1982 in case 25/81 C.H.W, para. 2 of the operative part).

(Available, only in Latvian, at the website of the Supreme Court, <http://www.at.gov.lv/downloadlawfile/137>, visited on 15 October 2018; translated by the editor)

4/9

In its decision of 4 February 2016 in case no. SKK-53/2016 the Criminal Cases Department of the Supreme Court of the Republic of Latvia addressed the issue of incitement which has drawn extensive case-law of the ECtHR. Insofar as is relevant, the Supreme Court held as follows:

> ... The importance of fundamental principles of criminal proceedings, including human rights guarantees and the right to a fair trial and the need to abide by these principles has already previously been stressed in several decisions of the Supreme Court that have analysed the case-law of the European Court of Human Rights with regard to the use in criminal

proceedings of information obtained through the employment of operational measures and special investigative actions ...

The ECtHR has pointed out that the principle of fair proceedings has to be applied towards the investigation of any criminal activity. The guarantees of Article 6 of the [Convention] need to be observed in all criminal proceedings, irrespective of the severity of the criminal offence; however, the interests of society may under no circumstances serve as an excuse for using such data that have been obtained by means of police incitement (*see* the judgment of 5 February 2008 of the ECtHR in *Ramanauskas* v. *Lithuania*, application no. 74420/01 and the judgment of 21 February 2008 in *Pyrgiotakis* v. *Greece*, application no. 15100/06).

With respect to incitement the ECtHR has indicated that the element of incitement is inherent in the very nature of investigative tests, and there is only a slight difference between incitement and legitimate undercover techniques. In such circumstances the role of the courts' scrutiny of whether the evidence was obtained without the use of incitement becomes even more important, in order to eradicate any reasonable doubts in that regard (*see* the judgment of 8 January 2013 of the ECtHR in *Baltiņš* v. *Latvia*, application no. 25282[/07]) ...

In assessing the case-law of the ECtHR and the Supreme Court jointly, it is possible to discern three important factors that have to be taken into account and weighed by courts when deciding whether there has been an incitement to commit a crime. First, whether before conducting the operative experiment the police officers were in possession of information that a person is committing specific crimes. Second, whether the police officers were active or passive. Third, whether the person would have committed the criminal offence even in the absence of the involvement of the police.

The Supreme Court concludes that in the case under review the appeal court has not fully evaluated these factors which were also indicated in the appeal ...

The ECtHR has pointed out that special investigative measures may be undertaken only with respect to a person about whose criminal activities there already is information. Furthermore, rumours or comparable unverifiable information cannot be found to be sufficient (*see* the judgment of 9 June 1998 of the ECtHR in *Teixeira de Castro* v. *Portugal*, application no. 25829/94, the judgment of 5 February 2008 in *Ramanauskas* v. *Lithuania*, application no. 74420/01, and the judgment of 1 July 2008 in *Malininas* v. *Lithuania*, application no. 10071/04).

(Available, only in Latvian, at the website of the Supreme Court, <http://www.at.gov.lv/downloadlawfile/3599>, visited on 16 October 2018; translated by the editor)

4/10

In its decision of 9 December 2016 in case no. SKK-566/2016 the Criminal Cases Department of the Supreme Court of the Republic of Latvia dealt with, *inter alia*, the issue regarding the need to provide the services of an interpreter in criminal proceedings. Insofar as is relevant, the Supreme Court held as follows:

... Article 6(3)(e) of the [Convention] provides that everyone has the right to have the free assistance of an interpreter.

Paragraph 21 [of the preamble] of the Directive 2010/64/EU of the European Parliament and of the Council of 20 October 2010 on the right to interpretation and translation in criminal proceedings provides that Member States should ensure that there is a procedure or mechanism in place to ascertain whether suspected or accused persons speak and understand the language of the criminal proceedings and whether they need the assistance of an interpreter. Such procedure or mechanism implies that competent authorities verify in any appropriate manner, including by consulting the suspected or accused persons concerned, whether they speak and understand the language of the criminal proceedings and whether they need the assistance of an interpreter. Paragraph 22 of the preamble states that interpretation and translation under this Directive should be provided in the native language of the suspected or accused persons or in any other language that they speak or understand in order to allow them fully to exercise their right of defence, and in order to safeguard the fairness of the proceedings ...

The ECtHR has pointed out that knowledge of languages by the accused is an essential element and that the court, in order to verify whether it is necessary to involve an interpreter in the proceedings, ought to consult with the accused person (*see* the judgment of 14 September 2002 of the ECtHR in *Cuscani* v. *the United Kingdom*, application no. 32771/96, para. 38).

The court also has to assess the severity of the criminal offence with which the accused has been charged, the complexity of the prosecution's case as well any prior communications addressed to him by the domestic authorities (see the judgment of 18 October 2006 of the Grand Chamber of the ECtHR in *Hermi* v. *Italy*, application no. 18114/02, para. 71).

(Available, only in Latvian, at the website of the Supreme Court, <http://www.at.gov.lv/downloadlawfile/627>, visited on 17 October 2018; translated by the editor)

Part Four: III. Relationship between International Law and Internal Law – Remedies under Internal Law for Violations of International Law

4/11

In its judgment of 29 April 2016 in case no. 2015-19-01 the Constitutional Court dealt with issues pertaining to reopening of criminal proceedings due to newly discovered circumstances. The judgment also touched upon the reopening of criminal proceedings after a finding of a violation by the ECtHR.

> 12.3. It has been recognised in the case-law of the Constitutional Court a number of times that the norms of human rights included in international human rights documents might be used to interpret the right to a fair trial defined in Article 92 of the [Constitution]. On the level of constitutional law international norms of human rights and the practice of application thereof serve as a means of interpretation to establish the content and scope of fundamental rights and the principle of a state governed by the rule of law, insofar as this does not lead to decreasing or restricting fundamental rights that are included in the [Constitution].
>
> It follows from Article 4 § 2 of Protocol 7 to the Convention that in some cases a repeated examination of a case is permissible; namely, if there is evidence of new or newly disclosed circumstances or if significant errors had been made in the previous proceedings which could have influenced the outcome of the case. Whereas the ECtHR ... has recognised in a number of cases that examination of a case *de novo* or, if a respective request

has been submitted, renewing legal proceedings is to be considered as the most appropriate way to eliminate a violation of Article 6 of the Convention (*see, for example,* the judgment of 20 April 2010 of the ECtHR in *Laska and Lika* v. *Albania,* application nos. 2315/04 and 17605/04, para. 74).

Moreover, the ECtHR notes that in some cases renewal of legal proceedings allows to eliminate in full a manifest violation of a person's right to a fair trial, for example, using in criminal proceedings evidence which has been obtained by breaching the prohibition of torture or inhumane treatment (*see, for example,* the judgment of 11 February 2014 of the ECtHR in *Cēsnieks* v. *Latvia,* application no. 9278/06, para. 65 and 78). This point is based upon the conclusion that the use of such evidence for verifying facts that are essential in criminal proceedings always causes serious doubts about the fairness of criminal proceedings as a whole and requires to consider these proceedings as a whole unlawful (*see, for example,* the judgment of 1 June 2010 of the Grand Chamber of the ECtHR in *Gäfgen* v. *Germany,* application no. 22978/05, para. 66).

Pursuant to Article 46 of the Convention every final judgment of the ECtHR is binding upon member states where the respective member state is one of the parties. The enforcement of the ECtHR judgment is monitored by the Committee of Ministers of the Council of Europe. Article 15(b) of the Statute of the Council of Europe provides that the Committee of Ministers has the right to adopt recommendations addressed to member state governments. Although these recommendations are not legally binding, they are adopted on issues that are recognised as being issues of the member states' common policy. On 19 January 2000 the Committee of Ministers of the Council of Europe adopted recommendation no. R (2000)2 'On the re-examination or reopening of certain cases at domestic level following judgment of the European Court of Human Rights'.

In this recommendation the Committee of Ministers encourages member states to examine their legal systems to verify whether they provide an appropriate possibility to re-examine cases (*inter alia*, by renewing legal proceedings) in those cases where the ECtHR has recognised that the Convention has been violated, in particular in those cases, where: (1) the injured party continues to suffer very serious negative consequences because of the decision by a state institution which violated the person's fundamental rights, which cannot be adequately remedied by paying compensation, and which cannot be rectified except by re-examination or reopening the case; (2) the ECtHR judgment leads to the conclusion that (a) the impugned domestic decision is on the merits contrary to the Convention; (b) the violation of the Convention found is based on procedural errors or shortcomings of such gravity that a serious doubt is cast on the outcome of the domestic proceedings complained of.

It has been recognised also in legal literature that in those cases where valid court rulings can be considered as being unfair, preference should be given to the principle of justice over the principle of legal certainty (*see, for example:* Hoffmann R., *Verfahrensgerechtigkeit. Studien zu einer Theorie prozeduraler Gerechtigkeit.* Paderborn: Schöningh, 1992, S. 132–133).

Thus, cases where legal proceedings must be renewed in a case in which the final ruling has been adopted to ensure the right to a fair trial are possible.

(An unofficial translation by the Constitutional Court available at the website of the Constitutional Court, <http://www.satv.tiesa.gov.lv/wp-content/uploads/2015/08/2015-19-01_Spriedums_ENG.pdf>, visited on 25 September 2018)

4/12

The Civil Cases Department of the Supreme Court had to examine the question of reopening the proceedings in its decision of 31 March 2016 in case no. SJC-13/2016. The case came before the Supreme Court in the aftermath of the judgment of the ECtHR of 13 January 2015 in *Rubins* v. *Latvia*, application no. 79040/12. The Supreme Court ruled, insofar as it is relevant, as follows:

[4] ... Pursuant to Article 479(6) of the Civil Procedure Law, newly discovered circumstances are[, *inter alia*,] a ruling of the ECtHR from which it follows that the proceedings in the case have to be restarted. In such a situation a court that is adopting a ruling in the restarted case ought to rely on the facts established by the ruling of the ECtHR or another international or supranational court and the legal assessment of the facts.

The cited legal provision does not provide that in all situations when the ECtHR has adopted a ruling by which a violation of the Convention has been found, the judgment which formed the basis for the application to the ECtHR has to be quashed.

The Convention does not provide that the national court has to restart the examination of the case anew whenever the ECtHR has found a violation of the Convention. The national court ought to decide on the reopening of the proceedings in the light of the circumstances of the particular case. This is also confirmed by Recommendation No. R (2000) 2 of the Committee of Ministers to member states on the re-examination or reopening of certain cases at domestic level following judgments of the European Court of Human Rights which indicates in which situations (in exceptional circumstances) a re-examination of a case would be desirable.

From the text of the recommendation it may be concluded that the main criterion for re-examination or reopening of cases is related to the possibility to ensure the situation that existed initially (*restitutio in integrum*), namely, if in exceptional circumstances the re-examination of a case or a reopening of proceedings is the most efficient, if not the only, means of achieving *restitutio in integrum* (paragraph 6 of the preamble of the Recommendation). Re-examination of cases or reopening of proceedings is recommended in cases in which the injured party continues to suffer very serious negative consequences which are not adequately remedied by the just satisfaction and cannot be rectified except by re-examination or if grave violations of the Convention have been committed in the ruling or procedure of the domestic court (para. 11 of the Recommendation). Hence, in deciding the issue of re-examination of the case, the national court is guided by the criterion of whether a re-examination of the case will be capable of reinstating the initial situation and of redressing the negative consequences which have not been sufficiently rectified by just satisfaction and are not adequately remedied by just satisfaction and cannot be rectified except by re-examination.

The ECtHR has repeatedly indicated in which situations imposing an obligation to re-examine the case is the individual measure chosen for rectifying the violation. For instance, in the judgment of 9 January 2013 in *Oleksandr Volkov v. Ukraine*, [application] no. 21722/11, para. 206, the ECtHR has indicated that when it considers that the most appropriate form of individual measure would be the reopening of the domestic proceedings it so indicates in the judgment.

From the judgment of 26 January 2006 of the ECtHR in *Lungoci v. Romania*, [application] no. 62710/00, paras. 55–56, it may be concluded that the finding of a violation of the Convention legally obliges the respondent state not only to transfer the sums of money awarded but also to select, under supervision of the Committee of Ministers of the Council of Europe, general or individual measures in order to cease the violation and to, as far as is possible, diminish its consequences in a way that insofar as possible would restore the previous situation (see also the judgment of the Grand Chamber (of the ECtHR) in *Ilascu and Others v. Moldova and Russia*, application no. 48787/99, para. 487).

[In the applicant's case the ECtHR] found a violation of Article 10 of the Convention ... The Court ... awarded compensation of 8000 EUR ... and awarded 2280 EUR for costs and expenses...

There is no indication in the judgment that it is necessary to restore the previous situation and that therefore the case ought to be re-examined.

The Department of Civil Cases concludes that no circumstances relating to the consequences of the violation derive from the judgment of 13 January 2015 of theECtHR that would be the basis for restarting the examination of the case. Acting in equity, the ECtHR has awarded just satisfaction. However, the judgment of 13 January 2015 of the ECtHR in itself is not to be considered as a newly discovered circumstance within the meaning of Article 479(6) of the Civil Procedure Law.

(Available, only in Latvian, at the website of the Supreme Court, <http://www.at.gov.lv/downloadlawfile/709>, visited on 19 October 2018; translated by the editor)

Part Five: I.B.6. Subjects of International Law – States – Recognition – Non-recognition (including non-recognition of governments) and Its Effects

5/1

On 20 February 2016 the Ministry of Foreign Affairs issued a statement to mark two years that had passed since the "Crimean referendum".

Two years ago, on 20 February 2014, Russia's military activities triggered the process of the illegal annexation of Crimea leading up to the illegitimate referendum on 16 March on Crimea joining the Russian Federation.

> On 18 March, the Russian Federation took a decision on the incorporation of Crimea.
>
> By continuing the process of illegal annexation, Russia is in gross violation of its international commitments and acting contrary to international law.
>
> Up till now and also in future, Latvia together with the international community will consistently condemn this action thereby continuing the policy of non-recognition of the illegal annexation of Crimea. Latvia is a staunch supporter of the restoration of Ukraine's territorial integrity and sovereignty...

(Available at the website of the Ministry of Foreign Affairs, <https://www.mfa.gov.lv/en/news/latest-news/49801-latvia-remains-committed-to-its-non-recognition-policy-concerning-the-annexation-of-crimea>, visited on 3 November 2018)

5/2

On 26 January 2016 the point of Latvia's policy of non-recognition of annexation of Crimea was made by the Minister of Foreign Affairs Edgars Rinkevičs during the annual foreign policy debate at the Parliament of the Republic of Latvia.

> Latvia will be unrelenting in its pursuit of a policy of non-recognition of the illegitimate and illegal annexation of Crimea. Crimea is Ukraine! Latvia's support for Ukraine's sovereignty, territorial integrity and the reform process will be unwavering.

(Available at the website of the Ministry of Foreign Affairs, <https://www.mfa.gov.lv/en/brussels/latvijas-darbiba-es/373-speeches-and-interviews/49504-speech-by-latvian-foreign-minister-edgars-rinkevics-at-annual-foreign-policy-debate-in-the-latvian-parliament-saeima-on-26-january-2015>, visited on 3 November 2018)

5/3

The Crimean annexation was also invoked by the President of Latvia, Mr. Raimonds Vējonis, during his speech at the 71st session of the United Nations General Assembly:

Latvia together with the international community will continue to stand for the sovereignty and territorial integrity of Ukraine. The illegal annexation of Crimea by the Russian Federation will not be recognized and must end.

(Available at the website of the Ministry of Foreign Affairs, <https://www.mfa.gov.lv/en/news/latest-news/speeches-and-interviews/55106-statement-by-h-e-mr-raimonds-vejonis-president-of-the-republic-of-latvia-at-the-71st-session-of-the-united-nations-general-assembly>, visited on 4 November 2018)

Part Five: 11.A.2.(a) Subjects of International Law – International organisations – In General – Participation of States and International Organisations in International Organisations and in Their Activities – Admission

5/4
On 1 July 2016 Latvia finalised the accession process to the Organisation for Economic Co-operation and Development.

[O]n 1 July, the Instrument of Accession of Latvia to the Organisation of Economic Co-operation and Development was deposited with the Ministry of Foreign Affairs of the French Republic. In accordance with Article 16 of the OECD Convention, as from this date, Latvia is a full-fledged Member of the OECD.

(Available at the website of the Ministry of Foreign Affairs, <https://www.mfa.gov.lv/en/news/latest-news/54182-latvia-officially-becomes-the-35th-member-of-the-oecd>, visited on 5 November 2018)

Part Five: 11.A.2.(d) Subjects of International Law – International Organisations – In General – Participation of States and International Organisations in International Organisations and in Their Activities – Representation of States and International Organisations to International Organisations, including Privileges and Immunities

5/5
At a working lunch hosted by the Ambassador of Switzerland to Latvia, Markus Niklaus Paul Dutly, for Ambassadors of non-European Union (EU) countries

residing in Latvia on 30 September 2016 the Minister of Foreign Affairs, Mr. Edgars Rinkēvičs:

> expressed support for the reform of the United Nations Security Council. Minister Rinkēvičs pointed out the need for increasing the number of the Security Council's permanent and non-permanent members and encouraged the permanent members to refrain from exercising their veto power in cases involving war crimes and crimes against humanity.

(Available at the website of the Ministry of Foreign Affairs, <https://www.mfa.gov.lv/en/news/latest-news/54993-foreign-minister-rinkevics-syrian-conflict-cannot-be-resolved-without-the-engagement-of-the-region-s-countries>, visited on 6 November 2018)

5/6

The President of Latvia, Mr. Raimonds Vējonis, during his speech at the 71st session of the United Nations General Assembly also invoked the need to reform the UN Security Council:

> The United Nations' capacity to address the current challenges also depends on the political will to move forward the necessary reforms of the Security Council. This is long overdue and we should all aim for strengthening the legitimacy of this important body. For the Security Council to react accordingly, its members should restrain from using their veto in situations of atrocity crimes. Latvia supports this important initiative, as well as the Code of Conduct regarding Security Council action against genocide, crimes against humanity, or war crimes.

(Available at the website of the Ministry of Foreign Affairs, <https://www.mfa.gov.lv/en/news/latest-news/speeches-and-interviews/55106-statement-by-h-e-mr-raimonds-vejonis-president-of-the-republic-of-latvia-at-the-71st-session-of-the-united-nations-general-assembly>, visited on 4 November 2018)

Part Six: VIII.B. Human Rights and Fundamental Freedoms – Under United Nations Treaty System

6/1

On 26 January 2016 Latvia presented the National Report of Latvia in the framework of the 2nd cycle of the United Nations Universal Periodic Review.

Significant improvements have been achieved in various areas including gender equality, prevention of domestic violence, the fight against trafficking in human beings and sham marriages.

Latvia ranks among the countries most successful in terms of women's involvement in decision-making, in science and the justice system. Furthermore, 31% of companies listed on Latvia's stock exchange were managed by women in 2014, which is the second highest rating in the European Union. According to data gathered by the World Economic Forum, Latvia scores in the top 20 countries on the Forum's Global Gender Gap Index which estimates levels of gender equality.

To prevent domestic violence, amendments have been made to legislation ensuring provision of short-term shelter. In 2015, the state-funded rehabilitation and recovery for adults who have suffered from violence became available.

Legislation has been amended in regard to human trafficking, for example, providing for the right of a victim of human trafficking to receive government compensation. Active work is under way on the implementation of the National Guidelines for the prevention of human trafficking (2014–2020) approved in 2014. To help victims of human trafficking, the government has considerably increased funding for rehabilitation, recovery and reintegration of the victims.

Significant improvements have also been achieved in regard to persons with disabilities, children's rights and progress continued with regard to national minority rights and citizenship.

In 2015, the Ombudsman's Office of Latvia was accredited by the International Coordinating Committee for National Human Rights Institutions (ICC) being granted 'A' status; this is the highest internationally recognized valuation of the compliance of national human rights institutions to international standards. 'A' status accreditation also grants the Ombudsman's Office participation in the work and decision-making of the ICC, as well as the work of the Human Rights Council and other UN mechanisms.

(Available at the website of the Ministry of Foreign Affairs, <https://www.mfa.gov.lv/en/news/latest-news/49328-latvia-to-present-its-progress-in-the-field-of-human-rights>, visited on 5 November 2018)

6/2

On 23 June 2016 a representative of Latvia was elected to the United Nations Human Rights Committee for the term 2017–2020.

On 23 June in New York, Ilze Brands-Kehris was elected to the United Nations Human Rights Committee for the term 2017–2020. This is the first time that a representative from Latvia was a candidate for a post on the committee. Candidates from 22 countries had been nominated for nine positions of independent experts. Ilze Brands-Kehris is the first expert from the Baltic States who will work on the UN Human Right Committee.

The election of Ilze Brands-Kehris to the UN Human Right Committee means high appreciation of her knowledge and experience, said Ambassador Jānis Mažeiks, Permanent Representative of Latvia to the United Nation in New York, after the elections. At the same time, he noted, this is also acknowledgement by the UN member states of Latvia's achievements in the human rights sector, since the UN Human Rights Committee is the most important and prestigious structure of elected UN experts.

Ilze Brands-Kehris is a human rights expert with more than twenty years of experience. Over this time, she has occupied important posts such as Director of the Latvian Centre for Human Rights (2002–2011), Chairperson of the Management Board of the EU Fundamental Rights Agency (2010–2012), and Director of the Office of OSCE High Commissioner on National Minorities in The Hague (2011–2014). Ilze Brands-Kehris is currently Visiting Scholar at the Harriman Institute, Columbia University, New York, on Conflict Prevention and Human Rights, Including Minority Rights.

(Available at the website of the Ministry of Foreign Affairs, <https://www.mfa.gov.lv/en/news/latest-news/54126-ilze-brands-kehris-elected-to-the-un-human-rights-committee>, visited on 5 November 2018)

Part Six: VIII.C. Human Rights and Fundamental Freedoms – Under Council of Europe Treaty System

From the fourteen judgments adopted in cases against Latvia in 2016 by the ECtHR, two highlighted particularly novel aspects of the interplay between the Convention and the Latvian (and not only Latvian) legal system.

6/3

On 23 May 2016 the Grand Chamber of the ECtHR adopted a judgment in *Avotiņš* v. *Latvia* (application no. 17502/07), which *prima facie* pertained to issues related to recognition and enforcement of a Cypriot court judgment in Latvia. However, the real significance of the judgment lies in the fact that the ECHtR used it to clarify the relationships between the potentially conflicting obligations that the Member States of the European Union might have deriving from the EU legal system and the Convention. In particular, the Court had an opportunity to review the continued validity and scope of the so-called *Bosphorus* presumption which states that the protection of fundamental rights afforded by the European Union is in principle equivalent to that provided by the Convention (deriving from the judgment of 30 June 2005 of the Grand Chamber of the ECtHR in *Bosphorus Hava Yolları Turizm ve Ticaret Anonim Şirketi* v. *Ireland*, application no. 45036/98). The Court described its task in the following way:

> 112. ... the Court concludes that the presumption of equivalent protection is applicable in the present case, as the Senate of the Supreme Court [of Latvia] did no more than implement Latvia's legal obligations arising out of its membership of the European Union ... Accordingly, the Court's task is confined to ascertaining whether the protection of the rights guaranteed by the Convention was manifestly deficient in the present case such that this presumption is rebutted. In that case, the interest of international cooperation would be outweighed by observance of the Convention as a 'constitutional instrument of European public order' in the field of human rights. ...
>
> ...
>
> 115. [T]he Court observes that where the domestic authorities give effect to European Union law and have no discretion in that regard, the presumption of equivalent protection set forth in the *Bosphorus* judgment is applicable. This is the case where the mutual recognition mechanisms require the court to presume that the observance of fundamental rights by another Member State has been sufficient. The domestic court is thus deprived of its discretion in the matter, leading to automatic application of the *Bosphorus* presumption of equivalence. The Court emphasises that this results, paradoxically, in a twofold limitation of the domestic court's review of the observance of fundamental rights, due to the combined effect of the presumption on which mutual recognition is founded and the *Bosphorus* presumption of equivalent protection.

116. In the *Bosphorus* judgment the Court reiterated that the Convention is a 'constitutional instrument of European public order' ... Accordingly, the Court must satisfy itself, where the conditions for application of the presumption of equivalent protection are met ..., that the mutual recognition mechanisms do not leave any gap or particular situation which would render the protection of the human rights guaranteed by the Convention manifestly deficient. In doing so it takes into account, in a spirit of complementarity, the manner in which these mechanisms operate and in particular the aim of effectiveness which they pursue. Nevertheless, it must verify that the principle of mutual recognition is not applied automatically and mechanically ... to the detriment of fundamental rights – which, the CJEU has also stressed, must be observed in this context ... In this spirit, where the courts of a State which is both a Contracting Party to the Convention and a Member State of the European Union are called upon to apply a mutual recognition mechanism established by EU law, they must give full effect to that mechanism where the protection of Convention rights cannot be considered manifestly deficient. However, if a serious and substantiated complaint is raised before them to the effect that the protection of a Convention right has been manifestly deficient and that this situation cannot be remedied by European Union law, they cannot refrain from examining that complaint on the sole ground that they are applying EU law.

The ECtHR eventually came to the conclusion that 'the protection of fundamental rights was [not] manifestly deficient such that the presumption of equivalent protection is rebutted' (para. 125 of the judgment); however, the significance of judgment lies in the conclusion that because of the Convention requirements, 'if a serious and substantiated complaint is raised before [courts of the member states] to the effect that the protection of a Convention right has been manifestly deficient and that this situation cannot be remedied by European Union law, they cannot refrain from examining that complaint on the sole ground that they are applying EU law'. Thus the *Bosphorus* presumption remained standing but was eroded to a certain extent.

6/4

The other judgment adopted in 2016 in a case brought against Latvia by the Grand Chamber of the ECtHR was the judgment of 5 July 2016 in *Jeronovičs* v. *Latvia* (application no. 44898/10). The judgment dealt with a very topical issue in Latvia, namely, the obligation to renew examination of cases subsequent to rulings of the ECtHR, in this case subsequent to a decision to strike a case out of the Court's list of cases due to a unilateral declaration conceding violation that had been submitted by the Latvian Government. The Court included the following points in its judgment:

> 108. With regard to Article 13 of the Convention, the Court reiterates that it guarantees the availability at national level of a remedy by which to complain about a breach of the Convention rights and freedoms. Although Contracting States are afforded some discretion as to the manner in which they conform to their obligations under this provision, there must be a domestic remedy allowing the competent national authority both to deal with the substance of the relevant Convention complaint and to grant appropriate relief. The scope of the obligation under Article 13 varies depending on the nature of the applicant's complaint under the Convention, but the remedy must in any event be 'effective' in practice as well as in law, in particular in the sense that its exercise must not be unjustifiably hindered by the acts or omissions of the authorities of the State...

> 109. Furthermore, the Court's rulings serve not only to decide those cases brought before it but, more generally, to elucidate, safeguard and develop the rules instituted by the Convention, thereby contributing to the observance by the States of the engagements undertaken by them as Contracting Parties. Although the primary purpose of the Convention system is to provide individual relief, its mission is also to determine issues on public-policy grounds in the common interest, thereby raising the general standards of protection of human rights and extending human rights jurisprudence throughout the community of the Convention States ...

> 116. ... The payment of compensation, be it a result of a unilateral declaration or following domestic proceedings for damages, cannot suffice, having regard to the State's obligation under Article 3 to conduct an effective investigation in cases of wilful ill-treatment by agents of the State ...

> 117. Therefore, the Government's interpretation, as stated in their unilateral declaration, that the payment of compensation constituted the final resolution of the case cannot be accepted. Such an interpretation would extinguish an essential part of the applicant's right and the State's obligation under the procedural limb of Article 3 of the Convention ...

> ...

> 123. Having regard to the authorities' refusal to reopen the discontinued criminal proceedings concerning the applicant's ill-treatment as

acknowledged by the Government's unilateral declaration ..., the Court considers in the instant case that the applicant did not have the benefit of an effective investigation as required by Article 3 of the Convention.

Part Six: VIII.D. Human Rights and Fundamental Freedoms – Other Aspects of Human Rights and Fundamental Freedoms

6/5

On 22 March 2016 during an interactive dialogue with Ivan Šimonović, the United Nations Assistant Secretary-General for Human Rights, Latvia expressed its concern with the human rights situation in the Russian-annexed Crimea:

> The representative of Latvia also expressed his concern over the dire human rights situation in Crimea, violations perpetrated by *de facto* Russia's institutions against the human rights of Crimean Tatars and Ukrainians including discrimination, intimidation, harassment, arbitrary arrests for alleged membership in terrorist organisations, and called on Russia to grant the Human Rights Monitoring Mission unfettered access to Crimea. Latvia shared the concerns of the UN Monitoring Mission regarding the recent request filed with the Crimean Supreme Court by the Prosecutor of Crimea, appointed by Russia, to recognise the Mejlis, the self-governing body of the Crimean Tatars established in 1991, to be an extremist organization and to ban its activities.

(Available at the website of the Ministry of Foreign Affairs, <https://www.mfa.gov.lv/en/news/latest-news/50200-at-the-un-the-international-community-expresses-its-doubts-about-deterioration-of-the-human-rights-situation-in-illegally-annexed-crimea>, visited on 5 November 2018)

Part Seventeen: I.9. The Law of Armed Conflict and International Humanitarian Law – International Armed Conflict – Conventional, Nuclear, Bacteriological, and Chemical Weapons

17/1

On 18 January 2016 the Ministry of Foreign Affairs released a statement concerning Iran's nuclear programme:

Latvia welcomes the statement of 16 January by Yukia Amano, Director General of the International Atomic Energy Agency (IAEA), confirming that Iran has completed the necessary preparatory steps to begin implementation of the Joint Comprehensive Plan of Action, namely, the gradual lifting of international sanctions. This development caps long standing efforts of the international community to address Iran's nuclear issues by diplomatic means and demonstrates that abiding by international norms contributes to national welfare and prosperity and its standing on the international stage. This step will also enable Iran to proceed in building full bilateral relations with the European Union Member States including in the area of business cooperation.

Latvia commends the members of the E3+3 format for their efforts invested in solving problems related to the Iranian nuclear issue and also commends Iran for honouring its obligations and commitments. Iran is called upon to ensure due implementation of the Joint Comprehensive Plan of Action to strengthen international confidence in the exclusively civilian purposes of its nuclear programme. Latvia also wishes to thank the IAEA for the verification measures undertaken in regard to Iran's nuclear programme as well as expecting further broader access by the iaea to the infrastructure of Iran's nuclear programme.

(Available at the website of the Ministry of Foreign Affairs, <https://www.mfa.gov.lv/en/news/latest-news/49415-latvia-welcomes-iran-s-direction-on-its-nuclear-programme>, visited on 4 November 2018)

17/2

The President of Latvia, Mr. Raimonds Vējonis, during his speech at the 71st session of the United Nations General Assembly referred to the progress made with respect to the nuclear program of Iran but at the same time expressed concern with the nuclear activities carried out by North Korea:

Iran's diligent implementation of the Joint Comprehensive Plan of Action and cooperation with the International Atomic Energy Agency will contribute to greater stability in the Middle East. On the other hand, the irresponsible actions of North Korea, including repeated nuclear tests, undermine the security of all countries in the region and beyond

(Available at the website of the Ministry of Foreign Affairs, <https://www.mfa.gov.lv/en/news/latest-news/speeches-and-interviews/55106-statement-by

-h-e-mr-raimonds-vejonis-president-of-the-republic-of-latvia-at-the-71st-session-of-the-united-nations-general-assembly>, visited on 4 November 2018)

Part Seventeen: I.10. The Law of Armed Conflict and International Humanitarian Law – International Armed Conflict – Treaty Relations between Combatants (cartels, armistices, etc.)

17/3

The importance of the Minsk agreements for ceasing the conflict in eastern Ukraine was underlined by the President of Latvia, Mr. Raimonds Vējonis, during his speech at the 71st session of the United Nations General Assembly:

> The international community must work to facilitate the peaceful resolution of the conflict in the eastern Ukraine. All parties must fulfil their commitments under the Minsk Agreements and make the Minsk process work.

(Available at the website of the Ministry of Foreign Affairs, <https://www.mfa.gov.lv/en/news/latest-news/speeches-and-interviews/55106-statement-by-h-e-mr-raimonds-vejonis-president-of-the-republic-of-latvia-at-the-71st-session-of-the-united-nations-general-assembly>, visited on 4 November 2018)

ANNEX I.A Agreements signed by Latvia before 2016 but entered into force in regard to Latvia in 2016 – Bi- and multilateral agreements

Title	Conclusion	Entry into Force
Agreement between the Government of the Republic of Latvia and the Government of the Islamic Republic of Iran on International Transport of Passengers and Goods by Road	22.05.2000	09.01.2016
Agreement between the Government of the Republic of Latvia and the Government of the Republic of Kazakhstan on the Readmission of Persons	16.09.2011	04.02.2016

ANNEX I.A   Agreements signed by Latvia before 2016 but entered into force in regard to Latvia in 2016 – Bi- and multilateral agreements (*cont.*)

Title	Conclusion	Entry into Force
International Road Transport Agreement between the Government of the Republic of Latvia and the Government of Turkmenistan	12.12.2015	07.08.2016

ANNEX II   Agreements signed by Latvia in 2016 – Bi- and multilateral agreements

Title	Conclusion	Entry into Force
Agreement between the Government of the Republic of Latvia and the Government of the Hong Kong SAR of the People's Republic of China for the Avoidance of Double Taxation and the Prevention of Fiscal Evasion with Respect to Taxes on Income	13.04.2016	24.11.2017
Agreement on the Terms of Accession of the Republic of Latvia to the Convention on the Organisation for Economic Co-operation and Development	29.04.2016	01.07.2016
Agreement on Economic Cooperation between the Government of the Republic of Latvia and the Government of the United Arab Emirates	08.05.2016	08.05.2018
Convention between the Government of the Republic of Latvia and the Government of the Republic of Cyprus for the Avoidance of Double Taxation and the Prevention of Fiscal Evasion with Respect to Taxes on Income	24.05.2016	27.10.2016
Protocol of 2014 to the Forced Labour Convention, 1930	11.06.2016	09.11.2016
Universal Postal Convention	06.10.2016	01.01.2018

Title	Conclusion	Entry into Force
Agreement between the Government of the Republic of Latvia and the Government of the Kyrgyz Republic on Co-operation in the Field of Education and Science	17.10.2016	20.06.2017
Strategic Partnership Agreement between Canada, of the One Part, and the European Union and its Member States, of the Other Part	30.10.2016	
Cooperation Agreement between the Government of the Republic of Latvia and the European Organization for Nuclear Research (CERN) concerning Scientific and Technical Cooperation in High-Energy Physics	31.10.2016	31.10.2016
Memorandum of Understanding between the Government of the Republic of Latvia and the Government of the United States of America on the Fulbright Academic Exchange Program	16.12.2016	16.12.2016

CHAPTER 12

Republic of Lithuania Materials on International Law 2017

Edited by *Andrius Bambalas and Saulius Katuoka*

[*Editorial Notes:*

1. Republic of Lithuania Materials on International Law 2017 (RLMIL2017) are drafted and classified pursuant to Recommendation (97)11 of 12 June 1997 of the Committee of Ministers of the Council of Europe.

2. For ease of reading a number of abbreviations are used in RLMIL2017, namely ECHR – Convention for the Protection of Human Rights and Fundamental Freedoms, 1950; ECtHR – European Court of Human Rights; *Seimas* – Parliament of the Republic of Lithuania; Government – Government of the Republic of Lithuania. Unless explicitly provided for otherwise, references to cases or decisions in RLMIL2017 are references to acts of national courts and institutions. Cases decided by national courts referred to herein are available in Lithuanian free of charge at the following website: https://eteismai.lt/paieska. The case law of the Constitutional Court is available on its website http://www.lrkt.lt/index_e.html. Case law of the European Court of Human Rights is available through the website http://www.echr.coe.int/echr/. Bilateral agreements of Lithuania are mostly available in Lithuanian at the following website: https://www.urm.lt/default/lt/uzsienio-politika/tarptautines-sutartys/dvisales-sutartys. Universal and regional international instruments mentioned in RLMIL2017 do not bear any reference to their source, as these may be easily accessed from various pages on the internet. Due to limited scope, RLMIL2017 does not reproduce entire texts, therefore certain information is omitted and marked as […].

3. RLMIL2017 consists mainly of translations of texts made by the authors; therefore, translations should not be regarded as official and should be used for information purposes only. Documents the translations of which are provided by national institutions and are available in English on the internet are attached with a particular link.

4. A rather technical remark should be made in regard to ratifications by the *Seimas* and approvals by the Government, noted in the Appendix hereto, meaning expression of consent to be bound under national law, rather than meaning an international act, attributed to the notion "ratification" in Article 2 part 1(b) of the Vienna Convention on the Law of Treaties, 1969.]

Part Three: 11.B. The Law of Treaties – Observance, Application and Interpretation of Treaties – Application of Treaties

3/1

In case No. e3K-3-123-219/2017 of 7 March 2011, the Supreme Court of Lithuania provided a detailed and step by step application of various provisions of the CMR Convention in a dispute regarding compensation for damaged goods exceeding the limits laid down in Article 23 of the CMR Convention. Relevant extracts of the case are reproduced below:

Regarding limits of the carrier's liability

The CMR Convention strictly regulates the liability of the carrier, establishing a presumption of the guilt of the carrier when the goods are lost, damaged or delivered with delay (Articles 17 and 18 of the CMR Convention) and establishes certain guarantees which limit compensation of liability (Article 23 Paragraphs 1–3, Article 28 of the CMR Convention). However Article 29 Paragraph 1 of the CMR Convention establishes exclusions from such limitations: the carrier is not entitled to avail himself of exclusion or limits of liability if the damage was caused by his wilful misconduct or by such default on his part as, in accordance with the law of the court or tribunal seized of the case, is considered as equivalent to wilful misconduct. If the guilt of the carrier which meets the conditions of Article 29 Paragraph 1 of the CMR Convention, is established, the carrier cannot avail himself of the provisions of the Convention which exclude or limit his liability [...]

[...]

According to the case law of the Supreme Court of Lithuania, negligence equivalent to wilful misconduct by a carrier encompasses actions which he could have avoided if he had undertaken at least the minimum requirements of care and diligence, or inactivity, namely failure to carry out all possible actions that could have reduced or averted the risk of damage [...]. Under Article 29 Paragraph 1 of the CMR Convention such actions on the part of the carrier should be wilful and sufficiently purposeful to cause risk as to preservation of the cargo. Deciding on application of Article 29 of the CMR Convention requires an assessment of whether the actions of the driver had an impact on the emergence of damage, i.e. whether his actions directly resulted in or significantly increased the risk of damage to or loss of cargo. [...]

When developing the case law of interpretation and application of Article 29 Paragraph 1 of the CMR Convention the cassation court has emphasised that [...] in order to find wilful inappropriate conduct by the carrier, both objective and subjective criteria have to be considered. The objective criterion encompasses disregard or breach of established rules (traffic rules, rules concerning safety of the cargo, rules on work and rest time, instructions regarding delivery of cargo). The subjective criterion involves wilful conduct by the carrier (activity or inactivity) with the knowledge that such conduct would likely cause negative consequences [...].

[...]

The panel of judges does not agree [...] that the mere fact that the cargo was reloaded is sufficient ground to find that the carrier breached its general obligation of care, i.e. that the conduct of the carrier can be regarded as knowledge that due to such conduct some negative consequences would likely follow and its wilful conduct contributed to the emergence of such consequences. [...] Reloading the cargo did not necessarily lead to damage to the cargo.

The panel of judges – taking into account the subjective criterion (according to the circumstances of the case the objective criterion is not important because there was no breach of any rules) – determines that there is no ground in the present case to find wilful misconduct by the carrier. The respondent's behaviour while reloading the cargo manifested itself as negligent; however, this should not be regarded as wilful negligence.

As the actions of the carrier that fall within the sphere of liability prescribed by the CMR Convention cannot be regarded as wilful misconduct, the carrier is not precluded from availing itself of the grounds of limitation or exemption from liability as prescribed in the CMR Convention.

Regarding release of the carrier from liability

Article 17 Paragraph 1 of the CMR Convention enshrines a general provision that the carrier shall be liable for total or partial loss of the goods and for damage thereto occurring between the time when he takes over the goods and the time of delivery, as well as for any delay in delivery.

[...]

Under Article 18 Paragraph 2 of the CMR Convention, when the carrier establishes that in the circumstances of the case the loss or damage could be attributed to one or more of the special risks referred to in Article 17, Paragraph 4, it shall be presumed that it was so caused.

In the current case it was was established that damage to the cargo occurred during the carriage of goods [...]. The respondent recognised such circumstance as it retracted its claims that the goods were not properly packed and (or) loaded by the sender. For this reason, the panel of judges determines that in this case the circumstance which relieves the carrier of the liability, as prescribed in Article 17 Paragraph 4 subparagraph b of the CMR Convention, was not proven and determined. In the present proceedings Article 17 Paragraph 4 Subparagraph c also cannot be applicable because the carrier reloaded the goods. [...]

Based on these reasons the panel of judges determines that no circumstances have been determined that could relieve the carrier from liability under the CMR Convention.

Regarding limitation of the liability of the carrier and the amount of damages

Damage to the cargo means deterioration in the quality of the goods resulting in the diminution of their value, or when they become unsuitable for use. In the case of total loss of goods, the carrier has to pay compensation calculated by reference to the value of goods under Article 23 of the CMR Convention.

[...]

The respondent does not agree with the amount of compensation established by the courts, i.e. that part of the cargo was totally lost because the damage to the goods was small (scratches), so that a partial loss of value of the goods cannot be established as the full value of the aluminium framework. Moreover, the respondent maintains that the courts should have applied compensation limits as prescribed in Article 23 Paragraph 3 of the CMR Convention. [...]

In the present case it was established that in Article 3.4 of the Contract for single carriage of goods the parties agreed that the respondent as the carrier was informed that the value of the cargo exceeds the SDR provisions laid down in Article 23 of the CMR Convention; the declared value of the cargo was indicated in the agreement and (or) accompanying documents; an additional surcharge for the carriage, which changes the declared value of the cargo, exceeding the limit laid down in Article 23 of the CMR Convention, was included in the overall amount of freight; the carrier confirms that it knows the declared value of the cargo. [...] Considering these circumstances and on the basis of the provisions referred to in Article 24 and Article 26 Paragraph 1 of the CMR Convention the panel of judges establishes that in the present proceedings the courts, when determining the amount of compensation to be awarded to the claimant, rightly decided not to apply the limits laid down in Article 23 Paragraph 3 of the CMR Convention and the determination of the weight of cargo highlighted by the respondent did not have legal significance in determining the amount of compensation to be awarded.

3/2

In case No. 3K-3-98-687/2017 of 7 March 2017, the Supreme Court of Lithuania elaborated on the burden of proof under the CMR Convention, when during the carriage a breach of the temperature regime indicated in the CMR consignment note is established and on the possibility to transport food goods and dangerous goods in the same vehicle. Relevant extracts from the case are reproduced below:

Under the provisions of the CMR Convention the carrier is liable for total or partial loss of the goods and for damage thereto occurring between the time when he takes over the goods and the time of delivery (Article 17 Paragraph 1). Under the case law of the Supreme Court this provision of the CMR Convention establishes strictly (objective) liability of the carrier:

the carrier is liable in all cases unless he proves circumstances that relieve him of liability under Article 17 Paragraphs 2 and 4 [...].

Although the CMR Convention establishes a presumption of carrier's liability for total or partial loss of the goods and any delay (Articles 17 and 18 of the CMR Convention) which must be rebutted by the carrier, nevertheless the fact that goods were actually lost, damaged or delivered late must be proven by the sender.

[...]

In the present case the claimant seeks an award of compensation for loss of the goods (food products) and indicated the following circumstances as proof that the goods were damaged: 1) the goods (food products) were transported together with batteries and for this reason the food products perished; 2) the goods (food products) were transported in violation of the temperature regime prescribed in the CMR consignment note and for this reason the food products perished.

[...]

In the present case it was established that food products and dangerous goods (batteries, whose identification number under AFR is JT no. 2794) were transported together in the same vehicle.

The batteries transported by the respondent are recognised as dangerous goods the transportation of which is regulated under the European Agreement concerning the International Carriage of Dangerous Goods by Road (ADR). Section 7.5.4 of the ADR [...] does not prescribe a prohibition on carrying food products together with batteries JT no. 2794, nor does it provide for special safety measures that are required to carry food products. The accompanying transportation documents of the batteries indicate that they were packaged in accordance with packing instruction for dangerous goods P801.

[...]

As mentioned, transport of food products was allowed together with batteries, so that the mere fact is insufficient to prove the fact of damage to the goods. [...]

[...]

The panel of judges [...] determines that in the present proceedings, if the temperature indicated in the CMR consignment note is in compliance with the temperature set by the manufacturer of the food products, which was determined in the manner prescribed by law, and in which the goods remain safe for use until their expiry date and if the claimant provides evidence that the temperature regime indicated in the CMR consignment note was breached, then it can be recognised that breach of the temperature regime indicated in the CMR consignment note means insecurity of and damage to the food products. In that case the respondent is under obligation to prove that the breach of the temperature regime did not cause a risk to health and that the food products could still be safely used during their whole expiry period, i.e. that the food products in question did not perish.

The panel of judges [...] determines that in the present proceedings, if the temperature indicated in the CMR consignment note was not in compliance with the temperature established by the manufacturer of the food products, which was determined in the manner prescribed by law, and in which the goods remain safe for use until their expiry date and if the claimant provides evidence that the temperature regime indicated in the CMR consignment note was breached, then an assessment is required as to whether the temperature deviated from the temperature established by the manufacturer of goods under which those goods remain safe to use during their whole expiry period. If there was no deviation from the temperature established by the manufacturer, then the claimant is under obligation to provide evidence that deviation of the temperature regime for the transported goods from the temperature indicated in the CMR consignment note, considering the degree of deviation as well as its length, is such that the food products in question pose a risk for health and for those reasons are not fit for use (perished).

3/3

In case No. e3K-3-461-378/2017 of 18 December 2017, the Supreme Court of Lithuania reiterated that the CMR Convention is not applicable in a carrier's dispute with its insurance company regarding the insurance payout. Relevant extracts from the case are reproduced below:

The claimant requested the court to recognise an event that took place in Spain on 5 November 2015, wherein part of the cargo which was accepted for carriage under CMR consignment note [....] was stolen as an insured event and to award an insurance claim amounting to EUR 8,236.96.

[...]

The panel of judges establishes that the CMR Convention does not regulate the rights and obligations of the parties arising out of relations involving the carrier's liability insurance. Therefore, a dispute concerning recognition of the event as an insured event and payment of the sum insured must be resolved under legal acts that regulate insurance legal relations and the provisions of the particular insurance contract. Thus, in the present case the dispute has to be heard according to the legal norms for insurance legal relations instead of the rules established in the CMR Convention.

Therefore, in the event of a dispute concerning recognition of an event as an insured event, payment of insurance shall be governed by the legal relationship of insurance law and the specific provisions of the insurance contract.

Part Three: II.C. The Law of Treaties – Observance, Application and Interpretation of Treaties – Interpretation of Treaties

3/4
In case No. E3K-3-60-421/2017 of 6 January 2017, the Supreme Court of Lithuania interpreted Article 21 Paragraph 2 of the Agreement between the Republic of Lithuania and the Republic of Belarus on legal assistance and legal relations in civil, family and criminal cases and established that this rule provides for two alternative jurisdiction rules in non-contractual disputes and the claimant is entitled to choose either of them. Relevant extracts from the case are reproduced below:

Principles on interpretation of international treaties are set out in the Vienna Convention, which states in Article 31 that a treaty shall be interpreted in good faith in accordance with the ordinary meaning to be given to the terms of the treaty in their context and in the light of its object and purpose (Paragraph 1); a special meaning shall be given to a term if it is established that the parties so intended (Paragraph 4).

As mentioned in accordance with the provisions of the bilateral treaty, jurisdiction to hear the case belongs to the court of the Contracting State in whose territory the event giving rise to the damage or other circumstances giving grounds to claim damages has occurred (Article 41 (2)). [...] There is no need to provide further interpretation of the notion of 'event giving rise to the damage' that is enshrined in the bilateral treaty, whereas the legal category of 'other circumstances giving grounds to claim damages' should be interpreted as including the very fact of occurrence of damage as a ground for the claim, which bestows jurisdiction to examine the dispute on the courts of the country where the damage occurred. Therefore Article 41 Paragraph 2 of the bilateral treaty prescribes two jurisdictional alternatives and the claimant has the prerogative to choose between them.

3/5

In case No. E3K-7-73-421/2017 of 7 March 2017, the Supreme Court of Lithuania determined whether the wording in the contract "arbitration courts of the Russian Federation" referred to arbitration or courts and decided that it refers to the court system and thus applied the relevant provisions of the Agreement between the Republic of Lithuania and the Russian Federation on Legal Assistance and Legal Relations in Civil, Family and Criminal Cases. Moreover, the court analyzed the scope of application of the Agreement and decided that the provision on agreed jurisdiction is not limited only to nationals of the Contracting Parties of the Agreement and is to be applied whenever the contract between the parties refers to the courts of the Contracting Parties of the Agreement. Relevant extracts from the case are reproduced below:

> The courts have determined in this case that the challenged contracts contained an agreement on dispute settlement, which specifies the arbitration courts of the Russian Federation.
>
> [...]
>
> Therefore, the courts of the Russian Federation – notwithstanding the existence of the word 'arbitration' in their title – cannot be regarded as an arbitral tribunal (a court constituted by the parties) as understood under the 1958 New York Convention and the Law on Commercial Arbitration of the Republic of Lithuania and should be regarded as part of the judiciary of the said country.
>
> [...]

Therefore, the enlarged panel of judges notes that neither the 1958 New York Convention, nor the Law on Commercial Arbitration is applicable in this case, where the court has to decide on the legal consequences of agreements regarding international jurisdiction.

The Republic of Lithuania and the Russian Federation are bound by their Agreement on Legal Assistance and Legal Relations in Civil, Family and Criminal Cases [...] (hereinafter – International Treaty, Treaty).

Article 1 Paragraph 1 of the Treaty prescribes that citizens of each Contracting Party have the right to use the same legal protection of their personal and property rights on the territory of the other Contracting Party as citizens. Article 1 Paragraph 2 of the Treaty prescribes that such rules are also applicable to legal entities established in the territories of the Contracting Parties in accordance with their laws.

Pursuant to Paragraph 2 of the same article, citizens of each Contracting Party have the right to turn freely and without obstacles to courts and other agencies whose competence covers civil, family and criminal cases; they may participate in hearing such cases, submit requests, bring suits and fulfil their procedural activities on the same conditions as native citizens.

[...] The legal provisions prescribed in the general part of the International Treaty grant nationals of the Contracting Parties certain rights that arise from the Treaty. There are no provisions in the general part of the International Treaty which explicitly prescribe that this legal act is applicable exclusively to relations arising between nationals of the Republic of Lithuania and the Russian Federation.

Limitations on application of a particular legal provision due to the subject's citizenship, residence, fact of granting asylum, stay in the territory of the respective country, and so on, are enshrined in special provisions that govern particular spheres falling within the application of the International Treaty (see e.g. Article 25 Paragraph 1, Articles 27, 28, 59, 61, 62, etc. of the International Treaty). Thus, in principle the International Treaty can govern the rights and obligations of nationals not of the Contracting Parties and (or) obligations of the Contracting Parties towards those nationals.

The general rule for allocation of international jurisdiction between the courts of the Contracting Parties is enshrined in Article 21 of the Treaty, Paragraph 1 of which prescribes that the courts of a Contracting Party have jurisdiction to hear civil and family matters if the respondent has his place of residence in the territory of that Contracting Party, unless otherwise provided for in the Treaty. The courts also have jurisdiction to hear claims raised against juridical persons if there is an administrative organ, representation or branch of that juridical person in the territory of that Party.

Paragraph 2 of the same Article lays down a special rule regarding Article 21 Paragraph 1 of the International Treaty, which governs agreements on international jurisdiction. This legal provision prescribes that the courts of the Contracting Parties shall hear cases in other instances too, if there is an agreement between the parties in writing. When there is such an agreement, the court shall terminate the proceedings at the respondent's request if such request was received before submission on the substance of the claim. The parties to the agreement cannot change the exclusive jurisdiction of the courts.

The panel of judges notes that the text of Article 21 Paragraph 2 of the International Treaty does not refer to the need for the parties to an agreement on jurisdiction to be limited to nationals of the Contracting Parties. The mere fact that some provisions of the International Treaty specify what nationals they are subject to [...], whereas some other provisions do not make such references, implies the conclusion that the scope of the analysed Article 21 Paragraph 2 of the International Treaty covers individuals, irrespective of their place of living (residence) and citizenship.

By concluding the International Treaty in question, Lithuania assumed obligations arising from it to the other Contracting State and *vice versa*. One of those obligations is not to hear cases which parties to the dispute by their agreement assigned to the jurisdiction of the courts of the other Contracting State and in the manner prescribed in the International Treaty to refer the parties to resolve their dispute in the agreed way.

Therefore when the provision in question does not contain limitations on the composition of nationals, a court of Lithuania considering the issue of referring the disputing parties to a court of the other country shall apply the laws applicable to the Republic of Lithuania and to such other country indicated in the agreement on jurisdiction, as well as procedural rules, conditions and assumptions that enforce the specific obligation in question which are prescribed in those laws.

In the light of the above the enlarged panel of judges formulates the following rule on interpretation and application of the law: the Lithuanian court shall decide on referring the parties to the dispute – irrespective of their nationality, domicile or residence – to the courts of the country specified in their agreement on international jurisdiction in the manner and in accordance with the procedures such as those prescribed in the legal acts of the Republic of Lithuania and the respective country (Regulation of the European Union, international agreement, etc.).

3/6

In case No. 3K-3-267-611/2017 of 15 June 2017, the Supreme Court of Lithuania interpreted Article v(2)(b) of the 1958 New York Convention and evaluated the notion of 'public order'. The court found that the time limit of five years to submit a document for enforcement prescribed in the Civil Procedure Code of the Republic of Lithuania does not constitute public policy under the 1958 New York Convention. Relevant extracts from the case are reproduced below:

> Article v paragraph 2 Subparagraph b of the 1958 New York Convention sets out the possibility to refuse recognition and enforcement of a foreign arbitral award if a competent authority in the country where recognition and enforcement is sought finds that recognition and enforcement of the award would be contrary to the public policy of that country.
>
> It is stated in consistently developed case law of the cassation court that the notion of 'public policy' in the doctrine and practice of international arbitration is interpreted as international public policy, which encompasses fundamental principles of fair proceedings, as well as mandatory norms establishing fundamental and universally recognised principles of law [...]. The cassation court has emphasized that not every violation of mandatory norm of the Republic of Lithuania can be considered as sufficient ground to refuse recognition and enforcement of a foreign arbitral award. Violation of public policy can be recognised in cases where it is established that recognition and enforcement of a foreign arbitral award violates internationally recognised fundamental legal principles and moral norms enshrined in the Constitution of the Republic of Lithuania,

as well as in cases when an agreement to arbitrate was obtained by coercion, fraud, threat, etc. [...]. It is not only the cassation court, but also foreign supreme courts, who in their case law formulate limits of the criterion on conformity to public policy in a narrow manner. Only arbitral awards which violate fundamental and clear principles of justice and fairness, main norms of morality can be found as contrary to public policy [...].

There is no basis to recognise a period of five years to submit an enforceable document prescribed in Article 606 Paragraph 2 of the Civil Procedure Code as a fundamental principle of fair proceedings or mandatory norm establishing fundamental and universally recognised principles of law, because that period is not a mandatory time-limit: under Article 608 of the Civil Procedure Code it can be restored; besides, only a foreign arbitral award that has been recognised obtains *res judicata* force in the Republic of Lithuania [...]. Therefore, the panel of judges decides that there is no legal ground to refuse recognition and enforcement of a decision adopted by the Stockholm arbitration tribunal on 31 May 2006 on the public policy ground in accordance with Article 606 Paragraph 2 of the Civil Procedure Code.

3/7

In case No. 3K-3-75-916/2017 of 11 January 2017, the Supreme Court of Lithuania interpreted and applied Article 31 Paragraph 1 of the CMR Convention and discussed conditions for successive carriers to be bound by a single contract of carriage. Relevant extracts from the case are reproduced below:

Courts that can hear disputes that fall within the scope of the CMR Convention are prescribed in Article 31 Paragraph 1 of the CMR Convention. Assessment of which courts have jurisdiction to hear such disputes has to be based on not only the Lithuanian version of the text of the CMR Convention but also on text in other languages. The Lithuanian version of Article 31 Paragraph 1 of the CMR Convention provides that in all contentious matters arising out of carriage, the plaintiff – in addition to the courts of the Contracting States – can bring action in the courts: (a) of a country within whose territory the respondent has a permanent residence, headquarters of firm or subsidiary through which the contract of carriage was made, or (b) in the courts of a country within whose territory the place where the goods were taken over or the place designated for delivery is situated. Assessment of the text of the relevant provision in

English and French reveals that jurisdiction is conferred not on any court situated in the Contracting State of the Convention, but the courts of the Contracting State designated by agreement between the parties (in English – in any court or tribunal of a Contracting State designated by agreement between the parties; in French – *des juridictions des pays contractants désignées d'un commun accord par les parties*). [...]

Thus, two categories of courts can hear disputes that fall within the scope of application of the CMR Convention. First, the courts of a country which is a party to the CMR Convention appointed by common agreement between the contracting parties, secondly the courts prescribed in Article 31 Paragraph 1 Subparagraphs a and b. The commentary to the CMR Convention as well as doctrine indicate that such courts have jurisdiction to hear cases that fall within the scope of application of the cmr Convention; however, the agreement between the parties does not prevail over the courts prescribed in this provision and does not undermine their jurisdiction to hear the case (see 1975 Commentary on the Convention on the Contract for the International Carriage of Goods by Road, UN Inland Transport Committee document ECE/TRANS/14; Clarke, M.; Yates, D. Contracts of Carriage by Land and Air, Second edition, London, 2008, pp. 52–54).

Based on the above [...] the court hearing a case must assess whether it has jurisdiction to hear the case or some of the claims raised in the case, taking into account all criteria prescribed in Article 31 of the CMR Convention. In order to do so, it must qualify all relations that arose in the case. The mere existence of a potential agreement for international carriage of goods between the parties is not sufficient to limit the jurisdiction of the courts of the Contracting States under other grounds prescribed in Article 31 Paragraph 1 of the CMR Convention.

In order to determine that parties participating in international carriage are contracting parties to one agreement, it must be established that they have mutual obligations towards each other and have reached mutual consensus, have agreed on the essential terms of their contract for international carriage [...].

The commentary on the CMR Convention as well as some other sources of doctrine support the position that carriage shall be governed by a single contract performed by successive road carriers only in cases where a single carriage document (consignment) is issued and where every successive carrier joins it by accepting the goods and the consignment note.

When there is a single consignment note for the carriage, it is deemed that by accepting the goods under the consignment note each carrier joins a single contract of carriage and together with other carriers undertakes the obligation for the whole operation. Other sources of doctrine recognise the possibility that carriage can also be performed by a single contract in cases involving separate consignment notes, provided that the sender (consignor) knows about particular persons participating (going to participate) in the carriage and those persons on their own behalf and at their own risk undertake the obligation towards the sender (consignor) to deliver the goods and be aware of the terms of the carriage contract concluded between the sender (consignor) and contracting carrier (see 1975 Commentary on the Convention on the Contract for the International Carriage of Goods by Road, UN Inland Transport Committee document ECE/TRANS/14; Clarke, M.; Yates, D. *Contracts of Carriage by Land and Air*, Second edition, London, 2008, 75–76 [...].

3/8

In cases No. e3K-3-60-421/2017 of 6 January 2017 and 3K-3-121-687/2017 of 7 March 2017, the Supreme Court of Lithuania decided on the effect of Regulation No. 1215/2015 on an Agreement between the Republic of Lithuania and the Republic of Belarus on legal assistance and legal relations in civil, family and criminal cases. The relevant extracts from the case are reproduced below:

As this case contains an international element and one of the respondents resides in a Member State of the European union (in Lithuania), the need arises to decide on the application and scope of application of Regulation (EU) No 1215/2012 of the European Parliament and the Council of 12 December 2012 on Jurisdiction and the Recognition and Enforcement of Judgments in Civil and Commercial Matters (hereinafter – Regulation No. 1215/2012) in the current proceedings (see e.g. Judgment of the Court of Justice of the European Union of 1 March 2005 in *Andrew Owusu v. N.B. Jackson, trading as 'Villa Holidays Bal-Inn Villas' and Others*, paragraphs 24–35).

When deciding on application of the above-mentioned regulation in a particular case, it is necessary to analyse the conflict rules. Paragraph 36 of the recitals to Regulation No. 1215/2015 and Article 73 Paragraph 3 prescribe that the Regulation does not affect application of bilateral conventions and agreements between a third State and a Member State concluded before the date of entry into force of Regulation (EC) No 44/2001 which concern matters governed by the Regulation. This rule is also laid down in the first paragraph of Article 351 of the Treaty on the Functioning of the European Union.

It is recognized in the practice of the Supreme Court of Lithuania, that, in view of the fact that the agreement between the Republic of Lithuania and the Republic of Belarus on legal assistance and legal relations in civil, family and criminal cases was concluded on 10 October 1992, i.e. before the entry into force of Regulation No. 44/2001 (and respectively Regulation No. 1215/2012), therefore Regulation No. 1215/2012 does not affect jurisdictional matters prescribed therein [...].

In addition, in case No. 3K-3-121-687/2017 of 7 March 2017 the court decided on application of the Agreement between the Republic of Lithuania and the Republic of Belarus on legal assistance and legal relations in civil, family and criminal cases when one of a number of defendants is domiciled in the Republic of Belarus, whereas the rest are domiciled in EU Member States. The relevant extracts from the case are reproduced below:

The Bilateral Treaty on Legal Assistance governs the rules on court jurisdiction in cases where the dispute is related to another Contracting State. It contains general and special rules on international jurisdiction. Article 20 Paragraph 1 of the Bilateral Treaty on Legal Assistance establishes a general rule on jurisdiction, which prescribes that the courts of the country where the respondent has his residence shall have jurisdiction to hear civil and family matters, unless otherwise provided for in the Bilateral Treaty.

Article 20 Paragraph 2 of the Bilateral Treaty on Legal Assistance prescribes a legal institute on agreement for international jurisdiction. This provision prescribes that the courts of contracting countries shall have competence to hear disputes in other cases too provided there is a written agreement between the parties. The loan contract does not contain agreement on international jurisdiction; therefore it is necessary to analyse whether the Bilateral Treaty contains other special rules which might allow the jurisdiction of the courts of Lithuania. This verification should be performed by analysing, interpreting and evaluating the provisions of the Bilateral Treaty.

Questions related to the binding nature of international treaties, their interpretation, etc. are regulated by the 1969 Vienna Convention on the Law of Treaties. Articles 26 and 27 of the Vienna Convention on the Law of Treaties of 23 May 1969 enshrine the principles of binding force of international treaties and their supremacy over national law; Articles 31–33 enshrine principles and rules on interpretation of international treaties. Under Article 31 Paragraph 1 of the Convention, a treaty shall be interpreted in good faith in accordance with the ordinary meaning to be given to the terms of the treaty in their context and in the light of its object and purpose.

The panel of judges notes that the Bilateral Treaty on Legal Assistance does not contain provisions that give grounds to conclude that the Contracting States intended to determine court jurisdiction in cases, such as currently under consideration, based under internal law, general national or international jurisdiction rules, or other international or regional documents of one of the countries. There is no such information in the remaining preparatory works (in French *travaux préparatoires*) of this treaty either.

The Bilateral Treaty on Legal Assistance does not contain any special jurisdiction rules for disputes arising out of loan legal relations. The Bilateral Treaty also does not contain any special jurisdiction rules for instances, when the plaintiff submits a claim for recovery of debt under a loan agreement against a number of defendants (principal debtor and guarantors), one of whom resides in another Contracting State.

The Bilateral Treaty does not contain any other provision which could be interpreted so that in the case of a number of defendants would allow for the court of one country to 'attract' jurisdiction to the place of residence of one of the defendants, provided the claims are so closely connected that it is expedient to hear and determine them together to avoid the risk of irreconcilable judgments resulting from separate proceedings. It should be noted that such a situation has arisen in the present proceedings. Therefore, the court must assess its jurisdiction over the plaintiffs' claim against one of the defendants – a citizen of the Republic of Belarus – separately from jurisdiction over the other defendants.

[...]

As there are no exceptions in the International Treaty regarding this question, international jurisdiction against the guarantor has to be established assessing such claim separately under the rules of personal jurisdiction (in Latin – *in personam* – directed against a particular person).

In a dispute regarding recovery of debt under a loan agreement the jurisdiction of the court of a Contracting State shall be determined by the place of residence of the defendant, being a natural person. When deciding on the jurisdiction of the court, it is sufficient for the court to determine the place of residence of the defendant in the territory of the country of that court.

3/9

In case No. 3K-3-173-686/2017 of 13 April 2017, the Supreme Court of Lithuania interpreted Article 32 of the CMR Convention in the light of authentic texts of the CMR Convention and found that the claimant failed to institute action arising out of carriage within the period of limitation prescribed in the CMR Convention. Relevant extracts from the case are reproduced below:

Article 32 Paragraph 1 of the CMR Convention prescribes that the period of limitation for an action arising out of carriage under this Convention is one year. In the case of wilful misconduct, or such default as in accordance with the law of the court or tribunal seized of the case is considered as equivalent to wilful misconduct, the period of limitation shall be three years. Subsection a of the said article prescribes that in case of partial loss, damage or delay in delivery the period of limitation shall begin to run from the date of delivery of the goods.

According to Article 32 Paragraph 2 of the CMR Convention a written claim suspends the period of limitation until such date as the carrier rejects the claim by notification in writing and returns the documents attached thereto.

The official translation of Article 32 Paragraph 3 in Lithuanian contains the following wording: 'without prejudice to the provisions of paragraph 2 of this article, the court hearing the case shall have a right to suspend as well as terminate the limitation period thereof'. Authentic texts of Article 32 Paragraph 3 of the CMR Convention, which prescribes the right of the court to suspend or terminate the period of limitation, contain the following wording: *Sous réserve des dispositions du paragraphe 2 ci-dessus, la suspension de la prescription est régie par la loi de la juridiction saisie. Il en est de même en ce qui concerne l'interruption de la prescription (in French)*; Subject to the provisions of paragraph 2 above, the extension of the period of limitation shall be governed by the law of the court or tribunal seized of the case. That law shall also govern the fresh accrual of rights of action (*in English*). In a judgment of 29 March 2013, case No. 3K-7-28/2013, the extended panel of judges of the Supreme Court of Lithuania noted that this provision of the Convention is not translated accurately. It would be more precise to translate it as: 'Without prejudice to the provisions of paragraph 2 of this article, the law of the court hearing the case shall be applicable to the suspension of the limitation period. Such law shall also apply to the termination of the limitation period'. The CMR Convention in German also prescribes the right for the court to suspend, as well as terminate, the period of limitation: *Unbeschadet der Bestimmungen des Absatzes 2 gilt für die Hemmung der Verjährung das Recht des angerufenen Gerichtes. Dieses Recht gilt auch für die Unterbrechung der Verjährung.*

The commentary on the Convention on the Contract for the International Carriage of Goods by Road (CMR) of 1975 indicates that the French terms 'suspension' and 'interruption' cover all situations in which the period of limitation is either prolonged by a certain time or is prevented from running or ceases to run (Loewe, R. *Commentary on the Convention of 19 May 1956 on the contract for the international carriage of goods by road (CMR)*. Geneva, 1975, p. 69, 267 para.) [...].

In the present case the claimant sought to renew the elapsed period of limitation, whereas the respondent sought to apply the consequences of the period of limitation that had ceased to run and to reject the claim.

When interpreting the rule on the moment of the beginning of the period of limitation as prescribed in Article 32 Paragraph 1 Subparagraph a of the CMR Convention, it is important to determine the moment of delivery of the cargo, i.e. the moment of transfer of the delivered goods.

Under Article 17 Paragraph 1 of the CMR Convention the carrier is liable for total or partial loss of the goods and for damage thereto occurring between the time when he takes over the goods and the time of delivery, as well as for any delay in delivery.

The CMR Commentary indicates that delivery takes place at the time when the carrier allows the consignee to unload the goods which are at that moment still on the vehicle [...]. [...] delivery takes place at the moment when the goods leave the carrier's control and pass under the control of the consignee (Loewe, R. *Commentary on the Convention of 19 May 1956 on the contract for the international carriage of goods by road (CMR)*. Geneva, 1975, p. 42, 149 para.) [...].

[...]

The last sentence of Article 32 Paragraph 1 of the CMR Convention prescribes that the day on which the period of limitation begins to run shall not be included in the period. On that basis, the period of limitation of one year started the day following delivery of the cargo – 25 February 2012 – while the last day of this period was 24 February 2013.

On 1 July 2013 the claimant submitted to the respondent (carrier) a written claim with evidence proving the damage: invoices signifying acquisition of lost and damaged goods, documents of payment. At the date of submission of the written claim, the one-year period of limitation prescribed in Article 32 Paragraph 1 of the CMR Convention had expired. [...] The claimant submitted a claim to the court on 1 April 2015 and from submission of the claim on 1 July 2013 until submission of the claim to court on 1 April 2015 it did not address the respondent requesting compensation for damage.

According to the case law of the Supreme Court of Lithuania, negligence equivalent to wilful misconduct by a carrier encompasses actions which he could have avoided if he had undertaken at least the minimum requirements of care and diligence , or inactivity – failure to carry out all possible actions that could have reduced the risk of damage or avert it [...].

In order to find wilful inappropriate conduct by the carrier, both objective and subjective criteria have to be taken into account. The objective criterion encompasses disregard or breach of established rules (traffic rules, rules concerning safety of the cargo, rules on work and rest time, instructions regarding delivery of cargo). The subjective criterion means wilful conduct by the carrier (activity or inactivity) with the knowledge that such conduct will likely cause negative consequences [...].

> In this case no violation of the rules on carriage of goods or wilful default conduct by the respondent (carrier) was established; his conduct was not considered to be wilful misconduct, therefore there is no ground to apply the period of limitation of three years prescribed in Article 32 Paragraph 1 of the CMR Convention.
>
> [...] In its claim the claimant sought to renew the elapsed period of limitation but did not provide any reasons that would justify expiration of the period and the length of the delay. From the day of delivery to submission of the claim the claimant did not undertake actions to recover damages.
>
> [...]
>
> As the claimant's claim for an award of damages for partial loss of goods and for damage was submitted after the expiration of the one year period of limitation prescribed in Article 32 Paragraph 1 of the CMR Convention, the claim is rejected and the court need not determine the other arguments concerning the respondent's (carrier's) relief from liability under Article 17 Paragraph 2 of the cmr Convention, which were provided by the claimant in the cassation claim, as they have no legal significance for the legal result in this case.

3/10

In case No. e3K-3-427-915/2017 of 23 November 2017, the Supreme Court of Lithuania elaborated that the Convention Providing a Uniform Law For Bills of Exchange and Promissory Notes (Geneva, 1930) provides an additional and independent instrument of assurance – aval – which is not the same as a guarantee under national civil law. Relevant extracts from the case are reproduced below:

> The instrument of guarantee under a promissory note as well as the majority of other rules prescribed in the Law on Bills of Exchange and Promissory Notes of the Republic of Lithuania (Law on Bills of Exchange) were transferred from the 1930 Geneva Convention Providing a Uniform Law for Bills of Exchange and Promissory Notes. Article 34 Paragraph 2 of the Law on Bills of Exchange establishes an analogous rule as prescribed in Article 32 Paragraph 2 of the Convention, which prescribes that an undertaking is valid even when the liability which it has guaranteed is inoperative. The only exception to this rule is a defect of form of a bill of exchange. The Convention uses the notion of 'aval' to describe a guarantee under a bill of exchange.

> Legal jurisprudence recognises that an aval as a method to guarantee performance of an obligation under the Convention should not be regarded as a guarantee under civil law, i.e. it is an independent and separate instrument to guarantee performance of an obligation; therefore general rules on guarantees are not applicable to it (see Heremann, G. *Background and salient features of the United Nations Convention of International Bills of Exchange and International Promissory Notes*. Published by Penn Law: Legal Scholarship Repository, 2014, p. 532).

3/11

In case No. 3K-3-270-687/2017 of 15 June 2017, the Supreme Court of Lithuania elaborated on the scope and meaning of 'literary and artistic works' under the Berne Convention for the Protection of Literary and Artistic Works. Relevant extracts from the case are reproduced below:

> International and EU legal acts do not directly provide the meaning of object of copyrights. Article 2 Paragraph 1 of the Berne Convention for the Protection of Literary and Artistic Works provides that 'literary and artistic works' shall include every production in the literary, scientific and artistic domain, whatever may be the mode or form of its expression, such as books, pamphlets and other writings, etc. The purpose of Article 2 Paragraph 1 of this Convention is to define the expression 'literary and artistic works'. Two criteria are employed for this purpose: first – to include all literary, artistic and scientific works in this expression, second – to reject any restrictions relating to the methods and forms of expression of works. For instance, regarding the first criterion it should be noted that the expression also includes scientific works, even though they are not directly mentioned in the Convention. Protection for these works is provided not due to their scientific character (medical textbook, treatise on physics or scientific work), but because they exist as books or films about medicine, physics, the topography of the surface of the moon or the geography of outer space. The contents of the work are not a precondition for protection. By referring to the literary, artistic and scientific domain the Convention also includes scientific works in its remit of protection providing protection for their mode of expression [...].

> Expressions used in the Berne convention should be understood as all-inclusive: the expression 'literary and artistic works' should be understood as including all works which can be afforded protection. Article 2 Paragraph 1 of the Convention provides a list of such works. Neither the contents nor size, nor purpose (entertainment, informational, discussion,

promotional, propaganda or other publication), nor form (manuscript, typescript, typographic text, bound or unbound etc.) of the work affects protection of such work.

Part Four: 11.A. Relationship between International Law and Domestic Law – Application and Implementation of International Law in Domestic Law

4/1

In case No. 3K-3-111-686/2017 of 20 February 2017, the Supreme Court of Lithuania assessed a claim to compensate the litigation costs of the Government in expropriation proceedings, which consisted of an expert evaluation to assess the market value of the land plots and indicated that such claim should satisfy the requirements of Article 1 of Protocol 1 of the ECHR. Relevant extracts from the case are reproduced below:

> [...] the claimant stated that the fact of her application to the court itself did not prove the alleged failure to determine just compensation for land taken for public purposes, as prescribed by law, and did not give a privilege to the former owner to be discharged from the obligation to cover the claimant's litigation costs that amount to EUR 10,136.70 (for expert assessment of the market value of the expropriated land plots). It is stated that if the respondents had accepted the amount of compensation indicated by the claimant for the land, which is taken for public purposes, such litigation costs would not have been incurred at all.
>
> [...]
>
> Article 23 Paragraph 3 of the Constitution of the Republic of Lithuania prescribes that property may be taken only for the needs of society according to the procedure established by law and shall be justly compensated for. Article 4.93 Paragraph 4 of the Civil Code of the Republic of Lithuania prescribes that property may be taken for public needs only upon just compensation. The instances, manner and compensation for taking land for public purpose are prescribed in the Land Law. The case law of the ECtHR establishes that interference with the right to the peaceful enjoyment of possessions (Article 1 of Protocol No. 1 of the ECHR) must always strike a fair balance between the demands of the general

interest of the community and the requirements of protection of the individual's fundamental rights. There must be a reasonable relationship of proportionality between the means employed and the aim sought to be realised by any measure depriving a person of his possessions (see judgment of the Grand Chamber in *Vistinš and Perepjolkins v. Latvia*, application no. 71243/01, § 108, 25 October 2012; judgment of the Grand Chamber in case of *Scordino v. Italy (no. 1)*, application no. 36813/97, § 93, 29 March 2006). The conditions for compensation are significant in assessing whether the challenged measure has ensured the right balance and, in particular, did not create a disproportionate burden for the applicants. The ECtHR has recognized that taking possessions without paying an amount reasonably related to their value usually results in a disproportionate restriction on the applicant's rights.

The panel of judges considers that in this particular case it is very important to respect the principle of fair balance of interests, which reveals the need for a more sensitive approach when dealing with determination of the value of property and of the amount of fair compensation. When dealing with allocation of costs and considering the aspect of protection of human rights (property), attention should be drawn to the fact that in the present case allocation of costs occurs in a dispute that is not private in nature, but within the framework of State-led expropriation; the costs of expert assessments were incurred due to the fact that the State did not offer the respondents fair compensation for land plots taken for public needs, and as a result, there was a need to establish the amount of compensation before the court.

The panel of judges notes that, as can be seen from the case law of the ECtHR, the compliance of national law with Article 1 of Protocol No. 1 of the Convention (protection of property) in regard to allocation of court fees has been addressed in a case decided by the Grand Chamber: *Perdigao v. Portugal* (application no. 24768/06, judgment of 16 November 2010). In this judgment a violation was found because in essence the compensation for expropriation awarded to the applicants had ultimately been fully absorbed by the amount they had to pay to the State in court fees.

On the one hand the ECtHR recognises that the State enjoys a wide margin of appreciation with regard both to choosing the means of enforcement and to ascertaining whether the consequences of the measures taken are justified in the general interest for the purpose of achieving the object of the interference in question (see cited *Perdigao*). On the other hand, the ECtHR recognises the special nature of cases involving the State. According to the case law of the ECtHR rules regarding legal costs must avoid placing an excessive burden on litigants where their action is justified as it is paradoxical that, by imposing various taxes the State takes away with one hand what it has awarded with the other (see judgment of the Grand Chamber in *Scordino v. Italy (no. 1)*, § 201; cited *Perdigao*; judgment in *Harrison Mc Kee v. Hungary*, application no. 22840/07, § 31, 3 June 2014).

It should be noted that the ECtHR in cases concerning compliance of allocation of court fees with the requirements of the Convention evaluates the actions of the applicant himself and his responsibility in regard to the particular sum of court fees (e.g. whether claims were frivolous and grossly exaggerated). The case law of the ECtHR reveals that even if it is established that the behaviour of a person had an effect on the costs of litigation, it is of utmost importance that the effect of allocation of court fees would not be considered as imposing an excessive burden, for example by fully 'absorbing' or substantially reducing the compensation awarded for the expropriation (see cited *Perdigao*, judgment in *Klauz v. Croatia*, application no. 28963/10, 18 July 2013).

According to the assessment of the panel of judges in the present case when assessing the behaviour of the respondents whose property has been expropriated it should be noted that they have reasonably disagreed with the amounts proposed by the applicant (which led to the dispute in court), since the courts finally adjudged much larger compensation. Therefore, the argument of the cassation claim that it was precisely the will of the respondent that caused the applicant to go to court, because if they had agreed with the amount of compensation for the land taken for public purposes the litigation costs would not have been incurred at all is unfounded. The panel of judges is of the opinion that in the present case the respondents are entitled to full compensation of their damages.

4/2

In case No. e3K-3-134-969/2017 of 16 March 2017, the Supreme Court of Lithuania interpreted Labour Code provisions in the light of the international obligations of the Republic of Lithuania in the field of rights of workers. Relevant extracts from the case are reproduced below:

According to Article 2 Paragraph 1 Subparagraph 4 of the Labour Code the following principles apply to the relations referred to in Article 1 of this Code: <...> equality of subjects of labour law irrespective of their gender, sexual orientation, race, national origin, language, origin, citizenship and social status, religion, intention to have a child (children), marital and family status, age, opinions or views, membership of political party or public organisation, factors unrelated to the employee's professional qualities.

The above-mentioned provision of the Labour Code reflects the international obligations of the Republic of Lithuania in the sphere of rights of workers:

An obligation to undertake all necessary and appropriate measures to ensure that workers and employers may freely exercise the right to organise, which is enshrined in Article 11 of International Labour Organization Convention No. 87, the Freedom of Association and Protection of the Right to Organise Convention.

The principle of adequate protection of workers against acts of antiunion discrimination in respect of their employment is enshrined in Article 1 of International Labour Organization Convention No. 97 on the Right to Organise and Collective Bargaining Convention. According to Article 1 Paragraph 2 of this Convention, protection for workers shall be applicable more particularly in respect of acts calculated to: (a) make the employment of a worker subject to the condition that he shall not join a union or shall relinquish trade union membership; (b) cause the dismissal of or otherwise prejudice a worker by reason of union membership or because of participation in union activities outside working hours or, with the consent of the employer, within working hours.

In the sphere of discrimination against workers on the basis of their membership in a trade union, the following provisions of the ECHR are relevant: Article 11 (freedom of association) together with Article 11 of the Convention (prohibition of discrimination). The ECtHR in its decision of 30 July 2009 in *Danilenkov and others v. Russia* (application no. 67336/01), when interpreting Article 11 of the Convention (freedom of association), recalled that Paragraph 1 of this article enshrines trade union freedom as one form of or as a special aspect of freedom of association. The words 'for the protection of his interests' in Article 11 Paragraph 1 are not redundant, and the Convention safeguards freedom to protect the occupational interests of trade union members by trade union action, the conduct and development of which the Contracting States must both permit and enable. As to the substance of the right of association enshrined in Article 11, the ECtHR has emphasised that it takes into consideration the totality of the measures taken by the State concerned in order to secure trade union freedom, subject to its margin of appreciation. An employee or worker should be free to join or not join a trade union without being sanctioned or subject to disincentives.

The wording of Article 11 of the Convention explicitly refers to the right of 'everybody', and this provision clearly includes a right not to be discriminated against for choosing to avail oneself of the right to be protected by a trade union, given also that Article 14 of the Convention (prohibition of discrimination) forms an integral part of each of the Articles of the Convention, laying down rights and freedoms whatever their nature. Thus, the totality of the measures implemented to safeguard the guarantees of Article 11 should include protection against discrimination on the ground of trade union membership; according to the ILO's Freedom of Association Committee such discrimination constitutes one of the most serious violations of freedom of association, capable of jeopardising the very existence of a trade union. The ECtHR has also emphasized that individuals affected by discriminatory treatment should be provided with an opportunity to challenge it and should have the right to take legal action to obtain damages and other relief. Therefore, States are required under Articles 11 and 14 of the Convention to set up a judicial system that ensures real and effective protection against anti-union discrimination. In the abovementioned case the ECtHR found that the negative effects of respective membership on the applicants were sufficient to constitute a *prima facie* case of discrimination in the enjoyment of the rights guaranteed by Article 11 of the Convention and decided that the State failed to fulfil its positive obligations to adopt effective and clear judicial protection against discrimination on the ground of trade union membership (various techniques were used in order to encourage employees to relinquish their trade union membership, which resulted in a dramatic reduction in membership).

4/3

In administrative case No. 2AT-2-489/2017 of 14 February 2017, the Supreme Court of Lithuania applied the proportionality principle enshrined in Article 1 of Protocol No. 1 of the ECHR while interpreting a mandatory provision of the Code of Administrative Offences, which prescribes seizure of vehicles which have been used to hunt animals. Relevant extracts from the case are reproduced below:

> In the present proceedings involving an administrative offence, wherein a property that belongs to a company established and controlled by the municipal council was seized, the proportionally of limitations on such legal entity's ownership right is of relevance.
>
> It should be noted that protection of ownership is also guaranteed in Article 1 of Protocol No. 1 to the Convention on Fundamental Human Rights and Freedoms. Article 1 Paragraph 1 of the Convention prescribes that every natural or legal person is entitled to the peaceful enjoyment of his possessions. No one shall be deprived of his possessions except in the public interest and subject to the conditions provided for by law and by the general principles of international law. Under Paragraph 2 of this article the preceding provisions shall not, however, in any way impair the right of a State to enforce such laws as it deems necessary to control the use of property in accordance with the general interest or to secure the payment of taxes or other contributions or penalties.
>
> According to the case law of the ECtHR confiscation of things by means of which an offence was committed usually constitutes an instance of control of the use of property within the meaning of the second paragraph of Article 1 of Protocol No. 1 of the Convention (e.g. judgment in *B.K.M. Lojistik Tasimacilik Ticaret Limited Sirketi v. Slovenia*, application no. 42079/12, § 38 with further references, 17 January 2017). The second paragraph of Article 1 of Protocol No. 1 has to be interpreted with consideration for the principle set out in the first sentence of this article; therefore under this provision in every interference with property rights a balance has to be struck between the demands of the general interest and the imperative of protecting the fundamental rights of the individual, which means that the relationship of proportionality between the means employed and the aim or aims sought has to be realised (e.g. decision on admissibility in *Yildirim v. Italy*, application no. 38602/02, 10 April 2003). The State has a wide margin of appreciation with regard both to choosing the means of enforcement and to ascertaining whether the consequences of enforcement are justified in the general interest for the purpose of achieving the object of the law in question. While recognising the

importance of the fight against dangerous and prohibited activities it is also stated that confiscation of property used in the commission of such offences may, as in the present case, impose a significant burden on the third parties to whom the property belongs. The exercise of balancing the general interests of crime prevention and protection of the affected individual's rights in these circumstances thus means that imposing such a burden on the owner of the property concerned can be justified only if his interest in having the property returned to him is outweighed by the risk that its return would facilitate drug trafficking and undermine the fight against organised crime (*B.K.M. Lojistik Tasimacilik Ticaret Limited Sirketi* v. *Slovenia*, § 47).

In assessing the proportionality of confiscation of property in criminal matters, ECtHR case law also mentions that such interference should correspond to the severity of the infringement; the sanction should correspond to the gravity of the offence it is designed to punish (e.g. with corresponding amendments, judgment in *Boljević* v. *Croatia*, application no. 43492/11, § 44 and others, 31 January 2017; judgment in *S.C. Fiercolect Impex S.R.L.* v. *Romania*, application no. 26429/07, § 69–72, 13 December 2016; judgment in *Sud Fondi srl and others* v. *Italy*, application no. 75909/01, § 140, 20 January 2009).

4/4

In case No. 3K-3-75-916/2017 of 11 January 2017, the Supreme Court of Lithuania reiterated that the issues that fall within the scope of CMR Convention governed by the CMR Convention and national law in such a case can be applicable in a subsidiary manner. Relevant extracts from the case are reproduced below:

> The CMR Convention is an international treaty which governs issues related to contracts for the carriage of goods by road in vehicles for reward, when the place of taking over the goods and the place designated for delivery, as specified in the contract, are situated in two different countries, of which at least one is a Contracting State of the CMR Convention.
>
> Article 1.13 Paragraph 1 of the Civil Code establishes the principle of supremacy of international treaties. It has been clarified in the case law of the cassation court that the CMR Convention has a strict, special regulatory effect; thus issues falling within its scope of regulation are deemed to be comprehensively regulated and no derogations from this Convention are permitted (Articles 40–41 of the CMR Convention). When relations

fall within the scope of the CMR Convention, national law is applicable in a subsidiary manner.

4/5

In case No. 3K-3-4-916/2017 of 30 January 2017, the Supreme Court of Lithuania interpreted the provisions dealing with the impartiality of the judge in the light of Article 6 Paragraph 1 of the ECHR and found that the mere fact that the same panel of judges have heard a dispute involving the applicant does not by itself prove lack of impartiality on the part of the tribunal. The relevant extracts from the case are reproduced below:

> The cassator submits in his claim that the appellate court was improperly constituted because one of the judges [...] participated in rendering judgment in a civil case [...] which had involved the same relations between the claimant and respondents and dealt with such relations in detail.
>
> [...]
>
> It is emphasised in the practice of the ECtHR that impartiality usually means lack of personal prejudice or bias and within the context of Article 6 Paragraph 1 of the ECHR should be regarded in two aspects – subjective and objective. The subjective impartiality of the judge and tribunal means that no member of the tribunal holds any personal prejudice or bias (see judgment of ECtHR in *Hauschildt* v. *Denmark*, application no. 10486/83). In regard to the objective aspects of the impartiality of the judge and tribunal, the ECtHR has emphasised that ascertainable facts raising doubt about the impartiality of the judge have to be established. When it is being decided whether in a given case there is a legitimate reason to fear that a court lacks impartiality, the standpoint of the party to the dispute claiming that it is not impartial is important but not decisive (see judgment of ECtHR in *Gautrin* v. *France*, application no. 38/1997/822/1025–1028). What is decisive is whether the fear can be held to be objectively justified (see judgment in *Wettstein* v. *Switzerland*, application no. 33958/96, 21 December 2000; judgment in *Ferrantelli and Santangelo* v. *Italy*, application no. 19874/92, 7 August 1996). The objective test is usually related to hierarchical or other relationships between the judge and other participants in the proceedings (see e.g. judgment in *Miller and others* v. *the United Kingdom*, application nos. 45825/99, 45826/99 and 45827/99, 26 October 2004; judgment in *Mežnarić* v. *Croatia*, application no. 71615/01, 15 July 2005).

It has been clarified by the cassation court that the mere fact that a court of the same composition had heard another civil case initiated by the cassator concerning acquisition of ownership resulting from acquisitive prescription does not in itself confirm the existence of bias on the part of the court.

4/6

In case No. 3K-3-44-969/2017 of 15 February 2018, the Supreme Court of Lithuania analysed whether the owner of a semi-trailer which was seized during criminal investigations as evidence and then sold to cover the costs of its storage should be compensated the costs of such storage, when the criminal investigation was discontinued without bringing any charges against the claimant. The Court decided that the provisions of national law must be interpreted in the light of Article 1 Paragraph 1 of Protocol No. 1 of the ECHR. The relevant extracts from the case are reproduced below:

> Article 1 Paragraph 1 of Protocol No. 1 of the Convention on Fundamental Human Rights and Freedoms (hereinafter – the Convention) establishes that every natural or legal person is entitled to the peaceful enjoyment of his possessions. No one shall be deprived of his possessions except in the public interest and subject to the conditions provided for by law and by the general principles of international law. According to Paragraph 2 of the said article the preceding provisions shall not, however, in any way impair the right of a State to enforce such laws as it deems necessary to control the use of property in accordance with the general interest or to secure the payment of taxes or other contributions or penalties.
>
> In the case law of the ECtHR temporal limitation of property rights for the purposes of criminal proceedings usually constitutes an interference falling within the scope of the second paragraph of Article 1 of Protocol No. 1 concerning 'control of the use of property' in accordance with the general interest (e.g. judgment in *Zosymov* v. *Ukraine*, application no. 4322/06, § 72, 7 July 2016; judgment in *Borzhonov* v. *Russia*, application no. 18274/04, § 57, 22 January 2009).
>
> In many cases, confiscation of things by means of which a criminal offence had been committed is regarded similarly (e.g. judgment in *B.K.M. Lojistik Tasimacilik Ticaret Limited Sirketi* v. *Slovenia*, application no. 42079/12, § 38 with further references, 17 January 2017, judgment in *Jucys* v. *Lithuania*, application no. 5457/03, § 34, 8 January 2008). The panel of

judges is of the opinion that although the plaintiff has finally lost his semi-trailer but retained his right to claim its value, control of the use of property analysed in the present proceedings should also be regarded as interference with his property rights under the second paragraph of Article 1 of Protocol No. 1 of the Convention. According to the case law of the ECtHR the legality of the purpose of confiscating means of transport that were used to commit a criminal offence – to combat the respective criminal offences and prevent them – as well as its compliance with the general interest basically are not questioned even when such property belongs to a third party and not to the accused (e.g. judgment in *B.K.M. Lojistik Tasimacilik Ticaret Limited Sirketi* v. *Slovenia*, § 42, judgment in *Vasilveski* v. *Former Yugoslav Republic of Macedonia*, application no. 22653/08, § 54, 28 April 2016; decision on admissibility in *Yildirim* v. *Italy*, application no. 38602/02, 10 April 2003).

According to ECtHR case law interference for the purposes of the second paragraph of Article 1 of Protocol No. 1 must be interpreted considering the principle established in the first sentence of this article. All interference has to strike a balance between the demands of the general interest and the interest of the individual or individuals concerned, which means that there must be a reasonable relationship of proportionality between the means employed and the aim or aims sought to be realised (e.g. *Yildrim* v. *Italy*). The State has a wide margin of appreciation with regard both to choosing the means of enforcement and to ascertaining whether the consequences of enforcement are justified in the general interest for the purpose of achieving the object of the law in question. The character of interference, the aim pursued, the nature of property rights interfered with, and the behaviour of the applicant and the interfering State authorities are among the principal factors material to the assessment whether the contested measure respects the requisite fair balance and, notably, whether it imposes a disproportionate burden on the applicant (see judgment in *Forminster Enterprises Limited* v. *Czech Republic*, application no. 38238/04, 9 October 2008).

[...]

On the basis of the aforementioned legal regulation, the panel of judges establishes that when a pre-trial criminal investigation fails to identify the perpetrators of a criminal offence, the claimant as the legal owner of the property who has not been charged with any suspected offences should not suffer any negative financial consequences related to storage and sale of his property which was seized during the criminal investigations.

4/7

In case No. 3K-3-112-690/2017 of 7 March 2017, the Supreme Court of Lithuania determined that according to ECtHR practice on application of Article 1 Paragraph 1 of Protocol No. 1 of the ECHR, fair compensation encompasses statutory annual interest of 5 per cent on unpaid monetary compensation for property taken in the public interest. The relevant extracts from the case are reproduced below:

> Various aspects of establishment of fair compensation have been widely discussed in the case law of the ECtHR. [...].
>
> The ECtHR has recognised that taking property without payment of an amount reasonably related to its value would normally constitute a disproportionate interference (see judgment of Grand Chamber in *Former King of Greece* v. *Greece*, application no. 25701/94, § 78, 28 November 2002; etc.). When the property of a person is expropriated, there has to be a procedure ensuring comprehensive evaluation of all the consequences of expropriation, including determination of individuals who have a right to claim compensation and resolving any other questions related to expropriation (see judgment of the Grand Chamber in *Guiso-Gallisay* v. *Italy*, application no. 58858/00, § 94–95, 22 December 2009).
>
> According to general principles, the adequacy of compensation is likely to be diminished if it were to be paid without reference to various circumstances liable to reduce its value, such as the lapse of a considerable period of time (*see Stran Greek Refineries and Stratis Andreadis* v. *Greece*, § 82, Series A no. 301-B).
>
> When the ECtHR was deciding on the depreciated value of compensation for property that was expropriated in pursuance of the public interest (the difference between the value of compensation for expropriation on the date of the application to the court and its value at the time of the actual payment was due to lack of default interest) it took into account various circumstances: what was the extent of depreciation of compensation, whether the applicant's ability to continue using the land during the proceedings is sufficient to offset such loss, could the applicant have

claimed default interest, whether the legitimate public-interest consideration could have justified payment of an amount lower than the market value of the land, etc. (see judgment in *Yetis and others* v. *Turkey*, application no. 40349/05, 6 July 2010; judgment in *Dokmeci v. Turkey*, application no. 74155/14, 6 December 2016, and others).

The Supreme Court also formulated a rule that if for a long period of time a person fails to receive monetary compensation (or part of it) for a land plot that was taken from him, such compensation depreciates and cannot generate additional income for him. Therefore, according to general principles of law and by analogy applying Article 6.210 Paragraph 1 of the Civil Code, statutory annual interest of five per cent on unpaid monetary compensation should be recognised as a part of just compensation for such person [...].

Without prejudice to the explanations provided above, the panel of judges states that Article 47 Paragraph 1 of the Law on Land and the case law of the cassation court, as well as ECtHR interpretations, obliges the State (its authorised institutions) to pay the owner fair remuneration (compensation) for property taken from him. In this context, it should be noted that, in addition to interest on payment, the compensatory function can be performed by procedural interest, which was awarded to the plaintiff in the present proceedings, on condition that the courts determine the factual circumstances which prove that the interests of the owner of the property that was taken for public purposes are served best by awarding such interest.

4/8

In case No. e3K-3-128-469/2017 of 20 March 2017, the Supreme Court of Lithuania interpreted the right to an oral hearing under the ECHR. Relevant extracts from the case are reproduced below:

Cassator 1 requests in her cassation claim to refer the case to the enlarged panel of judges and conduct the hearing by way of oral proceedings.

It is indicated in the case law of the cassation court that according to legal regulation an oral hearing is conducted when it is established that such proceedings are necessary, and it is the court that has the exclusive right to decide on this. A request by participants in proceedings to hear a case in oral proceedings does not, in itself, imply that oral proceedings are necessary; the court must prevent legal proceedings from delays and participants in proceedings must honestly use and not abuse their procedural rights, seek prompt examination of the case (Article 7 of the Civil Procedure Code) (by analogy decision of the Supreme Court of Lithuania in civil case No. 3K-3-539/2013 of 4 November 2013).

Such practice by the cassation court correlates to the case law of the ECtHR regarding application of the ECHR, where in some circumstances (when the issue which is to be decided raises no questions of fact or law which cannot be adequately resolved on the basis of the case file and the parties' written observations) the court of appellate instance (in a broad sense meaning a court of higher instance) ensuring effective administration of justice can decide the dispute based on the materials in the case file. Thus the right to hold an oral hearing is not an absolute one – the absence of a hearing in a court of higher instance may be justified by the special features of the proceedings at issue, issues which are to be decided provided a hearing has been held at first instance (see judgment in *Oganova* v. *Georgia*, application no. 25717/03, § 27, 28, 13 November 2007).

4/9

In cases Nos. 3K-3-142-701/2017 of 23 March 2017 and 3K-7-74-313/2017 of 4 April 2017 the Supreme Court of Lithuania considered whether appellate courts respected the principle of adversarial proceedings under Article 6 of the ECHR, in particular when they rejected or approved an appeal on the basis of matters raised by the court of its own motion. The relevant paragraphs read:

> The case law of the ECtHR concerning the right to fair trial (Article 6 of the ECHR (hereinafter – the Convention)) demonstrates that from the point of view of the Convention there may be a danger of violation of rights enshrined in the Convention where courts adopt surprise judgments both in terms of examining and evaluating evidence, and in terms of application of law. Article 6 of the Convention enshrines the concept of fair trial in accordance with which the parties must have the opportunity not only to adduce evidence in support of their claims, but also to have knowledge of, and comment on, all evidence or observations filed, with a view to influencing the court's decision (see judgment in *Nideröst-Huber* v. *Switzerland*, application no. 18990/91, § 24, 18 February 1997; judgment in *K.S.* v. *Finland*, application no. 29346/95, § 21, 31 May 2001; judgment in *Duraliyski* v. *Bulgaria*, application no. 45519/06, § 30, 3 March 2014; etc.). The ECtHR has recognised that judges themselves must

respect the principle of adversarial proceedings, in particular when they reject an appeal or decide a claim on the basis of a matter raised by the court of its own motion (see judgment in *Prikyan and Angelova* v. *Bulgaria*, application no. 44624/98, § 42, 16 February 2006; judgment in *Clinique des Acacias and others* v. *France*, application nos. 65399/01, 65406/01, 65405/01, 65407/01, § 38, 13 October 2005; etc.).

In case No. 3K-3-142-701/2017 of 23 March 2017 the court found:

The case before the appellate court was heard in written proceedings. Although the court did not exceed the limits of the case, the matter regarding establishment of usufruct was raised by the court of appellate instance and was not directly raised by the claimant. The parties did not have an opportunity to adduce evidence, arguments or observations in appellate proceedings related to the question whether there is a legal and factual basis to establish usufruct.

[...]

It should be held that part of the judgment of the appellate court that was passed failed to ensure proper protection of the rights of participating parties established in [...] Article 6 Paragraph 1 of the Convention.

In case No. 3K-7-74-313/2017 of 4 April 2017 the court decided:

As mentioned, after the court decided to exceed the boundaries of the appeal, the appellate court gave the parties an opportunity to submit arguments regarding conformity of the Additional Agreement with public policy (Article 12 of the Civil Procedure Code). Assessment of the validity of the Additional Agreement was conducted on the basis of the facts and circumstances that were known to the parties and their compliance with public order was assessed considering the explanations of the parties that were provided before the court of first instance, as well as in additional written explanations before the appellate court.

[...]

On the basis of such arguments the panel of judges finds that in the current case the right of fair trial has been ensured and the appellate court did not deviate from the practice of the cassation court concerning notification of the participants in the case about the intention to go beyond the limits of the appellate claim.

4/10

In case No. 3K-3-125-219/2017 of 30 March 2017, the Supreme Court of Lithuania elaborated on the purpose of renewal of process in the light of requirements under Article 6 of the ECHR. The relevant paragraphs read:

> It is reiterated in the case law of the ECtHR that the right to a fair hearing before a tribunal as guaranteed by Article 6 § 1 of the Convention must be interpreted in the light of the Preamble to the Convention, which, in its relevant part, declares the rule of law to be part of the common heritage of the Contracting States. One of the fundamental aspects of the rule of law is the principle of legal certainty, which requires, among other things, that where the courts have finally determined an issue, their ruling should not be called into question. This principle underlines that no party is entitled to seek a review of a final and binding judgment merely for the purpose of obtaining a rehearing and a fresh determination of the case. The review should not be treated as an appeal 'in disguise', and the mere possibility of there being two views on the subject is not a ground for re-examination (see e.g. judgment in *Ryabhkh v. Russia*, application no. 52854/99, § 51–52, ECHR 2003-IX).

4/11

In case No. e3K-3-184-415/2017 of 5 April 2017, the Supreme Court of Lithuania applied Article 6 of the ECHR considering that improper service of documents on the respondent constitutes a violation of Article 6 of the Convention and thus can be used as a ground to renew proceedings. The relevant paragraphs read:

> The right to a fair hearing before a tribunal as guaranteed by Article 6 § 1 of the Convention must be interpreted in the light of the Preamble to the Convention, which, in its relevant part, declares the rule of law to be part of the common heritage of the Contracting States. One of the fundamental aspects of the rule of law is the principle of legal certainty, which presupposes respect for the principle of *res judicata* (finality of judgments). According to this principle, where the courts have finally determined an issue, their ruling should not be called into question, thus ensuring legal certainty (see e.g. judgment in *DRAFT – OVA a.s. v. Slovakia*, application no. 72493/10, § 77, 9 June 2015; judgment in *Amirkhanyan v. Armenia*, application no. 22343/08, § 33, 3 December 2015).

A departure from that principle is justified only when made necessary by circumstances of a substantial and compelling character (see e.g. judgment in *Solomun v. Croatia*, application no. 679/11, § 47, 2 April 2015; judgment in *Kot v. Russia*, application no. 20887/03, § 24, 18 January 2007). Higher courts' powers to quash or alter binding and enforceable judicial decisions should be exercised for the purpose of correcting fundamental defects (see judgment in *Protsenko v. Russia*, application no. 13151/04, § 26, 31 July 2008). That power must be exercised so as to strike, to the maximum extent possible, a fair balance between the interests of the individual and the need to ensure the effectiveness of the system of justice (see cited *DRAFT – OVA a.s. v. Slovakia*, § 77).

[...]

AB bank Finasta delivered court documents to the mother of the applicant at his old address, but she refused to accept the documents. Notwithstanding such circumstances the courts of first instance and appellate instance decided that the applicant had knowledge about the proceedings.

In accordance with the factual circumstances established in the case, it should be assessed whether the applicant was duly served with procedural documents and whether the respondent's right to be duly informed about the proceedings and to defend himself before the court in the context of the application of the Convention has not been violated.

The ECtHR has reiterated in its case law that the possibility for parties to take part in proceedings flows from the objectives and purpose of Article 6 of the Convention (see judgment in *Gyuleva v. Bulgaria*, application no. 38840/08, § 35, 9 June 2016). The principle of equality of arms, which is one of the elements of the broader concept of a fair hearing, requires each party to be given a reasonable opportunity to present its case under conditions that do not place it at a substantial disadvantage *vis-à-vis* its opponent (see e.g. judgment in *Gakharia v. Georgia*, application no. 30459/13, § 32, 17 January 2017).

If court documents, including summonses to hearings, are not served in person, then the applicant might be prevented from defending himself in the proceedings (see judgment in *Aždajić v. Slovenia*, application no. 71872/12, § 48, 8 October 2015). The ECtHR's consistent interpretation of the Convention implies that the national court should not just formally 'summon the applicant to the hearing', but should demonstrate that it had made a reasonable effort 'to duly summon the applicant to the hearing' and evaluate the evidence confirming such summons (see e.g. judgment in *Vorobyev* v. *Russia*, application no. 15722/05, § 23, 9 October 2012; judgment in *Puzyrevskiy* v. *Russia*, application no. 41603/05, § 20, 9 October 2012).

[...]

[...] when performing preliminary service of documents it was known that the respondent declared his residence in the United Kingdom on 3 April 2014 [...] such a procedural legal situation is not compatible with the requirements of the Convention [...], therefore it is established that Article 6 of the Convention has been violated (failure to duly summon the respondent).

4/12

In case No. e3K-3-164-421/2017 of 7 April 2017, the Supreme Court of Lithuania assessed service of documents by means of public notice in light of Article 6 of the Convention and elaborated on the limitations of such service of documents under Article 6 of the ECHR. The relevant paragraphs read:

The right to a fair hearing before a tribunal is guaranteed by Article 6 § 1 of the Convention: for the right to be effective, an individual must have a clear, practical opportunity to challenge an act that is an interference with his rights (see decision on admissibility of 10 April 2003 in *Nunes Dias* v. *Portugal*, application nos. 69829/01 and 2672/03).

The ECtHR has reiterated in its case law that the possibility for parties to take part in proceedings flows from the objectives and purpose of Article 6 of the Convention (see judgment of 9 June 2016 in *Gyuleva* v. *Bulgaria*, application no. 38840/08, par. 35). The principle of equality of arms, which is one of the elements of the broader concept of a fair hearing, requires each party to be given a reasonable opportunity to present its case under conditions that do not place it at a substantial disadvantage *vis-à-vis* its opponent (see e.g. judgment of 17 January 2017 in *Gakharia* v. *Georgia*, application no. 30459/13, par. 32).

Article 6 Paragraph 1 of the Convention does not provide for a specific form of service of documents (see e.g. judgment of 16 February 2017 in *Karakutsya* v. *Ukraine*, application no. 18986/06, par. 53; decision on admissibility of 5 February 2004 in *Bogonos* v. *Russia*, application no. 68798/01); however, the general concept of a fair trial, encompassing the fundamental principle that proceedings should be adversarial, requires that all parties to civil proceedings should have the opportunity to have knowledge of and comment on the observations filed or evidence adduced with a view to influencing the court's decision. This presupposes that a person against whom proceedings have been initiated should be informed of that fact (see e.g. judgment of 9 June 2016 in *Gyuleva* v. *Bulgaria*, application no. 38840/08, par. 35; judgment of 21 May 2015 in *Zavodnik* v. *Slovenia*, application no. 53723/13, par. 70; judgment of 4 March 2014 in *Dilipak and Karakaya* v. *Turkey*, application nos. 7942/05, 24838/05, par. 77). If court documents, including summonses to hearings, are not served in person, then an applicant might be prevented from defending himself or herself in the proceedings (see judgment of 8 October 2015 in *Aždajić* v. *Slovenia*, application no. 71872/12, par. 48).

It is also continuously noted in the case law of the ECtHR that various restrictions on the right to fair trial can be applied. In this regard the ECtHR has noted that Article 6 requires and allows States to organize their legal systems in a manner which facilitates expeditious and efficient judicial proceedings, including provision for the possibility of issuing default judgments (see, e.g. judgment of 17 January 2017 in *Gakharia* v. *Georgia*, application no. 30459/13, par. 34; judgment of 31 May 2016 in *Gankin and others* v. *Russia*, application nos. 2430/06, 1454/08, 11670/10 ir 12938/12, par. 26), however, that cannot be done at the expense of other procedural guarantees, notably the principle of equality of arms (see judgment of 21 May 2015 in *Zavodnik* v. *Slovenia*, application no. 53723/13, par. 72). The limitations applied must not restrict the access left to the individual in such a way or to such an extent that the very essence of the right is impaired. Furthermore, a limitation will not be compatible with Article 6 Paragraph 1 of the Convention if it does not pursue a legitimate aim and if there is not a reasonable relationship of proportionality between the means employed and the aim sought to be achieved (see judgment of 21 May 2015 in *Zavodnik* v. *Slovenia*, application no. 53723/13, par. 73; judgment of 16 February 2017 in *Karakutsya* v. *Ukraine*, application no. 18986/06, par. 44).

[...]

The panel of judges considers the factual circumstances established in the case, i.e. that procedural documents (claim and notice from the court to submit a reply to the claim), which were sent to the incorrect address indicated in the claim, returned undelivered; there was an attempt to deliver documents through the workplace, but it was determined that the respondent did not work there any more; thus it was decided to deliver the documents to the respondent by means of public notice (Article 130 of the Civil Procedure Code). The respondent learnt about the decision of the court and its contents on 31 May 2016 when he came to the court. Considering all this the court follows the interpretation of the ECtHR, which notes that service of documents by means of public notice should be used only after the national court is satisfied that the person's address could not be found and such person is not totally without remedy against such decision (e.g. submit a claim to renew proceedings or to provide arguments regarding improper service) (see, e.g. decision on admissibility of 10 April 2003 in *Nunes Dias* v. *Portugal*, application nos. 69829/01 and 2672/03).

The ECtHR has also recognized that the national courts were not sufficiently diligent when they served documents by means of public service immediately after failure to service documents at the place of registered residence, did not check available information about the whereabouts of the applicant in the territory of another State, made no attempt to contact the local police to ascertain the applicant's whereabouts, made no effort to request such information from the other party to the dispute (see, e.g. judgment of 17 January 2017 in *Gakharia* v. *Georgia*, application no. 30459/13, par. 39–44).

[...]

In such circumstances the respondent did not have a chance to submit a reply to the default judgment within the period of 20 days prescribed by law, because it did not know the contents of the decision and did not know about adoption of the judgment.

4/13

The Constitutional Court of the Republic of Lithuania in ruling No. KT4-N3/2017 on criminal liability for illicit enrichment, dated 15 March 2017, reiterated that the jurisprudence of the ECtHR is important for interpretation and application of Lithuanian law and elaborated on the criteria established therein related to criminal liability for illicit enrichment. The relevant paragraphs read:

The Constitutional Court has held on more than one occasion that the jurisprudence of the ECtHR is also important for the interpretation and application of Lithuanian law. Therefore, as far as the aspects relevant for this constitutional justice case are concerned, it is necessary to take into consideration the rights set out in Articles 6 and 7 of the Convention and Article 4 of Protocol No. 7 as they are interpreted and applied in the case law of the ECtHR.

Paragraph 1 of Article 7, titled 'No Punishment without Law', of the Convention stipulates that no one shall be held guilty of any criminal offence on account of any act or omission which did not constitute a criminal offence under national or international law at the time when it was committed; nor shall a heavier penalty be imposed than the one that was applicable at the time the criminal offence was committed.

This guarantee, established in Article 7 of the Convention, should be interpreted and applied, as follows from its object and purpose, in such a way as to provide effective safeguards against arbitrary prosecution, conviction, and punishment. This article of the Convention also embodies the principle that only the law can define a crime and prescribe a penalty (*nullum crimen, nulla poena sine lege*). The provisions of Article 7 of the Convention imply quality requirements, including those of accessibility and foreseeability, for a legal regulation that defines criminal acts (*inter alia*, the ECtHR, judgment of 12 February 2008 in *Kafkaris v. Cyprus* [GC], no. 21906/04, paragraph 140; judgment of 19 September 2008 in *Korbely v. Hungary*, no. 9174/02, paragraph 70).

Offences and the relevant penalties must be clearly (precisely) defined by law. It should be held that this requirement is satisfied where the individual can know from the wording of the relevant provision, if need be with the assistance of the courts' interpretation of it and after taking appropriate legal advice, what acts and omissions will make him/her criminally liable and what penalty he/she faces on that account. However clearly drafted a legal provision may be, in any system of law, including criminal law, there is an inevitable element of judicial interpretation. The role of adjudication vested in the courts is precisely to dissipate such interpretational doubts as remain (*inter alia*, ECtHR, judgment of 21 October 2013 in *Del Rio Prada v. Spain* [GC], no. 42750/09, paragraphs 77–79, 92, and 93; judgment of 27 January 2015 in *Rohlena v Czech Republic*, no. 59552/08, paragraph 50).

Paragraph 1 of Article 4, titled 'The Right Not to Be Tried or Punished Twice', of Protocol No. 7 to the Convention states: 'No one shall be liable to be tried or punished again in criminal proceedings under the jurisdiction of the same State for an offence for which he has already been finally acquitted or convicted in accordance with the law and penal procedure of that State'.

The ECtHR, interpreting the right established in this paragraph, has held a number of times that proceedings for imposition of certain tax surcharges should be treated as criminal proceedings for the purposes of Article 4 of Protocol No. 7 to the Convention (ECtHR, decision on admissibility of 8 April 2003 in *Manasson v. Sweden*, no. 41265/98; judgment of 27 November 2014 in *Lucky Dev v. Sweden*, no. 7356/10).

The ECtHR has also held that States have the right legitimately to choose complementary legal responses to socially offensive conduct (such as non-payment/evasion of taxes) through different procedures forming a coherent whole so as to address different aspects of the social problem involved, provided that the accumulated legal responses do not represent an excessive burden for the individual concerned. The object of Article 4 of Protocol No. 7 to the Convention is to prevent the injustice of a person's being prosecuted or punished twice for the same criminalised conduct. It does not, however, outlaw legal systems which take an 'integrated' approach to the social wrongdoing in question, and in particular an approach involving parallel stages of legal response to the wrongdoing by different authorities and for different purposes (ECtHR, judgment of 15 November 2016 in *A and B v. Norway* [GC], nos. 24130/11 and 29758/11, paragraphs 121–123).

Article 4 of Protocol No. 7 to the Convention does not exclude the conduct of dual proceedings regarding the same conduct provided that certain conditions are fulfilled. The State must demonstrate convincingly that the dual proceedings in question have been 'sufficiently closely connected in substance and in time'. This implies that the purposes pursued and the means used to achieve them should in essence be complementary and linked in time, and also that the possible consequences of organising the legal treatment of the conduct concerned in such a manner should be proportionate and foreseeable for the persons affected (ECtHR, judgment of 15 November 2016 in *A and B v. Norway* [GC], nos. 24130/11 and 29758/11, paragraph 130).

The ECtHR has noted that determining whether offences investigated and examined in different proceedings are the same depends on a facts-based assessment rather than on a formal assessment consisting of comparing only the essential elements of the offences (ECtHR, judgment of 10 February 2009 in *Zolotuhin* v. *Russia* [GC], no. 14939/03, paragraph 84; judgment of 15 November 2016 in *A and B* v. *Norway* [GC], nos. 24130/11 and 29758/11, paragraph 108).

Paragraph 2 of Article 6, titled 'The Right to a Fair Trial', of the Convention states that everyone charged with a criminal offence shall be presumed innocent until proved guilty according to law. The ECtHR, while interpreting in its jurisprudence the content of the presumption of innocence enshrined in this paragraph, has noted a number of times that this presumption is one of the elements of a fair trial required in Paragraph 1 of Article 6 of the Convention.

The ECtHR has also stated that a person's right to be presumed innocent and to require the prosecution to bear the onus of proving the allegations against him/her is not absolute. The Convention does not, in itself, prohibit presumptions of fact and law that operate in each national criminal system, but requires States to confine presumptions within reasonable limits that take into account the importance of what is at stake and effectively ensure the persons' right to defence (ECtHR, *inter alia*, judgment of 7 October 1988 in *Salabiaku* v. *France*, no. 10519/83, paragraph 28; judgment of 18 March 2010 in *Krumpholz* v. *Austria*, no. 13201/05, paragraph 34).

4/14

The Constitutional Court of the Republic of Lithuania in ruling No. KT6-N5/2017, on the grounds for revoking the validity of a licence for organising waste management, dated 30 May 2017 noted the case law of the ECtHR and CJEU in the sphere of positive obligations of States in the waste disposal sphere. The relevant paragraph reads as follows:

In this context the case law of the ECtHR in regard to respect for everyone's private and family life and his home enshrined in Article 8 of the ECHR should be mentioned. The ECtHR in paragraph 110 of the judgment in *Di Sarno and others* v. *Italy* (application No. 30765/08) of 10 January 2012 established that the collection, treatment and disposal of waste are without a doubt dangerous activities; therefore the State is under a positive obligation to take reasonable and adequate steps to protect the right of the people concerned to respect for their homes and their private life and, more generally, to live in a safe and healthy environment (see also judgment in *Tătar* v. *Romania*, application no. 67021/01, 27 January 2009). When establishing a violation of Article 8 in *Di Sarno and others* v. *Italy* for failure to fulfil the positive obligations of the State under Article 8 of the Convention, the ECtHR took note of the judgment of the Court of Justice of the European Union in *European Commission* v. *Italy* (case C-297/08) concerning the positive obligations of State in the waste disposal sphere, where it had also been emphasised that the accumulation of large quantities of waste could potentially expose the health of the local inhabitants and the environment to certain danger.

4/15

The Constitutional Court of the Republic of Lithuania in ruling No. KT8-N6/2017 on consideration of criminal cases under the appeal procedure upon the coming to light of essentially different factual circumstances, dated 26 June 2017, indicated the importance of the case law of the ECtHR related to the right to a fair trial and the power of the court to change the qualification of a criminal offence of its own motion. The relevant paragraphs read:

> In the context of this case of constitutional justice the case law of the ECtHR related to the right to a fair trial and the power of the court to change the qualification of a criminal offence of its own volition is of importance.
>
> The ECtHR, when explaining the contents of the right to fair trial enshrined in Article 6 of the ECHR, has noted in its case law *inter alia* that this right includes the obligation of the court to not only thoroughly and comprehensively examine all the circumstances of the case, which would enable an independent and impartial tribunal to make a just and well-founded decision in each case, but also to take that decision within the shortest possible time; the courts have a duty to ensure a fair balance between the different elements of the content of the right to a fair trial (judgment in *Boddaert* v. *Belgium* of 12 October 1992 (application no. 12919/87)).
>
> It should be noted that the criteria which the ECtHR employs to assess compliance of the length of proceedings with the requirements of Article 6 Paragraph 1 of the Convention are the complexity of the case, the

conduct of the person in criminal proceedings and that of the authorities before which the case was brought, and what was at stake for the applicant in the dispute (judgment in *Pedersen and Baadsgaard* v. *Denmark* of 17 December 2004 (application no. 49017/99); judgment in *Sorvisto* v. *Finland* of 13 January 2009 (application no. 19348/04)). The conclusion on compliance of particular proceedings with the requirements of Article 6 Paragraph 1 always depends on an assessment of the totality of criteria.

It should be noted that Article 6 of the Convention does not prescribe the right to appeal. This right in criminal cases is established in Article 2 of protocol No. 7 of the Convention. The ECtHR has noted that although Article 6 of the Convention does not compel the Contracting States to set up courts of appeal, nevertheless a State which does institute such courts is required to ensure that persons amenable to the law shall enjoy before these courts the fundamental guarantees contained in Article 6 (judgment in *Delcourt* v. *Belgium* of 17 January 1970 (application no. 2689/65)).

How these guarantees apply depends on the peculiarities of the appellate proceedings; account must be taken of the entirety of the proceedings conducted in the domestic legal order, the role of the appellate court therein, the powers it possesses, the peculiarities of protection of the interests of the parties to the proceedings (judgment of 2 March 1987 in *Monnell and Morris* v. *the United Kingdom* (application no. 9562/81, 9818/82)). Provided that the appellate court has the power to review both questions of law and of fact, normally in such a process the person must be afforded the same level of protection of the right to a fair trial as in the court of first instance (judgment of 26 May 1988 in *Ekbatani* v. *Sweden* (application no. 10563/83); judgment of 22 May 2007 in *Muttilainen* v. *Sweden* (application no. 18358/02)).

It should be noted that according to the case law of the ECtHR the right to a reasoned decision is an integral part of the right to a fair trial under Article 6 paragraph 1 of the Convention. The right to a reasoned decision reflects a wider guarantee – the proper administration of justice. Moreover, knowing the specific reasons on which the decision is based affords a party the possibility to appeal against it, as well as the possibility of having the decision reviewed by an appellate body (judgment of 22 February 2007 in *Tatishvili* v. *Russia* (application no. 1509/02)). A reasoned decision ensures the right of the public to know whether in a particular case justice was properly administered (see, *mutatis mutandis*, judgment of 27 September 2001 in *Hirvisaari* v. *Finland* (application no. 49684/99)).

According to the practice of the ECtHR the power of the court to change the classification of a criminal offence of its own initiative, *inter alia*, by applying a criminal law which prescribes a heavier offence, is not in itself contrary to the Convention.

It is recognised in the case law of the ECtHR that the rights enshrined in the Convention are violated if by the decision of the lower court a criminal offence is re-qualified and the accused had not been informed about it in advance and thus did not have sufficient opportunity to defend himself and when the court of higher instance decides only on legal aspects of the case, i.e. the accused does not have sufficient opportunity to determine facts that are important to qualify the offence (judgment of 20 April 2006 in *I.H. and others* v. *Austria* (application no. 42780/98), judgment of 19 December 2006 in *Mattei* v. *France* (application no. 34043/02)). However if the defence has a possibility to challenge such new qualification on a factual and legal basis, it is recognised that such rights are protected (judgment of 21 February 2002 in *Sipavičius* v. *Lithuania* (application no. 49093/99), judgment on admissibility of 24 June 2004 in *Balette* v. *France* (application no. 48193/99), judgment on admissibility of 7 February 2006 in *Virolainen* v. *Finland* (application no. 29172/02))

Thus, according to the case law of the ECtHR a court is entitled to change the legal characterisation of a criminal offence of its own motion and *inter alia* to apply criminal law that prescribes a heavier sentence. However, the defendant must be informed about it in advance and he should be given an opportunity to present defence arguments in regard to such new characterisation. When the defendant was not informed about the possible change of the legal characterisation of criminal charges and did not have a chance to provide defence arguments in this regard, the essential criteria shall be the possibility for the defendant to challenge such change of legal characterisation of criminal charges in the light of the facts or the law before a court of higher instance.

4/16

The Constitutional Court of the Republic of Lithuania in ruling No. KT9-N7/2017, on exempting priests from mandatory military service, dated 4 July

2017 addressed the notion of conscientious objection to military service under international and EU law. The relevant paragraphs read:

> In the context of this constitutional jurisprudence case the notion of conscientious objection to military service under international and EU law should be taken into account.
>
> The ECtHR has clarified that implementation of conscientious refusal to perform mandatory military service due to beliefs but ensuring the possibility to perform alternative (non-military) service has to be assessed under Article 9 of the Convention 'freedom of thought, conscience and religion'. In this respect, the ECtHR noted that Article 9 did not explicitly refer to a right to conscientious objection. However, it considered that opposition to military service, where motivated by a serious and insurmountable conflict between the obligation to serve in the army and a person's conscience or his deeply and genuinely held religious or other beliefs, constituted a conviction or belief of sufficient cogency, seriousness, cohesion and importance to attract the guarantees of Article 9 of the Convention (judgment of Grand Chamber of 7 July 2011 in *Bayatyan v. Armenia*, application no. 23459/03, § 110).
>
> The ECtHR also pointed out that the right to refuse to perform military service as an aspect of freedom of thought, conscience and religion has been recognised by the United Nations Human Rights Committee when assessing the limitation of such right under Article 18 of the International Covenant on Civil and Political Rights, which lays down freedom of thought, conscience and religion. The same notion of such right is provided in various documents of the Council of Europe.
>
> It should be noted that Article 10 Paragraph 2 of the Charter of Fundamental Rights of the European Union on Freedom of thought, conscience and religion explicitly states that the right to conscientious objection is recognised, in accordance with national laws governing the exercise of this right.

4/17

The Constitutional Court of the Republic of Lithuania in conclusion No. KT20-I1/2017 on the actions of Seimas member Kęstutis Pūkas, dated 19 December 2017, reiterated that the obligation to protect and defend human dignity and the inviolability of private life and the prohibition on discrimination based on sex or social status are enshrined in numerous international legal acts on the protection of human rights. The relevant paragraphs read as follows:

> In the context of the constitutional justice case at issue, it should be noted that the obligation to protect and defend human dignity and the inviolability of private life and the prohibition on discrimination based on sex or social status are enshrined in numerous international legal acts on the protection of human rights, such as:
>
> – the Universal Declaration of Human Rights of 1948, Article 1 whereof provides that all human beings are born free and equal in dignity and rights; Article 5 whereof states, among other things, that no one shall be subjected to degrading treatment; Article 7 whereof stipulates that all are equal before the law and are entitled without any discrimination to equal protection of the law, and that all are entitled to equal protection against any discrimination and against any incitement to such discrimination; and Article 12 whereof prescribes, inter alia, that no one shall be subjected to arbitrary interference with his/her privacy, family, nor to attacks upon his/her honour and reputation;
>
> – the International Covenant on Civil and Political Rights of 1966, Article 3 whereof prescribes that States Parties undertake to ensure the equal right of men and women to the enjoyment of all civil and political rights; Article 7 whereof states that no one shall be subjected to degrading treatment; Article 17(1) whereof provides, among other things, that no one shall be subjected to arbitrary or unlawful interference with his/her privacy or family, nor to unlawful attacks on his/her honour and reputation; and Article 26 whereof states that all persons are equal before the law and are entitled without any discrimination to the equal protection of the law, which, in this respect, shall prohibit any discrimination and guarantee to all persons equal and effective protection against discrimination on any ground such as race, colour, sex, language, religion, political or other opinion, national or social origin, property, birth or other status;
>
> – the International Covenant on Economic, Social and Cultural Rights of 1966, Article 2 whereof obliges States Parties to guarantee that the rights enunciated in this Covenant will be exercised without discrimination of any kind as to race, colour, sex, language, religion, political or other

opinion, national or social origin, property, birth, or other status, and Article 3 whereof obliges States Parties to ensure the equal right of men and women to the enjoyment of all economic, social, and cultural rights;

– the United Nations Convention on the Elimination of All Forms of Discrimination against Women of 1979, condemning all forms of discrimination against women; according to Article 11 whereof, on the basis of equality of men and women, women must be ensured the right to the same employment opportunities, including the application of the same criteria for selection in matters of employment, and, according to Article 15 whereof, women are accorded equality with men before the law;

– the International Labour Organisation Convention (No 111) concerning Discrimination in Respect of Employment and Occupation of 1958, Article 1 whereof provides that discrimination means any distinction, exclusion, or preference made, *inter alia*, on the basis of sex, which has the effect of nullifying or impairing equality of opportunity or treatment in employment or occupation, where 'employment' and 'occupation' include terms and conditions of employment, access to employment and to particular occupations, and access to vocational training;

– the ECHR of 1950, Article 3 whereof, *inter alia*, provides that no one shall be subjected to degrading treatment; Article 8 whereof states that everyone has the right to respect for his/her private and family life; and Article 14 whereof prohibits discrimination on any ground such as sex, race, colour, language, religion, political or other opinion, national or social origin, association with a national minority, property, birth, or other status;

– the European Social Charter (revised) of 1996, Article 26 whereof provides that, with a view to ensuring the effective exercise of the right of all workers to protection of their dignity at work, the parties undertake, *inter alia*, to promote awareness, information and prevention of sexual harassment in the workplace or in relation to work, and of recurrent reprehensible or distinctly negative and offensive actions directed against individual workers in the workplace or in relation to work and to take all appropriate measures to protect workers from such conduct;

– the Council of Europe Convention (2011) on preventing and combating violence against women and domestic violence, Article 40 whereof consolidates a prohibition on sexual harassment, obliges the parties to take the necessary legislative or other measures to ensure that any form of unwanted verbal, non-verbal or physical conduct of a sexual nature with the purpose or effect of violating the dignity of a person, in particular when creating an intimidating, hostile, degrading, humiliating, or offensive environment, is subject to criminal or other legal sanction.

It should also be noted that the protection of personal dignity, the right to inviolability of private life, as well as a prohibition on discrimination based on gender, are also enshrined in EU primary law:

– Article 2 of the Treaty on European Union provides, *inter alia*, that the European Union is founded on the following values: respect for human dignity, freedom, democracy, equality, the rule of law, and respect for human rights; these values are common to the Member States in a society in which non-discrimination, tolerance, justice, solidarity, and equality between women and men prevail;

– according to Article 1 of the Charter of Fundamental Rights of the European Union, human dignity is inviolable, it must be respected and protected; Article 7 of the Charter stipulates that everyone has the right to respect for his/her private and family life; Article 20 thereof states that everyone is equal before the law; Article 21 thereof prohibits any discrimination based on any ground such as sex, race, colour, ethnic or social origin, genetic features, language, religion or belief, political or any other opinion, membership of a national minority, property, birth, disability, age or sexual orientation; under Article 31 thereof, every worker has the right to working conditions that respect, inter alia, his/her dignity.

EU secondary legislation consolidates *expressis verbis* a prohibition on conduct that has the characteristics of harassment and sexual harassment:

[...]

Summing up the above-mentioned international and EU legislation, which is relevant to the constitutional justice case at issue, it should be held that both international law and EU law guarantee the protection and defence of the dignity of each individual, the inviolability of private and family life, as well as protection from any discrimination, inter alia, discrimination based on gender.

According to EU law, one of the forms of discrimination is harassment, *inter alia*, harassment based on gender, as well as sexual harassment; harassment degrades human dignity (inter alia, the personality of an individual), as well as disturbs the private life of an individual (*inter alia*, his/her physical and psychological integrity). Under EU law, harassment is understood as unwanted conduct that is expressed by physical actions or gestures, verbally, or in writing, and takes place over a period of time (*inter alia*, such conduct is repetitive or systematic) and that violates human dignity and creates an intimidating, hostile, humiliating, or offensive environment for an individual, regardless of whether or not such an environment was intended to be created; harassment based on gender is related to the sex of a person, and conduct of such a nature is understood as sexual harassment (sexual harassment is understood in the same way as in the Council of Europe Convention (2011) on preventing and combating violence against women and domestic violence).

4/18

In case No. 3K-3-167-684/2017 of 6 April 2017, the Supreme Court of Lithuania assessed the contents of its positive obligation to ensure proper and adequate criminal investigation in light of international obligations, namely Article 1 of Protocol No. 1 of the Convention. The relevant paragraphs read:

> The Cassation court has noted that the legal system of the Republic of Lithuania comprises national legal acts and international treaties, under which the Republic of Lithuania undertook the obligation to ensure protection of certain rights and interests and to consider actions that violate such rights as infringements. When an individual indicates potentially illegal actions by officers, which are not prescribed in special legal norms that regulate the liability of such officers, the courts assess such facts about potential violations in the context of general principles of law, the Constitution of the Republic of Lithuania and international agreements [...].
>
> Article 1 of Protocol No. 1 to the Convention on Protection of Human Rights and Fundamental Freedoms (hereinafter – the Convention) establishes that every natural or legal person is entitled to the peaceful

enjoyment of his possessions. No one shall be deprived of his possessions except in the public interest and subject to conditions provided for by law and by general principles of international law.

The Convention became a part of the system of State legal acts; Lithuania undertook the obligation to guarantee the human rights and freedoms enshrined in the Convention to any person within its jurisdiction; State organs that perform legal protection of human rights and freedoms must directly apply the provisions of the Constitution and enforce the provisions of the Convention [...]. The provisions of the Convention are interpreted and applied in line with the case law of the ECtHR.

The ECtHR in its judgment of 14 October 2008 in *Blumberga v. Latvia* (application no. 70930/01) indicated that effective exercise of the right protected by Article 1 of Protocol No. 1 does not depend merely on the State's duty not to interfere, but may require positive measures of protection, particularly where there is a direct link between the measures an applicant may legitimately expect from the authorities and effective enjoyment of his possessions. When interference with the right to peaceful enjoyment of possessions is perpetrated by a private individual, a positive obligation arises for the State to ensure in its domestic legal system that property rights are sufficiently protected by law and that adequate remedies are provided whereby a victim of interference can seek to vindicate his rights, including, where appropriate, by claiming damages in respect of any loss sustained. Furthermore, where the interference is of a criminal nature, this obligation will in addition require that the authorities conduct an effective criminal investigation and, if appropriate, prosecution.

The ECtHR in the abovementioned decision also noted that the obligation on the part of the authorities to investigate and prosecute such acts cannot be absolute, as it is evident that many crimes remain unresolved or unpunished notwithstanding reasonable efforts by the State authorities. Rather, the obligation incumbent on the State is to ensure that a proper and adequate criminal investigation is carried out and that the authorities involved act in a competent and efficient manner. Moreover, the Court reiterated that it was sensitive to the practical difficulties which the authorities may face in investigating crime and to the need to make operational choices and prioritise investigation of the most serious crimes. Consequently, the obligation to investigate is less exacting with regard to less serious crimes, such as those involving property, than with regard to more serious ones, such as violent crimes, and in particular those which would fall within the scope of Articles 2 and 3 of the Convention. In cases involving less serious crimes the State will only fail to fulfil its positive obligation in that respect where flagrant and serious deficiencies in the criminal investigation or prosecution can be identified.

4/19

In case No. 2K-87-942/2017 of 13 April 2017, the Supreme Court of Lithuania elaborated on the criteria for the wording of a court judgment in criminal cases which were terminated due to the limitation period to ensure the presumption of innocence guaranteed under Article 6 paragraph 2 of the ECHR. The relevant paragraphs read:

> It is indicated in the cassation claim that the court of first instance terminated criminal case [...] due to elapse of the limitation period to adopt a judgment; however, the judgment of the court of appellate instance failed to avoid expressions which are not compatible with the principle of innocence, i.e. the court elaborated on objective and subjective features of the criminal offence that R.V. was charged with.

> [...]

> The case law of the ECtHR interpreting Article 6 Paragraph 2 of the Convention has an important place in case law when applying and interpreting Article 44 paragraph 6 of the Criminal Procedure Code. When clarifying the provisions of Article 6 Paragraph 2 of the Convention the ECtHR has noted that the presumption of innocence is infringed if a judicial decision concerning a person charged with a criminal offence reflects an opinion that he is guilty before he has been proved guilty according to law. It suffices, even in the absence of any formal finding, that there is some reasoning suggesting that the court regards the accused as guilty (*Minelli*; *Englert*; *Nölkenbockhoff*; *Capeau v. Belgium*, no. 42914/98, § 25, ECHR 2005-I). According to the ECtHR there is a fundamental distinction to be made between a clear judicial declaration, in the absence of a final conviction, that the individual has committed a crime and a statement that someone is merely suspected of having committed the crime in question (i.e. a description of the suspected crime). The first type of decision violates the presumption of innocence, whereas the second type of decision has been recognised as in compliance with Article 6 of

the Convention (*Vulakh and others* v. *Russia*, no. 33468/03, judgment of 10 January 2012).

Such provisions of the ECtHR entail that in cases when it is decided that a judgment of acquittal should be annulled but the criminal case is discontinued due to elapse of the limitation period, the judgment of the appellate court cannot be based on statements which essentially mean that the person is guilty of a crime. Nevertheless, it does not undermine the possibility for the court of appellate instance to state the factual circumstances of the crime, as long as such statement does not exceed a description of the suspected crime and become a declaration of the person's guilt.

4/20

In case No. 2K-80-976/2017 of 25 April 2017, the Supreme Court of Lithuania elaborated on the nature of ensuring effective execution of court decisions under Article 6 of the ECHR. The relevant paragraphs read:

A State must guarantee an effective system of judgment enforcement, otherwise there is a risk of violating both the procedural and substantive rights of the ECHR. In its case law the ECtHR has reiterated several times that execution of a judgment given by any court must therefore be regarded as an integral part of the 'trial' for the purposes of Article 6 (right to fair trial) (see., e.g.., *Hornsby* v. *Greece*, judgment of 19 March 1997, Reports 1997-II, p. 510, par. 40).

Under Article 6 Paragraph 1 of the Convention a State must make use of all the means at its disposal in order to execute a final decision, even in cases involving only private persons; the State has a positive obligation to organise a system for enforcement of judgments that is effective both in law and in practice and ensures their enforcement without any undue delay (see *Fuklev* v. *Ukraine*, no. 71186/01, par. 84, 7 June 2005, *Sovtransavto Holding* v. *Ukraine*, no. 48553/99, ECHR 2002-VII, par. 96.

4/21

In case No. 2K-7-183-648/2017 of 28 November 2017 the Supreme Court of Lithuania found that criminal charges against the defendant who had been fined by the Tax Authorities constituted a violation of the *non bis in idem* principle and Article 4 of Protocol 7 of the ECHR. The relevant extracts from the case are reproduced below:

V.K. was sentenced [...] because from 15 June 2007 to 28 October 2008 while working in V.K.'s personal company, which he owned, he organised the import of 66 cars from the USA [...] and seeking to avoid import taxes [...] he submitted to the customs officials counterfeit invoices containing a reduced price of the cars that did not meet the factual price of their purchase.

[...]

According to a report of 26 June 2012 Kaunas territorial customs office imposed against the defendant a fine of EUR 14,687.21 EUR.

[...]

The court of appellate instance [...] indicated that V.K. was charged with smuggling under Article 199 Paragraph 1 of the Criminal Code, whereas Kaunas territorial customs office [...] imposed a fine against V.K.'s company under Article 139 of the Law on Tax Administration and Article 123 of the Law on Added Value Tax for violation of tax laws.

[...]

The cassators disagree with the conclusions of the appellate court and one of the essential arguments of the claim concerns the *non bis in idem* principle, which was violated when the court of appellate instance found V.K. guilty under Article 199 Paragraph 1 of the Criminal Code.

[...]

No one can be punished twice for the same crime (Article 31 Paragraph 5 of the Constitution of the Republic of Lithuania). The prohibition on being punished twice for the same offence for which he has already been finally acquitted or convicted in accordance with the law and penal procedure of the State is enshrined in Article 4 Paragraph 1 of Protocol No. 7 of the ECHR. Such provisions establish the principle of *non bis in idem* (prohibition on being charged and punished twice for the same offence).

In the case law of the ECtHR this principle must be interpreted as prohibiting the prosecution or trial of a second 'offence' after the final judgment in the case (in so far as it arises from identical facts or facts which are substantially the same) and inextricably linked together in time and space (decision in *Gradinger* v. *Austria* of 23 October 1995, application no. 15963/90; decision in *F.F.* v. *Austria* of 29 May 2001, application no. 37950/97; decision of Grand Chamber in *S.Z.* v. *Russia* of 10 February 2009, application no. 14939/03; decision in *Routsalainen* v. *Finland* of 16 June 2009, application no. 13079/03 and others).

[...]

According to the practice of the ECtHR, when evaluating whether in a particular case an offence is considered as 'criminal', three criteria should be applied: the legal classification of the offence under national law, the nature of the offence, and the severity of sanctions which can be imposed against the offender. It should be noted that in the ECtHR's practice of application of such criteria, violations of tax law, which attract tax fines, are considered as 'criminal' within the meaning of the Convention (decision in *Janosevic* v. *Sweden* of 23 July 2002, application no. 34619/97; decision in *Jussila* v. *Finland* of 23 November 2006, application no. 73053/01; decision in *Impar LtD.* v. *Lithuania* of 5 January 2010, application no. 13102/04; decision in *Steininger* v. *Austria* of 17 April 2012, application no. 21539/07). [...]

[...]

Neither Article 4 Paragraph 1 of Protocol No. 7 of the Convention, nor the national law of the Republic of Lithuania prohibits execution of two processes regarding the same offence; however, repeated prosecution or trial is prohibited. Assessment of whether in a particular case the principle of *non bis in idem* is violated has to be based on the following circumstances: (1) whether the sanction imposed against a person is a criminal charge; (2) whether the person was punished for the identical or essentially the same legally significant facts (same conduct); (3) whether the person was punished repeatedly; (4) whether the same person was punished repeatedly (same person). These criteria cannot be applied formally: violation of the said principle can be determined only after examination of all the significant factual circumstances of the case.

[...] The tax fine that was imposed is even higher than the possible maximum penalty – a fine amounting to EUR 11,295.18 – which can be imposed against V.K. for a criminal offence. Thus, considering the type and severity of the fine imposed against V.K.'s company for violations of tax laws, the fine constituted a criminal penalty within the meaning of Article 4 Paragraph 1 of Protocol No. 7 of the Convention.

Part Four: III. Relationship between International Law and Domestic Law – Remedies under Domestic Law for Violations of International Law

4/22

In case No. e3K-3-184-415/2017 of 5 April 2017, the Supreme Court of Lithuania decided that a violation of Article 6 of the ECHR – failure to duly summon to the hearing – can be rectified by renewal of process and starting fresh proceedings. The relevant paragraphs read:

> If the cassation court finds a violation of Article 6 of the Convention (failure to duly summon to the hearing) the renewal of proceedings based on new essential circumstances in the case is the legal instrument to ensure an effective legal balance between the interests of the parties and the effectiveness of the legal system.

4/23

In case No. 2K-87-942/2017 of 13 April 2017, the Supreme Court of Lithuania assessed whether prolonged length of criminal proceedings constitutes a ground to terminate criminal proceedings or reduce the sentence under Article 6 Paragraph 1 of the ECHR. The Court found that in the present case there was no ground to reduce the sentence or terminate criminal proceedings because the prolonged length of the proceedings was mostly caused by the behaviour and actions of the accused. The relevant paragraphs read:

> The cassator submits in the cassation claim that unreasonably lengthy criminal proceedings against her constitute a separate ground to terminate criminal proceedings or apply Article 54 Paragraph 3 of the Criminal Code and reduce the penalty imposed against her.

> According to the practice of the Supreme Court of Lithuania, excessive length of criminal proceedings, depending on the circumstances related to the individualisation of the penalty (Article 54 Paragraph 2 of the Criminal Code) and to violation of the right to trial within the shortest

possible time, can serve as a ground to reduce the sentence within the limits of sanction of the respective applicable article of the Criminal Code. Such case law is formed in line with the case law of the ECtHR, whereas reduction of sentence for violation of the right to trial within the shortest possible time is considered a sufficient redress for serious breach of the reasonable-time requirement, therefore an individual who used such redress can no longer claim to be a victim of a violation of the Convention [...].

According to the rulings of the ECtHR and the case law of the Lithuanian courts, the possibility to reduce the sentence due to the unreasonable length of the proceedings is not based on the length of proceedings as such, but on the unreasonable length under the particular circumstances of the case, which violate the right to a fair trial within a reasonable time enshrined in Article 6 Paragraph 1 of the Convention and Articles 2, 44 Paragraph 5 of the Criminal Procedure Code. Criteria which serve as a basis for the ECtHR to assess whether the length of proceedings meet the requirements of the Convention have been formulated in many of the cases heard by this court. Such criteria usually are that the reasonableness of the length of proceedings must be assessed in the light of the circumstances of the case and by reference to the following criteria: the complexity of the case, the conduct of the prosecuted person and relevant authorities in criminal proceedings, and what was at stake for the prosecuted person (e.g. severity of procedural coercive measures applied and their duration) etc. (*Sorvisto* v. *Finland,* no. 19348/04, judgment of 13 January 2009; *Meilus* v. *Lithuania,* no. 53161/99, judgment of 6 November 2003).

[...]

It should be noted that in the jurisprudence of the ECtHR it has been stated several times that, when it is recognised that the proceedings failed to observe the requirement of reasonable time, one of the adequate and sufficient remedies is to provide redress in relation thereto by reducing the sentence for the accused (*Einarsson* v. *Iceland,* no. 22596/93, decision of 5 April 1995; *Beck* v. *Norway,* no. 26390/95, judgment of 26 June 2001; *Wejrup* v. *Denmark,* no. 49126/99, decision of 7 March 2002; *Tamás Kovács* v. *Hungary,* no. 67660/01, judgment of 28 September 2004; *Ohlen* v. *Denmark,* no. 63214/00, judgment of 24 May 2005 and other).

[...]

The panel of judges of the cassation court notes that firstly the cassator was accused of criminal offences prescribed in Article 25 Paragraph 2, Article 184 Paragraph 1 and Article 189 Paragraph 1 of the Criminal Code. [...] It should be noted that the information contained in the criminal case allows the conclusion that pre-trial criminal proceedings in this case took longer because it took a long time to receive a conclusion from a specialist regarding corrections in the journal; R.V. did not come to inquiry meetings claiming that her defender could not participate or presenting a medical certificate justifying failure to come to the pre-trial criminal investigation office; it also took a long time to receive a reply from UAB Sveikatos centras on whether any procedural actions can be conducted in regard to R.V.

Whereas a pre-trial criminal investigation under Article 300 Paragraph 1 and Article 228 Paragraph 2 of the Criminal Code was started only on 29 November 2013 [...]. The criminal case was referred to Kaunas District Court on 10 September 2014. Once Kaunas District Court started examination of the criminal case, the accused R.V. did not come to the court hearing, the court imposed an order bringing R.V.to court; after failure to find the accused at the address of her residence, she was contacted by phone but refused to indicate her current residential address though promised to come to court voluntarily. At the court hearing on 2 January 2015 R.V. submitted a medical certificate about illness. The attorney for R.V. explained that she did not know the recent residential address of R.V. Later R.V.'s defending attorney [...] terminated the legal services agreement and at a court hearing on 4 February 2015 R.V. announced that she was in a need of a defence attorney. Therefore, the trial in the criminal case started only on 14 May 2015.

Considering these circumstances, the court of cassation instance determines that although the proceedings were prolonged, the delay was caused mostly by the actions and behaviour of the cassator herself. That being the case the process is considered to be optimal and does not give grounds to impose a penalty in accordance with Article 54 Paragraph 3 or terminate criminal proceedings.

4/24

In case No. 2K-289-693/2017 of 28 November 2017, the Supreme Court of Lithuania noted the importance of the practice of the ECtHR under Articles 3 and 10 of the Convention in cases where individuals are accused of making false accusations against police officers or alleging non-existent criminal offences by the officers. The relevant paragraphs read:

> It should be noted that courts which hear cases where individuals are accused of submitting false accusations against police offers or non-existent criminal offences by officers, should take into account the case law of the ECtHR. Under the case law of this court concerning Article 3 of the Convention, which establishes a right to be protected against ill-treatment (torture or inhuman or degrading treatment) by police officers, when a person raises an arguable claim that he or she has been seriously ill-treated by the police, the Government is under obligation to ensure an effective official investigation (inter alia, judgment of 27 November 2008 in *Spinov* v. *Ukraine*, no. 34331/03). Moreover, assessing complaints by individuals regarding their liability for defamation of officials in the context of interference with the individual's freedom of expression (Article 10 of the Convention), the ECtHR emphasised that one of the precepts of the rule of law is that citizens should be able to notify competent State officials about the conduct of civil servants which to them appears irregular or unlawful. Unlike politicians, other officers and public servants are considered to be less open to public scrutiny; however, interference with freedom of expression can be justified only where there is a real threat that such expression of such opinion threatens the need to enjoy public confidence in conditions free of undue perturbation when on duty, i.e. public officials and officers should be sufficiently open to criticism (judgment of 8 April 2010 in *Bezymyannyy* v. *Russia*, no. 10941/03; a contrario judgment of 27 May 2003 in *Skałka* v. *Poland*, no. 43425/98). Disproportionate criminal persecution and conviction of individuals for the sole reason that their complaints against officers for their irregular or unlawful conduct were rejected, would limit the rights enshrined in Articles 3 and 10 of the Convention and would deter protection of such rights.

Part Five: I.A.2. Subjects of International Law – States – Sovereignty and Independence

5/1
[17/1]

Part Five: 11.A.2.C. International Organizations – General – Participation of States and International Organizations in International Organisations and in Their Activities – Obligations of Membership

5/2
The Constitutional Court of the Republic of Lithuania in decision No. KT14-N7/2017 on the interpretation of the provisions of the Constitutional Court's rulings of 30 December 2003 and 13 November 2006 and its decision of 13 March 2013 that are related to the prohibition of dual (multiple) citizenship, dated 20 October July 2017, elaborated on the scope of international obligations related to membership in the European Union and the North Atlantic Treaty Organisation and found that such obligations do not entail dual citizenship:

> The geopolitical orientation of the Lithuanian State as prescribed in the Constitution implies European and Transatlantic integration chosen by the Republic of Lithuania (rulings of the Constitutional Court of 24 January 2015 and 9 November 2015); 'the geopolitical orientation of the Lithuanian State' means the membership of the Republic of Lithuania in the European Union and the North Atlantic Treaty Organisation and the need to comply with international obligations related to such membership (rulings of 7 July 2011, 24 January 2016 and 19 November 2015).
>
> It should be noted that neither the obligations of the Republic of Lithuania arising out of and related to membership of the European Union and the North Atlantic Treaty Organisation, nor the geopolitical orientation of the Lithuanian State enshrined in the Constitution constitute an obligation on the part of the Republic of Lithuania to create preconditions to obtain dual (multiple) citizenship for citizens of the Republic of Lithuania who have left and obtained the citizenship of an EU or NATO member State. It should be also noted that European Union law also does not prescribe an obligation for Member States to create preconditions for its citizens to have citizenship of other Member States.

Part Six: VI. The Individual (including the corporation) in International Law – Refugees

6/1
In cases Nos. eA-3511-822/2017 of 17 May 2017 and eA-3888-822/2017 of 5 October 2017 the Supreme Administrative Court reiterated that the risk of torture in

asylum cases has to be based on substantial grounds and a general situation of violence normally does not entail a violation of Article 3 of the Convention. The relevant paragraph reads:

> According to the case law of the ECtHR in asylum cases, in assessing whether the request of an asylum seeker is credible, substantial grounds have to been shown for believing that the person concerned, if deported, faces a real risk of being subjected to treatment contrary to the prohibition of torture enshrined in Article 3 of the ECHR. Assessment of such risk has to be established based on substantial grounds and considering each individual case (see e.g. judgment in *NA v. the United Kingdom*, application no. 25904/07, 6 August 2008). In the judgment in *H.L.R. v France*, application no. 24573/94, 29 April 1997 the ECtHR noted that a general situation of violence will not normally in itself entail a violation of Article 3 in the event of expulsion.

Part Six: VIII.C. Human Rights and Fundamental Freedoms – Under the Council of Europe Treaty System

6/2

In a judgment of 17 January 2017 in *Jankovskis* v. *Lithuania*, application no. 21575/08 the ECtHR found a violation of Article 10 of the ECHR, considering that by preventing an inmate from receiving education-related information via the Internet the Government violated the applicant's right to receive information. The ECtHR reasoned a violation of Article 10 of the ECHR, as follows:

> The Court has consistently recognised that the public has a right to receive information of general interest. Furthermore, the Court has held that the right to receive information basically prohibits a government from preventing a person from receiving information that others wished or were willing to impart (see *Kalda*, cited above, §§ 41 and 42).
>
> In the present case, however, the question at issue is not the authorities' refusal to release requested information (compare and contrast *Magyar Helsinki Bizottság* v. *Hungary* [GC], no. 18030/11, §§ 149–156, 8 November 2016); the applicant's request concerned information that was freely available in the public domain. Rather, the applicant's complaint concerns a particular means of accessing the information in question: namely, that he, as a prisoner, wished to be granted access – specifically via the

Internet – to information published on a website belonging to the Ministry of Education and Science [...].

In this connection, the Court reiterates that in the light of its accessibility and its capacity to store and communicate vast amounts of information, the Internet plays an important role in enhancing the public's access to news and facilitating the dissemination of information in general (see *Delfi AS* v. *Estonia* [GC], no. 64569/09, § 133, ECHR 2015; *Ahmet Yıldırım* v. *Turkey*, no. 3111/10, § 48, ECHR 2012; and Times Newspapers Ltd v. the United Kingdom (nos. 1 and 2), nos. 3002/03 and 23676/03, § 27, ECHR 2009).

Nevertheless, the Court notes that imprisonment inevitably entails a number of restrictions on prisoners' communications with the outside world, including on their ability to receive information. It considers that Article 10 cannot be interpreted as imposing a general obligation to provide access to the Internet, or to specific Internet sites, for prisoners (see *Kalda*, cited above, § 45). However, in the circumstances of the present case, since access to information relating to education is granted under Lithuanian law, the Court is ready to accept that the restriction of access to the Internet site to which the Ministry referred the applicant in reply to his request to provide information constituted an interference with the right to receive information.

[...]

The Court notes that the website to which the applicant wished to have access contained information about learning and study programmes in Lithuania. The information on that site was regularly updated to reflect, for example, admission requirements for the current academic year. It also provided up to date information from the Lithuanian Labour Exchange about job vacancies and unemployment [...]. It is not unreasonable to hold that such information was directly relevant to the applicant's interest in obtaining education, which is in turn of relevance for his rehabilitation and subsequent reintegration into society. As underlined by the CPT, a satisfactory programme of activities, including education, is of crucial importance for the well-being of all detainees, including prisoners awaiting trial. This is all the more relevant in relation to sentenced prisoners [...], and the applicant, who was serving a sentence in the Pravieniškės Correctional Home, was one such prisoner [...]. In fact, as regards the Pravieniškės Correctional Home, the CPT specifically noted after its 2008 visit that steps should be taken to ensure that all sentenced prisoners in that prison were able to engage in purposeful activities of a varied nature, such as educational programmes ([...] in fine of the CPT report, quoted in *Mironovas and Others* v. *Lithuania*, nos. 40828/12, 29292/12, 69598/12, 40163/13, 66281/13, 70048/13 and 70065/13, § 65, 8 December 2015).

The Court also considers that accessing the AIKOS website in the manner advised by the Ministry of Education and Science – namely browsing through it in order to find information that was relevant – was more efficient than making requests for specific information, as was proposed by the Government [...]. Indeed, in order to make a specific request to an educational institution one would need to be aware of the competencies of that institution and the services provided by it. Such preliminary information would be provided by the AIKOS website. The Court furthermore notes the applicant's argument that information about study programmes was of a constantly evolving nature [...]. This fact is also highlighted on the AIKOS website itself [...].

Turning to the Lithuanian authorities' decisions, the Court cannot but observe that they essentially focused on the legal ban on prisoners having Internet access as such, instead of examining the applicant's argument that access to a particular website was necessary for his education [...]. It is true that the Pravieniškės Correctional Home authorities pointed out the presence of a secondary school in that prison, as well as the possibility of following computer courses at Elektrėnai vocational school [...]. However, this appears to be a very remote proposition in relation to the applicant's wish to acquire a second university degree [...]. In the present case the Court also observes that the prison authorities or the Lithuanian courts did not even go so far as to argue that extended Internet access might incur additional costs for the State [...]. Whilst the security considerations arising from prisoners' access to Internet, as such, and cited by the prison authorities [...] may be considered as relevant, the Court notes that the domestic courts failed to give any kind of consideration to the fact that the applicant asked for access to a website created and administered by the Ministry of Education and Science, which was a State institution. In fact, both courts were completely silent on the matter of education [...].

Lastly, the Court is mindful of the fact that in a number of the Council of Europe and other international instruments the public-service value of the Internet and its importance for the enjoyment of a range of human rights has been recognised. Internet access has increasingly been understood as a right, and calls have been made to develop effective policies to achieve universal access to the Internet and to overcome the 'digital divide' (see Kalda, [...]). The Court considers that these developments reflect the important role the Internet plays in people's everyday lives, in particular since certain information is exclusively available on the Internet. Indeed, as has already been established in this case, the AIKOS website provides comprehensive information about learning possibilities in Lithuania. In this connection it is also noteworthy that the Lithuanian authorities did not even consider the possibility of granting the applicant limited or controlled Internet access to this particular website administered by a State institution, which could have hardly posed a security risk.

In these circumstances, the Court is not persuaded that sufficient reasons have been put forward in the present case to justify interference with the applicant's right to receive information. Moreover, having regard to the consequences of that interference for the applicant [...], the Government's objection that the applicant had not suffered significant disadvantage [...] must be dismissed.

The Court concludes that the interference with the applicant's right to receive information, in the specific circumstances of the present case, cannot be regarded as having been necessary in a democratic society.

6/3

In a judgment of 24 January 2017 in *Fridman* v. *Lithuania*, application no. 40947/11 the ECtHR found a violation of Article 6(1) of the ECHR, considering that by failing to serve notice on the applicant about an oral hearing in appellate proceedings in a civil case and simply putting a notice in his letter box after the hearing, the Government violated the claimant's defence rights and the principle of equality of arms. The ECtHR reasoned a violation of Article 6 Paragraph 1 of the ECHR, as follows:

The Court firstly reiterates that Article 6 § 1 of the Convention does not guarantee the right to be present in court in cases which do not concern determination of a criminal charge, but rather a more general right to present one's case effectively before a court and to enjoy equality of arms with the opposing side. Article 6 § 1 leaves States a free choice as to the means to be used in guaranteeing litigants those rights (see *Steel and Morris* v. *the United Kingdom*, no. 68416/01, § § 59–60, ECHR 2005-II; *Artyomov* v. *Russia*, no. 14146/02, § 201, 27 May 2010; and *Buterlevičiūtė* v. *Lithuania*, no. 42139/08, § 55, 12 January 2016).

The Court also reiterates that the Convention is intended to guarantee rights that are practical and effective and not those that are theoretical or illusory (see, among many other authorities, *Cudak* v. *Lithuania* [GC], no. 15869/02, § 58, ECHR 2010). It considers that the right to a public hearing would be devoid of substance if a party to a case were not apprised of a hearing in such a way as to have an opportunity to attend it, should he or she decide to exercise the right to appear established in domestic law (see *Yakovlev* v. *Russia*, no. 72701/01, § 21, 15 March 2005).

The Court further reiterates that Article 6 § 1 cannot be construed as conferring on litigants a right to obtain a specific form of service of court documents, such as by registered post (see *Kolegovy* v. *Russia*, no. 15226/05, § 40, 1 March 2012; *Perihan and Mezopotamya Basın Yayın A.Ş.* v. *Turkey*, no. 21377/03, § 39, 21 January 2014; and *Avotiņš* v. *Latvia* [GC], no. 17502/07, § 119, ECHR 2016). Nonetheless, the Court considers that in the interests of the administration of justice a litigant should be notified of a court hearing in such a way as to not only have knowledge of the date and place of the hearing, but also to have enough time to prepare his or her case and to attend the court hearing. Formal dispatch of a notification letter without any confidence that it will reach the applicant in good time cannot be considered by the Court as proper notification (see *Kolegovy*, cited above, § 40, and the cases cited therein).

In the present case there is no dispute that notification of the hearing of 11 October 2010 before the Court of Appeal was sent to the applicant's home address and that the applicant eventually received it. However, the applicant argued before the domestic courts and this Court that the notification had not been put in his letter box until 14 October 2010 ([...]). The Government contested that argument, claiming that the notification had been sent on 21 September 2010 and most likely reached the applicant within five days at the latest. However, they were unable to provide any evidence to that effect because the relevant case material had already been destroyed [...]. The Court observes that in previous cases it has considered that it was incumbent on the Government to submit evidence showing that notification had reached an applicant in good time (see *Mokrushina v. Russia*, no. 23377/02, § 20, 5 October 2006; *Prokopenko v. Russia*, no. 8630/03, § 18, 3 May 2007; *Kolegovy*, cited above, § 41; and *Buterlevičiūtė*, cited above, § 59), and it sees no reason to adopt a different approach in the present case. Accordingly, in the light of the material in its possession, the Court concludes that the applicant was not notified of the hearing of 11 October 2010 in due time. The Court also notes that domestic law did not require the applicant to identify a legal representative at the appeal stage or to look up the schedule of hearings on the Court of Appeal website [...], so the fact that he did not do so cannot relieve the Government of the obligation it had to duly notify the applicant of the hearing.

The Court further observes that the Court of Appeal at the hearing of 11 October 2010 merely noted that the applicant 'had been notified of the hearing' [...] but there is nothing in the transcript of the hearing or in the text of the judgment to suggest that the court examined whether the applicant had been notified in due time. The Court notes that domestic law states that employees of the post office, bailiffs or couriers serving notification must record its delivery in the relevant registers, indicating, inter alia, the date [...]. It also notes that domestic law lays an obligation on a court to verify whether a party who is absent from a hearing has been duly notified [...]. In those circumstances, the Court is of the view that the Court of Appeal had both the obligation and the possibility to examine whether the applicant had been duly notified of the hearing on 11 October 2010, and, if he had not been, whether examination of the appeal should have been adjourned (see, *mutatis mutandis, Yakovlev*, cited above, § 22; *Gusak v. Russia*, no. 28956/05, § 26, 7 June 2011; and *Kolegovy*, cited above, § 41). Although the Government argued that if there had been any shortcomings in the proceedings before the Court of Appeal, the Supreme Court would have examined the applicant's appeal on points of law [...], the Court reiterates that it is not its role to speculate whether the Supreme Court should have examined the applicant's appeal, or for what reasons it may have decided not to do so (see, mutatis mutandis, *Pyrantienė v. Lithuania*, no. 45092/07, § § 75–76, 12 November 2013).

Lastly and most importantly, the Court does not lose sight of the fact that the other party's representative was present at the hearing of 11 October

2010 and provided submissions in reply to the applicant's appeal [...]. Contrary to the Government's arguments [...], the Court considers that it should not speculate on whether the hearing before the Court of Appeal was important to the applicant, because the very fact that the other party had the opportunity to submit observations on the applicant's appeal – whereas the applicant was not able to express his views on those observations – was sufficient to undermine his confidence in the workings of justice (see, *mutatis mutandis, Švenčionienė v. Lithuania*, no. 37259/04, § 29, 25 November 2008, and *Gusak*, cited above, § 27).

6/4

In a judgment of 24 January 2017 in *Liatukas v. Lithuania*, application no. 27376/11 the ECtHR found that there was no violation of Article 6(1) of the ECHR. The Court decided that the mere mistake of accepting the applicant's appellate claim that had not been lodged in accordance with domestic procedural rules does not constitute arbitrariness or denial of justice. The ECtHR reasoned the non-violation of Article 6 Paragraph 1 of the ECHR, as follows:

> Turning to the circumstances of the present case, it is not disputed that D.L.'s appeal had not been lodged in accordance with domestic procedural rules [...]. The Government submitted that, on the one hand, the appeal had been referred for examination before the appellate court because of 'a clerical error' [...] and, on the other hand, that its examination had been justified by the public interest [...]. In this respect the Court agrees with the applicant that the Kaunas Regional Court, which examined the case on appeal, did not mention either the public interest or any other reason for examining D.L.'s appeal despite its formal deficiencies [...]. Indeed, it appears that the Kaunas Regional Court was not aware of any reasons why the appeal should not have been accepted for examination. In such circumstances, the Court is more inclined to accept the Government's first submission that D.L.'s appeal was referred to the Kaunas Regional Court by mistake.

> In that connection, the Court reiterates that it is not its function to deal with errors of fact or law allegedly committed by a national court unless and in so far as they may have infringed rights and freedoms protected by the Convention (see *Scordino v. Italy* (no. 1) [GC], no. 36813/97, § 190, ECHR 2006-V, and *Bochan v. Ukraine* (no. 2) [GC], no. 22251/08, § 61, ECHR 2015). In previous cases the Court has found a violation of Article 6 § 1 where domestic courts committed 'a manifest error of assessment' (see *Dulaurans v. France*, no. 34553/97, § 34, 21 March 2000), where

decisions by domestic courts could be regarded as 'grossly arbitrary' (see *Khamidov v. Russia*, no. 72118/01, § 174, 15 November 2007, and *Bochan*, cited above, § 64), or where such decisions amounted to a 'denial of justice' (see *Anđelković v. Serbia*, no. 1401/08, § 27, 9 April 2013).

In the present case, the Court cannot disregard the fact that the appeal submitted by D.L. formed the foundation for the appellate proceedings which resulted in a judgment that was to the applicant's detriment [...]. At the same time, the Court observes that D.L.'s appeal was communicated to the applicant and that he had an opportunity to reply to it [...]. Contrary to the applicant's submissions, the foregoing means that there are therefore no grounds to find that the principle of equality of arms was disregarded [...], and compare and contrast *Gürkan v. Turkey*, no. 1154/04, §§ 34–35, 29 March 2011). The applicant did not allege that the civil proceedings were unfair for any other reason, and the Court, having examined the material submitted to it, sees no grounds to hold otherwise. Having regard to the proceedings taken as a whole, the Court is of the view that the error committed by the domestic courts was not so significant as to make the proceedings arbitrary or to result in a denial of justice, and that in any event it was counterbalanced by granting the applicant sufficient opportunity to become acquainted with D.L.'s appeal and to comment on it.

6/5

In a judgment of 24 January 2017 in *Paulikas v. Lithuania*, application no. 57435/09 the ECtHR found that there was no violation of Article 6(1) and 6(2) of the ECHR, even though the applicant complained that he had not received a fair trial because of media reports and comments by State officials concerning the criminal case against him, in particular because those reports and comments had breached the right to the presumption of innocence. The ECtHR reasoned non-violation of Article 6 Paragraphs 1 and 2 of the ECHR, as follows:

(a) As to public statements by State officials

(i) General principles

The Court reiterates that the presumption of innocence enshrined in paragraph 2 of Article 6 is one of the elements of a fair criminal trial that is required by paragraph 1 (see, among many other authorities, *Deweer v. Belgium*, 27 February 1980, § 56, Series A no. 35; *Allenet de Ribemont v.*

France, 10 February 1995, § 35, Series A no. 308; and *Natsvlishvili and Togonidze* v. *Georgia*, no.9043/05, § 103, ECHR 2014 (extracts)). Article 6 § 2 prohibits premature expression by the tribunal of the opinion that the person 'charged with a criminal offence' is guilty before he or she has been so proved according to law (see, among many other authorities, *Minelli* v. *Switzerland*, 25 March 1983, § 37, Series A no. 62, and *Peša* v. *Croatia*, no. 40523/08, § 138, 8 April 2010). It also covers statements made by other public officials about pending criminal investigations which encourage the public to believe the suspect guilty and prejudge assessment of the facts by the competent judicial authority (see *Allenet de Ribemont*, cited above, § 41; *Daktaras* v. *Lithuania*, no. 42095/98, § § 41-43, ECHR 2000-X; and *Butkevičius*, cited above, § 49).

The Court also reiterates that the freedom of expression guaranteed by Article 10 of the Convention includes the freedom to receive and impart information, including, to a certain extent, the right to seek and access information (see *Maygar Helsinki Bizottság* v. *Hungary* [GC], no. 18030/11, § § 155-156, 8 November 2016). Article 6 § 2 cannot therefore prevent the authorities from informing the public about criminal investigations in progress, but it requires that they do so with all the discretion and circumspection necessary if the presumption of innocence is to be respected (see *Allenet de Ribemont*, cited above, § 38, and *Karakaş and Yeşilırmak* v. *Turkey*, no. 43925/98, § 50, 28 June 2005). The Court has previously considered that in a democratic society it is inevitable that information is imparted when a serious charge of misconduct in office is brought or where an applicant was an important political figure at the time of the alleged offence. However, this circumstance cannot justify every possible choice of words by officials in interviews with the press (see *Butkevičius*, cited above, § 50; *Arrigo and Vella* v. *Malta* (dec.), no. 6569/04, 10 May 2005; and *Fatullayev*, cited above, § 161). Nevertheless, judging whether a statement by a public official is in breach of the principle of the presumption of innocence must be determined in the context of the particular circumstances in which the impugned statement was made (see *Daktaras*, cited above, § 43; *Böhmer* v. *Germany*, no. 37568/97, § 60, 3 October 2002; and *Peša*, cited above, § 141).

(ii) Application of the above principles in the present case

At the outset the Court notes that in the present case the impugned statements were made by the President, the Minister of the Interior, several other politicians and the Police Commissioner General in a context that was independent of the criminal proceedings themselves, that is, by way of public statements or interviews in the national press [...]. The Court acknowledges that the circumstances of the accident of 7 November 2007 – the deaths of three children and the involvement of a police officer, which followed the pattern of several similar accidents caused by officers – created a legitimate public interest to be informed about the alleged offence and the ensuing criminal proceedings [...]. The Court is also of the view that those same circumstances justified the wish of high-level State officials to express their reaction to the accident, particularly as seen in its broader context of several other similar accidents, as well as to keep the public informed about the institutional reforms carried out in its aftermath. However, the Court reiterates that those circumstances in and of themselves could not justify any and every use of words by officials in their statements to the press (see, *mutatis mutandis, Butkevičius*, cited above, § 50).

The Court observes that the public statement issued by the Minister of the Interior on 8 November 2007 did not specifically discuss the applicant's case but stated that 'this was not the first time police officers, who are supposed to stop traffic violations, have caused terrible accidents' [...]. While that statement implied that the applicant had 'caused' the accident of 7 November 2007, the Court notes that by the time the statement was made the applicant had confessed to driving the car [...], so his involvement in the accident could not be disputed. Given the status of the Minister of the Interior, the Court is of the view that he should have exercised particular caution in his choice of words (see, *mutatis mutandis, Peša*, cited above, § 150). Nonetheless, the Court considers that the Minister's statement, seen in context, cannot be construed as a declaration of the applicant's guilt of the criminal offence he was suspected of, nor could it have influenced courts examining the case against the applicant.

The Police Commissioner General, in his interview with the press on 8 November 2007, the President's spokesperson, in her statement given that same day, and the politicians who provided comments to a newspaper on 9 November 2007, expressed their opinion as to who should take political responsibility for the accident and the overall situation concerning road traffic safety, but they did not specifically discuss the applicant's criminal liability [...]. The Court considers that the statements were of a general nature related to shortcomings within the police and problems concerning road traffic safety, and could not be seen as breaching the applicant's right to the presumption of innocence (see, *mutatis mutandis, Natsvlishvili and Togonidze*, § 104, and *Konstas*, § 41, both cited above).

The Court further observes that the resignation of the Minister of the Interior and the Police Commissioner General five days after the accident [...] cannot be seen as a declaration of the applicant's guilt. The Court notes that in line with domestic law the resignation of a minister or the Police Commissioner General is not necessarily related to criminal liability on the part of either those individuals themselves or of anyone else [...], and the applicant did not argue that they expressed any views as to his guilt in their resignation statements. Accordingly, the Court is of the view that by resigning from their posts the Minister of the Interior and the Police Commissioner General took political responsibility for a series of events which had occurred within the police, and that their resignation could not have affected the applicant's right to the presumption of innocence.

As to the President's statement issued on 12 November 2007, the Court notes that it was not disputed by the parties that it directly related to the criminal case in question: it mentioned the date and location of the accident and the names of the victims' families, thereby making it very easy to identify the applicant (see, *mutatis mutandis, Konstas*, cited above, § § 39–40). At the same time, the Court observes that the President's statement did not discuss the applicant's case in isolation but placed it in the context of inappropriate behaviour by police officers and recurring problems within the police, stressing the need to ensure an adequate level of criminal liability and political responsibility [...]. The Court considers that the President's decision to make a public statement is understandable not only in the light of the public attention to such accidents but also in the aftermath of the resignation of the two highest-level State officials responsible for the work of the police – the Police Commissioner General and the Minister of the Interior – who were appointed by and reported to the President [...].

The Court also reiterates that although the President's statement implied that the applicant had 'caused' the accident of 7 November 2007, the applicant had by that time already confessed to driving the car [...], so his involvement in the accident could not be disputed. The Court emphasises that the President did not make any specific statements about the factual or legal aspects of the criminal case against the applicant, for example, that he had driven while being drunk or that he had exceeded the speed limit, which were the key circumstances in determining his guilt [...], or that he had been guilty of any particular criminal offence (compare and contrast *Allenet de Ribemont*, § 41; *Lavents*, § § 119 and 127; *Butkevičius*, § 53; *Fatullayev*, § 162; and *G.C.P.* v. *Romania*, § 57, all cited above). The President's statement spoke of the need to 'thoroughly examine' and 'especially strictly evaluate' offences committed by police officers, criticising the past trend of 'relatively mild punishments' [...]. The Court has some concerns about the choice of wording, as the call to 'strictly evaluate' offences caused by police officers and to avoid 'mild punishments' could be regarded as expressing an opinion about the sentence to be handed down to the applicant and thus implying his guilt, and reiterates that the President should have exercised particular caution in his choice of words (see, *mutatis mutandis, Peša*, cited above, § 150). However, the Court reiterates that each statement must be seen in the context of the particular circumstances in which it was made (see, among other authorities, *Daktaras*, cited above, § 43). In the present case, regard being had to the history of traffic accidents caused by police officers who had then avoided criminal liability, as well as the ongoing discussion concerning the political responsibility of high-level officials for problems within the police, the Court is unable to conclude that the President's statement of 12 November 2007, taken as a whole, should be seen as prejudging the criminal proceedings against the applicant.

Accordingly, the Court considers that the public statements by State officials made in relation to the accident did not breach the applicant's right to a fair trial and to the presumption of innocence under Article 6 § § 1 and 2 of the Convention.

(b) As to media publications

(i) General principles

The Court reiterates that, in certain situations, a virulent media campaign can adversely affect the fairness of a trial and involve the State's responsibility. This is so with regard to the impartiality of courts under Article 6 § 1, as well as with regard to the presumption of innocence embodied in Article 6 § 2 (see *Ninn-Hansen* v. *Denmark* (dec.), no. 28972/95,

ECHR 1999-V; *Shuvalov* v. *Estonia*, no.39820/08 and 14942/09, § 82, 29 May 2012; and *Natsvlishvili and Togonidze*, cited above, § 105). At the same time, the Court notes that press coverage of current events is an exercise of freedom of expression, guaranteed by Article 10 of the Convention. If there is a virulent press campaign surrounding a trial, what is decisive is not the subjective apprehensions of the suspect concerning the absence of prejudice required of the trial courts, however understandable, but whether, in the particular circumstances of the case, his or her fears can be held to be objectively justified (see *Butkevičius* v. *Lithuania* (dec.), no. 48297/99, 28 November 2000, and *G.C.P.* v. *Romania*, cited above, § 46).

The Court also reiterates that a fair trial can still be held after intensive adverse publicity. In a democracy, high-profile criminal cases will inevitably attract comment by the media; however, that cannot mean that any media comment whatsoever will inevitably prejudice a defendant's right to a fair trial – otherwise the greater the notoriety of a crime, the less likely that its perpetrators will be tried and convicted. The Court's approach has been to examine whether there are sufficient safeguards to ensure that the proceedings as a whole are fair. It will require cogent evidence that concerns about the impartiality of judges are objectively justified before any breach of Article 6 § 1 can be found (see *Craxi* v. *Italy* (no. 1), no. 34896/97, § § 99 and 103, 5 December 2002, and *Mustafa (Abu Hamza)* v. *the United Kingdom* (dec.), no. 31411/07, § 39, 18 January 2011, and the cases cited therein).

The Court has previously identified some of the factors relevant to its assessment of the impact of a media campaign on the fairness of a trial. Such factors include the time which has elapsed between the press campaign and the commencement of the trial, and notably the determination of the trial court's composition; whether the impugned publications were attributable to, or informed by, the authorities; and whether the publications influenced the judges and thus prejudiced the outcome of the proceedings (see *Sutyagin* v. *Russia* (dec.), no. 30024/02, 8 July 2008, and *Beggs* v. *the United Kingdom* (dec.), no. 15499/10, § 124, 16 October 2012).

(ii) Application of the above principles in the present case

Turning to the circumstances of the present case, the Court observes that there was extensive media coverage of the accident and the criminal proceedings against the applicant [...]. Taking note of the Government's submission as to the existence of a legitimate public interest to be informed about the applicant's trial [...]; see also, *mutatis mutandis, Ninn-Hansen, Daktaras* and *Craxi*, § 102, all cited above), the Court accepts that the media interest in the case was largely the result of the serious consequences of the accident, the fact that it had involved a police officer, and the fact that it had followed the pattern of several similar accidents. Therefore, although various State officials discussed the applicant's case in the media, it cannot be said that the coverage was prompted by the authorities (see *Butkevičius and Beggs*, § 127, both cited above); nor did the applicant allege otherwise (see, *mutatis mutandis, Craxi*, cited above, § 105).

The Court notes that the media coverage began immediately after the accident and coincided in time with the domestic court proceedings. It also observes that the language used in the publications was strong and unambiguous – the applicant was called 'a killer of children' and 'the man who caused the horrific accident' [...] – so even though those same publications referred to him merely as a suspect in the case, such language could nonetheless have influenced the public's perception of the applicant's guilt.

However, the Court emphasises that the charges against the applicant were determined by professional judges who would have been less likely than a jury to be influenced by the press campaign against the applicant on account of their professional training and experience, which allows them to disregard improper external influence (see *Craxi*, § 104, and *G.C.P. v. Romania*, § 48, both cited above). Furthermore, domestic courts at three levels of jurisdiction issued well-reasoned judgments based on the testimony of several witnesses, expert opinions, and other evidence [...]. The appellate court upheld some of the applicant's arguments and reduced his sentence ([...]; see, *mutatis mutandis, Mustafa (Abu Hamza)*, cited above, § 38). Accordingly, there is no evidence in the case file to suggest that the judges who assessed the arguments put forward by the applicant and who examined the charges brought against him were influenced by any of the publications in the press (see *Ninn-Hansen, Daktaras, Butkevičius* and *Craxi*, § 104, all cited above).

The foregoing considerations are sufficient to enable the Court to conclude that the media coverage of the accident and the criminal proceedings against the applicant did not breach his right to a fair trial and the presumption of innocence under Article 6 § § 1 and 2 of the Convention.

6/6

In a judgment of 21 February 2017 in *Šimaitienė* v. *Lithuania*, application no. 55056/10 the ECtHR found that there was no violation of Article 1 of Protocol No. 1 to the Convention. The Court decided that neither the protracted process of restitution nor the amount of compensation paid to the applicant constitute a violation of the applicant's rights. The ECtHR reasoned the non-violation of Article 1 of Protocol No. 1 to the Convention of the ECHR, as follows:

(a) The overall length of the restitution process

The Court takes cognisance of the fact that the present case concerns the restitution of property and is not unmindful of the complexity of the legal and factual issues that a State faces when resolving such questions (see *Aleksa* v. *Lithuania*, no. 27576/05, § 86, 21 July 2009; *Igarienė and Petrauskienė* v. *Lithuania*, no. 26892/05, § 58, 21 July 2009, and *Paukštis* v. *Lithuania*, no. 17467/07, § 84, 24 November 2015). It follows that certain impediments to the realisation of the applicants' right to the peaceful enjoyment of their possessions are not in themselves open to criticism (*ibid.*). It is true that in restitution proceedings the executive authorities are required to carry out a complex set of actions under the domestic legislation on restitution of property, rather than to perform a clear one-off act, such as payment of a particular amount of money (see *Nekvedavičius* v. *Lithuania*, no. 1471/05, § 62, 10 December 2013). Even so, the Court has emphasised that that uncertainty – be it legislative, administrative or arising from the practices applied by the authorities – is a factor to be taken into account in assessing the State's conduct. Indeed, where an issue in the general interest is at stake, it is incumbent on the public authorities to act in good time and in an appropriate and consistent manner (see *Paukštis*, cited above, § 84; and *Beyeler* v. *Italy* [GC], no. 33202/96, § § 110 *in fine*, and 120 *in fine*, ECHR 2000-I).

In the instant case the Court is of the view that contrary to the statements of the applicant, the restitution process had not taken 25 years because the applicant's legitimate expectation that her property rights would be restored in a certain way stemmed from the decision of the authorities of 9 October 2003 [...]. The Court notes that before that date the applicant had no legitimate expectation to restore her property rights. The Court considers that the fact that the authorities delayed in providing compensation to the applicant until 2011 amounted to interference with her right to property, within the meaning of the first sentence of the first paragraph of Article 1 of Protocol No. 1 (see *Lyubomir Popov* v. *Bulgaria*, no. 69855/01, § 119, 7 January 2010). Furthermore, the Court is not insensitive to the complexities inherent in the restitution process and accepts that this interference was lawful, as there were no special time-limits for providing compensation under the relevant legislation, and was legitimately undertaken in the public interest, namely with the aim of protecting the rights of others, as the authorities needed to accommodate the claims of other owners in the rather complex restitution process.

Turning to the question of proportionality, the Court has to examine whether the delay in awarding the compensation due meant that the applicant must have borne a special and excessive burden (see *Lyubomir Popov*, cited above, § 120).

The Court notes that the applicant was always aware that she would be paid compensation as a form of restitution, and did not object to that. To the contrary, she explicitly requested to be paid her compensation in the form of securities [...]. The Court also observes that the delay in the applicant's case amounted to approximately seven years and four months, that is to say, from the decision of 9 October 2003 to restore her property rights [...] until the finalisation of the transfer of securities on 1 February 2011 [...].

The Court notes that a number of administrative decisions were taken by the authorities during the period between 9 October 2003 and 1 February 2011 [...]. As the applicant challenged the compensation indicated in the decision of 9 October 2003, the court proceedings were ongoing from 10 June 2004 [...] until 21 September 2007, when it was decided to annul the amount of the compensation indicated in the decision of 9 October 2003 [...]. The Court also notes that the applicant started several sets of court proceedings even later, repeatedly challenging the assessment of the value of the buildings [...]. After the amendment to the decision of 9 October 2003 was adopted on 5 June 2009 [...], it was for the applicant to submit a request for compensation in securities to the State Property Fund. However, she only did so on 16 August 2010 [...]. In view of the above considerations, the Court considers that the restitution process was protracted in great part because of the conduct of the applicant. The Court therefore accepts that the Lithuanian authorities took the necessary actions in order to finalise the process of restitution for the applicant without undue delays [...].

There has accordingly been no violation of Article 1 of Protocol No. 1 on this account.

(b) The amount of the compensation paid to the applicant in securities

The Court notes that the applicant was paid compensation in the form of securities at the beginning of 2011. The Court observes, however, that the applicant was dissatisfied with the amount of the compensation paid to her. It thus cannot be said that the matter had been resolved and the Court therefore rejects the Government's request for this part of the application to be struck out under Article 37 § 1 (b) of the Convention [...].

It has been noted in the Court's case law that while Article 1 of Protocol No. 1 requires that the amount of compensation granted for property taken by the State be 'reasonably related' to its value, the same rule does not apply to situations in which compensatory entitlement arises not from any previous taking of individual property by the respondent State, but is designed to mitigate the effects of a taking or loss of property not attributable to that State – in such situations, the State is entitled to reduce, even substantially, levels of compensation provided for by law (see *Broniowski* v. *Poland* [GC], no. 31443/96, § 186, ECHR 2004-V, and *Nekvedavičius* v. *Lithuania* (just satisfaction), no. 1471/05, § 19, 17 November 2015). The Court has also held that in regulating the restitution process the Contracting States have a wide discretion, including over the rules of how compensation for long-extinguished property rights should be assessed (see *Jantner* v. *Slovakia*, no. 39050/97, § 34, 4 March 2003, *Bergauer and Others* v. *the Czech Republic* (dec.), no. 17120/04, 13 December 2005, and *Paukštis*, cited above, § 74).

In numerous rulings that have already been analysed and accepted by the Court, the Constitutional Court held that fair compensation for property which could not be returned was compatible with the principle of protection of property and that the notion of restitution of property rights in Lithuania essentially denoted partial reparation (see relevant domestic practice, [...]). The Court has also already accepted that Lithuania has chosen the principle of partial restitution to rectify old wrongs (see *Paukštis*, cited above, § 81). The Court finds that as the first assessment of value was undertaken on 14 July 2003 and the decision to restore the applicant's property rights was taken on 9 October 2003 [...], the assessment of the value of the buildings was at the value that they had in that particular year. In this context the Court cannot accept the applicant's claim that she should be compensated for the full market value of the buildings, since no such right had been guaranteed to her under the applicable domestic law or in the judgment of 21 September 2007 ([...]; see also, *mutatis mutandis, Nekvedavičius*, cited above, § 20). The Court thus finds no reason to conclude that the compensation calculated was not pertinent.

Finally, as regards the actual compensation transferred to the applicant, the Court notes that the applicant received the exact level of compensation indicated in the decision of the authorities of 5 June 2009 [...]. The applicant did not use her opportunity to challenge this decision before the domestic courts [...]. Having regard to the margin of appreciation that Article 1 of Protocol No. 1 affords national authorities [...], the extensive jurisprudence of the domestic courts (see the relevant domestic practice, cited in [...]) and the line of reasoning that the Court has already taken regarding restitution of property in Lithuania (see *Paukštis*, cited above, § 81), from which it sees no reason to depart, the Court considers that as a result of the amount of compensation paid to the applicant in securities, she did not have to bear a special and excessive burden.

Accordingly, there has been no violation of Article 1 of Protocol No. 1 to the Convention on this account. This conclusion absolves the Court from examining this same question also from the standpoint of Article 6 § 1 of the Convention.

6/7

In a judgment of 18 April 2017 in *Valančienė v. Lithuania*, application no. 2657/10 the ECtHR found that there was no violation of Article 1 of Protocol No. 1 to the Convention. The Court decided that neither inability to receive a plot of land in nature, nor the amount of compensation paid to the applicant, nor the length of proceedings constituted a violation of Article 1 of Protocol No. 1 to the Convention. The ECtHR reasoned the non-violation of Article 1 of Protocol No. 1 to the Convention of the ECHR, as follows:

The Court notes that the applicant complained about several different aspects of the domestic proceedings. Firstly, she complained about her inability to receive the plot of land *in natura* or to receive a plot of land of equivalent value. Secondly, she complained about the amount of monetary compensation for the plot of land. Thirdly, she complained about overall delays in the restitution process. The Court will examine each of those complaints separately.

(a) As to recovery of a plot of land in natura or a plot of land of equivalent value

The Court notes that while in the present case the option to receive the land *in natura* never existed, there was a possibility for V.V. and later the applicant to obtain a plot of land of equivalent value [...], which was later changed to monetary compensation by the authorities [...]. Even assuming that that situation amounted to interference with the applicant's property rights, the Court notes that such interference struck a 'fair balance' between the demands of the general interest of the community and the requirements of protection of the individual's fundamental rights (see *Sporrong and Lönnroth* v. *Sweden*, 23 September 1982, § 69, Series A no. 52), for the reasons set out below.

Firstly, the Court notes that the Lithuanian authorities' decision to restore V.V.'s property rights by paying monetary compensation instead of returning the plot of land *in natura* [...] was based on Article 21 of the Law on Restitution and Point 3 of the Resolution; thus it was provided for by law, as required by Article 1 of Protocol No. 1 to the Convention.

Moreover, the decision to restore V.V.'s property rights by paying monetary compensation was based on 'public interest' to protect the rights of others, a ground which has already been upheld by the Court (see *Pyrantienė* v. *Lithuania*, no. 45092/07, § 48, 12 November 2013; and *Paukštis*, cited above, § 80). Indeed, the Court has declared that, finding it natural that the margin of appreciation available to the legislature in implementing social and economic policies should be a wide one, it will respect the legislature's judgment as to what is 'in the public interest' unless that judgment is manifestly without reasonable foundation. This logic applies to such fundamental changes in a country's system as the transition from a totalitarian regime to a democratic form of government and reform of the State's political, legal and economic structure, phenomena which inevitably involve the enactment of large-scale economic and social legislation (see *Pyrantienė*, § 46; and *Paukštis*, § 80, both cited above,).

Lastly, the Court notes that it was highlighted in the judgment of 21 September 2009 of the Supreme Administrative Court [...] that, contrary to V.V.'s and later the applicant's allegations, there was no possibility to recover the plot of land *in natura* because it was already being used by other people. This approach is not unreasonable. Moreover, although there was a possibility of providing her with a plot of land of equivalent value, the applicant had made it impossible for the authorities by tying that form of restitution to her own rules and requirements. In particular, the applicant firstly asked the authorities to conclude a preliminary agreement, which was not provided for by domestic law, and, secondly, asked to be provided with a plot of land before she had signed the document on the transfer of land, which the authorities were also unable to do [...]. As a result, the authorities took the only decision possible – they themselves chose what form restitution should take. They were only required to take such measures as were appropriate to provide compensation for the applicant as set out in domestic law. The Court is therefore of the opinion that the decision to pay monetary compensation reached a fair balance between the competing interests at stake.

The Court thus concludes that there has been no violation of Article 1 of Protocol No. 1 to the Convention in respect of the applicant's complaint that she was not able to recover the plot of land *in natura* or obtain a plot of land of equivalent value.

(b) As to the amount of compensation

It has been noted in the Court's case law that while Article 1 of Protocol No. 1 requires that the amount of compensation granted for property taken by the State be 'reasonably related' to its value, the same rule does not apply to situations in which compensatory entitlement arises not from any previous taking of individual property by the respondent State, but is designed to mitigate the effects of a taking or loss of property not attributable to that State – in such situations, the State is entitled to reduce, even substantially, levels of compensation provided for by law (see *Broniowski* v. *Poland* [GC], no. 31443/96, § 186, ECHR 2004-V, and *Nekvedavičius* v. *Lithuania* (just satisfaction), no. 1471/05, § 19, 17

November 2015). The Court has also held that in regulating the restitution process the Contracting States have a wide discretion, including over the rules of how compensation for long-extinguished property rights should be assessed (see *Jantner* v. *Slovakia*, no. 39050/97, § 34, 4 March 2003, *Bergauer and Others* v. *the Czech Republic* (dec.), no. 17120/04, 13 December 2005, and *Paukštis*, cited above, § 74).

In numerous rulings that have already been analysed and accepted by the Court, the Constitutional Court held that fair compensation for property which could not be returned was compatible with the principle of the protection of property and that the notion of restitution of property rights in Lithuania essentially denoted partial reparation (see the relevant case law, [...]). The Court has also already accepted that Lithuania has chosen the principle of partial restitution to rectify old wrongs and has already found it pertinent that a similar methodology adopted by the Lithuanian Government on the land-price calculation was used in a high percentage of cases in Lithuania (see *Paukštis*, cited above, § 81).

The Court cannot accept the applicant's claim that the compensation counted was too low, since no right to receive a higher amount of compensation had been guaranteed under the applicable domestic law or by the judgment of 21 September 2009 of the Supreme Administrative Court [...]. Having regard to the margin of appreciation that Article 1 of Protocol No. 1 affords national authorities, the extensive jurisprudence of the domestic courts [...] and the line of reasoning that the Court has already taken regarding restitution of property in Lithuania (see *Paukštis*, cited above, § 81), from which it sees no reason to depart, the Court considers that the amount of compensation calculated did bear a reasonable relation to the property in question.

The Court therefore finds no violation of Article 1 of Protocol No. 1 to the Convention with respect to the amount of the compensation calculated.

(c) As to the overall length of the restitution process

The Court turns to the applicant's complaint that even though the restitution request had been submitted in 1991, the decision to restore V.V.'s property rights had only been taken in 2008, and that even then she had not received any compensation to the present day [...].

The Court takes cognisance of the fact that the present case concerns restitution of property and is not unmindful of the complexity of the legal and factual issues that a State faces when resolving such questions. It is true that in restitution proceedings the executive authorities are required in particular to carry out a complex set of actions under domestic legislation on restitution of property, rather than to perform a clear one-off act, such as payment of a particular amount of money (see *Nekvedavičius v. Lithuania*, no. 1471/05, § 62, 10 December 2013). It follows that certain impediments to the realisation of applicants' right to the peaceful enjoyment of their possessions are not in themselves open to criticism (see *Aleksa v. Lithuania*, no. 27576/05, § 86, 21 July 2009, *Igarienė and Petrauskienė v. Lithuania*, no. 26892/05, § 58, 21 July 2009, and *Paukštis*, cited above, § 84). Even so, the Court has emphasised that that uncertainty – be it legislative, administrative or arising from the practices applied by the authorities – is a factor to be taken into account in assessing the State's conduct. Indeed, where an issue involving the general interest is at stake, it is incumbent on the public authorities to act in good time and in an appropriate and consistent manner (see *Paukštis*, cited above, § 84).

In the present case the Court finds that the restitution process was indeed long. Active steps towards the restitution of V.V.'s property rights began in 1999 [...] and compensation was paid to the applicant in 2016 [...]. The restitution process thus lasted for around seventeen years. In this context, the Court notes that the authorities claimed there had been a mistake with the information they had given to the applicant that compensation had been paid [...] and the Court finds such a mistake regrettable. However, in the first place, the Court does not consider that that mistake had a major impact on the overall length of the restitution process. Moreover, V.V., and later the applicant, contributed to a large extent to making the process protracted. Firstly, they kept changing their minds about the form of restitution [...]. In addition, although V.V. and the applicant stated that they did not understand why the authorities kept asking her to make a new choice on the form of restitution, the Court observes that the authorities based their requests on the provisions of domestic law and that both V.V. and the applicant failed properly to express their wish on that issue. Secondly, although the decision to restore V.V.'s property rights by paying monetary compensation was taken by the relevant authorities on 13 May 2008 and the applicant was duly informed, she failed to provide all the relevant documents to the notary, which would have allowed her to inherit the money. In particular, the Court cannot understand why it took the applicant eight years to make a request to the authorities for that money. It also appears that the applicant only started contacting the authorities after the case had been communicated to the Government. In that regard, the Court notes that as soon as the applicant provided the authorities with the relevant documents and her account number, they fulfilled their duty and paid the applicant her compensation [...].

In the Court's opinion, those facts are demonstrative of a lack of due diligence. Having regard to the applicant's own inactivity, the Court considers that the delays in the payment of compensation were not such as to amount to a violation of Article 1 of Protocol No. 1 to the Convention.

There has been accordingly no violation of Article 1 of Protocol No. 1 to the Convention on this account.

6/8

In a judgment of 2 May 2017 in *Lisovskij v. Lithuania*, application no. 36249/14 the ECtHR found a violation of Article 5 Paragraph 3 of the Convention. The Court decided that continued detention that lasted four years, five months and seven days had been excessively long and unjustified and thus constituted a violation of Article 5 Paragraph 3 of the Convention and reasoned such finding as follows:

> The applicable general principles have been recently summarised in *Buzadji v. the Republic of Moldova* [GC], no. 23755/07, § § 84–91, ECHR 2016 (extracts).
>
> The Court reiterates in particular that the question whether or not a period of detention is reasonable cannot be assessed in the abstract but must be assessed in each case according to its special features. Accordingly, there is no fixed time-frame applicable to each case (see *McKay v. the United Kingdom* [GC], no. 543/03, § 45, ECHR 2006-X). The responsibility falls in the first place to the national judicial authorities to ensure that, in a given case, the pre-trial detention of an accused person does not exceed a reasonable time. To this end they must, paying due regard to the principle of the presumption of innocence, examine all the facts arguing for or against the existence of a public interest which justifies a departure from the rule in Article 5 and must set them out in their

decisions on the applications for release. It is essentially on the basis of the reasons given in these decisions and of the established facts stated by the applicant in his appeals that the Court is called upon to decide whether or not there has been a violation of Article 5 § 3 (see *Idalov* v. *Russia* [GC], no. 5826/03, § 141, 22 May 2012).

The Court also reiterates that cases which concern organised crime inevitably present more difficulties for the investigative authorities and courts in determining the facts and the degree of responsibility of each member of the criminal organisation (see *Pastukhov and Yelagin* v. *Russia*, no. 55299/07, § 44, 19 December 2013, and the cases cited therein). In cases of this kind, continuous control and limitation of the defendants' ability to contact each other and other individuals may be essential to avoid their absconding, tampering with evidence and influencing or threatening witnesses. Accordingly, longer periods of detention than in other cases may be reasonable (see *Bąk* v. *Poland*, no. 7870/04, § § 56–57, 16 January 2007; *Tomecki* v. *Poland*, no. 47944/06, § 29, 20 May 2008; and *Luković*, cited above, § 46).

Lastly, the Court reiterates that Article 5 § 3 of the Convention requires the competent national authorities to display 'special diligence' in the conduct of criminal proceedings against the accused in detention (see *Labita* v. *Italy* [GC], no. 26772/95, § 153, ECHR 2000-IV). In assessing whether the 'special diligence' requirement has been met, the Court will have regard to, *inter alia*, the overall complexity of the proceedings, any periods of unjustified delay and the steps taken by the authorities to speed up proceedings to ensure that the overall length of detention remains 'reasonable' (see *Suslov* v. *Russia*, no. 2366/07, § 93, 29 May 2012, and the cases cited therein). While very long periods of detention do not automatically violate Article 5 § 3, the Court notes that exceptional circumstances are usually required to justify them (see *Bulatović* v. *Montenegro*, no. 67320/10, § 143, 22 July 2014, and the cases cited therein).

(b) Application of the above principles in the present case

(i) Period to be taken into consideration

In the present case the applicant's detention on remand started on 15 December 2009 when he was arrested [...]. He was detained for the purposes of Article 5 § 3 of the Convention until his conviction by the Vilnius

Regional Court on 22 May 2014 [...]. Although to date that conviction has not become final, the Court reiterates that the period to be taken into consideration for the purposes of Article 5 § 3 ends on the day when the criminal charge is determined, even if only by a court of first instance (see *Buzadji*, cited above, § 85, and the cases cited therein). From 22 May 2014 the applicant was detained 'after conviction by a competent court', within the meaning of Article 5 § 1 (a) and therefore that period of his detention falls outside the scope of Article 5 § 3 (see *Kudła v. Poland* [GC], no. 30210/96, § 104, ECHR 2000-XI; *Piotr Baranowski v. Poland*, no. 39742/05, § 45, 2 October 2007; and *Dragin v. Croatia*, no. 75068/12, § 111, 24 July 2014).

During the period from 11 to 24 September 2013 the applicant's detention was replaced by house arrest [...]. In this connection the Court reiterates that where detention on remand is broken into several non-consecutive periods and where applicants are free to lodge complaints about detention while they are at liberty, those non-consecutive periods should be assessed separately (see *Idalov*, cited above, § 129, and *Chuprikov v. Russia*, no. 17504/07, § 61, 12 June 2014).

On many previous occasions the Court has held that house arrest, in view of its degree and intensity, amounted to deprivation of liberty within the meaning of Article 5 of the Convention (see *Buzadji*, cited above, § § 104–05), and thus a period of house arrest between periods of detention on remand was not considered as breaking the detention into several non-consecutive periods (see, among others, *Nikolova v. Bulgaria (no. 2)*, no. 40896/98, § 60, 30 September 2004, and *Süveges v. Hungary*, no. 50255/12, § 77, 5 January 2016). In this connection the Court observes, however, that conditions of house arrest under Lithuanian law [...] differ rather significantly from those which it has previously assessed. Whereas the applicants in the other cases cited above were prohibited from leaving their place of residence save for specific exceptions indicated by the authorities (see *Nikolova*, § 53; *Süveges*, § 53; and *Buzadji*, § 42, all cited above), by contrast, the applicant in the present case was allowed to leave his home for most of the day (except from 10 p.m. to 8 a.m.), he was allowed to work, and there were only limited restrictions to his public and social life [...].

However, despite the relatively low 'degree and intensity' of the house arrest in the present case, the Court is of the view that there are other circumstances which warrant assessing the applicant's detention on remand from 15 December 2009 to 22 May 2014 as a single period. Firstly, the duration of the applicant's house arrest was very short – thirteen days. In this respect the Court has previously acknowledged that if a period of liberty in between repeated remands in custody was negligible, it might not break the detention into separate periods (see *Velichko v. Russia*, no. 19664/07, § 80, 15 January 2013). Secondly, the applicant's release was terminated not by a new detention order but by an extension of an already existing detention order [...]. The decision to release the applicant from detention never became final because it was revoked by a higher court on the grounds that the reasons for keeping him in detention persisted (contrast with *Idalov*, cited above, in which the applicant's release on bail was discontinued due to his failure to comply with bail conditions, and *Süveges*, also cited above, in which the applicant's house arrest was replaced by detention on remand ordered in connection with different criminal proceedings). Thus, at the domestic procedural level the applicant's detention was not broken into separate periods. Accordingly, the Court considers that, on the basis of the above elements, in must assess the applicant's detention as a single period.

Accordingly, the period of the applicant's detention on remand, to be considered in the present case, was four years, five months and seven days (from 15 December 2009 to 22 May 2014).

(ii) Reasonableness of the length of detention

At the outset the Court observes that the inordinate length of the applicant's detention on remand – more than four years – is a matter of grave concern and requires the domestic authorities to put forward very weighty reasons in order for it to be justified (see *Tsarenko v. Russia*, no. 5235/09, § 68, 3 March 2011; *Trifković v. Croatia*, no. 36653/09, § 121, 6 November 2012; and *Dragin*, cited above, § 112).

The Court sees no reason to doubt the findings of the domestic courts that during the entire period under consideration there was a reasonable suspicion that the applicant had committed the offences with which he had been charged [...]. Although in the domestic proceedings the applicant argued to the contrary, the Court reiterates that 'reasonable suspicion' requires the presence of facts or information which would satisfy an objective observer that the person concerned may have committed the offence (see *Gusinskiy* v. *Russia*, no. 70276/01, § 53, ECHR 2004-IV, and the cases cited therein) and the facts which raise a suspicion justifying arrest under Article 5 of the Convention do not need to be of the same level as those necessary to bring charges or secure a conviction (see *Murray* v. *the United Kingdom*, 28 October 1994, § 55, Series A no. 300-A). The Court considers that that level was reached in the applicant's case.

The domestic courts re-examined the grounds for the applicant's detention every three months and gave reasons why the detention should be further extended. They relied on the following grounds [...]:
(1) the risk of absconding, based on the severity of punishment that the applicant was facing, his lack of strong social ties, and his connections abroad (see also *Sopin* v. *Russia*, no. 57319/10, § § 41–42, 18 December 2012);
(2) the risk of reoffending, based on the seriousness, nature and number of the charges against the applicant, his alleged leading role in the criminal organisation, his prior convictions, and the allegation that criminal activity had been his main source of income (see also *Merčep* v. *Croatia*, no. 12301/12, § 96, 26 April 2016; compare with *Šoš* v. *Croatia*, no. 26211/13, § 95, 1 December 2015);
(3) the particular complexity and large, constantly increasing volume of the case, resulting from a high number of charges, defendants and witnesses (contrast *Kalashnikov* v. *Russia*, no. 47095/99, § 119, ECHR 2002-VI).

The Court considers that the Lithuanian courts thoroughly evaluated all the relevant factors and that they based their decisions on the particular circumstances of the applicant's case, his personal and financial situation, his criminal history and his connections abroad, among others. The reasons relied upon by the domestic courts cannot be said to have been stated *in abstracto*, nor can it be said that they ordered or extended the applicant's detention on identical or stereotypical grounds, using some pre-existing template or formalistic and abstract language (compare and contrast *Khudoyorov* v. *Russia*, no. 6847/02, § § 185–86, ECHR 2005-X; *Boicenco* v. *Moldova*, no. 41088/05, § 143, 11 July 2006; and *Qing* v. *Portugal*, no. 69861/11, § 67, 5 November 2015). Accordingly, the Court is satisfied that the domestic courts did not use 'general and abstract' arguments for the applicant's continued detention and that their reasons were relevant and sufficient.

It remains to be ascertained whether the domestic authorities displayed 'special diligence' in the conduct of the criminal proceedings against the applicant. The Court firstly observes that during the pre-trial investigation, which lasted for almost a year after the applicant's arrest (from 15 December 2009 to 3 December 2010 – [...]), the authorities interviewed over fifty witnesses and other suspects, and carried out multiple other investigative measures which appear to have been necessary and were carried out with sufficient frequency ([...]; compare and contrast *Kalashnikov*, cited above, § 119). Having regard to the fact that the pre-trial investigation concerned multiple crimes allegedly committed by a criminal organisation and was thus of considerable complexity, the Court is of the view that the actions of the domestic authorities during that period could be considered as falling within the standard of special diligence under Article 5 § 3 of the Convention.

However, after the case was transferred to the first-instance court for examination on the merits, the applicant remained in detention on remand for another three years, five months and nineteen days (from 3 December 2010 to 22 May 2014 [...]), during which period fifty-seven hearings were scheduled on a monthly or nearly monthly basis [...]. Bearing in mind that at the start of the court proceedings the applicant had already been detained for a year, the Court is not convinced that scheduling on average one hearing per month displayed sufficient diligence on the part of the authorities (see, *mutatis mutandis*, *Čevizović v. Germany*, no. 49746/99, § 51, 29 July 2004, and *El Khoury v. Germany*, nos. 8824/09 and 42836/12, § 69, 9 July 2015; compare and contrast *Chraidi v. Germany*, no. 65655/01, § 44, ECHR 2006-XII, and *Rażniak v. Poland*, no. 6767/03, §§ 10 and 33, 7 October 2008). The Court further notes that twenty-six of those hearings were adjourned, mainly because of the authorities' failure to ensure the presence of other co-accused or witnesses ([...]; see also *Malkov v. Estonia*, no. 31407/07, § 51, 4 February 2010, and Kobernik v. Ukraine, no. 45947/06, § 62, 25 July 2013; compare and contrast Shikuta v. Russia, no. 45373/05, § 49, 11 April 2013). None of the adjournments or any other delays were imputable to the applicant (see *Kuibishev v. Bulgaria*, no. 39271/98, § 69, 30 September 2004, and *Grujović v. Serbia*, no. 25381/12, § 53, 21 July 2015). As a result of the repeated adjournments, there were several long periods when no hearings were held – from 3 December 2010 to 31 March 2011, from 23 June 2011 to 7 December 2011, from 15 June 2012 to 3 October 2012, from 30 November 2012 to 3 March 2013, from 26 March

2013 to 6 October 2013, and from 26 November 2013 to 16 February 2014 – amounting to a total period of more than two years without a single hearing ([...]; see, *mutatis mutandis, Dervishi* v. *Croatia*, no. 67341/10, § 144, 25 September 2012, and *Süveges*, cited above, § 101; compare and contrast *Sigarev* v. *Russia*, no.53812/10, § 56, 30 October 2014, and *Topekhin* v. *Russia*, no. 78774/13, § 109, 10 May 2016).

While the Court accepts the Government's submission that the criminal proceedings against the applicant were complex and of a large scale, it nonetheless considers that neither their complexity nor the fact that they concerned organised crime can justify detention of such length as in the present case (see, *mutatis mutandis, Veliyev* v. *Russia*, no. 24202/05, § 157, 24 June 2010, and *Chyła* v. *Poland*, no. 8384/08, § § 122–23, 3 November 2015). The authorities have not advanced any exceptional circumstances able to demonstrate otherwise, such as, for example, the need to collect evidence abroad or to request international legal assistance (compare and contrast *Łaszkiewicz* v. *Poland*, no. 28481/03, § 61, 15 January 2008; *Ereren* v. *Germany*, no. 67522/09, § 62, 6 November 2014; and *Merčep*, cited above, § 110). Furthermore, although the domestic courts acknowledged on several occasions that the period of the applicant's detention had been very long [...], it does not appear that any measures were taken to speed up the proceedings. The Court observes that hearings were adjourned mainly because of the absence of witnesses or co-accused [...], and acknowledges that in certain situations that could be justified; however, in the present case the Court does not discern any attempts on the part of the domestic authorities to fix a tighter and more efficient hearing schedule in order to avoid the repeated adjournments (see, *mutatis mutandis, Dzelili* v. *Germany*, no. 65745/01, § 80, 10 November 2005, and *Baksza* v. *Hungary*, no.59196/08, § 38, 23 April 2013). In such circumstances, the Court considers that the domestic authorities did not display special diligence in the conduct of the criminal proceedings against the applicant during the lengthy period of his detention on remand.

Accordingly, there has been a violation of Article 5 § 3 of the Convention.

6/9

In a judgment of 23 May 2017 in *Matiošaitis and others* v. *Lithuania*, application nos. 22662/13, 51059/13, 58823/13, 59692/13, 59700/13, 60115/13, 69425/13 and 72824/13 the ECtHR found a violation of Article 5 Paragraph 3 of the Convention. The Court decided that the applicants' life sentences in the Republic of

Lithuania cannot be regarded as reducible for the purposes of Article 3 of the Convention, thus violating Article 3 of the Convention. The Court reasoned such finding as follows:

> The relevant principles as to imposition of life sentences and rehabilitation and the prospect of release for life prisoners have been summarised in *Murray v. the Netherlands* ([GC] no. 10511/10, § § 99–104, 26 April 2016; see also the case law referred to therein), and, most recently, in *Hutchinson v. the United Kingdom* ([GC], no. 57592/08, § § 42–45, 17 January 2017).
>
> The Court notes at the outset that the applicants in the instant case did not seek to argue that their sentence was, as such, grossly disproportionate to the gravity of their offences, or that there were no longer any legitimate penological grounds for their continued incarceration (see *Vinter and Others*, cited above, § 102). Their grievance was rather directed against the effects of their life sentences.
>
> [...]
>
> In Lithuania, the penalty of life imprisonment has existed since 1990, when the old Criminal Code of 1961 continued to be applied. Although life imprisonment for aggravated murder, a criminal offence of which all the applicants in the present case have been found guilty, was not mentioned in Article 105 of that Code, a court could still impose life imprisonment instead of the death penalty, pursuant to Article 24 thereof. Indeed, this was the situation of the first and sixth applicants, K. Matiošaitis and A. Kazlauskas [...]. Life imprisonment was then introduced as the heaviest punishment for aggravated murder in December 1998, following formal abolition of the death penalty, and remains so according to the new Criminal Code [...].
>
> In the light of its case law, the question for the Court is whether the penalty imposed on the applicants in the present case should be classified as irreducible, or whether there is a prospect of release (see *Vinter and Others*, § 110, *Murray*, § 99 and *Hutchinson*, § 44, all cited above).
>
> *(i) Parole, terminal illness, amnesty and reclassification of sentence*
>
> The Court firstly notes that Lithuanian law does not permit life prisoners to be released on parole, a measure that applies only to prisoners serving

fixed-term sentences [...]. In this connection the Court also observes that life prisoners, including some of the applicants in this case, attempted to raise this issue with the domestic courts of administrative and criminal jurisdiction. Although alleged unconstitutionality underpinned their complaints, those courts either did not consider it necessary to refer the matter to the Constitutional Court of their own motion, or denied such explicit requests by life prisoners altogether [...]. It can likewise be noted that life prisoner R.P. also relied on the Committee of Ministers' Recommendation Rec(2003)22 on conditional release (parole) of 24 September 2003, paragraph 4.a of which clearly indicates that the law should make conditional release available to all sentenced prisoners, including life-sentenced prisoners (the Recommendation is summarised at length in *Kafkaris v. Cyprus* ([GC], no. 21906/04, § 72, ECHR 2008). Furthermore, and contrary to what has been suggested by the Government [...], the Court also considers that the life prisoners' complaints about being discriminated against as well as about being *de facto* condemned to die in prison do not appear to be an *actio popularis* [...]. Indeed, those requests concerned the very situation they were in. The complaint by life prisoner R.P. was lodged with the criminal courts with a view to annulling the prison authorities' concrete refusal to perform a particular action – to collect materials for R.P.'s parole request [...].

The Court has also consistently held that commutation of life imprisonment because of terminal illness, which only means that a prisoner is allowed to die at home or in a hospice rather than behind prison walls, cannot be considered as a 'prospect of release', as the notion is understood by the Court (see *Vinter and Others*, cited above, § 127, and *Öcalan v. Turkey* (no. 2) (nos. 24069/03 and 3 others, § 203, 18 March 2014).

The Court further shares the applicants' and the third-party intervener's view that amnesty may not be regarded as a measure giving life prisoners a prospect of mitigation of their sentence or release. The seven amnesties so far declared by the Seimas did not apply to prisoners convicted of the most serious crimes. Moreover, three of those amnesties explicitly excluded life prisoners from the scope of their application, this fact also having been underlined by the life prisoners [...]. The Government have not provided any information or produced evidence showing that any new draft law on amnesty would be drafted which would include life prisoners and would give them a 'prospect of release' (see *Öcalan*, cited above, § 204). The Court reiterates that European penal policy currently places emphasis on the rehabilitative aim of imprisonment, even in the case of life prisoners (see *Harakchiev and Tolumov* v. *Bulgaria*, nos. 15018/11 and 61199/12, § 245, ECHR 2014 (extracts)). Amnesty, which is an act of general rather than individual application, does not appear to take into account the rehabilitation aspect of each individual prisoner.

The Government argued that the courts could reduce a prisoner's life sentence by reclassifying the sentence under Article 3 of the new Criminal Code. The Court acknowledges that that remedy was successfully used by Mr I.A., whose life sentence was firstly commuted to a fixed-term sentence of twenty-five years, and who was subsequently released on parole [...]. Be that as it may, commutation of a life prisoner's sentence under the new Criminal Code is a one-off possibility [...]. All eligible applicants have asked for it, without success as to the reduction of the duration of their sentence [...]. Accordingly, even if those applicants reformed, Article 3 of the new Criminal Code would not give them any 'prospect of release'.

(ii) Presidential pardon

Having excluded all the other possibilities for mitigating life sentences in Lithuania, the Court finds that a stricter scrutiny of the regulation and practice of presidential pardon, which the Government saw as the most effective measure, is required (see *László Magyar* v. *Hungary*, no. 73593/10, § 56, 20 May 2014).

The Court firstly observes that the present cases are substantially different from that of *Harakchiev and Tolumov* (cited above, § 262), as the legal framework for presidential pardon in Lithuania has remained consistent since it was set up in 1993. The criteria applicable to pardon pleas have remained identical throughout its operation, with the exception of the term which a life prisoner must have served before he can submit a pardon plea, which was extended in 2003 from ten to twenty years. In 2011, that term was reduced by a presidential decree to ten years [...]. That notwithstanding, even a term of twenty years after the imposition of a sentence is shorter than the maximum indicative term of twenty-five years which the Court has found to be acceptable (see *Vinter and Others*, § 120, and *Murray*, cited above, § 99).

The Court further notes that the Pardon Commission regulations had been adopted on 11 January 1993, that is, before any of the applicants in the instant case had been sentenced to capital punishment or to life imprisonment and also before the Convention had entered into force in respect of Lithuania in 1995 [...]. Those regulations were and remain publicly accessible, and all life prisoners are able to consult them, thus increasing the transparency of the pardon procedure and constituting a guarantee contributing to consistency in the exercise of the President's powers in that respect.

Since the day of their approval in 1993, the Pardon Commission regulations have retained the same list of criteria to be taken into account when exercising presidential pardon: the nature of the crime committed, the danger of that crime to society, the personality of the life prisoner, his behaviour and attitude towards work, the time already served, the prison authorities' opinion, the opinion of non-governmental organisations and the prisoner's former employer, as well as other circumstances. The authorities have a general duty to collect the following information about the prisoner and enclose it with the pardon request: the court decisions convicting the prisoner; a detailed assessment (*išsami charakteristika*) of the prisoner's behaviour, including a recommendation by the prison administration. As of 2003, a new criterion has been added: whether the prisoner has compensated for the pecuniary damage caused by the crime he committed [...]. That being so, the Court finds that there is nothing ambiguous or misleading in those rules such as to make the applicants' situation uncertain as to the factors that guide the President in the exercise of his or her power of pardon. The above list can be seen as a set of criteria allowing the President to assess whether a life prisoner's continued imprisonment is justified on legitimate penological grounds. The Court cannot criticise the non-exhaustive nature of the list, for it permits the President to evaluate any other relevant factors, which may be to a life prisoner's benefit. Lastly, the President is advised by the Pardon Commission, including persons that represent the interests of justice, those of prisoners' and crime victims, in order to give a fair recommendation to the President [...].

The Court next turns to the question whether presidential pardon could be regarded as making life sentences reducible *de facto*.

The applicants argued that, in the absence of reasons given to them when their pardon pleas had been refused, they had had no guidance as to how to reform in order to try to persuade the President to pardon them. The Court would emphasise that the opportunity for a prisoner to reform was central to its finding in *Vinter and Others* (cited above). Under Lithuanian law, however, neither the Pardon Commission nor the President of the Republic is bound to give reasons why a life prisoner's pardon plea has been refused (compare and contrast *Hutchinson*, cited above, § 51). Furthermore, and notwithstanding certain hypothetical arguments to the opposite by the Government [...], the Court considers it clear that because of the principle of separation of powers the President's pardon decrees are not subject to judicial review (compare and contrast *Hutchinson*, cited above, § 52). Above all, they cannot be challenged by prisoners directly [...]. This state of affairs is confirmed by the administrative court's response to a complaint by the applicant K. Matiošaitis as well as by the criminal court's reply to life prisoner R.P. [...]. The Government have not proven the legal regulation to be otherwise.

As to the question of transparency of the Pardon Commission's work, the Court recalls that it examined a similar issue in the case of *Harakchiev and Tolumov* (cited above). In that case the Court noted that in Bulgaria in its work the Pardon Commission must explicitly take into account, *inter alia*, relevant case law of international courts and other bodies on the interpretation and application of international human rights instruments in force in respect of that country, to assess whether the prisoner's continued imprisonment is justified on legitimate penological grounds. To increase the transparency of the pardon procedure, the Commission also publishes comprehensive activity reports where it summarises the reasons for its recommendations in individual cases to the authority exercising the power of pardon, as well as relevant statistical information (see *Harakchiev and Tolumov*, cited above, § § 91–107; see also *Hutchinson*, cited above, § 61). In contrast, no such information is made public in Lithuania, except for a general outline of the criteria relevant for the examination of pardon pleas [...], to demonstrate how, if at all, those criteria are practically applied by the President of the Republic. The Court lastly notes that although the latter takes a decision only after the Pardon Commission has provided its recommendations, those recommendations are not legally binding on the President [...].

The applicants gave much weight to the statement on the President's webpage to the effect that 'murderers and other perpetrators of violent crime can hardly expect to be granted pardon'. Although the Court is ready to concede that the aforementioned statement shows the strict stance of the President, who took office in 2009, towards those convicted of the most heinous crimes, it cannot fail to observe that that phrase has been taken out of context. The President's policy statement equally stipulates that 'even persons on whom a life sentence has been imposed may appeal for pardon' [...]. More important for the Court is to note that there is an example of one person in the applicants' situation who has already benefited from the President's discretionary power: in May 2012 the incumbent President granted life prisoner J.B.'s plea by commuting his sentence to a fixed term of twenty-five years [...]. The Court must note, however, that four years have passed since J.B.'s pardon, without one single other life prisoner having been fully or partially pardoned. The Court has already held that in assessing whether the life sentence is reducible *de facto* it may be of relevance to take account of statistical information on prior use of the review mechanism in question, including the number of persons having been granted a pardon (see *Murray*, cited above, § 100, with further references). According to the statistical information provided by the Government, only one out of thirty-five life prisoners who have asked for pardon has received a positive response, whereas in general about one out of five of all pardon pleas are granted [...]. Accordingly, and although the Court is careful not to hold that the President of the Republic should periodically pardon life prisoners, it attaches a certain weight to the applicant's argument that J.B.'s pardon was an isolated exception.

In the light of the above, the Court considers that in Lithuania the presidential power of pardon is a modern-day equivalent of the royal prerogative of mercy, based on the principle of humanity (also see *Harakchiev and Tolumov*, cited above, § 76), rather than a mechanism, with adequate procedural safeguards, for review of the prisoners' situation so that the adjustment of their life sentences could be obtained.

The Court has constantly held that the prisoner's right to a review entails an actual assessment of the relevant information whether his or her continued imprisonment is justified on legitimate penological grounds (see *László Magyar*, § 57, and *Murray*, § 100, both cited above), and the review must also be surrounded by sufficient procedural guarantees (see *Kafkaris*, § 105; *Harakchiev and Tolumov*, § 262; and *Murray* § 100, all cited above). To the extent necessary for the prisoner to know what he or she must do to be considered for release and under what conditions, it may be required that reasons be provided (see *Murray*, cited above, § 100). The Court further observes the CPT's view to the effect that discretionary release from imprisonment, as with its imposition, was a matter for the courts and not the executive, a view which had led to proposed changes in the procedures for reviewing life imprisonment in Denmark, Finland and Sweden (see *Murray*, cited above, § 61). The Statute of the International Criminal Court also states that that court shall review a life sentence if more than twenty-five years have passed since the life prisoner's conviction [...].

In their observations to the Court, the Government suggested that the same criteria as those considered within the pardon proceedings were also relevant when the courts decide the question of life prisoners' transfer to Pravieniškės Correctional Institution. The Court does not dispute this argument. It is ready to accept that during court proceedings for transfer a life prisoner is provided with sufficient procedural guarantees to make his case to prove his repentance and capacity to change [...]. Even so, a life prisoner's transfer to Pravieniškės Correctional Institution changes nothing as concerns the length of his sentence, which remains for life, without raising his hope of being released from prison [...]. The Court also observes that in 2013 two of the applicants, V. Beleckas and R. Lenkaitis, used their right to apply for the President's pardon, albeit without success [...]. Both of them later asked to be transferred to a correctional home, and the Vilnius Regional Court granted their requests, having concluded that these applicants had indeed repented [...]. At this juncture the Court also notes that the Vilnius Regional Court, on the one hand, and the Pardon Commission and/or the President of the Republic, on the other, came to opposite conclusions as to those applicants' capacity to distance themselves from their criminal past, whilst it was only the court which made its reasoning transparent and thus available to these applicants. In this connection the Court underlines that regard must be had to the need to encourage the rehabilitation of offenders (see *James, Wells and Lee v. the United Kingdom*, nos. 25119/09, 57715/09 and 57877/09, § 218, 18 September 2012; *Murray*, cited above, § 102), and that '... a whole-life prisoner is entitled to know ... what he or she must do to be considered for release and under what conditions' (see *Vinter and Others*, cited above, § 122). The Court also observes that the principle of rehabilitation, that is, the reintegration into society of a convicted person, is reflected in international norms [...] and has not only been recognised but has over time also gained increasing importance in the Court's case law under various provisions of the Convention (see *Murray*, cited above, § 102).

As the Government acknowledged, transfer to the Pravieniškės Correctional Home is not a precondition for a pardon plea. Moreover, one cannot disregard the possibility that a life prisoner does not wish to be transferred to a correctional home [...]. In this connection the Court also observes that even in the Pravieniškės Correctional Home life prisoners are held segregated, and separately from other prisoners [...]. Accordingly, and even assuming that the President's reasoning to grant a pardon plea could coincide with the court's reasoning to permit a life prisoner's transfer to Pravieniškės on account of that prisoner's reformed personality, which is not always the case (see the preceding paragraph), a life prisoner who chooses to repent in Lukiškės Prison is left with a conundrum as to what he or she must do to prove to the President his or her rehabilitation.

That said, in the present case the applicants also make a complaint that the regime and conditions of their incarceration did not give them a genuine opportunity to reform themselves in order to try to persuade the President to pardon them [...]. The Court has already held that while Article 3 cannot be construed as imposing on the authorities an absolute duty to provide prisoners with rehabilitation or reintegration programmes and activities, such as courses or counselling, it does require the authorities to give life prisoners a chance, however remote, to some day regain their freedom. The regime and conditions therefore need to be such as to make it possible for the life prisoner to endeavour to reform himself, with a view to being able one day to seek an adjustment of his or her sentence (see *Harakchiev and Tolumov*, cited above, § § 264–265; also see *Murray*, cited above, § 104).

Turning to the situation of life prisoners in Lithuania, the Court observes that at Lukiškės Prison, where life prisoners must first serve ten years of their sentence, a number of social rehabilitation programmes have been set up [...]. Contrary to what has been claimed by the applicants, there is nothing in the file to suggest that the aim of those programmes is to get life prisoners used to spending their entire lives in prison, rather than their social rehabilitation for successful correction and transformation of their personality. Indeed, as the internal prison rules state, the programme of social rehabilitation starts immediately when a convict enters the prison and is aimed at his social rehabilitation with a view to eventual reintegration in society after having served the sentence [...]. In 2012 the CPT also noted that a certain number of positive measures had been taken to expand the programme of life prisoners' activities, and that material conditions in the unit for life-sentenced prisoners remained unchanged since the CPT's visit in 2008 and were acceptable [...].

Without undermining these positive aspects, the Court nevertheless observes that since its visit to Lukiškės Prison twelve years ago the CPT has also constantly highlighted shortcomings in life prisoners' regime which stood in the way of their reform. [...]. Although the CPT had advocated extending the possibilities to have long-term visits to all prisoners, including those serving life sentences, they do not have such a possibility (see point 75 of the cpt report, [...]). In the Court's view, the deleterious effects of such life prisoners' regime must have seriously weakened the possibility of the applicants reforming and thus entertaining a real hope that they might one day achieve and demonstrate their progress and obtain a reduction in their sentence.

The Court reiterates that the mere fact that a prisoner has already served a long term of imprisonment does not weaken the State's positive obligation to protect the public, and that no Article 3 issue could arise if a life prisoner continues to pose a danger to society. This is particularly so for those convicted of murder or other serious offences against the person (see *Vinter and Others*, § 108; also see *Murray*, § 111, both cited above). However, it equally considers that even those who commit the most abhorrent and egregious of acts nevertheless retain their essential humanity and carry within themselves the capacity to change. Long and deserved though their prison sentences may be, they retain the right to hope that, some day, they may have atoned for the wrongs which they have committed. They ought not to be deprived entirely of such hope. To deny them the experience of hope would be to deny a fundamental aspect of their humanity and to do that would be degrading.

The Court also acknowledges that having regard to the margin of appreciation which must be accorded to Contracting States in matters of criminal justice and sentencing, it is not its task to prescribe the form (executive or judicial) which that review should take (see *Vinter and Others*, cited above, § 120; also see *Hutchinson*, cited above, § § 46–50). That being so, the Court nevertheless considers that in order to guarantee proper consideration of the changes and the progress towards rehabilitation made by life prisoners, however significant they might be, the review should entail either the executive giving reasons or judicial review, so that even the appearance of arbitrariness is avoided. The Court has also stated that to the extent necessary for a prisoner to know what he or she must do to be considered for release and under what conditions, it may be required that reasons be provided, and this should be safeguarded by access to judicial review (see *Murray*, cited above, § 100). The Court has already established that presidential pardon in Lithuania *de facto* does not allow a life prisoner to know what he or she must do to be considered for release and under what conditions. It has also noted the absence of judicial review which could lead to full or partial commutation of a life sentence. Accordingly, the Court finds that, at the present time, the applicants' life sentences cannot be regarded as reducible for the purposes of Article 3 of the Convention (see *László Magyar*, cited above, § 58). Last but not least, it transpires that no reform will take place in Lithuania until the Court has resolved this case [...].

In the present case the Court lastly notes that the applicant P. Gervin has served seven years of his life sentence. Therefore, he does not yet fulfil the legislative requirements for applying for presidential pardon [...]. Even so, the Court has already held that in the absence of effective review of a life sentence the incompatibility with Article 3 of the Convention already arises at the moment of the imposition of the life sentence and not at a later stage of incarceration (see *Vinter and Others*, cited above, § 122).

There has accordingly been a violation of Article 3 of the Convention in respect of each of the six applicants.

In a Joint Concurring Opinion Judges Lemmens and Spano Reasoned

We concur in the judgment. However, we consider it necessary to write separately as parts of the reasoning do not, in our opinion, fully reflect the scope and content of the Court's case law in this area as it has developed since the Grand Chamber delivered its judgment in *Vinter and Others v. the United Kingdom* in 2013 ([GC], nos. 66069/09, 130/10 and 3896/10, ECHR 2013 (extracts)).

The fundamental requirement in the Court's case law under Article 3 of the Convention is that life sentences be *de facto* and *de jure* reducible. The crucial element in the assessment of reducibility is whether domestic law provides a person serving a life sentence with a prospect of release based on a dedicated mechanism of review. The review mechanism must be formulated in a manner which mandates that the assessor, whether it be an executive or a judicial organ, examines after a certain period of time whether legitimate penological grounds justify continued imprisonment (see *Vinter and Others*, cited above, § § 119–20). The review mechanism must also take account of progress towards rehabilitation, as the Court emphasised in *Murray v. the Netherlands* ([GC], no. 10511/10, § 100, ECHR 2016).

In the recent Grand Chamber judgment in *Hutchinson v. the United Kingdom* ([GC], no. 57592/08, 17 January 2017), the Court elaborated further on the nature of the review mechanism, its scope and the criteria and conditions for its assessment (§ § 46–65). Firstly, the Court explained that, although the system of review does not necessarily have to be judicial in nature, it has to guarantee the independence and impartiality of the assessor, as well as certain procedural safeguards, and provide protections against arbitrariness. Secondly, the review mechanism must impose a duty on the authority to consider whether legitimate penological grounds justify continued imprisonment, and must not leave the decision fully to that authority's discretion. Thirdly, and in line with the Court's findings in *Murray* (see paragraph 2 above), there needs to be a degree of specificity or precision as to the criteria and conditions attaching to sentence review, in keeping with the requirements of legal certainty. Lastly, to the extent necessary for the prisoner to know what he or she must do to be considered for release and under what conditions, it may also be required that reasons be provided, and this requirement should be safeguarded by access to judicial review (see *Murray*, cited above, § 100).

In two important judgments the Court has applied these fundamental requirements, as regards a Convention-compliant post-conviction review mechanism for those serving life sentences, to presidential pardon or clemency systems in certain Contracting States. In the case of *László Magyar v. Hungary* (no. 73593/10, 20 May 2014), the Court found a violation of Article 3 of the Convention on the basis that the Hungarian presidential pardon system did not conform to the requirements of post-conviction *Vinter* review for three reasons. Firstly, domestic law did not impose any obligation on the President to perform a *Vinter*-type review of the sentence. Secondly, although there was a duty to collect certain information about the prisoner, no criteria had been published in that regard. Thirdly, domestic law did not impose a duty on the Minister of Justice or the President to give reasons.

Subsequently, in the case of *Harakchiev and Tolumov* v. *Bulgaria* (nos. 15018/11 and 61199/12, ECHR 2014 (extracts)), the Court examined the Bulgarian presidential clemency system under Article 3 of the Convention. In so far as the complaint concerned the period between 2004 and 2012, the Court found firstly that it was not clear whether domestic law provided *de jure* for the reducibility of life sentences. Secondly, the life sentence was not *de facto* reducible as the applicant in question could not have known that a mechanism existed that would actually permit him to be considered for release. The Court noted, however, that in 2012 the incumbent President had set up a Clemency Commission. The rules governing the work of the Commission provided that in its work it had to take account of the relevant case law of international courts and other bodies on the interpretation and application of the international human rights instruments in force in respect of Bulgaria. The Commission had published the criteria that would guide it in the examination of clemency requests, as well as the reasons for its recommendations to exercise the power of clemency in individual cases. Also, the Court considered it important that the Constitutional Court had in April 2012 given a binding interpretation of the Constitution that defined the scope of the power of clemency and held that it should be exercised in a non-arbitrary way, taking into account equity, humanity, compassion, mercy and the health and family situation of the convicted offender, and any positive changes in his or her personality. The Constitutional Court had gone on to say that while the President or the Vice-President could not be required to give reasons in individual cases, they were expected to make known the general criteria guiding them in the exercise of the power of clemency. Lastly, the Constitutional Court had held that a clemency decree was open to legal challenge before it, albeit subject to some restrictive conditions, in particular relating to standing. That ruling of the Constitutional Court had thus provided weighty guarantees that the presidential power of clemency would be exercised in a consistent and broadly predictable way. The Court concluded that if the President's power of clemency was exercised in line with the practices adopted by the Clemency Commission and the precepts laid down by the Constitutional Court, then whole-life sentences could be regarded as *de facto* reducible.

In the light of the fundamental requirements of the *Vinter* post-conviction case law of the Court [...], and their application to presidential pardon or clemency systems [...], we consider that the examination by the Court in this type of case should be limited to an abstract review of the general elements of the domestic system for its conformity with the structural requirements for *de jure* and *de facto* reducibility of life sentences. Therefore, the Court's references in the reasoning to the individual circumstances of the applicants in the present case or other life prisoners in Lithuania should not have formed part of the Court's analysis [...]. In other words, in our view, it would have sufficed for the Court to find a violation of Article 3 of the Convention for the following three reasons.

Firstly, while we are prepared to accept that the Pardon Commission Regulations from 1993, as subsequently amended, may conform, as such, to the requirements of clarity under the Court's case law, we note that the Lithuanian system affords the President full and unlimited discretion to grant pardon. His power is not circumscribed by any procedural safeguards, nor are the President or the Parole Commission under a duty to give reasons for their decisions. Also, the practice of the Pardon Commission or the President is not publicly accessible as no reports are issued providing insights into the manner in which they perform their functions.

Secondly, neither domestic law nor judicial practice imposes a positive duty on the Pardon Commission or the President to examine whether legitimate penological grounds justify continued imprisonment, in conformity with the *Vinter* standards.

Thirdly, and importantly, the decisions of the Pardon Commission or the President – the latter enjoying full discretion and neither of these organs providing reasons for its decisions – cannot be subjected to judicial review providing the necessary protection against arbitrariness.

The Court notes at the outset that the applicants in the instant case did not seek to argue that their sentence was, as such, grossly disproportionate to the gravity of their offences, or that there were no longer any legitimate penological grounds for their continued incarceration (see *Vinter and Others*, cited above, § 102). Their grievance was rather directed against the effects of their life sentences.

In a Concurring Opinion Judge Kūris Reasoned

Having dissented in a very recent similar case, *T.P. and A.T.* v. *Hungary* (nos. 37871/14 and 73986/14, 4 October 2016), where the Court found a violation of Article 3 of the Convention on account of the irreducibility of life prison sentences under Hungarian law, I am, however, not able to maintain the same legal position in the instant case, because the present judgment is based on the law of the Convention as it stands today. I am far from being satisfied with that law; to be more precise, I am critical not so much with regard to *what* it says, but more with regard to *how* it has arrived at saying it.

Since *T.P. and A.T.* v. *Hungary* [...], the Court adopted the landmark judgment in *Hutchinson* v. *the United Kingdom* ([GC], no. 57592/08, 17 January 2017), in which (although no violation of Article 3 was found) the Court consolidated its doctrine as to life prisoners' 'right to hope' that their life prison sentences will be reviewed and that, as a consequence, they may be released earlier. *Hutchinson*, just like the instant judgment, goes on to refer to and cite not only *Vinter and Others* v. *the United Kingdom* ([GC], nos. 66069/09, 130/10 and 3896/10, ECHR 2013 (extracts)) and one of the most important post-*Vinter* judgments, *Murray* v. *the Netherlands* ([GC] no. 10511/10, ECHR 2016), but also the earlier judgment in *Kafkaris* v. *Cyprus* (no. 21906/04, ECHR 2008). Applying *Kafkaris* standards (had these (or at least some of them) not become by now a dead letter, one which nevertheless continues to adorn many judgments pertaining to life imprisonment), the examination of the instant case could – and should – have brought about a different result, namely that no violation of Article 3 was to be found. However, under the Court's case law as it has been developed to the present day (most recently in *Hutchinson*), such a finding is no longer possible.

The Court's case law pertaining to life imprisonment continues to be developed further. This has been a breathtakingly fast process. One of the elements of this development, albeit not yet an outstanding one (at least to the outside observer), is the slow but steady and purposeful movement from the admission – as in *Vinter and Others* ([...], § 120), which is, to a much greater extent than the post-*Vinter* case law, permeated with the spirit of the then still recent judgment in *Kafkaris* [...] – that the review of life prison sentences 'should entail *either* the executive giving reasons *or* judicial review, so that even the appearance of arbitrariness is avoided'

([...], emphasis added) to the effective rejection, whenever possible, of the 'executive alternative'. This is so despite repeated verbal assurances that the 'executive alternative' is not impossible, at least in theory. If one looks more attentively at what arguments, employed in earlier cases pertaining to life imprisonment, are selected for recapitulation in later cases or at how the emphasis at times shifts from some arguments to others (even without any of them being rephrased), or at how prominence is given to certain provisions of hard or even soft law that are 'external' to the Convention (see, for instance, paragraph 174 of the judgment), one could perhaps predict that sooner or later this movement will arrive at its logical destination. As to *when*, at last, this will take place, is a matter for the prophets. It is also true that today this logical destination has not yet been reached. For instance, in *Hutchinson* (cited above) the 'executive alternative' was not dismissed, in particular owing to the fact that in the British system the executive *does* provide reasons for not commuting life prison sentences; moreover, these reasons are *amenable to judicial review*. Be that as it may, one cannot but observe how far the case law has moved away from *Kafkaris* (cited above).

Contrary to the British legal and administrative situation, in a legal setting such as that of Lithuania the possibility of Convention-compatible 'executive review' in the (sole) form of presidential pardon no longer seems to be fit for the purposes of compatibility with Article 3, especially given the fact that, as a rule, *no presidential decree* is issued in cases where the life prisoner's plea for pardon is rejected by the President – either following the advice of the Pardon Commission or even in disregard of it. As a former constitutional judge, I am tempted to observe that such a practice of abstention would, to put it mildly, give rise to doubts as to its compatibility with the Lithuanian Constitution, under which '[t]he President of the Republic, implementing the powers vested in him, *shall issue* acts-decrees' (Article 85, emphasis added), but such considerations would be beyond the scope of the instant case. On the other hand, the introduction into the Lithuanian legal system of periodic judicial review of life prison sentences does not appear to be an insurmountable task, albeit one which, for some reasons (to which I shall briefly come back later), the authorities have not yet undertaken. Moreover, introduction of the said judicial review would not require any change to the national Constitution or any fundamental alteration of the institution of presidential pardon, the essence of which, so far, has been clemency or grace. Most importantly, such introduction would be *in conformity with the law of the Convention* as it stands now and even as it will become – if not in theory (the soothing mantra about the possibility of the 'executive alternative' will continue to be repeated), then almost inevitably in practice – in the (perhaps foreseeable) future.

'It is emphatically the province and duty of the judicial department to say what the law is' (*Marbury v. Madison*, 5 U.S. 1 Cranch 137 (1803)). It is a 'dogma or systematized prediction [of what the courts will do] which we call the law' (Oliver Wendell Holmes, Jr., 'The Path of the Law', 10 *Harvard Law Review* 457 (1897)). Or, to cite one of the former US Chief Justices (in a speech before he was made a Justice), Charles Evans Hughes, 'the Constitution is what the judges say it is' ('Addresses and Papers of Charles Evans Hughes, Governor of New York, 1906–1908' (1908), p. 139).

In the same vein, and whether one likes it or not, *the Convention is what the Strasbourg Court says it is*. The 'systematized prediction' (which for O.W. Holmes was the synonym of 'dogma') as to how cases pertaining to life prisoners' 'right to hope' *will* be decided after *Vinter and Others* and *Hutchinson* (both cited above) is there.

Frankly, some ambiguity remains – and is not insignificant. In the science of logic, this ambiguity has a name. It is just one version of what is known as the Cretan (or Epimenides) paradox. *Vinter and Others* and *Kafkaris* (both cited above) – at least those parts of them which deal with the compatibility with Article 3 of an executive pardon as the main instrument for the commutation of life prison sentences (or even the only one, if release on compassionate grounds is not taken into account) – are to some extent at odds with each other and do not cohabit peacefully. They cannot both be relied upon at the same time. To wit, *either* a discretionary executive pardon, which gives no reasons for rejection and is not amenable to judicial review, is sufficient for the purposes of Article 3 (as in *Kafkaris*), *or* it is not (as in *Vinter and Others*). Yet the Court has never acknowledged that *Kafkaris* has been overruled.

But it has.

Under the Court's case law as it stands today, in cases such as the instant one it is the overall 'quality' of the domestic law which is decisive for finding a violation of Article 3, and not so much the conduct of a particular applicant. In fact, that conduct is *completely immaterial* to finding the said violation: if no other form of review of a life prison sentence is provided for in the domestic legislation, offering life prisoners 'hope' for review of their life prison sentences and, consequently, for earlier release, besides pardon by the Head of State or release on compassionate grounds, Article 3 *will* be found to have been violated *from the very moment of imposition of the sentence* on the applicant, with no regard being had as to *when that sentence was imposed*. Such a violation *will* be found irrespective of whether the applicant made *any progress* towards rehabilitation, whether there was *sufficient time* to make such progress and even when he or she *made no efforts at all* towards his or her own rehabilitation. If this sounds like a drastic exaggeration, see *P. and A.T.* v. *Hungary* (cited above). Such is the case law as it has been developed up to the present day.

As to the *contradictio in temporis* whereby such violations may be – and actually *are* – found by the Court to have been committed in the pre-*Vinter* era, that is to say, when the *Kafkaris* principles *really* applied, I dealt with this in my dissenting opinion in *T.P. and A.T.* v. *Hungary* (cited above). With regard to the respondent State in that case, Article 3 was found to have been violated at the time of the imposition of life sentences on the applicants in that case, even in disregard of the Court's own assessment in *Törköly* v. *Hungary* ((dec.), no. 4413/06, 5 April 2011), in which the Court had found the relevant domestic legislative framework *to have complied* with the requirements of Article 3.

In the instant case, the applicants were sentenced to life imprisonment (or to death, but their death sentences were changed to life imprisonment) between 1993 and 2010. At that time the prospects for their earlier release, as provided for in the domestic legislation, were no higher than they are now. Perhaps lower. Yet, under the Court's pre-*Vinter* case law, such a situation *was compatible* then with Article 3. It no longer is.

In my dissenting opinion in *T.P. and A.T.* v. *Hungary* (cited above), I argued that 'the Hungarian courts violated Article 3 *because this Court changed its approach*' and asked whether the domestic courts could and should have foreseen such a development (see paragraph 11 of the dissenting opinion). I doubted it.

The same applies, to a very great extent, to the instant case. Many of my arguments in the said dissenting opinion also apply to the instant judgment, and I shall not repeat them all here.

Still, one important aspect distinguishes the instant case from *T.P. and A.T.* v. *Hungary* (cited above). In that case, the Hungarian authorities could have quite reasonably expected that, in similar subsequent cases against that State, the Court would remain faithful to itself and coherently follow the line of reasoning it had adopted in *Törköly* (cited above) and would not declare that the domestic legislative framework, which was found to be in compliance with the Convention only five years earlier, was no longer in harmony with the latter (this was one of the reasons for my disagreement with the majority in that case). However, the Lithuanian authorities did not have this advantage ('right to hope'?), because the instant case happens to be the first one against Lithuania in which the alleged irreducibility of life imprisonment is challenged.

The Lithuanian authorities clearly had to be aware of the prevailing – and very strong – trend in the post-*Vinter* development of the Court's case law pertaining to the alleged irreducibility of life imprisonment. They were obliged not to dismiss or disregard this trend, but to take it into account, even if this enters into the domain of pro-active penal policy rather than being strictly confined to the domain of the law of the Convention, as interpreted in the pre-*Vinter* case law.

After *Vinter and Others* (cited above), the Court adopted a series of judgments which made it glaringly obvious that the Government's case was doomed to failure. To highlight just a few: *Öcalan* v. *Turkey (no. 2)* (nos. 24069/03, 197/04, 6201/06 and 10464/07, 18 March 2014); *László Magyar* v. *Hungary* (no. 73593/10, 20 May 2014); *Harakchiev and Tolumov* v. *Bulgaria* (nos. 15018/11 and 61199/12, ECHR 2014 (extracts)); *Čačko* v. *Slovakia* (no. 49905/08, 22 July 2014); *Trabelsi* v. *Belgium* (no. 140/10, ECHR 2014 (extracts)); *Murray* (cited above); *T.P. and A.T.* v. *Hungary* (cited above); and, finally, *Hutchinson* (cited above).

It is hard to understand therefore why the Lithuanian authorities chose to tarry until the Court delivered its judgment *in the applicants' case*. They explicitly acknowledged the deliberate character of their procrastination in introducing the indispensable legislative changes [...]. One could surmise that the said procrastination was due to a lack of political will on the part of the legislative authority (and the executive authority, too, because it is the executive branch which initiates most of the bills), as well as to subservience to public opinion which, as publicly available research allows us to conclude, would have been and probably still is very much against the introduction of even a formal possibility of periodic review of life prison sentences. So much against that it could not be comforted by the reminder, as in *Öcalan v. Turkey (no. 2)* (cited above, § 207), that the 'finding of a violation [of Article 3] cannot be understood as giving the applicant the prospect of imminent release' and that the 'national authorities must review, under a procedure to be established by adopting legislative instruments and in line with the principles laid down by the Court in paragraphs 111–113 of its Grand Chamber judgment in the case of *Vinter and Others* ..., whether the applicant's continued incarceration is still justified after a minimum term of detention, either because the requirements of punishment and deterrence have not yet been entirely fulfilled or because the applicant's continued detention is justified by reason of his dangerousness'?

One can speculate as to which will come first: whether the necessary legislative changes will be introduced into the domestic legal system, which would allow for judicial (!) review of life prison sentences, or whether a new case against Lithuania, pertaining to the alleged irreducibility of life imprisonment, will be decided by the Court, in which a violation of Article 3 is found on the same account as in the instant case. Given that, according to the Government's submissions, there are well over a hundred life prisoners in Lithuania [...], such new cases are not at all unlikely.

I have no problem with the Court pointing out to the respondent State in the instant case (as it did with a number of other respondent States in previous cases) that its penal legislation *must* be amended. After all, such amendment would be an important step toward the *humanisation* of the domestic penal law. This is the positive side – undoubtedly so.

What raises concerns is that although the judgment describes in detail – and correctly! – the factual situation of each of the applicants (in the 'Facts' section of the judgment; in this respect the instant judgment is quite some way ahead of and less openly dogmatic, less blinkered than, say, the judgment adopted in *T.P. and A.T. v. Hungary* (cited above)), that factual situation is *in no way taken into account* in the reasoning and the overall assessment of the applicants' individual situation. The Court follows reasoning which (as I already argued in my dissenting opinion in *T.P. and A.T. v. Hungary*) migrates from one case to another and 'uncritically makes personal self-improvement, in essence a moral phenomenon, virtually a matter of a legal trade-off, devoid of the element of sincere repentance' [...] by asserting that 'in cases where the sentence, on imposition, is irreducible under domestic law, it would be *capricious* to expect the prisoner to work towards his own rehabilitation without knowing whether, at an unspecified, future date, a mechanism might be introduced which would allow him, on the basis of that rehabilitation, to be considered for release' (see *Vinter and Others*, cited above, § 122; *László Magyar*, cited above, § 53; and *Harakchiev and Tolumov*, cited above, § 246; emphasis added). The 'capriciousness' clause exempts the Court from examining whether an applicant made any progress on 'working toward his rehabilitation'.

In the instant judgment, the Court did not incorporate verbatim the doctrinal statement quoted above (at least it did not use the word 'capricious' when speaking on its own behalf; but see the arguments of the third-party intervener in paragraph 152 of the judgment). Still, that idea is there.

The applicants complained that although a 'life prisoner was entitled to know, at the start of his sentence, what he must do to be considered for release', the Government 'provided no indication that ... a rehabilitation plan had been drawn up for each applicant to provide the necessary guidance for meaningful reform' and that '[i]n the absence of any such tangible plan for release at least at some point in the future and with no clear indications from the rejection of the pardon plea, [they] had been left in ultimate uncertainty and despair' [...]. The Court uncritically agreed, by the way, without even taking a closer look at these rehabilitation plans so that their 'tangibility' could be examined. What is more, although the Code for the Execution of Sentences and the Rules for Correctional Facilities explicitly require that such plans *must be* in place, and the Government assert that they *are* in place, and although a number of social rehabilitation programmes providing life prisoners with assistance and guidance for meaningful reform are organised at the prison in which the applicants are being held, and the applicants themselves were involved in various programmes of adaptation, social rehabilitation and personality transformation (see paragraphs 101–03 and 144–46 of the judgment), none of this is taken into consideration. The applicants assert that they do not 'know' what they 'must do' – and the Court believes them, whatever the Government say. The Government submit that information about prisoners' personality and behaviour, and the results of their social rehabilitation, is kept in their prison file [...], but the applicants (two of them) argue that they were not shown their character assessments [...]. But did the applicants ask for this information? They do not say so. Which means that they did not ask. Still, the Court prefers the applicants' assertion to that of the Government. As if it were obvious that one can win the lottery without buying a ticket. The applicants' progress toward rehabilitation, if any, was likewise not looked into by the Court. It was not even considered, even incidentally, whether, objectively, there had been sufficient time for them to make such progress, at least with regard to some of the applicants who, at the time their applications were lodged with the Court, had served only three and a half years of their prison sentence [...]. The Court merely found it established that 'presidential pardon in Lithuania *de facto* does not allow a life prisoner to know what he or she must do to be considered for release and under what conditions' [...].

To say that expecting a prisoner to work towards rehabilitation if he is not promised the prospect of release is 'capricious' is an *overstatement* (here I repeat what I wrote in my dissenting opinion in *T.P. and A.T.* (paragraph 15)). If it is 'capricious' to expect a prisoner to work towards his own rehabilitation without what amounts to a 'legislative promise' that he will be 'considered for release', and if, moreover, it is 'capricious' to expect that a life prisoner himself should know, from the outset of his sentence, 'what he must do to be considered for release and under what conditions, including when a review of his sentence will take place or may be sought' (see *Vinter and Others*, cited above, § 122), then really *nothing else matters*. Neither *when* the life prison sentence was imposed, nor *for what* it was imposed, *nor* whether the prisoner made *any progress* towards rehabilitation, nor whether he *made any efforts* towards rehabilitation, nor the *legitimate expectations of society*, whatever they may be. What matters is the 'legislative promise' (or the absence thereof) and the predictability of its being kept.

Thus, the finding of a violation of Article 3 in this case (as well as in a number of other similar cases) is – and *will* be – based on the fact that the 'quality' of the domestic law was insufficient for the purposes of Article 3, as interpreted in the Court's case law, because the domestic law does not provide for the possibility of review of life imprisonment sentences. *The applicant's conduct does not matter at all, let alone his progress towards rehabilitation.*

But that conduct warrants being looked into – both as a matter of principle and in the instant case.

If and when one looks into the *actual* conduct of the applicants, one can hardly continue to believe, let alone aver, that they did not 'know what [they must] do to be considered for release and under what conditions' [...]. Even conceding that some of them might not know everything they *must do*, they definitely knew – or should have known! – what they must *not do*, but nevertheless *did*. The things that some of the applicants *actually* did would *disqualify* them from being considered for release *in any legislative setting*.

[...]

So if any life prisoner (not necessarily any of the five [...]) argues that his personality has been transformed for the better to the extent that he is now ready for fully-fledged reintegration into society as a valuable member, but does not know what to do in order to be eligible for earlier release, albeit by way of presidential pardon, here – in a nutshell – are some tips. Begin by erasing the criminal sub-culture from your personality by not regarding other people as belonging to lower castes. Fully admit your guilt for the crimes committed. Feel remorse for what you have done. Make serious resolutions about it. Do not commit disciplinary violations. Do not hide prohibited objects in your cell, especially knives or sharpened pieces of tin. Do not consume alcohol in prison – it is illegal. Do not behave in such a way that the authorities have reasonable grounds to believe that you will attempt to escape. And, of course, do not use physical violence against anyone. Trying to kill someone is also a no-no. Is it 'capricious' to expect that persons spending their life behind bars ought to know this? Of course, the list is not exhaustive.

I do not want to generalise and to draw the same conclusion as to the disqualifying nature of the applicants' conduct regarding each and every one of them. In particular, the case file does not contain any *prima facie* disqualifying information regarding the second applicant, Mr Maksimavičius. Still, having been sentenced to death in 1993 and having had this sentence changed to life imprisonment in 1995 (*a propos*, by way of a presidential pardon(!), see paragraphs 16 and 17 of the judgment), this applicant (the longest-serving of all of them) has not yet completed the period of twenty-five years which, according to the Court's case law, is the maximum indicative term after which the sentence has to be first reviewed (see *Vinter and Others*, cited above, § 120, and *Murray*, cited above, § 99). This, however, does not mean that the review of his sentence, albeit by way of presidential pardon, could not take place earlier (and, indeed, he could plead for presidential pardon after serving ten years of his sentence, as provided for by the domestic legislation). It is not clear, however, why his pleas for pardon were rejected in 2012 and 2014 (see paragraph 20 of the judgment). This applicant claims that his plea was rejected despite a positive character assessment, and that he was left with an 'open question as to *what else* he must do, and *how* and *in what manner* he should *seek to improve in order to demonstrate* that he posed no danger to society and was ready to be re-integrated' [...]. This is rather convincing, even very convincing (at least, if the eternal philosophical question as to the goals of punishment is set aside). Here, one might say, a *real* problem exists – and not only that of the particular prisoner's rights, but also of the transparency of executive decisions.

As to the other two applicants not yet mentioned, Mr Gervin and Mr Svotas (the seventh and eighth applicants), they were sentenced to life imprisonment in 2010 and are still not entitled to apply for presidential pardon. At the time their applications were lodged with the Court, they had served only three and a half years each [...]. Could they realistically expect to be released at that stage? Most likely not.

Are the complaints of these two applicants also rooted in the fact that they do not 'know what [they must] do to be considered for release and under what conditions' [...]? Well, there are two things which they *really* know – or at least *should* know – that they must *do*: (i) serve some considerable period of time in prison (yes, considerable, because, after all, it was not the theft of a bike that they were convicted of) and (ii) do it without breaking prison rules. It is not 'capricious' at all to expect them to have *this* knowledge. As it transpires from the case file – and I observe this to the benefit of these two applicants – they have successfully complied, so far, with the second condition. As to the first one, it *must* be met too, and it is not 'capricious' at all for the State to require this, especially bearing in mind that the State – let it not be forgotten – also represents the victims of the crimes of life prisoners, including those whose lives were deprived of *any hope* when their dear ones were murdered by those who claim their 'right to hope' (not only the two applicants dealt with here). What about some balancing of these two hopes? Unfortunately, there is not a trace of such remembrance of the victims in the Court's post-*Vinter* case law.

Also, Mr Katkus [...], although eligible, did not apply for presidential pardon. Had he applied for it, it is very unlikely that his plea would have been granted, given that he admitted his guilt only 'partly' [...].

How then is it possible *in all seriousness* (?!) to believe and assert that, at least with regard to these three applicants (Mr Gervin, Mr Svotas and Mr Katkus), there were 'no clear indications from the *rejection* of the pardon plea' and that it was the absence of these 'clear indications' which left the applicants 'in ultimate uncertainty and despair' [...]? And how is it possible *with no less seriousness* to believe and assert that the other applicants, with the possible exception of Mr Maksimavičius, especially given their disciplinary record while in prison (and in the case of Mr Kazlauskas even his criminal record), did not know what the factual basis was for the rejection of their pleas? Did they not themselves contribute to their alleged 'despair'?

I do not intend to suggest that all the applicants should necessarily have had their pleas for presidential pardon rejected on certain disqualifying grounds, or that those of the applicants who fully admitted their guilt and showed remorse and whose conduct was not tainted by various disciplinary violations, let alone crimes, should have had to wait for an inordinate number of years to submit such pleas. The Lithuanian legal framework is really in great need of improvement as regards the very restricted possibility for commutation of life prison sentences.

My major concern (in addition to the *contradictio in temporis* dealt [...] above, but also – even more extensively – in my dissenting opinion in *T.P. and A.T.* v. *Hungary* (cited above)) is that the Court's case law pertaining to the alleged irreducibility of life imprisonment has been developed to the point where the Court confines itself to the examination and assessment *not of the actual infringement* of an applicant's rights under the Convention, but of the 'quality' of domestic law alone. Which equates, in Hans Kelsen's words, to be(com)ing not a 'court of men' but a 'court of norms' – a characteristic which, so far, has been reserved for constitutional courts. Was that the intention of the founders?

One does not need to re-read David Hume to appreciate that there is a great difference between 'ought' and 'is', between *Sollen* and *Sein*, between *devoir-être* and *être*. It goes without saying that the application, to a particular person, of even a 'very good' law does not guarantee that that person's right under the Convention will not *actually* be violated. In the same vein, the application of even a 'very bad' law does not automatically mean that the right of a particular person has actually been violated. It is by no means impossible that that person himself or herself may have contributed to the fact that the right in question *cannot be enforced* in his or her case, *whatever legislative framework is in place*. Nor is it impossible that the actual conduct of a person and the lack of efforts and progress (which – let it be stressed once again – requires time) towards changing that conduct to make it more socially acceptable may mean that what, in the abstract sense, is the right under the Convention is not the enforceable right which *that* person *actually* enjoys.

By construing and applying the Convention, in so far as the latter sets forth requirements pertaining to life imprisonment (but, alas, also in relation to an increasing number of other aspects), in such a manner that *the facts pertaining to the applicants' situation no longer matter* (even if they are absolutely correctly described in the relevant part of the judgment), and confining itself to the examination and assessment – effectively, *in abstracto* – of the domestic legislative setting, the Court resembles – time and again, and more and more – *the supranational constitutional court which it was not meant to be(come)*.

6/10

In a judgment of 13 June 2017 in *Šimkus* v. *Lithuania*, application no. 41788/11 the ECtHR found a violation of Article 4 § 1 of Protocol No. 7 to the Convention. The court found a violation of the *ne bis in idem* principle because the applicant had been tried in criminal proceedings, for the same offence, for which he had been given an administrative penalty. The Court reasoned as follows:

(a) Whether proceedings for minor hooliganism were criminal in nature

The Court reiterates that the legal characterisation of the procedure under national law cannot be the sole criterion of relevance for the applicability of the *ne bis in idem* principle under Article 4 § 1 of Protocol No. 7. Otherwise, the application of this provision would be left to the discretion of the Contracting States to a degree that might lead to results incompatible with the object and purpose of the Convention. The notion of 'penal procedure' in the text of Article 4 § 1 of Protocol No. 7 must be interpreted in the light of the general principles concerning the corresponding words 'criminal charge' and 'penalty' in Articles 6 and 7 of the Convention respectively (see *Igor Tarasov* v. *Ukraine*, no. 44396/05, § 24, 16 June 2016, and the case law cited therein).

The Court's established case law sets out three criteria, commonly known as the 'Engel criteria', to be considered in determining whether or not there was a 'criminal charge' for Convention purposes. The first criterion is the legal classification of the offence under national law, the second is the very nature of the offence, and the third is the degree of severity of the penalty that the person concerned risks incurring (see *Engel and Others* v. *the Netherlands*, 8 June 1976, § § 82–83, Series A no. 22, and *A and B* v. *Norway* [GC], nos. 24130/11 and 29758/11, § § 105–07, 15 November 2016, ECHR 2016).

Under Lithuanian law, the offence of minor hooliganism under Article 174 of the Code of Administrative Offences was characterised as 'administrative'. Nonetheless, the Court is of the view that its nature can be regarded as criminal within the meaning of Article 4 § 1 of Protocol No. 7. As submitted by the Government, punishment for minor hooliganism served to protect public order and peace [...] – values and interests which often fall within the sphere of protection of criminal law (see *Sergey Zolotukhin* v. *Russia* [GC], no. 14939/03, § 55, ECHR 2009). Furthermore, that provision of the Code of Administrative Offences was directed towards all citizens rather than towards a group possessing a special status, and its primary aims were punishment and deterrence, which are recognised as characteristic features of criminal penalties (see *Sergey Zolotukhin, ibidem*, and *Milenković* v. *Serbia*, no. 50124/13, § 35, 1 March 2016). The Court also observes that the reference to the 'minor' nature of the act does not in itself exclude its classification as 'criminal' in the autonomous sense of the Convention, as there is nothing in the Convention to suggest that the criminal nature of an offence necessarily requires a certain degree of seriousness (see *Ezeh and Connors* v. *the United Kingdom* [GC], nos. 39665/98 and 40086/98, § 104, ECHR 2003-X, and *Sergey Zolotukhin, ibidem*).

As to the severity of the measure, the Court reiterates that it is determined by reference to the maximum potential penalty provided for in the relevant law. Where that penalty involves the loss of liberty, there is a presumption, which can be rebutted entirely exceptionally, that the charges against the applicant are 'criminal'. While the actual penalty imposed on the applicant is relevant to the determination, it cannot diminish the importance of what was initially at stake (see *Sergey Zolotukhin*, cited above, § 56). In the present case, Article 174 of the Code of Administrative Offences provided for thirty days of detention as the maximum penalty [...]. Thus, irrespective of the fact that the applicant was given a warning (see paragraph 11 above), the Court considers that the maximum potential penalty for the offence of minor hooliganism was of sufficient severity to make those proceedings 'criminal' within the meaning of Article 4 § 1 of Protocol No. 7 (see *Milenković*, cited above, § 36). The Court also observes that the Government did not submit any arguments to the contrary.

Accordingly, the Court concludes that the administrative proceedings against the applicant concerning minor hooliganism fell within the ambit of 'penal procedure' for the purposes of Article 4 § 1 of Protocol No. 7 to the Convention.

(b) Whether there was a duplication of proceedings (*bis*)

The Court reiterates that the aim of Article 4 § 1 of Protocol No. 7 is to prohibit the repetition of criminal proceedings that have been concluded by a 'final' decision, that is to say a decision which has acquired the force of *res judicata* and against which no further ordinary remedies are available (see *Gradinger v. Austria*, 23 October 1995, § 53, Series A no. 328-C; *Franz Fischer v. Austria*, no.37950/97, § 22, 29 May 2001; and *Sergey Zolotukhin*, cited above, § § 107–08).

In the present case, the administrative proceedings against the applicant were concluded when he was given a penalty on 18 December 2006. That decision of the Jurbarkas District Court was not appealed against and became final within ten days [...]. Meanwhile the criminal proceedings against him, which had been opened on 23 July 2006 [...], continued until 6 September 2011, before being terminated as time-barred [...]. Thus, the two sets of proceedings coincided in time, and the criminal proceedings continued after the decision ordering the administrative penalty had become final. The Court observes that the domestic authorities acknowledged on multiple occasions that the applicant had already been given an administrative penalty, although they eventually decided that it did not preclude the continuation of the criminal proceedings ([...]; compare and contrast *A and B v. Norway*, cited above, § § 121–34 and 144–47). Accordingly, it finds that the domestic authorities permitted the duplication of proceedings against him in the full knowledge of his previous administrative penalty. In this connection the Court also observes that, contrary to the Government's submissions [...], it is immaterial that the criminal proceedings did not end in conviction because Article 4 § 1 of Protocol No. 7 contains not only the right not to be punished twice but also extends to the right not to be prosecuted or tried twice (see *Sergey Zolotukhin*, cited above, § 83, and *Kapetanios and Others v. Greece*, nos. 3453/12 et al., § 63, 30 April 2015).

(c) Whether the offences for which the applicant was prosecuted were the same (*idem*)

The Court reiterates that Article 4 § 1 of Protocol No. 7 prohibits the prosecution or trial of a second 'offence' in so far as it arises from identical facts or facts which are substantially the same (see *Sergey Zolotukhin*, § 82, and *A and B v. Norway*, § 108, both cited above). The Court has also held that the approach which emphasises the legal characterisation of the two offences is too restrictive on the rights of the individual and risks undermining the guarantee enshrined in Article 4 § 1 of Protocol No. 7 (see *Sergey Zolotukhin*, cited above, § 81, and *Boman v. Finland*, no. 41604/11, § 33, 17 February 2015). Accordingly, it cannot accept the Government's argument (see paragraph 38 above) that the duplication of proceedings in the present case was justified by the distinct legal characteristics of the administrative and criminal offences (see also *Rivard v. Switzerland*, no. 21563/12, § 26, 4 October 2016).

The Court notes that in the administrative proceedings the applicant was punished for using swearwords in the presence of law enforcement officers, and in the criminal proceedings he was charged with threatening to murder or seriously injure law enforcement officers and with insulting those officers. Both proceedings referred to the words and statements spoken by the applicant in the hospital on the night of 23 July 2006 in the presence of the border officers guarding K.B. [...], while the criminal charges additionally included the telephone conversation between the applicant and an officer on that same night [...].

The Government submitted that the administrative offence of minor hooliganism was committed when a person used swearwords in a public place, irrespective of whether those swearwords were threatening or insulting to anyone in particular, whereas the criminal offences with which the applicant had been charged consisted of threats and insults directed at other persons but did not require the use of swearwords [...]. The Court observes, however, that the administrative and criminal proceedings against the applicant addressed the same words and statements spoken in the hospital on the same night in the presence of the same officers – it was alleged that the swearwords had contained threats and insults towards those officers. It cannot therefore be said that the applicant was given an administrative penalty for some of his statements and charged with criminal offences for some other statements (see, *mutatis mutandis*, *Sergey Zolotukhin*, cited above, § 97; *Butnaru and Bejan-Piser* v. *Romania*, no. 8516/07, § § 37–38, 23 June 2015; and *Milenković*, cited above, § § 40–41; contrast with *Dungveckis* v. *Lithuania*, no. 32106/08, § 44, 12 April 2016). Furthermore, although the criminal charges also included additional facts, namely the telephone conversation between the applicant and an officer [...], that does not change the fact that the criminal charges embraced the facts of the administrative offence of minor hooliganism in their entirety and that, conversely, the administrative offence did not contain any facts not contained in the criminal charges (see, *mutatis mutandis*, *Sergey Zolotukhin*, cited above, § 97, and *Khmel* v. *Russia*, no. 20383/04, § 65, 12 December 2013).

Accordingly, the Court concludes that the facts which constituted the basis for the administrative and the criminal proceedings against the applicant were substantially the same for the purposes of Article 4 § 1 of Protocol No. 7.

(d) Conclusion

The foregoing considerations are sufficient to enable the Court to conclude that the applicant was tried twice for the same offence. It stresses in this respect that neither the text of Article 4 of Protocol No. 7 nor the Court's case law allows for any exceptions to the *ne bis in idem* principle. While it is in the first place for the Contracting States to choose how to organise their legal systems, including their criminal justice procedures (see *A and B* v. *Norway*, cited above, § 120), the system chosen must not contravene the principles set forth in the Convention (see *Taxquet* v. *Belgium* [GC], no. 926/05, § 83, ECHR 2010, and the case law cited therein). In this connection the Court also observes that Lithuanian law appears unambiguous in stating that a person who has been held administratively liable cannot be held criminally liable for the same offence [...] and that the annulment of a previous administrative penalty after a criminal conviction would not render the proceedings in compliance with the *ne bis in idem* principle [...]. The Court therefore cannot accept the Government's submission [...] that the duplication of proceedings against the applicant for the same offence was justified.

There has accordingly been a violation of Article 4 § 1 of Protocol No. 7 to the Convention.

6/11

In a judgment of 13 June 2017 in *Kosteckas* v. *Lithuania*, application no. 960/13 the ECtHR assessed whether the authorities had failed to effectively investigate and prosecute the individuals who had assaulted the applicant. The ECtHR found a violation of Article 3 of the Convention under its procedural limb and provided reasoning as follows:

> The Court notes at the outset that during the assault the applicant sustained multiple contusions on his face and head, his nose was broken, and he was granted four days off work on sick leave [...]. In addition, the assault on the applicant occurred in a public place – a petrol station – with more than ten witnesses present [...], which was bound to arouse in him feelings of humiliation and helplessness, diminishing his dignity (see, *mutatis mutandis, Ceachir* v. *the Republic of Moldova*, no. 50115/06, § 47, 10 December 2013, and *Basenko* v. *Ukraine*, no. 24213/08, § 60, 26 November 2015). The Court also notes that the Government did not question the extent of the applicant's injuries, nor did they argue that those injuries had not been sufficiently grave to fall within the scope of Article 3 of the Convention. Accordingly, the Court concludes that the violent treatment to which the applicant was subjected on 17 February 2007 reached the minimum level of severity under Article 3 of the Convention and raised the Government's positive obligations under that provision.

> In this connection the Court reiterates that Article 3 of the Convention requires that the authorities conduct an effective official investigation

into alleged ill-treatment even if such treatment has been inflicted by private individuals (see *O'Keeffe*, cited above, § 172). The procedural obligation under Article 3 of the Convention requires that any investigation should in principle be capable of leading to the establishment of the facts of the case and to the identification and punishment of those responsible for an offence. This is not an obligation of result, but one of means. The authorities should have taken the reasonable steps available to them to secure the evidence concerning the incident, such as by taking witness statements and gathering forensic evidence (see *N.D. v. Slovenia*, no. 16605/09, § 57, 15 January 2015, and the cases cited therein).

The Court also reiterates that promptness by the authorities in reacting to complaints is an important factor. In previous judgments the Court has given consideration to matters such as the time taken to open investigations, delays in identifying witnesses or taking statements, and the unjustified protraction of criminal proceedings, resulting in expiry of the statute of limitations (ibid.). Moreover, where the investigation leads to charges being brought before the national courts, the positive obligations under Article 3 of the Convention extend to the trial stage of the proceedings. In such cases the proceedings as a whole, including the trial stage, must meet the requirements enshrined in Article 3. In this respect, the Court reiterates that, regardless of the final outcome of the proceedings, the protection mechanisms available under domestic law should operate in practice in a manner allowing for examination of the merits of a particular case within a reasonable time (ibid., § 58, and the cases cited therein).

Turning to the circumstances of the present case, the Court notes that the case before the domestic authorities does not appear to have been particularly complex: it concerned one incident between two relatively small groups of individuals, the incident had been recorded on the petrol station's camera, and the number of witnesses was not excessive. The investigating authorities established the relevant circumstances and identified three suspects within a few months [...]. The duration of the pre-trial investigation was less than eleven months (from the applicant's complaint on 17 February 2007 until the issuing of the indictment on 10 January 2008 [...]) and thus cannot be considered excessive. In addition, the applicant himself explicitly stated that he did not have any complaints concerning the pre-trial investigation [...]. In those circumstances, the Court sees no reason to find that the pre-trial investigation by the domestic authorities was ineffective.

After the indictment was issued, examination of the criminal case before the domestic courts lasted for more than four years and five months, until it was finally discontinued as time-barred on 28 June 2012 [...]. Although it cannot be said that the courts were inactive during that period, the delay was mainly caused by re-examination of the case after it had been remitted by a higher court. The Skuodas District Court's judgment of 17 December 2009, which convicted the alleged perpetrators [...], was quashed by the higher court on the grounds that the district court had committed grave breaches of the Code of Criminal Procedure – it had not provided sufficient reasons for the conviction but had merely copied the description of the charges from the indictment, it had not assessed all the testimony and other evidence in detail, and had not explained why some evidence had been considered reliable and some not [...]. After the Skuodas District Court re-examined the case and adopted a new judgment on 5 May 2011 [...], the higher court once again quashed the judgment because of grave breaches of the Code of Criminal Procedure – this time it held that the district court had violated the rights of the accused by *de facto* changing the charges against them, and that it had failed to make any findings in respect of one of the victims [...]. The Court sees no reason to doubt the assessment of the Klaipėda Regional Court that those errors were indeed grave, and considers that they cannot be classified as being of a purely procedural nature. It reiterates that the repetition of orders for remittal within the same set of proceedings, where such orders have been given because of errors committed by the lower courts, may reveal a serious deficiency in the judicial system (see *Wierciszewska v. Poland*, no. 41431/98, § 46, 25 November 2003; *Huseinović v. Slovenia*, no. 75817/01, § 25, 6 April 2006; *Marini v. Albania*, no. 3738/02, § 145, 18 December 2007; and *Kaçiu and Kotorri v. Albania*, nos. 33192/07 and 33194/07, § 154, 25 June 2013; see also *Ceachir*, cited above, § 50). In this particular case the Government have not provided any explanation that would lead the Court to reach a different conclusion.

The Court also notes that after the case was remitted for re-examination for the second time on 5 August 2011, less than seven months remained until the expiry of the statute of limitations [...]. In such circumstances the Court considers that the domestic courts should have acted diligently and at a reasonable pace in order to examine the merits of the case and adopt a judgment before the prosecution became time-barred (see, *mutatis mutandis, Velev v. Bulgaria*, no. 43531/08, § 58, 16 April 2013). However, the statute of limitations eventually expired and the criminal proceedings were discontinued, without a final judgment on the merits [...]. In this connection the Court reiterates that the purpose of providing effective protection against acts of ill-treatment cannot be achieved where the criminal proceedings are discontinued owing to the fact that the prosecution has become time-barred and where this has occurred, as in the present case, as a result of flaws in the actions of the relevant State authorities (see *Valiulienė v. Lithuania*, no. 33234/07, § 85, 26 March 2013).

In those circumstances, the Court finds that the examination of the criminal case against the alleged perpetrators of the assault on the applicant before the domestic courts was not consistent with the State's positive obligations under Article 3 of the Convention.

The Government also argued that the shortcomings in the criminal proceedings had been remedied by the compensation awarded to the applicant from the alleged perpetrators in subsequent civil proceedings, and cited the Court's case law under Article 2 of the Convention in which civil-law remedies had been considered sufficient [...]. However, the Court observes that the cases invoked by the Government (*Calvelli and Ciglio*, *Vo* and *Šilih*, all mentioned above) concerned injuries caused by the negligent acts of private individuals. In contrast, in cases such as the present one, where the applicants were injured by the deliberate, violent acts of other individuals, the Court has repeatedly held that compensation awarded in civil proceedings could not be considered sufficient for the fulfilment of the State's positive obligations under Article 3 of the Convention, as it is aimed at awarding damages rather than identifying and punishing those responsible (see *Biser Kostov v. Bulgaria*, no. 32662/06, § 72, 10 January 2012; *Dimitar Shopov v. Bulgaria*, no. 17253/07, § 39, 16 April 2013; *Aleksandr Nikonenko v. Ukraine*, no. 54755/08, § 41, 14 November 2013; and *Stoev and Others v. Bulgaria*, no. 41717/09, § 50, 11 March 2014). The Court sees no reason to depart from that approach in the present case.

The foregoing considerations are sufficient to enable the Court to conclude that there has been a violation of Article 3 of the Convention under its procedural limb.

6/12

In a judgment of 27 June 2017 in *Jankauskas v. Lithuania* (No. 2), application no. 50446/09, the ECtHR found no violation of Article 8 of the ECHR, considering that dismissal of the applicant from the list of trainee advocates and restrictions on him practising law as an advocate due to lack of high moral character had not interfered with his right to respect for his private life, because such measure did not exceed what was "necessary in a democratic society" for pursuing the legitimate aim of protecting the rights of others by ensuring the good and proper functioning of the justice system. The ECtHR reasoned the non-violation of Article 8 of the ECHR, as follows:

> The parties have disputed whether the decision to dismiss the applicant from the list of trainee advocates had an impact on his professional activities and thus on his private life. Whilst acknowledging that the applicant, who had a degree in law [...], could practise law in the private sector both before and after his dismissal, the Court nevertheless notes that even before his dismissal as a trainee advocate, there were certain strains over his working in that role in Šiauliai [...]. It is not unreasonable to hold that the Bar Association's decision to dismiss the applicant, together with the reasons given by the Court of Honour and the civil courts, only additionally dented the applicant's name [...], which must have further hampered his professional reputation (see *Milojević and Others v. Serbia*, nos. 43519/07 and two others, § 60, 12 January 2016, and *Oleksandr Volkov v. Ukraine*, no. 21722/11, § 166, ECHR 2013).
>
> That being so, the Court will proceed on the assumption that the applicant's dismissal as a trainee advocate constituted an interference with his right to respect for his private life within the meaning of Article 8 of the Convention.
>
> [...]
>
> The above-mentioned interference will be in breach of Article 8 of the Convention unless it can be justified under paragraph 2 of Article 8 as being 'in accordance with the law', pursuing one or more of the legitimate aims listed therein, and being 'necessary in a democratic society' in order to achieve the aim or aims concerned (see *S.H. and Others v. Austria* [GC], no. 57813/00, § 89, CEDH 2011).
>
> [...]
>
> The Court firstly notes that the Court of Honour and the civil courts relied on Article 8 (4) of the Law on the Bar when holding that the applicant was not of high moral character [...]. Contrary to the applicant's assertion, the disciplinary sanction was not based on Article 8 (1) of that

law, which at the material time read that a person may not become an advocate because of a criminal conviction [...]. Furthermore, the Court of Appeal also relied on points 12.1 and 13.2 of the Code of Ethics, which also applies to trainee advocates [...], and which, as considered by the Court of Appeal and the Supreme Court, also applied to the applicant's situation [...]. The courts also referred to numerous other provisions of the Law on the Bar, of the Code of Ethics, and the Supreme Court's case law to explain their decisions that the applicant did not meet the criteria applicable to candidates to the bar [...]. The Court therefore finds that the interference was prescribed by law within the meaning of Article 8 § 2 of the Convention.

[...]

The Court also accepts the Government's argument [...] that the interference in question served the aim of protecting the rights of others. That was also noted by the Court of Honour, and reiterated by the Vilnius Regional Court and the Supreme Court, which underlined advocates' obligations towards society and the need to safeguard the good functioning of the justice system overall [...].

[...]

At the outset the Court reiterates the most important role played by lawyers in the administration of justice (see, on this point, *Schöpfer v. Switzerland*, 20 May 1998, § § 29–30, Reports 1998-III; *Nikula v. Finland*, no. 31611/96, § 45, ECHR 2002-II; *Amihalachioaie v. Moldova*, no. 60115/00, § 27, ECHR 2004-III; *Kyprianou v. Cyprus* [GC], no. 73797/01, § 173, ECHR 2005-XIII; and *André and Another v. France*, no. 18603/03, § 42, 24 July 2008; all cited in *Morice v. France* [GC], no. 29369/10, § 132, ECHR 2015). The Court has also held that for members of the public to have confidence in the administration of justice they must have confidence in the ability of the legal profession to provide effective representation (see *Kyprianou*, cited above, § 175).

That special role of lawyers, as independent professionals, in the administration of justice entails a number of duties and restrictions, particularly with regard to their professional conduct, which must be discreet, honest and dignified (see *Casado Coca v. Spain*, 24 February 1994, § 46, Series A no. 285-A; *Steur v. the Netherlands*, no. 39657/98, § 38, ECHR

2003-XI; *Veraart* v. the *Netherlands*, no. 10807/04, § 51, 30 November 2006; and *Morice*, cited above, § 133).

The Court has also held that any criminal proceedings entail certain consequences for the private life of an individual who has committed a crime. They are compatible with Article 8 of the Convention provided that they do not exceed the normal and inevitable consequences of such a situation (see *Karov*, cited above, § 88).

Turning to the circumstances of this case, the Court notes that the domestic courts' findings that the applicant was not of high moral character were based on consistent domestic case law, which emphasises the high standards applicable to the profession of advocate [...]. In fact, the domestic authorities underlined that the applicant had committed his crimes while working in law enforcement, and that those crimes had been extremely cynical in nature, which obviously contradicted the requirements of professional ethics [...]. The Court also notes that in 2000, in finding the applicant guilty, the Šiauliai Regional Court also prohibited him from working in law enforcement and the justice system for five years [...]. Given the nature of the crimes the applicant committed, the Court does not consider it unreasonable that first the Court of Honour and then the civil courts found that it was inappropriate to regard the applicant as being a person of high moral character so as to qualify to work in the justice system. In that connection, the Court notes that in its Recommendation R (2000) 21, the Committee of Ministers of the Council of Europe has emphasised that the profession of an advocate must be exercised in such a way that it strengthens the rule of law [...]. Furthermore, the principles applicable to the advocate's profession contain such values as the dignity and honour of the legal profession, the integrity and good standing of the individual advocate, respect towards professional colleagues, as well as respect for the fair administration of justice [...]. The Court has already noted that the applicant's crimes caused strains with his former colleagues [...]. It therefore inclines to the view that the reasons given by the domestic courts can be regarded as relevant in terms of the legitimate aims pursued [...].

Examining further, the Court does not fail to observe that the applicant's prior conviction and the nature and scope of his crimes was only one of the grounds to hold that he lacked high moral character. The Bar Association, the Court of Honour and the civil courts also noted that a person who wished to become an advocate had an obligation to cooperate honestly and fully with the Bar Association and to disclose all relevant information, which the applicant had failed to do [...]. Notwithstanding the absence of an explicit, written requirement to indicate previous, even expired, convictions when applying to the bar, the Court does not find it unreasonable that the domestic authorities should conclude that such an obligation flowed from notions of honesty and ethics and the idea that the relationship between an advocate and the Bar Association must be based on mutual respect and good-will assistance [...]. Likewise, the Court shares the Court of Honour's conclusion that the applicant should have understood the significance of such information for his application and therefore the need to provide it to the Bar Association when his aptness for the bar was being considered [...]. In that connection, the Court also reiterates that professional associations of lawyers play a fundamental role in ensuring the protection of human rights and must therefore be able to act independently [...], and that respect towards professional colleagues and self-regulation of the legal profession are paramount [...]. It is plain that the Bar Association could never perform that self-regulation function effectively if it was deprived of full information about a person wishing to become an advocate.

The Court also notes that neither the Court of Honour, nor any civil court ever stated that the applicant was permanently barred from becoming an advocate. Indeed, it transpires from Article 8 of the Law on the Bar as it stands today [...], as well as from the Supreme Court's case law [...], that the applicant in principle remains free to prove, with time, that he has restored his reputation. The applicant's contention that the domestic courts held that he could never hold a position as trainee advocate for lack of high moral character [...] is therefore devoid of any basis. Neither has the applicant claimed that after the Supreme Court's decision in his case in 2009 he again approached the Bar Association to become an advocate because his reputation had improved. The Court therefore is satisfied that in the present case the domestic courts carried out a careful analysis and sought to strike a balance between the protection of the applicant's private life and the need to protect the rights of others and the justice system as a whole.

The applicant also contended before the domestic courts and before the Court that the requirement on him to be of good name was too high when compared with representatives of other legal professions and other lawyers [...]. However, the Court cannot but note the statement of the president of the Court of Honour that those other lawyers, unlike the applicant, had not hidden a previous conviction from the Bar Association [...]. As to the reputational requirements applicable to bailiffs or civil servants, an argument explicitly relied on by the applicant during the domestic proceedings [...], the Court observes that the requirements on reputation applied to them were somewhat comparable to those applied to advocates because the severity and nature of the crime, or expiry of the conviction, determined whether a person could be held as being morally fit to take up those jobs [...]. Moreover, Lithuania's reputation-related restrictions on judges and prosecutors were at the relevant time even stricter than those applicable to advocates. In particular, a person who had been convicted of any crime, irrespective of its seriousness or whether it was intentional or due to negligence, could not become a judge or prosecutor [...].

Lastly, the Court turns to the applicant's argument about bias on the part of the President of the Court of Honour. The applicant was able to put that complaint to the civil courts, which examined and dismissed it as unfounded [...]. The Court finds that the applicant therefore had the possibility to have the Bar Association's findings reviewed by the civil courts, an independent and impartial judicial authority [...]. There is nothing in the procedure followed by those courts that would lead this Court to the conclusion that the applicant was deprived of an opportunity to prove his complaints under Article 8 and/or that the decision-making process leading to measures interfering with his Article 8 rights was unfair (see, *mutatis mutandis, McMichael v. the United Kingdom,* 24 February 1995, § 87, Series A no. 307-B).

In these circumstances, the Court considers that the interference with the applicant's right to respect for his professional activity, as part of his private life, did not exceed what was 'necessary in a democratic society' for pursuing the legitimate aim of protecting the rights of others by ensuring the good and proper functioning of the justice system.

6/13

In a judgment of 27 June 2017 in *Lekavičienė* v. *Lithuania,* application no. 48427/09, the ECtHR found no violation of Article 8 of the ECHR, considering that refusal to readmit the applicant to the bar due to lack of high moral character constituted an interference with her right to respect for her private life;

however, such measure did not exceed what was "necessary in a democratic society" for pursuing the legitimate aim of protecting the rights of others by ensuring the good and proper functioning of the justice system. The ECtHR reasoned the non-violation of Article 8 of the ECHR, as follows:

> The Court reiterates that Article 8 of the Convention 'protects a right to personal development, and the right to establish and develop relationships with other human beings and the outside world' (see *Pretty* v. *the United Kingdom*, no. 2346/02, § 61, ECHR 2002-III), and that the notion of 'private life' does not in principle exclude activities of a professional or business nature (see *C.* v. *Belgium*, 7 August 1996, § 25, *Reports of Judgments and Decisions* 1996-III). Although no general right to employment can be derived from Article 8, the Court has previously had occasion to address the question of the applicability of Article 8 to the sphere of employment (see *Travaš* v. *Croatia*, no. 75581/13, § 52, 4 October 2016). It is, after all, in the course of their working lives that the majority of people have a significant opportunity to develop relationships with the outside world (see *Mateescu* v. *Romania*, no. 1944/10, § 20, 14 January 2014). It would be too restrictive to limit the notion of 'private life' to an 'inner circle' in which the individual may live his or her own personal life as he or she chooses and to exclude therefrom entirely the outside world not encompassed within that circle (see *Niemietz* v. *Germany*, 16 December 1992, § 29, Series A no. 251-B, and *Fernández Martínez* v. *Spain* [GC], no. 56030/07, § 109, ECHR 2014 (extracts)).
>
> The Court has further held that restrictions on registration as a member of certain professions (for instance, lawyer or notary), which could to a certain degree affect the applicant's ability to develop relationships with the outside world, undoubtedly fall within the sphere of his or her private life (see *Campagnano* v. *Italy*, no. 77955/01, § 54, ECHR 2006-IV). In the case of *Bigaeva* (cited above, § § 23–25) the Court held that Article 8 could also cover employment, including the right of access to a profession, specifically that of lawyer.
>
> In the present case, the Court observes that from September 1996 to December 2003 the applicant practised law as an advocate [...]. Taking into account her prior professional experience, the Court considers that the Lithuanian authorities' refusal, in 2007, to readmit the applicant to the bar [...] undeniably affected the applicant's ability to pursue her professional practice as an advocate and that there were consequential effects

on her enjoyment of the right to respect for her 'private life' within the meaning of Article 8 (ibid; see also, *mutatis mutandis* and regarding a ban to be reinstated as a civil servant, *Naidin* v. *Romania*, no. 38162/07, § 34, 21 October 2014, with further references). The Government's objection that the complaint is inadmissible *ratione materiae* must therefore be dismissed.

[...]

The Court is prepared to accept that the Bar Association's refusal to readmit the applicant to the bar affected a wide range of her relationships with other persons, including relationships of a professional nature. It is also clear that this refusal, based on the findings by the Bar Association, the Court of Appeal and the Supreme Court that the applicant's prior criminal conviction had cast a shadow on her name [...], must have had affected her professional reputation (see, *mutatis mutandis*, *Milojević and Others* v. *Serbia*, nos. 43519/07 and two others, § 60, 12 January 2016, and *Oleksandr Volkov* v. *Ukraine*, no. 21722/11, § 166, ECHR 2013).

That being so, the Court acknowledges that the refusal to accept the applicant to the bar constituted an interference with her right to respect for her private life within the meaning of Article 8 of the Convention.

The above-mentioned interference will be in breach of Article 8 of the Convention unless it can be justified under paragraph 2 of Article 8 as being 'in accordance with the law', pursuing one or more of the legitimate aims listed therein, and being 'necessary in a democratic society' in order to achieve the aim or aims concerned (see *S.H. and Others* v. *Austria* [GC], no. 57813/00, § 89, CEDH 2011).

The Court observes that the Bar Association and the Court of Appeal relied on Article 8 (4) of the Law on the Bar [...] when holding that the applicant had not regained an irreproachable reputation. The Bar Association and the appellate court also noted numerous other provisions of the Law on the Bar, as well as the Code of Ethics for Advocates as the bases of their conclusion that the applicant did not meet the criteria set out for the bar [...]. The Court therefore finds that the interference was prescribed by law within the meaning of Article 8 § 2 of the Convention.

The Court also accepts the Government's argument [...] that the interference in question served the aim of protecting the rights of others. This was also noted by the Court of Appeal and the Supreme Court, which underlined the advocates' obligations towards clients, courts and society and the need to safeguard the good functioning of the justice system overall [...].

At the outset the Court reiterates the most important role played by lawyers in the administration of justice (see, on this point, *Schöpfer* v. *Switzerland*, 20 May 1998, § § 29–30, *Reports* 1998-III; *Nikula* v. *Finland*, no. 31611/96, § 45, ECHR 2002-II; *Amihalachioaie* v. *Moldova*, no. 60115/00, § 27, ECHR 2004-III; *Kyprianou* v. *Cyprus* [GC], no. 73797/01, § 173, ECHR 2005-XIII; and *André and Another* v. *France*, no. 18603/03, § 42, 24 July 2008; all cited in *Morice* v. *France* [GC], no. 29369/10, § 132, ECHR 2015). The Court has also held that for members of the public to have confidence in the administration of justice they must have confidence in the ability of the legal profession to provide effective representation (see *Kyprianou*, cited above, § 175).

The special role of lawyers, as independent professionals, in the administration of justice entails a number of duties and restrictions, particularly with regard to their professional conduct, which must be discreet, honest and dignified (see *Casado Coca* v. *Spain*, 24 February 1994, § 46, Series A no. 285-A; *Steur* v. *the Netherlands*, no. 39657/98, § 38, ECHR 2003-XI; *Veraart* v. *the Netherlands*, no. 10807/04, § 51, 30 November 2006; and *Morice*, cited above, § 133).

The Court has also held that any criminal proceedings entail certain consequences for the private life of an individual who has committed a crime. They are compatible with Article 8 of the Convention provided that they do not exceed the normal and inevitable consequences of such a situation (see *Karov* v. *Bulgaria*, no. 45964/99, § 88, 16 November 2006).

Turning to the circumstances of this case the Court notes that the domestic courts' findings that the applicant had not yet regained high moral character are in line with their consistent case law, which underlines high standards applicable to the advocate's profession [...]. In fact, the domestic authorities emphasised the nature of the applicant's crime – forgery of documents and misappropriation of State funds while ostensibly providing legal aid services and submitting forged documents to the court, as well as the fact that the applicant had more than thirty times used her professional practice to commit a crime – which obviously contradicted the requirements of professional ethics [...].

In this connection the Court notes that in its Recommendation R (2000) 21, the Committee of Ministers of the Council of Europe has emphasised that bar-admitted lawyers must carry out their practice in order to strengthen the rule of law [...]. Furthermore, the principles applicable to lawyer's profession contain such values as the dignity and honour of the legal profession, the integrity and good standing of the individual lawyer, respect towards professional colleagues, as well as respect for the fair administration of justice [...]. Before being accepted to the bar for the first time, the applicant swore an oath to observe the laws and to honestly perform her duties as an advocate [...], but later committed a grave breach of these duties. It is true that because of the size of the criminal sanction the offences for which the applicant was convicted were not categorised as serious crimes, and the applicant was let off with a fine [...]. That notwithstanding, it is not unreasonable to hold that the applicant's behaviour when systematically cheating the court system and the State out of sums of money also showed her disrespect for her colleagues and peers, thus undermining the entire ideal of justice. The Court therefore inclines to the view that the reasons given by the Court of Appeal and the Supreme Court not to hold the applicant as being of high moral character [...] can be regarded as relevant in terms of the legitimate aims pursued.

The Court further notes that, in line with the Lithuanian courts' practice, absence of conviction, or its expiry do not mean *ipso facto* that a person has or has regained high moral character [...]. In this particular case the Court of Appeal and the Supreme Court considered that insufficient time – four years – had passed since the applicant's conviction for forgery of documents and fraud [...]. It is not for the Court to substitute its view of what would be the appropriate interval until the applicant could claim to have regained her good name. Even so, the Court of Appeal underlined that this in no way prevented the applicant from reapplying for admission to the bar in future, or from asking a court to reconsider whether she had regained high moral character [...]. The Court therefore is satisfied that in the present case the domestic courts carried out a careful analysis and sought to strike a balance between the protection of the applicant's private life and the need to protect the rights of others and the justice system as a whole.

[...]

In these circumstances, the Court considers that the interference with the applicant's right to respect for her professional activity, as part of her private life, did not exceed what was 'necessary in a democratic society' for pursuing the legitimate aim of protecting the rights of others by ensuring the good and proper functioning of the justice system.

6/14

In a judgment of 11 July 2017 in *Mardosai v. Lithuania*, application no. 42434/15, the ECtHR found no violation of Article 2 of the ECHR, considering that although criminal investigations into the alleged medical negligence which had led to their newborn daughter's death could not regarded as effective for the purpose of Article 2 of the Convention, the civil proceedings were concluded without undue delay and ended with adequate compensation by Convention standards. The ECtHR reasoned the non-violation of Article 2 of the ECHR, as follows:

> The Court reiterates that the procedural obligation under Article 2 of the Convention requires States to set up an effective independent judicial system so that the cause of death of patients in the care of the medical profession, whether in the public or the private sector, can be determined and those responsible made accountable (see *Šilih v. Slovenia* [GC], no. 71463/01, § 192, 9 April 2009, and the cases cited therein). This procedural obligation is not an obligation of result but of means (see *Paul and Audrey Edwards v. the United Kingdom*, no. 46477/99, § 71, ECHR 2002-II).

> The Court also reiterates that, although the Convention does not guarantee a right to have criminal proceedings instituted against third parties, the effective judicial system required by Article 2 may, and under certain circumstances must, include recourse to criminal law. However, if the infringement of the right to life is not caused intentionally, the procedural obligation imposed by Article 2 does not necessarily require the provision of a criminal-law remedy in every case. In the specific sphere of medical negligence the obligation may also be satisfied if the legal system affords victims a remedy in the civil courts, either alone or in conjunction with a remedy in the criminal courts, enabling any responsibility on the part of the doctors concerned to be established and any appropriate civil redress, such as an order for damages and/or for publication of the decision, to be obtained (see *Calvelli and Ciglio v. Italy* [GC], no. 32967/96,

§ 51, ECHR 2002-I; *Vo* v. *France* [GC], no. 53924/00, § 90, ECHR 2004-VIII; and *Šilih*, cited above, § 194).

Lastly, the Court reiterates that, apart from the concern for respect for the rights inherent in Article 2 of the Convention in each individual case, more general considerations also call for a prompt examination of cases concerning death in a hospital setting. Knowledge of the facts and possible errors committed in the course of medical care is essential to enable the institutions and medical staff concerned to remedy potential deficiencies and prevent similar errors. Prompt examination of such cases is therefore important for the safety of users of all health services (see *Byrzykowski* v. *Poland*, no. 11562/05, § 117, 27 June 2006, and *Šilih*, cited above, § 196).

[...]

The pre-trial investigation in the case lasted more than four years and nine months [...], a period which the Court considers excessive even taking into account the complexity of the case. As seen from the case file, there were several periods of inactivity (almost four months from October 2009 to February 2010, three months from June to September 2010, almost four months from September 2010 to January 2011, more than five months from December 2011 to May 2012, and more than two months from July to October 2012), which together amounted to about one year and six months of inactivity imputable to the authorities. The Court also notes that for the rest of the time the investigation was conducted very slowly and the investigative measures were sparse.

The Government submitted that many of the delays in the investigation had been caused by the workload of specialists and experts, but the Court cannot accept that argument and reiterates that it is for the State to organise its judicial system in such a way as to enable its institutions to comply with the requirements of the Convention (see, *mutatis mutandis*, *O'Reilly and Others* v. *Ireland*, no.54725/00, § 33, 29 July 2004; *Rakhmonov* v. *Russia*, no. 50031/11, § 60, 16 October 2012; and *W.* v. *Slovenia*, no. 24125/06, § 69, 23 January 2014). The Government also argued that the applicants had themselves prolonged the investigation by requesting additional specialist opinions and forensic examinations. The Court acknowledges that the applicants' request for an additional specialist opinion [...] appeared to have been based on their disagreement with the conclusions of the previous opinion rather than on any shortcomings therein. However, it notes that the authorities were not obliged to satisfy the applicants' request for an additional opinion if they did not consider it necessary (see *Mustafa Tunç and Fecire Tunç v. Turkey* [GC], no. 24014/05, § 180, 14 April 2015). The Court further observes that the applicants' request for an additional forensic examination [...] resulted from the fact that their questions had not been forwarded to the experts conducting the previously ordered examination, without any reasons being provided [...], so in the Court's view the applicants cannot be reproached for asking for another examination which would address their questions.

Of particular concern to the Court is the authorities' failure to forward an order for a forensic examination to the relevant experts for one year and two months, for which nobody was held responsible [...]. Although the Government submitted that that failure had prolonged the investigation by 'only five months' [...], the Court considers such a delay to be significant, especially in view of the total length of the pre-trial investigation and the fact that the proceedings eventually became time-barred.

The Court further notes that, following the lengthy pre-trial investigation, the case was transferred to the Jurbarkas District Court for examination on the merits when only slightly more than one month remained until the expiry of the statute of limitations [...]. In such circumstances, the Court considers that there was little that the domestic court could do to avoid the case becoming time-barred, especially as domestic law at that time did not allow suspending the statute of limitations [...]. It nonetheless observes that, after the first two hearings were adjourned as a result of the illness of the accused, the Jurbarkas District Court scheduled the next hearing on 25 June 2014 – a date which was already after the expiry of the statute of limitations – because of the defence lawyer's schedule, without examining the possibility of finding another date before 21 May 2014 or suggesting that the accused appoint a different lawyer [...].

Accordingly, the Court is of the view that in the present case the criminal proceedings could not be regarded as effective for the purpose of Article 2 of the Convention.

However, the Court observes that there is no dispute that the death of the applicants' daughter was not intentional. It reiterates that, in cases concerning medical negligence, the procedural obligation under Article 2 of the Convention does not necessarily require criminal liability, and civil liability may be sufficient (see *Calvelli and Ciglio*, § 51; *Vo*, § 90; and *Šilih*, § 194, all cited above). In the present case, the applicants lodged a civil claim against Jurbarkas Hospital and were awarded compensation for pecuniary and non-pecuniary damage caused by the inadequate medical services which had contributed to their daughter's death [...].

The applicants lodged their civil claim in September 2011 (and revised it in December 2011 and August 2013 [...]), but the first-instance judgment was only issued in November 2014 [...], thereby raising the question as to whether the proceedings were sufficiently prompt. No information was provided to the Court as to the reasons for that delay. However, it may be assumed that the civil proceedings were stayed pending the outcome of the criminal proceedings, especially as the courts in the former proceedings relied on the evidence obtained in the course of the latter ([...]; see, *mutatis mutandis, Koceski v. the Former Yugoslav Republic of Macedonia* (dec.), no. 41107/07, § 27, 22 October 2013). After the criminal proceedings became time-barred, the civil proceedings were concluded without undue delay [...].

The Court further observes that the amount awarded to the applicants in the civil proceedings (EUR 23,170 in respect of non-pecuniary damage and EUR 1,945 in respect of pecuniary damage) corresponded to the degree of the hospital's liability [...], and was adequate by Convention standards.

Lastly, the Court notes that the applicants complained only about the ineffectiveness of the criminal proceedings, but did not allege that the civil proceedings had been unfair or ineffective in any way, or that the amount awarded to them in the latter proceedings had been inadequate.

The foregoing considerations are sufficient for the Court to conclude that the State complied with its procedural obligations under Article 2 of the Convention. There has therefore been no violation of that provision in the present case.

6/15

In a judgment of 11 July 2017 in *Šidlauskas* v. *Lithuania*, application no. 51755/10, the ECtHR found a violation of Article 1 of Protocol No. 1 of the ECHR, considering that the courts failed to strike a fair balance between the applicant's right to the peaceful enjoyment of his property and any competing general interest, and that awarding the applicant compensation which was several times below the market value of his apartment and which was insufficient for him to obtain a new comparable apartment imposed an individual and excessive burden on him. The ECtHR reasoned the violation of Article 1 of Protocol No. 1 of the Convention as follows:

> The Court notes at the outset that the applicant's apartment was sold at a public auction in 2004, that is, more than six months before the present application was submitted to the Court (6 August 2010). Therefore, it cannot assess compliance of that sale with Article 1 of Protocol No. 1 (see *Vinniychuk* v. *Ukraine*, no. 34000/07, § 49, 20 October 2016). However, the domestic courts acknowledged that the sale had been unlawful [...] and, in line with domestic law [...], the applicant was entitled to compensation. Accordingly, the Court considers that the applicant's entitlement to compensation for the unlawful sale of his apartment was sufficiently established to constitute 'possession' within the meaning of Article 1 of Protocol No. 1 to the Convention. That provision is therefore applicable.

> As to which part of that provision applies in the present case, the Court observes that the applicant's complaint concerned the amount of compensation awarded to him, which was insufficient for him to buy a new comparable apartment. The Court considers it most appropriate to examine this complaint under the first sentence of the first paragraph of Article 1 of Protocol No. 1, which lays down in general terms the principle of the peaceful enjoyment of property (see *Kirilova and Others* v. *Bulgaria*, nos. 42908/98 and 3 others, § § 104-5, 9 June 2005).

> The Court reiterates that Article 1 of Protocol No. 1 to the Convention requires a fair balance to be struck between the demands of the general interest of the community and the requirements of protection of the individual's fundamental rights. Such a balance will not be achieved where an individual has had to bear a disproportionate and excessive burden (see, among many other authorities, *Broniowski* v. *Poland* [GC], no. 31443/96, § 150, ECHR 2004-V).

The Court also reiterates that compensation terms under the relevant legislation are material to assessment of whether the contested measure respects the requisite fair balance, and notably whether the measure imposes a disproportionate burden on the applicant. In this connection, the Court has held that the taking of property without payment of an amount reasonably related to its value will normally constitute a disproportionate interference (see *Vistiņš and Perepjolkins v. Latvia* [GC], no. 71243/01, § 110, 25 October 2012, and the cases cited therein). It has also considered that, where there is 'an extreme disproportion' between the value of the expropriated property and the compensation awarded to the applicants, only very exceptional circumstances can justify such a situation (ibid., § 119, and the cases cited therein).

Turning to the circumstances of the present case, the Court observes that the amount of damages awarded to the applicant by the Supreme Court in its judgment of 8 February 2010 (EUR 3,504) was about four times lower than the amount he claimed (EUR 14,770). It was not disputed by the parties that the amount claimed by the applicant corresponded to the apartment's market value at the time when he had submitted that claim, nor was it disputed that EUR 3,504 had not been sufficient for him to acquire a new comparable apartment at the time when that award was made [...]. While the Court does not consider that the disproportion between the market value of the apartment at the time when the applicant submitted his claim and the compensation received by him was 'extreme' [...], it is nonetheless of the view that the domestic courts needed to provide adequate reasons to justify that difference.

In this connection, the Court notes that the rule established in Article 6.249 § 5 of the Civil Code was to assess the amount of damages on the basis of market prices at the time when the award for damages was made, unless there were reasons to rely on market prices at a different time [...]. When making the award, the Supreme Court considered that 'the nature of the obligation and the principles of equity, reasonableness and good faith' warranted relying on market prices at the time when the apartment had been sold at a public auction [...]. However, the Supreme Court did not provide any explanation as to how those principles applied in the applicant's case, nor why they justified such a decision in the particular circumstances. The Court reiterates that, according to its established case law reflecting a principle linked to the proper administration of justice, judgments of courts and tribunals should adequately state the reasons on which they are based (see *Albergas and Arlauskas* v. *Lithuania*, no. 17978/05, § 67, 27 May 2014, and *Paliutis* v. *Lithuania*, no. 34085/09, § 45, 24 November 2015; see also the relevant practice of the Lithuanian Constitutional Court [...]). It considers that, in the present case, a reiteration of principles without any accompanying reasoning was clearly inadequate to justify rejection of the applicant's claim.

The Government argued that the Supreme Court had implicitly based its judgment on the defendants' submissions that the applicant had acted in bad faith because he had not asked for restitution *in integrum*, and because he had deliberately waited until the last day to submit his claim in order to obtain a higher monetary award than he would have received in 2004 [...]. However, the Court is not convinced by the Government's argument. It firstly observes that the applicant submitted his claim within the time-limit provided in domestic law, and his exercise of his procedural rights cannot be interpreted as evidence of bad faith (see, *mutatis mutandis, Kolomiyets* v. *Russia*, no. 76835/01, § 29, 22 February 2007). The Court further notes that the Supreme Court explicitly held that, according to its own case law, restitution *in integrum* should not have been applied in the applicant's case [...]. Furthermore, the Supreme Court did not make any mention of the applicant's alleged bad faith, either in relation to the reasons presented by the Government, or in relation to anything else (contrast with the judgment of the first-instance court in the applicant's case [...]). Therefore, in the absence of adequate reasons in the final judgment, the Court considers the Government's position that that judgment relied on the applicant's alleged bad faith to be purely speculative and does not accept it (see, *mutatis mutandis, Albergas and Arlauskas*, cited above, § § 66–67).

The Court further observes that the Supreme Court, when determining the amount of damages to be awarded to the applicant, did not assess the balance between his right to the peaceful enjoyment of his possessions and any competing interests – in fact, it did not even specify whether any such competing interests existed in the applicant's case (see, *mutatis mutandis, Tuleshov and Others* v. *Russia*, no. 32718/02, § 47, 24 May 2007). In particular, although the applicant made it clear that he had not had a home following the unlawful sale of his apartment, and that the amount of damages which he claimed was intended to cover the purchase of a new comparable apartment [...]), it does not appear that the Supreme Court took any account of the applicant's ability to obtain a new home (see, *mutatis mutandis*, *Rousk* v. *Sweden*, no. 27183/04, § 140, 25 July 2013; compare and contrast *Zrilić* v. *Croatia*, no. 46726/11, § 69, 3 October 2013). In such circumstances, the Court considers that the domestic courts failed to strike a fair balance between the applicant's right to the peaceful enjoyment of his property and any competing general interest, and that awarding the applicant compensation which was several times below the market value of his apartment at the time when he submitted his claim to the domestic courts and which was insufficient for him to obtain a new comparable apartment imposed an individual and excessive burden on him.

It therefore concludes that there has been a violation of Article 1 of Protocol No. 1 to the Convention in the present case.

6/16

In a judgment of 30 October 2017 in *Grigolovič* v. *Lithuania*, application no. 54882/10, the ECtHR found a violation of Article 1 of Protocol No. 1 of the ECHR, considering that the Government upset the peaceful enjoyment of the applicant's possession because since 5 February 2009 a procedure to restore the applicant's property rights was at a standstill. The ECtHR reasoned the violation of Article 1 of Protocol No. 1 of the ECHR, as follows:

> The Court notes that the applicant complained about two different aspects of the domestic proceedings. Firstly, he complained about his inability to receive the plot of land *in natura*. Secondly, he complained about the inability to receive a plot of equal value or fair compensation for the land. The Court will address each of these complaints separately.
>
> [...]
>
> As concerns the applicant's complaint that he was unable to recover the original plot *in natura*, the Court reiterates that the Convention does not guarantee, as such, the right to restitution of property. 'Possessions' within the meaning of Article 1 of Protocol No. 1 can either be 'existing possessions' or assets, including claims, in respect of which an applicant can argue that he has at least a 'legitimate expectation' that they will be realised. The hope that a long-extinguished property right may be revived cannot be regarded as 'possession' within the meaning of Article 1 of Protocol No. 1, nor can a conditional claim which has lapsed as a result of failure to fulfil the condition (see *Polacek and Polackova* v. *the Czech*

Republic [GC] (dec.), no. 38645/97, § 62, 10 July 2002, and *Nekvedavičius v. Lithuania*, no. 1471/05, § 73, 10 December 2013).

It follows that the applicant has no 'possessions' with regard to his claim to recover the original plot in natura, and this complaint is incompatible *ratione materiae* with the provisions of Article 1 of Protocol No. 1 within the meaning of Article 35 § 3 of the Convention.

[...]

As regards the applicant's complaint about his inability to obtain a plot of equal value or fair compensation for his father's land, the Court notes that the authorities continually highlighted the fact that the applicant could have his property rights restored to his father's land, and that his right of restitution was never contested by the authorities [...]. In 2009 he was granted a plot of land, which confirms that he satisfied the criteria for restitution of the land that his father had, totalling 9.5705 hectares, in whatever form that restitution might take ([...], see also, *mutatis mutandis, Paukštis v. Lithuania*, no. 17467/07, § 68, 24 November 2015). More specifically, the domestic courts observed that the process of restoring the applicant's property rights had not been completed and that he could still have his rights restored [...]. In view of those judgments, the applicant's claim to have his property rights restored by means other than *in natura* constituted a 'proprietary interest' which has sufficient basis in domestic law and is covered by the notion of a 'possession' under Article 1 of Protocol No. 1 to the Convention (see *Nekvedavičius*, cited above, § 76). The Court thus finds that the Government's objection as to this complaint being inadmissible *ratione materiae* must be dismissed.

[...]

The Court notes that the applicant applied to have his property rights restored in 2000. And although the opportunity to recover the whole plot of land *in natura* never existed, his right to have his property rights restored in the form of land of equal value or money was never contested by the authorities [...]. This was also confirmed by the decisions of the domestic courts. Even though that right was created in an inchoate form, it clearly constituted a legal basis for the State's obligation to implement it. The Court thus holds that the applicant had an enforceable right and a legitimate expectation to have his property rights restored in some form.

However, the procedure seemed to be at a standstill, as no particular decision had been adopted since 5 February 2009, when the authorities decided to restore the applicant's property rights to 0.18 hectares of his father's land [...]. In particular, it had not been determined whether and when the applicant would receive a new plot of land or compensation, and for what value.

It follows that there was an interference with the applicant's right to peaceful enjoyment of his possessions, as set out in the first sentence of the first paragraph of Article 1 of Protocol No. 1 to the Convention. It remains to be ascertained whether or not that interference was justified.

For the purposes of the above-mentioned provision, the Court must determine whether a fair balance was struck between the demands of the general interest of the community and the protection of the individual's fundamental rights (see *Sporrong and Lönnroth* v. *Sweden*, 23 September 1982, § 68, Series A no. 52, and *Nekvedavičius*, cited above, § 86). The requisite balance will not be struck where the person concerned bears an individual and excessive burden (see *Străin and Others* v. *Romania*, no. 57001/00, § 44, ECHR 2005-VII, and *Tunaitis* v. *Lithuania*, no. 42927/08, § 31, 24 November 2015).

In the context of property rights, particular importance must be attached to the principle of good governance (see *Nekvedavičius*, cited above, § 87). It requires that where an issue in the general interest is at stake, in particular when the matter affects fundamental human rights such as those involving property, the public authorities must act in good time and in an appropriate and, above all, consistent manner (see *Bogdel* v. *Lithuania*, no. 41248/06, § 65, 26 November 2013).

The Court takes cognisance of the fact that the present case concerns the restitution of property and is not unmindful of the complexity of the legal and factual issues that a State faces when resolving such questions. It follows that certain impediments to the realisation of an applicant's right to the peaceful enjoyment of his possessions are not in themselves open to criticism (see *Aleksa* v. *Lithuania*, no. 27576/05, § 86, 21 July 2009; *Igarienė and Petrauskienė* v. *Lithuania*, no. 26892/05, § 58, 21 July 2009; *Paukštis*, cited above, § 84; and *Šimaitienė* v. *Lithuania*, no. 55056/10, § 45, 21 February 2017).

45. Even so, the state of uncertainty in which an applicant might find himself as a result of delays attributable to the authorities is a factor to be taken into account in assessing a State's conduct (see *Broniowski* v. *Poland* [GC], no. 31443/96, § § 151 and 185, ECHR 2004-V, and *Igariene and Petrauskiene*, cited above, § 58). The Court notes that in 2007 the applicant was 4,055th on a list of people waiting to have their property rights restored, and that it is still not certain when that will happen.

As to the Government's argument that the applicant himself contributed to the fact that his property rights to the remaining plot of land had not yet been restored by failing to change his mind as to the form of restitution, the Court notes that he was not under any obligation to do so under domestic law [...]. The applicant did not respond to the authorities' letter of November 2014 [...], but that did not absolve the Government from their duty to complete the restitution process in the applicant's case, since the applicant had clearly expressed his wish to restore his property rights by obtaining a plot of land of equal value [...]. In these circumstances the Court does not see any grounds for finding that the applicant was responsible, in whole or in part, for the fact that his property rights to the remaining plot had not yet been restored.

Even though the domestic authorities were not completely inactive, the Court considers that they did not display due diligence in their attempts to restore the applicant's property rights to the remaining plot of land. More specifically, although the Government stated that the law had been amended in order to accelerate the restitution process, the Court notes that no effective action to accelerate the restitution process had been taken since November 2014, when the applicant was asked to change his mind as to the form of restitution [...].

Having regard to the circumstances of the case, the Court concludes that the domestic authorities did not act in line with the principle of good governance to ensure that the applicant's property rights were protected. Moreover, the applicant's legitimate expectation to have his property rights restored to the remaining plot of land was unjustifiably affected by failure of the authorities to act. As a result, the balance which had to be struck between the general interest and the applicant's personal interest was upset, and he has had to bear an individual and excessive burden, which is incompatible with Article 1 of Protocol No. 1 to the Convention.

Accordingly, there has been a violation of that provision in the present case.

6/17

In a judgment of 31 October 2017 in *Činga* v. *Lithuania*, application no. 69419/13, the ECtHR found a violation of Article 1 of Protocol No. 1 of the ECHR, considering that awarding the applicant the amount of LTL 15 for an expropriated land plot of 0.05 hectares did not sufficiently mitigate the negative consequences of the applicant's losing title to the property in question. The ECtHR reasoned the violation of Article 1 of Protocol No. 1 of the Convention, as follows:

> The relevant general principles on Article 1 of Protocol No. 1 are set out in *Pyrantienė* v. *Lithuania* (no. 45092/07, § § 37–40, 12 November 2013).
>
> [...]
>
> There is no dispute between the parties in the present case that there has been a 'deprivation of possessions' within the meaning of the second sentence of Article 1 of Protocol No. 1. The Court must therefore ascertain whether the deprivation in question was justified under that provision.
>
> [...]
>
> The Court notes that the domestic courts' decisions to order the applicant to return 0.05 hectares of land to the State and to annul the orders by which that plot was allocated to him and part of the land purchase agreement signed in 1993 was based on the provisions of domestic law [...].
>
> [...]
>
> The Court has held that because of their direct knowledge of local society and its needs, the national authorities are in principle better placed than international judges to appreciate what is 'in the public interest'. Under the system of protection established by the Convention, it is thus for the national authorities to make an initial assessment as to the existence of a problem of public concern warranting measures of deprivation of property. Here, as in other fields to which safeguards of the Convention extend, the national authorities accordingly enjoy a certain margin of appreciation (see *Moskal* v. *Poland*, no. 10373/05, § 61, 15 September 2009;

Pincová and Pinc v. *the Czech Republic*, no. 36548/97, § 47, ECHR 2002-VIII; and *Pyrantienė*, cited above, § 45).

As stated above, the measure complained of was designed to correct mistakes by the authorities and to protect the process of sale of State land by ensuring that individuals were not given more property than they were entitled to at the expense of the State (see, *mutatis mutandis, Misiukonis and Others* v. *Lithuania*, no. 49426/09, § 57, 15 November 2016). In those circumstances, and having regard to the State's margin of appreciation, the Court accepts that the deprivation of property experienced by the applicant not only served his neighbours' interests, but also the general interests of society as a whole (see, *mutatis mutandis, Bečvář and Bečvářová* v. *the Czech Republic*, no. 58358/00, § 67, 14 December 2004).

[...]

The Court reiterates that any interference with property must, in addition to being lawful and having a legitimate aim, also satisfy the requirement of proportionality. A fair balance must be struck between the demands of the general interest of the community and the requirements of protection of the individual's fundamental rights, the search for such a fair balance being inherent in the whole of the Convention. The requisite balance will not be struck where the person concerned bears an individual and excessive burden (see *Sporrong and Lönnroth* v. *Sweden*, 23 September 1982, § § 69–74, Series A no. 52; *Brumărescu* v. *Romania* [GC], no. 28342/95, § 78, ECHR 1999-VII; and *Anthony Aquilina* v. *Malta*, no. 3851/12, § § 58–59, 11 December 2014, and the cases cited therein).

There is no dispute in the present case that the national authorities' decisions to allocate and later sell to the applicant the impugned 0.05 hectares of land had breached substantive provisions of the relevant legislation [...]. At this point, the Court reiterates that the principles of good governance should not, as a general rule, prevent the authorities from correcting occasional mistakes, even those resulting from their own negligence. However, the risk arising from any mistake made by a State authority must be borne by the State itself, and errors must not be remedied at the expense of the individuals concerned (see *Romankevič* v. *Lithuania*, no. 25747/07, § § 38–39, 2 December 2014; *Albergas and Arlauskas* v. *Lithuania*, no. 17978/05, § 59, 27 May 2014 and the cases cited therein).

In that connection, the Court notes that the procedures for the sale of the land to the applicant were conducted by official bodies exercising the authority of the State. There are no indications that the applicant had somehow contributed to the adoption of the unlawful decisions. The Court considers that the applicant did not have sufficient reasons to doubt the validity of those decisions and was entitled to rely on the fact that they would not be retrospectively declared invalid to his detriment (see, *mutatis mutandis, Gladysheva* v. *Russia*, no. 7097/10, § § 79–80, 6 December 2011; *Tunaitis*, cited above, § 39; and *Misiukonis and Others*, cited above, § 59).

The domestic courts in the present case held that the applicant should have known that the disputed part of the land would block the road and that the applicant had not been diligent enough [...]. The Court finds that conclusion difficult to accept. The Court takes note of the domestic court's conclusion that ignorance of the law does not absolve anyone of responsibility and that the Zujūnai settlement plans had shown that there was a continuing passage which was part of the applicant's 0.05 hectares of land [...]. However, the Court observes that there was no detailed plan of Vilnius County at the time of purchase of the land [...] and that the rules for the Register of Territorial Planning Documents were only approved in 1996 [...]. The Court thus does not see convincing reasons to find that the applicant should have questioned the actions of the competent public authorities rather than expecting them to take all the necessary measures to avoid mistakes in applying legislation (see, *mutatis mutandis, Misiukonis and Others*, cited above, § 60). In particular, the Court takes into account the fact that the domestic courts had already adopted decisions favourable to the applicant [...], where they indicated that the applicant's neighbours could access their own land (compare and contrast *Răchită* v. *Romania*, no. 15987/09, § § 69–70, 17 May 2016) and these findings had acquired *res judicata* effect and could not have been called into question (see, *mutatis mutandis, Brumărescu*, cited above, § 61; *Esertas* v. *Lithuania*, no. 50208/06, § § 20–21, 31 May 2012; and *Nekvedavičius* v. *Lithuania*, no. 1471/05, § 74, 10 December 2013).

The Court further observes that the Supreme Court held that the applicant was a *bona fide* owner of the land [...]. The Court sees no reason to question those findings (see, *mutatis mutandis, Vistiņš and Perepjolkins* v. *Latvia* [GC], no. 71243/01, § 120, 25 October 2012, and *Žilinskienė* v. *Lithuania*, no. 57675/09, § 51, 1 December 2015).

Moreover, the Court considers that the applicant had no reasons to fear that he would lose his land or to anticipate that the prosecutor and later the Prosecutor General would persevere to such an extent [...].

Moreover, the Court notes that after losing his title to the land, the applicant was paid LTL 15, the nominal equivalent of the price he had paid in 1993. According to an assessment submitted by the applicant, the market value of the improvements he had made to the disputed plot was LTL 74,972 (EUR 21,713) in October 2008. While no estimates were provided by the domestic authorities, the Court finds it reasonable to conclude that the market value of the land in 2008, when the first judgment in favour of the prosecutor was adopted, and in 2014, when the applicant's request to reopen proceedings was dismissed, was higher than the nominal price he had paid in 1993. It should also be noted that the LTL 15 returned to the applicant had obviously suffered considerable depreciation and could not reasonably be related to the value of the land fifteen or, even more so, twenty-one years later. Accordingly, the Court finds that the amount of as little as LTL 15 paid to the applicant in 2008 was clearly insufficient for the purchase of a comparable plot of land (see, *mutatis mutandis, Velikovi and Others v. Bulgaria*, nos. 43278/98 and 8 others, § 207, 15 March 2007; and *Padalevičius v. Lithuania*, no.12278/03, § 69, 7 July 2009).

The Court takes note of the Government's argument that the applicant has not yet removed his constructions from the disputed plot. However, it cannot ignore the fact that the land has been entered in the State Register as property of the State, and that the applicant has been refused permission to rent it [...], which means that the constructions will be removed in connection with the binding domestic court decisions in the case [...].

The Court reiterates that the taking of property without the payment of an amount reasonably related to its value will normally fail to respect the requisite fair balance between the demands of the general interest of the community and the requirements of protection of the individual's fundamental rights and will constitute a disproportionate burden on the applicant (see *The Holy Monasteries v. Greece*, 9 December 1994, § 71, Series A no. 301-A; *Former King of Greece and Others v. Greece* [GC], no. 25701/94, § 89, ECHR 2000-XII; *Padalevičius*, cited above, § 66; and *Albergas and Arlauskas*, cited above, § 73). In line with the Court's case law in similar cases concerning expropriation of property, the balance mentioned above is generally achieved where compensation paid to the person whose property has been taken reasonably relates to its 'market' value as determined at the time of the expropriation (see *Pincová and Pinc*, cited above, § 53; *Vistiņš and Perepjolkins*, cited above, § 111; and *Guiso-Gallisay* v. *Italy* (just satisfaction) [GC], no. 58858/00, § 103, 22 December 2009). It follows that the amount of money for the applicant's loss of title to the land must be calculated using the value of the property on the date ownership was lost.

In the present case, the Court considers that awarding the applicant the amount of LTL 15 did not sufficiently mitigate the negative consequences of losing his title to the property in question. The lack of proportion between the land's market value and the amount awarded is too significant for the Court to find that a 'fair balance' was struck between the interests of the community and the applicant's fundamental rights (see, *mutatis mutandis, Pyrantienė*, cited above, § 71, and *Vistiņš and Perepjolkins*, cited above, § 130).

The foregoing considerations are sufficient to enable the Court to conclude that the conditions under which the applicant had his title to the land removed imposed an individual and excessive burden on him, and that the authorities failed to strike a fair balance between the demands of the public interest on the one hand and the applicant's right to peaceful enjoyment of his possessions on the other. There has, accordingly, been a violation of Article 1 of Protocol No. 1 to the Convention.

6/18

In a judgment of 31 October 2017 in *Bauras* v. *Lithuania*, application no. 56795/13, the ECtHR found no violation of Article 6 Paragraph 2 of the ECHR, considering that the domestic courts had *de facto* found him guilty of having instigated the murders of two individuals, and had thereby prejudged the ongoing criminal case against him. The ECtHR found no violation of the principle of innocence and Article 6 Paragraph 2of the Convention. The relevant paragraphs read:

The Court reiterates that the presumption of innocence enshrined in paragraph 2 of Article 6 is one of the elements of a fair criminal trial that is required by paragraph 1 (see, among many other authorities, *Deweer* v. *Belgium*, 27 February 1980, § 56, Series A no. 35; *Allenet de Ribemont* v. *France*, 10 February 1995, § 35, Series A no. 308; and *Natsvlishvili and*

Togonidze v. *Georgia*, no.9043/05, § 103, ECHR 2014 (extracts)). Article 6 § 2 prohibits the premature expression by the tribunal of the opinion that a person 'charged with a criminal offence' is guilty before he or she has been so proved according to law (see, among many other authorities, *Minelli* v. *Switzerland*, 25 March 1983, § 37, Series A no. 62, and *Peša* v. *Croatia*, no. 40523/08, § 138, 8 April 2010). It also covers statements made by other public officials about pending criminal investigations which encourage the public to believe the suspect guilty and prejudge assessment of the facts by the competent judicial authority (see *Allenet de Ribemont*, cited above, § 41; *Daktaras* v. *Lithuania*, no. 42095/98, §§ 41–43, ECHR 2000-X; and *Butkevičius* v. *Lithuania*, no. 48297/99, § 49, ECHR 2002-II (extracts)).

[...]

The Court further reiterates that a fundamental distinction must be made between a statement that someone is merely suspected of having committed a crime and a clear declaration, in the absence of a final conviction, that an individual has committed the crime in question. In this connection the Court has emphasised the importance of the choice of words by public officials in their statements before a person has been tried and found guilty of a particular criminal offence (see *Daktaras*, cited above, § 41; *Böhmer* v. *Germany*, no. 37568/97, § 56, 3 October 2002; and *Khuzhin and Others* v. *Russia*, no. 13470/02, § 94, 23 October 2008). While the use of language is of critical importance in this respect, the Court has further pointed out that whether a statement of a public official is in breach of the principle of the presumption of innocence must be determined in the context of the particular circumstances in which the impugned statement was made (see *Daktaras*, cited above, § 43; *A.L.* v. *Germany*, no. 72758/01, § 31, 28 April 2005; and *Paulikas* v. *Lithuania*, no. 57435/09, § 55, 24 January 2017). When regard is had to the nature and context of the particular proceedings, even the use of some unfortunate language may not be decisive. The Court's case law provides some examples of instances where no violation of Article 6 § 2 has been found even though the language used by domestic authorities and courts was criticised (see *Allen* v. *the United Kingdom* [GC], no. 25424/09, § 126, ECHR 2013, and the cases cited therein).

Lastly, the Court has previously acknowledged that the principle of the presumption of innocence may in theory also be infringed on account of premature expressions of a suspect's guilt made within the scope of a judgment against separately prosecuted co-suspects (see *Karaman* v. *Germany*, no. 17103/10, § 42, 27 February 2014). It has held that such statements, notwithstanding the fact that they are not binding with respect to the applicant, may have a prejudicial effect on the proceedings pending against him or her in the same way as a premature expression of a suspect's guilt made by any other public authority in close connection with pending criminal proceedings (ibid., § 43).

[...]

Turning to the circumstances of the present case, the Court firstly observes that the applicant and D.A. were accused of the same criminal offence – it was suspected that D.A. had murdered two individuals at the applicant's instigation [...]. The Court therefore has no reason to doubt that the facts established in the proceedings against D.A. and the legal findings made therein were directly relevant to the applicant's case, which was pending at that time (see, *mutatis mutandis, Navalnyy and Ofitserov* v. *Russia*, nos. 46632/13 and 28671/14, § 103, 23 February 2016). It further observes that one of the key pieces of evidence against D.A. was his letter in which he had confessed to the murder and accused the applicant of ordering him to commit that murder [...]. In such circumstances, the courts examining the case against D.A. could hardly avoid mentioning the applicant's alleged involvement in the murder (see, *mutatis mutandis, Karaman*, cited above, § 66). Accordingly, the Court has to assess whether safeguards were in place to ensure that the decisions taken in the proceedings against D.A. would not undermine the fairness of the subsequent proceedings against the applicant (see *Navalnyy and Ofitserov*, cited above, § § 103–04).

In this connection, the Court takes note of the grounds on which the prosecutor separated the proceedings against the applicant from those against D.A. – namely the applicant having a different procedural status with regard to the two different accusations against D.A., and the case against D.A. being ready for trial, unlike the one against the applicant [...] – and sees no reason to consider those grounds unjustified [...]. As to the court judgments delivered in the proceedings against D.A., the Court observes that some statements in the Vilnius Regional Court's judgment of 20 June 2011 were worded in a way which may have raised doubts as to a potential prejudgment about the applicant's guilt. In particular, that court stated 'the statement in [D.A.'s] letter that [D.A.] – upon the orders of the individual in respect of whom a separate pre-trial investigation was opened – killed [R.Ž.] so that all the profit would go to that individual alone ... must be considered true' [...]. However, the Court reiterates that whether a statement is in breach of the principle of the presumption of innocence must be determined in the context of the particular circumstances in which that statement was made (see, among other authorities, *Paulikas*, cited above, § 55). In the present case, assessing the impugned statements in their context, the Court considers that, in the proceedings against D.A., the courts made it clear that they were not determining the applicant's guilt. The Vilnius Regional Court referred to the applicant as 'the individual in respect of whom a separate pre-trial investigation [had been] opened' [...], and the Court of Appeal explicitly stated that only the investigation which had been opened against the applicant could determine his guilt [...]. The Court is thus satisfied that the domestic courts avoided, as far as possible, giving the impression that they were prejudging the applicant's guilt (see *Karaman*, § § 69–70; compare and contrast *Navalnyy and Ofitserov*, § 106, both cited above).

The Court further observes that, in accordance with domestic law, the courts in the proceedings against D.A. were called to examine only the latter's guilt, and the legal effect of their judgments was limited to those proceedings ([...]; see also *Karaman*, § 65; compare and contrast *Navalnyy and Ofitserov*, § 107). It underlines that the courts which examined the case against the applicant carried out a new assessment of all the evidence, including D.A.'s letter, and the applicant had the opportunity to contest the truthfulness of its contents [...]. Furthermore, the Court of Appeal explicitly rejected the prosecutor's argument that the findings of the courts in the proceedings against D.A. had to be followed in the proceedings against the applicant [...]. The Court therefore has no reason to doubt that the state of the evidence admitted in the case against D.A. remained purely relative and that its effect was strictly limited to that particular set of proceedings, as further demonstrated by the applicant's acquittal (see *Navalnyy and Ofitserov*, cited above, § 105).

Accordingly, assessing all the circumstances of the present case as a whole, the Court is of the view that the judgments delivered in the proceedings against D.A. did not breach the principle of the presumption of innocence and did not preclude the applicant from having a fair trial in the proceedings against him.

There has therefore been no violation of Article 6 § 2 of the Convention.

Part Nine: 1.B. State Territory – Territory – Good Neighbourliness

9/1

On 22 June 2017, the Seimas adopted a resolution on the Unity and Cooperation of the Baltic States Seeking to Protect Themselves against Threats Posed by Unsafe Nuclear Power Plants in Third Countries, which reads as follows:

> The Seimas of the Republic of Lithuania,
>
> *having regard* to the fact that the EU and NATO are seeking to expand the area of security and trust in the Eastern Neighbourhood;
>
> *taking* into account the conclusions of the European Council of 24/25 March, 2011 to introduce the obligation for all EU Member States to carry out 'stress tests' in their nuclear power plants and a call for similar 'stress tests' to be carried out in existing and planned plants in the neighbouring countries and worldwide;
>
> *seeking* that, in developing nuclear power plant construction projects, neighbouring third countries of the EU would take account of the interests of the Republic of Lithuania and other States in the region, in particular regarding the selection of construction sites, and comply with the highest international requirements for environmental protection as well as nuclear safety and radiation protection and their commitments in these areas;
>
> *supporting* the EU's objectives to strengthen the safety of operation and decommissioning of nuclear power plants in the EU and third countries and control of storage of spent nuclear fuel and nuclear materials;
>
> *having* regard to the assessment presented by the Government of the Republic of Lithuania regarding the nuclear power plant under construction in the Ostrovets District of the Republic of Belarus which, on the basis of requirements laid down in international conventions, recognises the nuclear power plant under construction in the Ostrovets District as an unsafe nuclear power plant which poses a threat to the national security of the Republic of Lithuania, its environment and public health;
>
> *recalling* the solidarity between the Baltic States and the Republic of Poland on major issues concerning foreign policy and military and energy security,

calls on the Riigikogu of the Republic of Estonia, the Saeima of the Republic of Latvia and the Sejm of the Republic of Poland to get acquainted with the Law on Necessary Measures of Protection against the Threats Posed by Unsafe Nuclear Power Plants in Third Countries adopted by the Seimas of the Republic of Lithuania;

urges the Riigikogu of the Republic of Estonia, the Saeima of the Republic of Latvia and the Sejm of the Republic of Poland to take decisions that will prevent electricity supplied by developers of unsafe nuclear power plants from entering the electricity systems of the Baltic States and Poland;

calls on the Riigikogu of the Republic of Estonia, the Saeima of the Republic of Latvia and the Sejm of the Republic of Poland to support international initiatives aimed against the construction of unsafe nuclear power plants, including the Ostrovets Nuclear Power Plant, stressing that the lack of energy security is a key factor in retaining the Baltic States and Europe in Russia's sphere of influence;

calls on the Riigikogu of the Republic of Estonia, the Saeima of the Republic of Latvia and the Sejm of the Republic of Poland to jointly address the institutions of the European Union – the European Parliament and the European Commission – in order to shape a common policy of the European Union which would:
1) ensure the application of international requirements to all projects of nuclear power plants;
2) protect against the development of unsafe nuclear power plants in third countries in the EU neighbourhood;
3) prevent the entry of electricity generated in unsafe nuclear power plants in third countries into the EU market;
4) ensure in the future that spent nuclear fuel and other materials are stored or disposed of safely and in accordance with EU safety requirements;
5) ensure that developers of nuclear power plants developed in third countries in the EU neighbourhood comply with the principle of transparency and disclose the sources of funding of the decommissioning and fuel storage of such power plants.

(Available in English at the website of the *Seimas*, <https://e-seimas.lrs.lt/portal/legalAct/lt/TAD/fea37f205ca011e7a53b83ca0142260e?jfwid=14shvjobsx>)

Part Nine: III.A. State Territory – Territorial Sovereignty – General

9/2
[17/1]

Part Thirteen: IV.2.B. International Responsibility – International Armed Conflict – Consequences of Responsibility – Consequences other than Reparation

13/1

On 23 November 2017, the Seimas adopted a resolution on the Anniversary of the Death of Sergei Magnitsky, which reads as follows:

> The Seimas of the Republic of Lithuania,
>
> *commemorating* the anniversary of the death of Russian lawyer Sergei Magnitsky who uncovered financial fraud schemes involving the officials and citizens of the Russian Federation where the amount of USD 230 millions of taxpayers' money was fraudulently misappropriated, who was unlawfully arrested, detained for 358 days and subjected to torture, and who died on 16 November 2009, having been maliciously denied necessary medical care;
>
> *noting* that so far not a single responsible person has been convicted of this well-documented crime, while five officials have been honoured with State decorations;
>
> *stressing* the moral responsibility and obligation of democratic States to contribute to ending impunity for gross violations of human rights, large-scale financial fraud schemes and corruption, regardless of their occurrence, by adopting legal acts providing for targeted sanctions, namely, a visa ban for and a freezing of the assets and property of the perpetrators of such crimes;
>
> *having regard* to the fact that legal acts symbolically named after Sergei Magnitsky and providing for sanctions have already been adopted by the United States of America, Estonia, Great Britain and Canada;
>
> *recalling* that the European Parliament has been calling for a number of years for adoption of the Magnitsky sanctions at EU-level and reiterated

this call in its recent document – European Parliament resolution of 13 September 2017 on corruption and human rights in third countries (2017/2028 (INI)),

notes that the amendments of the Law of the Republic of Lithuania on the Legal Status of Aliens adopted by the Seimas of the Republic of Lithuania are an important step towards ensuring that aliens who have committed large-scale crimes in the areas of human rights, corruption or money laundering would be prohibited from entering the territory of the Republic of Lithuania, and contributing to the strengthening of the national security of Lithuania;

emphasises that this process will be completed only after the adoption of legal acts that prevent such persons from acquiring property in Lithuania or through Lithuania and from holding crime-related proceeds, and that ensure their freezing, and **invites** the Government of the Republic of Lithuania to submit, in the near future, proposals for relevant legal acts to the Seimas of the Republic of Lithuania;

expects the Minister of Foreign Affairs and the Minister of the Interior who are responsible for the implementation of the provisions of the Law of the Republic of Lithuania on the Legal Status of Aliens to take immediate action necessary to implement the said provisions and to initiate the appropriate consultations with the countries which have already adopted the Magnitsky legal acts;

urges to place the following persons on the list of persons banned from entering the Republic of Lithuania based on the US Sergei Magnitsky Rule of Law Accountability Act of 2012 and on the grounds provided for in the Law of the Republic of Lithuania on the Legal Status of Aliens:

DROGANOV, Aleksey O., born 11 October 1975;
KARPOV, Pavel, born 27 August 1977;
KOMNOV, Dmitriy, born 17 May 1977;
KHIMINA, Yelena, born 11 September 1953;
KRIVORUCHKO, Aleksey, born 25 August 1977;
KUZNETSOV, Artem, born 28 February 1975;
LOGUNOV, Oleg, born 4 February 1962;
PECHEGIN, Andrey I., born 24 September 1965;
PODOPRIGOROV, Sergei G., born 8 January 1974;

PROKOPENKO, Ivan Pavlovitch, born 28 September 1973;
SILCHENKO, Oleg F., born 25 June 1977;
STASHINA, Yelena, born 5 November 1963;
STEPANOVA, Olga G., born 29 July 1962;
TOLCHINSKIY, Dmitri M., born 11 May 1982;
UKHNALYOVA, Svetlana, born 14 March 1973;
VINOGRADOVA, Natalya V., born 16 June 1973;
BOGATIROV, Letscha, born 14 March 1975;
DUKUZOV, Kazbek, born 1974;
LITVINOVA, Larisa Anatolievna, born 18 November 1963;
KRATOV, Dmitry Borisovich, born 16 July 1964;
GAUS, Alexandra Viktorovna, born 29 March 1975;
TAGIYEV, Fikret, born 3 April 1962;
ALISOV, Igor Borisovich, born 11 March 1968;
MARKELOV, Viktor Aleksandrovich, born 15 December 1967;
KLYUEV, Dmitry Vladislavovich, born 10 August 1967;
STEPANOV, Vladlen Yurievich, born 17 July 1962;
KHLEBNIKOV, Vyacheslav Georgievich, born 9 July 1967;
VAKHAYEV, Musa, born 1964;
SUGAIPOV, Umar, born 17 April 1966;
KRECHETOV, Andrei Alexandrovich, born 22 September 1981;
DAUDOV, Magomed Khozhakhmedovich, born 26 February 1980;
ALAUDINOV, Apti Kharonovich, born 5 October 1973;
GRIN, Victor Yakovlevich, born 1 January 1951;
STRIZHOV, Andrei Alexandrovich, born 1 August 1983;
ANICHIN, Aleksey Vasilyevich, born 1 December 1949;
KIBIS, Boris Borisovich, born 20 November 1977;
URZHUMTSEV, Oleg Vyacheslavovich, born 22 October 1968;
LAPSHOV, Pavel Vladimirovich, born 7 July 1976;
ANTONOV, Yevgeni Yuvenalievich, born 1955;
PLAKSIN, Gennady Nikolaevich, born 31 August 1961;
LUGOVOI, Andrei Konstantinovich, born 19 September 1966;
KOVTUN, Dmitri, born 1965;
BASTRYKIN, Alexander Ivanovich, born 27 August 1953;
GORDIEVSKY, Stanislav Evgenievich, born 9 September 1977;

appeals to the national parliaments of the EU Member States and NATO countries inviting to adopt Magnitsky legal acts, thus strengthening a common area of justice, responsibility and transparency;

supports the initiative to adopt targeted Magnitsky sanctions at EU-level and **calls on** the Government of the Republic of Lithuania to raise these issues in relevant configurations of the Council of the EU;

invites the High Representative of the European Union for Foreign Affairs and Security Policy Federica Mogherini, the European Commission and the Council of Europe to listen to the calls of the European Parliament to adopt the Magnitsky sanctions at EU-level and to launch, in the near future, a comprehensive discussion on the relevant EU legal act.

(Available in English at the website of the *Seimas*, <https://e-seimas.lrs.lt/portal/legalAct/lt/TAD/d5a59510d38111e782d4fd2c44cc67af?jfwid=14shvjoc6x>)

Part Seventeen: I.D. The Law of Armed Conflict and International Humanitarian Law – International Armed Conflict – Belligerent Occupation

17/1

On 16 March 2017, the Seimas adopted a resolution on The Condemnation of the Ongoing Occupation and Annexation of Crimea, which reads as follows:

The Seimas of the Republic of Lithuania,

recalling that three years ago the Russian Federation, by using armed military force, occupied and annexed a part of the Ukrainian territory – the Autonomous Republic of Crimea and the city of Sevastopol;

having regard to the UN General Assembly Resolution of 27 March 2014 expressing support for the sovereignty and territorial integrity of Ukraine and affirming the commitment of the United Nations to recognize Crimea as part of the Ukrainian territory;

having regard to the International Criminal Court's Report on Preliminary Examination Activities of 14 November 2016 in relation to the international armed conflict in Ukraine, stating that the military aggression which was unleashed by the Russian Federation three years ago in the Autonomous Republic of Crimea and has currently expanded to Eastern Ukraine, gravely infringes the Charter of the United Nations, the provisions of the Helsinki Final Act, the 1994 Budapest Memorandum and other international agreements;

having regard to the UN General Assembly Resolution of 19 December 2016 on the situation of human rights in the Autonomous Republic of Crimea and the city of Sevastopol (Ukraine);

having regard to the OSCE Parliamentary Assembly Resolution of 4 July 2016 on violations of human rights and fundamental freedoms in Crimea;

expresses its strong support for the sovereignty, independence, unity and territorial integrity of Ukraine and the inviolability of its internationally recognized borders;

strongly condemns the ongoing occupation and annexation of part of the sovereign territory of Ukraine – the Autonomous Republic of Crimea and the city of Sevastopol – by the Russian Federation;

reiterates its call on the Russian Federation to end the illegal occupation and annexation of Crimea, withdraw its armed forces from the Ukrainian territory, immediately implement the Minsk agreements, and comply with international law and its own obligations under international law;

points out that the intensive militarisation of the Crimean peninsula carried out by the Russian Federation poses a threat to the security and stability of the whole of Europe;

declares that it does not recognise the results of the elections to the Russian Federation State Duma, held on 18 September 2016 in Crimea occupied by the Russian Federation and supports the decision of the European Union to add the representatives elected in Crimea to the list of persons subject to restrictive measures of the European Union;

strongly condemns gross and systematic violations of human rights with respect to the Crimean Tatars and ethnic Ukrainians in Crimea occupied by the Russian Federation: intimidation and persecution, unlawful detention and imprisonment, application of laws of a discriminatory nature, infringements of the right to property and expropriation of property, restrictions on the freedoms of the media, expression, peaceful assembly, religion and belief, urges to expand the list of persons subject to restrictive measures of the European Union, adding the persons who have committed serious violations of human rights;

urges the authorities of the Russian Federation and the occupying authorities in Crimea to ensure for international human rights organisations and independent experts unimpeded access to Crimea and information on the human rights situation in order to objectively investigate and evaluate the human rights violations committed by the occupying authorities, calls for the implementation of resolutions of the UN General Assembly and recommendations on the human rights situation in Crimea of the UN Human Rights Monitoring Mission, the OSCE High Commissioner on National Minorities and the Office for Democratic Institutions and Human Rights of the Organisation for Security and Cooperation in Europe and calls on the EU institutions and the Member States as well as the international community at large to take active steps to influence the decisions of the Russian Federation on these matters;

strongly condemns the ruling of the so-called Crimean Supreme Court of 26 April 2016, which found the Mejlis of the Crimean Tatar People, the highest executive and representative authority, to be an extremist organisation and banned its activity;

supports the call made in the European Parliament resolution of 12 May 2016 on the Crimean Tatars for the EU to provide financial support for the activities of the Mejlis while it is in exile as well as for increased financing for human rights organisations working in Crimea;

expresses support for the Ukrainian authorities raising the issues of recovery of the occupied and annexed territory and claims for damages incurred in the course of occupation and annexation in international organisations and courts;

appeals to the political leaders, parliaments and governments of the transatlantic community and the European Union urging them to pursue an active policy of non-recognition of the occupation and annexation of Crimea and to uphold the sanctions regime in a principled manner, preventing any attempts to evade it; to further unanimously uphold the position that the termination of the occupation and annexation of Crimea is one of the conditions for the resumption of full cooperation with the Russian Federation, and the sanctions applied by the Western democratic communities for the actions that undermine the independence of Ukraine and infringe its territorial integrity should be maintained until Ukraine's territorial integrity is restored in accordance with the principles enshrined in the Constitution of Ukraine and international law.

(Available in English at the website of the *Seimas*, <https://e-seimas.lrs.lt/portal/legalAct/lt/TAD/4fbed5c30b0811e78dacb175b73de379?jfwid=14shvjoawl>)

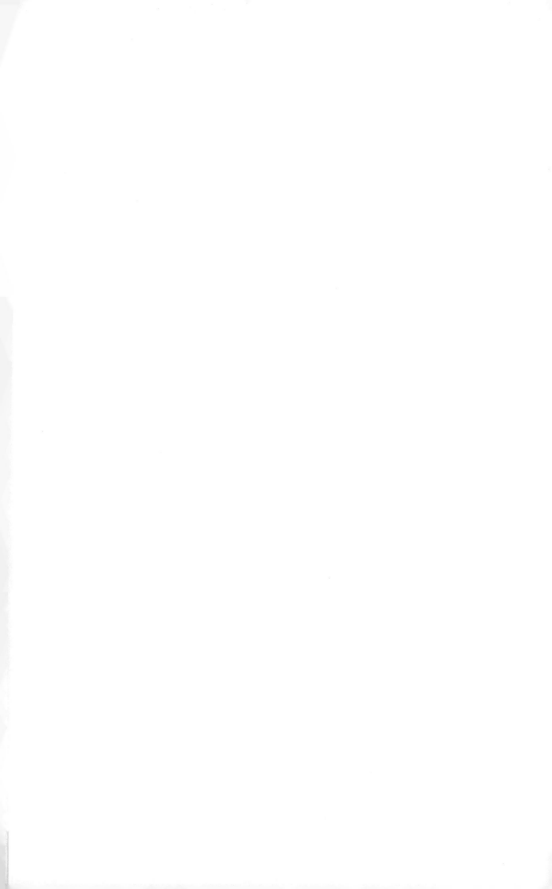